Social Theory at Work

Social Theory at Work

Edited by
Marek Korczynski
Randy Hodson
Paul K. Edwards

This book has been printed digitally and produced in a standard specification in order to ensure its continuing availability

OXFORD
UNIVERSITY PRESS

Great Clarendon Street, Oxford OX2 6DP

Oxford University Press is a department of the University of Oxford.
It furthers the University's objective of excellence in research, scholarship,
and education by publishing worldwide in

Oxford New York

Auckland Cape Town Dar es Salaam Hong Kong Karachi
Kuala Lumpur Madrid Melbourne Mexico City Nairobi
New Delhi Shanghai Taipei Toronto
With offices in
Argentina Austria Brazil Chile Czech Republic France Greece
Guatemala Hungary Italy Japan South Korea Poland Portugal
Singapore Switzerland Thailand Turkey Ukraine Vietnam

Published in the United States
by Oxford University Press Inc., New York

Reprinted 2009

ISBN 978-0-19-928598-3

Dedication

For Ursula and Anna

For Debbie Mei and Susie Xin

Contents

Contributors

James R. Barker is Professor of Organizational Theory and Strategy at the Waikato Management School, Waikato University, Hamilton, NZ. Jim studies the consequences of organizational control practices and is particularly concerned with critically analyzing the morality of control structures and applications. His work has been published in journals such as *Administrative Science Quarterly*. He is the author of *The Discipline of Teamwork* (Sage, 1999).

Thomas D. Beamish is an assistant professor, Department of Sociology, University of California at Davis. Dr Beamish's research reflects a substantive interest in the structuring influence that institutions and complex/formal/informal organization exert on interpretation and practice and, in turn, how interpretation and practice reproduce and change institutions and organizations. Dr Beamish's publications include a recently published book, *Silent Spill: The Organization of an Industrial Crisis* (MIT Press, 2002), chapters in edited volumes, and professional journal articles that have appeared in the *Journal of Social Problems*, the *Annual Review of Sociology*, and *Organization and Environment*, among others.

Jacques Bélanger is a professor in the Départment des Relations Industrielles at Université Laval, Quebec City. His research has focused on workplace industrial relations and, more generally, on the evolution of employment relations. The results of field research he conducted within multinational firms have appeared in various industrial relations and sociological journals. He is Co-director of the Centre de Recherche Inter-Universitaire sur la Mondialisation et le Travail (CRIMT).

Nicole Woolsey Biggart is Dean at the Graduate School of Management, and Professor of Management and Sociology at the University of California at Davis. She holds the Jerome J. and Elsie Suran Chair in Technology Management. Nicole is interested in the social structural foundations of industries and markets and has written about Asian business groups, the direct selling industry, and other topics related to the organization of economic activity. She has served as Chair of the Organizations, Occupations and Work and the Economic Sociology Sections of the American Sociological Association. She is Editor of *Readings in Economic Sociology* (Blackwell, 2002), and co-author of *The Economic Organization of East Asian Capitalism* (Sage, 1996).

Gibson Burrell is Head of the Management Centre at the University of Leicester. His main interests lie in social theory and how this connects to organization theory. Among the books he has authored are *Pandemonium: Towards a Retro-Organizational Theory* (Sage, 1996) and *Organisation, Space and Architecture* (with Karen Dale) (Palgrave/Macmillan, 2005).

Peter Cappelli is the George W. Taylor Professor of Management at the Wharton School and Director of Wharton's Center for Human Resources. He is also a Research Associate at the National Bureau of Economic Research in Cambridge. He is the Editor of the *Academy of Management Executive*. Professor Cappelli's more recent research examined changes in employment relations in the US. These publications include *Change at Work* (Oxford University Press, 1997), a major study for the National Planning Association which found that employees paid a considerable price for the restructuring of US industry, and *The New Deal at Work: Managing the Market-Driven Workforce* (Harvard Business School Press, 1999), which examines the challenges associated with the decline in lifetime employment relationships.

Paul Edwards is Professor of Industrial Relations at Warwick Business School, University of Warwick and is a fellow of the British Academy. He is conducting research, within the program of the UK Advanced Institute of Management Research, on employment relations in small firms. The most recent of his eight books (written with Judy Wajcman), is *The Politics of Working Life* (Oxford University Press, 2005).

Stephen Frenkel is a professor specializing in the sociology of work and organization in the Australian Graduate School of Management. His research focuses on several aspects of workplace relations including the impact of globalization on work and worker well-being. His recent research has examined the impact of global supply chains on codes of conduct and the way work organization and human resource practices influence the dynamics of service and knowledge work. Among many publications, he is joint author of *On the Front Line: Organization of Work in the Information Economy* (Cornell University Press, 1999). Steve is on the editorial board of the *Industrial & Labor Relations Review*, the *British Journal of Industrial Relations*, and the *International Journal of Human Resource Management*.

Heidi Gottfried is an associate professor of Labor Studies at Wayne State University, USA. Over the past several years her research (funded by the Center for Global Partnership, American Sociological Association/National Science Foundation; DAAD; the Social Science Research Council Abe Fellowship, Council for European Studies) has focused on gender and work in comparative perspective. Currently, she is engaged in two international projects: one examines flexible employment and labor regulation in the US, the UK, Germany, and Japan; and the other explores working women's networks and networking transnationally. She is Editor of *Feminism and Social Change: Bridging Theory and Practice* (University of Illinois Press, 1996), *Equity in the Workplace: Gendering Workplace Policy Analysis*, (with Laura Reese, Lexington Press, 2004), and the symposium on Gender and Globalization (with Joan Acker) in *Critical Sociology* (2004).

Didier Guillot joined the Organizational Behavior area at INSEAD, Paris, in 2003. He conducts research in the areas of organization theory and international/comparative management. His current projects examine the structure and evolution of organizational networks and their effect on firm performance in the Japanese electronics industry. He also conducts research on the role and emergence of organizational culture within and across firm boundaries.

Heather Haveman is currently Professor of Management and, by courtesy, Sociology at Columbia University. Her research examines the evolution of formal organizations, the industries in which they operate, and the careers of their employees. She investigates several questions that relate to stability and change in organizational systems: what causes change? what are its consequences for both organizations themselves and employees? Her studies of savings and loan associations, telephone companies, hotels, and magazines have been published in such scholarly journals as *Administrative Science Quarterly*, the *American Journal of Sociology*, the *American Sociological Review*, the *Academy of Management Journal*, and *Poetics*.

Geoffrey M. Hodgson is a research professor at the University of Hertfordshire Business School, in Hatfield, England. He was formerly a Reader in Economics at the University of Cambridge. He is the author of several books including *The Evolution of Institutional Economics* (Routledge, 2004), *How Economics Forgot History* (Routledge, 2001), *Economics and Utopia* (Routledge, 1999), *Economics and Evolution* (University of Michigan Press, 1993), and *Economics and Institutions* (Polity, 1988). He has published more than eighty articles in prominent academic journals and is currently the Editor-in-Chief of the *Journal of Institutional Economics.*

Randy Hodson is Professor of Sociology at Ohio State University. His research interests include worker citizenship and resistance, management behavior, and co-worker relations. He is also engaged in research on economic transformations in Eastern Europe and China. His recent books include *Dignity at Work* (Cambridge, 2001) and *Worlds of Work: Building an International Sociology of Work* (co-authored with Daniel B. Cornfield, Kluwer/Plenum, 2002). He is also co-author with Teresa A. Sullivan of *The Social Organization of Work*, 3rd edition (Wadsworth, 2001) and Editor of the JAI/Elsevier Science annual series on *Research in the Sociology of Work*.

Richard Hyman is a professor in the Department of Industrial Relations at the London School of Economics. His main research interests focus on the history and theory of trade unionism and the comparative political economy of industrial relations. He is Editor of the *European Journal of Industrial Relations* and author of a number of books including *Understanding European Trade Unionism: Between Market, Class and Society* (Sage, 2001).

Mukti Khaire is a faculty member in the Entrepreneurial Management Unit of Harvard Business School. Mukti is interested in understanding how sociological theories explain organizational characteristics and performance. In particular, she is interested in the relationship between intangible assets and new venture growth. Mukti's research focuses on firms in creative industries and firms that produce cultural and experience goods, such as advertising agencies, magazine publishing, and wineries.

Marek Korczynski is Professor of Sociology of Work at Loughborough University. His research centres on the sociology of service work, on social theory and work, and on music and work. He is the co-author of *On the Front Line: Organization of Work in the Service Economy* (Cornell University

Press, 1999) and author of *Human Resource Management in Service Work* (Palgrave/Macmillan, 2002).

Karen Legge is Professor in Organizational Behaviour, Warwick Business School. Until 2003, Karen was Joint Editor of *Journal of Management Studies* and has also served on numerous editorial boards including *British Journal of Industrial Relations, Industrial Relations, Human Resource Management Journal, Gender, Work and Organization* and *Organization*. Karen's research interests lie in the area of applying postmodern organization theory to HRM, change management, the development of the learning organization, and organizational ethics. She has published widely in these areas, a well-known publication being *HRM, Rhetorics and Realities* (Palgrave/Macmillan, 1995), an updated anniversary edition of which was published in 2005.

Robin Leidner is Associate Professor of Sociology at the University of Pennsylvania. She is the author of *Fast Food, Fast Talk: Service Work and the Routinization of Everyday Life* (University of California Press, 1993), as well as articles on emotion work, service work, and feminist organizations. She is currently investigating the work identities of stage actors.

James R. Lincoln is the Warren E. and Carol Spieker Professor of Leadership at the Walter A. Haas School of Business, University of California, Berkeley. He is also an affiliated faculty member of the Department of Sociology and the Center for Japanese Studies. His primary research and teaching interests include organizational design and innovation, Japanese management and industrial relations, and organizational networks. He is the author (with Michael Gerlach) of *Japan's Network Economy: Structure, Persistence, and Change* (Cambridge University Press, 2004), and (with Arne Kalleberg) *Culture, Control, and Commitment: A Study of Work Organizations and Work Attitudes in the U. S. and Japan* (Cambridge University Press, 1990). He has in addition published numerous articles and chapters on Japanese business and labor topics.

Keith Macdonald is currently Visiting Professor of Sociology in the Department of Sociology, University of Surrey, where he has held various post since 1964. He has published numerous articles on the sociology of occupations, especially the professions and the military. He is also author of *The Sociology of the Professions* (Sage, 1995). While continuing his interest in occupations, he is also working on studies in historical sociology.

Stephen Machin is Professor of Economics at University College London, Director of the DfES Centre for the Economics of Education and Research, and Director of the Centre for Economic Performance at the London School of Economics. He is currently one of the editors of the *Economic Journal*. He is the co-author of *What's the Good of Education? The Economics of Education in the UK* (Princeton University Press, 2004), and author of *The Age of Inequality* (Texere, 1999).

Graham Sewell is Associate Professor of Organization Studies and Human Resource Management in the Department of Management, University of Melbourne, Australia. Although he is best known for his research on the disciplinary effects of workplace surveillance and teamwork he has also published on topics as diverse as knowledge work, workplace resistance, evolutionary psychology, business ethics, foreign direct investment in the UK, and innovation processes in the international semiconductor industry. This work has appeared in a number of leading journals, including the *Administrative Science Quarterly*, the *Academy of Management Review, Organizational Studies, Sociology, Human Relations*, and *Research Policy.* Over the last five years Graham has been working with James R. (Jim) Barker on a long-term project that is attempting to take the critical energy of the 'postmodern turn' in social theory and refocus it on some of the perennial concerns of classical studies of work organizations, such as class, solidarity, and bureaucracy. His contribution to the chapter with Jim Barker in this volume was completed while he was at the University of Pompeu Fabra and he wishes to acknowledge the generous support of the Ministerio de Educación y Ciensiasde España during his stay in Barcelona.

Acknowledgements

We would like to express our appreciation of and gratitude to all the authors involved in this book—not least because of the patience we asked of them on this long project. In addition, thanks to David Mussor and Matthew Derbyshire at Oxford University Press for all their good work in helping the book towards completion. The work of Paul Edwards was supported by the UK's Advanced Institute of Management Research.

1

Introduction: Competing, Collaborating, and Reinforcing Theories

Marek Korczynski, Randy Hodson, and Paul K. Edwards

The sociology of work benefits from both strong empirical and theoretical traditions. Until now, however, there has been no available source that elaborates the various theoretical traditions in the study of work. This book is intended to fill that need. It grows out of our own pedagogical and research struggles to assemble readings for students and materials for ourselves that provide coherent overviews of the various theories of work. Such materials are particularly important in upper-division undergraduate classes and graduate seminars where students have a right to be presented with comprehensive visions of the theoretical terrain of the topics they are studying. The organization of this book is thus in terms of the major competing, collaborating, and reinforcing theories of work. It is our hope that through this book students, and instructors, will gain a much more grounded view of the theoretical foundations of workplace studies. We also hope that this book will provide an important benchmark representing the current theoretical state of workplace studies—an area which is incredibly vibrant and rapidly developing.

An alternative approach would have been to provide overviews of the many topics within workplace studies, such as alienation and job satisfaction, unionization and its challenges, women and work, globalization, and so on. This approach allows historical foundations and current issues and changes to be highlighted and is highly useful. Several excellent topical presentations of the sociology of work are already available, including Grint (1998), Hodson and Sullivan (2001), Krahn and Lowe

(1998), Rothman (1998), Thompson and McHugh (2002), and Watson (2001). Such books, however, do not facilitate an understanding of the *different theoretical approaches* to contemporary issues and changes. Achieving such understandings is a crucial developmental goal for students of the workplace as they grow and mature intellectually, whether they are undergraduates, graduates, or faculty at whatever career stage.

This introductory chapter is structured as follows: first, we address some fundamental questions about the focus and the shape of this book. Most basically, the question 'why focus on work' immediately arises, and we address this in the section below. Next, we lay out the criteria underpinning our choice of the social theories that are included in the book and outline the structure of the book. Finally, with these basic points covered, we offer an overview of some key themes in the comparative assessment of social theories' analyses of work.

1. Why Focus on Work?

The workplace is central to understanding society because it is a foundation for one's position in the social stratification system, for the meaning of one's life, for fulfilment, dignity, and health, and for the success of nations. Social theories address many aspects of life besides work, including relationships in families, religion, and politics. Why do theories of work merit special and separate attention? Besides the centrality of work to social life, another reason to focus on theories of work is the tremendous pace of change in work and the burgeoning of theories of work. These issues have been brought into sharp focus in recent years as a result of several developments that present clear challenges to contemporary theories of work. One is the apparent fall in the relevance of work-based concepts such as class. A second is the growing emphasis on consumption rather than production, together with an interest in personal identities as opposed to the structures that create work roles. Third, social roles are often seen as increasingly flexible and transient, so that one's work situation may be of less importance to one's identity and beliefs than was the case in the past.

An introduction is not the place to consider such changes in detail. That work is carried out much more effectively in the following chapters. The chapter on identity, for instance, discusses in detail the importance of work to the generation of identity, stressing that work may have lost some of its ways of shaping identity (perhaps with the decline of class-based solidarity), but has contributed to new ones as people turn to work for recognition when community and family ties may be weakening. But a few key facts should be briefly highlighted. First, it is not the case that the time that people typically spend at work has fallen markedly. Second, women have seen their labor market participation rise, so that any decline of the 'organizational man' is balanced against a growth of the 'organizational woman'. Third, the decline of class may be exaggerated, for there is evidence that class continues to predict key facts of people's lives and that class-based voting, for example, is about as common as ever. And in any event a decline of class would at most suggest a decline in a particular type of link with work, namely, one in which blue-collar workers form stable work communities that provide a basis of class identity. Fourth, many countries have witnessed concerns about long work hours, 'presenteeism', and work-based stress. Such trends scarcely suggest that work experience has ceased to be fateful for workers.

Such points suggest that what is happening to work may be less dramatic than is often thought. There is thus a clear rationale for looking at social theories with a long pedigree: the kinds of work relations currently dominant have many similarities with those prevailing when such theories were developed. A further fundamental point is that work in its broadest sense has in some respects become more important than ever. A major discourse throughout the advanced economies since the rise of liberal market economics in the 1980s has been the importance of competitiveness and the development of a 'knowledge economy'. The European Union (EU), for example, has developed targets for proportions of the population in paid work, and has more generally advanced a vision of competitive flexibility combined with fulfilling work. This discourse takes it for granted that the ability of a country to produce, and not just consume, goods and services is critical to its prosperity. The organization of work thus remains central, as the stress on skills and knowledge suggests.

It is clearly the case that the patterns of work are changing as manufacturing industry declines, but the importance of work is at least as great as ever. This is also true if we look at work as a lived experience. The white-collar organizational man and the blue-collar worker in a job for life were always extreme stereotypes but, to the extent that they captured something of workplace reality, it was of a reality in which work changed little, one could place clear boundaries around it, and its core requirements were ones of mere compliance with the demands of 'the system'. As organizations have come to demand commitment and even an entrepreneurial vision, and as they have measured performance more closely, workers find themselves required to display active engagement with organizational goals. An instrumental disengagement from work is less feasible than it was in the past.

Equally fundamental, the structure of economic activity says a great deal about how a society is organized. Social theories differ as to the nature of this linkage. Classical Marxism offered one picture, with the economic base 'determining' the superstructure of other aspects of social life. Other theoretical traditions have been more cautious and more prone to stress the contingency of relationships and the influence of the noneconomic on the economic. But they have not denied the importance of the ways in which the productive capacity of a society is organized. This book aims to review and assess how various theories have addressed this and other issues.

2. The Selection of Theories

Modern social science identifies a large and growing number of specialities, including economics, sociology, psychology, and politics, with subjects such as law also having social science aspects. Some scholarly works include assessments of the contribution of these (and indeed other) disciplines to the study of work, for example, a recent book on industrial relations (Ackers and Wilkinson 2003). Others consciously set out to provide *Handbooks* in such areas as organization studies and management thinking, while yet others are styled as *Encyclopaedic Dictionaries*, for example, of organizational behavior.

Our approach is different. First, we decided to be more selective. This allows contributors to write at more length and also to offer their own interpretations. The chapters in the book are original essays that are based on deep appreciation of their subjects, and yet that also bear the strong mark of their authors. They are not summaries or reviews.

Second, selection means omission. Of the disciplines mentioned above, politics, that is the study of power and influence, runs through much of the social analysis of work. Structures of power are key to many chapters in this book, including those on feminist thought (where male organizational power is theoretically central), technology (where the control of technology as a means of exerting power over people is a major theme), and the professions (with the power of professions to define themselves and to establish 'social closure' being a core strand of the literature).

Psychology, by contrast, is not covered in a central fashion. Aspects of social psychology appear in several places. Of the 'founding fathers', Durkheim was perhaps the most interested in belief systems, and his views on culture and its effects on individuals are addressed here, as are more recent studies in this tradition. The chapter on identity also considers the symbolic interactionist school and the study of occupations, and their identities as exemplified by Everett Hughes and Erving Goffman. But psychology as such is not directly addressed. The key reason is that this book is about social theories that address the structuring of work through social organization. Psychology is concerned with individual responses to such structuring. It makes a major contribution to the study of work, for example in relation to such issues as trust and commitment and through such concepts as the psychological contract. But it stands outside the traditions to which this book is devoted.

What, though, of economics, which is often accused of being based on individualistic models of behavior and also of saying nothing about politics and power? It is true that neoclassical economics in its most pure form assumes rational self-serving individuals. As many economists have remarked, such an approach cannot explain many of the core institutions of modern economies such as firms (for, if individuals can transact directly, there is no need for firms). Economics of a broadly conventional kind has sought answers to such questions, using concepts such as market failure and transaction costs—and in these studies the structuring of work relationships has thus been a central issue. Less conventional economists have made institutions central to their analysis, and here their work overlaps with the tradition of economic sociology. There is, in short, much within economics that addresses the concerns of this book and these contributions are fully reported and represented here.

The first main section of the book, Chapters 2–11, is made up of chapters giving overviews of the main social and economic theoretical traditions and their application to the analysis of work. The traditional 'founding fathers', Marx, Weber, and Durkheim are covered first, before more recent approaches of feminism and Foucault and postmodernism are considered. Next, two important economics schools are considered—the neoclassical school and the institutional economics tradition. This main section is completed by chapters on economic sociology, organizational sociology and ethics-based approaches to the analysis of work. The second section is made up of chapters focusing on technology and work, professions, globalization and work, and identity and work. In this section, we see how far important substantive issues have been advanced by social theories, and also see how far these advances have been based on some de facto integration between social theories. Whereas chapters in the first section generally examine specific social theories in isolation from each other, those in the second section allow us to begin to look for connections between social theories. The section below takes further the idea of the comparative analysis of social theories' approaches to work.

3. Comparative Analysis of Different Social Theories' Approaches to Work

The chapters in the first section of the book have been deliberately written to be free-standing. The reader, thus, should be able to turn to the chapter on feminism and work and come away with a holistic understanding of a feminist analysis of work without having any recourse to other chapters in the book. There is an obvious strength in this approach, but there is also the danger that the book, and the reader's knowledge, becomes fragmented. This structure makes it difficult for the reader to look across chapters, to assess the key differences and similarities between different social theories' analyses of work.

In an important sense, the concluding chapter by Peter Cappelli addresses the need for integration and synthesis. His overview carefully examines the degree to which different social theories have relevance in helping us understand what he sees as the key empirical trends within the contemporary workplace. In addition, we thought it appropriate that this introduction should help develop assessments *across* social theories at a more abstract level.

A good deal of literature on the metanalysis of social theory per se already exists of course. This literature ranges from the most ambitious comparison of a broad range of social theory, such as undertaken by Ritzer (1996; Ritzer and Smart 2001), to more focused in-depth comparisons of a small number of social theories. Important works of the latter kind include comparisons of the classic sociologists of emergent capitalism, Marx, Weber, and Durkheim, undertaken by Giddens (1971), the intriguing comparison of Marx and Foucault written by Marsden (1999), and the elegant framing put forward by Hirschman (1982).

There have also been some important studies that involve comparisons of social theory vis-à-vis *the arena of work*—our specific domain of interest. Burrell and Morgan (1979) present an overview, which plots a wide range of 'organizational theories' against two key dimensions: objective/subjective and sociology of radical change/sociology of regulation.[1] More recently, Reed (1996) has written an overview of what he calls 'metanarrative interpretative frameworks', or paradigms, underpinning the analysis of organizations in which he puts forward six broad paradigms, each of which is concerned with a different central problematic. He lists a rationality framework, concerned with order (e.g. classical organization theory); an integration framework concerned with consensus (e.g. Durkheim); a market framework concerned with liberty (e.g. neoclassical economics); a power framework concerned with domination (e.g. Marx and Weber); a knowledge framework concerned with control (e.g. Foucault); and a justice framework concerned with participation (e.g. ethics). While the approaches of Burrell and Morgan (1979) and Reed (1996) offer important insights, both can be accused of trying to categorize social theories rather too neatly. For instance, Reed discusses the Weberian tradition as centering on power and domination, but such a narrow categorization of this tradition hardly does justice to its wider focus—a point developed below.

We lay out three important considerations for understanding the role and impact of social theories of work. First, a theory may have relevance to a topic *even though its exponents do not make a connection explicitly.* Weber, for example, may have said nothing directly about front-line service work, but his ideas about rationality and bureaucracy have been used constructively to address this issue. Several chapters in this book show, moreover, that forgotten theorists are often rediscovered. The value of Durkheim in the analysis of contemporary 'corporate cultures' is a clear example.

Second, the intended *scope of a theory* must be taken into account. The theories addressed here all respond to the emergence of large-scale industry from the middle of the eighteenth century onward. This is most obvious in relation to the work of Marx, Weber, and Durkheim, but it is also true of modern economics, with Adam Smith's famous pin factory example plainly resting on the rationalized division of labor of the capitalist firm. Foucault offered a different vision of modern society, but was none the less concerned with rationality and what he termed the disciplinary society. And some of the more concrete themes addressed in this book, such as the relationship between technology and work and the nature of professional work, take much of their import from the context

[1] Similarly, Grint (1998) offers a mapping of organizational theories against the dimensions of determinist-interpretativist, and technocratic-critical.

of large organizations in modern societies. Consider the professions. It is of course true that the liberal professions predate the Industrial Revolution. But other 'professional' occupations such as accountancy not only emerged later but also did so specifically as products of the need for rationalized forms of knowledge. And the liberal professions have been powerfully shaped by the requirements of the modern state, for example, in the granting of licences to practise. The theories considered do not then, in the main, purport to explain work in all its possible forms but address, rather, the shaping of work by the rise of modern forms of social organization. The reader will have noticed several terms such as 'large-scale', 'capitalist', and 'modern'. This variety is deliberate, for different theorists stress different features of the societies in question. For some, there is a distinctively capitalist dynamic, others equally insist on the concept of modernity, while yet others prefer a looser reference to 'industrial' societies. The salience of these particular preferences is explained in the relevant chapters. Our present point is that there is a shared, if not always clearly defined, interest in forms of work characteristic of advanced modern economies in which the institution of the market plays a central role.

Third, there is what we may call the *depth of a theory*. Many of the theories addressed here focus on very large issues such as the relationship between rationality and freedom. They do not directly propose concrete hypotheses, and might more accurately be termed perspectives or paradigms. These latter terms can take various meanings: a 'perspective' can be a very loose idea, while the popularizer of 'paradigm', Thomas Kuhn, used the word in many different senses. For our purposes, such terms mean an intellectual approach that identifies some core concepts and the relationships between them without necessarily specifying concrete hypotheses. A Marxist paradigm for example uses concepts such as accumulation, exploitation, surplus value, and class. It may generate hypotheses such as 'the tendency of the profit rate to fall', but these do not reflect everything in the paradigm, and different users of it may legitimately disagree as to whether a particular hypothesis is directly entailed by the paradigm or is only consistent with it, as well as the conditions under which a hypothesis disconfirms the paradigm as a whole. To take a different example, neoclassical economics expects a single wage rate to exist for a given occupation in a given labor market. Repeated observations over many years that appear to conflict with this hypothesis do not of themselves disconfirm it, still less lead economists to abandon their whole approach, for there can be many reasons why wage rates do not equalize, and without a better theory to put in place of the original one the empirical observations lack any cogent explanation. 'It takes a theory to kill a theory', as the celebrated economist Samuelson (1951: 323) once remarked. The point here then is that theories as paradigms are not to be assessed solely as hypothesis generators.

Some of the approaches considered in this book, the Durkheimian one for example, do not say much directly about work, and their scope is of course much broader. But they say a great deal about the structure of society in which an organization of work is embedded. They do not, therefore, directly lead to hypotheses about, say, the degree of autonomy enjoyed by particular groups of workers or the ways in which people search for new jobs—though they may well contribute to such hypotheses. (In the case of Durkheim, for example, such contributions might be through underlining the importance of group norms and thus perhaps suggesting that job search is shaped by these norms as well as by individual preferences, and perhaps further arguing that what is a 'preference' is in fact socially shaped, and so on.) The *crucial task of a theory of work* is to analyze the structuring of society by forces including (depending on the theorist) the state, the rise of rationality and markets, and norms and traditions, with the implications then being pursued by analysts operating at a more concrete level. Various traditions of research, such as that of economic sociology, then follow through the implications of broader theories.

Turning, then, to how paradigms might be assessed, several criteria may be suggested. First, do the relevant ideas continue to stimulate analysis of contemporary problems? Do scholars return to the original texts? Second, is this interest more than a matter of curiosity or the writing of a history of ideas? The chapter on Durkheim, for example, shows that his ideas continue to be of use in relation to such issues as workplace culture. Third, do ideas constructively inform debate rather than simply being convenient pegs for arguments? Continuing with Durkheim, Lincoln and Guillot (see Chapter 4) show that his writings have profound implications about workplace culture that some current writings on the subject have failed to address; thus returning to Durkheim is not a matter of finding authority in ancient texts but of using those texts constructively to address issues that would otherwise be treated superficially.

It is helpful to distinguish broad paradigms from research programs. The former establish sets of ideas and ways of seeing. As several chapters, notably those on Marxism, feminism, and Foucault stress, paradigms gain much of their strength from being open and inclusive. Research programs, however, may be more suitable to more precisely defined questions and to empirical research that builds incrementally on previous knowledge. Some areas of the study of work, such as economic sociology, can point to the development of a clear program, whereas others may wish for such development, while yet others may prefer an approach that is more wide-ranging though possibly at the cost of finding it harder to point to the accumulation of knowledge around tightly defined questions.

The approach of the book, then, is to present theories that illuminate how work is organized and experienced. The reader will find explanation and discussion of these theories, with a wide range of supporting illustration. The chapters with particular substantive concerns, notably those on technology, the professions, identity, and globalization contain extended illustrations while those reviewing research traditions, such as that on economic sociology, point to the wide range of concrete empirical issues that have been addressed.

Our discussion takes as a starting point that it may not be useful or accurate to place social theories in tightly defined boxes. Accordingly, we offer the following six *dimensions* as being useful to consider when looking across the particular social theories of work. Some of the dimensions match those from previous overviews, while others are new. Some are particularly useful in comparing two specific approaches, but less so when comparing others. Our discussion under each of the subheadings below is meant to be suggestive, rather than definitive, seeking to open up, rather than close off, critical inquiry among readers.

Theme 1: Power, Market, and Social Norms—Their Centrality and Definition

A number of scholars have argued that *power* (hierarchy), *market*, and *social norms* (such as trust) are the three fundamental bases of social action in the economy. For instance, Ouchi (1979) has argued that firms rely on three basic forms of control—bureaucracies (i.e. hierarchy), markets, and clans (i.e. norms operating within peer groups); while Hirschman (1982) has argued that exit, voice, and loyalty (which map onto markets, power, and norms respectively) are the three central coordinating mechanisms for the modern corporation. If it is accepted that these are the three fundamental bases of social action within the economy, a first logical step in assessing social theories' analyses of work is to see which theories open up space for an examination of all three bases.

At one extreme, there are social theories which explicitly deny the existence of one or other of these bases. Take, for instance, Alchian and Demsetz's exemplary statement (1972) of neoclassical economic thinking that power does not function as a coordinating mechanism within the economy; and Williamson's argument (1993), within the closely allied transaction costs school of economics, that trust effectively only functions *outside* of economic activity. At a number of points, Marx also points to the vanishing of social norms as a significant basis of economic activity—the social relations of capitalism are *essentially* those of the bare cash nexus, he argued (e.g. *Communist Manifesto*). At the other extreme, there is the nascent school of economic sociology in which writers explicitly draw out this school's strength as involving a pluralist openness towards an examination of markets, hierarchy, and trust, and other social norms within the economy (Powell 1990). Also important in this regard is Durkheim's argument that simple economic contracting rests on the implicit functioning of important social norms.

But there are important issues at play here other than simply opening up space for an examination for all three bases. There are still crucial debates to be had over the substantive deeper social meanings of these concepts of market, power, and trust. One of the central arguments of Marx was, for instance, that while the free market ostensively coordinated the economy in a neutral way, these market forces were in effect a form of (class) power in action. As Lukes (1974) has argued, there may be more to the functioning of power than the simple visible rule of an organizational hierarchy. Similarly, feminist analyses have argued that the bureaucratic organizational form, the main form of hierarchy in at least Fordist economies, while appearing to be gender-neutral is, in fact, deeply inscribed with masculine norms (Acker 1990). The forms of social theory most closely tied with an analysis of political economy—neoclassical economists, Marx, Weber, Durkheim, economic sociology, institutional economic, institutional analysis—take part in crucial debates over which of the three bases tend to be most prevalent in particular periods and types of capitalism. Beside these debates, the analyses put forward from feminist, Foucauldian, postmodern, and different ethical school perspectives contribute to debates around the substantive meaning of these three bases of organization for peoples' work lives. So, for instance, Foucauldians may have something useful to say on how trust at work, for instance within a mentoring system, may actually function as part of a wider process of disciplinary domination in society (Covaleski et al. 1998).

Theme 2: Structure and Agency

The structure–agency debate is one of the key fault-lines that runs through discussions of social theory. Layder (1994: 4), who makes one of the most lucid contributions to this debate, argues that the debate 'concentrates on the question of how creativity and constraint are related through social activity—how can we explain their co-existence'. Substantive schools of social theory are often portrayed as more closely aligned to one or the other of the poles of structure or agency—as placing greater emphasis either on the potential for the agency of the individual actor (whether an individual person, or an organization such as a firm or a trade union), or on the constraints imposed on actors by the structures within which they act (for instance, by a bureaucracy for an individual employee). As Reed (1996) argues, within the specific terrain of social theories' analyses of work, the structure–agency fault line often emerges most clearly between a concept of organization as a determinate structure and a concept of organizing as an ongoing process in which individual agency is crucial. It has been common to place some schools of social theory as largely oriented towards the structure side of the divide. Weber, especially when placed next to his metaphor of an 'iron cage' of rationality, often emerges as an ideal candidate for such categorization. Marx has also often suffered a similar fate. Contingency theory, which as Haveman and Khaire (Chapter 10) on organizational structure argue, is the foundation stone of institutional analysis, has also been criticized for its overemphasis on structure, and its effective denial of a conceptual space for agency. On the other hand, a key criticism put forward of some postmodernist literature has been that, by highlighting the scope for creative agency, for instance in terms of identity-creation, it loses sight of wider structuring forces of society.

Such categorizations appear easy, but a careful analysis suggests that they may arise too readily. Consider, for instance, that it has been argued that the idea of Weber's iron cage metaphor rests on a mistranslation of his original German: 'ein stahlhartes Gehause'. Sayer (1991) and Smart (1999) argue that a more metaphorically appropriate translation of this might be 'a [steel] shell on a snail's back' which has intimations of both constraint and subjective experience related to everyday life—factors with which, they argue, Weber was centrally concerned (see also Baehr 2001). With its potential reference to subjectivity this metaphor now appears less clearly aligned to the structure-side of the structure–agency fault-line. Consider also a famous quotation from Marx ([1859]1954: ch. 1):

> Men make their own history, but they do not make it as they please; they do not make it under circumstances of their own choosing, but under circumstances existing already, given and transmitted from the past.

Such a clear acknowledgement by Marx of the structure–agency tension within social analysis should make us pause for reflection before simply labeling Marxism as crippled by an overemphasis on the structures of society and work.

In short, it appears that much of the substantive concerns of social theorists covered in this book can inform analysis at the level of both structure and agency. Problems may, of course, emerge in terms of a loss of conceptual space for structure or agency in how individual studies are conducted within a particular tradition of social theory. But it appears problematic to trace the root of the problem back to the social theory itself without careful analysis. As Ritzer puts it (1996: 650):

> To be avoided at all costs is the simple identification of a theory or a theorist with specific levels of social analysis. . . . It often does them [social theorists] an injustice simply to equate the breadth of their work with one or more levels [of analysis].

Thus, while it may be easy to tar contingency theory, for example, with the brush of structuralism, it is also the case that scholarship within the contingency theory tradition has given rise to the concept of 'strategic choice' (Child 1972), in which structural constraints are acknowledged, but space is also ceded for the agency of actors within these constraints. It is notable, indeed, that the many attempts to build a conceptual bridge across the structure–agency fault-line appear in themselves quite compatible with a range of social theory. The concepts of strategic choice, structuration (Giddens 1984), habitus and field (Bourdieu 1984), micro- and macro-coupling and decoupling (Goffman 1990), the tactics and strategies of everyday life (de Certeau 1984), and the idea of embeddedness (Granovetter 1985) have little which, intrinsically, stand in the way of their use by scholars from a range of theoretical traditions.

The embeddedness of institutions and behavior serves as a good example of a potential bridging theme across theoretical traditions. The concept of embeddedness—introduced, it is worth noting, by Granovetter (1985) specifically in the context of economic sociology as opposed to social theory in general—has value in two core respects. The first is ontological. Is human behavior determined by the structure in which it exists or is it a matter of free choice? Saying that behavior is embedded helps us move beyond this stark dualism: people are embedded in sets of institutions, each of which will help to shape how they think and act, but different institutions will have different, and possibly conflicting, sets of influences. Moreover, being embedded in an institution does not mean being its creature. People have choice, but how they exercise it, and indeed more fundamentally how they know what choices they have, depends on their social context.

Words such as 'determine' and 'shape' are often used quite loosely. There has been much debate as to how to render them more exact. At one time in Marxian circles, for example, the idea of 'determination in the last instance' was fashionable. What it meant was defined variously, and its vagueness was probably part of its appeal. But the broad idea was that institutions under capitalism have a degree of autonomy but that ultimately, 'in the last instance', their freedom is constrained by certain iron requirements of the capitalist mode of production. Though what the last instance in fact constituted was never clearly explained, the basic idea was sound: institutions shape behavior not by fixing exactly what people do but by establishing boundaries and limits. Just how rigid these limits are is a matter of difference between social theories. Orthodox Marxism would insist that they are hard constraints that stem from the requirements of the mode of production. A Durkheimian study of culture (see Chapter 4) would generally see cultures as more variable and changing, though the idea of culture must also claim, if it is to claim anything at all, that collective cultures do exert definite influences on how people behave.

The second contribution of the idea of embeddedness is epistemological. How do we establish the truth of a proposition? How in particular do we move beyond two extreme positions about social knowledge? The first is absolutist, which sees knowledge as certain and universal. The second is relativist, saying that what is known depends on the viewpoint of the observer. Much social science has disputed the first position, a line of argument given renewed force by interest in the work of Foucault (see Chapter 6) and others who criticize the certainties and 'grand narratives' of Enlightenment thought. But does this end up in pure relativism? In our view, some Foucault-inspired work does tend strongly in this direction. But this need not be the case. Saying that knowledge is socially shaped is not the same as saying that it is wholly a matter of choice or construction. Notions of embeddedness help us ask why particular groups define the world in certain ways and why they pursue certain forms of knowledge. New technologies, for example, are invented, not through an autonomous world of science generating ideas independently, but by attempts to resolve particular concrete problems as they arise at particular times and places.

Theme 3: Assumptions about Human Nature

As Grint (1998) has argued, there are a number of social theories that operate with an implicit assumption that human nature has a particular character. Here, we can point to important elements of Marx's key concept of alienation under capitalism as resting on the assumption that mankind's 'species being' resides in the sphere of labor. For Marx, there is an implicit image of the human as essentially *homo faber*. Humans find (and lose) themselves through labor. Against this, we have the neoclassical economics assumption of human nature as centering on the individual, self-interested, rational economic agent, or *homo economicus*.[2] Arguably, the (contested) feminist concept of patriarchy also rests on an assumption that half of the male population seeks to dominate women in the various spheres of social life. Going further, the human relations school, which has a number of close intellectual links with Durkheim's work, can be seen as resting on an assumption of *homo gregarious*. Here there is an emphasis on the essential sociality of humans. In the workplace context, human relations scholars followed this through to emphasize the importance of work groups and leadership behaviors.

Two points are worth emphasizing about paradigmatic assumptions about human nature. First, it is useful for these implicit assumptions to be made explicit. Core assumptions should always be examined in the clear light of day. Second, while we do not seek to suggest that human nature is 'a blank slate' (Pinker 2002), we think it appropriate to highlight the overwhelming evidence from a wide range of studies, both in and outside the workplace, that social context can and does have a very strong influence on human action and meaning-creation. For instance, we can point to studies which show that the nature and legitimacy of 'cheating' at work is centrally related to the workplace context (Browne 1973; Mars 1982: Clarke et al. 1994). Thus, overly bold assumptions about human nature run the clear risk of assuming as given what is in fact created.

[2] Williamson, founder of transaction cost economics, goes even further in assuming that individuals are 'self-seeking with guile'. A number of commentators have labelled this assumption as neo-Hobbesian (Bowles 1985; Marginson 1993)—recalling Hobbes' political–philosophical justification of the state being based on the assumption that left to themselves, essentially self-seeking individuals would exist in a permanent war of all against all.

Theme 4: Does a Social Theory Prioritize Work as the Core Domain of Society, and How Does it Conceptualize the Linkages between Work and Other Domains of Social Life?

A core issue for understanding a social theory's contribution to the analysis of work is whether the theory's understanding of work is fundamental to the theory itself, or whether work shares the stage with other life domains or is even theoretically marginalized as a social phenomenon. Does a theory say that there is something specifically relevant and unique about the sphere of work in comparison to other spheres of social activity—or does it present a general model of social behavior that can be applied to the domain of work like any other social domain? Within the approaches of Marx, Weber, and Durkheim, the three key analysts of emergent capitalism, there is a tendency to place an analysis of work as central to the whole social theory. The Marxian tradition is perhaps the clearest in its statement that social relations within the arena of production have a distinct quality compared to relations in other spheres—because of what is seen as the essentially exploitative and alienating nature of employment in capitalism. For Weber, the key tragedy of capitalist modernity is that while bureaucracies bring heightened efficiency, they also create an arena of arid, impersonal, formal rationality for people to work in. Durkheim was less pessimistic about the nature of society being created by changes in the nature of production under capitalism. He saw the possibility of societies cohering not despite the heightened division of labor within production, but *because* of it. What he termed 'organic solidarity' would emerge through people seeing their mutual interdependence within this heightened division of labor.

There are different strands of thought within feminist scholarship on how far work is central to understanding gender relations in society. Broadly, there are feminist schools that put different emphasis on the relations of *reproduction* and on the relations of *production* in understanding patterns of gender inequality in societies. Within feminist scholarship this debate revolves around how to understand the relationship between patriarchy and capitalism—as Heidi Gottfried's views (Chapter 5) in this book so ably bring out. Foucauldian analysis also suggests systemic linkages between the arena of work and other arenas. Foucault's famous statement (1979: 228) that 'prisons resemble factories, schools, barracks, hospitals which all resemble prisons' is clearly relevant here—but notice that there is also a deliberate avoidance of prioritizing the sphere of production over other spheres.

All these traditions of social theory, then, involve to an important degree an analysis of systemic linkages (Stone 1998) between the arena of work and other social arenas. Institutional analysis, by contrast, concerns itself solely with analyzing the arena of work, and does not seek to draw out ideas of systemic linkages between this and other arenas. Neoclassical economics explicitly denies the idea of the distinctive nature of work relations, assuming that all forms of economic exchange, whether in production or consumption, are of equal status and type. At the furthest extreme from the Marxian assumption of the centrality of production relations, are strands of postmodern thought which emphasize the centrality of relations of *consumption* for understanding the core nature of society. A good example of this approach is Baudrillard's argument (1970) that the central tragedy of contemporary society lies in individuals' search for 'distinction' from each other in the sign-values or meanings that are ascribed to consumption goods and services.

Theme 5: How Far Does a Theory Prioritize Social Order or Social Conflict at Work?

Dahrendorf (1959) highlighted what he saw as a key distinction among social theories—those that tended either to emphasize conflict or to emphasize order as central to the nature of contemporary society. A similar distinction can be applied when looking at the application of social theories to the arena of work. Again, it is easy to point to Marxian social theory as an exemplar of one extreme position here. Marx's overall analysis was underpinned by the adoption of Hegel's idea of society being driven forward by dialectical clashes between 'theses' and their 'antitheses'. Within the sphere of capitalist production, this dialectical tension was manifest in the essential clash of interests between employers and employees. This emphasis led to a considerable degree of criticism that this social theory was inadequate because it could not deal with the 'order' that seemed to prevail in very many workplaces. This, in turn, has led to a number of attempts by Marxian scholars to theorize why social order at work appears so common (Burawoy 1979). A similar trajectory can be seen within feminist scholarship, where an early emphasis on essential conflicts of interests between men and women within the sphere of work (Walby 1986) has been followed by attempts to understand why women have often acted in ways which stabilize, rather than challenge, the nature of gender relations at work.

Social theories that have been identified as emphasizing social order, both within and outside the arena of work, are the Durkheimian school, neoclassical economics, and contingency theory. With regard to Durkheim, Fox (1974) has argued that there is an essential unitarism to his analysis of work—an assumption that there is a fundamental harmony of interests between the employer and the employee. Chapter 4 by James Lincoln and Didier Guillot, however, suggests that a Durkheimian analysis of organizational culture can also allow an understanding of subcultural conflict as well as order. Within neoclassical economics the pivotal concept of equilibrium shows an emphasis on an essential tendency towards order, while in contingency theory a similar role is played by the concept of 'fit' between an organization and its environment. Taking the pluralist school of industrial relations scholarship as an example of institutional analysis, Ackers and Wilkinson (2003) raise a further important issue, however. The union bargaining literature within this school not only highlights conflict but also emphasizes that such conflict, if appropriately institutionalized (through collective bargaining) could be *functional* for social order within production and more generally within society (Fox 1966). In other words, some forms of conflict can also be seen as informing social order.

While many schools of social theory have attempted to allow space for an analysis of both conflict and order within the arena of work, perhaps the key question revolves around how the relationship between the two is conceptualized. Take the case of economic sociology, which claims as a key contribution its ability to allow a nuanced analysis of all three bases of economic action—power, market, and norms. It may be simple to show that some *conflict* exists in the operation of hierarchical power within organizations, and to highlight the integrative qualities of social norms towards consensus and social *order*. Key substantive questions to resolve, however, revolve around the *relationship* between conflict and order in relation to the three bases—in this case, between conflict in the operation of hierarchy and order in the operation of norms.

Theme 6: Does a Theory Suggest that Work in Contemporary Capitalism Civilizes or Degrades?

Hirschman (1982) offers an important examination of a range of social theories' analyses of capitalism. He entitled this piece: 'Rival interpretations of market society: civilizing, destructive, or feeble?' Here we revisit this question—in terms of how different social theories suggest that work in contemporary capitalism tends to either civilize or degrade people (see also Hodson 2001). We realize that the question itself begs an initial question about the meaning of 'civilizing' and 'degrading', and in the discussion below we sketch how different social theories implicitly approach this first-order question. For Marx, capitalism per se worked against human as *homo faber* and so to this degree necessarily degraded people's essential humanity. Contemporary scholarship in this tradition has tended to argue that there are also specifically contemporary currents in employment that further degrade people. Much of this is elegantly summarized by Richard Hyman (Chapter 2). Here we can point to the emphasis within this literature of the rise of work intensification (Bunting 2004) and of the increased commodification of emotional labor in contemporary capitalism (Hochschild 1983). Within a Weberian tradition, the key way to address the question of whether contemporary work civilizes or degrades is to look to discussions of post-Fordism and the postbureaucratic organization (Heckscher and Donnellon 1994), for it was the bureaucratic form that Weber saw as denying people's humanity—their value systems or value rationality—in its emphasis of impersonal formal rationality. The last two decades has seen a great deal of scholarship suggesting that the bureaucratic organizational form was tied to an overall Fordist form of economy, and that postbureaucratic forms are more prevalent in contemporary post-Fordist economies (Offe 1985; Lash and Urry 1987; Castells 1996). While this suggests a movement away from degradation, a key question still to be fully debated concerns exactly how 'new' are new organizational forms and are postbureaucratic organizational forms really less degrading? To take the examples of two central business trends of the last two decades, the question becomes—how far do Business Process Reengineering and Total Quality Management actually represent a reformulation rather than an abandonment of bureaucratic logic?

For the Durkheimian tradition the way to approach this question is to consider whether contemporary work tends to promote organic solidarity or whether it promotes *anomie*—the Durkheimian concept of an individual cut adrift from collective, social, and moral embeddedness. Sennett's book (1998), *The Corrosion of Character: Personal Consequences of Work in the New Capitalism,* is an examination of these very questions. His answer is largely a pessimistic one—he sees anomie as rising in contemporary workplaces in which flexibility has become the key defining feature. Individuals are shown as losing all sense of interdependence, as cut adrift from meaningful embeddedness both within and without the workplace because of the flexibility demanded within work. Other scholars, not necessarily from the Durkheimian tradition, have highlighted a rise in individualism in many Western societies (Bauman 2001; Beck and Beck-Gersheim 2001), but in these analyses the role ascribed to contemporary work in driving this increased individualism is not always clear. Again important debates are yet to be resolved here. On the one hand, we can point to increased individualization of payment and reward systems within contemporary work (Bacon and Storey 2000) but, on the other, there is also a rise in adoption of an integrative division of labor in the form of teamwork (Proctor and Mueller 2000).

Postmodernist scholars, in contrast, have tended to eschew the guiding question of this subsection. Postmodernist analysis has tended to emphasize the plasticity of identity creation and human nature and to highlight the dangers of scholarship informed by 'modernist metanarratives'. Through this lens, the very question of whether contemporary work civilizes or degrades carries with it implicit modernist assumptions that civilizing and degrading are meaningful concepts. There is no large story, no metanarrative, to be meaningfully told on this flawed subject. By contrast, the approach of the neoclassical economics school to the question is to sidestep the issue of civilizing versus degrading to concentrate on the utilitarian question of whether work allows people to meet higher or lower utility functions of their needs. Here, the easy approach is to point to rising income levels to show that people are able to meet more of their material needs. Two important riders need to be made here, however. One is that this assumes that material needs have a higher utility than the needs that people have regarding the process of work—for instance, the utility that people gain from having discretion in their work. The evidence on how contemporary work has an impact on the utility functions regarding work is much less clear-cut. Second, even with the first rider addressed, this utilitarian approach rests on an assumption of the essential commensurability of money with all forms of human action. Money and human action are on equal planes; human action can be commodified without qualm. If the market relations, economic exchanges, extend further and further into human behavior, for instance in the rise of sex tourism, this is not an issue that can be of concern within this school. As Radin (1996: 122) argues, however, 'something important to humanity is lost if market rhetoric becomes... the sole rhetoric of human affairs'. A key part of a debate on what 'civilizing' means, of what personhood means, is to consider where limits on the commodification of human action (within and without work) should lie. Readers can find further contributions to this important issue within two chapters in this book—Stephen Frenkel on globalization (Chapter 14) and Karen Legge on examination of ethics and work (Chapter 11). Indeed, the latter chapter makes a significant contribution to how different schools of ethical analysis allow us to understand how far the contemporary economy is a moral economy. We recommend interested readers to turn to that chapter.[3]

Returning to the original Albert Hirschman article that informs this discussion, it is worth recalling his conclusion—that social theory should allow for an understanding of ways in which a market society might be *simultaneously* a civilizing and degrading force—and his suggestion for future social theorizing (1982: 1483): 'after so many failed prophecies, is it not in the interest of social science to embrace complexity, be it at some sacrifice of its claim to predictive powers'. While the word 'contradiction' might stand better than 'complexity' here, the implications of the statement are important. For our purposes, the key outstanding question becomes how far different social theories open up an understanding of the ways in which contemporary work may *simultaneously* civilize and degrade people.

4. Integration or Incompatibility?

At the beginning of our social theory metanalysis, we briefly sketched the dimensions that other writers have used in their analyses. Here we end the discussion by reflecting upon the sorts of conclusions that are formed in the metanalysis literature on theories of work. Three broad approaches can be identified. One, exemplified by George Ritzer, is to seek to use this metanalysis to move social theory to a more *integrated* paradigm. Such concerns are prompted by an awareness that too much social analysis involves a dialogue of the deaf, with scholars from different traditions talking past, rather than to, each other. A second major approach is exemplified by Burrell and Morgan (1979) who use their metanalysis to effectively highlight crucial differences in assumptions between theories—differences which tend to make many of the theories fundamentally incompatible with each other. Such an approach is prompted

[3] A chapter on ethics, we would argue, is essential to any overview of social theories. That is, it is important for scholars to take seriously Bauman's arguments (1989) about how 'most sociological narratives do without reference to morality'. A related way of thinking about this issue is to consider how far the social theories prioritize conceptualizing the *means* of work without reference to the *ends* of work—in ways analogous to the way in which bureaucracy prioritizes means over ends (reaching its ultimate expression, as Bauman brilliantly shows, in the Nazi bureaucrat's credo, 'I was following orders').

by a concern that too little social analysis goes back to consider the core assumptions of theoretical approaches. A final major approach is exemplified by later work by Morgan (1997). This approach, developed so that practitioners can make more use of social theory, argues that it is appropriate for practitioners to pick and choose from the different social theories that have been laid out within the metanalysis. Morgan thus lays out an array of metaphors of organizations within different social theories, and concludes his book by suggesting that having understood these different metaphors and their different assumptions, managers should be able usefully and creatively to pick and choose between metaphors according to the context and the problem facing them. As Morgan (1997: 429) himself admits, this approach 'has a distinctly postmodern flavor'—a reference to the postmodern position that knowledge cannot be integrated, and we, therefore, should be playful in our creation of pastiches of knowledge forms. A clash of assumptions between social theories does not matter; indeed such a clash can even be celebrated.

Our approach is rather different from these three. We have sketched out what we regard as six important questions/dimensions. Within a given set of social theories there may be crucial differences in answering some of these questions, while for other questions there can be a great deal of consensus. We have also highlighted that, even within a given theoretical tradition, there can often be a range of answers to the questions. These points bring us back to a recurring motif in our discussion—the importance of context. In short, more integration between social theories, more dialogue between them, may or may not be useful depending on the specific issue being addressed—because differing substantive issues being investigated will tend to suggest different dimensions as centrally salient. Not all dimensions will be centrally relevant in the examination of a given topic. Consider for instance the chapters in this book focusing on different substantive issues, rather than theoretical traditions per se—the chapters on globalization, technology, identity, and professions. In these chapters our understanding of some (but not all) important issues is shown to have been moved forward by a de facto integration among different theoretical traditions. To take two examples, in the chapter on professions, Keith Macdonald makes a strong argument (Chapter 13) that the concept of the professional project is central to an adequate understanding of professions, and he lays out clearly how a range of insights from different theoretical traditions have, in practice, informed this analytical lens. Note also that this is not part of a utopian search for theoretical integration, for he also clearly shows how other social theory traditions have tended *not* to be helpful in the development of this concept.

The second example comes from Jacques Bélanger (Chapter 12) on technology and work. In his discussion of the role of technology in call center work, Belanger shows how an adequate analysis of this issue needs to be informed by three concepts deriving from different theoretical traditions—the concept of the Panopticon, the centrality of labor agency within the labor process, and the concept of the customer-oriented bureaucracy. The first of these concepts comes from Foucault, the second derives from the Marxian labor process tradition, and the third from an attempt to update Weberian conceptualizations of ideal types of work organization. Integration of elements of social theories, then, can take forward our understanding of the world of work. Indeed, it is tempting to see economic sociology as occupying a strong position to take forward potential areas of integration. But much detailed analysis of specific issues concerning work needs to be done before that potential is fulfilled.

In short, in view of the variations in social theories across the dimensions that we have identified, an integrated theory is unlikely unless it is one that is so bland as to empty analysis of excitement and controversy. But constructive engagement from different perspectives is essential. We hope that this book stimulates such engagement.

References

Acker, J. (1990). 'Hierarchies, Jobs, Bodies: A Theory of Gendered Organizations', *Gender and Society*, 4(2): 139–58.

Ackers, P. and Wilkinson, A. (ed.) (2003). *Understanding Work and Employment*. Oxford: Oxford University Press.

Alchian, A. and Demsetz, H. (1972). 'Production, Information Costs and Economic Organization', *American Economic Review*, 62: 777–95.

Bacon, N. and Storey, J.(2000). 'New Employee Relations Strategies in Britain: Towards Individualism or Partnership', *British Journal of Industrial Relations*, 38(3): 407–28.

Baehr, P. (2001). 'The "Iron Cage" and the "Shell as Hard as Steel": Parsons, Weber and the *stahlartes gehause* Metaphor in the *Protestant Ethic and the Spirit of Capitalism*', *History and Theory*, 40: 153–69.

Baudrillard, J. (1970). *Consumer Society*. Paris: Gallimard.

Bauman, Z. (1989). *Modernity and the Holocaust*. Cambridge: Polity Press.

—— (2001). 'Foreword', in U. Beck and E. Beck-Gernsheim (eds.), *Individualization*. London: Sage.

Beck, U. and Beck-Gernsheim, E. (2001). *Individualization*. London: Sage.

Bourdieu, P. (1984). *Distinctions: A Social Critique of the Judgement of Taste*. Cambridge: Cambridge University Press.

Bowles, S. (1985). 'The Production Process in a Competitive Economy: Walrasian, noe-Hobbesian and Marxian Models', *American Economic Review*, 75: 16–36.

Browne, J. (1973). *The Used-Car Game*. Lexington: Lexington Books.

Bunting, M. (2004). *Willing Slaves*. London: HarperCollins.

Burawoy, M. (1979). *Manufacturing Consent*. Chicago, IL: University of Chicago Press.

Burrell, G. and Morgan, G. (1979). *Sociological Paradigms*. London: Heinemann.

Castells, M. (1996.) *The Rise of the Network Society*. Cambridge, MA: Blackwell.

Child, J. (1972). 'Organizational Structure, Environment and Performance: The Role of Strategic Choice', *Sociology*, 6: 1–22.

Clarke, M., Smith, D., and McConville, M. (1994). *Slippery Customers: Estate Agents, the Public and Regulation*. London: Blackstone.

Covaleski, M. A., Dirsmith, M. W., and Heian, J. B. (1998) 'The Calculated and the Avowed: Techniques of Discipline and Struggles Over Identity in Big Six Public Accounting Firms', *Administrative Science Quarterly*, 43(2): 293–327.

Dahrendorf, R. (1959). *Class and Class Conflict in Industrial Society*. London: Routledge.

De Certeau, M. (1984). *The Practice of Everyday Life*. London: University of California Press.

Foucault, M. (1979). *Discipline and Punish*. London: Penguin.

Fox, A. (1966). *Industrial Sociology and Industrial Relations*, Donovan Commission Research paper 3. London: HMSO.

—— (1974). *Beyond Contract: Work, Power and Trust Relations*. London: Faber.

Giddens, A. (1971). *Capitalism and Modern Social Theory*. Cambridge: Cambridge University Press.

—— (1984). *The Constitution of Society: Outline of the Theory of Structuration*. Cambridge: Polity Press.

Goffman, E. (1990). *The Presentation of Self in Everyday Life*. London: Penguin.

Granovetter, M. (1985). 'Economic Action and Social Structure: The Problem of Embeddedness', *American Journal of Sociology*, 91: 481–510.

Grint, K. (1998). *The Sociology of Work*. Cambridge: Polity Press.

Heckscher, C. and Donnellon, A. (eds.) (1994). *The Post-Bureaucratic Organization*. Thousand Oaks, CA: Sage.

Hirschman, A. (1982). 'Rival Interpretations of Market Society: Civilizing, Destructive, or Feeble?' *Journal of Economic Literature*, 20: 1463–84.

Hochschild, A. (1983). *The Managed Heart*. London: University of California Press.

Hodson, R. (2001). *Dignity at Work*. Cambridge: Cambridge University Press.

—— and Sullivan, T. (2001). *The Social Organization of Work*. New York: Wadsworth.

Krahn, H. J. and Lowe, G. S. (1998). *Work, Industry, and Canadian Society*, 3rd edn. Toronto: ITP Nelson Canada.

Lash, S. and Urry, J. (1987). *The End of Organized Capitalism*. Cambridge: Polity Press.
Layder, D. (1994). *Understanding Social Theory*. London: Sage.
Lukes, S. (1974). *Power: A Radical View*. London: Macmillan.
Marginson, P. (1993). 'Power and Efficiency in the Firm', in C. Pitelis (ed.), *Transaction Costs, Markets and Hierarchies*. Cambridge: Cambridge University Press.
Mars, G. (1982). *Cheats at Work: An Anthropology of Workplace Crime*. London: Allen & Unwin.
Marsden, R. (1999). *The Nature of Capital*. London: Routledge.
Marx, K. ([1859] 1954). *The Eighteenth Brumaire of Louis Bonaparte*. London: Progress.
Morgan, G. (1997). *Images of Organization*. London: Sage.
Offe, C. (1985). *Disorganized Capitalism*. Cambridge: Polity Press.
Ouchi, W. (1979). 'A Conceptual Framework for the Design of Organizational Control Mechanisms', *Management Science*, 25: 833–48.
Pinker, S. (2002). *The Blank Slate: The Modern Denial of Human Nature*. London: Allen Lane.
Powell, W. (1990). 'Neither Market Nor Hierarchy', *Research in Organizational Behavior*, 12: 295–336.
Proctor, S. and Mueller, F. (ed.) (2000). *Teamworking*. Basingstoke: Macmillan.
Radin, M. (1996). *Contested Commodities*. Cambridge, MA: Harvard University Press.
Ritzer, G. (1996). *Modern Sociological Theory*. New York: McGraw-Hill.
—— and Smart, B. (2001). *Handbook of Social Theory*. London: Sage.
Reed, M. (1996). 'Organizational Theorizing', in S. Clegg, C. Hardy, and W. Nord (eds.), *Handbook of Organization Studies*. London: Sage.
Rothman, R. A. (1998). *Working: Sociological Perspectives*, 2nd edn. Upper Saddle River, NJ: Prentice-Hall.
Samuelson, P. A. (1951). 'Economic Theory and Wages', in D. M. Wright (ed.), *The Impact of the Union*. New York: Harcourt, Brace.
Sayer, D. (1991). *Capitalism and Modernity*, London: Routledge.
Sennett, R. (1998). *The Corrosion of Character: Personal Consequences of Work in the New Capitalism*. London: W. W. Norton.
Smart, B. (1999). 'Introduction', in B. Smart (ed.) *Resisting McDonaldization*, London: Sage.
Stone, R. (ed.) (1998). *Key Sociological Thinkers*. Basingstoke: Macmillan.
Thompson, P. and McHugh, D. (2002). *Work Organizations*. Basingstoke: Palgrave.
Walby, S. (1986). *Patriarchy at Work*. Cambridge: Polity Press.
Watson, T. J. (2001). *Sociology, Work and Industry*, 4th edn. London: Routledge.
Williamson, O. E. (1993). 'Calculativeness, Trust and Economic Organisation', *Journal of Law and Economics*, 36: 453–86.

2

Marxist Thought and the Analysis of Work

Richard Hyman

Marx was anything but a detached academic observer of the world of work: he was passionately engaged in the struggles of the emergent labor movements within, and against, the new capitalist society in which wage-labor was becoming the dominant form of work. As he famously declared, the task was not only to interpret the world but to change it. The unity of theory and practice was to be a fundamental maxim of all variants of Marxism—of which there were many—and hence intellectual and political controversies were intermingled. The writings by, and about, Marx are voluminous. In a short overview it would be impossible to reference every argument; the reader is advised to seek more detailed information elsewhere (for example, Bottomore and Rubel 1956; Lichtheim 1961; Tucker 1961; Giddens 1971; McLellan 1971; Howard and King 1976). Like most great thinkers of the nineteenth century, he aspired to a comprehensive understanding of all areas of social life. Few sociologists writing about work—at least if their writings are in any way interesting—can have failed to be influenced in some degree by ideas and interpretations derived from Marx. But this chapter does not aspire to offer a comprehensive survey of such influences. Any brief discussion of the relevance of Marx to the analysis of work is bound to be selective.

According to one biographer (Wheen 1999: 5), 'Karl Marx was a philosopher, a historian, an economist, a linguist, a literary critic and a revolutionist'. This catalogue does not include sociology; an earlier analyst (Lefebvre 1968: 22) asserted that 'Marx is not a sociologist', insisting however that 'there is a sociology in Marx'. Marx was a social theorist (had the term social scientist existed in English in his lifetime he might well have embraced it), but at the same time a political activist, and neither aspect of his achievements (and perhaps his failures) can be understood in isolation from the other.

It is common to speak of 'Marxism'. The label might imply an integrated, consistent, and systematic body of thought. Many of Marx's followers (as well, often, as his detractors) assumed that such an integrated theoretical system existed. Were that the case, it would be easy to outline the implications of Marxist thought for the analysis of work and to identify (according to tastes) its strengths and weaknesses. Unfortunately, exploring Marxist thought involves many difficulties. 'Moi, je ne suis pas marxiste,' was the famous and irritated rejoinder by Marx to French admirers towards the end of his life.[1] There is no unambiguous body of thought called Marxism; and most of those who have called themselves Marxists have fashioned a selective vision which has matched their own circumstances and objectives. The meaning of Marxism varies, often markedly, according to time, place, and political affiliation.

Why is this? First, uniquely among social theorists, Marx's theories inspired a mass movement. They became the dominant point of reference for most European social-democratic parties in the late nineteenth century, were firmly embraced by the Russian Bolsheviks, and after the 1917 revolutions were inscribed in the programs of the communist parties created around the world. As different political factions fought for supremacy, so the heritage of Marx became an object of contest. All too often, 'Marxism' became ossified as dogma: an ironical fate for a theorist for whom *criticism*—initially of idealist political philosophy, subsequently of bourgeois political economy—was a driving principle of thought. In the twentieth-century states which tendentiously claimed Marx as their inspiration, to be a heretic at the wrong time and in the wrong place could bring imprisonment or even death—not a risk faced by those with unorthodox interpretations of Durkheim or Weber.

Marx's written output was immense. The 'official' communist publication of an English edition of the collected works of Marx and his collaborator Friedrich Engels, which commenced in 1975, encompasses fifty volumes (forty-nine of which had appeared when this chapter was written). In the first volume the editors wrote that Marx and Engels 'were the authors of an integrated body of philosophical, economic and social–political views, the ideology of communism . . . '. This is a travesty of the truth. One may debate whether their writings constituted an ideology

[1] For a critical note on the misuse of this quotation see Draper 1978: 5–11.

(this is partly a question of definition) and, more importantly, whether the orthodox communist parties of the latter twentieth century were recognizably Marxist in their theory or practice. Some have questioned how far Engels (and writers like the 'father of Russian Marxism', Plekhanov)—who in the years after Marx died in 1883 did much to 'systematize' his theories in a manner which suppressed many of their complexities—really worked on the same wavelength. One writer (Bender 1975) has referred to a 'betrayal of Marx' initiated by Engels and continued by Lenin and his successors. A similar argument has been developed more recently by Desai (2002). On the specific issue of the interaction of productive systems, managerial authority, and worker subordination, Avineri (1968: 235–8) has suggested that Engels imposed a form of technological determinism on the much more complex conceptions of Marx himself. In any event, there is a vast literature giving many different interpretations of 'what Marx really meant'.

Born in 1818, Marx lived through an epoch of immense social, economic, and political transformation. After beginning a law degree in Bonn he moved to Berlin and Jena to study philosophy, joining the iconoclastic 'Young Hegelian' circle. In 1843 his political radicalism took him into exile in Paris and Brussels; after returning briefly to Germany he moved again to France, then settled in England in 1849. His intensive studies of political economy in the British Museum ran in parallel with his vehement engagement with the fevered controversies of European revolutionaries, particularly after the formation of the 'First International' in 1864. Three years afterwards the first volume of his magnum opus, *Das Kapital*, was published. A second volume appeared just after Marx died and a third, far from complete, a decade later. It is now clear that this massive enterprise was only the first of six projected studies, which were to encompass not only capital but landed property, wage labor, the state, international trade, and the world market (Nicolaus 1973: 53–5). This was almost certainly an impossible objective; in any case Marx suffered serious illness from the early 1970s and never accomplished more than a fraction of his intellectual ambitions. But he left volumes of unpublished notebooks, a mass of correspondence, many years of newspaper articles, and a range of publications ranging from complex theoretical explorations to heated polemics.

As an activist striving to make sense of revolutionary events, Marx was never static in his theories: whether or not one accepts a dichotomy between a 'young Marx' and an old, there were certainly shifts in perspective which have allowed posterity to erect many different models of

'Marxism'. His analysis evolved and his emphases varied, partly according to the issues addressed, partly according to the nature of immediate political and polemical debates, partly because he was living through such revolutionary times. Some of his most quoted arguments were in works designed to rally mass support, such as the *Manifesto of the Communist Party* written with Engels in 1848; for dramatic effect, many of the nuances of analysis which he provided elsewhere were omitted. As a combatant in the internecine struggles of emigré revolutionaries, Marx also presented many of his ideas in letters and pamphlets, typically marked by the enthusiasm (and ill temper) of the moment. More than a century later, it is often impossible to be confident which judgments were hasty and ephemeral, which were more soundly considered.

For the modern social theorist another crucial problem is that Marx's most powerful ideas involved a high level of abstraction. Of his massive intellectual project, what he came closest to completing was his study of the dynamics of the production and exchange of value within capitalism, often conceptualized in terms barely comprehensible to English-speaking empiricists. Hence as Nichols and Beynon have pointed out (1977: viii), 'much of what passes for "theory" (even Marxist theory) fails to connect with the lives that people lead'. To move from this abstract focus to exploring the concrete realities of work (though this too was certainly of key importance for Marx) involves a shift of several gears. Add to this the fact that capitalist manufacturing was still an emergent system when Marx wrote (in Britain, the 'first industrial nation', the small workshop rather than the factory predominated, while the largest single occupational group comprised domestic servants), and the difficulties of applying his ideas to modern times are considerable. Some disciples have argued that all the key elements of the present can be found in germ in Marx's writings, and he was indeed prescient enough to make this notion not wholly ridiculous; but Marx was not a prophet, and when he did act as such he was often wrong. Moreover, his emphasis on class led him to neglect, or underemphasize, other societal features such as gender or ethnicity which sociologists today would surely highlight. Applying his ideas to the world of work in the twenty-first century allows, and requires, considerable scope for imaginative extrapolation. This means in particular that if Marxism is to be set to work by sociologists today, it must be complemented by theories and insights which are not distinctively Marxist. And the question then arises: do such additions sustain, or undermine, what was integral to Marx's analysis? For example (to take a question to which I will return), is the work of Foucault in principle compatible with

Marxism, a potential source of enrichment, or does it negate Marx's fundamental insights? There can be no innocent answer to such a question.

1. Marx at Work

Given the existence of a variety of possible Marxisms, and the imprecise boundaries between what is and is not Marxist thought, any catalogue of the 'key' elements of Marxist theory is bound to be idiosyncratic. Nevertheless the following themes would be widely regarded as of central importance.

First, Marx was a materialist. He contested the view prevailing within early nineteenth-century German philosophy that ideas, beliefs, and moral values possessed a timeless quality and could be viewed as the driving force of history; on the contrary, he insisted, they were the products of circumstance, of time and place. More fundamentally, he argued that people's practical activity in securing their physical existence—producing food and shelter, caring for children—and the social relationships created through such activities, shaped their ideas and understandings. 'Life is not determined by consciousness, but consciousness by life,' he wrote with Engels in *The German Ideology*; 'consciousness is from the very beginning a social product'.

In its starkest expression, this materialist perspective took the form of *economic determinism*. Many of his writings were determinist in the sense that they stressed the 'external coercive laws' driving human behavior, in ways which seemed to leave little or no space for deliberate choice and influence. This determinism was economic in that the system of property ownership and the organization of production were seen as the causal force behind 'the social, political, and intellectual life process in general'—a relationship at times expressed in the metaphor of 'base' and 'superstructure'. Occasionally Marx's approach seemed to involve, more narrowly, a kind of *technological* determinism: the 'forces' of production (which included not only physical machinery but also the available repertoire of skills and scientific understanding) shaped the more general 'relations' of production. Famously (or notoriously), Marx wrote in *The Poverty of Philosophy* that 'the hand-mill gives you society with the feudal lord; the steam-mill, society with the industrial capitalist'.

Often, however, Marx was far more cautious. Economic (or technological) causation was decisive only 'in the final instance' (as Engels later put it); in any given situation, political, legal, and ideological factors could exert their own autonomous influence. Such a cautious formulation clearly weakens the force of the arguments of some critics that Marx totally neglected the extent to which political institutions or beliefs and values could shape the course of history, but by the same token also weakens the predictive power of the 'materialist conception of history'. Nor did Marx always stress the external coercion of social forces: repeatedly he pointed to the *interaction* between material context and the conscious interventions of social actors. The much quoted opening of *The Eighteenth Brumaire of Louis Bonaparte* insists that 'people make their own history, but they do not make it just as they please; they do not make it under circumstances chosen by themselves, but under circumstances directly encountered, given and transmitted from the past'.

Determinism is qualified in much of Marx's writing by his emphasis on *contradiction*. He insisted that any society—whether local, national, or global—could only be adequately understood as a totality. No area of social life can be properly comprehended in isolation (as is presumed by the creation of demarcated social science disciplines); social phenomena are interrelated, so that work, politics, law, family have to be analyzed in terms of their interconnections. Yet in no way did Marx regard societies as harmoniously integrated systems; on the contrary, institutions inherited from the past could prove 'fetters' inhibiting dynamism elsewhere; while the logic of one set of social relations could be incompatible with those prevailing in another. For example, traditional bonds of hierarchical authority in the political system or the family were completely at odds with the principles of a market society in which buyers and sellers met at least notionally as equals, however unequal in reality their power might be. Indeed the capitalist employer might exert as much, or even more control over the workforce than did the feudal lord; but whereas the latter had often tended to accept some responsibility for the welfare of those subject to his rule, such principles of *noblesse oblige* were less likely to operate in the 'free' labor market where competition drove even well-meaning employers to treat waged workers as disposable resources.

The disjuncture between different institutional elements of nineteenth-century societies was for Marx the key explanation of the revolutionary transformations which preoccupied all social analysts of the time. As the *Communist Manifesto* declared, 'the bourgeoisie cannot exist without constantly revolutionising the instruments of production, and thereby the relations of production, and with them the whole relations of society.... Constant revolutionising of production, uninterrupted disturbance of all social conditions, everlasting uncertainty and agitation distinguish the bourgeois epoch from all earlier ones.... All that is solid melts into air.'

The existence of contradictory forces helped to negate any crude determinism in Marx's analysis: precisely because different social and economic developments pointed in different directions, there was scope for human choice to make a difference in terms of outcomes. It was because Marx identified irresoluble contradictions within the capitalist system which was coming to dominate the world that he predicted its own collapse. Yet here too there was a tension in his analysis: was the transition (perhaps violent) from capitalism to socialism an objective inevitability? At times Marx said precisely this. But in this case, by what logic did Marx endure hardships for much of his life in working for revolution, and why were others subsequently prepared to risk their lives for the cause? Conversely, if the socialist revolution required active mass commitment and skilled political leadership, how could it be considered inevitable? Many (probably most) twentieth-century Marxists were to argue that without effective political intervention by the labor movement (or more specifically, the revolutionary party), capitalist contradictions might lead not to socialism but to new, more barbaric, social and political 'solutions': fascism was one example, and some would see the current brutalities of global capitalism as another. Hence is Marxism really a 'predictive theory' (Edwards 1986; Thompson 1990) whereby analysis of the contradictions of capitalism is inseparable from the scenario of socialist revolution? Undeniably this defines the unity of Marx's own thought and action, at least in many of his works; but there is no logical inconsistency in endorsing much of what Marx wrote as social analyst without embracing Marx as prophet.

2. The Context of Work under 'Modern Industry': Capitalism and Class

A central element in Marxist analysis was the importance of *class*. 'The history of all previously existing society is the history of class struggles,' wrote Marx and Engels in the *Communist Manifesto*.

> Freeman and slave, patrician and plebeian, lord and serf, guild-master and journeyman, in a word, oppressor and oppressed, stood in constant opposition to one another, carried on an uninterrupted, now hidden, now open fight, a fight that each time ended, either in a revolutionary reconstitution of society at large, or in the common ruin of the contending classes.

The distinctive feature of class society in the nineteenth century, in their view, was a weakening of the moral cement which held previous societies together through a reciprocal web of rights and obligations, and a more overt clash of material interests between workers dependent on their wages for their existence and employers whose own success depended on reducing costs and maximizing profits. The transparency of class antagonism would inevitably bring an increasingly concerted and confident resistance which would result in the creation of a new, socialist (or communist—at that time the terms were often interchangeable) society.

What exactly is meant by class? The word itself derives from the census categories applied in ancient Rome; and classification of social groups according to key common attributes has been familiar ever since. Ownership (or lack) of different types of property was always an important criterion, but in precapitalist societies so also were noneconomic attributes of status. Marx (unlike Weber) assumed that within capitalism, the latter would lose their significance; and also that there would be an increasing polarization between 'two great camps': the bourgeoisie who owned and controlled the means of production, and the proletariat who in order to live were obliged to work for wages; intermediate classes would increasingly be subsumed within the one or the other. However we may note ambiguities in his treatment. Despite the vital role of class in his analysis and in his political interventions, Marx never offered a systematic theory. It is an irony that the incomplete third volume of *Capital*, published more than a decade after his death, ends with a chapter 'On Classes' which breaks off after two pages. Yet here Marx speaks of 'wage-laborers, capitalists and landowners' as the 'three big classes of modern society based upon the capitalist mode of production': an interesting contrast to his thesis elsewhere of a polarization into two classes. In other of his writings, when discussing the political dynamics of specific countries, he often stressed the distinctive position of such groups as the peasantry or the petty bourgeoisie, and the different interests of financial and industrial capitalists. Perhaps what unites Marx's approach despite such differences is his insistence that class involves a *relationship*. Societies are not simply hierarchically stratified, which is what many sociologists have meant when using the concept of class; it is the conflicts and alliances between different economic groups which give them a social meaning and identity, bridging the 'objective' and 'subjective' dimensions of class structure.[2]

[2] There is not space in this chapter to discuss historical approaches to social theory at work; but here one should note two very different applications of Marxist analysis to the early formation of the working class in Britain, both stressing the social relationships involved: Foster (1974) and Thompson (1963).

A crucial difference between Marx's approach to class and that of Weber is his emphasis on production as the primary dynamic of social relationships. This is, no doubt, one consideration which has made Marxism attractive to students of work and employment (and, conversely, has encouraged Marxists to focus on this field of research). As was seen above, an important element in his analysis was the thesis that any specific economic system—or mode of production—was constituted by an interaction between the 'forces of production' (which comprised not only technical hardware but also skills and scientific knowledge) and 'relations of production' (for example, patterns of ownership and the division of labor). Class relations were shaped by—but could in turn redefine—this material–institutional matrix. Most famously, Marx as activist insisted that in creating and oppressing a growing class of propertyless workers—proletarians—capitalism was constructing the force that would destroy it. As the *Communist Manifesto* resolutely declared, 'what the bourgeoisie therefore produces, above all, is its own gravediggers. Its fall and the victory of the proletariat are equally inevitable.' The first volume of *Capital* ends with a similarly ringing prediction of the overthrow of capitalism by 'the revolt of the working class, a class constantly increasing in numbers, and trained, united and organized by the very mechanism of the capitalist process of production'. We will return to this core aspect of Marx's work in a later section.[3]

3. The Fetishism of Commodities

For Marx, a defining characteristic of the capitalist mode of production was the predominance of commodity production. What does this mean? That even though, for Marx, production is the basic process in any economic system, under capitalism its conduct is subordinated to the dynamics of market exchange. In all societies of which historical records exist, markets played some role, initially through barter, subsequently also through the medium of money. But before capitalism, many products

[3] As I was completing this chapter I came across a contribution by Gall, who kindly provides a definition of my current position. Readers should be aware that the basis is a one-page handout I prepared for a 20-minute talk. Be that as it may, Gall insists (2003: 318–19) that one of 'three indispensable elements which are missing from Hyman's conceptualization of Marxism' is that 'a social class exists which is the potential "gravedigger" of capitalism'. Let us note that Marx actually wrote not of potential but of inevitability. It is possible to be sceptical of this prophetic core of Marx—and some of the reasons for scepticism are discussed below—while accepting the value and validity of much of the corpus of his work.

were directly consumed by the collective group (extended family, local community) involved in their production, or were directly exchanged for other products (so much flour for so much woollen cloth, for example). Money of course existed from ancient times, but the money economy encompassed only a minor proportion of total productive activity. Capitalism expanded this proportion enormously: market exchange, and market calculation, came to dominate relations of production. And this reversed the causal relationships: previously, a tailor, miller, or blacksmith produced their goods, then took the products to market if there was not an immediate consumer to hand; now, increasingly, the price obtaining in the market determined whether the product would be made at all. And this was also because, under capitalism, the dominant form of production was no longer by independent artisans or farmers who owned their own tools and (in the latter case) land but by wageworkers employed by a capitalist who owned the means of production and whose priority was to achieve a profit on this capital.

Marx distinguished two faces of any product, a distinction fundamental to capitalism. The first was its utility, or use value. This was a quality independent of the economic system: things in every society were made because they were useful (a concept to be understood broadly: art and culture may not be 'useful' in a narrow sense but contribute to human welfare). The second was exchange value (often simply termed value), the price that a product would attain in the market.

While markets, as indicated above, existed in precapitalist societies, production was not normally driven by considerations of the price which a product would fetch as a commodity. But under capitalism, exchange value became more important a factor in driving the economic system than use value. If poor people needed shoes or houses, but could not pay for them, they would not be produced; conversely, luxury commodities with little intrinsic utility would be produced if the rich were willing to pay the price. More than this: increasingly, the measure of any object or activity became its price ticket. From this insight, Marx developed the notion of the 'fetishism of commodities'. A fetish was an object which so-called 'primitive' people constructed and then regarded as a god. For Marx, exactly the same occurred with commodities in capitalist society. A carpenter produces a table, a tailor produces a pair of trousers, but each regards what they produce primarily as the equivalent of the money they will obtain in the market. The social relationship between people with different skills and capacities is turned into a 'fantastic relation between things': so many tables are the equivalent of so many pairs of trousers, as if their price in the market is a reflection of qualities intrinsic to their existence as tables and as trousers, rather than the outcome of far broader social relations of production and hence cumulatively of the activities of those involved in their production and consumption. The market becomes regarded, not as an institution which is socially created, but as a force independent of human intermediation.

4. The Duality of Labor and the Rediscovery of the Labor Process

Classical political economy confronted a puzzle: how can value expand if all products are exchanged at their value, which is how markets are assumed to operate? Many writers before Marx had identified labor as the creative process which generated what would later be called economic growth; yet if workers were paid the value of their labor, where did profits come from? The solution, Marx argued in Volume 1 of *Capital* (as noted above, the only one he completed), can be grasped only by analyzing the ambiguous character of labor itself. Under capitalism the typical worker is an employee, performing work for an employer and receiving in return a wage or salary. At first sight, what is involved is an exchange (in the 'labor market') between work and wages. Not so, insisted Marx. Rarely is a worker employed to perform a precise set of tasks which can be specified in detail in advance. Rather, what workers sell through the contract of employment is their *ability* to work—as Marx termed it, their 'labor power'—thereby authorizing the employer to set them to work and to assume ownership of whatever they produce.

Marx argued (to simplify a complex story) that the (exchange) value of the commodity which workers sold, their labor power, reflected the socially recognized standard of living for a particular type of worker. The use value of their labor power—the value added by their work to the materials and machinery provided by the employer—was typically greater, perhaps much greater, generating what Marx termed surplus value. Hence the explanation of capitalist expansion was to be found in the 'hidden abode' of production. And just as there was a dualism in the character of labor, so there was in the function of the capitalist employer. On the one hand, the latter performed a productive role in coordinating what became an increasingly complex organization involving the interaction of numerous workers with differentiated tasks and competences; but, on the other, to survive and prosper it was necessary to increase the amount of surplus which workers produced, in the face of their own resistance. This necessitated a coercive apparatus of supervision and control.

How could employers—competing against each other—maximize the proportion of surplus value in their production? One method was to increase the number of hours worked by employees. But at the time when Marx was writing, this option was being restricted in England both by legislative rules (though these contained many loopholes) and by workers' own collective resistance through trade unions. A second was to cut wages; at times Marx seemed to suggest that 'immiseration', in an absolute sense, was integral to the dynamic of capitalism. But there were many ambiguities in his discussion, and here too he recognized that unions could make wage cutting difficult (and by implication, that expectations of rising subsistence standards could actually lead to *higher* wages). A third was to make labor more productive, either by mechanization or by managerial pressure (or both). A fourth was to displace more skilled, and more expensive labor by less qualified and cheaper workers, partly again through mechanization and partly through the subdivision of tasks (an approach previously identified by Adam Smith).

In volume 1 of *Capital* Marx analyzed what he termed the *labor process*. Workers' productive activity was the way in which their labor power was consumed by the employer in order to create use-values, and at one and the same time a process of creating surplus value (a 'valorization process'), 'which, for the capitalist, has all the charms of something created out of nothing'. Marx explored this process in detail in notes apparently intended to form part of *Capital* but not published until the 1930s (and in English, only in the 1970s). Here, he argued that the development of capitalism displayed a qualitative shift from an initial phase when work organization reflected precapitalist social relations—what Marx termed the 'formal subordination' (or as precise translations of the German rendered it, 'subsumption') of labor—to a process of 'real subordination', or 'capitalist production proper', in which the whole system of production is structured in order to minimize workers' autonomy and discretion and maximize the creation of surplus for the employer.

Labor process analysis exploded into English-language sociology of work in the 1970s with the publication of Harry Braverman's *Labor and Monopoly Capital* (1974). Central to Braverman's thesis was the 'degradation' of the labor process: the competitive forces always inherent in capitalism, but combined with the organizational power generated by modern monopoly capitalism, both required and enabled a cheapening of labor by the erosion of the skills which (in an era of 'formal subordination') made key workers both relatively expensive and relatively autonomous. Twentieth-century capitalism attacked these surviving, essentially precapitalist forms of organization of the labor process. One weapon was mechanization and the division of labor, extolled by Adam Smith as the route to enhanced productivity (and thus surplus); another, closely related, was the 'Babbage principle', named after the early nineteenth-century advocate of the strategy of stripping craft labor of all ancillary tasks which might be adequately accomplished by lower-skilled, and cheaper workers. A twentieth-century approach highlighted by Braverman was the 'scientific management' propagated by F. W. Taylor, who called on employers to separate the design of the labor process ('conception') from its actual performance ('execution') in order to ensure the single most efficient technique and also to eliminate the discretion which enabled workers to determine their own pace and method of work, potentially as a means of resistance to employer authority.

Braverman did not claim to have developed a new theory of work under capitalism; rather, he argued (correctly) that Marx's analysis of the labor process had been largely neglected for much of the twentieth century. His objective was thus to restate this aspect of Marxism, and to set it to work to interpret the dynamics of management–worker relations in a very different economic context and within a very different occupational structure from when Marx wrote. In Britain, his study stimulated intense discussion of the labor process, first among Marxists (e.g. Brighton Labor Process Group 1977), then among sociologists of work more generally. A by-product was the series of annual labor process conferences which commenced in the early 1980s, and the succession of edited volumes which resulted. Some referred disparagingly to 'Bravermania'.[4]

Critical discussion of Braverman's account (among relatively early examples see Littler 1982 and Salaman 1986) focused in particular on two related issues: the inevitability of deskilling and the status of Taylorism as the 'ideal' management approach to labor. In both cases, a consequence was to stimulate extensive empirical research, by Marxists, non-Marxists, and anti-Marxists alike. Such research led in turn to increasing efforts to revise and reformulate labor process analysis in what became frequently a debate with, or often against, both Braverman and Marx (see, notably, Knights and Willmott 1990).

[4] Today, a Google search for labor process will yield over two million results. Some references are obstetric in content, but most relate to the post-Braverman debate.

The deskilling issue arose in the context of what, in the 1970s, was still very much 'new' technology, or as Braverman termed it, the 'scientific–technical revolution'. In his view, the application to industrial production of computer technology enabled the definitive separation of conception from execution, to a degree impossible in practice when devised in principle by Taylor and his successors. As Braverman added in a concluding chapter, 'A Final Note on Skill', existing trends were confusing: technological change was indeed creating some new skills—though in his view, many of these might prove precarious—but on balance the erosion of many traditional skills was the dominant tendency. Critics argued, first, that Braverman offered an idealized account of traditional craft work, and failed to appreciate the complex character of skill. This was only partly correct: an important element of his argument was that much work traditionally viewed as unskilled in fact required considerable experience and learned capacity, and that occupations of this kind were particularly vulnerable to 'new technology'. The second objection was that the transformation of work in the late twentieth century actually involved, on balance, an 'upskilling' of labor. The strong version of this argument was that in what would today be called the 'knowledge economy', enhanced education and training were more extensively required than in the past. The weaker version was that 'tacit skills' remained important in any kind of labor process: electronics could never displace human discretion, and in some respects the introduction of expensive hardware and software made employers even more dependent on workers' initiative when systems failed.

How should one evaluate this debate? Noon and Blyton (2002: ch. 6) provide a useful overview, and I will not attempt to cover the same ground here. One key issue concerns levels of generalization and abstraction. As Armstrong has insisted (1988: 157), Braverman (like Marx himself) 'regarded the deskilling tendencies of technical change as a system-wide dynamic which could, temporarily and locally, be interrupted or reversed'. Technological innovation inevitably creates a need for new competences which are initially in short supply, as was the case with the invention of the computer, or the typewriter more than half a century earlier; but such competences tend rapidly to become routinized and devalued. Also at issue is the relationship between the notions of, and evidence for, 'deskilling' and 'degradation'. The notion of skill can encompass the range of competences required in a specific occupation; the degree of training and experience necessary for effective performance; the amount of judgment and discretion routinely exercised (with the benchmark provided by 'the unity of conception and execution'); and the relative scarcity of these capacities. In treating 'craft mastery' as the paradigm of skill, Braverman assumed perhaps too easily that these elements were typically complementary; whereas much subsequent literature has focused on the disjunctures between them.

Much empirical work in the Marxist tradition (see the studies in Pollert 1991) has explored the ambiguities inherent in occupational change since Braverman wrote, but has also endorsed the broad sweep of his argument. Smith and Thompson (1998: 554) summarize the essence of most 'new work systems' as the creation of 'an enlarged number of interchangeable tasks carried out by interchangeable labour'. What recent research has also emphasized is evidence of a contradictory combination of work intensification and new areas of employee responsibility: what in management-speak is 'empowerment' is more accurately described as degradation through stress. This contradiction is perhaps especially evident in service work, which Braverman (like Marx) discussed, but relatively briefly; this large but extremely heterogeneous category of employment has attracted substantial empirical and theoretical scrutiny within the framework of labor process analysis. An important addition to the analytical repertoire is the concept of emotional labor (Hochschild 1979, 1983): the constraints on (typically female) workers, from shop assistants to nurses to airline cabin crew, to sustain a facial expression, form of address, and body language pleasing to the client or customer. Such behavior represents in some respects a distinctive skill, but its enforced production can be viewed more fundamentally as a form of degradation. It is interesting to note that in her initial article on 'emotion work', Hochschild made no reference to Marx and drew primarily on the interactionist social psychology of Goffmann; in her subsequent book she commenced with a reference to *Capital* and made Marx's analysis of alienation an important point of reference. This is another indication of the imprecise boundaries between Marxist and non-Marxist sociology.

The debate over Braverman's focus on 'scientific management' connects to that over de-skilling but raises more fundamental issues. In effect, Braverman agreed with Taylor that there was 'one best way' for the employer to organize the labor process in order to maximize surplus value, and this involved the elimination of employee discretion and the imposition of 'scientific' controls over performance. This perspective links directly to the fact that he intentionally made 'no attempt . . . to deal with the modern working class on the level of its consciousness, organization, or activities' (1974: 26–7); and also perhaps to an exaggerated conception of the disciplining capacity of innovative technology.[5] Yet if there is no foolproof technological shortcut to the translation of labor power into profitable production, 'real subordination' can never be fully achieved (Cressey and MacInnes 1980); hence 'at some level workers' cooperation, creative and productive powers, and consent must be engaged and mobilised' (Thompson 1990: 101). Put differently, workers' capacity to resist and disrupt cannot be wholly eliminated and therefore requires in addition more subtle countermeasures. Management strategy necessarily involves a *dialectic* between capital and labor: an attempt by employers to impose control while still evoking consent, with both elements of this contradictory set of objectives conditioned by the actual and potential recalcitrance of their employees.

From this understanding—certainly not inconsistent with much that Marx wrote on the contradictory dynamics of capitalism, even if at odds with his (and Braverman's) somewhat unilinear reading of the evolution of the labor process—have stemmed many attempts to explore a diversity of managerial strategies and their evolution over time. An early, binary classification was provided by Friedman (1977) who argued that capitalism tended to divide workers between a comparatively privileged segment enjoying relative job security and a measure of task discretion, benefits dependent on their 'voluntary' compliance with managerial objectives; and a more vulnerable segment subject to oppressive discipline. The 'responsible autonomy' of the former was reinforced by the risk of falling into the latter category, whose insecurity was matched by subjection to the 'direct control' of the employer. This analysis can be seen as a precursor of the notion of the 'flexible firm' proposed by Atkinson (1985).

Other writers in the Marxist tradition have attempted to periodize changes between different modes of labor control. For example, Edwards (1979) suggests (like Braverman) a historical evolution in management strategies, largely on the basis of US experience. In the early phase of industrial capitalism, the typical mode was arbitrary, authoritarian 'simple control'; more sophisticated forms of work organization in the twentieth century resulted in 'technical control', in which the system of production itself (notably, the assembly line) imposed its own disciplines; subsequently, when confronted with the rise of worker collectivism, employers

[5] In Volume 1 of *Capital*, Marx accepted the accuracy of Andrew Ure's remark, with reference to technological innovation in cotton-spinning in the early nineteenth century, that 'when capital enlists science into her service, the refractory hand of labor will always be taught docility'. Yet contrary to the expectations of both Marx and Ure, relatively skilled and highly paid male spinners were not displaced by cheaper female workers when new 'self-acting' machinery was introduced (Lazonick 1979).

introduced a system of partially negotiated 'bureaucratic control'. In a later work of which he was a coauthor (Gordon et al. 1982), there is an ambitious attempt to relate the evolution of forms of labor management to long-wave changes in 'social structures of accumulation'. Much subsequent critique, however, has argued the limitations of such ideal-typical classifications as instruments for analyzing changes over time as well as differentiations both within and between societies. The same criticisms have often been made of Burawoy (1979, 1985), whose work is in some respects nevertheless sophisticated in combining both cross-national and historical analysis. While he also offers a simple distinction—between 'despotic' and 'hegemonic' regimes, and a possible synthesis of the two in an era of intensified global competition—a crucial element in his work is the exploration of the contradictory dynamics of coercion and consent: in his terms, the need for capital simultaneously to secure and to obscure the production of surplus value. We may note, in passing, that some of the studies which have built critically on such contributions have evident affinities with recent 'varieties of capitalism' writings (for example, Hall and Soskice 2001) which focus on the cross-national institutional structuring of a diversity of modes of labor management. As Smith and Thompson have suggested (1998: 563–70), such non-(and often anti-) Marxist approaches can in principle offer a valuable complement to Marxist analysis of the labor process. Such complementarity can be found, for example, in the wide-ranging historical and cross-national study by Tilly and Tilly, who link Marxism to other varieties of interactionist and institutionalist analysis in order to explore 'the triad of compensation, commitment and coercion' in the world of work (1998: 3)

Another development in labor process analysis is less readily compatible. Criticisms of Braverman's neglect of 'subjectivity' coincided with the accelerating impact on English-speaking sociologists of the work of Foucault, and in particular his *Discipline and Punish* (1977). Whether or not Foucault's explorations of the dynamics of power and discipline in prison and workplace should be seen as a negation of Marx, many of those who have applied his work to labor process analysis (for an early example see Knights and Willmott 1989) have explicitly rejected Marxism. There are some potential complementarities, however. Marx wrote of the 'barrack-like discipline' inherent in the new factory system:

[I]n the factory code, the capitalist formulates his autocratic power over his workers like a private legislator.... This code is merely the capitalist caricature of the social regulation of the labor process which becomes necessary in co-operation on a large scale and in the employment in common of instruments of labor, and especially of machinery. The overseer's book of penalties replaces the slave-driver's lash.

Marsden (1999), in his meticulously researched comparison of the theoretical writings of Marx and Foucault, insists not only that the two are compatible but that their analytical complementarities are so strong that each illuminates the complexities of the other. In terms of empirical research, the influential account by Sewell and Wilkinson (1992: 283) of the 'electronic Panopticon' imposing 'surveillance systems using computer-based technology' could in principle be read as a modern elaboration of Marx's analysis.

Typically, however, such approaches mark a sharp break with Marxism in at least four respects. First, they often merely reverse the objective/subjective disjuncture criticized in Braverman: an exaggerated emphasis on linguistic and discursive practices is disconnected from the macrosocial and institutional dynamics in which they are embedded. Second, there is commonly a one-sided focus on the individualization of human subjects, neglecting the degree to which production is necessarily a social and collective process. Third, the production of 'docile bodies' is often treated as unproblematic for modern capitalism: it is assumed that the contradictions inherent in any strategy to maintain both control and consent have now been transcended. Fourth, while the some of the language of labor process analysis may be retained, it is emptied of content: 'any distinctive features of the relations between capital and labor in the workplace or larger political economy are largely set aside' (Smith and Thompson 1998: 562).[6] This is to reduce the labor process to a decorative label, innocent of theoretical meaning or purchase.

5. Collectivism, Control, and Resistance

'The proletarians have nothing to lose but their chains. They have a world to win. Proletarians of all countries, unite!' The ringing conclusion of the *Communist Manifesto* is commonly regarded as the crystallization of Marx's analysis of the world of work, and ever since it has inspired an important

[6] Kelly (1985: 32) criticized Braverman, and the early literature which followed the publication of *Labor and Monopoly Capitalism*, for neglecting the 'full circuit' of capitalist production and *reducing* capitalism to the labor process alone. This seems unfair to Braverman: he explicitly presented his study (1974: 11) as a corrective to twentieth-century Marxist analysis in which 'the critique of the mode of production gave way to the critique of capitalism as a mode of distribution'. But Kelly's objection clearly applies to most 'labor process' writing of more recent times.

stream of the labor movements which emerged in the following decades. In London he developed close links with many of the more politically advanced leaders of British craft unions, while maintaining relationships with many of the continental socialists involved in the creation of unions elsewhere in Europe; and these culminated in the formation in 1864 of the International Working Men's Association, later known as the 'First International', within which he played a dominant role throughout its turbulent existence (Collins and Abramsky 1965).

Yet somewhat surprisingly, Marx never produced an extended and systematic theoretical analysis of trade unionism and of workers' collective struggles more generally. A Marxist account can indeed be compiled from his numerous writings, and many have attempted to synthesize their insights (Hyman 1971; Kelly 1988); but most of what Marx wrote was colored by the immediate circumstances with which he was concerned, and the tactical polemics in which he was engaged. In consequence, as with so much of his work, many conflicting 'Marxist' theories may be proposed.

Central to Marx's analysis was the principle that capitalism itself organized workers collectively: the division of labor made them interdependent units in a collective production process—a 'collective laborer'; the factory gathered numerous workers together under a single roof; the slums and tenements of the rapidly expanding urban proletariat formed a seething new working-class community. Trade unionism gave this organic collectivity a formal character. Engels, in his *Condition of the Working Class in England in 1844*, had written of the struggles of the early unions of cotton factory workers; and Marx drew on his account in 1847 in *The Poverty of Philosophy*, when he declared that 'large-scale industry concentrates in one place a crowd of people unknown to one another.... The maintenance of wages, this common interest which they have against their boss, unites them in a common thought of resistance—*combination*.'

Though the impetus to combination was economic, Marx largely discounted the economic potential of trade unions. While he did not accept the idea of an 'iron law of wages'—a thesis which is often attributed to him but was actually devised by Lassalle, whom Marx sharply criticized—he felt that capitalist competition imposed constant downwards pressure on workers' pay and conditions, which unions could only partially withstand. Yet the counterpart of unions' relative economic weakness was their potential political force. Engels had been impressed by the outbreak of strikes which, though usually defeated, served 'to nourish the bitter hatred of the workers against the property-holding class.... As schools of war, the Unions are unexcelled.' Marx went on to draw a historical analogy between the combinations among the rising bourgeoisie which led eventually to a successful challenge to the feudal regime, and the emerging combinations of workers. 'That union, to attain which the burghers of the Middle Ages, with their miserable highways, required centuries, the modern proletarians, thanks to railways, achieve in a few years.' The revolutionary upsurge across much of Europe in 1848, when the *Communist Manifesto* appeared, was seen as vindicating this analysis.

But the revolutionary wave ebbed, and much of Marx's subsequent writings suggested reasons why trade unionism failed to live up to his early expectations. One, particularly associated with Engels, was the argument that trade unionism primarily encompassed a 'labor aristocracy', relatively secure and advantaged groups of skilled workers, who did not identify their own interests with the working class more generally. Another, which Lenin would later elaborate, was that trade unionism was most firmly established in imperialist nations and that the profits from colonial exploitation allowed some of the benefits to 'trickle down' (as might be said today) to organized workers who underwent a process of 'embourgeoisement'.[7] A third, also to be developed by Lenin in his theory of 'economism', was that trade unions tended to formulate their demands and to bargain—and on occasion fight—with employers on terrain shaped by the existing capitalist society. In terms used by Marx in 1865, unions were 'fighting with effects, but not with the causes of those effects'; in contradiction to his earlier prognosis, unions seemed more comfortable fighting economically within than politically against capitalism.

What can a modern student of industrial relations learn from Marx? At a time when union membership and effectiveness are in decline in almost all countries where unions were formerly strong, Allen's proposition (1966: 11) that 'wherever labour is freely bought and sold trade unionism is endemic, universal and permanent' seems less convincing than when he wrote almost four decades ago. Likewise, the falling levels of collective militancy in most countries entail that the thesis of Lane and Roberts (1971), that 'strikes are normal,' requires significant qualification.[8]

[7] When Engels wrote to Marx in 1858 of an apparent trend in Britain towards the emergence of a 'bourgeois proletariat', this was an exasperated flight of rhetoric in no way consistent with Marxist class theory; a century later, the concept of 'embourgeoisement' was embraced far more seriously by some British sociologists.

[8] The work of Kelly (1998) is important in offering an analytical model for the explanation of the *contingent* nature of collective resistance. Yet it is interesting that one of his core explanatory variables, the perception of injustice, was central to a previous, and not specifically Marxist historical comparison by Moore (1978).

Nevertheless, Marx retains his relevance in pointing to the omnipresent *potential* of collective resistance, since the employment relationship is inherently conflictual. Edwards (1986) developed the same theme in identifying a 'structured antagonism' between labor and capital. He terms his approach materialist but non-Marxist, and this is correct: not only because he rejects the inevitability of proletarian revolution (which, as suggested earlier, many of those who otherwise follow Marx have disputed), but also because his analysis of conflicting interests in the workplace is not embedded in a broader political economy of class relations. Even so, his emphasis on exploitation as central to the dynamic of capitalist production places him closer to Marx than is the case with a writer like Dahrendorf (1959), who defines 'class conflict' in Weberian terms as an outcome of hierarchical authority relations alone.

From this it follows that worker resistance is rational (Hyman 1989: ch. 5): there is no need for psychoanalysis to explain why workers strike, work to rule, take the odd day off, or disregard management instructions. Traditionally, Marxists have tended to document, analyze, and celebrate the apparent historical advance in the strength and cohesion of collective struggle, exploring the ways in which the point of production constitutes, in the words of Goodrich (1920)—not himself a Marxist—a 'frontier of control' over which workers and employers battled for supremacy.[9] But in recent decades they have been forced to search for explanations for the *limits* to collective resistance. Four main arguments may be noted, in addition to those indicated above.

First, Marx himself was forced to recognize (in his 1847 lectures on *Wage–Labour and Capital*) that workers *do* have something to lose but their chains; or, to put it differently, though the relationship between capital and labor is exploitative it involves interdependence: 'so long as the wageworker is a wageworker his lot depends upon capital'. Hence workers are bound by 'golden chains'; and if the employment relationship appears precarious—as has been increasingly the case for many employees in recent times—its material advantages may dominate workers' attitudes and actions. As Desai has commented (2002: 65–6), the logic of Marx's own analysis appears to entail that 'if employability depends on high

[9] As well as examining overt forms of collective action such as the strike, Marxists have also provided valuable analyses of 'hidden forms' of resistance, the term Cohen (1991: ch. 6) uses in his study of African workers. In developed industrial societies, Marxist writers some decades ago analyzed sabotage (Taylor and Walton 1971; Beynon 1973; Dubois 1979). Perhaps surprisingly, this theme seemed for a long time to have disappeared from the concerns of sociologists of work, but it has resurfaced under the guise of 'organizational misbehavior' (Ackroyd and Thompson 1999).

profitability, workers would want to *co-operate* with employers in keeping profits high'.

This connects with a second emphasis, on consciousness and ideology. When Marx began to write, capitalism was a novel social experiment which many believed soon would be reversed. Today, capitalism is hegemonic and alternatives to the capital–labor relationship are remote from popular imagination. Fighting the system thus commonly appears futile (though, significantly, some of the most substantial recent examples of mass resistance have been in the countries of the south and east where capitalism still represents a disruptive innovation). In consequence, conflict and resistance may themselves be self-limiting; a central theme of the work of Burawoy, mentioned above, was how workers' successes in imposing limits to the day-to-day exercise of managerial control could cement their assent to the basic structure of the capitalist employment relationship.

Third, Marxists have developed more sophisticated analyses than those of Marx or Lenin of the role of trade unions themselves in 'manufacturing consent'. At a theoretical level, Zoll (1976) has explored what he terms the 'dual character' of trade unionism: at one and the same time, unions disrupt capitalist exploitation and function as a source of social order which helps stabilize capitalist society.[10] Detailed empirical accounts of this process, leading even militant trade union representatives to recognize limits to the possibility of resistance, were produced in studies in the 1970s by Beynon (1973) of the Ford Halewood car factory and by Nichols and Armstrong (1976) and Nichols and Beynon (1977) of the ICI Severnside fertilizer factory. These studies, written in a period of trade union advance and near-full employment, still provide a basis for understanding the dynamics of union–management relations in times of recession and union retreat.

Fourth, a major controversy among Marxists for over a century has concerned the role of *leadership*. For Marx and Engels, in many of their writings at least, and for many of their successors (notably Rosa Luxemburg), workers' experience of class oppression would lead more or less spontaneously through a process of collective learning to a struggle against capitalist society. For others, notably Lenin, as indicated above, workers'

[10] Though Zoll draws on the writings of Marx himself to elaborate this analysis, non-Marxists have developed a similar interpretation of trade unionism. A notable example is the work of Mills (1948), a sociologist more influenced by Weber than by Marx, who described unions as 'managers of discontent'. More explicitly Marxist is the analogous (though more abstract) exploration of a dualism in trade union action by Offe and Wiesenthal (1985).

fragmented revolts were unlikely to lead spontaneously to a concerted anticapitalist movement; this would occur only through coordinated leadership. In Lenin's view, this required a disciplined, elite revolutionary party; other communists such as Gramsci thought differently. But as many recent writers on social movements have insisted (for an overview see Barker et al. 2001), successful insurgent struggles always involve some internal strategic leadership, and others fail for lack of this. How such strategic capacity emerges—or can be created—remains deeply problematic.

6. The Injuries of Class

Underlying the debates over the nature, limits, and indeed existence of class struggle is the question of consciousness. In *The Poverty of Philosophy*, Marx distinguished between the emergence of a proletariat with 'a common situation, common interests . . . as against capital', and workers' development through collective organization and struggle into 'a class for itself'. This distinction was subsequently elaborated by many followers of Marx (and to some extent by Marx himself) into a rather mechanical formula: an objectively defined 'class in itself' will, with the addition of class consciousness, become a (revolutionary) 'class for itself'. Conversely, any failure of the proletariat to exercise its revolutionary potential must be a reflection of 'false consciousness'. Yet many Marxists have questioned this account. Gorz (1982), for example, argues that there is a fundamental contradiction between Marx's analysis of the dynamic of degradation and subordination of labor within capitalist production, and his confidence in the revolutionary creativity of the proletariat. For Gorz, this confidence was a product of Hegelian mysticism, a belief that history possesses an immanent teleology, according to which the proletariat would perform its historical mission regardless of the circumstances and aspirations of actual workers. While this critique is in important respects exaggerated (Hyman 1983), it does indeed identify a genuine problem in Marxist analysis, one which relates to the question, already discussed, of the inevitability of revolution.[11]

[11] Some of Gorz's criticisms had been anticipated by Draper (1978: 70–80) and (to his satisfaction at least) refuted. One should note that throughout his life, Marx was keenly concerned to establish the actual circumstances and reactions of real workers. Particularly interesting was the 100-item questionnaire which he drafted in French in 1880 (the *enquête ouvrière*): an ambitious sociological enterprise which achieved no known outcome.

A concept also deriving from Marx's early critical engagement with Hegel, which has entered the mainstream of the sociology of work, is that of alienation. Its meaning and significance are complex and contested: partly because the term is conventionally used in English to denote two distinct concepts in Marx's analysis (*Entäusserung* and *Entfremdung*, literally meaning externalization and estrangement); partly because it simultaneously combines references to the philosophy of religion, to law, and to political economy; and partly because it is central to debates on how much the ideas of the 'young Marx' persisted in his mature work (Mészáros 1970; Ollman 1971; Torrance 1977). Here it is unnecessary to pursue these questions. To simplify, one can identify three key applications of Marx's idea of alienation. First, the wage laborer surrendered to the employer the legal ownership of what he/she produced. Today this may seem inevitable and self-evident, but in the early phase of capitalism it could appear strange and shocking; independent artisans or peasants did own what they produced, and for early social theorists such as Locke the right of ownership was intrinsically linked to the performance of work. Second, and as a corollary, was the loss of autonomy over the labor process, discussed earlier: the capitalist acquired the right to control the worker's attendance and work performance. Third, and crucially, Marx saw this as a negation of the human condition. His theoretical premise was that self-conscious creative activity was a defining characteristic of humanity, a form of self-affirmation which set humankind apart from other animals. Capitalist wage-labor, by contrast, turned 'life-activity, productive life itself' into a mere means of physical survival; in consequence, 'as soon as no physical or other compulsion exists, labour is shunned like the plague'.

Some modern applications of the concept of alienation have trivialized Marx's meaning. For example, a well-known study by Blauner (1964) in effect reduced alienation (or its absence) to task discretion and job satisfaction. Evidently Marx did indeed focus on the loss of autonomy in work as a key element in the capital–labor relation, and regarded dissatisfaction as an inevitable outcome. But his more fundamental concern was with the political economy which resulted in alienated labor, and its impact on workers' sense of personal identity, their relations with one another, and their role within society. Many sociologists, often but not always Marxist, *have* made such themes central to their analysis, whether or not they tie this explicitly to the concept of alienation.

Methodologically such studies have often involved the ethnographic construction of life narratives. For example Sennett and Cobb (1972), in their account of urban workers in the USA, identify a frustrated effort to achieve freedom, dignity, and self-respect, if not through their own careers then through those of their children. They summarize the findings thus (1972: 75): 'the search for respect is thwarted; the individual feels personally responsible for the failure; the whole attempt accustoms him to think that to have individual respect you must have social inequality.' Gouldner (1969: 355) developed a parallel argument: capitalism 'incorporates [people] primarily as utilities useful for performing functions' and all other aspects of their capacities and identities are 'subordinated to their efficient employment'. More recently, Sennett (1998) has explored how the corrosion of identity and respect is reinforced by growing employment insecurity; a theme also developed by Beck (2000: ch. 5) with his thesis that 'the work society is becoming risk society'. In France, very similar interpretations have been offered by Dejours (1998).

Other writers have interpreted such systematic suppression of human capacities as a major source of divisions among different categories of workers, resulting for example in sexism, racism, and xenophobia. The title of the Severnside study by Nichols and Armstrong (1976), *Workers Divided*, encapsulates such analysis. Sennett and Cobb (1972: 83) write of 'male solidarity' as the medium through which oppressed working men attempt to assert personal worth and dignity: an analysis paralleled in Britain by studies such as Willis (1977) and Collinson (1992). Marxist feminists such as Cockburn (1983) and Rubery (1978) have shown how such gender-based conceptions of solidarity have informed trade union practices which exclude, marginalize, or demean women workers. Pollert (1981: 171) has indicated the contradictory reactions among women themselves: 'from their male trade-union "brothers" they received a constant stream of conflicting messages: on the one hand they were second-rate workers who should really stay at home; on the other hand, they should be better trade unionists. Caught between two stools, they blamed themselves.' Analogously, Lamont (2000) has explored (though not from a specifically Marxist perspective: she terms her approach 'cultural materialist') how the quest for dignity on the part of working-class men in France and the USA can lead to expressions of racial difference and division: though she insists that principles of class solidarity can still transcend these.

As indicated in the introduction to this chapter, Marx's central focus on class led him largely to neglect the role of ethnicity or gender both within the workplace and in society more generally. Marx and Engels tended to assume that capitalism itself created, or exacerbated, divisions within the working class and that socialism would transcend these. In his 'Origin of the Family, Private Property and the State', Engels attributed women's subordination to their treatment, in effect, as a form of private property; he assumed that capitalism would increasingly absorb women within the ranks of wage labor, leading to their integration in the struggle for socialism, which when successful would result in their emancipation.

Marx himself noted, in the *Grundrisse* and later in Volume 1 of *Capital*, that the exchange value of labor power encompassed both the day-to-day maintenance of the worker (food, shelter, clothing) *and* the cost of reproducing a new generation of children to become workers in their turn. He failed, however, to explore the nature of the household as a (re)productive unit, or the ways in which gender relations within the household carry over into the sphere of capital–labor relations. Feminist approaches to the analysis of work are discussed elsewhere in this volume, but cannot be neglected in this context. Most sociologists today would agree with Wajcman (2000: 196) that

> [T]he workplace and the labour market cannot be understood in isolation from the private sphere of the household and the labour of social reproduction that goes on there.... The very nature of jobs and the organization of the labour market are intimately tied to the nature of gender relations within the family. In other words, the employment contract presupposes the sexual contract.

Can Marxism in principle incorporate feminism, so that class and gender receive complementary attention as axes of differentiation, oppression, and struggle, or must a theoretical (and political) choice be made between the two? This issue has been debated within sociology in general for several decades, and figured prominently in the labor process debates from the 1980s onwards (for example Beechey 1982; Knights and Willmott 1986; West 1990). As yet, what Hartmann (1979) termed the 'unhappy marriage' between Marxism and feminism appears to persist.

7. Marxism and Beyond

In the decade and a half since the fall of the Berlin Wall, some have argued that Marxism itself no longer deserves attention: regime change has eclipsed its relevance. On the contrary. The collapse of the former 'communist' bloc has relieved Marxism of the anomalous burden of serving as an official ideology of state. At the same time, the system of global capitalism which has filled the void seems to outdo Marx's own dystopian vision of a world in which 'all that is solid melts into air', with a growing subordination of production itself to the anarchy of financial markets, intensification of the fetishism of commodities, and consequential accentuation of insecurity and stress in work. In the twenty-first century, the relevance of Marxist theory is more evident than ever.

Nevertheless, the discussion throughout this chapter has emphasized that though Marxist analysis offers an indispensable contribution to the understanding of work, on its own it is insufficient. Marx was a great thinker; but only those who regard him as a saint would agree with all he wrote (which is itself problematic, given the variations in his analysis over time) or accept that he provides all the answers to the questions which preoccupy us today. Sociologists can scarcely ignore Marx; but they must choose what of Marx they apply, and what theories developed by other social analysts are used to complement his. As a corollary, in the case of many of the sociologists whose relevance has been asserted in this chapter it is not clear from their work whether or not they should be regarded, or would regard themselves, as Marxists.

Does this matter? Can we live with theoretical ambiguity and eclecticism? Almost certainly, Marx himself would have given a resounding negative. Personally, I have come to sympathize with the argument of Galtung (1990: 102): 'a good theory should never leave us with the idea that the world is made once and for all. A good theory will always have some empty spaces for the reality not yet there, for potential as opposed to empirical reality.' In important respects this sums up Marx's own dialectical imagination, but seems to indicate additionally that theory itself, however brilliant, must always require innovation.

References

Ackroyd, S. and Thompson, P. (1999). *Organizational Misbehaviour.* London: Sage.

Allen, V. L. (1966). *Militant Trade Unionism*. London: Merlin.

Armstrong, P. (1988). 'Labour and Monopoly Capital', in R. Hyman and W. Streeck (eds.), *New Technology and Industrial Relations*. Oxford: Blackwell.

Atkinson, J. (1985). *Flexibility, Uncertainty and Manpower Management*. Brighton: IMS.

Avineri, S. (1968). *The Social and Political Thought of Karl Marx*. Cambridge: Cambridge University Press.

Barker, C., Johnson, A., and Lavalette, M. (2001). 'Leadership Matters: An Introduction', in C. Barker, A. Johnson, and M. Lavalette (eds.), *Leadership and Social Movements*. Manchester: Manchester University Press.

Beck, U. (2000). *The Brave New World of Work*. Cambridge: Polity Press.
Beechey, V. (1982). 'The Sexual Division of Labour and the Labour Process', in S. Wood (ed.), *The Degradation of Work?* London: Hutchinson.
Bender, F. L. (ed.) (1975). *The Betrayal of Marx*. New York: Harper & Row.
Beynon, H. (1973). *Working for Ford*. Harmondsworth: Penguin.
Blauner, R. (1964). *Alienation and Freedom*. Chicago, IL: University of Chicago Press.
Bottomore, T. B. and Rubel, B. (1956). *Karl Marx: Selected Writings in Sociology and Social Philosophy*. Harmondsworth: Penguin.
Braverman, H. (1974). *Labor and Monopoly Capital*. New York: Monthly Review.
Brighton Labour Process Group (1977). 'The Capitalist Labour Process', *Capital and Class*, 1: 3–42.
Burawoy, M. (1979). *Manufacturing Consent*. Chicago, IL: University of Chicago Press.
—— (1985). *The Politics of Production*. London: Verso.
Cockburn, C. (1983). *Brothers: Male Dominance and Technological Change*. London: Pluto.
Cohen, R. (1991). *Contested Domains*. London: Zed.
Collins, H. and Abramsky, C. (1965). *Karl Marx and the British Labour Movement*. London: Macmillan.
Collinson, D. L. (1992). *Managing the Shopfloor: Subjectivity, Masculinity, and Workplace Culture*. Berlin: De Gruyter.
Cressey, P. and MacInnes, J. (1980). 'Voting for Ford: Industrial Democracy and the Control of Labour', *Capital and Class*, 11: 5–33.
Dahrendorf, R. (1959). *Class and Class Conflict in Industrial Society*. London: Routledge.
Dejours, C. (1998). *Souffrance en France: La banalisation de l'injustice sociale*. Paris: Seuil.
Desai, M. (2002). *Marx's Revenge: The Resurgence of Capitalism and the Death of Statist Socialism*. London: Verso.
Draper, H. (1978). *Karl Marx's Theory of Revolution*, vol. 2. New York: Monthly Review.
Dubois, P. (1979). *Sabotage in Industry*. Harmondsworth: Penguin.
Edwards, P. K. (1986). *Conflict at Work: A Materialist Analysis of Workplace Relations*. Oxford: Blackwell.
—— (1986). *Conflict at Work*. Oxford: Blackwell.
Edwards, R. (1979). *Contested Terrain*. London: Heinemann.
Foster, J. (1974). *Class Struggle in the Industrial Revolution*. London: Weidenfeld.
Foucault, M. (1977). *Discipline and Punish*. Harmondsworth: Penguin.
Friedman, A. L. (1977). *Industry and Labour*. London: Macmillan.
Gall, G. (2003). 'Marxism and Industrial Relations', in P. Ackers and A. Wilkinson (eds.), *Understanding Work and Employment: Industrial Relations in Transition*. Oxford: Oxford University Press.

Galtung, J. (1990). 'Theory Formation in Social Research', in E. Øyen (ed.), *Comparative Methodology*. London: Sage.
Giddens, A. (1971). *Capitalism and Modern Social Theory*. Cambridge: Cambridge University Press.
Goodrich, C. L. (1920). *The Frontier of control*. London: Bell.
Gordon, D., Edwards, R., and Reich, M. (1982). *Segmented Work, Divided Workers*. Cambridge: Cambridge University Press.
Gorz, A. (1982). *Farewell to the Working Class: An Essay on Post-Industrial Socialism*. London: Pluto.
Gouldner, A.W. (1969). 'The Unemployed Self', in R. Fraser (ed.), *Work 2*. Harmondsworth: Penguin.
Hall, P. A. and Soskice, D. (eds.) (2001). *Varieties of Capitalism: The Institutional Foundations of Comparative Advantage*. Oxford: Oxford University Press.
Hartmann, H. (1979). 'The Unhappy Marriage of Marxism and Feminism', *Capital and Class*, 8: 1–33.
Hochschild, A. R. (1979). 'Emotion Work, Feeling Rules and Social Structure', *American Journal of Sociology*, 85(3): 551–75.
—— (1983). *The Managed Heart: Commercialization of Human Feeling*. Berkeley, CA: University of California Press.
Howard, M. C. and King, J. E. (eds.) (1976). *The Economics of Marx*. Harmondsworth: Penguin.
Hyman, R. (1971). *Marxism and the Sociology of Trade Unionism*. London: Pluto.
—— (1983). 'André Gorz and his Disappearing Proletariat', *Socialist Register 1983*, pp. 272–95.
—— (1989). *Strikes*, 4th edn. London: Macmillan.
Kelly, J. (1985). 'Management's Redesign of Work', in D. Knights, H. Willmott, and D. Collinson (eds.), *Job Redesign*. Aldershot: Gower.
—— (1988). *Trade Unions and Socialist Politics*. London: Verso.
—— (1998). *Rethinking Industrial Relations*. London: Routledge.
Knights, D. and Willmott, H. (eds.) (1986). *Gender and the Labour Process*. Aldershot: Gower.
—— and—— (1989). 'Power and Subjectivity at Work', *Sociology*, 23: 535–58.
—— and—— (eds.) (1990). *Labour Process Theory*. London: Macmillan.
Lamont, M. (2000). *The Dignity of Working Men: Morality and the Boundaries of Race, Class, and Immigration*. Cambridge: Harvard University Press.
Lane, T. and Roberts, K. (1971). *Strike at Pilkingtons*. London: Fontana.
Lazonick, W. (1979). 'Industrial Relations and Technical Change: The Case of the Self-Acting Mule', *Cambridge Journal of Economics*, 3: 231–62.
Lefebvre, H. (1968). *The Sociology of Marx*. Harmondsworth: Penguin.
Lichtheim, G. (1961). *Marxism: An Historical and Critical Study*. London: Routledge.
Littler, C. R. (1982). *The Development of the Labour Process in Capitalist Societies*. London: Heinemann.
McLellan, D. (1971). *The Thought of Karl Marx*. London: Macmillan.

Marsden, R. (1999). *The Nature of Capital: Marx after Foucault.* London: Routledge.
Mészáros, I. (1970). *Marx's Theory of Alienation.* London: Merlin.
Mills, C. W. (1948). *The New Men of Power.* New York: Harcourt Brace.
Moore, B. (1978). *Injustice: The Social Bases of Obedience and Revolt.* New York: Sharpe.
Nichols, T. and Armstrong, P. (1976). *Workers Divided.* London: Fontana.
—— and Beynon, H. (1977). *Living with Capitalism.* London: Routledge.
Nicolaus, M. (1973). 'Foreword', in K. Marx, *Grundrisse: Foundations of the Critique of Political Economy (Rough Draft).* Harmondsworth: Penguin.
Noon, M. and Blyton, P. (2002). *The Realities of Work.* London: Palgrave.
Offe, C. and Wiesenthal, H. (1985). 'Two Logics of Collective Action', in C. Offe, *Disorganized Capitalism.* Cambridge: Polity Press.
Ollman, B. (1971). *Alienation.* Cambridge: Cambridge University Press.
Pollert, A. (1981). *Girls, Wives, Factory Lives.* London: Macmillan.
—— (ed.) (1991). *Farewell to Flexibility?* Oxford: Blackwell.
Rubery, J. (1978). 'Structured Labour Markets, Worker Organisation and Low Pay', *Cambridge Journal of Economics,* 2(1): 17–36.
Salaman, G. (1986). *Working.* London: Tavistock.
Sennett, R. (1998). *The Corrosion of Character.* New York: Norton.
—— and Cobb, J. (1972). *The Hidden Injuries of Class.* New York: Knopf.
Sewell, G. and Wilkinson, B. (1992). ' "Someone to Watch over Me": Surveillance, Discipline and the Just-in-Time Labour Process', *Sociology,* 26: 271–89.
Smith, C. and Thompson, P. (1998). 'Re-Evaluating the Labour Process Debate', *Economic and Industrial Democracy,* 19: 551–77.
Taylor, L. and Walton, P. (1971). 'Industrial Sabotage', in S. Cohen (ed.), *Images of Deviance.* Harmondsworth: Penguin.
Thompson, E. P. (1963). *The Making of the English Working Class.* Harmondsworth: Penguin.
Thompson, P. (1990). 'Crawling from the Wreckage', in D. Knights and H. Willmott (eds.), *Labour Process Theory.* London: Macmillan, pp. 95–124.
Tilly, C. and Tilly, C. (1998). *Work under Capitalism.* Boulder, CO: Westview Press.
Torrance, J. (1977). *Estrangement, Alienation and Exploitation.* London: Macmillan.
Tucker, R (1961). *Philosophy and Myth in Karl Marx.* Cambridge: Cambridge University Press.
Wajcman, J. (2000). 'Feminism Facing Industrial Relations in Britain', *British Journal of Industrial Relations,* 38: 183–201.
West, J. (1990). 'Gender and the Labour Process', in D. Knights and H. Willmott (eds.), *Labour Process Theory.* London: Macmillan.
Wheen, F. (1999). *Karl Marx: A Life.* London: Fourth Estate.
Willis, P. (1977). *Learning to Labour.* Farnborough: Saxon House.
Zoll, R. (1976). *Der Doppelcharakter der Gewerkschaften.* Frankfurt: Suhrkamp.

3

Max Weber and the Irony of Bureaucracy

Graham Sewell and James Barker

> Unless bureaucracy is to become the graveyard of democracy, freedom must learn the lessons of power as a normal tendency that moves through institutions in silent stealth.
>
> (Diggins 1996: 76)

> Logic is merely slavery within the fetters of language. But language includes within itself an illogical element: metaphor, etc. The initial power produces an equation between things that are unequal, and is thus an operation of the imagination. The existence of concepts, forms, etc. is based upon this.
>
> (Nietzsche 1979: §177)

We should be eternally grateful to Hans Gerth and C. Wright Mills for bringing Max Weber (1864–1920) to the wider attention of the Anglophone world. It is fitting then that the volume containing their selection of Weber's sociological essays is still recognized as an indispensable guide to the man and his work (Gerth and Mills 1948). Given the legacy of Gerth and Mills and so many prominent others, any contemporary scholar taking on Weber faces a rather daunting task: What can be said about him that no one else has already said? For our part, we seek here to articulate a vision of Weber's work from a perspective grounded in today's discursive and representational theorizing. We first reflect on the major theoretical and methodological elements of Weber's thinking which helps us to develop the basis of Weberian thought as it relates to the study of work organizations. Then, consistent with our discursive and representational outlook, we set about developing a contemporary reading of Weber that can serve as the basis for criticizing organizational power and domination. Our basic approach depends on exploring the connections between Nietzsche, Weber, and Foucault. This allows us to argue for a discourse-sensitive, figurative analysis, which we refer to as an ironical approach. The subsequent ironical analysis of power and domination in today's organizations identifies and assesses the competing grammars and vocabularies of organizational discourse. With Weber's ideal type of bureaucracy serving as our exemplar, we then discuss how a grammar must pass through four stages—from inaugurating gesture to metaphor, from metaphor to metonymy, from metonymy to synecdoche, and from synecdoche to irony—in order to build up a coherent representation of the character, purpose, and operation of this familiar form of organization. Using an ethnographic analysis of ISE Communications—an organization that was ostensibly trying to overcome to the stultifying effects of bureaucracy through the introduction of teamwork (Barker 1993, 1999)—we then illustrate the continuing usefulness that this discursively based Weberian approach has for the study of work life in today's allegedly 'postbureaucratic' era.

1. Contextualizing Weber: The Importance of the German Tradition

Max Weber's fate has long been to be judged in terms of his position vis-à-vis Marx (Blau 1963). Thus, he has been denounced both as an apologist for bourgeois liberalism and as a fellow traveller of the workers' struggle. With this point in mind, we can see the continuing debate on the significance of Weber as a continuing struggle for his 'soul'; an attempt to adduce his original intent and claim him for liberalism or radicalism, for the status quo or social emancipation. Thus, whether we consider Talcott Parsons' theorizing (1949) of unified and stable social systems or Alvin Gouldner's attempts (1980) to reconcile the critical and scientific impulses of Marxism, Weber has been a touchstone for the 'ideology' wars of the second half of the twentieth century. However, there is much more to Weber than simply being the bourgeois Marx. We will show below that in developing his complex and expansive approach to a range of organizational problems he was responding to several currents that had dominated German thinking for much of the nineteenth and early twentieth century. In particular, his engagement with the ideas of Friedrich Nietzsche will serve as our inspiration for re-evaluating Weber's familiar bureaucratic ideal type in order to develop a *tropological* account of the broader concept of bureaucracy. First, however, we need to review Weber's German intellectual influences that prefigured his Nietzschian turn.

2. Hegel, Kant, and the Morality of Organizational Conduct

Our starting point is Knapp's identification (1986) of the commonalities in the thinking of Weber and Georg Wilhelm Friedrich Hegel (d. 1831). These include, *inter alia*, the eight elements summarized in Table 3.1.

Reflecting on these common elements, we find that, ontologically and epistemologically speaking at least, Weber was principally Hegelian in his outlook. Here we can see the origins of what Turner (1991) sees as Weber's primary objective: 'getting at the nature of Modernity' through an interpretive analysis of the values that underpin ostensibly rational systems of domination. Ontologically, Weber had no notion of a social structure (such as an organization) existing *sui generis*. Instead of being 'things in themselves' with their own powers of agency, social structures should be seen as complex and more or less organized 'flows of action' that cannot be grasped by universal scientific concepts (Lopez 2003). Epistemologically, as we shall see below, this thought points to the origin of *Verstehen*—Weber's extension of Wilhelm Dilthey's interpretive methodology that seeks to understand the particularities of organizations by studying the subjective values, motives, and actions of the individuals that make them up (Lopez 2003).

Table 3.1. Common elements in Weber and Hegel

1. Social structures are constellations of interacting individual roles
2. An actor's subjective understanding of their individual role constitutes a form of self-consciousness.
3. Structures of organization cannot be considered independently of the systematic theories that inspire them.
4. Structures of domination generate systems of rules.
5. The exact composition of these rules depends on the particular arrangements of a structure of domination.
6. The transformation of a system of domination is a historical process brought about by intentional action (usually by charismatic leaders).
7. Systems of rules represent an attempt by dominant interests to enshrine those interests through rational means.
8. Complex rational structures of rules are increasingly undermined by irrationalities.

Source: Adapted from Knapp (1986).

Bringing these ontological and epistemological dimensions together, to a large extent 'getting at the nature of Modernity' will involve the study of individuals in organizations that pursue varying objectives in view of the empirical fact that so much of modern life is conducted in or through such social structures. This point immediately brings to the fore the matter of the underlying morality of individual conduct within specific organizations and, in terms of ethics, Weber diluted the moral absolutism of Immanuel Kant (d. 1804) to encompass a degree of moral relativism. Thus, whereas Kant's maxim was that you should act in such a way that the aim of your will could always hold as the principle of universal legislation, Weber offered the maxim that you should act in such a way that the aim of your will, *as the true expression of an explicit rule*, could always hold as the principle of universal legislation (Schluchter 1996).

While the former maxim is founded on an internal monologue (i.e. 'Am I doing the right thing in terms of my observation of eternal moral principles?'), by interposing a rational system of rules, Weber introduces an element of dialogue and temporality (i.e. 'Have I fulfilled my obligations under the rules that have been collectively drawn up at a particular historical moment, based on a socially acceptable interpretation of eternal moral principles?'). Responding to Goethe's question, 'How can you get acquainted with your own conviction?' Weber seems to be answering, 'Never on your own through internal reflection but only in discussion with others' (Schluchter 1996). Such a move goes straight to the heart of Weber's concept of legitimate authority for, so long as organizational actors recognize the general legitimacy of the rules that govern their conduct (say, because they reflect a consensus of values established through dialogue), they will have no misgivings about those rules being enforced. However, the introduction of a specific temporal dimension suggests that those rules are, potentially at least, subject to change; say, when a collectivity deems it necessary to strengthen or relax them in the face of an apparently irrational intrusion.

Such a position immediately suggests the potential for the existence of competing interpretations of morality rather than a single order, enshrined in universally applicable rules. Indeed, it is not uncommon to worry about the extent to which Weber's refinement of Kant's 'Practical Reason' opens the door to an infinitely regressive moral relativism and, on this very point, accusations of nihilism have been levelled against Weber from the political Left and Right.

3. Dilthey and the Problem of Positivism

The conventional way to present the development of Weber's post-Hegelian thinking is to point to his original training in jurisprudence which expanded to incorporate, in succession, subsequent interests in history, economics, and, eventually, sociology. This gives the impression that Weber was on an incremental journey of discovery that culminated in the systematic and holistic study of society. However, an alternative view is that Weber was above all what we would today call a philosopher of the social sciences who, in grappling with enduring ontological, epistemological, and methodological problems, turned his attention to a number of disciplines. Thus, rather than seeing Weber as a 'sociologist in waiting', merely biding his time while he sated his historical and economic appetites, we can see his career unfolding as a project aimed at developing a critique of positivism in all of the main 'human sciences' of the time. This response to the growing influence of positivism in the nineteenth century is important because it allies Weber with a broader movement in Germany centered on the activities of Wilhelm Dilthey (d. 1911), Wilhelm Windelband (d. 1915), and Hienrich Rickert (d. 1936).

Auguste Comte (d. 1857) and, later in the Anglophone world, Herbert Spencer (d. 1903) are widely credited with popularizing positivism within the then emerging discipline of sociology, although earlier prominent figures such as Francis Bacon (d. 1626) and John Locke (d. 1704) also looked forward to a world where all knowledge—including intellectual pursuits that we now label 'human' or 'social sciences'—would be founded on unambiguous and universal scientific principles. According to Giddens (1974) the 'positivistic attitude' toward sociology advocated by Comte and his successors is still evident and can be characterized as follows:

1. The methodological procedures of scientific investigation can be directly applied to sociology. This carries with it the implicit assumption that the investigator can be an impartial observer of social reality.
2. The end product of such investigation can be expressed in universal law-like statements.
3. Sociological knowledge generated in this way is 'neutral' and value-free.

Dilthey's response to positivism was to draw a distinction between *explanation* and *understanding*. According to Dilthey, explanation was the ultimate aim of the natural sciences which involves identifying universal causal mechanisms that are independent of our subjective experience of events. In contrast, understanding ought to be the ultimate aim of the human sciences through a historical appreciation of the subjective experience of our interpretation of the meaning of events. Unlike explanation, which tends to be the exclusive domain of specialist scholars, understanding saturates everyday life and makes up the very fabric of culture; without it a coherent society would be impossible (Swingewood 1984). This is why understanding was crucial for Dilthey; it meant getting at the inner experiences that make up our *Erlebnis* or 'lived experience' and, because positivism explicitly repudiated understanding in favor of explanation, it left out much of what is important to the study of society.

Windelband extended Dilthey's historical approach by focusing on matters of epistemology and methodology. Thus, he characterized explanation as *nomothetic* and instrumental in that it relies on methods of investigation to generate law-like knowledge that allows us to master nature. In contrast, understanding is ultimately a quest for human self-affirmation, achieved through generating *ideographic* knowledge obtained using in-depth descriptions of unique and individual aspects of *Erlebnis* (Günther and Windelband 1988). Rickert turned his attention to an obvious question which stems from Windelband's definition of *ideographic* knowledge: How can we determine which unique and individual events are historically significant and which are merely trivial? He was concerned that, if we could not make such a determination, we ran the risk of descending into meaningless relativism or, worse, that we would get distracted by the inconsequential. His response anticipated later developments in disciplines like cultural anthropology in that an observer's judgment on this matter should be guided by the prevailing values of the society they were observing rather than his own values (Rickert 1962).

Although Weber concurred with much of this developing critique, significantly his own attitude toward positivism was ambivalent. For example, although he advocated the pursuit of ideographic knowledge, he was confident that it could be as systematic and as ostensibly value-free as the natural sciences, even if it did not necessarily deploy the same methods. In effect, Weber only explicitly repudiated Giddens' second feature of positivism—that sociological knowledge can be expressed in universal law-like statements. Thus, while Weber accepted positivism's distinction between 'facts' and 'values' he was also confident that we could come to 'know' both of them objectively by gaining knowledge of *Erlebnis* through an integration of understanding and explanation. Although values are produced intersubjectively through social action, the act of *Verstehen* or interpretation first allows us to know individual subjective states through empathy and then render this knowledge objective through its integration with causal explanation that addresses the characteristic modes of social behavior we associate with familiar institutions like the state, the corporation, or the family (Weber 1962). In this sense, Weber was proposing that we can systematically account for recurrent types of social action by comparing individual examples of recognizable forms of behavior in particular institutions with the sequence of events that lead up to them. Thus, *Verstehen* involved developing a *meaningfully adequate level of understanding* (i.e. a subjective interpretation of a coherent course of behavior) that informed a *causally adequate level of explanation* (i.e. an objective interpretation of a sequence of events that, on the basis of past experience, will probably recur in the same way—Weber 1962). For Weber, it was this combination of qualitative and quantitative knowledge that made sociological research distinctive; especially its ability to go beyond the demonstration of functional relationships and uniformities found in physics and biology. Thus:

> [A] correct causal interpretation of a concrete course of behavior is achieved when such overt behavior and its motives have been correctly ascertained and if, at the same time, their relationship has become intelligible in a meaningful way. A correct causal interpretation of a typical course of behavior then can be taken to mean that the process which is claimed to be typical is shown to lend itself to both meaningful and causally adequate interpretation. If no meaning attaches itself to such typical behavior, then regardless of the degree of uniformity or the statistical preciseness of probability, it still remains an incomprehensible statistical probability, whether it deals with an overt or subjective process. On the other hand, even the most perfectly adequate meaning is causally significant from a sociological point of view if we have proof that in all likelihood the conduct in question normally unfolds in a meaningful way. In order for this to occur there must be determinable to some degree of frequency of approximation to an average or an ideal type. (Weber 1962: 40)

We will return to the epistemological and methodological significance of the ideal type later in our chapter but, at this stage, we would point out that one interesting way of getting some measure on the influence that Weber has subsequently exercised on social science is to determine the extent to which researchers have emphasized the nomothetic or ideographic aspects of his approach. It will become evident later that we concentrate on building ideographic knowledge.

4. Marx and the Problem of Ideology

Weber's critique of positivism was a direct response to the attempts of people like Spencer to put the social sciences on the same footing as the natural sciences. Similarly, Weber's critique of ideology was a response to the attempts of political groups like the German Social Democratic Party in the late nineteenth and early twentieth century to put Marxism on an equally scientific footing (Ricoeur 1994). In particular, Weber was dismissive of the extreme economic reductionism of the German Marxists who took Marx's distinction between science and ideology contained in *Capital*, Volume 1 (1976) to heart yet failed to appreciate the more subtle aspects of his discussion of the dialectical nature of the relationship between knowledge and interests. Nevertheless, Marx *did* see ideology (along with cultural and political practices) as being a mere epiphenomenon of the 'economic base' and it was this that convinced Weber that all subsequent forms of Marxism were founded on the strict functional relationship between the way we see the world and our location in a systems of class interests—because we live in a capitalist society the dominant ideology of the capitalist class promotes a 'false consciousness' that obscures the proletariat's 'true' interests (Swingewood 1984). This notion of ideology as a distortion of the truth of the matter was unsatisfactory for Weber, because it analytically privileged an explanation of its underlying causes over an understanding of its effects. This is evident in his famous observation that, although a consideration of our immediate material interests may well govern our conduct, the emergence of particular ideas have historically acted like a 'switchman' to direct society in certain directions (Weber 1991). Most obviously, the emergence of the Protestant work ethic influenced the characteristic moral order of capitalism, supplying what Weber described in a letter to Rickert as the asceticism necessary for the 'foundation of modern vocational civilization—a sort of "spiritualist" construction of the modern economy' (quoted in Gerth and Mills 1948: 18–19). Although Weber accepted that ideology served as a weapon in the struggle between interest groups—for example, the Protestant work ethic clearly favored certain members of society who could justify their privileged position on the grounds that it was a combination of their own abilities and unstinting efforts—the focus of a historical study of such a struggle should not be the role of ideology in obscuring 'real' interests but the attempts of groups to assert the hegemony of one coherent ideas at the expense of others. This exploration of the relationship between idea and social power exerted considerable influence on subsequent exponents of the sociology of knowledge like Karl Mannheim and Robert Merton and, as we shall see below, it also bears some comparison with certain aspects of Foucault's genealogical method (see also Burrell, Chapter 6, this book).

5. Weber, Nietzsche, and the Will to Power

Weber's apparent moral relativism, his critique of positivism and his opposition to Marx's conception of ideology puts him squarely in the company of another major commentator on the problems of Modernity, Friedrich Nietzsche (d. 1900), and over the years Weberian scholars have increasingly come to recognize the parallels between these scholars' work, especially towards the end of Weber's career. According to Giddens (1995), Weber's experience of the German state leading up to, during, and after the War made him a late convert to the view that democracy offered the only viable check on despotic institutional power. Before that he held the common bourgeois view that Germany was a nation largely comprised of 'brutes' who had neither the inclination nor the abilities to be entrusted with enfranchisement.

We have difficulty determining precisely the extent to which Nietzsche directly influenced Weber and the extent to which they were both simply responding in a similar manner to the anxieties of their age. As Gerth and Mills (1948) demonstrated, the pessimistic view of disenchantment and rationalization—later taken to the extreme by Burnham (1941)—was established in the German tradition well before Weber and Nietzsche turned their minds to it. According to Coser (1971), the issue that more obviously bound Nietzsche and Weber directly on this particular matter was their shared distrust of the abilities of bureaucratic officers to maintain the required degree of moral rectitude and personal discipline of conduct in order to avoid the despotism of what Michels (1915) later famously described as the 'Iron Law of Oligarchy'.

We find more than a little of the Nietzschian 'Overman' in this pessimism. We see, however, one subtle point of departure between Weber and Nietzsche here, at least in terms of degree rather than substance. Weber's distrust of bureaucracy was based on a common bourgeois belief that there were just not enough people who possessed the necessary skills to exercise good judgment (Coser 1971), although he later hoped that appropriate training institutions might ultimately be able to rectify what he came to see as a simple problem of supply and demand (Giddens 1995).[1] In contrast, Nietzsche's objection was much more fundamental in that he believed that no one (but *especially* the morally weak German bourgeoisie) could ever come close to the irreproachable Zarathustrian ideal that was required to exercise leadership over others (Hayman 1980).[2]

In matters such as moral relativism, the disenchantment of the world, and a general pessimism about the prospects of Modernity, we can argue that Weber and Nietzsche were providing similar (if not identical) interpretations of the general intellectual preoccupations of their day. From an organizational perspective, however, we find one point of commonality that has become increasingly important. Weber was particularly struck by Nietzsche's insight that, for all practical purposes, human relations must be seen as relations of *power*, regardless of the context in which they occur. According to Turner (1991), we can see Weber as systematically 'sociologizing' Nietzsche's notion of the will to power—focusing on the actual disciplinary mechanisms that we use in our ceaseless attempts to reorganize the world in pursuit of our desire to subsume all aspects of human life under a totalizing rationalism (Schacht 1995).

For us, these foregoing observations help explain the sustained interest that organization studies has exhibited in that more recent Nietzschian analyst of power relations, Michel Foucault (see Burrell, Chapter 6, this book).[3] Nietzsche, Weber, and, more recently, Foucault have inspired us to question how reason is used *instrumentally* to justify certain preferred systems of morality. In other words, instead of taking reason for granted and seeing how close forms of organizational rationality get to this ideal, we must recognize that reason is itself a political device, tendentiously used to justify certain types of practice (Foucault 2000). As Turner (1991: xxvii) puts it, the key question that Weber addresses is, 'How can reason be rationally justified?'

Turner's observation leads us to one of our principal contentions: when analyzing relations of power in organizations, our task is more than simply a matter of identifying the practices that maintain the status quo in order

[1] This sentiment has not died away. Indeed, it could be the mantra for innumerable Business Schools that justify themselves on the basis that they need to train the next generation of managers.

[2] Nietzsche's contempt for the German bourgeoisie was not unique. Indeed, Hayman (1980) argues that Nietzsche got much of his inspiration for *Thus Spoke Zarathustra* from Carl Spitteler's *Prometheus und Epimetheus*, where the latter character is used to personify the backsliding mediocrity of much of German society.

[3] Interestingly, Foucault (1998) was, by his own admission, largely ignorant of much post-Weberian German social theory (especially the 'Frankfurt School') and rarely made direct reference to Weber except in his later interviews.

to determine whether they measure up to some a priori rational ideal (although this is, of course, a crucial element of critique). Thus, although a concern for the perceived rationality of the practices of organizational power is important, we should also examine the grammar and vocabulary of the systems of knowledge that provide the justification for those very practices to be enacted. We contend that these grammars provide the means by which we understand the effects of power on the body, especially how embodied individuals can (or ought to) become useful and productive members of an organization. Indeed, humans work together efficiently and productively only after they have been 'caught up in a system of subjectification' (Foucault 1979: 26).

The analytical key is what we style, after White (1978) and Harvey Brown (1989), an *ironical* approach that not only recognizes the incompleteness of competing representations of the same object or process (Rorty 1989)—say organizational power—but also recognizes that ostensibly contradictory representations are frequently 'indebted' to each other (Burke 1969). Gouldner (1955) alluded to such an occurrence in his discussion of the Radical and Liberal perspectives on bureaucracy. Gouldner saw the former perspective as being wedded to a view in which the raison d'être of bureaucracy is nothing short of class domination, while the latter perspective sees bureaucracy, potentially at least, as an efficient form of organization operating in the interests of all citizens (so long as it is managed well). Thus, even if we see bureaucracy as a technology (cast in its broadest sense)—that is, a means to an end—when we pursue those ends we are revealing what we believe to be true in terms of purpose, necessity, and morality (Heidegger 1977). Thus, Weber's interest lay in the vocabulary and grammar of organizations—systems of knowledge or discourses, if you will—and their relation to issues of how we are to conduct ourselves in those organizations, which is the preoccupation that links him most directly with Nietzsche's legacy.

The approach we set out above effectively focuses on the epistemological role of discourse. This allows us to identify the key elements of a specific discourse of organizations and organizational conduct (Hall 2001):

(i) coherent and systematic statements about an organization that delineate our knowledge about it and construct its 'objects'—i.e. what the components of the organization (individuals, systems, etc.) are and how they interact;
(ii) rules which prescribe certain ways of talking about organizations and proscribe others—i.e. a justification as to why, say, bureaucracy is the preferred means of achieving organizational objectives;

(iii) 'subjects' who in some way personify the discourse—e.g. the 'fair' manager, the 'hard working' employee, the 'reliable' supplier, the 'committed' employee, etc.;
(iv) how this knowledge of organization acquires authority—i.e. why one discourse becomes accepted as a representation of the 'truth of the matter' while others do not; and,
(v) details of the specific technologies and practices of organization that not only supply practical knowledge about how it is to be run but also provide the normative basis by which organizational members are expected to regulate their own conduct and that of others—e.g. systems of coercion, reward, training, etc.

The above scheme comprises our first step towards developing an *ironical* analysis. Starting with the familiar bureaucratic ideal type, we will next discuss how different modes of subjectification follow on from a representation of what is ostensibly the same object—that is, organizational control achieved through the operation of rules enacted through hierarchical referral—that attribute to it different purposes and, therefore, different modes of rational (and irrational) behavior.

We will then see how these different modes of subjectification align with contrasting concepts of 'interests' and, therefore, systems of domination, that are constituted under different systems of knowledge about organization. Following Heidegger (1977), this move must ultimately incorporate a consideration of the morality that underpins these modes of rationality, which brings us back to Weber's discussion of the bureaucratic ideal type. We now proceed by turning to a genealogical mode of inquiry (Foucault 1979) and ask: Under what circumstances might one way of understanding bureaucracy prevail over the other and lead to a change in the rules of organizational conduct?

6. What Do Bosses Really, Really Do? The Grammar and Vocabulary of Bureaucracy

In his famous essay, 'What Do Bosses Do?' Stephen Marglin (1975) provided a Marxist economist's commentary on the role of the manager as the servant of capital, which we take as our exemplar of what Gouldner (1955) called the Radical view of bureaucracy. In his belated but equally famous rejoinder, 'What Do Bosses Really Do?', David Landes (1986) provided a liberal economist's response, presenting managers as selfless servants of everyone in an organization who exercise authority only by dint of the fact that they have a privileged access to a body of managerial skills and knowledge. We take the latter positions as our exemplar of what Gouldner (1955) called the Liberal view of bureaucracy. But how can two such starkly contrasting views of the same ostensibly objects—managers or 'bosses' going about their business in commercial organizations—come about? Our response is that each perspective—Radical and Liberal—constitutes a set of discursive rules (i.e. a 'grammar') that allows us to make meaningful and mutually intelligible statements using what is effectively a Weberian vocabulary of organization.

But what of this vocabulary? In his magnum opus, *Wirtschaft und Gesellschaft*, Weber develops some of his most concise definitions of many of the objects that we would still find recognizable in organizational studies today—such definitions that, under the general rubric of research on bureaucratic institutions, have come to form the basic and enduring vocabulary of organization studies. These main definitions are set out in Table 3.2.

Because Weber saw that concept of power as being 'sociologically amorphous' (i.e. there are many different social relationships in which individuals can demand compliance with their will), then the probability that a command will be obeyed relates to the context of domination. For example, a superior might expect a subordinate to obey a command in the workplace, but if the same individuals met outside the workplace then the superior is unlikely to have the same expectation of obedience.

Presenting the above definitions in this manner should not be taken to indicate that we consider them to have remained completely stable and uncontested. In particular, Weber's parsimonious statements on power have consistently been subjected to systematic refinement, augmentation, and elaboration by prominent scholars such Emerson (1962), Wrong (1968), Lukes (1974), Foucault (1979), and Clegg (1975, 1989). Despite this wrangling, however, many of the debates on matters of power, discipline, and domination have been less about the definition of these basic sociological units and more about how they relate to each other under the rubric of competing views of political economy that attribute purpose and necessity to organizations. In Foucault's terms this is the link between the higher order discourse of 'Governmentality' (i.e. the desire make diverse and potentially 'unruly' people 'useful' members of society) and localized techniques of disciplinary power (i.e. the competing practices used to ensure that an individual's actions are congruent with the goals of an organization). In this respect, we would argue that we *can* still

Table 3.2 Weber's definition of basic organizational objects

Organizational Object	Weber's definition
The Corporate Group	A social relationship that is closed to outsiders or restricts their admission by regulations, and whose authority is enforced by the actions of specific individuals charged with this function. These functionaries will also exercise plenary powers [i.e. the functionaries in question are charged with enforcing conduct in line with laws and regulations governing the corporate group] (Weber 1962: 107).
Organization	A system of continuous activity pursuing a goal of a specified kind. A 'corporate organization' is an aggregative social relationship characterized by an administrative staff whose activity is oriented exclusively and continuously to achieving the goals of the organization (Weber 1962: 115).
Power	That opportunity existing within a social relationship which permits one to carry out one's own will even against resistance and regardless of the basis upon which this opportunity rests (Weber 1962: 117).
Domination[4]	The opportunity to have a command of a given specified content obeyed by a given group of persons (Weber 1962: 117).
Discipline	The opportunity to obtain prompt and automatic, obedience in a predictable form from a given group of persons because of their practiced orientation toward a command . . . the concept of 'discipline' includes the practiced nature of uncritical and *mass* obedience (Weber 1962: 117—emphasis in original).

study how basic sociological objects (i.e. those established through the classic vocabulary of organization studies set out by Weber) have been incorporated into coherent systems of knowledge about organizations through the application of competing grammars.

Take, for instance, 'domination'. According to Weber's narrow definition, any organization that attempts to get a more or less diverse group of individuals to act in a concerted manner towards the achievement of some goal must necessarily be engaged in a form of domination, whether it is ultimately through coercion or consent (Diggins 1996). Moreover, organizationally speaking, within a corporate group then domination is usually what Weber called 'administered domination'—that is, domination is enshrined in rules whose authority is enforced by the actions of specific

[4] Interestingly, throughout his career Talcott Parsons persisted in translating *Herrschaft*, not as 'domination' but as 'leadership' (e.g. Parsons 1942). Reflecting on the nature of Weber's definition, it is not surprising then that Parsons saw 'leadership' as the quality of an individual who was able to discern and represent collective interests—that is, for Parsons *Herrschaft* automatically implied legitimate authority (Cohen et al. 1975).

individuals charged with this function.[5] Along these lines, even a committed Marxist like Wright (1997) has to concede that within noncapitalist organizations there will still be a functional division of labor where some individuals are charged with directing the actions of others, based on their superior skills and abilities.

In the narrow sense of Weber's definition, this still reflects a form of domination, albeit one that is not premised on furthering the interests of one class at the expense of the other. However, as Gouldner (1955) showed, the key question is not so much what occurs in the absence of domination, but how we justify the presence of domination for different political ends. In this sense, Radical and Liberal perspectives both involve grammars that provide a rationale for bureaucracy in the name of efficiency (Gouldner 1955): The Liberal view is happy for efficient organizations to serve the political and economic status quo (with some checks and balances to avoid the worst excesses of domination) while the Radical view aspires to a transformed political and economic situation in which efficient organization does not perpetuate exploitation. These grammars are not mutually exclusive; indeed, they are what Burke (1969) describes as 'mutually indebted' in the sense that they share many discursive features. This indebtedness, as we shall demonstrate in due course, is because they are both dependent on characteristic grammars of organization that are founded on a figurative use of the bureaucratic ideal type.

7. Developing a Grammar of Organization: The Ideal Type as an Interpretive Device

The debate over Weber's true intentions apropos the ideal type has been intense and protracted. It is fair to say, however, that there is now a good deal of agreement over the status of the bureaucratic ideal type as an act of figuration rather than as a model, archetype, or blueprint for developing social structures. That the ideal type was ever considered otherwise seems odd, given that Weber repeatedly referred its specific ontological and methodological roles. Weber based his argument on his concern that the

[5] It is important to note that Weber is not using 'corporate' as a synonym for a commercial organization here. Rather, he is relying on a much older sense of bringing people together in this manner as a form of 'incorporation'. For example, in order to covey this particular sense of incorporation, for the frontispiece of *Leviathan* Thomas Hobbes (1651) used an etching of the single body of the eponymous giant sea monster that is, on closer inspection, made up of the interlocking bodies of individual citizens.

'positivist sociology' promoted in the late nineteenth century by the likes of Herbert Spencer—with all its pretensions to scientific generalizability—was unable to capture the diversity of subjective experiences associated with being an individual engaged in a complex set of social relations (see Weber 1978: 56–7).

In response, Weber called for a multidisciplinary approach made up of what he labeled the 'sciences of concrete reality' that would investigate the diversity of social experience, in preference to a monist approach that imputes universal, law-based structures (Weber 1978: 57).[6] The ideal type is an important means of generating such knowledge specifically because it is *not* a neutral or universal model of a social structure that is apprehended by everyone in exactly the same way. Rather, an ideal type reflects the attempt to represent patterns or 'constellations of conduct' arising from an explicitly normative perspective (Lopez 2003). Weber captures this view in what is undoubtedly one of his most famous passages:

> An ideal type is formed by the one-sided *accentuation* of one or more points of view and by the synthesis of a great many diffuse, discrete, more or less present and occasionally absent *concrete individual* phenomena, which are arranged according to those one-sidedly emphasised viewpoints into a unified analytical construct... In its conceptual purity, this mental construct...cannot be found empirically anywhere in reality. It is *utopia*. (Weber in Gerth and Mills 1948: 90)

Here it is evident that the ideal type, as conceived by Weber, is an interpretive device that allows us to apprehend something as intangible as a complex nexus of social relations *as if it were a singular and stable entity* and, moving beyond solipsistic experience, also allows us to convey this state of affairs to others.[7] In the language of the philosophy of science, Weber's was anticipating what was later coined the 'theory lead' status of observation (Hanson 1959)—that is, ontologically speaking, our conceptualization of bureaucracy leads us to conceive of specific social relationships like power, domination, and discipline in a coherent and

[6] The term 'science' is restricted by a rather limited translation of *Wissenschaft*. A broader definition yields the term 'knowledge' rather than 'science'. Of course, it was Weber's contention that there were ways of generating knowledge other than slavishly aping the natural sciences.

[7] In his discussion of Weber's contribution to economics, Diehl (1923) describes the ideal type as a 'fiction' that allows us, not to deduce laws that contain the 'true reality of things' by analogy with physical principles, but to characterize historical phenomena in their cultural significance. According to Diehl (1923: 94), 'The concept of culture is a value concept. All value judgements are subjective and change in the course of history with the character of the culture and the ideas controlling men.'

unified yet partial way.[8] In other words, the ideal type is a 'structure of understanding for the historian who seeks to integrate, after the fact, a certain set of data' (Foucault 2000: 231).

Weber's oft-quoted caveat—subsequently restated by the likes of Alfred Schutz right through to Michel Foucault—has failed to prevent many scholars from taking the bureaucratic ideal type quite literally as an immanent (not to say desirable) social structure. Taking Weber literally was not, however, only the preserve of the functionalist systems builders; as Gouldner (1955) demonstrated, many other researchers of a more radical hue demonstrated similar literalist tendencies. Indeed, a literal reading of the bureaucratic ideal type as an enduring social object rather than as a merely ephemeral conceptualization is seductive in two specific ways: (*a*) it provides researchers of contrasting political perspectives with a degree of *ontological* stability—that is, effort expended in studying bureaucracy over an extended time would not be wasted; and, (*b*) it provides those researchers with *epistemological* stability because it allows them to study bureaucracy as a universal feature of modern life, thereby avoiding the theoretical and methodological problems associated with particularity, discontinuity, and ambiguity.

From here on we develop a less literal reading of bureaucracy: a tropological approach which takes as the primary function of the bureaucratic ideal type its role as an 'inaugurating gesture' (White 1978) for subsequent theory building about organizations that includes 'the delineation of concepts, the specification of objects and borders, the provision of argument and justifications, etc.' (Lemke 2001: 44). This inaugurating gesture allows us to build mutually intelligible knowledge of the world by using tropes: standard figures of speech that allow us to move between the private and public realm (cf. Burke 1969; Manning 1979). The more important challenge for us, however, is to answer the question: How do we move beyond this (admittedly crucial) ontological function of the bureaucratic ideal type to embrace theoretical and methodological concerns such as particularity, discontinuity, and ambiguity.

Starting with the familiar trope of metaphor, we establish common experiential ground by taking what is for most people an abstract or intangible entity that is difficult to apprehend (such as, how individuals

[8] We use the term, 'partial' in an intentionally ambiguous way here. An ideal type is 'partial' in that it is necessarily incomplete (in the same way that a road map is only useful insofar as it leaves out most of the topographical detail) and it is also 'partial' in that it represents a particular perspective on an entity or object.

are subjected to domination, discipline, and control in an organization) and describing it as a concrete or tangible entity that most people find familiar and easier to apprehend (such as, how we relate to each other in an organization through rules, stratification, and hierarchical referral).

The next figurative transition in developing a grammar of organization is the move from metaphor to metonymy. In effect this is a shift in emphasis from general form to specific substance that allows us to apprehend the concrete physicality of an entity associated with a particular metaphor. Thus, bureaucracy as a root metaphor not only provides us with particular conceptual configuration of domination, discipline, and control in organizations; in its metonymical form it also presents bureaucracy as having a physical structure made up of discrete components that play a part in a dynamic process—that is, bureaucracy helps us represent the practices of domination, discipline, and control (although these structures and processes need not be identical to the bureaucratic ideal type). Moreover, peoples' understanding of their relation to these structures and processes and how they might respond to them are captured through the attitudes and repertoires associated with characteristic subject positions, such as the dutiful and obedient worker or the difficult and recalcitrant worker.

The third figurative transition—from metonymy to synecdoche—is a way of dividing the world into classes of objects by comparing the extent to which discrete entities share similar structures and processes. Thus, we could say that an organization belongs to the class of objects we call bureaucracy because it shares some (if not all) of the characteristics we associate with the bureaucratic ideal type. This taxonomic move is particularly powerful from an epistemological perspective because it enables us to generate deductive knowledge about the extent of bureaucracy in the world through comparative research—that is, if we can classify an organization as a bureaucracy (to a greater or lesser extent) we can draw conclusions about the operation of certain aspects of its social structure.

In this respect, one way that the bureaucratic ideal type serves as the inspiration for comparative organizational studies is to undertake what Flyvbjerg (2001) calls the empirical study of 'maximum variation' cases on an organization-by-organization basis. Here the objective is not to confirm the actual practices of domination, discipline, and control to be always and everywhere the same (in other words, to take the bureaucratic ideal type literally as a universal social structure), but rather to explore all their subtleties and nuances in settings ranging from those in which we are most likely to encounter them (say, in highly rationalized call center work—Garson 1988; Bain and Taylor 2000) to those in which their presence may be surprising (e.g. under conditions of nominal autonomy associated with teamwork—Sewell 1998; Barker 1999).

For us to understand how these figurative transformations can form individually coherent and competing yet mutually indebted systems of representation of the 'truth of the matter', we turn to the final figurative transformation: irony. This involves seeing particular depictions of bureaucracy as offering what Rorty (1989) calls a 'final vocabulary' that enables researchers to link statements of fact about how, as they presently see it, the world *is* with normative statements about how it *ought* to be. We might reasonably expect these final vocabularies to be mutually exclusive; talking about bureaucracy in one way would seem to preclude the other. However, Burke (1969) shows how, by dogmatically adhering to a particular final vocabulary in this mutually exclusive manner, we are being relativist in the most basic sense in that we see the truth claims of all other final vocabularies on the same topic in terms of the extent to which they diverge from our own. In contrast Burke advocates developing an *ironical disposition* that acknowledges the 'indebtedness' of opposing discursive formations—that in some ways each discursive formation is anticipating and responding to the other's position. Adopting an ironical disposition allows us to gain a 'perspective on perspectives' that appreciates the way in which competing discursive formations help us to *create* truths, in all their ambiguity and contestability, rather than *reveal* universal and transcendental Truth (Burke 1969; Rorty 1989).

Consequently, ironists (*a*) have doubts about the validity of their current final vocabulary, not least because they recognize the merit, no matter how slight, of competing final vocabularies; (*b*) recognize that an argument exclusively phrased in their own final vocabulary can never completely allay these doubts; and, (*c*) recognize that their final vocabulary is a contestable representation of the world rather than an unambiguous statement of reality (after Rorty 1989). We advocate adopting an ironical disposition toward bureaucracy along these lines and, in order to 'gain a perspective on perspectives', we explore what Burke calls the 'indebtedness' of competing discursive formations. Our way into this is to explore representations of the paradoxes of bureaucracy that are not easily incorporated into either formation without reference to the other. This is not, however, a merely academic exercise: personal feelings of frustration with bureaucracy (as internal members or external 'clients') can be seen as an inevitable by-product of other objectives we value highly, such as procedural fairness and protection against management fiat or capricious whim (du Gay 2000). In this way, focusing on the ambiguities and paradoxical experiences of bureaucracy—for example, that it both constrains and protects or that the failure of rules to account for every eventuality is often used to justify the drafting of even more rules—is essential in developing an understanding of the impact that competing grammars of organization have on organizational conduct.

8. Toward an Ironical Reading of Competing Grammars of Bureaucracy

The conventional way of dealing with the ambiguities surrounding the concept of right conduct in bureaucracies has been to reflect on its Janus-faced character. This has generally involved the attribution of discrete dichotomous states that prevail at certain times and under certain conditions (see Bendix 1947; Eisenstadt 1959; Burns and Stalker 1961; Alder and Borys 1996). For example, Bendix (1947) identified mutually exclusive 'democratic' and 'authoritarian' forms of bureaucracy, each with its own characteristic ethos. Thus, democratic bureaucracy is associated with discretion, mutual respect, and loyalty established through camaraderie while authoritarian bureaucracy is associated with the obedience, fealty, and loyalty established through unquestioning compliance. The logic of this is that we should classify bureaucracy as being *either* democratic *or* authoritarian: a discrete choice also reflected in Eisenstadt's identification (1959) of bureaucracy as an instrument of public service or malign power and Alder and Borys's discussion (1996) of 'constraining' or 'enabling' bureaucracies.

Bendix relied on the familiar image of the court of the absolutist and autocratic monarch, Frederick the Great of Prussia, to illustrate the ethos of authoritarian bureaucracy but we find his choice of the civilian police force as an example of the ethos of democratic bureaucracy much more interesting. For this he took Smith's counterintuitive observation (1940) that effective policing depended, not on the universal and unfaltering enforcement of the letter of the law by every officer, but on individual officers exercising their discretion on a case-by-case basis to ensure that the greatest degree of social protection will be secured. Thus,

> [T]he degree of enforcement and the method of its application will vary with each neighbourhood and community. There are no rules, nor even general guides to policy, in this regard. Each policeman [*sic*] must, in a sense, determine the standard

which is to be set in the area for which he is responsible.... Thus he is a policy-forming police administrator in miniature, who operates beyond the scope of the usual devices of popular control. (Smith 1940: 20)

Notwithstanding Smith's prescient comments on the now fashionable concept of self-management, his observations are also interesting because they demonstrate the moral dilemma faced by officers individually charged with invoking the concept of the greater good through the exercise of discretion. Most obviously, this can be in direct conflict with the concept of procedural fairness exactly because there are no hard and fast rules to follow when an officer is faced with applying the law on a case-by-case basis. This opens up opportunities for various forms of venality (e.g., turning a blind eye to one's fellow officers who use legally dubious means to get 'results') or even more sinister and irrational abuses (e.g., an officer focusing his or her attention on one group in society on the basis of personal prejudice). Other instances of this dilemma are also to be found in organizations that we might reasonably expect to be the very model of rational/legal order such as prison or the military, but for us the significance of Bendix's example of the police is that it draws attention to du Gay's paradox (2000): personal feelings of frustration with bureaucracy are often by-products of our desire for procedural fairness.

According to Gouldner (1955) this characteristic tension between higher order discourses of coercion versus consent or domination and care was played out through contrasting Radical and Liberal grammars of bureaucracy. Our contention, however, is that neither of these grammars adequately captures the experience of organizational members: we find it quite conceivable that an organizational member may simultaneously cavil at being constrained by rules yet yearn for protection against fiat or capricious whim. Thus, rather than classifying specific organizations in either/or terms, we see it as much more analytically fruitful to seek out such moments of paradox in which the grammars offered by dichotomous typologies—be they dominative or caring, democratic or authoritarian, constraining or enabling—are in tension yet, at the same time, mutually indebted. In other words, we should seek out the moments when employees are faced with the dilemma of deciding when certain local techniques of disciplinary power are a legitimate form of coercion (and, therefore, to be supported) or an illegitimate intrusion into their autonomy (and, therefore, to be resisted).

Such an ironical enterprise would throw into sharp relief the ethical terrain of the debates that surround questions of the success (or otherwise) of specific legal/rational rules enacted in organizations. For example, we can reasonably expect these moments of contradiction to be all the more confronting and (potentially, at least) destabilizing if, say, an organization emphatically espoused the rhetoric of 'teamwork' and 'empowerment' yet was also the site of disciplinary techniques that attempted to ensure that any nominal discretion was used in the pursuit of that organization's expressed goals (Sewell 1998). With this comment in mind, we now, through the use of a case study that made much of its non-coercive credentials, go on to explore how we might use an ironical approach to address the paradoxical experiences of bureaucracy.

9. Tightening the Iron Cage: An Ironical Reading of Concertive Control

Our case illustration comes from a long-term ethnographic study of teamwork in ISE Communications—a small North American assembler of electronic circuit boards that took an almost evangelical approach to the perceived benefits of teamwork, empowerment, and increased employee discretion (Barker 1993, 1999). Indeed, the presence of such an explicit discourse of mutual dependency and consensual values at ISE constitutes what Flyvbjerg (2001) would call a 'least-likely' case—that is, prima facie, we might be surprised to find discourses of coercion and consent or domination and care coming into conflict. As we proceed, we will point to instances at which such conflicts were indeed evident and where an ironical approach can provide important insights into how competing models of right conduct impacted on employees' actions 'on the ground'.

Barker described the implementation of a new teamwork program that appeared to be a significant deviation from ISE's previous operating practices. The impetus for the changes was heavily influenced by contemporary management texts that exhorted managers to 'loosen their employees' reins' or 'set them free' so as to develop a neglected resource: the ingenuity, creativity, and knowledge of those very employees, people who had rarely been consulted in the past on operational matters. This exhortation followed the familiar logic associated with movements that emerged in the 1980s such as quality circles and, later, total quality management: 'Nobody is better equipped to solve the problems arising on the production line than those nearest to the point when such problems occur'.

To the subjects of the ISE study—hourly-paid shift workers undertaking repetitive assembly tasks—this must have been an attractive proposition;

after experiencing years of the minutest managerial control, the promise of increased freedom, of 'being your own boss', or of 'having a say in how things are done' acted as a powerful motivator that was likely to overcome predictable feelings of cynicism. Over a number of years, however, local techniques of disciplinary power at ISE moved away from a familiar combination of technical and bureaucratic control (cf. Edwards 1979) and towards a new peer-based form that emulated many of the aspects of rule-based coercion; although the rules themselves were ostensibly arrived at and, therefore, legitimated, through processes of mutual agreement within the teams themselves. After Tompkins and Cheney (1985), this was characterized as a process of 'concertive' control (Barker 1993). We shall now explore concertive control's unfolding at ISE through a tropological approach that culminates in an ironical analysis of competing representations of the problem of right conduct in organizations.

The Bureaucratic Ideal Type as an Inaugurating Gesture

Weber's discussion of bureaucracy served as the inaugurating gesture for Barker's study as he set out to contrast how the experiences of concertive control were a manifestation of the will to power yet diverged from the bureaucratic ideal in important ways. Most significantly, the Weberian concept of the 'corporate group' (see Table 3.2) was primarily articulated at the level of the team, rather than the organization as a whole. From this modification of the inaugurating gesture, the teams ended up being even more constrained by the systems of peer-and rule-based control of their own devising than they would have been under the more traditionally bureaucratic form it replaced.

Metaphor in Use: The Team Ought to Behave Like a Family

Early in their transition to teamwork, ISE's employees often referred to their own team as a 'family'. This metaphorical usage articulated the idea of a tightly knit corporate group while introducing the concept of a 'natural' hierarchy of authority traditionally associated with the nuclear family. This move created an ethos that impacted on how the new team members were to think of themselves and to act towards each other. Liz, a key informant in ISE, regularly returned to the metaphorical value of the team as a means of conveying matters such as mutual dependency and the obligation this placed on members to submit themselves to its collective will. For example,

> [S]ee teams grow just like families do. Say you're divorced with kids, and you get remarried. There's this growth time when you have to learn how to get along together. You have to work at it each day. But after a while, you either find a way of making it work or things fall apart. It takes constant work. Same thing happens with the teams. You figure that you spend eight to ten hours a day here, and you only spend how much with your family? We are truly a family here. We are all in this together. We have to make it work together. So, we have to grow together. (Barker 1999)

This initial metaphorical move was very effective in establishing the legitimate basis for subsequent techniques of disciplinary power that were developed by the team members themselves.

Metaphor to Metonymy: Now We Are a 'Real' Team

Over time employees increasingly began to consider matters such as the team's physical structure as a collection of individually discrete components. Through a discourse of codependency and mutual obligation all team members came to see themselves as being a key part of a coherent corporate group. For example, there was intense pressure to learn how to undertake each other's jobs so that personnel could be interchangeable. More importantly, with the team as metonym, its members came to see interdependency in terms that could be reduced to the specific performance of individuals. This led team members to exert peer pressure on each other as a means of control. Being 'on the team' meant being functionally controlled as an individual component of a greater whole. They had become more than a family; they were a 'community of team mates'.

Moreover, during this metonymical move, the value systems of the team became enshrined in formal requirements enforced through rule-based discipline. For example,

> [O]ther values included the need for everyone to contribute fully. The team members called this 'saying your piece' at team meetings so that the team's decision would be better (and their consensus stronger). Another part of this value was the need for all team members to learn all of the jobs required by the team so that they could fill in and cover for each other. ISE's team workers were beginning to piece together the discursive formations they needed to build a useful and readily discernible concertive discipline. (Barker 1999)

Of key importance, the metonymical move allowed for specific techniques of disciplinary power to be enacted between individuals according to the team's substantive rationality, which provided their boundaries of action and interest. The emergence of rational rules during this developmental phase made concertive control concrete; almost as tangible as their old supervisor's book of job descriptions. The key element here was that the locus of authority rested with the teams themselves, which gave the rules their disciplinary power.

Metonymy to Synecdoche: ISE Is One Big Family

With this move *all* of ISE's teams began to see themselves as a collective set of discrete entities sharing similar structures and processes. Thus, the notion of 'team' came to represent the dynamic of working together as a corporate group across the whole organization. All the teams developed similar methods of working and disciplinary processes and they acted in concert to meet the wider goals of the organization. This is clearly a synecdochical move in that the local disciplinary practices of individual teams became standardized. In effect, ISE was seen as a confederation of individual teams who, on the basis of their shared value systems, could legitimately intervene in each other's activities. For example, although it was always expected that longer-tenured team members would help to integrate and train new temporary workers into existing teams (with the teams themselves deciding who would ultimately be retained as a full-time employee), experienced workers were also appointed to new teams to socialize the new workers into the existing teams' established value systems. This was especially evident in team meetings which became a forum for discussing established norms and creating rules *within and between* ISE's teams.

Ultimately, all the teams converged around a consistent pattern of disciplinary techniques enforced through peer monitoring. Here is the synecdochical move—seeing ISE as a whole made up of individual teams, each sharing similar value systems—that led to an organization-wide concertive control, creating an 'Iron Cage' even stronger and more effective than the former orthodox bureaucratic control (Barker 1993).

Irony: The Paradox of Concertive Control

If concertive control at ISE is a highly effective means of establishing discipline in Weber's sense (see Table 3.2), then how can we understand the potentially paradoxical experiences of team members at ISE who are promised empowerment but find themselves coerced into certain behaviors? This concern leads us to our final tropological move of irony. It was clearly evident to some team members that they were creating their own systems discipline. Even those who were alert to this paradox, however, consistently expressed the feeling that these rules were good for them and their work. For example, many of ISE's team members readily understood that they had created a more powerful form of control than had existed under the old hierarchy, but none of these workers was willing to contemplate a return to their previous ways of working. When Barker asked Lee Ann about the stress of working within the new team structure she commented:

> No way [laugh]. I've worked damn hard. We've worked damn hard for this. We've made this thing work. Yeah, we get super involved. We work the long hours. But it works. The company works. I'm proud of that, and I don't want to go back [to a traditional management system]. We have self-management here, and I don't want to give that up. No way. (Barker 1999)

Thus, ISE's workers found concertive control to be simultaneously constraining *and* liberating, coercive *and* protective. Over and above reported benefits like perceived autonomy, concertive control provided them with tangible rewards like increased job security and protection from opportunistic, free-riding coworkers (see Sewell and Wilkinson 1992).

In this paradoxical situation, the team members made sense of their working lives through two conflicting modes of subjectification; competing systems of knowledge, each of which was constructed on the basis of objects drawn from the bureaucratic ideal, yet resulted in quite different sets of subject positions. More importantly, the experience of ISE demonstrates that competing models of right conduct associated with teamwork are articulated through familiar grammars of bureaucracy. In the case of ISE, however, individual organizational personalities were highly conflicted exactly because neither grammar held sway to the complete exclusion of the other—that is, in responding to the emergence of the specific disciplinary practices of concertive control, team members decided for themselves whether those practices were overwhelmingly constraining or protective, coercive or caring, and so forth.

Such conflicting experiences clearly demonstrate the difficulty we face in conclusively determining whether teamwork at ISE was excessively coercive or 'empowering'. Certainly team members regularly reported acute feelings of the type: 'We believe we're participating in our own coercion but it's better than the alternative'. But, if we attempt to determine who benefits from a move away from bureaucratic control, we would make a serious mistake by dismissing such sentiments as the ruminations of dupes in thrall to false consciousness. Likewise, we do not have to prove that ISE's managers were consciously serving the interests of shadowy 'capitalists' by playing some sophisticated Machiavellian game that involved tricking their employees into a form of intense self-exploitation (indeed, we have no doubt that Jack Tackett—ISE's vice president of manufacturing, who instigated the shift to teamwork—was acting in good faith when he spoke of 'empowerment' and 'autonomy'). This is why an ironical analysis of techniques of disciplinary power reveals the difficulty of arguing against programs such as empowerment and teamwork when they accord with employees' everyday concepts of procedural justice and autonomy, even though the result may also be an increase in relative levels of coercion and work intensification.

Moving Organizational Research Forward Through Irony

Our ISE case demonstrates how the conflicting experiences of team members at ISE help account for the force of du Gay's bureaucratic paradox: we may yearn for protection and justice but still object vociferously when we perceive that our autonomy and freedom are being constrained. This paradox comes as no surprise since Weber's famous depiction of creeping rationalization as a potential 'Iron Cage' is, of course, ambiguous: a cage protects as well as constrains. Indeed, this very ambiguity has enabled scholars like Bendix (1947), Gouldner (1955), Eisenstadt (1959), and Alder and Borys (1996) to focus on bureaucracy's dualistic nature. In this way it will always be difficult to exercise a discrete choice between 'good' or 'bad' forms of bureaucracy, even when the prospects for an ostensibly 'good' form to prevail seem strong, such as in the context of teamwork. For example, Bauman (2002) argues that, at its extreme, a team's principal purpose is clearly exploitative in that it is an effective way for its 'strongest' member to serve their own interests at the expense of weaker colleagues.

Under these conditions, polarized and static conceptions of organizational power, domination, and discipline become less persuasive. Indeed, as we found through the experiences of ISE's teams, in breaking the fetters of traditional superior/subordinate relations, team members became enmeshed in new relations of power, domination, and discipline. In this sense, rather than becoming emancipated through 'post-bureaucratic' structures, teams come to function as a basic unit of organization; a development which compels us to reconsider the technical and moral status of bureaucracy but this time at a lower level of incorporation. Here we concur with du Gay (2000) in that, generally speaking, bureaucracy should be seen as an 'instituted style of ethical life' but we would add that distinct 'styles' align with particular grammars of bureaucracy, competing with each other in providing the ethical 'script' to the conduct of team life. It is irony that allows us to understand how these competing scripts play out in organizations with all the problems of ambiguity, paradox, and contradiction that this entails.

10. Concluding Remarks

At the start of our chapter, we stated the daunting task facing any contemporary scholar taking on Weber: What can be said about him that no one else has already said? For our part, we have sought to articulate a discursive and representational vision of Weber's work that is grounded in the connections between Nietzsche, Weber, and Foucault. As a result, we have offered a figurative analytical perspective on Weber's work that enables current scholars to expand his thinking more into the discursive realm.

Finally, we are left with one remaining observation. Clearly and unequivocally, Weber has an enduring and robust influence on how we understand our experience of organizations. All organizational scholars have been, are being, and will be shaped by his thought. Just the simple fact that taking on Weber is such a daunting task speaks volumes about his influence. Why is Weber so enduring, so useful, so embraced? The answer lies in his ability to engage that which must be engaged—developing a critical appreciation of the practical and ethical implications of a life primarily lived in and through organizations. Said another way, Weber's enduring legacy is to point scholarly thinking towards the organizational 'anxieties of the age'. Weber directs our attention towards important issues that face us in organizational studies, be they the continuing debate on whether positivistic studies can capture the diversity of subjective experience in social relations or the desire to critique power and domination in an organizational world. By reflecting on Weber's massive contribution to the study of work organizations from a discursive perspective, we have continued the powerful, useful, and necessary stream of thought we call Weberian.

References

Adler, P. S. and Borys, B. (1996). 'Two Types of Bureaucracy: Enabling and Coercive', *Administrative Science Quarterly*, 41(1): 61–89.

Bain, P. and Taylor, P. (2000). 'Entrapped by the Electronic Panopticon? Worker Resistance in a Call Centre', *New Technology, Work, and Employment*, 15(1): 2–18.

Barker, J. R. (1993). 'Tightening the Iron Cage: Concertive Control in Self-Managing Teams', *Administrative Science Quarterly*, 38(3): 408–37.

—— (1999). *The Discipline of Teamwork: Participation and Concertive Control*. Thousand Oaks, CA: Sage.

Bauman, Z. (2002). *Modernity and the Holocaust*. Cambridge: Polity Press.

Bendix, R. (1947). 'Bureaucracy: The Problem and Its Setting', *American Sociological Review*, 12(5): 493–507.

Blau, P. M. (1963). 'Critical Remarks on Weber's Theory of Authority', *The American Political Science Review*, 57(2): 305–16.

Burke, K. (1969). *A Grammar of Motives*. Berkeley, CA: University of California Press.

Burnham, J. (1941). *The Managerial Revolution: What is Happening in the World*. New York: John Day & Co.

Burns, T. and Stalker, G. M. (1961). *The Management of Innovation*. London: Tavistock Publications.

Burrell, G. (2002). 'Twentieth-century Quadrilles: Aristocracy, Owners, Managers, and Professionals', *International Studies of Management and Organization*, 32(2): 25–50.

Clegg, S. R. (1975). *Power, Rule, and Domination: A Critical and Empirical Understanding of Power in Sociological Theory and Organizational Life*. London: Routledge & Kegan Paul.

—— (1989). *Frameworks of Power*. London: Sage.

Cohen, J., Hazelrigg, L. E., and Pope, W. (1975). 'De-Parsonizing Weber: A Critique of Parsons' Interpretation of Weber's Sociology', *American Sociological Review*, 40(2): 229–41.

Coser, L. (1971). *Masters of Sociological Thought: Ideas in Historical and Social Context*. New York: Harcourt Brace Jovanovich.

Diehl, C. (1923). 'The Life and Work of Max Weber', *Quarterly Journal of Economics*, 38(1): 87–107.

Diggins, J. P. (1996). *Max Weber: Politics and the Spirit of Tragedy*. New York: Basic Books.

Du Gay, P. (2000). *In Praise of Bureaucracy: Weber • Organization • Ethics*. London: Sage.

Edwards, R. (1979). *Contested Terrain: The Transformation of the Workplace in the Twentieth Century*. London: Heinemann.

Eisenstadt, S. N. (1959). 'Bureaucracy, Bureaucratization, and Debureaucratization', *Administrative Science Quarterly*, 4(3): 302–20.

Emerson, R. M. (1962). 'Power-Dependence Relations', *American Sociological Review*, 27(1): 31–41.

Flyvbjerg, B. (2001). *Making Social Science Matter*. Cambridge: Cambridge University Press.

Foucault, M. (1979). *Discipline and Punish: The Birth of the Prison*. Harmondsworth: Penguin.

—— (1998). 'Structuralism and Post-Structuralism', in J. Faubion (ed.), *Michel Foucault: The Essential Works, 2*. New York: The New Press.

—— (2000). 'Question of Method', in James D. Faubion (ed.), *Michel Foucault: The Essential Works, 3*. New York: The New Press.

Garson, B. (1988). *The Electronic Sweatshop: How Computers are Transforming the Office of the Future into the Factory of the Past*. New York: Simon & Schuster.

Gerth, H. H. and Wright Mills, C. (eds.) (1948). *From Max Weber: Essays in Sociology*. Oxford: Oxford University Press.

Giddens, A. (1974). *Positivism and Sociology*. London: Heinemann.

—— (1995). *Politics, Sociology and Social Theory: Encounters with Classical and Contemporary Social Thought*. Cambridge: Polity Press.

Gouldner, A. W. (1955). 'Metaphysical Pathos and the Theory of Bureaucracy', *American Political Science Review*, 49(2): 496–507.

—— (1980). *The Two Marxisms: Contradictions and Anomalies in the Development of Theory*. New York: Seabury Press.

Günther, S. and Windelband, W. (1988). *Geschichte der antiken Naturwissenschaft und Philosophie*. Nördlingen: C.H. Beck.

Hall, S. (2001). 'Foucault: Power, Knowledge and Discourse', in M. Wetherell, S. Taylor, and S. J. Yates (eds.), *Discourse Theory and Practice: A Reader*. London: Sage.

Hanson, N. R. (1959). *Patterns of Discovery*. Cambridge: Cambridge University Press.

Harvey Brown, R. (1989). *A Poetic for Sociology*. Chicago: University of Chicago Press.

Hayman, R. (1980). *Nietzsche: A Critical Life*. Oxford: Oxford University Press.

Heidegger, M. (1977). *The Question Concerning Technology*. New York: Harper Torchbooks.

Hobbes, T. (1651). *Leviathan, or, the Matter, Form, and Power of a Common-wealth Ecclesiastical and Civil*. London: Andrew Crooke.

Knapp, P. (1986). 'Hegel's Universal in Marx, Durkheim and Weber: The Role of Hegelian Ideas in the Origin of Sociology', *Sociological Forum*, 1(4): 586–609.

Landes, D. S. (1986). 'What Do Bosses Really Do?', *Journal of Economic History*, 46(3): 585–623.

Lemke, T. (2001). ' "The Birth of Bio-Politics": Michel Foucault's Lectures at the Collège de France on Neo-Liberal Governmentality', *Economy and Society*, 30(2): 190–207.

Lopez, J. (2003). *Society and its Metaphors: Language, Social Theory, and Social Structure*. London: Continuum Books.

Lukes, S. (1974). *Power: A Radical View.* London: Macmillan.

Manning, P. (1979). 'Metaphors of the Field: Varieties of Organizational Discourse', *Administrative Science Quarterly*, 24(3): 660–71.

Marglin, S. (1975). 'What Do Bosses Do?', in A. Görz (ed.), *The Division of Labour: The Labour Process and Class-Struggle in Modern Capitalism.* Brighton: Harvester Press.

Marx, K. (1976). *Capital*, Volume 1. Harmondsworth: Penguin.

Michels, R. (1915). *Political Parties: A Sociological Study of the Oligarchical Tendencies of Modern Democracy.* Glencoe, IL: Free Press.

Nietzsche, F. (1961). *Thus Spoke Zarathustra.* London: Penguin.

—— (1979). *Philosophy and Truth: Selections from Nietzsche's Notebooks of the Early 1870s.* Atlantic Heights, NJ: Humanities Press.

Parson, T. (1942). 'Max Weber and the Contemporary Political Crisis', *Review of Politics*, 4(1): 61–76.

—— (1949). *The Structure of Social Action.* Glencoe, IL: Free Press.

Rickert, H. (1962). *Science and History: A Critique of Positivist Epistemology.* Princeton, NJ: Van Nostrand.

Ricoeur, P. (1994). 'Althusser's Theory of Ideology', in G. Elliott (ed.), *Althusser: A Critical Reader.* Oxford: Blackwell.

Rorty, R. (1989). *Contingency, Irony, Solidarity.* Cambridge: Cambridge University Press.

Schacht, R. (1995). 'Nietzsche', in R. Audi (ed.), *The Cambridge Dictionary of Philosophy.* Cambridge: Cambridge University Press.

Schluchter, W. (1996). *Paradoxes of Modernity: Culture and Conduct in the Theory of Max Weber.* Stanford, CA: Stanford University Press.

Sewell, G. (1998). 'The Discipline of Teams: The Control of Team-Based Industrial Work Through Electronic and Peer Surveillance', *Administrative Science Quarterly*, 43(2): 397–429.

—— and Wilkinson, B. (1992). 'Someone to Watch Over Me: Surveillance, Discipline and the Just-in-Time Labour Process', *Sociology*, 26(2): 271–90.

Smith, B. (1940). *Police Systems in the United States.* New York: Harpers.

Spitteler, C. (1945). 'Prometheus und Epimetheus', in *Gesammelte Werke.* Zurich: Artemis.

Swingewood, A. (1984). *A Short History of Sociological Thought.* New York: St Martin's Press.

Tompkins, P. K. and Cheney, G. (1985). 'Communication and Unobtrusive Control in Contemporary Organizations', in R. D. McPhee and P. K. Tompkins (eds.), *Organizational Communication: Traditional Themes and New Directions.* Beverly Hills, CA: Sage.

Turner, B. S. (1991). 'Preface', in H. H. Gerth and C. Wright Mills (eds.), *From Max Weber: Essays in Sociology.* London: Routledge.

Weber, M. (1962). *Basic Concepts in Sociology.* London: Peter Owen.

—— (1978). *Economy and Society: An Outline of Interpretive Sociology.* Berkeley, CA: University of California Press.

—— (1991). 'The Social Psychology of the World Religions', in H. H. Gerth and C. Wright Mills (eds.), *From Max Weber: Essays in Sociology.* London: Routledge.

White, H. (1978). *Tropics of Discourse: Essay in Cultural Criticism.* Baltimore, MD: Johns Hopkins University Press.

Wright, E. O. (1997). *Classes.* London: Verso.

Wrong, D. (1968). 'Some Problems in Defining Social Power', *American Journal of Sociology*, 73(6).

4

A Durkheimian View of Organizational Culture

James Lincoln and Didier Guillot

> *The degree of consensus over, and intensity of, cognitive orientations and regulative cultural codes among the members of a population is an inverse function of the degree of structural differentiation among actors in this population and a positive, multiplicative function of their (a) rate of interpersonal interaction, (b) level of emotional arousal, and (c) rate of ritual performance.*
> (Durkheim's theory of culture as rendered axiomatically by Jonathan Turner 1990)

This chapter examines the significance of Emile Durkheim's thought for the study of organization, with particular attention given to the concept of organizational culture. We are not the first to take the project on—a number of scholars have usefully addressed the extent and relevance of this giant of Western social science for the study of organization and work. Even so, there is no denying that Durkheim's name appears with vastly less frequency in the literature on these topics than is true of Marx and Weber, sociology's other founding fathers. Some intriguing sociology of knowledge reasons exists for this neglect to which we give attention in the pages to follow. It is also true that matters of work and organization per se were less central to Durkheim's concerns than to those of Marx and Weber. Little of his writing directly engages the problem of the private sector firm and the employment relationship. Yet, in our view, the indirect significance of Durkheim's ideas for organizational study is substantial.

The chapter is organized as follows. We begin with a review of Durkheim's theory of culture and its position in the social sciences. We then consider the implications of Durkheim's perspectives for the following problems in organizational culture research: (*a*) whether organizations genuinely have *cultures* as opposed to *ideologies*; (*b*) the role of culture as a force in social solidarity; (*c*) the relevance of Durkheim's *anomie* to the problem of corporate malfeasance; (*d*) whether culture determines structure or vice versa; (*e*) the role of ritual and ceremony in organizational life; (*f*) whether culture gestates slowly or explodes into existence in a 'big bang;' and (*g*) culture and cultural effects as emergent from and channeled through social networks.

1. Durkheim and Social Science

Durkheim is *the* classical social theorist of culture (Emirbayer 1996), celebrated, in particular, for his analyses of how 'collective representations' derive from and, in turn, support social structures. His standing in social anthropology has remained high across the near-century since his death (Peacock 1981). Yet in sociology, his status as founding father notwithstanding, his reputation and the use of his writings in contemporary work has waxed and waned with the times. One reason is the early refraction of his thought through the prism of Parsons' social action theory (1949). In recent years, various scholars have argued that Durkheim's ideas were distorted, not only by Parsons, but even by Merton (1968) and others in the structural-functional tradition (see, *inter alia*, Pope 1973; Mestrovic 1987). Beyond his association with functionalism, Durkheim's fortunes rose and fell with the prominence in Western social science of cultural themes and concepts. Both sociology and anthropology moved away from cultural analysis in the 1960s. In the first case, the shift was to Marxist and more generally materialist or structuralist interpretations of social reality. In the second, the shift was also to structuralism, but of a markedly different sort: the 'cultural' or ideational structuralism of Claude Levi-Strauss (Lemert 1994). Yet in reducing linguistic patterns and other cultural forms to societally invariant structures, Levi-Strauss downgraded the Durkheimian conception of culture as a system of representations rooted in and reflective of distinct social groups.

Sociology of the post-1960s also stayed clear of Durkheim because, aside from the taint of functionalism, he was portrayed by Nisbet (1967) and others as 'conservative', committed to an intellectual and public agenda of preserving moral community before the rationalizing and individuating forces transforming Western society (Giddens 1976). Weber, too, was troubled by the disintegrative effects of capitalism, bureaucratization, and democracy. But Durkheim's more explicit concern with cohesion and moral order, combined with his strong claims for culture's part in fostering them, made it easy to label him a nostalgist for the past.

Yet as new cultural frames of reference and modes of inquiry arose, Durkheim's writing again drew attention. Emirbayer (1996: 110) writes:

> Most responsible for this development was... a heightened interest in cultural theory and in the systematic analysis of symbolic structures and discourses.... Other developments fed as well into this turn back to Durkheim: a new concern with mechanisms of social solidarity, inspired partly by the emergence of a new (micro) sociology of the emotions; a keen new interest in the substantive topic of civil society; and a growing tendency to see social life as networks of relations and transactions, rather than as either 'a substantial entity having corporate existence'... or a mere aggregation of individuals.

Moreover, the critical twist on cultural themes typical of humanistic Marxism and postmodernism mostly disposed of any residual scholarly concern that to invoke Durkheim was to embrace homogeneity and tradition (Archer 1985: 335). Traces of Durkheim are readily apparent in postmodernist and poststructuralist writings. Bourdieu cites Durkheim in portraying the economy as a symbolic order, integral to the cultural sphere of sentiments, constructions, and beliefs, thus in no way abstracted or decoupled from society (LeBaron 2001: 24). Foucault's discussion (1972: 20) of how ritual and taboo constrain discourse creation draws heavily on Durkheim's analysis of how 'the categories of the understanding' emerge from the totemic rites of tribal society.

It is the privilege and pleasure of each new generation of scholars to reappraise the classics and in so doing demolish the interpretations of prior generations. Marx and Weber, needless to say, have inspired a myriad dissertations and other scholarly tracts, but Durkheim's work is uniquely suited to endless rounds of critical assessment because of his oblique and polemical style. Durkheim seemed to revel in cryptic prose, particularly in his discussion of such thorny topics as the objective reality of social facts, the externality and unity of culture, and the etiology of culture vis-à-vis society (Lukes 1973). He also incensed readers with provocative assertions, for example, in *The Elementary Forms of the Religious Life* that '... god and society are one'. Yet a detailed reading of Durkheim also reveals many passages that are utterly clear and tightly reasoned on the mechanisms—most of them network-based—whereby culture emerges from social structure and process, how it is constituted and sustained, and how it feeds back to motivate and channel individual and collective action.

2. The Meanings of Organizational Culture

Given Durkheim's profile in culture studies generally, it behooves students of organizational culture to give some serious consideration to how this interesting problem of recent vintage might be viewed through a Durkheimian lens.

The concept of organizational—often 'corporate'—culture, has a peculiar history and standing in organization research. While several scholars had earlier applied the term to the values, beliefs, and sentiments associated with a single organization (Pettigrew 1979), what gave the topic real impetus was a series of practitioner-oriented books published in the late 1970s to early 1980s.[1] Moreover, as Barley and Kunda (1992: 381) observe, much of the inspiration for those writings was the discovery of and rapid infatuation with Japanese styles of management and organization. By the late 1970s, Japan's burgeoning global competitiveness was drawing broad attention from business researchers, journalists, and practitioners, yet the organization of the Japanese firm seemed to fly in the face of Western theories of economic and administrative modernity, rationality, and efficiency.

Culture is arguably the most pervasive buzzword in the popular management lexicon, routinely invoked in casual business discourse to sum up all that is distinctive in a company. Prominent Japanologist Chalmers Johnson is not alone among scholars in dismissing it as a 'weasel word,' devoid of academic legitimacy.[2] Many in organization studies and social science more broadly have resisted its use. This is truer of the sociological or macro-organization side of the field than the micro- or psychology side, where the bulk of self-described organization culture research is concentrated (e.g. Schein 1996). Yet there is an abundance of work in organizational sociology that deals directly with the substance of what the culture concept seems to comprise, even as it avoids this label. As we observe below, the 'institutional' school (both old and new variants) addresses, implicitly or explicitly, such cultural components as symbols, myth, and ceremony (Meyer and Rowan 1977; Perrow 1986). The same might be said of certain strains of organizational economics. The mystical 'routines' of Nelson and Winter's evolutionary economics smack (1982) of cultural codes as does Oliver Williamson's

[1] See, in particular, Ouchi (1981); Pascale and Athos (1982), and Peters and Waterman (1982).

[2] Lecture given at Berkeley *c.*1993.

sometime contemplation (1975) of the role of 'atmosphere' in mitigating the firm's transaction costs.

Moreover, the concept of ideology has absorbed much of the content that in organization study might otherwise fall to culture. Selznick (1949) alludes to the grass-roots 'ideology' of the Tennessee Valley Authority in his study of the New Deal agency's efforts to establish itself as a force in the region. A comparable sociological classic is Bendix's analysis (1956) of the historical evolution of managerial ideology in England, Russia, and the USA as a device for reconciling systems of hierarchy and domination with societal ideals of democracy and equality. Rohlen's rich ethnography (1974) of *Uedagin*, his pseudonym for a Japanese bank, is an extraordinary inquiry into how cultural patterns shape management action and employee motivation and behavior. Yet Rohlen favors the concept of ideology in discussing the doctrines, symbols, rules, and rituals whereby the bank conducted its business and molded its people. More recently, Kunda (1992: 228–9) describes the culture of the high-tech firm in his thorough observational study as ideology.

> Underlying all the verbiage of managerially mandated texts is an elaborate and highly articulated managerial ideology that portrays the company as a non-hierarchic, humanistically inclined, moral collective. More crucially, the ideology constructs a distinct view of employees...that prescribes not only their behavior but runs much deeper, offering elaborate scripts for their cognitive and emotional life.

Is there substantive reason to prefer 'ideology' to 'culture' as a label for the ideational superstructure of an organization (Morgan 1986: 139)? Ideology connotes the purposive crafting of ideas and values so as to advance the agenda of a class or interest group. Swidler (1986) argues that as long as the ideology is clearly identified with a 'special cadre within a society', it 'will resist being absorbed into common sense', which is to say, culture. Thus, culture refers holistically to the entrenched and encompassing value, belief, and symbolic systems of a natural collectivity, such as the tribal societies Durkheim studied. The occasional corporation may have something of this character as well, but typically the term 'membership' is only meaningfully applied to the executive and professional echelons, lower ranking support and production people mostly functioning as substitutable factors of production (Kunda 1992; Linstead and Grafton-Small 1992). With respect to such settings, claims to the effect that the organization is a community whose members have evolved and share a distinctive and persistent culture bear a heavy burden of proof.[3]

3. Do Organizations Have Cultures? A Durkheimian View

Can corporations in fact take on cultures in the Durkheimian sense of coherent, exterior, and constraining collective consciousness? From his perspective, culture attaches to society or, within it, families, communities, and voluntary associations, not, it appears, to specialized functional units such as firms or industries. Individuals are inextricably bound to society, and (most clearly in the primitive case) it is the whole of their reality. Culture, in Durkheim's view, is the outcome of human beings' collective efforts to come to grips symbolically with a complex world that surrounds and overwhelms them.

Durkheim's model of culture has been criticized as: (*a*) holistic, seamless, and homogenous—admitting to no divisions or conflicts; (*b*) reified or hypostasized—existing outside people and society; (*c*) deterministic—making little room for human agency. As we later discuss, some of these attributions mischaracterize his work. Still, the Durkheimian model stands in sharp contrast with Archer's (1985), Swidler's (1986), and other conceptions of culture as a loosely knit, semicoherent 'tool kit' that people apply selectively and adaptively as coping strategies in navigating social life (DiMaggio 1997). From their perspective, culture is neither Parsonsian programing stamped on individuals by an irresistible socialization mechanism, nor is it an externalized and constraining Durkheimian social force. Instead, publicly available meanings and preferences are proactively and creatively assembled and exploited in the rational pursuit of chosen courses of action.[4]

Do the cultures of any of today's firms and bureaus approximate the tightly woven ideational systems that preoccupied Durkheim? The

[3] In the writings of Gramsci (1990) and others, all 'culture' serves an ideological purpose, as, once accepted, it reinforces inequalities and blinds the powerless to alternative possibilities. Still, as applied to contemporary organizational research, the culture–ideology distinction is sharply drawn.

[4] By contrast, the 'new institutionalism' in organizational sociology is criticized by Stinchcombe (1997: 2) as: 'Durkheimian in the sense that collective representations manufacture themselves by opaque processes, are implemented by diffusion, are exterior and constraining without exterior people doing the creation or the constraining. . . . [It is a]contrast with the old institutionalism in which people built and ran institutions.'

employment relation that binds people to work organizations in advanced societies, perhaps the USA most of all, is today a tenuous one—subject to severance by either party at any time. Further, more than is true, for example, of Japan, Germany, or Sweden, work-life in the Anglo-American societies tends to be segregated from the competing social milieux of home and local community (Lincoln and Kalleberg 1990; Dore 2000).

Yet this is precisely the problem that those who embrace the concept of organization culture seek to address. Weak employment ties and uncommitted workers need not, these writers suggest, be the rule. There are organizations where people develop collective purpose, experience a real sense of community, and participate, not merely for the extrinsic rewards, but for the intrinsic ones of involvement in an enterprise that they believe has deep and lasting value. Some streams of organization culture writing go farther in proposing that inspired executives can overcome the frailties of the employment relation and build community by crafting a system of transcendent values and vision that the cultural devices of stories, ceremony, and folklore support and sustain.

4. What Does Culture Do? For Durkheim, Build Cohesion

There is little clear consensus among students of organization as to just what culture 'does'. Kanter (1983: 119), who early in her career wrote widely on the nature and origins of community, offers a Durkheimian view of organizational culture in suggesting that in companies where it is strong, people: 'gain an experience of... communitas... which lifts them out of the humdrum... of their... place. [It] may be the closest to an experience of community.'

Durkheim's own overarching intellectual, as well as moral and political, interest was the problem of community, which he saw reflected in and enhanced by cultural forms. Marx, too, understood the cohesion-building role of ideas, religion in particular, which he took to be an ideological 'opiate' contrived by a ruling class to blind ordinary people to the reality of their oppression and shift their aspirations for a better life to the heavenly hereafter. The view of culture as tool of exploitation—the imposition on the powerless of the discourse of an elite—is key to postmodernist thought. However, Durkheim's cultural representations, in contrast not only with Marx but also with Weber, do not mirror interests and domination (Bottomore 1981). If not the conservative some claimed, Durkheim was no radical, and he worried about the deterioration of moral consensus and social cohesion he saw progressing in the advanced societies of his day. Class conflict, portrayed by Marxists as liberating and progressive, was for Durkheim merely one more disintegrative force in social life.

Durkheim specifically believed that the atomizing thrust of modernization might be blunted with various cohesion-building mechanisms, among them: ceremonial activity; new moral ideology (e.g. of individualistic humanism: the 'cult of man'); and participation in membership organizations, occupational groups, in particular, such as guilds, unions, or professional associations. He wrote:

> A nation can be maintained, only if, between the State and the individual, there is intercalated a whole series of secondary groups near enough to the individuals to attract them strongly in their sphere of action and drag them, in this way, into the general torrent of social life... occupational groups are suited to fill this role, and that is their destiny. (Durkheim [1915] 1961: 23)

Durkheim did not appear to entertain the possibility that business firms might similarly serve as intervening loci of community. A probable reason is his sense that homogeneity of type and purpose, as in the mechanical solidarity of the tribal 'clan', is structurally prerequisite to the formation of strong collective consciousness (Durkheim [1897] 1966: 378). Yet historical instances of companies taking on the integration role are not difficult to find. The postwar Japanese corporation and the Chinese state-owned enterprise (the 'iron rice bowl') are examples of the workplace as near-total enterprise community, functioning as Durkheim envisioned to bridge the gap between individual and state. The USA, as Tocqueville documented, may be the best realization of the Durkheimian thesis that membership organizations anchor people to society, while the US private sector firm with notable exceptions (e.g. the 'company town'; the AT&T and IBM of the 1950s), has played this role to a relatively small historical degree (Jacoby 1997; Dore 2000).

Like Marx and Weber, Durkheim saw cultural forms reflecting and sustaining social structure (*The Protestant Ethic*'s suggestion that cultural ideas independently shape social action was Weber's exploration of an exceptional case). We later suggest that there is room in the Durkheimian canon for an interpretation that cultures sometimes form and grow within short spans of time, such that a visionary corporate leader bent on sweeping change might deliberatively and expeditiously engineer one.

Durkheim's focus on the challenges posed by division of labor for cohesion and community finds a parallel in contemporary organizational research. The more segmented the organization, the weaker is apt to be its culture and the greater become the problems of integration and coordination. Organization designs that splinter activities into functional subunits have drawn much attention from scholars and practitioners for the barriers to communication and cooperation they erect. Such walls are best understood as competing cognitive frames, each group seeing the company through its own narrow technical and professional lens (Martin 1992: 103). This, as Wuthnow and Witten (1988) suggest, is the chief source of subculture in work organizations:

> While subcultures may reinforce integration with the overall organization, they may also provide centers of dissent. Cultural cleavages are likely to occur on occupational, status, or divisional lines. Evidence for the existence of subcultures is found in different discursive practices in organizations: in the divergent accounts workers on different organizational levels give of organizational events...; in specialized language that professionals in some organizations share more fully with colleagues outside the organization than those within it; and in different expressive symbols around which subgroups converge in the production of their collective sense of mission.

The differentiation/integration model of Lawrence and Lorsch (1967) and other organizational researchers in the 'structural contingency' tradition is usefully re-examined in this context. Their conclusion is that, while differentiation does foster interdependence, it also *diminishes* corporate solidarity. While the specialized subunits are in Durkheimian fashion 'joined at the hip' by functional complementarity, the lack of common working culture—goals, values, language—renders boundary-spanning communication and cooperation difficult and conflict-prone. The usual structural solution is to reduce the interdependence by arranging the units into quasi-independent divisions (e.g. along product or regional lines). Yet this does little for cohesion, as the divisions then go their own way, losing sight of common purpose and affiliation. As Freeland (1996: 484) writes of General Motors: 'Because division managers have partisan interests in specific operations, they tend to promote policies that benefit those units rather than the corporation as a whole.' One Durkheimian solution (for which the Japanese company is renowned) is the creation of mediating structures such as cross-functional teams (Galbraith 1973). Still another is the deployment of the cultural devices of myth, symbols, and ceremony to build common understanding and sentiment across disparate units (Bartlett and Ghoshal 1989).

5. Durkheim as Social, not Cultural, Determinist

For all his interest in the structure, content, and consequences of culture, Durkheim was not a cultural determinist. 'Durkheim,' Rawls (1996) observes, 'is interpreted as arguing that ideas and representations are the real social facts, when actually he argued the reverse: that social processes generate both the social person and their basic categories of thought.' Similarly, Giddens (1976: 290) writes that Durkheim was 'always careful to insist that such propositions as "society is the ideal" must be interpreted to mean that ideals are *creations* of human society, not 'given' forces which determine social conduct'.

In holding that culture stems from social structure and process, Durkheim advanced a view quite different in substance from that of Parsons and most mainstream sociological and anthropological thought. The latter, according to Peterson (1979), asserts that: 'culture is to social structure roughly what the genetic code is to a species of living organisms'. But for Durkheim ([1897] 1966: 387) society is fundamental and culture is derivative or emergent:

> (A) people's mental system ... depends really on the grouping and organization of social elements. Given a people composed of a certain number of individuals arranged in a certain way, we obtain a definite total of collective ideas and practices which remain constant so long as the conditions on which they depend are themselves the same.

To make sense of culture, then, the analyst must first attend to the social structural configurations that beget and sustain it. Organizational research, however, has directed scant attention to these. More has been paid to attributes of the membership and styles of leadership conducive to a culture's growth and strength (Carroll and Harrison 1998; Chatman et al. 1998). The Japanese firm is again an instructive case in how a distinctive mix of human resource and organization design practices provided the hard skeletal frame on which the soft tissue of strong culture could be hung: permanent employment, wage compression, job rotation, broad and frequent training, teams as functional units, and consensus decision-making (Lincoln and McBride 1987).

Yet Durkheim ([1897] 1966: 130) also acknowledged that 'once (cultural representations) exist, they are, by that very fact, realities *sui generis*, autonomous and capable of producing new phenomena'. Culture may originate with social structure, but people experience structure through cultural frames and filters (Fine 1984: 245; Martin 1992: 34–5). Culture is:

'the way in which the group thinks of itself in its relationships with the objects that affect it' (Durkheim [1938] 1982: 40). 'Durkheim asserts that concrete symbols, such as myths, are necessary for solidarity', Ouchi and Wilkins (1985) write, 'because [quoting Durkheim] 'the clan is too complex a reality to be represented clearly in all its complex unity'. That culture, typically through myth, legend, and metaphor, render organizational life comprehensible is a central theme in organizational culture research. Morrill (1991: 586) puts it well:

> In this sense, 'structure' and 'symbolic systems' interact and persist as overlapping social phenomena: social structure cannot exist without symbolic systems, which individuals use to make sense of, maintain, and change social structure, while symbolic systems cannot exist for long without 'plausibility structures, which root symbols in behavioral patterns.

An implication is that the significance of structural change is conditioned on cultural patterns. CEO Carly Fiorina's aggressive restructuring of Hewlett-Packard (HP) in a functionally centralized format was reportedly wrenching for HP managers (Hamilton 2000), as the technology firm's long-time configuration as a loose network of business divisions—each run by an entrepreneur-manager—was a pillar of HP's oft-touted culture ('The HP Way').[5] Even the hard incentives of making money and keeping a job have meaning for people largely in the symbolism they convey—sky-high executive pay is not mere money but a signal that the company loves its leader; a layoff is not mere loss of income and security but humiliating loss of face for a Japanese salaryman (that all too often brings on suicide).

6. Durkheim on Ritual and Ceremony

One of Durkheim's best known contributions is his treatment of the role of rite and ceremony in creating and sustaining solidarity and culture. A much-noted paradox of organizational life is that formal structures and processes take on ceremonial meaning. Further paradoxical is the Durkheimian inference that ceremonial activity, seemingly so at odds with Weber's legal–rational model, could, by fostering community and energizing the

[5] More rigorous testimony for the same is Lincoln, Hanada, and Olson's finding (1981) that the job attitudes and social integration of Japanese and American employees of a sample of twenty-eight Japanese-owned firms reacted differently to the same organizational structures. Specifically, the Japanese' job satisfaction and social integration rose with structures typical of Japanese-style organization (higher vertical differentiation combined with lower functional differentiation).

membership, render the organization *more* effective in competitive market terms than if it were entirely true to the principles of technical rationality.

Ritual, in Durkheim's theory, is also key to the creation of knowledge and thought. The study of culture generally and that of the organization-specific sort in particular has been marked by a debate over content: are the cathectic and valuative components more or less important than the cognitive/symbolic/belief elements? Drawing on the enthnographic literature of his time, Durkheim sought the origins of religious ideas—which he took to be the root of all ideas—in the social 'effervescence' of ritual. In dancing, chanting, and other heated celebration, individual identities melt away, and the collective passions so aroused are transferred to objects, anointing them as sacred or profane. Thus, it is not that charismatic religion inspires social emotion that the vehicle of ceremony then conveys. Durkheim saw the process reversed—ritual binds individuals to the group while simultaneously constructing the cognitive categories whereby reality is made meaningful in symbolic terms.[6]

The neo-institutionalist school of organizational sociology has actively sought to distinguish the cognitive face of culture from the cathectic systems that absorbed an earlier generation of (chiefly structural-functional) institutionalists (Powell and DiMaggio 1991). While cathexis and values were indeed central to Parsons' view of culture's role in ordering and stabilizing society, culture for Durkheim is mostly cognitive—classification systems, ontological and etiological myths, and the symbolic forms that represent them. Yet the cognitive is sculpted on the template of the cathectic: collective thought originates with the ceremonial assignment of positive and negative emotions to objects and events.[7]

Also an issue for organizational research is the intensity, complexity, and formality that organizational rituals attain and whether they play the salutary role in cohesion and performance so often claimed. Early work on the problem—the studies of the ceremonial qualities of the Japanese firm

[6] Durkheim's analysis of contract (1933: 180) also highlights emotion-charged ritual. Blood convenants allowed 'two different individuals or groups, between whom no natural ties exist, [to] agree to be associated in some common aim: in order that this covenant should be binding, they bring about the physical blood relationship considered to be the source of all obligations. They mingle their blood.'

[7] This attribution, while accurate on the role of culture in Parsons' social action scheme, is largely off the mark when applied to the rich case studies for which the latter tradition is justly renowned (see, *inter alia*, Selznick 1949, 1996; Gouldner 1954; Blau 1955; Crozier 1964). In a way that far too little qualitative research in the interim has matched, the 'old' institutionalists scrutinized the processes whereby whole organizations and the occupational and status groups within them cognitively structured their worlds.

by Rohlen (1974) and Dore (1973) or the attention to the cult-like qualities of strong culture corporations in the popular management writings of Peters and Waterman (1982) or Deal and Kennedy (1982)—paint a picture of ceremonial activity as vibrant and gripping, infusing organizational routines with charisma and transporting people out of their fragmented workaday roles into cohesive and committed communities.

Ornate tapestries of ritual are on conspicuous display in many Japanese companies. To be sure, Japanese society itself is more laden with ceremonial baggage than is true, say, of US society (Dore 2000). Whether it is the checkout clerks chanting their singsong customer service refrains; the salutes and calisthenics of construction workers about to begin the day's job; the *shinto* ceremonies sanctifying the opening of a new branch; or the symbolically consensual *ringi* system of decision-making; Japan is the *shikata* society—everything is done in a ceremonial way.[8]

The Japanese describe their culture in general and business culture in particular as *uetto*—wet with emotion—as against the *dorai* calculatedness of Western ways. The teaching of organizational culture in US business schools is taken seriously by MBA students if only because the language of culture so pervades US business discourse. But cynicism toward the topic abounds, and the published pretensions of companies to transcendent values and far-reaching visions easily draw sneers and laughter (Martin 1992: 70). That cynicism, if on the rise in recent years, is much less prevalent in Japan. That again says something about the larger culture. Yet it also speaks to the social construction of the Japanese firm as a stable institution in which employees—not only executives and stockholders—see themselves and are seen by others as the real stakeholders. Thus, ritual in the Japanese company—as in the weepy entrance ceremony at Uedagin described by Rohlen—has the emotion-charged character Durkheim saw engendering culture and cohesion in tribal 'clans'.[9]

[8] There is also an impersonal quality to the superpolite demeanor of clerks and other service personnel in Japanese enterprise. The melodic recitation of polite, indeed obsequious, phrases substitutes for real conversation. Some of this stems from the Japanese obsession with order and efficiency. Another part is conflict avoidance. Real interaction with customers introduces the risk that the encounter might prove awkward or embarrassing.

[9] Rohlen's description (1974) of a *nyusha-shiki*—an employee entrance ceremony—dramatizes the thick ritual and sentiment-laden character of much Japanese corporate practice. In attendance, he writes, are the top officers of the corporation, the new employees, and the parents of the recruits. Corporate and Japanese flags are unfurled. Everyone stands and sings the company song. The principles of the bank are recalled—service to small and medium enterprises, contribution to public welfare and prosperity, emphasis on trust and enterprising spirit—and the president's teachings—harmony, sincerity, kindness, spirit, unity, responsibility, and purity. The new employees are introduced in turn. The president recalls the blood and sweat of prior generations whose labors elevated the bank to its present strength. The

Most research on rite and ceremony in organizational life, however, conveys an image rather different from Rohlen's portrait of Uedagin. An important body of organizational theory highlights the looseness of organizations—the randomness of action, the inconsequentiality of leadership, the decoupling of cause and effect (Cohen et al. 1972; Weick 1976; Meyer and Rowan 1977). Such images—so at odds with the classical model of organization as a tightly wound machine—are consistent with a view of structure and process as symbolic and ceremonial versus instrumental and utlilitarian (Starkey 1998). Ritualized activity in this sense, engenders dry, cool, cognitive legitimacy, acceptance, whether by members or external constituencies, of the organization's purposes and practices (Morgan 1986: 123; Powell and DiMaggio 1991). These become taken-for-granted as normal and proper. People cannot think of the organization as configured another way.

The model of organizational ritual as hotly emotional is quintessentially Durkheimian. The alternative model of cool cognitive legitimacy, by contrast, is Weberian. This contrast is thoughtfully explored by Pope, Cohen, and Hazelrigg (1975: 421–2):

> In Durkheim's framework, moral obligation stems from an awe of the sacred and of society writ large. Moral sentiment, often awakened by ritual ceremonies, commands dutiful obedience. For Weber, on the other hand, a legitimate order has no more than equal footing with self interest in fostering behavioral regularities. Since legitimate orders are not necessarily ethical in nature and not common to society as a whole, they generally lack the power of Durkheim's collective sentiments and moral rules.

Of Weber's three types of legitimate domination, 'charismatic' best corresponds to Durkheim's moral obligation. Yet even this does not convey the moral and emotional force of the sacred in Durkheim's theory.

Thus, different rites have different functions. Some are socially turbulent (Durkheim's 'collective effervescence') and infused with moral significance and emotional resonance. Others are routinized and cerebral. They build solidarity, not by arousing collective passion, but by cultivating in members and external constituents an incapacity to contemplate alternative states of the world.[10]

assembled parents are promised that their offspring will be educated and nurtured. The president breaks down and cries, despite, Rohlen observes, having given the speech many times before. A spokesperson for the parents asks that the bank discipline and guide their children. The ceremony ends with the president leading everyone in banzai cheers for the survival and success of the company.

[10] Pertinent here is anthropologist Douglas's assessment (1968: 369) of the difference between 'spontaneous' and standard or 'routinized' rites in simple societies. Standard rites,

7. Durkheim's Anomie: Corporate Greed as Culture Breakdown

Durkheim's famous concept of anomie once informed a good deal of sociological research on work and organization, but applications to the problem of organizational culture have yet to be made. Anomie in this literature is tied to 'alienation', a main concern of the industrial and cultural sociology of the 1950s and 1960s. Converted to a social-psychological construct by Parsons (1949), Merton (1968), and Srole (1956), anomie became 'normlessness'—a term evocative of the structural–functional framework within which Durkheim's thought was situated at the time. Most uses of the anomie concept had structural as well as cultural overtones: isolation and detachment in the first instance and meaninglessness and purposelessness in the second. For Durkheim, however, anomie—a state of *dereglement*—disorganization or derangement—is an attribute of collectivities, not individuals. Orru (1983) writes:

Although Durkheim's concept of anomie underwent modifications from the earlier *Division of Labor*... to his later writings, his overriding concern was the inadequacy of socially generated goals and values in industrial societies. In *Suicide*, Durkheim ([1897] 1966: 254–7) viewed anomie as a condition that occurs when economic materialism becomes an end transcending itself... the supreme end of individuals and societies alike... Durkheim declared 'It is not true then that activity can be released from all restraint. Nothing in the world can enjoy such privilege.'

Besnard (1988) adds:

Anomie is a situation characterized by indeterminate goals and unlimited aspirations, the disorientation or vertigo created by confrontation with an excessive widening of the horizons of the possible, in a context of expansion or increasing upward mobility. It is loss in the infinity of desires.

she says, like the feast days of the Australian aborigines discussed by Durkheim, have strong moral content: 'The rite imposes order and harmony... Great rituals create unity in experience. They assert hierarchy and order. In doing so, it affirms the value of the symbolic patterning of the universe. Each level of patterning is validated and enriched by association with the rest. But jokes have the opposite effect... they destroy hierarchy and order. They do not affirm the dominant values, but denigrate and devalue. Essentially a joke is an anti-rite.' Douglas suggests that 'Dionysian' ritual, wherein laughter, jokes, and other ribaldry ridicule and thereby weaken hierarchy and classification, affirms the value of and commitment to unstructured community or 'network', defined by Barnes (1954) as 'an undifferentiated field of friendship and acquaintance'. Casual observation of Silicon Valley corporate culture regularly alludes to the ceremonial flavor of casual dress, disheveled offices, beer busts, basketball matches, and the like. From Durkheim's perspective, the loose-knit structure of high-technology enterprise, combined with the networked character of the Northern California industry, accords with the pattern of organizational ritual there.

Durkheim thus saw anomie as the dissolution of cultural restraint, arousing in persons restless, insatiable cravings—unbridled acquisitiveness—the inevitable consequence of which was frustration, stress, and depression. 'One does not advance when one proceeds towards no goal,' he wrote, 'or—which is the same thing—when the goal is infinity. To pursue a goal which is by definition unattainable is to condemn oneself to a state of perpetual unhappiness' (from *Suicide*).

The theory of anomie as loss of moral restraint is usefully applied to the timely problem of corporate malfeasance, placed in high relief by the US corporate governance and accounting scandals of 2001–2 (e.g. Enron, WorldCom, Adelphia). A common interpretation of the ethical/legal lapses that proliferated in this period is that the implicated firms were imbued with a fiercely competitive 'cowboy culture' (Raghavan, Kranhold, and Barrionuevo 2002). The implicit subtext is that, absent immersion in and corruption by such strong but errant cultures, the people involved would not have behaved in such ways. The business press is inclined to invoke the culture concept to explain almost any organizational behavior. But for culture to be a useful conceptual tool, it cannot account simultaneously for a phenomenon and its opposite. If strong culture is why some companies appear tight-knit communities pursuing 'transcendent' (i.e. nonfinancial) values (creativity, customer service, people), it cannot also explain the boundless material ambitions of Enron executives, which drove them to self-serving excesses that destroyed the firm and with it the fortunes of a multitude of employees and shareholders.

Thus, the Durkheimian take on corporate scandal is one of cultural *dereglement*, not strong and distinct culture of a gunslinging wild west sort. In comparison, for example, with Japan or continental Europe, where the corporation is socially constructed as a bona fide community of diverse stakeholders, the weaker institutionalization of US firms implies fewer normative constraints on business goals and tactics. Moreover, the image of the company in US economic theories of the firm—as mere tool for the profit-maximization of its owners—may have contributed to a climate in which the abandonment of restraint was easily rationalized (Selznick 1996: 272; Dore 2000; Ghoshal 2003; Lincoln and Gerlach 2004). In general, powerful people—corporate chieftains in particular, whose misdeeds are generally hidden from public scrutiny—feel themselves less bound by everyday convention. This speaks to an issue we later take up in some detail: the Durkheimian concept of culture as emergent 'social force', an irreducible collective property exhibiting the dual features of 'exteriority and constraint'. Some people internalize the culture and thus conform voluntaristically to its rules. The compliance of others is driven by external constraint. Such constraints, it goes without saying, are felt more keenly by persons of lesser means.

8. Can Culture Be Created Overnight? Durkheim's 'Big Bang'

A high-profile theme in the popular management literature is that cultures may be designed and constructed by charismatic CEO's or visionary executive teams. Such 'engineering' of culture might seem most compatible with the views of Weber who was more open than was Durkheim to a conception of social structure and culture as shaped by individual action (Pope et al. 1975). For Weber, charismatic authority is institutionalized into *traditional* authority (thus transferring the charisma of the prophet to the bureaucracy of the church). For Durkheim, cultural representations spring from the 'collective effervescence' of ritual. Durkheim, again, was strenuously opposed to reductionism: in his view, social facts originate with other social facts, not the motives, abilities, or behaviors of individuals.

Yet one can imagine from a Durkheimian standpoint that the mix of classifications, symbols, and sentiments peculiar to a group derive from the legendary myths surrounding a charismatic leader. This is particularly likely in an entrepreneurial organization whose success depends on the personal talents and heroic efforts of the founder. The persona of founder is a powerful symbol—a sacred totem—providing the group with a concrete object on which to center its representations of itself. Moreover, in a fledgling undertaking, the leadership of the founder and the culture of the organization may be so intertwined that the two cannot be isolated.

Those who argue that organizational cultures sometimes can be assembled by a committed leader will generally concede that the planting and cultivating of a coherent field of values and beliefs is a slow and evolutionary process. At the beginning of the corporate culture boom, *Business Week* (1980) eavesdropped on the conversation of a CEO and his subordinate as the two departed an executive seminar on the topic: 'This culture stuff is great,' the CEO reportedly said. 'Get me a culture by Monday!' Whatever the significance of culture for corporate performance, impatient, results-oriented executives are notoriously reluctant to make the investments necessary to prepare the ground, sew the seeds, and grow the culture.

Yet it was Durkheim's insight that cultural systems may arise or undergo radical transformation in relatively short order: a sociological 'big bang,' as it were. In his account of how intense ritual activity spawns religious ideas in aboriginal society, culture balloons into being:

> On feast days . . . their thoughts are centered upon their common beliefs, their common traditions, the memory of their great ancestors, the collective ideal of which they are the incarnation; in a word, upon social things. . . . So it is society that is in the foreground of every consciousness; it dominates and directs all conduct; this is equivalent to saying that it is more living and active, and consequently more real, than in profane times. . . . The individual soul is regenerated too, by being dipped again in the source from which its life comes; consequently it feels itself stronger, more fully master of itself, less dependent upon physical necessities. (Durkheim [1915] 1961: 390–1)

Furthermore, convulsive social change may ignite sufficient 'social effervescence' that large cultural shifts take place in short intervals. 'Under the influence of some great collective shock in certain historical periods social interactions become much more frequent and active', Durkheim wrote. 'Individuals seek out one another and come together more. The result is the general effervescence that is characteristic of revolutionary or creative epochs' (quote taken from Emirbayer 1996: 122). He cites as an example the vast transformation of French culture occasioned by the Revolution.

Durkheim also argued that culture must be reinvented regularly in order to counter the disintegrative tendencies endemic to secular modern life (Etzioni 2000: 45). He felt it is his responsibility as public intellectual to identify ritual activities and binding philosophies that might serve this end. Thus, culture not only can but must be (re)engineered in order to sustain solidarity and community.

Often overlooked in discussions of the ritualized solidarity of the Japanese firm is that much corporate ideology in that country, along with the management systems that support it, were in substantial part wartime and postwar creations, whatever the legitimacy they may have drawn from long-standing tradition (Cole 1971; Gordon 1985). Prewar labor markets and industrial relations resembled the West. To a notable degree the structures, processes, and cultures of postwar Japanese enterprise were deliberately constituted by management and labor with an eye to averting industrial strife and building enterprise community.

9. Culture as Sui Generis Social Fact: The Emergence Problem

For Durkheim, society presents itself to individuals as an external 'thing', a sui generis social fact that has an objective reality much like the objects that comprise the physical environment. Hilbert (1986: 2) provides a summary of the Durkheimian view:

> That modern society displays the famous twin features of exteriority and constraint no less so than elementary societies is no happenstance of history. Moral constraint is indeed the essence of collective life. When individuals confront moral reality, they are confronting society; society and morality are one.... Thus, a society lacking these twin features is inconceivable, as is a legal contract without a commitment to follow it... Yet as it happens, societies can vary with respect to the extent to which they display these twin features. Abrupt social changes, for example, can limit a society's regulating power, as can rapid evolutionary changes that outstrip the development of appropriate regulative morality.

Organization scholars commonly refer to 'shared values and beliefs' as the sine qua non of culture, although few are explicit on just what sharing means and how much is required for an organization to be said to have a culture (Morgan 1986: 135). 'Sharing' implies that most or all members, either through selection or socialization, hold personally to the values, beliefs, and sentiments peculiar to their organization. In practice, as Hermalin (2001) suggests, it is not easy to tell the difference between real sharing and external constraint. Do I comply with a rule to drive on the right side of the road because I have internalized it as a habit or merely because I consciously or unconsciously fear the sanctions that noncompliance will evoke? Work organizations may through an array of channels pressure members to conform with prescribed ways of doing things. Because of the short tenures and weak ties that workers often have to firms, one must question how much psychological internalization of firm-specific culture really figures in employees' proclivities to conform. Much such compliance is simply bowing to external constraint. That need not mean that the organization lacks a culture. But if the people who truly share the culture mostly hail from the executive ranks, ideology might be the preferable term (Goll and Zeitz 1991). For Durkheim, culture is an emergent property, a 'social fact' sui generis, irreducible to individual attributes and processes. Durkheim's cryptic and provocative pronouncements on these themes earned him sharp criticism both from his contemporaries and from later generations of scholars who saw him reifying culture and society and thus practising 'social metaphysics'. As his intellectual focus shifted over his lifetime to the cultural forms whereby societies cognitively classify and order the world, some saw him succumbing to idealism—the doctrine that cultural forms have a separate and detached existence.

Collective tendencies have an existence of their own—they are forces as real as cosmic forces, though of another sort... The proof that the reality of collective tendencies is not less than that of cosmic forces is that this reality is demonstrated in the same way, by the uniformity effects. [They] cause us to act from without, like physico-chemical forces to which we react.... They may be measured, their relative sizes compared, as is done with the intensity of electric currents or luminous foci. (quoted in Takla and Pope 1985: 75).

10. Culture Emergence as a Network Process

It is one thing to suggest that culture is an emergent social fact and quite another to imply, as the above quote seems to, that culture is a kind of Platonic ideal, divorced from—seemingly suspended above—society and the people who comprise it. Yet some of the criticism of Durkheim's emergence theory mistakes his meaning. An early critic attributed to him the view that, since culture is exterior to individuals, the network of human relations, like that of atoms in a compound, cannot be a social fact and so cannot explain another (Tosti 1898). On the contrary, as the following quote from Archer makes clear (1982: 475), for Durkheim the network is the locus and foundation of culture (see also Sawyer 2002: 233–4):

[E]mergent properties are therefore relational: they are not contained in the elements themselves, but could not exist apart from them. [They]... arise at all levels from small scale interaction upwards, although as the scope grows they are increasingly distanced from everyday psychological dispositions but never ultimately detached from interaction. The highest orders of emergence are nothing more than the relations between the results of interaction. Nevertheless these 'feedback' to condition subsequent interaction at lower levels.

Durkheim ([1897] 1966: 124) himself was explicit on the point:

In the midst of the same social group, all the elements of which undergo the action of a single cause or number of similar causes, a sort of leveling occurs in the consciousness of different individuals which leads everyone to think or feel in unison. The name of imitation has very often been given the whole number of operations resulting in this harmony. It then designates the quality of the states of consciousness simultaneously felt by a given number of different persons leading them so to act upon one another or combine among themselves as to produce a new state. Using the word in this sense, we mean that this combination results from reciprocal imitation of each of them by all and of all by each. 'In the noisy gatherings of our cities, in the great scenes of our revolutions,' it has been said, best appears the nature of imitation thus defined. There one sees best how men in union can mutually transform one another by their reciprocal influence.

Thus, culture materializes out of social network processes. Individuals' reactions to objects or events are not independent. Rather, each through his or her ties to others conditions those others' perceptions, cognitions, and emotions.[11] Moreover, the larger and denser the network, the stronger is the emergent culture and the more rapid the chain reaction of relational effects.[12]

Where collective sentiments are strong, it is because the force with which they affect each individual conscience is echoed in all the others, and reciprocally. The intensity they attain therefore depends on the number of consciences which react to them in common. For the same reason, the larger a crowd, the more capable of violence the passions vented by it. Consequently, in a family of small numbers, common sentiments and memories cannot be very intense; for there are not enough consciences in which they can be represented and reinforced by sharing them. In a sufficiently dense society, [the] circulation... of views and impressions from one person to another... is uninterrupted; for some social units are always in contact, whereas if there are few their relations can only be intermittent and there will be moments when the common life is suspended. (Durkheim [1897] 1966: 201)

The Durkheimian conception of culture as collective consciousness is congruent with the concept of 'group mind' that latter-day cognitive social psychologists have entertained. Weick and Roberts (1993) invoke the idea in their analysis of the tight coordination of action ('heedful interrelating') typical of high reliability organizations such as aircraft carrier flight decks. They quote Solomon Asch, famous for his experiments

[11] This imagery of the microsocial origins of culture in interpersonal interaction is extensively developed in the sociological traditions of symbolic interactionist and phenomenological sociology. Consider Berger and Luckmann's definition (1966: 109) of institutionalization: 'Institutionalization occurs whenever there is reciprocal typification of habitualized actions by types of actors. Put differently, any such typification is an institution. What must be stressed is the reciprocity of institutional typifications and the typicality of not only the actions but also the actors in institutions. The typifications of habitualized actions that constitute institutions are always shared ones.'

[12] The question of whether culture is a sui generis reality responsive only to macrolevel forces is an intellectual problem that has plagued anthropology as well. Kroeber (1948: 409) writes that Simmel grasped the conundrum in asserting that culture is: 'a "structure of independent reality, which leads its life after peculiar laws and by virtue of peculiar forces, independent of all its individual components... yet in the last analysis only individuals exist," and the "spiritual structures" of culture "have their existence only in personal minds" so that "to think of them outside of persons is a mysticism." [Thus] [c]ulture is credited with having a reality with laws and forces of its own, but also with existing only in persons. It is no wonder that nonphilosophers have floundered a bit in this area.'

on individual conformity in groups, in a passage that nicely complements Durkheim's sociological reasoning:

There are group actions that are possible only when each participant has a representation that includes the actions of others and their relations. The respective actions converge relevantly, assist and supplement each other only when the joint situation is represented in each and when the representations are structurally similar. Only when these conditions are given can individuals subordinate themselves to the requirements of group action. These representations and the actions they initiate bring group facts into existence and produce the phenomenal solidity of group process.[13]

Implicit in Asch's writing and, of course, explicit in Durkheim's, is that such representations of others themselves derive from prior rounds of interaction, reciprocation, and convergence. Consider the following from *Suicide* ([1897] 1966: 125–6):

Each [person] imperfectly imagines the state of those about him. What happens then? Once aroused in my consciousness, these various representations combine with one another and with my own feeling. A new state is thus formed, less my own than its predecessor, less tainted with individuality and more and more freed, by a series of repeated elaborations analogous to the foregoing, from all excessive particularity. Such combinations . . . then blend and fuse in a compound absorbing them but different from them. . . . This is indeed the only procedure by which the mind has the power of creation.

11. Culture's Consequences as 'Contextual Effects'

For Durkheim, not only the causes but the consequences of culture are embedded in social networks. To satisfy the Durkheimian criteria of 'exteriority and constraint', culture must shape human action through macrocausal (network) mechanisms, as contrasted with the microprocess of persons acting to realize individually held values and beliefs (Hilbert 1986).

To be sure, culture is at times equated with aggregate psychology, as in Ruth Benedict's remark (1932: 24) that 'cultures are individual psychology thrown large upon the screen, given gigantic proportions, and a long time

[13] Frank and Fahrbach (1999) offer an interesting and credible 'complex system' simulation of organization culture generation that makes use of these ideas. In their mathematical model, culture emerges as the cognitions and sentiments of individuals converge through interaction in networks and through the selection of others into the network to which each person is exposed.

span'. For Durkheim, however, culture emerges from a 'synthesis [that] has the effect of disengaging a whole world of sentiments, ideas and images, which once born obey laws of their own' ([1915] 1961: 471). The Durkheimian view of culture as emergent, external, and irreducible is generally accepted by sociologists, despite their disagreements over how integrated and constraining it may be (Martin 1992: 34; DiMaggio 1997).

When the socialization process imprints sufficient numbers of people with the same cultural codes, their coaligned actions may draw in others whose personal preferences may put them at odds with the group. Durkheim cites the phenomenon of social contagion ([1897] 1966: 96). If enough people are engaged in an action and that information is widespread, others will jump on the bandwagon—even one as extreme and personal as suicide.

In fads or social movements, such tipping effects usually appear when one set of true believers becomes a majority. In organizational settings, fewer persons acting on their own predilections may be required, particularly if they overrepresent from the organization's upper ranks. The costs for the individual of noncompliance—at a minimum in peer-group collegiality, at a maximum in exclusion, demotion, and job loss—are patently steep (Kunda 1992; O'Reilly and Chatman 1996; Kanter 1997; Martin 2002: 71, 99).

To warrant the label, 'culture', some number of individuals, via mutual influence processes, must come to share a set of values, sentiments, and understandings. Their 'collective consciousness', itself conveyed through networks, then constrains the actions of others. In this way, culture both emerges from the confluence of individual actions and is simultaneously experienced by individuals as an exterior and constraining social force.

Durkheim, it seems, was the first scholar to grasp these issues, which are fundamental to his model of culture as a 'total social fact'. The aggregation or distribution of values, beliefs, and sentiments in a group may channel behavior in ways quite distinct from that of persons acting to realize felt preferences. The famous example from *Suicide* was that, while Protestants in Europe killed themselves at four to five times the rate of Catholics—a pattern Durkheim attributed to the tighter integration and conformity demands of Catholic moral teachings—the ratio fell to three to one for Protestant minorities residing in Catholic countries. Members of a minority faith, he wrote ([1897] 1966: 156), 'facing the hostility of the surrounding populations . . . are obliged to exercise severe control over themselves and subject themselves to an especially rigorous discipline'. Their suicide rates were thus more a function of external constraint, less of internalized morality.

Another poignant Durkheimian example of group behavior diverging from individual disposition is the collective outpouring of grief in ceremonial rites of bereavement (Fisher and Chon 1989). Observing funeral services in Australian aboriginal society, he construed the ritual of mourning, not as an individual-level process of people giving vent to personal anguish, but as the macrophenomenon of a community reaffirming commitment and identity on the occasion of a member's loss. 'Grief', he wrote, 'is not a natural movement of private feelings wounded by a cruel loss' Rather it is 'a ritual attitude which [one] is forced to adopt out of respect for custom, but which is in large measure independent of his affective state' (Durkheim [1915] 1961: 443).[14]

A substantial empirical literature has addressed such emergent macroprocesses. First labeled 'structural effects' by Blau (1960), they are generally referred to as 'contextual' effects. As in the Durkheimian example of religion and suicide, their defining feature is that the average levels of two or more individual-level attributes (e.g. Protestant or Catholic affiliation) correlate over collectivities (e.g. nations) in a way that diverges from the individual-level correlations. This divergence is technically known as aggregation bias, a nuisance problem in economics and demography which generally posit individual-level causation but rely on data assembled for aggregates (e.g. industries, regions, and nations). But for Durkheim and the tradition of macrosociology he pioneered, aggregation bias bespeaks an emergent social fact: a macroprocess operating above and beyond its microlevel counterpart.

The study of emergent group effects was fundamental to Durkheim's sociology, and his writings here, in particular, had a polemical thrust. In asserting that collective properties and processes are not reducible to individual ones, he attacked the atomistic utilitarianism of Bentham, Mill, and Spencer. Durkheim's quarrel with the utilitarians finds a parallel

[14] An important stream of contemporary organizational culture research deserves mention here. In Hochschild's study (1983) of flight attendants, the pressures on these service workers to present smiling, cheerful demeanors to customers is portrayed as calculated (and dehumanizing) management policy. The ever-present threat of dismissal ensured that, no matter how tired the attendant or rude the passenger, the former kept an upbeat persona. Moreover, management sought to avert the formation of a subculture of resistance by warning attendants against airing gripes in the presence of coworkers. This company clearly had no bona fide customer-service 'culture' of friendly eager-to-please workers. By contrast, Martin et al.'s research (1998) on The Body Shop finds a genuinely emergent culture of emotionality. Some employees internalized a propensity to display emotionality in work settings; others seemingly did so in response to peer-group expectations.

today in the competing epistemologies of economics and sociology (Granovetter 1985). As Manski (1993) acknowledges in a creative paper on contextual effects models in the social sciences, economic reasoning is highly reductionist. Economists resist the idea of group or network phenomena that transcend the decisions and actions of individuals. In sociology, by contrast, a core theme—classically typified by Durkheim—is that groups and networks matter and macrolevel processes must be explicated with macrolevel causal laws.

Blau's article remains perhaps the best example of an emergent group effect readily interpretable in terms of external culture constraint. Commonplace in work organizations is a division between organization-centered and occupation-centered cultures, as our quote (p. 96) from Wuthnow and Witten (1988) testified. In human service agencies, this materializes in the tension between the client-service posture of human service workers and the bureaucratic orientation of the agencies that employ them. The agency sees clients as costs to be minimized or inputs to be processed. Many, if not all, caseworkers see them as people in need of the services that the caseworker was trained to provide in a spirit of sympathetic professional care. Blau's data showed that, irrespective of their own attitudes, caseworkers assigned to pro-client teams behaved in pro-client ways. Demonstrating the 'exteriority and constraint' of the group's pro-client culture, Blau's interpretation (1960: 182) is strongly Durkheimian:

> The structural effects of the prevailing values in a group are not necessarily parallel to the effects of the individual's value orientation. In some respects pro-client group values and the individual's own pro-client attitudes have opposite implications for his conduct.... These findings suggest that the social values that prevail in a work group do exert external constraints upon the thinking and acting of its members. If pro-client values prevail in a group, merely checking on the eligibility of clients meets with social disapproval while providing casework services gains a worker approval and respect. But this is not the case if pro-client values do not prevail. In other words, the pro-client values of the members of a group motivate them not only to furnish more intensive service to their own clients but also to express social approval of colleagues who are service-oriented and social disapproval of those who are not. In response to those sanctioning patterns, individuals tend to modify their approach to clients.

Thus, Durkheim's thoughts on the emergence problem illuminate the 'sharing' criterion for the presence and strength of organization culture. Sharing is requisite only up to some critical mass. Beyond that threshold, network-based normative constraints come into play, which induce further conformity and thus action in line with the culture even among those who cannot be said to 'share' it.[15]

In our view, the search for emergent macrolevel causal processes warrants high priority in organizational culture research.[16] Apart from specifying the mechanisms whereby cultural effects in actuality occur, they address the matter of whether a company's manifest system of values, symbols, and beliefs is better framed as 'culture' or 'ideology.' Culture in the oversocialized Parsonsian sense of most organizational culture research implies psychological absorption by each individual member of the same set of cultural codes. Organizational culture in the Durkheimian sense of externally constraining collective consciousness might be better characterized as 'ideology': some members share it, others do not but are constrained by the network to comply with its rules.[17]

Thus, the causes and consequences of culture rest on two distinct network mechanisms, both treated by Durkheim: (*a*) through reciprocated social influence people iteratively mold one another's cognitive and cathectic makeup so that more and more of them acquire, consequently share, the culture; (*b*) those same network constraints induce people to act in accordance with the culture/ideology even when the organization's socializing processes have failed to win their hearts and minds.

12. Conclusions

For the study of corporate culture to win broad social science acceptance, it requires better grounding in the vast scholarly literatures on culture in sociology and anthropology. 'Culture' in organizational study is a rich but

[15] Granovetter (1985) makes a similar argument against 'oversocialized' models of social action, such as Parsonsian and other varieties of cultural determinism. His 'embeddedness' theory is largely about the externally constraining properties of networks

[16] While commonplace in stratification and education research, contextual effects models have seen few applications of any sort in organizational study. In a sample of twenty social service agencies, Lincoln and Zeitz (1980) used an analysis of covariance technique to expose a strong pattern of organization-level (contextual) effects not apparent in the individual-level data. Measuring professionalization on a three-item scale given to employees, they found that, across individuals, professionals were apt to hold supervisory/administrative positions. With that tendency statistically netted out, however, the regression of the (adjusted) agency means took the opposite form: more professionalized agencies had lower supervisory densities. The emergent macropattern accords with theories of professional organization as a flexible 'organic' form distinct from bureaucracy.

[17] Some important recent work improves upon the contextual effects models used by Blau and Lincoln and Zeitz by explicitly incorporating network properties (Erbring and Young 1979; Manski 1993)

underspecified concept. While there are useful discussions of its content (i.e. specific values and beliefs); its significance for corporate performance; how best to observe it (whether qualitatively and quantitatively); and other matters, insufficient attention has been paid to an array of thorny questions, a number of which this essay has addressed: the culture versus ideology problem; the presence versus absence problem (does culture *always* exist?); the cognitive versus cathectic/evaluative problem; the questions of 'hot' versus 'cool' ritual and how much of each organizations really have; the structure versus culture problem–which drives which; and the level of causation problem–do culture effects operate through socialization and sharing or via external network constraint? The neglect of these and other issues is in substantial part a consequence of the broad decoupling of organization culture studies from that of mainstream culture theory and research. While greater 'coupling' of these literatures might be achieved in a number of ways, a first place to start, we suggest, is with careful attention to the work of Durkheim, a towering figure in the social sciences, whose writing has recently enjoyed a renaissance in several precincts of culture inquiry, but whose impact on organizational study on whole has been minimal.

Can a nineteenth-century theorist who devoted little explicit attention to matters of formal organization really have anything useful to offer on a problem that has drawn enormous research and journalistic attention since it appeared on the scene some twenty years ago? As our review hopefully demonstrates, many of Durkheim's ideas as applied to the organizational culture question seem not only creative and nuanced but also fresh and timely. Durkheim's writings on how ritual and ceremony serve to build cohesion and facilitate collective cognition is a novel take on a problem that has attracted wide interest but little theoretical closure (Trice and Beyer 1984). Our distinction between 'hot' and 'cool' ritual, rooted in the contrast between Durkheim's and Weber's thought, also seems a fruitful way to assess the ceremonial qualities of organizations. Durkheim's concept of anomie or culture breakdown is a helpful corrective to the pervasive tendency in organization studies to attach the culture concept to anything and everything as opposed to careful assessment of when it exists, when it does not, and what difference to the organization that makes.

Finally, Durkheim's insistence that culture (collective consciousness) is an 'exterior and constraining' social fact presents a challenge to organizational culture research, most of which assumes a highly reductionist etiology whereby culture affects behavior through processes of socialization so that individuals are psychologically programmed to comply with its rules and codes. Durkheim's writing here has been much criticized for appearing to embrace the opposite conception of a macroscopic 'collective mind', positioned outside people and society and determining human thought, feeling, and behavior from afar. Yet a fine-grained reading of Durkheim's work gives a different impression: all consciousness of necessity resides in individual minds but it converges and coalesces through a dynamic process of interaction and so becomes exterior and constraining in the incontrovertible sense that individuals find themselves enmeshed in thick and unyielding webs of social pressure that leave them little recourse but to join the crowd. Work organizations, as the careful studies by Kunda (1992) and Martin et al. (1998) show, often contrive to spin these ideological webs, which enable them to put aside the hard structural controls whose source is easily pinpointed and against which resistance can readily form. Some interesting and sophisticated organizational research and theory is now engaging the issue of the network basis for culture emergence and constraint. It would do well to examine Durkheim's pioneering contributions to these themes.

References

Archer, M. S. (1982). 'Morphogensis Versus Structuration: On Combining Structure and Action', *British Journal of Sociology*, 33: 455–83.

—— (1985). 'The Myth of Cultural Integration', *The British Journal of Sociology*, 36: 333–53.

Barley, S. R. and Kunda, G. (1992). 'Design and Devotion: Surges of Rational and Normative Ideologies of Control in Managerial Discourse', *Administrative Science Quarterly*, 37: 363–99.

Barnes, J. A. (1954). 'Class and Committees in a Norwegian Island Parish', *Human Relations*, 7: 39–58.

Bartlett, C. A. and Ghoshal, S. (1989). *Managing Across Borders: The Transnational Solution*. Boston, MA: Harvard Business School Press.

Bendix, R. (1956). *Work and Authority in Industry: Ideologies of Management in the Course of Industrialization*. New York: Harper & Row.

Benedict, R. (1932). 'Configurations of Culture in North America', *American Anthropologist*, 34: 1–27.

Berger, P. L. and Luckmann, T. (1966). *The Social Construction of Reality*. New York: Doubleday.

Besnard, P. (1988). 'The True Nature of Anomie', *Sociological Theory*, 6: 91–5.

Blau, P. M. (1955). *The Dynamics of Bureaucracy*. Chicago, IL: University of Chicago Press.

Blau, P. M. (1960). 'Structural Effects', *American Sociological Review*, 25: 178–93.

Bottomore, T. (1981). 'A Marxist Consideration of Durkheim', *Social Forces*, 59: 902–17.

Business Week (1980). 'Corporate Culture-the Hard to Change Values that Spell Success or Failure', October: 148–54.

Carroll, G. R. and Harrison, J. R. (1998). 'Organizational Demography and Culture: Insights from a Formal Model and Simulation', *ASQ*, 43: 637–67.

Chatman, J. A., Polzer, J. T., Barsade, S. G., and Neale, M. A. (1998). 'Being Different Yet Feeling Similar: The Influence of Demographic Composition and Organizational Culture on Work Processes and Outcomes', *Administrative Science Quarterly*, 43: 749–80.

Cohen, M. D., March, J. G., and Olsen, J. P. (1972). 'A Garbage Can Model of Organizational Choice', *Administrative Science Quarterly*, 17: 1–25.

Cole, R. E. (1971). *Japanese Blue Collar: The Changing Tradition*. Berkeley, CA: University of California Press.

Crozier, M. (1964). *The Bureaucratic Phenomenon*. Chicago, IL: University of Chicago Press.

Deal, T. E. and Kennedy, A. A. (1982). *Corporate Cultures: The Rites and Rituals of Corporate Life*. Reading, MA: Addison-Wesley.

DiMaggio, P. (1997). 'Culture and Cognition', *Annual Review of Sociology*, 23: 263–87.

Dore, R. P. (1973). *British factory, Japanese Factory*. Berkeley, CA: University of California Press.

—— (2000). *Stock Market Capitalism: Welfare Capitalism: Japan and Germany versus the Anglo-Saxons*. Oxford: Oxford University Press.

Douglas, M. (1968). 'The Social Control of Cognition: Some Factors in Joke Perception', *Man*, 3: 163–76.

Durkheim, E. (1933). *The Division of Labor in Society*. Glencoe, IL: Free Press.

—— ([1897] 1966). *Suicide: A Study in Sociology*. New York: Free Press.

—— ([1915] 1961). *The Elementary Forms of the Religious Life*. New York: Collier.

—— ([1938] 1982). *The Rules of the Sociological Method*. New York: Free Press.

Emirbayer, M. (1996). 'Useful Durkheim', *Sociological Theory*, 14: 109–30.

Erbring, L. and Young, A. A. (1979). 'Individuals and Social Structure: Contextual Effects as Endogenous Feedback', *Sociological Methods and Research*, 7: 396–430.

Etzioni, A. (2000). 'Toward a Theory of Public Ritual', *Sociological Theory*, 18: 44–59.

Fine, G. A. (1984). 'Negotiated Orders and Organizational Cultures', *Annual Review of Sociology*, 10: 239–62.

Fisher, G. A. and Chon, K. K. (1989). 'Durkheim and the Social Construction of Emotions', *Social Psychology Quarterly*, 52: 1–9.

Foucault, M. (1972). *The Archaeology of Knowledge*, trans. A. M. Sheridan-Smith. New York: Pantheon Books.

Frank, K. A. and Fahrbach, K. (1999). 'Organization Culture as a Complex System: Balance and Information in Models of Influence and Selection', *Organization Science*, 10: 253–77.

Freeland, R. F. (1996). 'The Myth of the M-Form: Governance, Consent, and Organizational Change', *American Journal of Sociology,* 102: 483–526.

Galbraith, J. (1973). *Designing Complex Organizations.* Reading, MA: Addison-Wesley.

Ghoshal, S. (2003). 'Schools Share Blame for Enron', *Financial Times,* July 17.

Giddens, A. (1976). 'Classical Social Theory and the Origins of Modern Sociology', *American Journal of Sociology,* 81: 703–29.

Goll, I. and Zeitz, G. (1991). 'Conceptualizing and Measuring Corporate Ideology', *Organization Studies,* 12: 191–207.

Gordon, A. (1985). *The Evolution of Labor Relations in Japan.* Cambridge, MA: Harvard University Press.

Gouldner, A. W. (1954). *Patterns of Industrial Bureaucracy.* New York: Free Press.

Gramsci, A. (1990). 'Culture and Ideological Hegemony', in J. Alexander and S. Seidman (eds.), *Culture and Society: Contemporary Debates.* New York: Cambridge University Press.

Granovetter, M. (1985). 'Economic Action and Social Structure: The Problem of Embeddedness', *American Journal of Sociology,* 91: 481–510.

Hamilton, D. P. (2000). 'At Hewlett-Packard, Carly Fiorina Combines Discipline, New-Age Talk', *Wall Street Journal Interactive Edition,* August 22.

Hermalin, B. (2001). 'Economics and Corporate Culture', in S. Cartweight et al. (eds.), *The International Handbook of Organizational Culture and Climate.* Chichester, UK: John Wiley & Sons.

Hilbert, R. A. (1986). 'Anomie and the Moral Regulation of Reality: The Durkheimian Tradition in Modern Relief', *Sociological Theory,* 4: 1–19.

Hochschild, A. R. (1983). *The Managed Heart: The Commercialization of Human Feeling.* Berkeley, CA: University of California Press.

Jacoby, S. M. (1997). *Modern Manors: Welfare Capitalism since the New Deal.* Princeton, NJ: Princeton University Press.

Kanter, R. M. (1983). *The Change Masters: Innovation and Entrepreneurship in the American Corporation.* New York: Simon & Schuster.

—— (1997). 'Some Effects of Proportions on Group Life: Skewed Sex Ratios and Responses to Token Women', *American Journal of Sociology,* 82: 965–90.

Kroeber, A. L. (1948). 'White's View of Culture', *American Anthropologist,* 50: 405–15.

Kunda, G. (1992). *Engineering Culture: Control and Commitment in a High-tech Corporation.* Philadelphia, PA: Temple University Press.

Lawrence, P. R. and Lorsch, J. W. (1967). *Organization and Environment.* Boston, MA: Harvard Business School Press.

LeBaron, F. (2001). 'Toward a New Critique of Economic Discourse (Review of Pierre Bourdieu's Le structure sociale de l'economie) Theory, *Culture & Society,* 18: 123–9.

Lemert, C. (1994). 'The Canonical Limits of Durkheim's First Classic', *Sociological Forum,* 9: 87–92.

Lincoln, J. R. and Zeitz, G. (1980). 'Organizational Properties from Aggregate Data: Separating Individual and Structural Effects', *American Sociological Review* 45: 391–409.

—— and McBride, K. (1987). 'Japanese Industrial Organization in Comparative Perspective', *Annual Review of Sociology*, 13: 289–312.

—— and Kalleberg, A. L. (1990). *Culture, Control, and Commitment: A Study of Work Organization and Work Attitudes in the U. S. and Japan*. New York: Cambridge University Press.

—— and Gerlach, M. L. (2004). *Japan's Network Economy: Structure, Persistence, and Change*. New York: Cambridge University Press.

——, Hanada, M., and Olson, J. (1981). 'Cultural Orientations and Individual Reactions to Organizations: A Study of Employees of Japanese Owned Firms', *Administrative Science Quarterly*, 26: 93–115.

—— , —— , and McBride, K. (1986). 'Organizational Structures in Japanese and U.S. Manufacturing', *Administrative Science Quarterly*, 31: 338–64.

Linstead, S. and Grafton-Small, R. (1992). 'On Reading Organizational Cultures', *Organization Studies* 13: 331–55.

Lukes, S. (1973). *Emile Durkheim: His Life and Work*. New York: Allen Lane.

Manski, C. (1993). 'Identification of Endogenous Social Effects—the Reflection Problem', *Review of Economic Studies*, 60: 531–42.

Martin, J. (1992). *Cultures in Organizations: Three Perspectives*. New York: Oxford University Press.

—— (2002). *Organizational Culture: Mapping the Terrain*. Thousand Oaks, CA: Sage.

——, Knopoff, K. and Beckman, C. (1998). 'An Alternative to Bureaucratic Impersonality and Emotional Labor: Bounded Emotionality at The Body Shop', *Administrative Science Quarterly*, 43: 429–69.

Merton, R. K. (1968). *Social Theory and Social Structure*. New York: Free Press.

Mestrovic, S. G. (1987). 'Durkheim's Concept of Anomie Considered as a "Total" Social Fact', *British Journal of Sociology*, 38: 567–83.

Meyer, J. W., and Rowan, B. (1977). 'Institutionalized Organizations: Formal Structure as Myth and Ceremony', *American Journal of Sociology*, 83: 340–63.

Morgan, G. (1986). *Images of Organization*. Beverly Hills, CA: Sage.

Morrill, C. (1991). 'Conflict Management, Honor, and Organizational Change', *American Journal of Sociology*, 97: 585–621.

Nelson, R. R. and Winter, S. G. (1982). *An Evolutionary Theory of Economic Change*. Cambridge, MA: Harvard University Press.

Nisbet, R. A. (1967). *The Sociological Tradition*. London: Heinemann.

O'Reilly, C. and Chatman, J. (1996). 'Culture as Social Control: Corporations, Cults, and Commitment', in B. M. Staw and L. L. Cummings (eds.), *Research in Organizational Behavior*, vol. 18. Greenwich, CT: JAI Press.

Orru, M. (1983). 'The Ethics of Anomie: Jean Marie Guyau and Emile Durkheim', *British Journal of Sociology*, 34: 499–518.

Ouchi, W. (1981). *Theory Z: How American Business Can Meet the Japanese Challenge*. Reading, MA: Addison-Wesley.

—— and Wilkins, A. L. (1985). 'Organizational Culture', *Annual Review of Sociology*, 11: 457–83.

Parsons, T. (1949) *The Structure of Social Action*. Glencoe, IL: Free Press.

Pascale, R. T. and Athos, A. (1982). *The Art of Japanese Management*. New York: Warner Books.

Peacock, J. L. (1981). 'Durkheim and the Social Anthropology of Culture', *Social Forces*, 59: 996–1008.

Perrow, C. (1986). *Complex Organizations: A Critical Essay*. New York: Scott, Foresman.

Peters, T. J. and Waterman, R. H. (1982). *In Search of Excellence: Lessons from America's Best-Run Companies*. New York: Warner Books.

Peterson, R. A. (1979). 'Revitalizing the Culture Concept', *Annual Review of Sociology*, 5: 137–66.

Pettigrew, A. M. (1979). 'On Studying Organizational Cultures', *Administrative Science Quarterly*, 24: 570–81.

Pope, W. (1973). 'Classic on Classic: Parsons' Interpretation of Durkheim', *American Sociological Review*, 38: 399–415.

——, Cohen, J., and Hazelrigg, L. E. (1975). 'On the Divergence of Weber and Durkheim: A Critique of Parsons' Convergence Thesis', *American Sociological Review*, pp. 417–27.

Powell, W. W. and DiMaggio, P. (eds.) (1991). *The New Institutionalism in Organizational Analysis*. Chicago, IL: University of Chicago Press.

Raghavan, A., Kranhold, K., and Barrionuevo, A. (2002). 'How Enron Bosses Created a Culture of Pushing Limits', *Wall Street Journal Interactive Edition*, August 26.

Rawls, A. W. (1996). 'Durkheim's Epistemology: The Neglected Argument', *American Journal of Sociology*, 102: 430–82.

Rohlen, T. P. (1974). *For Harmony and Strength: Japanese White-collar Organization in Anthropological Perspective*. Berkeley, CA: University of California Press.

Sawyer, R. K. (2002). 'Durkheim's Dilemma: Toward a Sociology of Emergence', *Sociological Theory*, 2: 227–47.

Schein, E. H. (1996). 'Culture: The Missing Concept in Organization Studies', *Administrative Science Quarterly*, 41: 229–40.

Selznick, P. R. (1949). *TVA and the Grass Roots: A Study in the Sociology of Formal Organization*. Berkeley, CA: University of California Press.

—— (1996). 'Institutionalism Old and New', *Administrative Science Quarterly*, 41: 270–7.

Srole, L. (1956). 'Social Integration and Certain Corrollaries: An Exploratory Study', *American Sociological Review*, 21: 709–16.

Starkey, K. (1998). 'Durkheim and the Limits of Corporate Culture: Which Durkheim? Whose Culture?', *Journal of Management Studies*, 35: 125–36.

Stinchcombe, A. L. (1997). 'On the Virtues of the Old Institutionalism', *Annual Review of Sociology*, 23: 1–18.

Swidler, A. (1986). 'Culture in Action: Symbols and Strategies', *American Sociological Review*, 51: 273–86.

Takla, T. N. and Pope, P. (1985). 'The Force Imagery in Durkheim: The Integration of Theory, Metatheory, and Method', *Sociological Theory*, 3: 74–88.

Tosti, G. (1898). 'The Delusions of Durkheim's Sociological Objectivism', *American Journal of Sociology*, 4: 171–7.

Trice, H. M. and Beyer, J. M. (1984). 'Studying Organizational Cultures Through Rites and Ceremonials', *Academy of Management Review*, 9: 653–69.

Turner, J. H. (1990). 'Emile Durkheim's Theory of Social Organization', *Social Forces*, 68: 1089–103.

Weick, K. E. (1976). 'Educational Organizations as Loosely Coupled Systems', *Administrative Science Quarterly*, 21: 1–19.

—— and Roberts, K. H. (1993). 'Collective Mind in Organizations: Heedful Interrelating on Flight Decks', *Administrative Science Quarterly*, 38: 357–81.

Williamson, O. E. (1975). *Markets and Hierarchies: Analysis and Antitrust Implications*. New York: Free Press.

Wuthnow, R. and Witten, M. (1988). 'New Directions in the Study of Culture', *Annual Review of Sociology*, 14: 49–67.

5

Feminist Theories of Work

Heidi Gottfried[1]

> So I take phosphates or phosphites—whichever it is, and tonics, and journeys, and air, and exercise, and I am absolutely forbidden to 'work' until I am well again.
>
> Gilman (1892).

As evocatively captured by Charlotte Perkins Gilman's lament in her short story, 'The Yellow Wall-Paper', work has a long, but troubled, history in women's lives and in feminist thought. Although written in the early twentieth century, Gilman anticipates many of the themes taken up by feminists in the late twentieth century. In this excerpt the female protagonist's fragile body dooms her to play the part of 'the weaker sex' in a Victorian drama. The treatment of middle- and upper-class women as physically unfit for labor confines work to and ultimately defines work against an implicit masculine standard. Women's situation has been intimately connected to the less visible work of reproduction. Feminist analysis has laid bare the male bias in the definition, constitution, and organization of work. Looking at work through a feminist lens exposes how restrictions on the type of work available, on where it happens, on its rewards, and even on what counts as work, is related to who does it (Brush 1999: 162–3).

It is important to note that feminism is neither a unified nor a singular theory. Feminism encompasses diverse political projects and varied theoretical claims about pervasive, ubiquitous, and persistent gender-based hierarchies in and at work. These multiple strands derive from their alignment with different theoretical traditions. Feminists disagree over the

[1] Special thanks to Joan Acker, Sylvia Walby, and David Fasenfest, and the three editors, Marek Korczynski, Paul Edwards, and Randy Hodson for their rounds of insightful comments on earlier drafts of this chapter.

causes and the mechanisms perpetuating male privilege and female disadvantage in the worlds of work. The chapter thus must perform double duty in order to capture the dual nature of feminism alternating between critical analysis and internal debate. Any single text, however, cannot represent the full range of feminist theories and the voluminous literature on the topic. Mapping the relationship between feminism and social theory necessarily is beyond the scope of this review (for excellent reviews, see Jackson 1998; and Evans 2003).

The chapter teases out the common threads, advancements, and variations in feminist scholarship on work and reviews these developments roughly in chronological order. Because a neat chronology would mask the ongoing dialogue shaping feminist discourses, each consecutive section progresses thematically within two historically relevant waves of feminist mobilization. Following this broad periodization, the initial section provides the historical context of first wave feminism as a movement for social change taking place in the midst of work transformation to large-scale manufacture. This first wave is not merely a relic of historical interest, but serves as a point of departure for second wave feminist thought. Reminiscent of a palimpsest, second wave feminists project new interpretations on the historical record in order to revise classical social theories, thereby uncovering the structures of patriarchy undergirding the structures of capitalism at its formative stage. What happens in the past has a bearing on present work configurations.

The bulk of the chapter documents alternative second wave feminist accounts in five sections covering a wide swath of approaches to the study of work, including those that focus on patriarchy and capitalism, labor markets, organizations to the self. The order reflects the theoretical move from an analysis of macrostructural factors towards an analysis of processual influences. In Section 3, feminist scholarship asks why some attributes become socially and culturally salient and typed in terms of gender differences within organizations and through organizational practices. By gendering organizational analysis and examining gendered work, Sections 4 and 5 make visible instances of emotional and aesthetic labor, and how gendered performances and embodiment are built into job requirements with different values depending on who does it.

Sections 6 and 7 discuss the influence of the postmodern turn and the return to earlier debates on patriarchy. Feminist postmodern theories posit diffuse power, multiple and fluid identities in analyses of gender differences at work. A materialist feminism salvages gender as a social structure as well as bringing class back into feminist theories of work. One variant on social practices is highlighted as an example that integrates the dynamic interplay between structure and process rather than forsake one for the other. And finally, the conclusion envisages feminist futures by reflecting on how far feminist scholarship has evolved and by considering to what extent feminists expect ongoing progress towards a degendering of work and a more equitable distribution of labor.

1. Social Theories and Feminist Waves

Political mobilization among women fertilized the growth of two major waves of feminism. A short history looks back at the first wave of feminist thought through which social reformers raised the question about women's economic insecurity and political disenfranchisement. From the earliest writings by Mary Wollstonecraft's vindication of the rights of woman written in the late eighteenth century, feminists have condemned separate and unequal treatment of women. Women's inability to fully participate in political and economic activities was connected to their reproductive burdens in the family. What has united an otherwise divided feminism is the shared recognition of the interrelationship between reproduction and production. Second wave feminism made this point clearer in their critique of narrow approaches to the study of work. Feminists took aim at the canon for giving priority to production over reproduction, public over private, paid over unpaid labor, and class over gender. Early second wave feminists criticized gender-neutral analysis of capitalism and other related economic categories, and developed the notion of patriarchy in relationship to capitalism.

First wave feminism, rising and abating from the late 1800s through the early 1920s, addressed the social ills of the day. Reformers posed 'the woman's question' to campaign against sweatshop conditions faced by women workers when large-scale manufacture altered traditional ways of working and agrarian rhythms of work. One of the few systematic theoretical contributions, *The Origin of the Family, Private Property, and the State* by Fredrick Engels (1968), offered a compelling historical–materialist conception linking women's oppression to class exploitation.[2] According to Engels, asymmetrical relations between men and women constituted the first-class relation. Under capitalism, Engels related male domination to

[2] Although little known today, the publication of *Woman and Labour* (1911) by Olive Schreiner made the connection between capitalism and social reproduction (cited in Wise and Stanley 2003: 3).

the bourgeois family in which men had an economic interest in controlling individual women's reproductive capacities in order to establish clear paternity lines for the transmission of private property to their male heirs. With rhetorical flourish Engels (1968: 495) intoned,

> The overthrow of mother right was the world-historic defeat of the female sex. The man seized the reigns in the house also, the woman was degraded, enthralled, the slave to the man's lust, a mere instrument for breeding children.

While the approach provided a historical rationale for the oppression of women, Engels narrowly reduced the woman's question to a class dynamic and the 'female sex' to a class relation.

As a counterpoint to Engels, Charlotte Perkins Gilman published her study of the 'economic relation between men and women as a factor in social evolution'. In the political ferment at the turn of the twentieth century, Gilman (1898: 2) juxtaposed women and economics in the title of her treatise on 'one of the most common and most perplexing problems of human life'.[3] Beginning with the story of genesis, she evoked the original state of equality between men and women until man succumbed to the tempting pleasures in the bountiful garden of delights.

> Close, close he bound her, that she should leave him never;
> Weak still he kept her, lest she be strong to flee

This prescient account brought unpaid domestic care work into economic analysis, thereby refusing to accept Marxist and neoclassical assumptions that housework created no economic value. By doing so, she perceptively gendered the concept of production and productive labor.

Feminist ideas flourished even after the peak of political activity from the end of the first wave to the commencement of the second wave. During the interwar period, labor feminists articulated principles and formulated reforms aimed at achieving gender equality by accommodating difference (Cobble 2004). The second wave swept in a more self-conscious feminism. As the women's movement gathered steam during the 1970s, Marxism, particularly the work of Engels, served both as an inspiration and as a foil to radical, socialist, and Marxist-feminists who drew on historical materialism and studied the architecture of capitalism to fashion structural accounts of patriarchal arrangements. Gilman's ideas about housework and domestic labor were also rediscovered. The debate over what constituted patriarchy forced feminists to rethink class analysis

[3] I am grateful to Sylvia Walby for reminding me of the impact of Charlotte Perkins Gilman on second wave feminism.

and to put gender relations and the gender division of labor in the forefront of work analyses.

The attempt to show that capitalism was not indifferent to the gender of individuals in the class structure gave rise to second wave feminist theories of patriarchy as a system of social relations that enabled men to control women's labor. Second wave feminists raised deeply historical questions in their search for the origins of patriarchy prior to and in articulation with capitalism. Three contributors exemplify what became known as the 'dual system's' approach. The French feminist, Christine Delphy (1977) identified separate spheres, locating the central dynamic of asymmetrical gender relations in a patriarchal domestic mode of production within families whereby men as a class exploited and benfited directly from the appropriation of women's labor. Like Gilman, she focused on housework and the household as a key to male domination, and insisted on the mainstreaming of gender into the concept of production. However, Delphy paid too little attention to women's paid labor outside of the home (Jackson 1998: 17). *Patriarchy at Work* by Sylvia Walby (1986) pushed forward the approach; it wove an intricate theory of patriarchy as relatively autonomous from other structures, with particular reference to a set of patriarchal relations permeating domestic work, paid work, state, male violence, and sexuality *in articulation* with capitalist relations. Hartmann (1979) traced women's disadvantage in the capitalist labor market to the organization of male workers in the late nineteenth century. The resulting occupational segregation concentrated women in low-wage work, which in turn kept women dependent on men for their economic survival, perpetuating a vicious cycle of patriarchy and capitalism. Both Walby and Hartmann historicized the connections between patriarchy and capitalism: the exclusion of women from paid work and the patriarchal relations in paid work, reinforced by state policies in Walby's account and by the family wage in Heidi Hartmann's model, represented the primary mechanisms for maintaining male superiority over women. This mode of theorizing implied 'abstract structuralism', reducing motivation, interests, and strategies for male domination of women either to the abstract needs of capital or to the equally abstract role of patriarchy (Pollert 1996: 641), thereby losing the dynamic tension between agency and structure.[4]

[4] This characterization overstates the case. *Patriarchy at Work* addresses collective agency to understand under what circumstances similar sorts of jobs (length of training, skill, heavy labor) became typed as either feminine or masculine, which Walby attributes to the outcome of a multifaceted struggle that involves different access to resources including state power.

Subsequent debates acknowledged the 'unhappy marriage' of Marxism and feminism (Sargent 1981), and expressed ambivalence about the category of patriarchy itself (Beechey 1979, 1987). Although ambivalent about the concept of patriarchy, many feminists reserved the concept for specific historical structures, that is, 'the patrilocal extended household in which the senior male holds authority' (Acker 1989: 236). While acknowledging the problems riddling the concept, Cockburn (1991) defended retaining the concept to define one form of sex-gender system in which fathers exercised customary or juridical rights to and over women. This 'father right' gave way to a more generalized 'male right' through a brotherhood of men under capitalism. Cockburn (1991: 8) sought to analyze the articulations of sets of social relations, that is the way they were lived and reproduced, and took care to distinguish patriarchy from other possible sex-gender systems. Acker (1989: 239) advocated applying less abstract concepts such as 'reproduction' to encompass 'all those activities that have to do with caring for human beings'. In *Gender Transformations* Walby (1997) revised her previous formulation to differentiate private from public patriarchy with the former rooted in family life and the latter in the labor market. The shift to public patriarchy occurred with the influx of women into the wage-labor force in large numbers, many of whom remained segregated in low-paying jobs. Walby addressed the implications of various forms of difference and politics for the transformation of gender relations, especially in employment.

While feminists disagreed on the usefulness of adopting particular terms such as reproduction, many opposed setting aside all references to patriarchal structures. No one advocated a return to macrostructural approaches. However, many expressed concern that the absence of any defining 'dynamic' deprived gender of distinctive social relations. Without the concept of patriarchy, feminism needed alternative concepts that appreciated the economic value of housework and unpaid domestic care work. Most feminists concluded that it was insufficient to merely add women to class analysis. Rather, it was necessary to examine gendered power relationships in the economy and the polity that affected the distribution of duties, rights, and rewards.[5]

In the wake of early second wave accounts, feminists introduced and refined the concept of gender in relationship to class and in distinction

[5] This paper primarily references Western feminist scholarship. However, feminist theories have traveled well to other regions of the world. In her cleverly titled article, 'Bye-bye Corporate Warriors', Mari Osawa (1994) translates the approach to understand the formation of a corporate-centered patriarchal society in Japan.

to sex.[6] To ask the question what was gender, challenged theories that had fixed sex in some natural, immutable essence. Within sociology, feminists dismantled the Parsonian assumptions that once dominated the field. The Parsonian systems' approach posited a dichotomy of differentiated sex roles that implied parallelism, which 'constantly collapse[d] into biological differences' (Connell 2002: 35). This binary of sex differences 'excluded patterns of differences among women and among men' and between alternative masculinities and femininities (Connell 2002: 9). The recognition that sex defaulted to biological differences led feminists to identify gender as a social relation and as a socially constructed category. By switching to a vocabulary of gender relationships, feminists analyzed the 'enduring patterns among social relations' (Connell 2002: 9).[7] Influenced by Weberian and Marxist class analysis, feminists argued that gender paralleled or intersected with class as a social structure that constituted 'a basic organizing principle in social life, a principle of allocation of duties, rights, rewards and power, including the means of violence' (Acker 2004: 20). As distinct from sex, patriarchal gender relations referred to 'inequalities, divisions and differences socially constructed around assumed distinctions between female and male' (Acker 2004: 20).[8] The social construction of gender was theorized as a complex process involving individual, structural and symbolic levels (see Scott 1986: 1067), that operated 'within institutions through interaction and [a]s a result of organizational practice' (Reskin and Padavic 1994: 12). Conceptualizing gender continued as a key concern of second wave feminist theory, leading to questions about the sources of male power, how work was gendered, and what constituted processes of gendering work organizations.

2. Deciphering Labor Market Structures

Using a less abstract model based on labor market structures, feminists have attempted to 'decipher' the causal forces driving the relative stability

[6] The initial impulse began with the philosophical work of Simone de Beauvoir in *The Second Sex*, which 'affirm[ed] that one is not born, but rather becomes, a woman' (paraphrased in Falasca-Zamponi 2003: 240).

[7] For a systematic discussion of gender, see Lorber 1994; Ferree et al. 1999; Connell 2002.

[8] Gender is not simply an object of study or a variable inserted into equations, but enters into the research process, into the selection of the problem and the methodology, into the conduct of the researcher, and into the assumptions guiding analysis. For a discussion of feminist methodology, see Gottfried 1996; Wolf 1996; Ramazanoglu with Holland 2002; and Wise and Stanley 2003.

of occupational sex segregation and related pay inequities despite greater female educational attainment, increasing participation both in the labor market and in politics (Charles 2003), and changing regulations over employment conditions. Persistent gender-based hierarchies presented feminists with a vexing puzzle to unravel: men and women not only worked in different occupations (horizontal segregation), but also occupied different positions in authority structures (vertical segregation). Enduring occupational segregation and pay inequities were seen as a function of either individual and/or structural characteristics, and these were related to decisions made by and preferences of either women or employers. Labor market analysis offered a toolkit for examining segmentation, emphasizing either demand-side or supply-side factors. In the ensuing debates, feminists took both sides.

On the demand side, a typology of dual or segmented labor markets distinguished primary from secondary sectors in terms of relative job characteristics. The primary labor market consisted of jobs paying higher wages, offering more promotional opportunities, and according greater job security, which for manufacturing jobs were associated with collective bargaining agreements negotiated by unions. The secondary labor market exhibited the opposite characteristics of low wages, low promotional opportunities, more job insecurity, and less access to union representation. These theorists observed that women were concentrated in the secondary labor market. Merely noting the gender composition of labor market segments was only the first step toward the development of an explanation to account for the differential allocation of men and women across occupations.

Demand-side models attributed segmentation to employers' decisions on hiring, placement, and promotion. Feminists specifically argued that occupational sex segregation was a function of employers' discriminatory policies and practices. Employers had engaged in 'disparate treatment' by discriminating against equally qualified men and women, and/or used gender-biased selection criteria having 'disparate impact' on men and women: the former becoming less salient due to regulatory reforms designed to address sex discrimination, and the latter being more tenacious and more difficult to uproot (England and Folbre 2003: 11). The persistence of what Reskin and Padavic (1994: 88) called a 'promotion gap' was related to the formation of firm-specific internal labor markets. Women more typically encountered truncated job ladders or dead-end jobs in contrast to men who enjoyed longer and broader career paths. Even as more women entered male work domains, women ended up in the lower ranks of professional occupations and in 'managerial ghettos' (Stone 1994: 410): 'Net of qualifications, women managers [w]ere lower in the chain of command, ha[d] limited decision-making power, and tend[ed] to supervise other women' (Stone 1994: 410). Vivid metaphors captured this uneven tempo of mobility by gender, including: sticky floors holding women back at lower levels, glass ceilings keeping women from shattering through to higher levels, escalators accelerating men's ascent to executive suites (Reskin and Padavic 1994: 88), and 'revolving doors' propelling men and women at different speeds and in different directions into high status positions (Jacobs 1989 cited in Stone 1994: 410).

Supply-side explanations emphasized cultural differences in occupational aspirations, choices, and preferences of men and women leading to occupational segregation. Catherine Hakim (1995) demarcated three basic types of women in relation to their commitments and orientations toward family and work: work-centered, home-centered, with the third and largest grouping made up of 'adaptive' women, including women who deliberately chose to combine work and family. Both home-centered and adaptive women's cumulative and collective preferences for less demanding 'female' occupations and/or part-time work contributed to their occupational segregation. This resurgence of 'preference theory' generated controversy and intense debate, especially in the UK (Bruegel 1996; Ginn and Arber 1996; Blackburn et al. 2002; Crompton 2002). Foremost among the many problems, the three categories reduced women's orientations and experiences to a narrow subset of possibilities (Blackburn et al. 2002: 524). Most critically, the emphasis on individual choice disregarded the social circumstances that constrained choices, such as availability and cost of childcare, attractiveness of available work, and relative pay levels (Blackburn et al. 2002).

The same labor market approaches also applied to analysis of the gender gap in earnings. No one disputed that the pay gap was clearly related to segregation, whatever the causes, although Anker (1998: 14) has warned that segregation was only one cause among many for pay differentials. Feminist theories of the gender pay gap followed similar lines of argument. Supply-side arguments proved less persuasive than demand-side arguments.

Human capital theory, a supply-side argument, assumed that pay differences reflected the actual human capital endowments men and women brought with them to the workplace. Thus, women earned less on average because they occupied different jobs with qualifications that were worth less. Mothers were particularly prone to earn low wages because their human capital depreciated when they either dropped out of the labor force or reduced the hours worked. Women made life choices to devote themselves to family, thereby reinforcing the traditional gender division of labor in which men with more human capital served as the principal earner. Empirically human capital endowments could not explain the full extent of gender differences in pay and failed to adequately account for discrimination. Women's occupational concentration in low-paying industries (particularly in the service sector), in small firms, and in the public sector resulted in an earnings differential even when controlling for human capital. In a rigorous panel study of earnings trajectories over a fifteen-year period in the USA, Rose and Hartmann (2004) found unequal pay despite similar educational achievements among men and women.

Perhaps more problematic, the approach narrowly defined human capital in terms of skill sets acquired through education, training, and on-the-job experience. Such empiricist approaches limited themselves to market-driven definitions of skills, qualifications, and competencies. Other labor activities associated with women's work, including caring labor, emotional labor, aesthetic labor, were unrecognized or devalued. Moreover, feminists questioned the assumption that domestic labor contributed zero value to the growth of an individual's human capital (Blackburn et al. 2002: 518). Which human capital characteristics were considered valuable and how skills and qualifications became valued were questions beyond the purview and concern of most supply-side theorists. The recognition and the valuation of skills and qualifications could not be reduced to a gender-neutral price mechanism in response to supply-side factors. Instead, demand-side factors have to be taken into account in order to explain the gender gap in earnings.

Building on demand-side labor market approaches feminists highlighted the role of discrimination in contributing to pay inequities by gender. Barbara Bergmann's 'crowding thesis' (1986) argued that women seeking to enter male occupations faced sex discrimination in hiring, leading to an excess of applicants for traditionally female-typed jobs (England and Folbre 2003: 24). The crowding of women into a small number of female-typed jobs lowered wages on average for those jobs. Men also suffered a wage penalty when they worked in female-typed occupations because employers set lower wages in such jobs (England and Folbre 2003: 25). While crowding of women helped explain occupational sex segregation, this thesis did not address the mechanisms that contributed to the devaluation of skills and the resulting pay gap. The approach was less successful in explaining why men still earned more on average than women in the same occupations (Rose and Hartmann 2004).

Ronnie Steinberg's 'devaluation thesis' (1990) located the source of pay inequities in labor market institutions. Devaluation was not simply an artifact of occupational segregation, but also related to gender bias in skill recognition and as a result of male-dominated wage-setting institutions. The devaluation thesis found that gender mattered to what counted as skill and as qualification. If skills were devalued due to gender and racial biases, then a reassessment of the 'true' value could correct pay levels. This assessment involved comparing male-typed and female-typed jobs to show the relative devaluation of women's work. By breaking down skill into component parts, it served the purpose of revaluing and recognizing devalued aspects of women's work. A comparable worth campaign gave women workers a political tool for demanding pay equity adjustments (Blum 1991). Comparable worth campaigns flourished in the public sector during the mid-1980s. The political principle of comparable worth, despite initial successes, fell victim to legal defeats (Nelson and Bridges 1999). These legal challenges plus strong employer opposition limited the use of comparable worth as a political mechanism for closing the pay gap.

The strength of structural models is their ability to identify and to operationalize variable clusters associated with occupational sex segregation and pay inequities. Large data sets culled from representative samples and sophisticated methods capture a panoramic view of persistent barriers and pervasive discrimination in the workplace. The models show the strong negative effect of gender (independent of and in interaction with other factors) on matching or 'queuing' of persons to sex segregated occupations and on determining income disparities. Demand-side approaches find employers' decisions remain a potent force shaping the gender distribution of employment opportunities. They insist that discrimination and devaluation of women's work are as important as human capital in explaining the gender wage gap (England 1992). Labor queues develop into gender queues as a result of employers' unexamined gender biases (Reskin and Roos 2002), such as the invisible discriminating assumptions in everyday communication at work (Reskin 2002). These strengths also are in part weaknesses. Relying on an inventory of structural-factors force all phenomena into quantifiable measures. One consequence is that reported gender differences are based on variables that are themselves gendered. The devaluation thesis has gone further than other labor market approaches to uncover the embedded gender biases in the recognition of skill, and to highlight the institutional arrangements and decisions behind lower wages experienced by women. 'Despite the centrality of gender... [such] accounts explain how gender works rather than why gender is such a major force in the organization of work' (Stone 1994: 416). To understand gendered work and the gendering of work demands a theory and a method attuned to cultural and political processes at the organizational level.

3. Gendering the Organization of Work and the Gendered Work Organization

Eclectic blending of neo-Marxism and neo-Weberian theories, with a dash of phenomenology, enabled feminists to unpack the cultural and political processes that contributed to the reproduction of male power in the economic sphere. Following neo-Marxism, feminists moved away from deterministic theories by no longer viewing cultural and political moments as epiphenomenal or as mere reflections of the economic base, but as relatively autonomous structures and processes. A more finely shaded analysis of organizationally based processes of social closure and bureaucracy drew on Weber's *Economy and Society* (1978). Regardless of the proportional weight given to each theoretical ingredient, with the shift to the mesolevel and microlevel it became possible to excavate the cultural meanings embedded in and attached to gendered work and gendered work identities in organizations and through organizational practices.

As one of the early works on gender and organizations, Rosabeth Moss Kanter's *Men and Women of the Corporation* (1977) became a touchstone for subsequent feminist research on gendering and gendered forms of work. Pioneering the study of gender and organizations, Joan Acker (1990: 140) identified, 'organizations [as] one arena in which widely disseminated cultural images of gender are invented and reproduced' and where individual gender identities were produced through organizational processes and pressures. By using the verb 'gendering' Acker emphasized the ongoing, active doing or organizing of gender relations in major institutions. Through an excavation of organizational processes, feminists further analyzed how jobs became gendered, that is, reserved and preserved for either men or women. 'To say that an organization is gendered means that advantage and disadvantage, exploitation and control, action and emotion, meaning and identity are patterned through and in terms of a distinction between male and female, masculine and feminine' (Acker 1990). Both gendering and gendered referred to processes that shaped the distribution of power and the division of labor in and through organizations.

Neo-Weberian approaches influenced feminist analyses of the ways in which organizational processes and practices created vertical and horizontal divisions of labor. Parkin (1982: 175) revised Weber's conceptualization of social closure as 'the process by which social collectivities seek to maximize rewards by restricting access to resources and opportunities to a limited circle of eligibles'. He added exclusionary closure as the attempt by one group to secure for itself a privileged position at the expense of some other group through a process of subordination and usurpation (Parkin 1982: 176). Parkin's linking of social closure to the distribution of power and closure strategies, both exclusionary and those adopted by the excluded, lent itself to feminist reinterpretation. Gendered divisions of labor, both formally structured and informally organized, occurred through processes of inclusion and exclusion, whereby women and men specialized in particular and different types of work (Hearn and Parkin 2001: 9–10). Walby (1990) extended the concept to 'patriarchal social closure' in order to argue that men excluded women from authority positions. Interaction between gendered divisions of labor and gendered divisions of authority, when consolidated, produced a formalized structure of gendered bureaucracy (Hearn and Parkin 2001). As a neo-Weberian, Frank Parkin recognized that authority constituted an organizational asset that was rarely exercised for its own sake, but rather was structured by property relations, linking his theory to Marxism.

Antonio Gramsci informed an important strand of neo-Marxist cultural theory that was applied to understanding mesolevel and microlevel processes reproducing class rule at the point of production (Burawoy 1985). Although Gramsci never directly addressed hegemony in relationship to the reproduction of male dominance, feminists appropriated the concept (Connell 1987; Acker 1989) for analysis of hegemonic masculinity in contemporary capitalism.[9] Feminist decoding of Gramsci's texts provided fruitful directions for analyzing the formation of sexualized cultures and hegemonic masculinity in organizational settings (Hearn and Parkin 1983;

[9] Gramsci's nonreductionist theory, giving centrality to politics and ideology with its area of hegemony, dissolved the static opposition of agency and structure. In the struggle for hegemony, ruling groups made concessions of a material kind in order to secure consent of subordinate groups. As a consequence, the dominant culture was never pure but became 'a mobile combination of cultural and ideological elements devised from different locations' (Bennett 1994: 225).

Cockburn 1991; Hearn 1993: 28).[10] In *Brothers*, Cockburn (1983) took the male working class as her subject revolutionizing the study of gender as more than an inquiry about women's lives. The study of hegemonic masculinity brought men back into sociological studies of work. Hegemonic masculinity operated *not* principally by legal coercion or economic compulsion, but by cultural means (Cockburn 1991: 170). Hegemonic masculinity was constructed in relationship to subordinated masculinities and femininities (Connell 1995). One study of a Japanese transplant in the USA found that job segregation predisposed male and female workers to 'use' gender differences in order to 'make' sense of their positions in class-based hierarchies that valorized hegemonic masculinity as the dominant form of rule in capitalist organizations. In the context of teamwork, 'The construction of hegemonic masculinity pushes workers to increase their workload in adopting a "manly" posture, thereby maintaining capitalist production as a well-oiled machine' (Gottfried and Graham 1993: 625). Their analysis brought the political concerns of Gramscian-informed cultural studies centrally into the new flexible factory but did not specify whether the dynamics it uncovered—wherein gender dynamics shaped the distribution of responsibilities—could have occurred in less innovative work contexts.

Feminist organizational analyses also criticized gender-neutral theories of technological development and skill. For example, technological innovation did not merely follow a Darwinian evolutionary trajectory of natural selection in which superior methods won out over less productive ideas, but also involved strategic choices on the part of (male) managers and engineers. Technology embodied a social process rather than being purely a scientific discovery. Technologies might be selected over others because they enhanced control over work and workers. Men controlled machines through the ideology of gender essentialism in which male mechanical prowess was naturalized. In relationship to skills, feminists asked why some skills and qualifications became socially and culturally valued and typed in terms of gender differences. As a result of their collective power, men could define what counted as qualifications and thereby could monopolize productive resources. For example, apprenticeships were institutional mechanisms assigning value to the skills necessary for practicing a particular trade. Skilled tradesman effectively restricted

[10] Like Burawoy (1979, 1985), Ching Kwan Lee (1998) and Lal (1998) choose local cases to reveal general principles. Through ethnographic studies, Lee excavates structural conditions from female workers' lived social worlds at the point of production in two regions of South China.

access to apprenticeships through requirements favoring skill sets and experience gained in male-typed jobs and training programs. In this system, women were at a disadvantage and often excluded from the 'skilled' trades. Those few women who successfully completed apprenticeship training faced other obstacles on-the-job as male coworkers treated them as less able or even disabled to perform the trade. The link between gender, class, and skill also was evident in female-typed jobs. Feminized jobs welded together femininity and skill 'in a construction that relies heavily on class imagery.... Office "lady" with its due overtones of gender and class encapsulates this ideal of a white and middle-class femininity' (Pringle 1988: 133).

Subsequent scholarship codified this gender paradigm in organizational studies (Hearn and Parkin 2001). A groundswell of new scholarship percolated from Foucault's preoccupation with the micropolitics and technologies of power. The Foucauldian rendering attended to sexual politics (Connell 1987) and discourses of power and sexuality in the workplace (Pringle 1989). With a particular focus on sexuality in organizations, Jeff Hearn (1993) deconstructed organizational cultures in order to 'name men as men' (also see Collinson and Hearn 1994). He rationalized a focus on sexuality in organizations to develop a 'more accurate conceptualization of patriarchy and public patriarchy' (Hearn 1993: 29). The adjectival use of 'patriarchal' combined with other descriptors such as 'patriarchal paternalism' (Collinson and Hearn 1994) summarized the concrete ways in which male power legitimized authority in capitalist organizations. Hearn, in collaboration with Wendy Parkin, developed their approach in a discussion of gender, sexuality, and violence. Viewing structural oppressions along with mundane everyday violence, such as disrespect and exclusion, as violations of persons the authors articulate the case for the organization's central and purposeful role in the existence and propagation of these violations (Keashley and Gottfried 2003: 275). Violence was a mechanism by which men maintained power in and through organizations.

A closer examination of organizational culture also highlighted the dynamic interplay between compliance and resistance practices and revealed the 'doing' and possible 'undoing' of unequal gender relations at work. As people produced culture at work, they generated a set of social practices that ran counter to hegemonic ones. Specifically, subjects might engage in small acts of antidiscipline as they created separate gendered subcultures. Unauthorized conduct or misconduct could act as a counterhegemonic force against alienation. For example, misconduct and unauthorized conduct by definition defied the dominant rationality since the behavior had been deemed improper or dysfunctional to organizational objectives.

The gender and organization perspective emphasizes how organizations operate to produce and reproduce gender differences. Through an excavation of organizational practices the analysis makes visible the active gendering processes and the gendered agents engaged in these processes, and grounds specific forms of male power in relationship to class and other hierarchies in organizations. Structure gives way to process in the proliferation of organizational studies disconnected from each other. Larger structures have tended to disappear in the richly detailed analyses of organizational cultures.

4. The Presentation of Self in Everyday Life, or the Drama of Self-Presentation

Appearing contemporaneously with, and cross-referencing organizational analysis of workplace culture, feminists examined the social construction of the gendered self as a microlevel phenomenon. With the publication of Hochschild's pioneering study (1983), *The Managed Heart*, feminist sociologists inherited a concept that addressed the absent (repressed) expressive rationality at the heart of commodity relations. One of the most far-reaching insights recognized the significance of 'emotional labor' in interactive service work (Leidner 1993). This stream of feminism flowed from Goffman's dramaturgical approach, viewing the presentation of self in everyday life as a kind of 'social' performance concerned with the creation and management of impressions and for 'doing gender' (West and Zimmerman 1987) and other differences (West and Fenstermaker 1995; Giuffre and Williams 2002).

Introducing the concept of emotional labor called attention to the management of impressions in ways consistent with occupations, and to employers' roles not only in directing employees' physical movements but emotional ones as well (Erikson and Wharton 1997: 189–90). Many female-typed occupations, such as those of secretaries, nurses, and flight attendants, required women workers to manage their own emotions and the feelings of others (Sotirin and Gottfried 1999). Whether or not employers intervened to reshape workers' moods, demeanor, appearance, and attitudes, Leidner (1993) convincingly argued that interactive service workers and their customers must negotiate interaction in which elements of manipulation, ritual, and genuine social exchange were subtly mixed. Workers managed customers through 'ethnomethodological competence', the capacity to make use of unspoken norms of behavior to control interactions (Stinchcombe 1990, cited in Leidner 1993: 7). This competency drew on emotional resources such as the use or 'withholding of personal charm and effort and vengeful retaliation against troublemakers' (Leidner 1993: 41). Leidner (1993: 201) also identified the gendered associations between the many skills for establishing and maintaining rapport—including drawing people out, bolstering their egos, displaying interest in their interests, and carefully monitoring one's own behavior so as not to offend—and the 'womanly arts'.

The concept of emotional labor highlighted an expressive rationality in which workers transformed feelings and sentiments into a serviceable commodity. In order to perform such labor, employees utilized skills as defined either as ethnomethodological competence, as interpersonal skills (i.e. perceptual skills), or as interactional skills (e.g. talking, hearing, dealing with people, communicating information). All of these terms implied social learning, interpretive capacities, and interpersonal abilities by which male and female actors enacted and reproduced gender in and at work.

An ethnomethodological approach viewed gender as a situational achievement rather than a fixed structural category. Workers accomplished more than tasks in the labor process; they 'do' gender and difference while doing work (West and Zimmerman 1987; West and Fenstermaker 1995). West and Zimmerman's proposal (1987) for an ethnomethodological approach emphasized the active production of gender. Similarly, Kessler and McKenna (1978: 5–7) asked, 'How do we "do" gender attributions? That is, what kinds of rules do we apply to what kinds of displays, such that in every concrete instance we produce a sense that there are only men and women, and that this is an objective fact, not dependent on the particular instance?' Gender was not simply a property of individuals (West and Zimmerman 1987: 126), but instead gender, along with race and class, were an 'on-going, methodological, and situated accomplishment' (West and Fenstermaker 1995). Categories and meanings associated with gender and work were interactional achievements. Extending this approach, 'Doing heterosexuality' investigated the negotiated, contested, and fluid boundary lines between legitimate and illegitimate behavior in a sexualized work culture. Social interactions, such as sexual banter and other public displays, normalized and naturalized, and thereby reproduced hegemonic heterosexuality and gender domination within work organizations (Giuffre and Williams 2002: 255).

For several decades from Goffman onwards, the symbolic interactionist perspective 'has fruitfully used the notion of the stage and performance as a way of understanding everyday behaviours and interactions' (McDowell 1997: 12). Doing gender put symbolic interaction and ethnomethodology front and center in interrogating the frozen smile on female flight attendants' faces in relationship to male passengers, the jockeying of door-to-door salesmen with their female customers, and the sexualized banter between waitresses and male short-order cooks. To say that work was meaningful carried the double sense of work as a process for producing gendered meanings as well as for producing goods and services. This focus on social exchange, however, upstaged structural factors.

Organizational structure retained a footing among feminists aligned with neo-Weberian and neo-Marxist approaches to the study of emotional labor (Steinberg and Figurt 1999). Rather than seeing emotions as banished from modern, bureaucratic organizations, feminists discovered a range of positive and negative emotions enacted by men and women in the corporation. A distinction was made between emotion work and emotional labor: emotion work involved the work on the self to feel and/or to present the self in certain ways, while emotional labor was seen as part of the work in the sense of providing counseling, comfort, protection, policing, doing social work, nursing, and so on.[11] This distinction combined the presentation of self from the symbolic interactionist perspective with the gendering of work from the gender and organizational perspective. Organizations sanctioned gender appropriate performances and determined the value of emotional labor and emotional work.

Emotional labor silently attached itself not only to many female-typed jobs, but also to many male-typed jobs. 'Rambo Litigators' cast the work of (male) litigators in a dramatic 'performance and presentation of an emotional self' tapping into cultural conceptions of masculinity with class inflections (Pierce 1999: 356–8). Gender and class appropriate codes of conduct, including tone of voice, cadence, body language, and dress codes were strategic choices, not simply individually selected but also institutionally constrained. The structure of the profession, including formal and informal professional norms, affected a 'style of self-presentation to create a desired impression' (Pierce 1999: 365). In their study of managerial careers, Martin and Wajcman (2003) investigated the understudied

[11] Joan Acker made this point in personal correspondence.

repertoire of positive emotions such as passion and enthusiasm emerging as more critical to managerial performance as a result of the erosion of mechanisms to secure organizational loyalty in the context of flexibilizing firms. Women had been at a disadvantage in managerial career tracks since gender displays coded as emotionality remained out of place in the 'rational' world of work. As positive emotions have gained importance to managerial performance, such symbolic resources either could become the basis of social closure fortifying the glass ceiling or could breakdown existing barriers to women's mobility in the firm.

In these studies, the workplace is a site not only for the making of things, but also for the 'making' of meanings about gendered workers and gendered jobs. Much is made of the significance of subtle social exchanges, utterances, displays, gestures, and emotional work as coded means of gender typing of jobs. It is this sustained attention to the microscopic that tends to narrow the focus on interactional processes at the expense of structural relationships. The doing of gender references cultural idioms framed within larger institutional contexts, but often takes for granted the structuring influence of institutional arrangements.

All the above studies make visible the cultural valuation associated with emotionality in job performance. As unrecognized, emotion work and emotional labor has been both undervalued and differentially rewarded, often depending on the gender expectations of the occupation. The performance of emotional labor and emotion work contributes to the reproduction of gender typing of occupations and helps to sustain horizontal and vertical segregation. The focus on emotion work hints at embodied forms of labor, but does not distinguish between different labor activities. Such feminist scholarship has paved the way for an appreciation of gendered embodiment in work styles and organizations.

5. Bodies at Work: Organizational Embodiment and Aesthetic Labor

The influential body of work on the body at work in bureaucratic organizations by Joan Acker (1990) drew attention to the process of gendering and embodiment to explain the fault lines of labor market segmentation (Witz et al. 1996; Halford et al. 1997; Tyler and Abbott 1998; Gottfried 2003). Building on this perspective, Halford et al. (1997) proposed a paradigm of 'gender and organizations' that sees gender as both embedded and embodied. Embodiment refers to modes of being in bodies

(Morgan 1998: 655); 'gender rests not only on the surface of the body, in performance and doing, but becomes *embodied*—becomes deeply part of whom we are physically and psychologically [and socially]' (Martin 1998: 495).

Feminist theory, under the influence of poststructuralism, mobilized the body to break up the 'unholy alliance' between sex and gender. Judith Butler moved feminist analysis beyond a notion of a sexed body as a substance upon which gender could work, but she failed to 'recuperate those lost matters of bodies that de Beauvior left in such a troubled state' (Witz 1997: 6). Grosz (1994: 63) argued that power in its discursive and material forms 'actively marks or brands bodies as social, inscribing them with the attributes of subjectivity'. The concept of gender, however, disappeared in her Foucauldian feminist rendering of the sex/sexuality pair (Witz 1997: 3). Rethinking the bodily roots of the female subject, Braidotti's nomadic wanderings (1994: 99) traversed theoretical borders to locate the double-sided process of subjectification by which the self-acquired subjectivity out of material (institutional) and discursive (symbolic) practices. Butler, among these other poststructuralists, failed to conceptualize 'the *social* construction of gendered bodies at the level of both social structural power relations and everyday social interaction and practices' (Jackson and Scott 2001, cited in Aiba 2004: 17). Staking out a position critical of poststructuralism with its emphasis on discourse, a number of sociologists opted for a materialist feminism to theorize men's use of gender difference to routinely exploit women's bodies (Cockburn 1991: 164).

A promising approach by Witz linked embodiment and gendered work to an analysis of new forms of labor market segmentation around 'aesthetic labor', particularly but not exclusively in service industries where employees were increasingly being called upon to develop particular forms of embodied skills in the service encounter. According to Witz (1998) 'aesthetic labor described the mobilization of embodied capacities and competencies possessed by organizational participants. This definition foregrounded the sensible components of social interaction'. Women must achieve and maintain a particular 'state of embodiment' (Tyler and Abbott 1998: 434), expressed through modes of speech, accent, and style that conform to a set of gender attributes that embodied socially sanctioned but variable characteristics of masculinity and femininity (McDowell 1997: 31). For example, temporary help agencies not only dispatched flexible employees to job placements, but they also selected, produced, and managed gendered bodies to fit people into organizational cultures. The treatment of body management in terms of aesthetic labor is particularly resonant in characterizing the Japanese work world where stylized uniforms, along with linguistic and gestural forms, marked workers' place in the social order. These practices burdened, excluded, and constrained female embodiment from the conception of full-time careers, and represented a good example of estheticized labor in which cultural idioms shaped bodies for temp(t)ing work (Gottfried 2003). The organization policed and demanded 'constant vigilance regarding gender self-presentation at work' (Wajcman 1998: 10).

Using the conception of embodiment feminist explored the ways that organizations shaped bodies at work and configured work around gendered bodies. A mesolevel analysis complemented such microlevel analysis of social interactions. Witz specifically called for a shift to the mesolevel as a means of 'confronting the possibility that modes of embodiment are not only mobilized by individuals but also are produced by organizations' (Witz 1998: 9). Bureaucratic organizations validated and permitted forms of male embodiment and invalidated or rendered impermissible forms of female embodiment (Witz 1998: 5). For women, the discursive construction of the reproductive body assumed particular importance in *disqualifying* them from authority positions and was continually evoked as the kernel of embodied difference (Halford et al. 1997: 213; Witz 1998: 6). The sexualized body represented another discursive construction of female embodiment whereby women had been included, *qualifying* them for certain front-stage and subordinate organizational functions (Witz 1998: 7; also see Adkins and Lury 1999). These dual processes of qualifying and disqualifying particular aspects of female embodiment shaped the development of sexualized cultures in which organizational gendering took place. Organizational practices were tied to embodied characteristics of gender, class, age, and race, and to notions of appropriate behavior and style (Halford and Savage 1997: 116).

In an effort to retrieve woman from the realm of biology, 'feminist sociology side-lined body matters and foregrounded gender matters' (Witz 1997: 2). One of the results was that feminists paid little attention to how bodies were used and misused at work. This neglect was especially notable given the centrality of bodywork and work on the body to the performance of women's work. For example, nursing assistants suffered high rates of back injuries in caring for their patients and carpel tunnel syndrome afflicted many keyboard users (Acker 2004). Women's work often involved the care of others' bodies as well as the management of their own body. Reproductive work most centrally dealt with women's bodies on both sides of the interaction. While Marx wrote passionately about the brutality of the capitalist machine destroying workers' bodies, he never linked the destruction of class bodies to gender meanings.[12] Bringing in the body mattered to our understanding of the value and the meaning of work.

During the 1990s, feminist theories of work and organization increasingly conceptualized embodiment as a new focus on the body at work and in organizations. Witz (1993: 32) 'points to some recent developments in feminist theory, in social theory and in organization theory more specifically, which pulled "the body" into the domain of "the social" . . . as a way of moving beyond "over socialized" and "desexualized" analyses of gender and bureaucracy . . . ', and of avoiding either 'the discursivization or the materialization of the body' (Witz 1997: 1). These developments exposed bodies as social matters, but how bodies matter resisted easy resolution. As yet, no one has fully accomplished the task of salvaging the gendered self by pulling bodies into the social domain.

Research on the body at work has provided a fresh look at the social construction of femininity and masculinity, a new exploration of the relations between sex and gender (see Aiba 2004), and a new focus on embodiment. Subsequent analyses emphasize the constitution of gender discursively and/or materially, bringing the body to bear on questions of gender and sexuality in organizational analysis, and conceptualizing gender as embedded and embodied in work styles and organizations. It reveals the implicit masculine standard by which employees are assumed to be free of attachments and responsibilities. This attention to bodies developed out of postmodernism and the deconstruction of sex and gender.

6. From the Postmodern Turn and the Return to Patriarchy

The second wave of Western feminist scholarship coalesced around tripartite divisions between liberal, socialist, and radical political theories, then splintered into multiple versions expressing the loss of confidence in conceptualizations of patriarchy, sex/gender distinctions, and gender. Any broad consensus around a feminist intellectual project centering

[12] 'Marx's portrait of the fractious and unruly links, cuts, and appropriations that characterise the structures of enjoining labourer and machine, labourer and labourer, labourer and the collective labourer, makes one wary of imagining that it has only been recently that theoretical work has superceded a nostalgia for an Arcadian corporeal integrity . . . ' (Callard 1998: 397)

around overwhelmingly structuralist discussions of 'gendered' and 'sexual' divisions of labor, whether in the labor market or in the household, were destabilized in a number of ways and for a number of reasons. The structuralist tone of this research was challenged by developments, particularly within feminist philosophy and postmodernism, which posed serious challenges to early feminist conceptualizations of power and—more significantly—of the very concept of gender itself. Moreover, intervention by black feminists criticized second wave feminist discussions of the interrelationship between gender and class for failing to integrate an analysis of race, and rendering black women invisible, just as traditional social science had, by and large, rendered all women invisible (Spelman 1988; Collins 1990).

Feminists ventured forward taking two directions: a 'postmodern turn' and a 'materialist' return. The postmodern turn marked a shift of analysis to 'words' from 'things' (Barrett cited in Jackson 1998: 12), and pulled feminism towards the fashion of deconstruction and the dissolution of the unified female subject on which much of second wave feminists' claims were founded. This sharp turn threatened to shipwreck studies of work perilously tipped toward the cultural side. Cultural studies like the Titanic failed to heed danger signs while crossing the disciplines at high speed. Navigating the icy waters required avoiding arguments that emphasized either cultural or discursive practices, and which 'le[d] to a preoccupation with cultural processes at the expense of an analysis of the structured conditions in which culture operate' (Wajcman 1993: 2–3). Another warning cautioned that the drift 'from a "gender paradigm" to a "sexuality paradigm" in organizational studies slight the concept of "gender" in a theoretical move that emphasized discursively constructed power relations' (Witz 1993: 32–3).

Feminists who disavowed the postmodern emphasis on discourse and representation also cautioned that the 'academic feminist gaze' had lost sight of class, a problem shared by structuralist and poststructuralist theories alike. This retreat from class was evident in the use of difference as a floating signifier as unanchored to historical and structural referents in postmodern thought (cf. Maynard 1994; Skeggs 1997: 7), and by neglect of the material conditions under which men and women worked (Kelly and Wolf 2001: 1245). One alternative called for an embrace of and return to historical materialism as both method and theory to capture tensions, contradictions, and oppositions within social processes (Pollert 1996). Class and gender were mutually constituting but representing two conceptually different types of irreducible social relationships. There was no ungendered class relations and no gender without class dimensions. These theoretical and methodological injunctions directed attention to 'the institutional embeddedness of different forms of male power' and the ways these 'two dynamics (class and gender) enmesh in practice' (Pollert 1996: 653–54).

A theory of social practice sought to avoid the trap of relativism and structuralism. By theorizing big structures from small acts, a theory of social practice directed attention to the efficacy of agency as well as structure.[13] De Certeau, Bourdieu, and Gramsci offered different solutions to the age-old problem of structuralism on the one hand, and voluntarism on the other, in studies of human practice. Rather than imposing abstract categories on lived experience, a theory of practice gave researchers tools for the excavation of lived experiences without sacrificing reference to structure for agency. The core concepts of habitus and hegemony were particularly attentive to the relationship between structure and agency. To a certain extent, habitus and hegemony mapped similar processes and derived from Bourdieu's and Gramsci's complementary interest in cultural (re)production. On closer inspection, this convergence masked deeper differences. There was more than a superficial distinction between Bourdieu as a microlevel theorist who 'makes sociological theory out of everything' and Gramsci as a macrolevel theorist who 'gives us a general theory of the imposition of hegemony' (Moi 1991: 1019). Despite similar preoccupations, each theory traversed different conceptual terrains on which to ground the production of practice. An excellent example of this new focus on social practices appeared in McDowell's study (1997) of The City in London. She examined The City through the lens of the daily social practices, careers, and interactions between individual men and women working in merchant banks. Focusing on the workplace level, although neither denying nor neglecting structural and institutional factors that sort men and women into different occupations, McDowell (1997: 182) suggested that 'uncovering the social construction of different masculinities and the relations between them is . . . a crucial element in revealing how the structural order of gender is maintained, reproduced or challenged'.

On the one hand, the postmodern turn sensitized researchers to discontinuity and difference. Even those unconvinced by or critical of postmodernism have internalized the theoretical insights about the complex and

[13] This excerpt comes from a longer article by Gottfried (1998) contrasting de Certeau, Bourdieu, and Gramsci theories of social practice.

fluid interactions between class, gender, race, and other differences. The postmodern suspicion of structural categories forced feminists to acknowledge differentiation among women, to problematize the notion of woman, and to appreciate the complication this has on solidarity around any singular identity. This concern with differences between women was not new, but rather had a long-standing role in the class/gender debates within socialist feminist theories of work. However, poststructuralists re-articulated the concept in a new way (Walby 2004*a*). On the other hand, the return to the concept of patriarchy appeared when feminism was in danger of coming unhinged without a female subject for grounding theory and practice. Revisiting the debate on the poverty of patriarchy crystallized the reasons why feminists had abandoned the problematic concept. It led feminists to rethink abstract structuralism and to develop more concrete, middle-range concepts such as gender regimes and gender orders (Connell 1995; Walby 2004*b*)

Feminism benefited from this exchange. Both approaches expressed skepticism about monocausal narratives of overarching forces, laws of motion, or other muscular engines propelling and sustaining male domination. While gender differences have been a principle for organizing the division of labor, neither approach posited male power as originating from a single source. Power might circulate through ever-present capillaries in the social system. Conversely, power might derive from and operate through particular ensembles of institutions. In either case, the favored mode of inquiry was more historical and allowed for contingency and unintended consequences. The past shaped the present but not necessarily in ways intended by the actors. Enduring patterns such as occupational sex segregation, pay inequities, and women's primary responsibility for care might be produced by different mechanisms at different times and in different places. Both gestures directed attention to embodied activity rather than sterile structures, shifting our gaze to gender, class, and race relations as embedded in everyday social practices and to the workplace as a site of cultural as well as material (re)production. Feminist theories of work needed both structure and agency to understand stability and change.

7. Feminist Futures

This review of feminist discourses supplies the conceptual vocabulary for gendering the sociology of work. Feminism serves as a lens through which to pose questions often ignored by or given secondary status in other theoretical approaches. Whether using a wide-angle lens to present a panoramic view or a telephoto lens to zoom in for a close-up picture, feminists have surveyed the field of work and the economic landscape in the shadows of male-biased models. Without feminist critiques, theorists of work would not likely have trained an eye on the intimate relationship and entanglements between production and reproduction.

Feminists have pried open the world of work to take account of asymmetrical gender divisions of labor. Regardless of the approach, feminist theories have highlighted the structuring influence of gender relations within and across households and firms. Applying gender only to discussions of women's work experiences and not to men's has limited our understanding of work. Likewise, the focus on men's paid employment has excluded a range of paid and unpaid labor activities, including emotional labor and care associated with women, from conceptions of work. The family and the household are clearly central to the distribution and valuation of paid labor and unpaid labor. To know where the family and the household fits into the analysis requires focusing beyond firms, markets, or formal work organizations, and broadening conceptualization of the economy to include activities and practices in the household and those involving care-giving.

Viewing work through the prism of gender relations illuminates the entanglements of, and the pressures between, work and family life. Research on care work has raised many of the same concerns and conceptual issues that preoccupied first and early second wave feminist scholars. An examination of the care sector, by crosscutting the family, paid employment, and the state, points out the necessity for examining the relationship between and within these institutions. There is a growing awareness of the need to integrate gendered welfare state analysis with gendered employment studies. The type of welfare state is consequential for women's ability to participate in the labor force and affects the conditions of their employment. Accounting for care also makes visible an activity distinct from emotional labor, but equally devalued as gendered work.

Feminists have introduced a grammar for parsing embedded gendered meanings in conceptions of work and labor, a lexicon for enunciating gender as an analytical category, and a new vocabulary for characterizing 'women's work'. While many deem the use of the noun patriarchy as inappropriately abstract, a feminist grammar that keeps the adjectival form of patriarchal relations or the noun of gender regimes neither fixes gender relations in a transhistorical totality nor relativizes claims about gender difference. By employing the active verb gendering, feminists have opened up the black box of organizational structures, and have revealed the ongoing, active process of embodied labor and emotional work that contributes to gender typing of jobs. The concept of gendering is better able to comprehend social change as well as the relative stability of male control over good jobs and their neglect of care. A more fluid and changing, although still structured, labor market analysis suggests that the process of organizational gendering need not only move in the direction of increasing segregation and differentiation. Analysis of degendering and regendering enables a discussion of the destabilization and reorganization of gender and sexuality in the workplace. This new grammar has extended the boundaries of what we study as work.

Despite the theoretical advances by feminists, the relentless focus on gender has eclipsed class analysis. A reassessment of class in relationship to gender has pushed forward reconciliation after the effective divorce of Marxism and feminism. No longer feisty combatants, the former partners have mellowed, yet tensions have not been resolved to the satisfaction of either party. Feminists reject prioritizing class over gender. Neither Marxists nor feminists have adequately theorized the social variability of class and gender relationships. Class often seems to refer only to economic inequality, with the processes that produce it being left unspecified. We are still left with the hard work of theorizing gender and class relationships.

What feminist futures are possible, even likely, in light of past practices and experiences? Ample evidence shows significant progress for women over the past four decades. Gender relations are changing as women enter the labor market in increasing numbers. Growing female labor force participation has enhanced women's independence but has not eradicated women's economic vulnerability. In assessing the likelihood of future changes in women's working time and earnings, several trends anticipate continued gains in women's economic achievement but suggest barriers will continue to limit overall progress. The host of new regulations for equal treatment makes the workplace more hospitable to women. Yet increasing income inequality and the stagnation of income for those at the bottom of income distribution have put new pressures on women to earn. Declining male incomes figure as a central factor here (Acker 2004, personal communication).

Women will not necessarily share gains equally. Several studies theorizing the complex articulation of gender and class and its global reach (Acker 2004; Ward et al. 2004; Walby 2005) find that women face diverse working conditions. Poor countries supply low-wage labor at the bottom of the production chain, which fuels demand for cheaper consumption in the metropoles. Immigration of women from poor to richer countries provides a cheap source of labor that frees global managers and members of the global elite from taking care of their own domestic tasks such as cleaning, laundry, child-rearing, and home care. Sassen (1996), for example, paints a chilling picture of the global male elite—clustered in a small handful of central business districts—concentrating power and income while devalued support occupations are characterized by a strong gender and ethnic marking. Global cities are also places where low wage women workers serve and service elite women. Many highly educated, single women living and working in central city districts enjoy similar amenities as men. Given these trends, class differences may widen the divide between rich and poor women both within and between countries.

A multi-scale approach including the international division of labor and globalization is important to analysis of working conditions in the future (Gottfried 2004; Ng 2004). Institutions such as the European Union through directives on part-time employment and equal treatment provisions can change the balance of power within and between nations, and create new possibilities for transnational women's lobbying efforts. Transnational women's organizations have mobilized effective movements for aligning equal employment regulations to internationally based standards. This interest in globalization brings feminists back to large structures and links micro- to macrolevels and local to global arenas.

Feminist thought has insisted on including reproductive work in any equation of the future of work. Women's work is still conditioned on their labor in families, where they often shoulder primary responsibility for child and elder care, and family and household maintenance. As long as women bear disproportionate responsibility for care, women workers will find it difficult to compete equally with their male counterparts. Acker (2004) puts the argument succinctly: 'as long as the workplace is organized on the assumption that workers have no other responsibilities, women will carry the responsibility for care'. Unless incentives change, fathers will not likely extend a hand to share caring responsibility with mothers and will not agitate for change to better balance work and family life.

Revisiting the troubled history of work in feminist thought reminds us of the distance already traveled and the journey ahead in order to craft theories for understanding social inequalities at the intersection of gender, class, and race. The past suggests an uneven path towards more equality between men and women vis-à-vis work. Since movement forward often is accompanied by backlash, feminism must continually renew theory and practice to both understand and alter patriarchal relationships. Feminism's utopian impulses as well as political projects can point the way towards what could be and what ought to be in a future society free of gender domination.

References

Acker, J. (1989). 'The Problem with Patriarchy', *Sociology*, 23: 235–40.

—— (1990). 'Hierarchies, Jobs, Bodies: A Theory of Gendered Organizations', *Gender & Society*, 4(2): 139–58.

—— (2004). 'Gender, Capitalism and Globalization', *Critical Sociology*, 30(1): 17–41.

Adkins, L. and Lury, C. (1999). 'The Labour of Identity: Performing Identities, Performing Economies', *Economy & Society*, 28: 598–614.

Aiba, K. (2004). 'Transformed Bodies and Gender: An Introduction to the Study of Professional Japanese Women Wrestlers'. Unpublished paper.

Anker, R. (1998). *Gender and Jobs: Sex Segregation of Occupations in the World*. Geneva: International Labour Office.

Beechey, V. (1979). 'On Patriarchy', *Feminist Review*, 3: 66–82.

—— (1987). *Unequal Work*, London: Verso.

Bennett, T. (1994). 'Popular Culture and the "Turn to Gramsci"', in J. Storey (ed.), *Cultural Theory and Popular Culture: A Reader*. New York: Harvester Wheatsheaf.

Bergmann, B. (1986). *The Economic Emergence of Women*. New York: Basic Books.

Blackburn, R., Browne, J., Brooks, B., and Jarman, J. (2002). 'Explaining Gender Segregation', *British Journal of Sociology*, 53: 513–36.

Blum, L. (1991). *Between Feminism and Labor: The Significance of the Comparable Worth Movement*. Berkeley, CA: University of California Press.

Braidotti, R. (1994). *Nomadic Subjects: Embodiment and Sexual Difference in Contemporary Feminist Theory*. New York: Columbia University Press.

Bruegel, I. (1996). 'Whose Myths Are They Anyway? A Comment', *British Journal of Sociology*, 47: 175–77.

Brush, L. (1999). 'Gender, Work, Who Cares?! Production, Reproduction, Deindustrialization, and Business as Usual', in M. M. Ferree, J. Lorber, and B. Hess (eds.), *Revisioning Gender*. Thousand Oaks, CA: Sage.

Burawoy, M. (1979). *Manufacturing Consent*. Chicago, IL: University of Chicago Press.

—— (1985). *The Politics of Production*. London: Verso.

Callard, F. (1998). 'The Body in Theory', *Environment and Planning D: Space and Society*, 16: 387–400.

Charles, M. (2003). 'Deciphering Sex Segregation: Vertical and Horizontal Inequalities in Ten National Labor Markets'. Unpublished paper presented at the

'Prospects for Women's Equality in a Changing and Global Political Economy: Varieties of Capitalism, Labor and Gender', Northwestern University, Chicago, IL, October 10–11.

Cobble, D. S. (2004). *The Other Women's Movement: Workplace Justice and Social Rights in Modern America*. Princeton, NJ: Princeton University Press.

Cockburn, C. (1983). *Brothers: Male Dominance and Technological Change*. London: Pluto Press.

—— (1991). *In the Way of Women: Men's Resistance to Sex Equality in Organisations*. London: Macmillan.

Collins, P. H. (1990). *Black Feminist Thought: Knowledge, Consciousness, and the Politics of Empowerment*. Boston, MA: Unwin Hyman.

Collinson, D. and Hearn, J. (1994). 'Naming Men as Men', *Gender, Work and Organisation*, 1: 2–22.

Connell, R. (1987). *Gender and Power: Society, the Person and Sexual Politics*. Cambridge: Polity Press.

—— (1995). *Masculinities*. Berkeley, CA: University of California Press.

—— (2002). *Gender*. Cambridge: Polity Press.

Crompton, R. (2002). 'Employment, Flexible Working and the Family', *British Journal of Sociology*, 53: 537–58.

Delphy, C. (1977). *The Main Enemy*. London: Women's Research and Resource Centre.

Engels, F. (1968). 'The Origin of the Family, Private Property and the State', in K. Marx and F. Engels (eds.), *Selected Works*. New York: International Publishers.

England, P. (1992). *Comparable Worth: Theories and Evidence*. New York: Aldine de Gruyter.

—— and Folbre, N. (2003). 'Gender and Economic Sociology'. Unpublished paper presented at the 'Prospects for Women's Equality in a Changing and Global Political Economy: Varieties of Capitalism, Labor and Gender', Northwestern University, Chicago, IL,October 10–11.

Erikson, R. and Wharton, A. (1997). 'Inauthenticity and Depression: Assessing the Consequences of Interactive Service Work', *Work and Occupations*, 24: 188–213.

Evans, M. (2003). *Gender and Social Theory*. Buckingham: Open University Press.

Falasca-Zamponi, S. (2003). 'Review of *Vichy and the Eternal Feminine*', *American Journal of Sociology*, 109: 240–2.

Ferree, M. M., Lorber, J., and Hess, B. (1999). *Revisioning Gender*. Thousand Oaks, CA: Sage.

Gilman, C. P. (1892). 'The Yellow Wall-Paper', *New England Magazine*, 5: 647–56. Now available at. Cornell University Library website.

—— (1898). *Women and Economics: A Study of the Economic Relation Between Men and Women as a Factor in Social Evolution*. Boston, MA: Small, Maynard & Co.

Ginn, J. and Arber, S. (1996). 'Feminist Fallacies: A Reply to Hakim on Women's Employment', *British Journal of Sociology*, 47: 167–77.

Giuffre, P. and Williams, C. (2002). 'Boundary Lines: Labeling Sexual Harassment in Restaurants', in A. Wharton (ed.), *Working in America: Continuity, Conflict, and Change, Second Edition*. Boston, MA: McGraw-Hill.

Gottfried, H. (ed.) (1996). *Feminism and Social Change: Bridging Theory and Practice*. Urbana, IL: University of Illinois Press.

—— (1998). 'Beyond Patriarchy? Theorising Gender and Class', *Sociology: Journal of the British Sociological Association*, 32: 451–68.

—— (2003). 'Temp(t)ing Bodies: Shaping Gender at Work in Japan', *Sociology: Journal of the British Sociological Association*, 37(2): 257–76.

—— (2004). 'Gendering Globalization Discourses', *Critical Sociology*, 30(1): 1–7.

—— and Graham, L. (1993). 'Constructing Difference: The Making of Gendered Subcultures in a Japanese Automobile Transplant', *Sociology: The Journal of the British Sociological Association*, 7: 611–28.

Grosz, E. (1994). *Volatile Bodies: Towards a Corporeal Feminism*. Bloomington, IN: Indiana University Press.

Hakim, C. (1995). 'Five Feminist Myths about Women's Employment', *British Journal of Sociology*, 46: 429–55.

Halford, S. and Savage, M. (1997). 'Rethinking Restructuring: Embodiment, Agency and Identity in Organizational Change', in R. Lee and J. Wills (eds.), *Geographies of Economies*. London: Arnold.

—— ,—— , and Witz, A. (1997). *Gender, Careers and Organisations*. London: Macmillan.

Hartmann, H. (1979). 'The Unhappy Marriage of Marxism and Feminism: Towards a More Progressive Union', *Capital and Class*, 8: 1–34.

Hearn, J. (1993). 'Men and Organisational Culture', in J. Wajcman (ed.), *Organisations, Gender and Power: Papers from an IRRU*. Workshop. Warwick Papers in Industrial Relations No. 48.

—— and Parkin, W. (1983). *'Sex' at 'Work': The Power and Paradox of Organization Sexuality*. New York: St Martin's Press.

—— and —— (2001). *Gender, Sexuality and Violence in Organizations*. London: Sage.

Hochschild, A. (1983). *The Managed Heart: Commercialization of Human Feeling*. Berkeley, CA: University of California Press.

Jackson, S. (1998). 'Feminist Social Theory', in S. Jackson and J. Jones (eds.), *Contemporary Feminist Theories*. New York: New York University Press.

Kanter, R. M. (1977). *Men and Women of the Corporation*. New York: Basic Books.

Keashley, L. and Gottfried, H. (2003). 'Fundamental Violations', *Psychology of Women Quarterly*, 27: 275–6.

Kelly, P. F. and Wolf, D. (2001). 'A Dialogue on Globalization', *Signs*, 26: 1243–9.

Kessler, S. and McKenna, W. (1978). *Gender: An Ethnomethodological Approach*. Chicago, IL: University of Chicago Press.

Lal, J. (1998). *Of Television and T-Shirts: The Making of a Gendered Working Class and the 'Made in India' Label*. D. Phil. dissertation, Department of Sociology, Cornell University.

Lee, C. K. (1998). *Gender and the South China Miracle*. Berkeley, CA: University of California Press.

Leidner, R. (1993). *Fast Food, Fast Talk: Service Work and the Routinization of Everyday Life*. Berkeley, CA: University of California Press.

Lorber, J. (1994). *Paradoxes of Gender*. New Haven, CT: Yale University Press.

McDowell, L. (1997). *Capital Culture: Gender and Work in the City*. Oxford: Blackwell.

Martin, B. and Wajcman, J. (2003). 'Fun, Excitement and Passion: Positive Emotions Amongst Men and Women Managers'. Unpublished paper presented at the 98th Annual Meeting of the American Sociological Association, Atlanta, Georgia, August 16–19.

Martin, K. (1998). 'Becoming a Gendered Body: Practices of Preschools', *American Sociological Review*, 63: 494–511.

Maynard, M. (1994). *The Dynamics of 'Race' and Gender: Some Feminist Interventions*. Bristol, PA: Taylor & Francis.

Moi, T. (1991). 'Appropriating Bourdieu: Feminist Theory and Pierre Bourdieu's Sociology of Culture', *New Literary History*, 22: 1017–49.

Morgan, D. (1998). 'Sociological Imaginings and Imagining Sociology: Bodies, Auto/Biographies and Other Mysteries', *Sociology*, 4: 647–63.

Nelson, R. and Bridges, W. (1999). *Legalizing Gender Inequality*. Cambridge: Cambridge University Press.

Ng, C. (2004). 'Globalization and Regulation: The New Economy, Gender and Labor Regimes', *Critical Sociology*, 30(1): 103–8.

Osawa, M. (1994). 'Bye-bye Corporate Warriors: The Formation of a Corporate-Centered Society and Gender-biased Social Policies in Japan'. University of Tokyo Institute of Social Science Occasional Papers in Labor Problem and Social Policy.

Parkin, F. (1982). *Marx Weber*. London: Tavistock Publications.

Pierce, J. (1999). 'Emotional Labor Among Paralegals', *The Annals of the American Academy of Political and Social Science*, 561: 127–42.

Pollert, A. (1996). 'Gender and Class Revisited; Or, The Poverty of 'Patriarchy', *Sociology*, 30: 639–59.

Pringle, R. (1988). *Secretaries Talk: Sexuality, Power and Work*. London: Verso.

—— (1989). 'Bureaucracy, Rationality and Sexuality: The Case of Secretaries', in J. Hearn, D. L. Sheppard, P. Tancred-Sheriff, and G. Burrell (eds.), *The Sexuality of Organization*. London: Sage.

Ramazanoglu, C. with Holland, J. (2002). *Feminist Methodology: Challenges and Choices*. London: Sage.

Reskin, B. (2002). 'Rethinking Employment Discrimination and Its Remedies', in M. Guillen, R. Collins, P. England, and M. Meyer (eds.), *The New Economic Sociology: Developments in an Emerging Field*. New York: Russell Sage.

—— and Padavic, I. (1994). *Women and Men at Work*. Thousand Oaks, CA: Pine Forge.

—— and Roos, P. (2002). *Job Queues, Gender Queues: Explaining Women's Inroads into Male Occupations*. Philadelphia, PA: Temple University Press.

Rose, S., and Hartmann, H. (2004). *Still a Man's Labor Market: The Long-Term Earnings Gap*. Washington, DC: Institute for Women's Policy Research.
Sargent, L. (ed.) (1981). *Women and Revolution. The Unhappy Marriage of Marxism and Feminism: A Debate on Class and Patriarchy*. London: Pluto.
Sassen, S. (1996). 'Toward A Feminist Analytics of the Global Economy', *Indiana Journal of Global Legal Studies*, 4: 7–41.
Scott, J. W. (1986). ' "Gender": A Useful Category of Historical Analysis', *American Historical Review*, 91(5): 1053–75
Skeggs, B. (1997). *Formations of Class and Gender: Becoming Respectable*. London: Sage.
Sotirin, P. and Gottfried, H. (1999). 'The Ambivalent Dynamics of Secretarial "Bitching": Control, Resistance, and the Construction of Identity', *Organization*, 6: 57–80.
Spelman, E. (1988). *Inessential Woman: Problems of Exclusion in Feminist Thought*. Boston, MA: Beacon Press.
Steinberg, R. (1990). 'The Social Construction of Skill: Gender, Power and Comparable Worth', *Work and Occupation*, 17: 449–82.
—— and Figurt, D. (1999). 'Emotional Labor Since *The Managed Heart', The Annals of the American Academy of Political and Social Science*, 561: 8–26.
Stone, P. (1994). 'Assessing Gender at Work: Evidence and Issues', in J. Jacobs (ed.), *Gender Inequality at Work*. Thousand Oaks, CA: Sage.
Tyler, M. and Abbott, P. (1998). 'Chocs Away: Weight Watching in the Contemporary Airline Industry', *Sociology*, 3: 433–50.
Wajcman, J. (ed.) (1993). *Organisations, Gender and Power: Papers From An IRRU Workshop*. Warwick Papers in Industrial Relations No. 48.
—— (1998). 'Personal Management: Sexualized Cultures at Work'. Paper presented at Work, Employment and Society conference, Warwick.
Walby, S. (1986). *Patriarchy at Work*. Cambridge: Polity Press.
—— (1990). *Theorizing Patriarchy*. Oxford: Basil Blackwell.
—— (1997). *Gender Transformations*. New York: Routledge.
—— (2004*a*). Personal Correspondence.
—— (2004*b*). 'Policy Strategies in a Global Era for Gendered Workplace Equity', in H. Gottfried and L. Reese (eds.), *Equity in the Workplace: Gendering Workplace Policy Analysis*. Lanham, MD: Lexington Books.
—— (2005). *Complex Modernities and Globalisation*. London: Sage.
Ward, K., Rahman, F. I., Saiful, A. K. M., Akhter, R., and Kama, N. (2004). 'The Effects of Global Economic Restructuring on Urban Women's Work and Income-Generating Strategies in Dhaka, Bangladesh', *Critical Sociology*, 30(1): 63–102.
Weber, M. (1978). *Economy and Society: An Outline of Interpretive Sociology*, 2 vols. Berkeley, CA: University of California Press.
West, C. and Zimmerman, D. (1987). 'Doing Gender', *Gender & Society*, 1: 125–51.
—— and Fenstermaker, S. (1995). 'Doing Difference', *Gender and Society*, 9: 8–37.

Wise, S. and Stanley, L. (2003). 'Review Article: Looking Back and Looking Forward: Some Recent Feminist Sociology Review', *Sociological Research* (online), 8. Available at: www.socresonline.org.uk.

Witz, A. (1993). 'Gender and Bureaucracy: Feminist Concerns', in J. Wajcman (ed.), *Organisations, Gender and Power: Papers From An IRRU Workshop*. Warwick Papers in Industrial Relations No. 48.

—— (1997). 'Embodying Gender: Society, Feminism and the Body'. Paper presented at European Sociological Society, University of Essex.

—— (1998). 'Embodiment, Organization, and Gender'. Paper presented at the International Conference on Rationalization, Organization and Gender, Sozialforschungsstelle, Dortmund.

—— , Halford, S., and Savage, M. (1996). 'Organized Bodies: Gender, Sexuality and Embodiment in Contemporary Organizations', in L. Adkins and V. Merchant (eds.), *Sexualizing the Social: Power and the Organization of Sexuality*. London: Macmillan.

Wolf, D. (1996). *Feminist Dilemmas in Fieldwork*. Boulder, CO: Westview Press.

6

Foucauldian and Postmodern Thought and the Analysis of Work

Gibson Burrell

The editors have been kind enough to give me the time and space to develop this chapter but there is a sense in which its inclusion in the current book reflects significant shifts in thinking about the role of certain types of social theory in the analysis of work. There was a time when neither Foucault nor postmodernism (what a leading figure in British sociology inclusively called 'Parisian fashions') were welcome in any Anglophone discussion of industrial sociology, or industrial relations, or organization theory.

In the (northern hemisphere) spring of 1987, I sent off a piece on the work of Michel Foucault to *Administrative Science Quarterly* (ASQ). Even in those long-off days there was some pressure on UK academics in all branches of the academy to publish in US journals. The three reviews were very similar in form and content and the crux of their positioning was, as reviewer 2 put it, 'why should we be interested in a dead French philosopher?' I had spent 8,000 words saying precisely 'why' but that was not the issue at hand. The reviewer's emphasis was on the word 'should'. The use of the adjectives in the sentence suggested that to be in possession of a death certificate and a European orientation were unwelcome blocks to knowledge. There was no intellectual curiosity in evidence in any complete line of the three reviews and so, out of spite, I started to use the text of the reviews as postgraduate teaching material. Luckily, for me at least, the same paper was taken by *Organisation Studies* in 1988 and achieved life as part of a curio series written with Robert Cooper.

However, the global picture of uninterested hostility in Foucault and in postmodernism within our field was matched by very local conditions.

The department I had joined in the summer of 1987 had a well-deserved reputation for excellence in industrial relations. Soon after my arrival, small cartoons from newspapers and magazines began to appear on my office door or under it. These were all designed to call into question the relevance of 'Parisian fashions' and to make fun of such 'high theory'. Twice posted was The Guardian newspaper's joke, 'Postmodernism is a term which means nothing. Use it on every occasion'. This anonymous 'mail' did not feel particularly welcoming but more importantly, the profound intellectual insecurity it reflected was very worrying to someone who had just joined the group. The defensiveness to all things new and different did not auger well for the intellectual future of industrial relations and suggested a closure which intriguingly mimicked that in the offices of ASQ.

So what has happened in the last twenty years or so to make Foucauldian ideas acceptable and even, in some circles, fashionable? How has postmodernism come and then gone and has it left any enduring imprint on the field? What can we learn from both 'Parisian fashions' in extending our curiosity about the world of work?

1. Terms of Engagement

Bruno Latour (2000) famously once said that Actor-Network Theory had only four problems; these were the words 'Actor', 'Network', 'Theory', and the hyphen. So in dealing with the title of this chapter, let us recognize there are a number of problems to face at the outset. First, there is clear evidence that Michel Foucault did not regard himself to be a postmodernist nor did he seek to promulgate postmodern thought. Thus it will be necessary later in the chapter to explain why these two bodies of works are placed together as bedfellows.

Second, I will not deal with the possible consequences of an insertion of a hyphen between 'post' and 'modern' and the issue of periodization that is raised thereby. Although very popular, the idea that the modern world has given way, via a caesura, to a world so fundamentally different that it requires a new label representing its rupturist nature is not what I wish to focus upon. The reader should consult Clarke and Clegg (1998) for an exposition of such gestalt thinking, where the left hand side of most pages in the introduction stands for the old and the right side of the page for the new. But while simple tables may be good for the undergraduate seeking to grasp a level of understanding of changes in the analysis of work, such a method does presuppose a seismic shift between systems just at the time the student is feeling their way into adulthood. Perhaps books sell more copies if the audience is flattered into thinking its members are more important because they play 'bit' parts in great historical shifts. I know that most of the great sociologists are 'great' precisely because they did witness and then comprehend the major fractures of industrialization. But might it be that there are too many contemporary thinkers who seek to follow in the pursuit of greatness by making claims for seismically intense slippages when there are none? For example, Bauman (1989), Beck (1992), and Giddens (1989) come to mind here. Social theorists who have not identified a cataclysmic movement and sought to put their name on it often fail to attract the epithet of 'major thinker'.

Third, if the postmodern does not mean something after modernity its meaning needs clarification outside of the drive for periodization. In this chapter it is taken to mean an 'epistemological turn' in which the object of reaction is not modernity, but modernism. We are speaking here of a mode of understanding and not an ontological rupture.

Fourth, if postmodernism is about a form of philosophically based understanding we must reflect what it has to say about the analysis of 'work'. Here there is relative silence. Indicatively, in 1810, Crabbe wrote:

> Trades and Professions–these are themes the Muse
> Left to her freedom, would forebear to choose.
> (Quoted in Thomas 1999: v)

Work as a concept has a very long tradition of being 'the primal curse' and those who seek amusement have eschewed dealing with it. The two cultures identified by C. P. Snow are not without some relevance at this juncture. Within the UK, Snow argued for the problematic existence of two separated worlds of the intellect, with the arts and humanities on one side, and the sciences on the other. Respect for one by the other was not high within these opposing cultures. Postmodernism emanates from the 'cultural' realm, we might contend, and not from the natural sciences. Science in the 'normal' sense then, stands opposed to much of what postmodernism represents. And the reverse is also to be found.

Following Crabbe, if (manual) work is seen as antithetical to reflection and 'higher' ideals, then following Snow, the humanities and the fine arts from which many postmodern notions emerge, are somewhat hostile to contemplating work at all. If it was 140 years ago when William Bell Scott's painting of 'Iron and Steel' was considered too mundane and not suitable as the subject of a serious work of art (McManners and Wales 2003: 37), there are still those today who believe the same. There is at least a sense in which the world of work is seen at odds with a quest to understand the strengths and defence of non-positivist epistemologies emanating from the *geisteswissenschaften*. Engineering, the natural sciences and the whole drive to performativity and an unthinking commercialized pragmatism are not natural feeding grounds for the epistemological turn. As Cooper and Burrell (1988) put it, the emphasis in postmodernism is not so much upon the 'organization of production' but upon the 'production of organization'. Here questions are asked at a 'deeper level' of existence about how it is that the world manages to be reproduced in its elemental entirety. What produces the organization we witness is the prime focus of attention. Questions of how economic production is itself organized are less central. Fifth then, the postmodern turn is less about economics, production, and work than it is about philosophy, consumption, and leisure. Having provided a very brief contextualization of the terms about to be used, let us begin to see how 'work' is seen differently using this set of lenses.

2. The Postmodern and the Analysis of Work

There are many available texts on the way in which the postmodern has influenced the world of work. As was mentioned earlier, many of these debate the rise of post-modernity (with the hugely important hyphen) but here I will concern myself only with the notion of the postmodern as a philosophical approach. The reader's attention is drawn to both sets of literature but what I aim to do here is to draw out the filaments of the latter. No real justice can be done to these elements in a chapter such as this so if the experienced reader finds huge leaps of argumentation, one only hopes the novitiate will not.

For this reader, we might say that postmodern thought in some ways is mounted upon four substantial corner posts. Rest assured that few would agree with this simplification but for ease of presentation let me adopt this relaxed attitude. The framework for postmodern analysis is embedded upon a foundation provided by the following elements. First, there is a pillar provided by the articulation of *The Postmodern Condition* by Jean Francois Lyotard (1984). Second, there is the pillar which takes the form of the issue of 'identity' as being deeply problematic to most Western understandings of that so-important notion—the self. The third support has been promulgated via the medium of Jacques Derrida's concept and articulation of 'deconstruction'. And fourth, within the furniture of postmodernism is the benefit it has derived from the insights of Michel Foucault. This pillared ordering is the one which this chapter will follow.

1. The assertion by Lyotard that 'I define postmodern as incredulity towards metanarratives' has a profound effect upon the sociology of work—if one believes in it. Marxism in all its strands has provided so much towards our understanding of the social theory of work precisely because it does provide a narrative. Within this narrative structure there is a plot, central characters, the possibility of reversals and climactic scenes, and the final denouement of successful societal transformation. No wonder this framework has exercised and continues to exercise, great sway over many thinkers and activists. Braverman (1974) provides a wonderfully described romp through this development in his thesis of the 'degradation of work' in which the roles of all actors are clear and the narrative thread direct and relatively unambiguous. Its potency is tangible. Leaving aside the moral and ethical appeal of Marxism, the notions seamlessly locked into modernism of progress, of enlightenment, of technological mastery (*sic*) over the natural world by humanity, and of the certain end of alienation created great appeal to most of its readership. But 'science' and 'progress' and 'mastery' and 'enlightenment' have all become terms of contestation. Just at the time when what passed for Marxism in the Soviet bloc was coming under threat from internal (and external) forces, Lyotard problematized the supposed achievements of the 'Enlightenment' which included a widely spread, scientistic Marxism–Leninism. Lyotard argued that science fragments into a set of games each of which seeks to be self-justifying by paralogy, a breaking of the rules. Science no longer seeks coherence, totalization, or integration into the whole. Science produces not the Truth but several truths. Metanarratives can no longer hold the center. They lose their impact.

What worries many is the contingent nature of knowledge that is thrown up by such a perspective. The search for a metanarrative in which all is placed into a rational and credible order is a very old one but the theses of industrialism fermented in California (Kerr et al. 1962), of postindustrialism concocted in Massachusetts (Bell 1972), of globalization hatched out everywhere, and of 'Empire' distilled in Italy (Hardt and Negri 2000), still show this desire for more certainty, for well-trodden paths and for the end of history (Fukuyama 1992). Postmodernism per se is not a disabling issue within such literature in the sense that it has not stopped in any way all those seeking a comprehensive theoretical coverage from carrying on their search. But just in case any disabling of the quest for the natural science Grail of a 'unified and unifying theory of everything' should be threatened, Callinicos (1989) feels the need to seek to maintain the universal power of persuasion of such approaches specifically in the face of the postmodern. However, the question is surely this. Why should we be so lazy as to believe faithfully in the stories that others have come up with? Is cynicism not healthy? Are not suspicious minds more abroad in the sceptical world? Are we not the producers of our own metanarratives?

However, the concept of 'we' itself is deeply problematic.

2. *Identities'R'Us*. In the same way as coherence has been sought in the realm of the geopolitical, yet been subject to intense questioning, the notion of identity as the 'entity which is the id' (in other words, a self-contained, unified, originary, and integral individual) has been opened up to debate. So much work has been done recently on the issue of 'identity' that one cannot begin to scratch the surface of this literature in the current chapter. Reflecting this flowering of work, within the UK the Economic and Social Research Council (ESRC) has recently funded a £3.5 million Program on identities in which some answers are being sought to questions of contemporary versions of identity. Both postmodernist and modernist orientations are apparently being supported. Very few of the projects derived from the sociology of work appear to have been funded, however, but one hopes that the research is, and will be, of likely significance to our field.

With regard to postmodern approaches to identity within our area some important reworkings have been undertaken. At the outset it is important to note that 'the question of subjectivity and its unconscious processes of formation has been developed within the discourse of psychoanalytically influenced feminism and cultural criticism' (Hall 1996: 1). Hall goes on to note that the self is seen within 'celebratory variants of postmodernism' as endlessly performative and as problematic from within an anti-essentialist critique of ethnic, racial, and national conceptions of cultural identity. The creation of identity is always conditional, always contingent. Once it has been secured there is never a proper fit between it and the self. There is always too much of one or the other and never an entity—never ever a totality. Identity at work, and identity through work thus become highly problematized notions (Collinson 2003). There can be no defensible metanarrative for the self.

Within this arena Knights and Willmott (1989, 1990) have proved to be able protagonists. Working with colleagues at the University of

Manchester Institute of Science and Technology (UMIST) they developed a whole series of research projects which problematized the concept of identity. One of the major limitations of Labor Process Theory they argue has been the so-called 'missing subject' where it is alleged there is little discussion of agency, subjectivity, or resistance. In an effort to bring in such dimensions, the UMIST group borrowed from Derrida, Foucault, and post-structuralism in other forms where crude materialist assumptions were not acceptable. Braverman was lumped in with those of a vulgar materialist bent, even if he explained in the first few pages of *Labor and Monopoly Capital* (1974) that he was more than aware of this danger. For a decade and beyond, the debate around Labor Process Theory raged, with the defenders of Braverman (e.g. Thompson 1993; Thompson and Smith 1998) rejecting the need to engage comprehensively with anything outside conventional Anglo-American sociology (albeit with its heavy dependence on very dead Europeans) while the other side of the debate (Knights, Willmott, and the UMIST researchers) turned to the European Continent in the guise of the still living or only recently dead theorists. In effect, these encampments were separated by both time and tide as much as by opposing views on the role of the subject in the world of work.

Catherine Casey (1995), in another hemisphere (i.e. the southern), also focused in her empirical work upon issues of the self and identity. The self, she argued, had become subject to siege and assault. This assault has been manifested in corporate culture approaches which often led to capitulation by the worker. The 'corporate designer self' is one in which the old certainties of class have disappeared. It is an 'emptied-out self' into which the clamor of narcissism has to be placed. Faced with these forces, the postmodernist emphasis on television, advertising, film, and on issues of style in general have become popular battlegrounds for theoretical debate (see Boje et al. 1996). It is important to note carefully that Casey (2002) has eschewed poststructuralism and the Foucauldian turn in social theory but yet she seeks to deal with questions that they raise. She argues serious challenges to conventional theorizing 'that the French thinkers offered, through disruption, disjuncture and disunity' were not taken up in the study of work which was monopolized by 'traditional economic, management and labour relations analysts' (Casey 1995: 9). Few of them were equipped, she said 'to critically, socially analyze the transformation of production practices and to read their broader implications for self and social life' (Casey 1995: 9).

Similarly, Paul du Gay (1996) has written on the 'enterprising self' and Flecker and Hofbauer (1998) on 'new model employees'. In both cases the emphasis is on the creation of new selves whose identity is more able to fit within the rigors of the capitalist enterprise. But the very notion that identity is malleable, fragmented, marginal, immediate, is a relatively recent development. Of course, it might be argued by the industrial sociologist that a critique of the orientations to work school that developed out of the affluent worker studies, saw as one of its objectives the destabilization of the notion of worker 'consciousness' (Nichols and Armstrong 1976). But in general there has been a willingness by those such as Sennett (1999) to indeed see identity as a thing fixed and stable in the minds of those analyzed. And it is this modernist concept, that the self was somehow primeval, a determinant of behavior, and historically rooted in the deep past, that does not sit well with its contingent treatment today. Rosenau (1992: 42) puts this point of differentiation well when she says of postmodernists:

> they consider the subject to be a fossil relic of the past, of modernity, an invention of liberal humanism, the source of the unacceptable object–subject dichotomy. They argue that personal identity of this sort, if it ever existed, was only an illusion, and it is no longer possible, today, in a post-modern context.

3. *'There is Nothing Outside of the Text.'* Let us now turn to theory and the key issue of deconstructionism. Again, Rosenau (1992: 118–19) is helpful here. She argues that postmodernists employ deconstruction to examine texts, 'and because everything is a text, the uses of deconstruction are unlimited'. Often, negative critical commentaries are a key part of the approach which allows some of its practitioners to claim they are anti-method, because conventional methods are so constrained and they too should be subject to deconstruction. However, deconstruction is often seen as a 'method' which is 'avowedly, intentionally, and intensely subjectivist and anti-objectivist by design. It hesitates to dismiss any perspective as entirely without interest. It precludes universal knowledge or global theory because it is itself an anti-theoretical enterprise. It refuses to institute hierarchies of good and bad theories.'

Whereas most forms of 'critique' (e.g. Alvesson and Willmott 2004) aim to supplant a previous form of knowledge by one which is truer or less inadequate, the deconstructive approach puts key concepts 'under erasure'. The implication is that such concepts in their original form require severe attention because they are unserviceable as presently constituted. The notion that 'progress' is recognizable through conceptual enhancement become problematized because of the very nature of 'concepts' themselves. There are contradictions inherent in all texts and in all concepts. Since every term exists by reference to something else, from which it differs, a term is necessarily inhabited by its opposite. However, since deconstruction does not assume a dialectical superiority and does not rest on a belief that one old concept can be replaced by a decidedly superior and more advanced one, it contemplates the continued use of the concept. Wrenched from the framework in which it was originally placed, it may be. Erased and transmogrified, definitely, but it is the same term nevertheless. Jacques Derrida (1981) speaks of this as thinking at the limit, of dislodged and dislodging writing, where an interval exists in which an inversion of the old concept takes place. What is produced is a new concept which the old regime would have found impossible to construct (Cooper 1989). Linstead (1993) and Hassard and Parker (1993) show that it would be easy for organization theorists simply to take the 'overturning' part of deconstructionism—and this alone. Here we must 'overturn the superordinate term' (quoted in Cooper 1989: 485) but, equally importantly, avoid the trap of replacing one side of the dichotomy with its previously 'inferior' partner. Bob Cooper points out the importance to Derrida of 'metaphorization' which is deconstructionism's key critical notion. These bipolar terms come to live in a place of undecidability where each inhabits the other and through which the reader gets carried along within a 'play of oppositions'. Unfortunately, there has been a plethora of works of 'vulgar deconstruction' which forget the need for the second part of the process over and beyond overturning.

Within the place where feminist writing and deconstructionism meet (Gherardi 2003: 225–7), there has been fertile ground for innovative work. Martin (1990) offers a fascinating deconstruction of the text of a story of a senior woman manager who, while she was in bed recovering from a Caesarian birth, watched closed-circuit television coverage of a new product launch for which she was deemed responsible. The organization had deliberately arranged the timing of the launch to fit in with the birth. Martin uses a line by line analysis of the press report to show how dichotomies work, where the silences are, what contradictions exist in the text, and to show where the biases are through the substitution of phrases in a 'reconstruction'. Notions of leadership too are relatively easy to deconstruct in this feminist/deconstructionist way. But in these analyses, such as that by Calas and Smircich (1995) where Mintzberg's textual approach to the topic is analyzed and presented as a seduction of organizational members in order that they pay obedience to the leader, the deep critique incurs the wrath of the leaders themselves (Mintzberg 1995) who reject as highly threatening to any such deconstruction.

Other attempts at 'deconstruction' within our field have been made with greater or lesser success by, for example, Legge, Doherty, Chia, and Cooper. The difficulty is that the term 'to deconstruct' has become so popular that it is used in places and on occasions when it is not appropriate. This is not an argument for conceptual purity and patrolled borders. But one sees a history of powerful terms losing their capacity to be inventive in the hands of the normalizing agents. However, this is what Derrida expected. Deconstructionism is a theoretical term which itself has been overturned.

4. And it is here that we come to Michel Foucault. Easy to say, but less easy to justify, is the periodization of his work into three phases; the archaeological, genealogical, and ethical. In the first, we might venture, Foucault argued that what was needed was not a theory of the knowing subject but rather a theory of discursive practice. Unlike post-Cartesian Western metaphysics, which has the subject at its very heart (or more correctly, its mind), what is required, says the early Foucault, is a decentering of the subject and a focus upon discourse. There is a degree of structuralism evident in this period and it produced some wonderful books on 'epistemes of truth'. Here Foucault was living up to his title as Professor of the History of Systems of Thought, which is so transgressive in itself. Organization theorists, however, in a less transgressive spirit, have drawn upon the 'middle period' of his work and upon common sense notions of the concrete organizational form (Knights 2002: 581). They have selectively appropriated the Foucault they desire. Typically, the notion of the 'genealogy' of a concept has proved to be very useful. Roy Jacques (1996) on the concept of the 'employee' for example, Nikolas Rose on subjectivity and the 'governed soul' (1999), and Grey on the concept of career (1992) have all used Foucauldian genealogy as a way of understanding how concepts came to be as they are. As we shall see they were not the only ones to come to appreciate the purchase that Foucault's middle period of output offered the social theorist of work. The third and final period of his work, on 'ethics', is the least satisfying and the most problematic. It returns to multiple sources in the Graeco-Roman period yet seeks to deal with contemporary issues of 'care of the self' which Foucault wished to address. We will deal with this period later but its direct relevance for the social theory of work needs much effort to pull it into view. Let us now turn to the second 'phase' in his writing.

3. Working with Foucault

There are a number of writers who have claimed, quite rightly, that the work of Foucault illuminates our world of work. It is at this point that one reaches for his single book that has affected our understanding in social science approaches to management more than any other. That book is *Discipline and Punish* and for all its intellectual power, it provides us with a very skewed understanding of what Foucault might have wished to say about organizing. For example, Keith Grint (1991: 148) sees the contribution of 'Foucault and Post-modernism' [*sic*] to the sociology of work as follows:

> Much of Foucault's and the other post-modernist writers' approach is fruitful in the different light it sheds on organizations. In particular, the contingent nature of organizations and the notion of power as a web within which all are held, are useful counterthrusts to the determinist and technocratic approaches of many managerialist and, indeed, orthodox Marxist approaches.

Grint here portrays Foucault as the unthreatening pluralist. McKinley and Starkey (1998: 1) state that: 'there has been a growing interest in the contribution of the work of Michel Foucault to our understanding of organizations, accounting and the control of work. In part this reflects the influence of postmodernism on organization theory and the social sciences in general'. Of their collection of essays to demonstrate this, McKinley and Starkey (1998: 3) state: 'all attempt to apply Foucauldian categories and procedures to throw fresh light on the history of the factory, management and the modern corporation'. Clegg (1999) focuses on disciplinary power and suggests that Foucault, Marx, and the Labor Process school associated with Braverman's book all concentrate on the themes of control and resistance in the capitalist workplace. Townley (1994) looks at the issue of the regulation of labor and shows how counselling and appraisals and a whole panoply of human resource management (HRM) techniques render the individual knowable within the workplace. The influence of Foucault upon accounting, perhaps, has been the most noticeable and even here the relevance of his work on 'work' has had profound effects. Hoskin and McVe (1988) are but one early example of a burgeoning literature.

Thus, there are many that see Foucault's work as important to their disciplines. Certainly, when I first read the book *Discipline and Punish* it was akin to experiencing a gestalt switch. The power of the text and the direct relevance to organization studies of Foucault's assertion that all organizations are like prisons had a profound effect upon my reading and writing thereafter. In a piece published in 1988, I made much of the two early 'periods' in Foucault's work which exhibited clear signposts for how and what organization studies should research. The focus on disciplinary technologies and the possibilities for developing 'genealogies' of the area were just two obvious ways forward. It is no surprise then that there has been a veritable explosion of work precisely on these features so that Townley (1994), Sewell and Wilkinson (1992), Jackson and Carter (1993), Zuboff (1988), McKinlay and Starkey (1998), Chan (2000), Knights and Willmott (1989), Hoskin and McVe (1988), and so on have developed this side of the argument in interesting and important ways.

Clearest of the impact craters upon the sociology of work is that left by the discussion in that book of the Panopticon. The description and analysis of the design by Jeremy Bentham for an all-seeing machine, 'the perfect managerial tool', is a brilliantly written section of the book and illuminates the sociology of work throughout. The way in which space is controlled and the inhabitants of the Panopticon 'disciplined' by bricks and mortar and social technologies of surveillance leave one gasping at Foucault's insight. It is difficult to read this part of the text and not feel that one is reading the work of an extraordinarily gifted mind. Much has been written on the Panopticon since 1977 when *Discipline and Punish* was published in English and it has become subsequently a metonymic representation of control. Reed carefully if unhappily (1999) demonstrates the temporal shift in analysis from Weberian concerns expressed in the spatial metaphor of an imprisoning 'iron cage' to the Foucauldian metaphor of the 'Benthamite Panopticon'. The notion that we are imprisoned by organizations is not a new one (Goffman 1959) but the sociology of work alighted on the surveillance society with vim and vigor. Close supervision was found to be operant everywhere and the concerns of many were reflected in the analysis of the ways in which people's working (and nonworking) lives were subject to the gaze. Key pieces to illustrate this focus here in our field were Sewell and Wilkinson (1992), Webster and Robins (1993), Townley (1994), Steingood and Fitzgibbon (1993), and Zuboff (1988). Various techniques, often Japanese in construction, were seen as offering disciplinary purchase on employees. Self-surveillance by workers in quality circles, in total quality management (TQM) regimes, and in other mechanisms of production control were given a Foucaultian twist as the Panopticon was found alive and well.

Let me just deal with one of these contributions to show how Foucault directly inspired research in the sociology of work. Townley (1994: 1) asks two questions at the outset of *Reframing Human Resource Management*. First, 'what gives the body of practices commonly understood as HRM their coherence?' Second, 'how can the academic study of HRM help people at work?' Her answer is as follows: 'The thesis of this book is that the work of Michel Foucault can help us address these two issues'. Later, (Townley 1994: 13) she claims 'Foucault provides the means of answering these questions. In the process, we can reconceptualise HRM'. Townley argues very convincingly for this reconceptualization, maintaining that HRM should be seen as a 'discourse' and a set of practices which construct knowledge about the worker in the analytical space of the employment relationship. Organizational participants are rendered 'calculable' and predictable by being subject to discipline within the interior of the organization. Time and space and movement become subject to technologies of discipline. One of the examples she gives of these technologies, recognized by the Catholic-born Foucault, is 'the confession'. Here the confessing individual is rendered up by attitude surveys seeking his/her views, by the selection interview, by self-assessment in the appraisal, and by mentoring. Each of these encourages the employee to confess to their weaknesses rendering them open to closer surveillance and discipline. Overall, the book's reconceptualization of HRM using Foucault is a good example of the way in which these ideas provided a different lens through which to look at employer/employee relations.

The 'Labor Process Theorists', of course, did not see Foucault as offering any more than Braverman; indeed they saw that particular Parisian fashion as decidedly inferior to the craftsmanship emanating from New York. And the complexities of Foucault's view that 'resistance' merely created more disciplinary attention meant that the Bravermaniacs distanced themselves from the Foucaultian view of power with alacrity (e.g. Thompson and Ackroyd 1995; Thompson et al. 2000. Thompson and McHugh 2003). Of great interest here, however, is the book by Richard Marsden (Marsden 1999) which approached *Discipline and Punish* as if it were a companion volume to Marx. This text, *The Nature of Capital*, is a very under-read book and this is unfortunate as it is exceptionally germane to the present task.

Far from seeing Marxism as opposed in central orientation to that of the Foucauldians, Marsden seeks in quite a sophisticated way to realign them. While it would be too great a leap to say that Marsden seeks to bring about an *entente cordiale* between Marxism and postmodernism, he does attempt to place a positive evaluation on Foucault from within a Marxist inspired position. In my view it is so much more constructive than the traditional

Labor Process perspective but it does pose Foucault as if he is in possession of a strong metanarrative.

4. The Compatibility of Foucault and Marx?

Many writers have felt that the challenge to historical materialism, fully in place by the 1880s, from a poststructuralism which arose in the 1980s and which gained force after the collapse of communism, has undermined the old notions of class, party, and state. In some senses, postmodernism has even been accused of accepting the assumption that we are postcapitalist. This belief has consequences for the sociology of work and its viability (Marsden 1999: 22), for what it does is to question the theoretical underpinnings of much activity. Is our lexicon of 'worker' and 'owner' and 'manager' reflective of a dead language? On the contrary, says Marsden. Foucault allows the reader to understand some of the problems first identified by Marx and moreover to address them with some success. Work may be better understood through the binocular vision afforded by Marxian and Foucauldian ideas. Put crudely, Marsden implies that while Marx explains *why* production is organized as it is, Foucualt explains *how* it is organized.

First, Richard Marsden seeks to rescue Foucault from the perdition he has been placed in by those within Labor Process Theory. The neglect of the material world in Foucault is asserted by many writers (e.g. Niemark 1990). Marsden (1999: 178), however, claims that this is mistaken and that materiality is alive and well within the corpus of Foucault's work. Moreover, Marsden claims that the nonfetishistic concept of 'forces' is taken from Althusser by Foucault and in return it helps Marxists deal with power (Marsden 1999: 23, 154–7). Third, Marsden tries to deal with a question that has concerned many Marxist thinkers. What purposes are docile bodies produced for? This is a question of some pertinence asked by Peter Armstrong. As already indicated above, Marsden turns it around to indicate that Foucault provides a conceptual mechanism by which surplus value is extracted. Foucault allows us to address the 'how' question.

Intriguingly, *Discipline and Punish* is a 'diagram of the mechanisms of power' or 'an explanation of the organization of production' according to Marsden (1999: 156). If so, this would make Foucault's book a key text of the sociology of work. This detailed description and referencing of units of production is why it is such a rich area for Marsden to hunt for connections with Marx. Despite Townley's assertion that Foucault does not ever directly address production (1994: 13) the text belies this. Marsden's analysis extends that of Dreyfus and Rabinow (1986: 153–60) which in itself is provocative.

Discipline and Punish is about how to organize movement, in space and through time. It deals with enclosure in the monasteries as a form of assembly allowing simple cooperation. The mechanisms of partitioning into linear cells, allocating each and every individual to a singular cell and thus fragmenting the collective body of the monastery, allows for much closer supervision to be put in train. The 'rule of sites' becomes coded and thus manageable by codifying space into a *tableau vivant*. The art of the rank is adumbrated where ranking of individual cell occupants takes place changing the 'multitude' into 'ordered multiplicities'. This creates ranks and files and hence 'cellular power'. Foucault describes how movement in time through the timetable and the temporal elaboration of the act was organized. He shows precisely how organization of the movement of the limbs and the mutilation of the worker are achieved. The direction is accepted to make each movement an efficient one and mesh it meticulously into the task. Then there is the organization of training aptitudes, of training the worker or the inmate. She/he thus becomes subject to the hierarchalization of observation and the power effect of normalizing judgments.

These principles might be thought to permeate the organized world of work. Wherever we seek to wander, we find enclosure, partition, the art of rank, the timetable. And what Foucault has shown us is the genealogy of these devices, these disciplinary technologies. He shows the reader the ways in which the past comes to exist in the present. As Dreyfus and Rabinow (1986: 155) suggestively indicate, it is also a way of Foucault making the point that structuralism has done this exact thing of placing codifying partitions onto the world in the years before *Discipline and Punish*. Structuralism itself had become a disciplinary technology for the laboring academician.

In discussing factories, Foucault explains how complex the arrangement is when it links control of the population to the production of goods. He describes the enormous building at Jouy which was erected in 1791 as the Oberkampf factory. A century before Taylorism was named,

> spread out in a perfectly legible way over a whole series of individual bodies, the work force may be analysed in individual units. At the emergence of large scale industry, one finds, beneath the division of the production process, the individualising fragmentation of labour power; the distributions of the disciplinary space often assured both. (Foucault 1977: 145)

Furthermore, he shows that the article on 'Manufacture' in the *Encyclopedie* cites surveillance as a major tool in the employers' armory against sabotage, poor workmanship, fraud, and laziness. Foucault is using the analysis of work as much, if not more than the analysis of custodial institutions, to make his points about disciplinary technologies. Carmona et al. (2002) use Foucault to further our understanding of the Royal tobacco factories of Seville where these disciplinary notions become manifest in the eighteenth century's attempts at accounting for space and time. Foucault wrote about factories when most people think he spoke only of asylums and of prisons. His examples from the industrial zones are often neglected. Famously he asks: 'Is it surprising that prisons resemble factories, schools, barracks, hospitals, which all resemble prisons?'

5. Foucault and Sexuality

Another impact crater upon the sociology of work is the area of 'sexuality'. Now writings on this by no means began with Foucault's publication (1979) of material on the topic in his *The History of Sexuality*, Part 1 but it did give impetus to feminists and non-feminists alike to research the field. Its aim was to 'define the regime of power-knowledge-pleasure' sustaining the discourse on human sexuality in the West (Foucault 1986: 11). Sexuality is an object and a target of power. The notion that the body, your body and my body, are sites of biopolitics creates a new way of seeing organizational politics (Martin 1990; Brewis and Linstead 2000; Hancock and Tyler 2001). The sociology of work perhaps, is traditionally based upon a history in which sexuality, and sex itself, has been controlled, channelled, and expelled from within the work environment (e.g. Acker 1990). Much recent work, however, has been on this process of channelling human sexual energy in ways which the organization sees as inclusively productive. The sexualization of the labor process in the airline industry, in tourism, in secretarial work, and so on is now well documented and Shere Hite's *Sex and Business* (1999) takes the analysis on a little by showing how corporations seek to harness the sexual energy which develops through gender difference. The Foucauldian notion of biopolitics, of course, has been criticized by many feminists for ignoring the gendered dimension to power (e.g. Diprose 2002: 79) and for his focusing in many places on male homosexual relationships to the apparent exclusion of other forms of sexual relations.

Brewis and Linstead together and separately have looked at the importance of sex at work and of sex work itself. The whole question of aesthetic labor and what that means about 'sex' in work has been studied by several authors (e.g. Hochschild 1983; Taylor and Tyler 1998; Brewis and Linstead 2000). The aestheticization of labor is a topic which sees presentation and feeling and emotion at the heart [*sic*] of the modern enterprise. Emotion at work is an area that Foucault played some part in developing because his later material on technologies of the self, although historically based, can be seen as very contemporary indeed. Thus, put crudely, *Discipline and Punish* raised issues of surveillance and disciplinary technologies while *The History of Sexuality* brought sex and biopolitics into the sociology of work. The former has stimulated more empirical fieldwork than the latter as a topic, but the latter continues to offer some impact of note.

By taking these twin dimensions to Foucault's work and the periodization which they possibly reflect, what I want to do very briefly at this juncture is to use (albeit in a very crude way) Derrida's notion of a binary hierarchy with which to unpick Foucault's material on the study of work. Following Derrida, we confront a play of *differance* in the work of Foucault. This neologism was coined by Derrida (1976: 23) to describe the relationship between two oppositional terms. At any one time, these terms *differ* from one another but one term also *defers* to the other within the binary relationship. Hence the notion of *differance* involves both deference and difference. By operating on a boundary between symbolic realms *differance* involves the privileging of one term and the subordination of another. As we have already seen, discourse is a signifying practice which constantly demarcates boundaries. But whatever is submerged, whatever is deferred, whatever is relegated to the other side of the line, then comes to play a role in constituting that which is left inside. And so it will be here.

Foucault's later approaches to leisure, to escape, to his project of the self, reveals a play of *differance*. Within this play of actions and play of words, it is possible to discern another view of the world of work. Through a dark glass certainly, but nevertheless the contours of bureaucratic organizations are discernible in his later writings by their very absence. His is a sociology of work perceived most clearly perhaps in the baroque mirror of his private life.

Binary hierarchies interpellate one term with another. Orientalism arises from the assumed superiority of Occidentalism (Said 1980). The center calls up the existence of the margin. Work begets leisure and the workplace begets the pleasure dome. The rhetoric of blame ensues and the subordinate term comes to exist within an authority relationship which Said calls a 'corporate institution'. But for some thinkers, the subordinate term engenders the dominant. The 'subaltern' is a term used by

Gayatri Spivak (herself an accomplished translator of Derrida and user of the deconstructionist method) to describe a locking in to 'imperialist values' of non-Western cultures and a subordinating of these cultures to some Western notion of 'hegemonic historiography'. Spivak (1999) wishes to create something out of the dominant. This would be noncolonized, totally new spaces where heterogeneity is the norm. And perhaps the subaltern Foucault has already been there.

6. The 'Differance' Between Non-work and Work

My focus here in this section is precisely on this possibility of an escape from the binary hierarchy of workplace/pleasure dome. It is my view that Foucault may well have striven in his private practices to create a noncolonized, totally new space in which to live and that his images of the everyday acts of 'to discipline and to punish' came from a binary hierarchy which, in no small measure, he was attempting to subvert. In other words, Michel Foucault's analysis of work is undertaken at the same time as he is seeking out a life of pleasure. And from the juxtaposition of the two comes a greater understanding of both.

It is not too much of an exaggeration perhaps to say that Foucault points us in the direction of alternative forms of management studies that escape 'the neo-Protestant bourgeois employee-self as its ideal employee' (Casey 1995: 196). As Foucault himself said of the dominant other, ' I am no doubt not the only one who writes in order to have no face. Do not ask who I am and do not ask me to remain the same: leave it to our bureaucrats and our police to see that our papers are in order. At least spare us their morality when we write' (Introduction to *The Archaelogy of Knowledge*, 1972: 17).

In looking at Foucault's writings we can learn something of work and something of leisure. If one considers *The Order of Things*, Foucault's translator does us a great disservice. There is an issue raised by the French *'l'organisation'* being translated into English as 'organization structure' in that a somewhat sterile and static notion of a bureaucratic parentage is put in the place of a more dynamic, processual concept. Foucault's conception of *'l'organisation'*—of how things come to be as they are and of the choices faced in arriving at them—is shaped possibly in some ways by his experiences within the San Franciscan bathhouses of the 1970s. While not addressing the world of work directly, Foucault's experiences in the San Franciscan bathhouses revealed to him forms of organization dedicated to the hedontics of desire. And in the same way as Veblen's analysis (1899) of the leisure class throws into much relief the world of the industrial poor through the use of contrast, Foucault's project of the self reveals many of the masked facets of a world of organized work. What he tells us about the sociology of work in the period in question is in the *differance*. What he privileges is leisure but in that deferring we can see how work is conceptualized. What he privileges is pleasure but in that *differance* we see the daily grind of the everyday life of the plebeian. What he describes is the care of the self but in that phrase comes a sense of *differance* in that there is a dangerous nature to modern day work. 'Care of the self' is 'the place one occupies among others', it is necessarily a relational concept involving how one relates ethically to fellow human beings and it is also hugely reliant upon the notion of 'freedom' (Foucault 1986: 9). None of these elements appear well established in the contemporary organization. It is in his opaque musings on the bathhouses that ones sees the other to work. And in seeing the other, light might be thrown upon the world of work itself.

The presence of the disciplinary technologies of dressage, the judges of normality, the confession, the gaze, and the Panopticon were remarkably absent (in the crucial sense of juridicial presence) within the bathhouses of San Francisco at the time of Foucault's visits. They were deferred. Let us briefly look at each of these in turn.

In some senses, the 'dressage' of the body which is sought by the management of large organizations was missing in these private clubs. The picture that Foucault chose to represent the concept of dressage in *Discipline and Punish* (Plate 10) is of the tree being bent back into straightness by the restraints of strong bonds. The English play here on 'bent' and 'straight' is not lost to the reader and I suspect that this imagery travels well. In the bathhouses, the body of the individual male could be used in whatever way they thought fit. Transformative, experimental, and transgressive 'bentness' was permitted and encouraged in some places without thought to the social mores which existed outside.

The 'confession' was not seen as desirable within the bathhouse for it was a place of action rather than contemplation, a locale of pleasure not of introverted introspection. Hedonism and the confession do not sit well with each other in the same physical space. Of course, they may be paired up with each other in proximity in that the morning-after-the-night-before may be the usual time for confession and possible forgiveness. But the Church in a post-Loyolan phase did not encourage physical homosexual bodily enjoyment in the sense of open *jouissance*. The love that dare speak its name was hidden and was therefore eminently confessionable.

Third, the conventional judges of normality were absent from the bathhouses—at least in their professional capacity. Public health inspections of the premises were fought off and resisted as best they could. What were regarded as 'normal', 'straight' sexual practices were deliberately subverted within the bathhouses and normality took on a different hue. Patient Zero (Gaetan Dugas) who was a French-Canadian air steward had a number of sexual partners each year which bore little resemblance to what most people would regard as 'normal'. But any judge of normality from public health, the police, or other state bureaucracy would have found this level of active sexual behavior to be remarkable and worthy of case-notes. In *Tales of the City*, Armistead Maupin (1978: 97) talks of Brian going to Valencia Street where a sign beckons 'FOR BETTER HEALTH—STEAM BATHS' and where the staff walk around with tee shirts bearing the legend 'WE DARE YOU'. It is difficult to imagine a conventional business organization that would ask staff to wear such invitations to provocation.

Fourth, the gaze and the Panopticon were missing from the bathhouses in a very deliberate sense. These pleasure domes were designed to provide a knowing sort of privacy. There was an ethos of strict confidentiality and names were not asked for, either by management or client. In Randy Shilt's *And the Band Played On* there is a clear way in which the spread of AIDS was associated in the minds of officialdom with the refusal of bathhouse owners to give names to police or implement a system to acquire them or even require names from anyone who entered the premises.

In summary then, the Foucault of *Discipline and Punish* had lived in the realm of the bathhouses and had felt perhaps their insulation as organizations from the mundanities of the organization of production. They were organizations that were as close to being 'beyond' discipline as one might wish to imagine and they were organizations of and for consumption. Moreover, for the Foucault of *The Use of Pleasure* they were sites of activity that reflected technologies of the self where small elite groups had banded together to create their own modes of understanding and behavior within their own communities.

But as Callinicos (1989: 90) argues, Foucault asks why:

> 'everyone's life couldn't become a work of art?' The answer, of course, is that most people's lives are still . . . shaped by their lack of access to productive resources and their consequent need to sell their labour power in order to live. To invite a hospital porter in Birmingham, a car-worker in Sao Paulo, a social security clerk in Chicago, or a street child in Bombay to make a work of art of their lives would be an insult.

This working at art was possible, however, in San Francisco. It was a world of pleasure and consumption. It was a world of escape and 'momentary slips through the fabric'. The use to which pleasure was put was not to radically transform society but to make life more bearable.

7. Conclusions

Bearing in mind yet again that Foucault was not a self-declared postmodernist, what possible conclusions can we draw from this all too brief excursus into this convoluted hinterland of the social theory of work?

Well, first is the question of how one might measure the impact of postmodernism on the high plains of the sociology of work? Impact may be measured perhaps both in terms of the immediate energy that something generates and by the longevity of the marks or traces that it leaves behind. As for the latter, who can say which of postmodernism's inscriptions that now lie upon the body of knowledge will endure? It is too early to tell. And no final answer is ever available to any significant question. If one adopts a cyclical view of knowledge then we are perpetually consigned to draw upon the same pools of insight, time and time again. As for the former, great energy was liberated by the postmodern turn but not necessarily within the encampment of industrial sociologists. Here the mining of data-sets using the well tried and tested technologies continued unabated and as the meteorite of postmodernism struck well to the east, little disturbance, let alone cratering, was felt. Where seismographical readings were registered, however, response teams swept into action.

Chan (2000: 91–2) tells us, 'Commentary and critique of Foucault's notions of power, freedom and resistance have become an intellectual industry itself.' The relatively well known criticisms have been collected in Barry Smart's anthology of essays on Foucault (1994). Leading opponents of Foucauldian approaches to power elsewhere include Ray (1993), Reed (1999), Miller (1993), and Hindess (1996). The world of work is seen by these Weberians as less illuminated by Foucault than by their own favored theorist of modernity. So the debates on work, the postmodern and Foucault carry on across space and time, representing a world of academic labor and travail itself. But now that the dust has settled, the impact of postmodernism upon the world of modernism, particularly in the sphere of the analysis of work, has not been spectacularly high. The crater is not that big.

Why? One might analyze the current state of affairs in a variety of ways. For the sake of simplicity let me suggest explanations that rest upon one of following—intellectual persuasiveness, parsimony, polyphony, or profundity. First, one might see this material exchange as a battle of the Titans in which the ideas of two dead European social scientists are pitted against each other according to firm rules of presidential debate. This is the terrain of intellectual persuasiveness in which neither Foucault nor the postmodernists are seen as having won the battle for the minds of the community. This is a view promulgated by Weberians and is shared, dare I say, by the current editors. Or, we might see this as the cultural capital of the established Weberians, accumulated in long nights poring over the books, being threatened by the need to read more texts from a different tradition requiring a heavy investment in time and the learning of a new vocabulary. This is the terrain of intellectual parsimony. And here the lack of conversion to the value of the postmodern is to do with the interest-led indolence of a possible readership. This is more of an assertion from those enamored with postmodernism. Or might it be that correct when Chan (2000: 45) claims that those inspired by a postmodernist turn have not formed any cohesive front against the Weberians, never mind the Marxists. They are at best a loose confederation. He is worth quoting at length.

> In terms of published work, a postmodern approach is in a developing stage (e.g., Hassard 1994; Boje, Gephart and Thatchenkery 1996; Kilduff and Mehra 1997; Calas and Smircich 1999) . . . theoretical preoccupation (e.g. Jeffcutt 1994; Chia 1996; Parker 1992, 1995; Kilduff and Mehra 1997) and quasi-deconstruction of organizational thematics like leadership (Calas and Smircich 1995); gender (Martin 1990; Gheradi 2003), decision making (Chia 1996); motivation (Jackson and Carter 1995), and the canons of great writers in organizations (Calas 1987; Kilduff 1993).

This, one might venture to say, is an argument around intellectual polyphony and is favored by those who see the academic world in terms of the professional orchestration of the political mobilization of bias. Politicization for career has been hindered then by postmodernists 'not singing from the same hymn sheet'. It is also a vaguely psephological approach around numbers of adherents to identifiable positions.

The fourth and final approach is one I cling to myself which is based upon intellectual profundity—a sense of a depth of feeling and an intensity of understanding. This is not measured by impact upon the field in terms of longevity nor the release of collective energy directed at the busyness of research, but by the excitement of reading something so fresh and thrilling that it changes one's life. And in this spirit of transgression, postmodernism has had a seismic impact upon many individuals.

So use whichever metric you will, be it intellectual persuasiveness or profundity or psephology, there can be no agreed metric that all will find acceptable. Who is better? Keats or Byron? The Stones or the Beatles? Perhaps such measurement is too reflective of the commodification of everything. Perhaps the real problem is that anyone balefully goes looking for a metric itself!

We can see this problematic notion of an intellectual commodity in the fact that Lash opined in 1990 (ix) that 'postmodernism is, patently, no longer trendy'. But note that he predated by fifteen years a very recent email from the publishers, Sage, plaintively asking academic suppliers, that now postmodernism was less trendy, what was coming after it! But we return here to intellectual capital. Foucault is a 'brand name' that has lasted well. It is said that the Foucault family, who now live largely in Italy, are controlling the drip-feed of new material in such a way as to give this industry a longevity which one might imagine Bourdieu's work will not possess. The commercialization of the produce of intellectuals is by no means new, of course, but when publishers (ever-present ghosts at the academics' feast) and controlling families get together in a knowing way, it is clear we are in the presence of intellectual 'capital'.

Bearing this in mind, we can see in Callinicos (1989) a description of some of the nonproletarian elements that alienate Foucault from conventional sociologists of work. Foucault's later work spoke not of the prisoner in the penitentiary, nor less still of the industrial worker. He wrote of the ancients more than of his contemporaries. It was the Greeks and Romans of patrician stock that appealed to him more than the sorts of workers that Callinicos describes. Echoing Callinicos, Catherine Casey (2002: 135) speaks for many when she says:

> Postmodernism is ineluctably part of the degradation of modernity and modern social thought in its dead-end, private resistance without sociality. Its uses for social theory and sociology are patently misguided.

Well, it would be nice to be so full of self-confidence and never to face a hint of angst. To know via some triangulated ordnance survey what is misguided and dead end without exploring the highways and byways oneself would be so reassuring. But some have not been so fortunate as Casey. Perhaps she did not sit through the Miners' Strike (and I choose my verb carefully here) and wonder how it was that the population of working men and women sided so much with the Thatcher Government. How was one to explain this end to class-based loyalties and identities? How was it possible that much greater cleavages had opened up within the working class than had previously seemed possible? It was at this point that Foucault's work started to explain the microphysics of power and the importance to the powerful of raising resistance to effect a restraining of resistance. The police rather than 'the management' became the source of discontent. At a time when the State showed its power most clearly and yet it did not disturb the working population, the question had to be raised 'how else were we disciplined'? It was this trauma that surfaced in a British interest in postmodernism. Casey's contemporary confidence reflects back on the old guard who 'wrote in a period in which they could see no effective oppositional actors and in which the old social movements had been dramatically defeated and converted into apparatuses of power' (Casey 2002: 182). Times change and so do fashions and so, of course, do underlying structures.

With great irony, Foucault also problematized the notion of the author. Indeed he spoke of 'the death of the author' (Foucault 1979) because he disliked the implied special status and ownership of ideas. In an attempt to escape from this privileging of his own position, Foucault sought to be highly mobile in his theoretical work, with one work contradicting the previous one. Like the classic proletarian resistor of Sillitoe's *Saturday Night and Sunday Morning* (1959), Arthur Seaton, who was never content to be pigeon-holed and categorized, and was never standing still long enough to be analyzed, Foucault too, perhaps sought nomadic status through which the judges of normality might be avoided. But death has fixed his work and the 'famille Foucault' have a great interest one might suppose in interpreting the death of the author in more conventional terms.

Foucault once said the following:

> It would be wrong to say that the soul is an illusion, or an ideological effect. On the contrary, it exists, it has a reality, it is produced permanently around, on, within the body by the functioning of a power... on those one supervises, trains and corrects, over madmen, children at home and at school, the colonized, over those who are stuck at a machine and supervised for the rest of their lives (quoted in Rose 1999: vi).

Perhaps we can conclude that he worked hard to shape his soul in a somewhat different fashion. And in that effort perhaps we can all take heart.

References

Acker, J. (1990). 'Hierarchies, Jobs, Bodies', *Gender and Society*, 4: 139–58.

Alvesson, M. and Willmott, H. (eds.) (2004). *Studying Management Critically*. London: Sage.

Bauman, Z. (1989). *Modernity and Ambivalence*. Cambridge: Polity Press.

Beck, U. (1992). 'From Industrial Society to Risk Society', *Theory, Culture and Society*, 9(1).

Bell, D. (1972). *The Coming of Postindustrial Society*. New York: Basic Books.

Boje, D., Gephart, R.,and Thatchenkery, T. (eds.) (1996). *Postmodern Management and Organization Theory*. London: Sage.

Braverman, H. (1974). *Labor and Monopoly Capital*. New York: Monthly Review Press.

Brewis, J. and Linstead, S. (2000). *Sex, Work and Sex Work*. London: Sage.

Calas, M. and Smircich, L. (1995). 'Voicing Seduction to Silence Leadership', *Organization Studies*, 12: 567–602.

Callinicos, A. (1989). *Against Postmodernism*. Cambridge: Polity Press.

Carmona, S., Ezzamel, M., and Gutierrez, F. (2002). 'The Relationship between Accounting and Spatial Practices in the Factory', *Accounting, Organisations and Society*, 27: 239–74.

Casey, C. (1995). *Work, Self and Society*. London: Routledge.

—— (2002). *Critical Analyses of Organizations*. London: Sage.

Chan, A. (2000). *Critically Constituting Organization*. Hague: John Benjamins.

Chia, R. (1996). 'The Concept of a Decision: A Deconstructive Analysis', *Journal of Management Studies*, 31: 781–806.

Clarke, T. and Clegg, S. (1998). *Changing Paradigms*: London HarperCollins.

Clegg, S. (1999). 'Weber and Foucault: Social Theory for the Study of Organizations', *Organization*, 11: 149–78.

Collinson, D. (2003). 'Identities and Insecurities', *Organization*, 10: 3.

Cooper, R. (1989). 'Modernism, Postmodernism and Organizational Analysis: The Contribution of Jacques Derrida', *Organization Studies*, 10: 3.

—— and Burrell, G. (1988). 'Modernism, Postmodernism and Organizational Analysis: An Introduction', *Organization Studies*, 9: 3.

Crabbe, T. Quoted in Thomas, K. (1999). *The Oxford Book of Work*. Oxford: Oxford University Press.

Derrida, J. (1976). *Of Grammatology*. Baltimore, MD: John Hopkins University Press.

—— (1981). *Positions*. Chicago, IL: University of Chicago Press.

Diprose (2002). *Corporeal Generosity*. Albany: State University of New York Press.

Dreyfus, R. and Rabinow, P. (1986). *Michel Foucault: Beyond Structuralism and Hermeneutics*. Chicago, IL: University of Chicago Press.

Du Gay, P. (1996). *Consumption and Identity at Work*. London: Sage.

Flecker, J. and Hofbauer, J. (1998). 'Capitalising on Subjectivity', in P. Thompson and C. Warhurst (eds.), *Workplaces of the Future*. Basingstoke: Palgrave.

Foucault, M. (1972). *The Archaelogy of Knowledge*. London: Tavistock.
—— (1977). *Discipline and Punish*. Harmondsworth: Penguin.
—— (1979). *History of Sexuality*, Part 1. Harmondsworth: Penguin.
—— (1986). *Care of the Self*. Harmondsworth: Penguin.
Fukuyama, F. (1992). *The End of History and the Last Man*. New York: Fress Press
Gherardi, S. (2003). 'Feminist Theory and Organization Theory', in H. Tsoukas and C. Knudsen (eds.), *The Oxford Handbook of Organization Theory*. Oxford: Oxford University Press.
Giddens, A. (1989). *The Consequences of Modernity*. Cambridge: Polity Press.
Goffman, E. (1959). *Asylums*. Harmondsworth: Penguin.
Grey, C. (1992). 'Career as a Project of Self', *Sociology*, 28(2): 479–97.
Grint, K. (1991). *The Sociology of Work*. Cambridge: Polity Press.
Hall, S. (1996). 'Who needs Identity?', in S. Hall and P. du Gay (eds.), *Questions of Cultural Identity*. London: Sage.
Hancock, P. and Tyler, M. (2001). *Work, Postmodernism and Organization*. London: Sage.
Hardt, M. and Negri. (2000). *Empire*. Cambridge MA: Harvard University Press.
Hassard, J. (1994). 'Postmodern Organizational Analysis', *Journal of Management Studies*, 31: 303–24.
—— and Parker, M. (eds.) (1993). *Postmodernism and Organization*. London: Sage.
Hindess, B. (1996). *Discourses of Power*. Oxford: Blackwell.
Hite, S. (1999). *Sex and Business*. London: Prentice-Hall.
Hochschild, A. R. (1983). *The Managed Heart*. Berkeley, CA: University of California Press.
Hoskin, K. and McVe, R. (1988). The Genesis of Accountability, *Accounting Organizations and Society*, 13(1): 37–73.
Jackson, N. and Carter, P. (1993). Modernism, Postmodernism and Motivation', in J. Hassard and M. Parker, *Postmodernism and Organizations*. London: Sage.
Jacques, R. (1996). *Manufacturing the Employee*. London: Sage.
Kerr, C., Dunlop, J., Harbison, and Myers. (1962). *Industrialism and Industrial Man*. Harmondsworth: Penguin.
Kilduff, M. and Mehra, A. (1997). Postmodernism and Organizational Research, *Academy of Management Review*, 22: 453–81.
Knights, D. (2002). 'Writing Organizational Analysis into Foucault', *Organization*, 9(4): 575–94.
—— and Willmott. (1989). 'Power and Subjectivity at Work', *Sociology*, 23(4): 535–58.
—— and —— . (eds.) (1990). *Labour Process Theory*. Basingstoke: Macmillan.
Lash, S. (1990). *Sociology of Postmodernism*. London: Routledge.
Latour, B. (2000). 'Actor Network Theory and After', in J. Law and J. Hassard (eds.), *After Actor Network Theory*. London: Sage.
Linstead, S. (1993). 'Deconstruction in the Study of Organization', in J. Hassard and M. Parker (eds.), *Postmodernism and Organization*. London: Sage.
Lyotard, J. (1984). *The Postmodern Condition*. University of Manchester Press.

McKinley, A. and Starkey, K. (eds.) (1998). *Foucault, Management and Organization.* London: Sage.
McManners, R. and Wales, G. (2003). *Shafts of Light.* Newcastle-upon-Tyne: Gemini.
Marsden, R. (1999). *The Nature of Capital.* London: Routledge.
Martin, J. (1990). 'Deconstructing Organizational Taboos', *Organization and Science,* 14: 339–59.
Maupin, A. (1978). *Tales from the City.* Harmondsorth: Penguin.
Miller, J. (1993). *The Passion of Michel Foucault.* New York: Simon & Schuster.
Minztberg, H. (1995). 'Reply to Calas and Smircich', *Organization Studies,* 12(4).
Nichols, T. and Armstrong, P. (1976). *Workers Divided.* London: Fontana.
Niemark, M. (1990). 'The King is Dead: Long Live the King', *Critical Perspectives on Accounting* 1(1): 103–14.
Ray, L. (1993). *Rethinking Critical Theory.* London: Sage.
Reed, M. (1999). 'From the Cage to the Gaze', in G. Morgan and L Engwall (eds.), *Regulation and Organizations.* London: Routledge.
Rose, N. (1999). *Governing the Soul,* 2nd edn. London: Free Association.
Rosenau, P. (1992). *Postmodernism and the Social Sciences.* Princeton, NJ: Princeton University Press.
Said, E. (1980). *Orientalism.* Harmondsworth: Penguin.
Sennett, R. (1999). *The Corrosion of Character.* New York: W.W. Norton.
Sewell, G. and Wilkinson, B. (1992). 'Someone to Watch Over Me', *Sociology,* 26(2): 271–89.
Sillitoe, A. (1959). *Saturday Night and Sunday Morning.* Harmondsworth: Pan.
Smart, B. (ed.) (1994). *Michel Foucault: Critical Assessments.* London: Routledge.
Spivak, G. (1999). *A Critique of Postcolonial Reason.* Cambridge, MA: Harvard University Press.
Steingood, D. and Fitzgibbon, D. (1993). A Postmodern Deconstruction of TQM, *Journal of Organisational Change Management,* 6(5): 27–42.
Taylor, S. and Tyler, M. J. (1998). 'The Exchange of Aesthetics: Women's Work and the Gift', *Gender, Work and Organization,* 5(3): 165–71.
Thomas, K. (1999). *The Oxford Book of Work.* Oxford: Oxford University Press.
Thompson, P. (1993). 'Fatal Distraction: Postmodernism and Organisation Theory', in J. Hassard and M. Parker (eds.), *Postmodernism and Organization.* London: Sage.
—— and Ackoyd, S. (1995). 'All Quiet on the Workplace Front', *Sociology,* 29(4): 615–33.
—— and Smith, C. (1998). 'Beyond the Capitalist Labour Process', *Critical Sociology,* 24(3): 193–215.
——, ——, and Ackroyd, S. (2000). 'If Ethics is the Answer, You've Been Asking the Wrong Questions', *Organization Studies,* 21(6): 1149–58.
—— and McHugh, D. (2003). *Work Organizations,* 3rd edn. Basingstoke: Palgrave.
Townley, B. (1994). *Reframing Human Resource Management.* London: Sage.
Veblen, T. (1899). *The Theory of the Leisure Class*: London: Macmillan.
Webster, F. and Robins, K. (1993). 'I'll Be Watching You', *Sociology,* 27(2): 243–52.
Zuboff, S. (1988). *In the Age of the Smart Machine.* Oxford: Heinemann.

7

The Economic Approach to Analysis of the Labor Market

Stephen Machin

Economics has always had a lot to say about the labor market. The labor market is a central feature of many macroeconomic models and has been analyzed in depth by at the microlevel by many leading economists dating back at least as far as Smith (1776). Having said that, the economic approach to analyzing labor markets has faced many dissenters in its time, with critical references to its assumptions and from people arguing that it treats labor as a good or service like any others in the economy. Yet, and despite this, relative to other social science disciplines the economic approach has one big, practical advantage. It offers a well-understood, coherent framework for looking at labor market behavior. One can clearly quibble with the assumptions that underpin the approach, and question their relevance to reality, but it is hard to deny that the framework is powerful in terms of generating empirical predictions regarding the operation of labor markets, and for giving a structure to develop empirical models to test these predictions.

In its starkest form the economic approach rests on its simplicity, coupled with a powerful predictive element. What may be lost from what some people think of as rather simplistic modeling of individual behavior is gained by the clarity of predictions. As Borjas' *Labor Economics* textbook puts it 'there is a trade off between realism and simplicity, and good economics hits the mark just right' (Borjas 1996: 6). There are also many useful generalizations of the orthodox economic approach. Some of these become much more complex, and therefore less focused with less empirical clarity and hence not so useful from a practical standpoint. Others purport to move closer to 'real world' behavior by deviating from the assumptions embodied in the classical economic approach.

In this chapter I focus on the usefulness, and sometimes the limitations, of the economic approach to analyzing labor markets. I argue that in some areas it is a powerful tool that sheds light on important behavioral questions that closely link to important issues of public policy. I also consider areas where the orthodox approach is less useful and where one needs to move away from the standard model to generate testable predictions that accord with the real world. However, moving away too far dilutes predictions too much and effectively becomes hopeless if one's aim is to say something general about labor market behavior.

I believe it is worth pointing out right at the start that the very simple textbook neoclassical model of the labor market—which I am thinking of as the orthodox approach—is not simply a straw man that can easily be knocked down and criticized. Of course, there are many (mostly non-economists, but also including some economists) who have tried to do this, but the bottom line is that they rarely come up with an alternative that has as powerful predictive ability.[1] Others, who build from this benchmark, seem to come up with relatively simple and concise ways of analyzing the labor market, retaining at least some of the predictive power from economic models formulated in this manner.

1. The Economic Approach to Labor Markets

The Orthodox Approach

What is the orthodox economic approach to analyzing the labor market? Picking up any undergraduate text makes it clear that, in its simplest form, it can be characterized by labor market equilibrium with equality of labor demand with labor supply. Labor demand, the employment demanded by employers, is a negative function of the wage on offer: a higher wage, all other things being equal, means an employer will take on fewer workers. Labor supply, the employment on offer by individuals for a given wage, is positively related to wages, in that more individuals will be prepared to supply their labor to the market if the wage is higher.

[1] There are debates on whether there is really any predictive power in the orthodox economic approach, or whether economic models are in fact tautological. Much of this debate rapidly moves into philosophical territory and I want to avoid this as a lot of the discussion is too negative and pessimistic. I prefer to look at the more positive side of economics as a discipline which, as Lazear (2000) notes, when done well is able to offer a relatively simple approach to obtaining behavioral predictions.

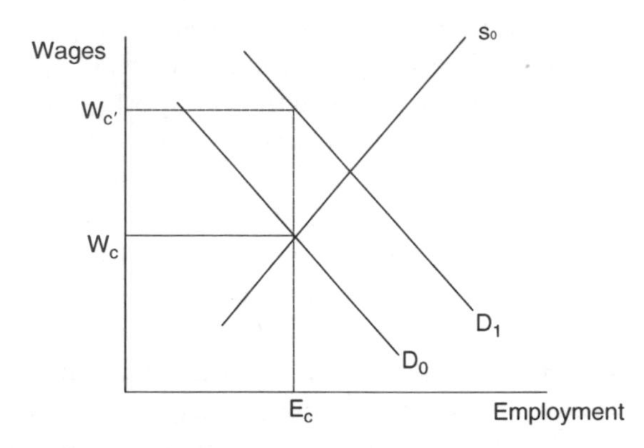

Figure 7.1 A perfectly competitive labor market

Equilibrium in the labor market occurs where the downward sloping labor demand curve intersects the upward sloping labor supply curve. This generates a wage W_c and an employment level E_c as shown in Figure 7.1. The subscript c is deliberately chosen to denote *competitive* since the model outlined here is a competitive labor market where the market wage W_c clears the market. That is, a higher wage would result in too many workers competing for jobs (supply exceeds demand) and a lower wage would result in there being too few workers to fill the job slots available (demand exceeds supply). The competitive equilibrium comes about, in Adam Smith's terminology (1776), through the 'invisible hand' that equilibrates demand and supply.

What are the assumptions underlying this model? The first is that the labor market is perfectly competitive. That is workers are free to switch between jobs costlessly in response to any wage changes and they possess full information about wages on offer. Second, all workers are the same (labor is homogeneous) so that their ability to produce output is the same. Third, there is a single competitive wage, and this wage is equal to the value of the marginal product of labor, the extra amount of output that an extra worker can produce.

None of these assumptions accord especially well with what we see in reality. So therefore it is interesting to ask: what are the implications of this model? The model clearly has certain predictions. Some of these are useful for what we see in the real world, some are less so. In terms of predictions from the model, one can see, for example, that a positive demand shock raises wages at a given employment level. To see this suppose that a positive demand shock moves the demand curve from D_0 to D_1.

At employment level E_c the wage moves up to $W_{c'}$. This seems plausible and sensible. Moreover, the magnitude of the wage increase depends on the slope of the labor demand curve and many researchers have tried to estimate the wage elasticity of labor demand, namely how sensitive employment is to wage changes (Hamermesh 1996).

This is but one example. It is evident that one can think more generally of shifts in demand and supply altering wage and/or employment levels. In this sense one has a clear framework about the way in which demand and supply shocks can alter wage and employment outcomes. And, if one has estimates of the slopes of the demand and supply curves, one can say something about the magnitude of such changes.

Taken at face value the assumptions themselves, of perfect competition, homogenous labor, and the resultant single wage equal to marginal products (with no dispersion) are much less defensible. It is therefore worth considering how economists have confronted this. They have done so by moving in several directions, some of which remain under the competitive framework, some of which move away and consider aspects of imperfect competition in the labor market.

2. Generalizations of the Orthodox Approach

The limitations of the orthodox approach have long been recognized by economists. I consider these in two main areas, the first set remaining in the competitive paradigm, the second based upon modeling imperfect competition in various ways.

Heterogeneous Labor

One can, in a reasonably straightforward manner, amend the orthodox approach to allow for workers with different productivity-related characteristics, while remaining in the competitive framework. Suppose we have workers of two skills types, high (H) and low (L). There will now be different demand and supply relations for H and L, but the logic of the orthodox model goes through. The extra dimension arising is that the degree of substitutability of workers becomes an issue for employers when making their demand decisions.

Of course the single wage feature now disappears. In this approach there will be different wages for high- and low-skill workers. A highly influential and important area of empirical labor economics has actually built upon

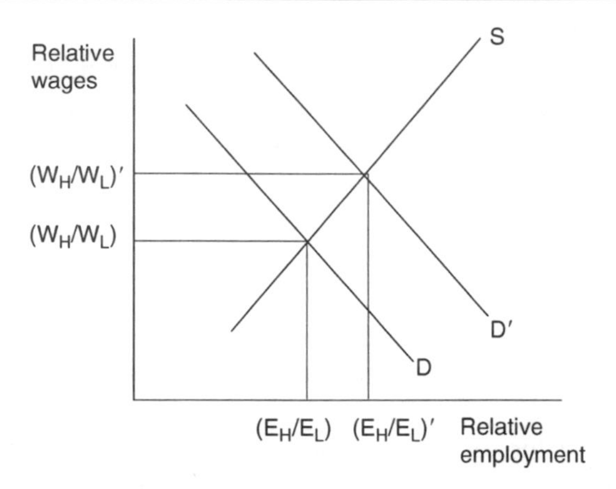

Figure 7.2 A model of relative demand and supply

simple supply–demand models with high- and low-skill workers to discuss important changes in the structure of wages that have occurred in recent years (Katz and Murphy 1992; Katz and Autor 1999).

Figure 7.2 shows a competitive labor market model where there are skilled and unskilled workers. The demand and supply schedules are now relative demand and supply curves and so the wage and employment outcomes are the relative wage between high- and low-skill workers (W_H/W_L) and their relative employment levels (E_H/E_L). One can use this framework to study what has happened to wage and employment structures over time, and how they have resulted in rising labor market inequality in many countries in the advanced world. Table 7.1 reports some information on shifts in the relative wages and employment of college graduates as compared to nongraduates in the UK and US labor markets between 1980 and 2000. The upper panel of the table shows the employment and hours shares of workers with a degree in the UK, together with the relative wage between graduates and nongraduates at five-year intervals between 1980 and 2000. The lower panel shows the same for the USA.

Table 7.1 very clearly confirms that rapid increases in the shares of the relatively skilled group of workers (graduates) have occurred in both countries. In the UK in 1980 5 percent of workers had a degree but this rose sharply through the 1980s and 1990s to reach 17 percent by the year 2000. In the USA there were many more graduates at the start of the 1980s, at around 19 percent, but there were also sharp rises over time that reached over 27 percent by 2000. In both countries, therefore, the relative supply of graduates increased very sharply between 1980 and 2000. If one considers

Table 7.1. Trends in graduate/nongraduate employment, hours, and relative wages, UK and USA, 1980–2000

	UK labour force survey/general household survey		
	% Graduate share of employment	% Graduate share of hours	Relative weekly wage (Full-timers)
1980	5.0	5.1	1.48
1985	9.8	10.5	1.50
1990	10.2	11.0	1.60
1995	14.0	15.4	1.60
2000	17.2	18.8	1.64
1980–2000 change	12.2	13.7	0.16
1980–1990 change	5.2	5.9	0.12
1990–2000 change	7.0	7.8	0.04
	US current population survey		
	% Graduate share of employment	% Graduate share of hours	Relative hourly wage (Full-timers)
1980	19.3	20.4	1.36
1985	22.0	23.6	1.47
1990	23.8	25.6	1.55
1995	25.5	28.1	1.61
2000	27.5	29.5	1.66
1980–2000 change	8.2	9.1	0.30
1980–1990 change	4.5	5.2	0.19
1990–2000 change	3.7	3.9	0.11

Notes: Sample is all people aged 18–64 in work and earning, except for relative wages which are defined for full-time workers. The relative wage ratios are derived from coefficient estimates on a graduate dummy variable in semilog earnings equations controlling for age, age squared, and gender (they are the exponent of the coefficient on the graduate dummy). The UK employment and hours shares are from the LFS. The relative wage gaps are from the GHS for 1980, 1985, and 1990 and the LFS in 1995 and 2000 (relative wages from regressions for the overlap year, 1995, were very similar in GHS and LFS). Weekly wages are used for the UK due to changes to the hours questions in the GHS in the 1980s, meaning that a consistent hourly wage cannot be defined through time. The CPS data is the Economic Policy Institute CPS ORG labor extracts data. I thank John Schmitt for making them available to me.

hours shares of graduates, rather than employment shares, one sees a similar pattern with there being a slightly bigger increase in the hours shares in both countries.

Table 7.1 also shows that, despite their increased numbers, the wages of more skilled workers (graduates) have not fallen relative to the less skilled (nongraduates). The final column of Table 7.1 actually shows the opposite to have occurred. The numbers given in this column are the relative wages of graduates versus nongraduates for full-time workers (after standardizing for age and gender in a least squares regression). In both countries the relative wage for graduates rose between 1980 and 2000. The increase is very sharp in the USA, going from 1.36 to 1.66, while the UK increase is less marked but shows a rise from 1.48 to 1.64.

But how do these changes square up with the relative supply and demand framework? At first glance, they do not seem to fit in well. One would normally think that, if there are more workers of a particular skill type (here the H type), their relative wage should fall, since employers are more able to pick and choose between a larger number of workers. In terms of the UK and US experience of the 1980s and 1990s what seems to have happened is that the ratio of skilled to unskilled wages has gone up at the same time as the ratio of skilled to unskilled employment. It becomes clear that, to rationalize such an outcome with the basic theory, there has to have been an outward shift in the relative demand curve. Suppose that in Figure 7.2 the demand curve shifts out to D′ (and supply is held fixed for convenience) one then ends up with simultaneously higher relative wages and employment for the skilled at $(W_H/W_L)'$ and $(E_H/E_L)'$.

A more general way of thinking about this kind of relative demand shift in favor of the skilled is in terms of an economic model where the wages and employment of skilled and unskilled workers are the outcomes of a race between supply and demand. Here the more general implication is that both demand and supply curves are shifting and the question is which curve has moved the most. To have generated simultaneously higher wages and employment for the skilled it seems that relative demand must have increased by more than relative supply. Put alternatively, over the period of rising wage inequality, demand has won the race so that employers are prepared to pay workers with appropriate skills more than less skilled workers, despite there being many more of them supplying their labor.

Thus a simple competitive model with two types of labor can shed light on the observed patterns of changing wage and employment differentials by skill types. It can also provide insight into what has driven such changes. A considerable research agenda has been devoted to try and ascertain what lies behind the relative demand shift, one needs to reconcile the facts. Researchers have looked at key possible drivers, including technical changes (Berman et al. 1994; Berman, et al. 1998; Machin and Van Reenen 1998), international trade (Johnson and Stafford 1999) and the decline of labor market institutions like unions (Freeman 1993). At the time of writing, there is a quite large body of evidence that technological changes that are biased in favor of more skilled workers, and against less skilled workers, are an important feature of the observed shifts in relative demand, and thus in labor market outcomes.

Contracts

Some other economic models of labor markets remain in the competitive paradigm, but start to look at particular aspects of employment contracts that relax some of the key assumptions of the orthodox approach. For example, it may be that workers are paid beneath their marginal productivity in some time periods (like early in the life cycle when they undergo training, as in Becker 1975) and above their marginal product in other periods. In models of deferred compensation these features operate, but the competitive approach is maintained so that an individual's wage equals his/her marginal product over the worker's lifetime.

These sorts of models can be thought of as useful for revealing other pertinent features of real labor markets. For example, it can be argued that a deferred compensation schedule can have a motivational impact on workers (Becker and Stigler 1974). A payment scheme here would have workers initially paid less than their marginal product, but after they have proven themselves to be hard working individuals, they will be paid more. Thus a long-term contract will be beneficial to workers as they will be guaranteed a higher payoff in future, but it is also of use to employers at their initial stage of hiring since they will be able to recruit more stable workers whom the firm can rely on.[2]

A sizable literature in economics looks at contracts that define wage payments between workers and firms. Malcomson (1999) provides a thorough survey of this work, much of which is of a fairly technical nature, especially when one starts to allow for information differences between workers and their employers (or prospective employers).[3] But the main point here is that one need not move very far away from simple neoclassical models to get to some of these approaches that emphasize real world aspects of the employment relationship, while retaining predictive power for empirical researchers to look at the labor market and at aspects of labor market policy.

[2] Of course, there is a possibility the firm may cheat and a body of work considers various aspects of how contracts can be enforced (e.g. since firms would lose reputations if they cheat), see Lazear and Moore (1984).

[3] The economics of information has become a highly important research area and is one that has had a very significant impact in many areas of economics. See Stiglitz (2000) for an in-depth discussion of this impact, and the potential for future significant developments.

Search Models

Another way to move away from the orthodox model is to recognize that full information is not available to workers and employers. In competitive search models (Pissarides 1990; Mortensen and Pissarides 1999) employers postwage offers and workers search among them until they find their match. As such one can have a situation where wages are not equal to marginal products while the search and matching process goes on, but, once employers and workers match, the competitive equilibrium returns. Unlike the orthodox approach, these models allow for unemployment in equilibrium and for wage dispersion, even where workers are of the same skill level.

One way of thinking about search models is that they are able to offer an equilibrium framework that is richer than the competitive model which has no frictions that generate search behavior on the part of workers and firms. The notion of labor market frictions is important in that the labor market is characterized by large flows of workers between labor market states and across firms when they move jobs, or flow into unemployment or inactivity. Again one gains in realism in this framework as search equilibrium models provide predictions that can be tested with data. There is a voluminous body of work that does so (see the comprehensive survey by Mortensen and Pissarides 1999), looking at aspects of wage dispersion and worker and firm turnover. These are often linked to policy debates on important questions like the relative effectiveness of policies towards unemployment (e.g. those that focus on individuals with longer unemployment durations) and on the role that can be played by employment subsidies from government to employers that can lower labor costs and promote increased labor demand.

Imperfect Competition

Something of a more substantive, and in economics more ideologically charged, move away from the orthodox approach occurs in models that explicitly recognize that markets may not clear due to imperfect competition in the labor market. The most natural of these occurs when firms bargain with trade unions, but in other approaches either workers or firms (or both) have market power which is exploited to yield noncompetitive equilibria.

Trade Unions

The presence of trade unions in the labor market means that workers have some degree of bargaining power that will generate wages that lie above the competitive wage. Over the years a great deal of attention has focused on models with unions and there are several ways to consider union behavior in labor market models. In the monopoly union approach, unions are monopoly suppliers of labor and thus they can exploit their monopoly power to raise wages above competitive levels (Oswald 1985). In union bargaining models, the key distinction that arises is whether or not unions bargain with employers over wages only or over both wages and employment. In the former, wage bargains occur between firms and unions, then employers set employment contingent upon the bargained wage. Thus one ends up in a situation on the labor demand curve where wages are above, and employment is below, competitive levels (this is frequently referred to as the right-to-manage model: Nickell and Andrews, 1983). In the case where employers and unions bargain over wages and employment—the so-called efficient bargaining model (McDonald and Solow 1981)—wages are above competitive levels, and employment may be higher or lower than competitive levels.

The typical way in which union models are set up is to specify firm and union objectives through utility functions.[4] So, in a very general sense, for the firm the utility function might be V(?) where ? is profits (equal to revenue, R, less wage costs, WE, if capital is assumed fixed in the short run) and for the union is U(W, E). In a union monopoly model the union sets a wage and the employer then sets employment on its labor demand curve. The monopoly union W–E outcome is given in Figure 7.3 at the point where the union indifference curve $\overline{U}$ (which shows a constant set of union utility levels for different wage–employment combinations) is at a tangent to the labor demand curve. Notice that the wage W_M is above the competitive wage and therefore that the employment level E_M is lower than it would be in the orthodox model.

In the bargaining approaches, the firm and the union bargain over wages or over wages and employment. The former case has the monopoly union model as a special case where the union has all the bargaining power: more typically the wage outcome will be somewhere between the competitive and monopoly union wages, as depicted in Figure 7.4, say at point A. In the latter case unions and firms bargain over wages and employment and the outcome is on a contract curve, denoted CC′, in Figure 7.4. This contract curve traces out the optimal, efficient

[4] It is, of course, controversial among some critics to even specify a utility function for trade unions. I abstract away from this discussion here so as to clearly describe the economic approach to analyzing union behavior.

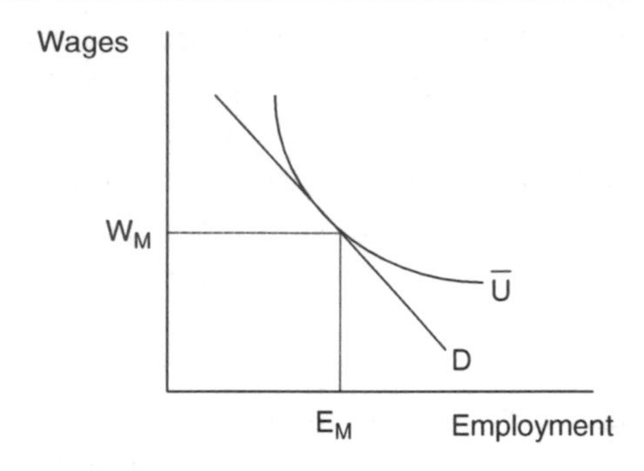

Figure 7.3 A monopoly union model

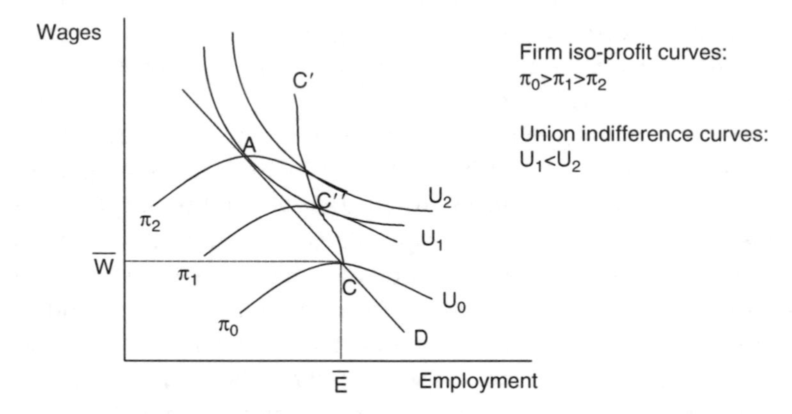

Figure 7.4 Union bargaining models

bargains.[5] The slope of CC′ can be negative or positive. If negative, employment is lower than in the competitive model, but if the slope of CC′ is positive then employment levels can actually be higher than competitive levels.

The key point for our purposes in illustrating how labor economics can function in noncompetitive environments is that the wage lies higher than the competitive wage owing to union bargaining power. This, of course, is consistent with what unions do to wages as there is a huge

[5] They are efficient in that either the firm can achieve higher profits given union utility, or the union higher utility for a given level of profits. In Figure 7.4 notice that point A is on union indifference curve U_1 and firm iso-profit curve π_2. By moving down the union indifference curve U_1 the firm can get on a higher iso-profit schedule, π_1. By moving along the firm iso-profit curve π_2 the union can get on a higher indifference curve U_2.

body of work showing that unions significantly raise wages above non-union levels (Lewis 1986; Booth 1995). Unionized models of labor markets have been used extensively in labor economics, and the development of a formal modeling approach yields a framework which can be used to generate testable predictions. Sometimes these refer to tests of the different union models (as in Brown and Ashenfelter 1986, or MaCurdy and Pencavel 1986, and a large literature that followed them.[6]) In other cases they are used as a key building block in a model of the labor market, Layard, Nickell, and Jackman's (1991) highly regarded work on unemployment being a case in point.

Other Noncompetitive Approaches

There are other noncompetitive models that generate higher than competitive wage outcomes, but not via union bargaining. For example, in efficiency wage models (Shapiro and Stiglitz 1984; Weiss 1991) it is optimal for employers to pay wages above competitive levels to elicit effort from workers. In these models there is a probability that workers will shirk on the job (perhaps due to imperfect monitoring) and higher wages are paid to ensure that a labor market equilibrium ensues where there is no shirking. The higher wage, the efficiency wage, lies above the competitive level so as to ensure productivity is higher and it is optimal for the employer to pay this wage.

There are different strands of efficiency wage models. Some, like the Shapiro-Stiglitz model, are based upon the notion that firms and workers possess different information sets and therefore the effort of workers can only be imperfectly observed by the employer. In others, aspects of fairness appear. For example, Akerlof (1982) and Akerlof and Yellen (1990) present models where employees receive a wage that is perceived to be fair on the grounds that fairness on the part of employers is able to generate workplace cohesiveness and thus higher productivity. This fair wage is then higher than the competitive wage.

The same feature, of wages above competitive levels, follows in rent sharing or insider–outsider models (for rent sharing see Abowd and Lemieux 1993 and Van Reenen 1996; for the insider–outsider approach see Lindbeck and Snower 1986). In these models firms earn above competitive

[6] These papers derive predictions from different union bargaining models about the determinants of wages and employment. Work that tries to distinguish between different approaches relies on empirical work, for example, estimating labor demand equations that have different wage variables as explanatory variables.

profits and workers with some degree of bargaining power (perhaps unionized workers, or skilled workers, or those who have accumulated some degree of insider power) are able to extract a share of these rents. This contrasts with the competitive case where firms do not share any profit increase with their employees.

Summary

This section has attempted to make clear how the economic approach can be used in the study of labor markets. It is worth pointing out that economics is much broader, and far more flexible in terms of how it has evolved as a discipline, than the 'straw man' stereotype of economics that many noneconomists like to criticize. It is certainly true that the reliance on market mechanisms forms the bedrock of the discipline. That said, many recent developments move on from this and much of the cutting-edge work in economics is fully aware of its limitations. But, as Lazear (2000: 99) points out, the fact that economics has a 'rigorous language that allows complicated concepts to be written in relatively simple, abstract terms' is important. This is true for people using economics everywhere, not only in academic research, but for professional economists and for policy makers wanting to look at the efficiency and equity of different policies. The beauty is in the simplicity, and the ability to generate clear, testable predictions that can be tested with data from the real world. Labor economics has been particularly active in this kind of venture over the years, by trying to consider how well or badly first order principles from economic theory correspond to what actually happens.

3. Applications of the Economic Approach to Analysis of Labor Markets

The economic approach has been widely used over the years to analyze labor market phenomena. So far the discussion has been on the most commonly utilized theoretical approaches to analyzing labor market behavior. But a very important aspect of the economic approach has been mostly overlooked. That is its usefulness in generating empirical predictions that can be tested with data. A large literature has taken first order economic principles like some of those discussed in Section 2 and attempted to assess which ones accord best with measured data. A very good and clear example of just how large scale this enterprise has been is evident if one takes a look at the volumes of the *Handbook of Labor Economics* (Ashenfelter and Layard 1986; Ashenfelter and Card 1999).

This is certainly one of the strong points of the economic approach and we have learnt a great deal from the empirical work in labor economics. It is probably fair to say that, as data collection and availability and computing power became much more widely available and accessible from the late 1960s onwards, labor economics was the first area in economics to systematically and intensively analyze data on individuals and employers. This has significantly contributed to knowledge, policy debates, and, most important for our purposes here, to shed light on the suitability (or otherwise) of the economic approach to analyzing labor markets.

The contribution of this research includes shedding light on the way in which labor markets function, but also on the applicability of the economic approach to labor market questions in the real world. I next consider two such examples.

Minimum Wages

One of the clearest predictions in labor economics arises from applying the textbook model of the labor market to minimum wage policy. Orthodox theory predicts that imposition of a minimum wage floor, or raising a minimum wage already in existence, results in job loss since workers are priced out of work. Moreover, the minimum wage is said to hurt the very workers it sets out to help, since the 'marginal' workers who are displaced from work are disproportionately more likely to be low-skill workers.

Consider Figure 7.5. In the figure, wages and employment are initially at the competitive labor market levels W_c and E_c. Imposition of a minimum wage floor at a wage higher than the competitive level, at say W_m, results in firms being moved up the labor demand curve. Thus employment falls to E_m (and unemployment rises by the distance E_u–E_m, a larger effect than the employment effect owing to more workers supplying their labor at the higher wage). The prediction about what happens to jobs is clear and unambiguous. Employment falls, and the only relevant question is: how negative is the negative employment effect? In this simple model the answer depends on the size of the minimum wage increase (W_m–W_c) and the sensitivity of employment to wage changes, given by the steepness of the labor demand curve, or the wage elasticity of labor demand (inelastic demand, where employment is not very sensitive to wages and the demand curve is relatively steep, leads to lower job losses as compared to more elastic demand).

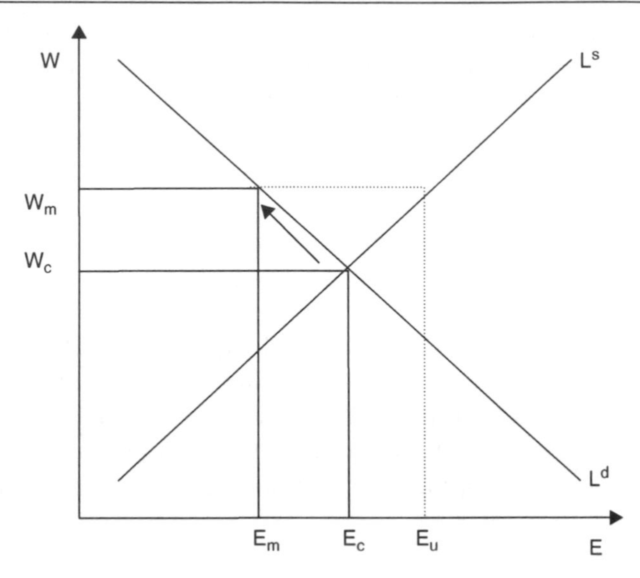

Figure 7.5 Minimum wages in a competitive labor market

One can develop more complex models, for example, with different sorts of workers, or in an economy where some sectors are covered by minimum wages and others are not (see Brown 1999). In these approaches, the size of any employment effect may be altered but the basic logic goes through. When the model is competitive, the prediction that job losses will occur always holds.

These very clear predictions have been confronted with a wide range of data. Most of the early work was in the USA, but more recently there is a growing international body of empirical work that looks at the economic effects of minimum wages. The area is a good one to illustrate the uses of empirical work in economics, since there is an older literature that tends to confirm the predictions of the standard model, and a newer 'revisionist' body of work that challenges that work.

The USA introduced a federal minimum wage in the Fair Labor Standards Act of 1938. It has been uprated on an irregular and infrequent basis since, and empirical researchers have looked at what happens to employment when minimum wages are altered as a means of testing the predictions of the model described above. Because demand and supply shocks may shift the demand and supply curves for reasons unrelated to the minimum wage, the empirical approach taken is to use a statistical regression framework to look at the relationship between employment and minimum wages over time, holding constant observable supply and demand factors.

Brown, Gilroy, and Kohen (1982) summarized this US literature on employment and minimum wages based upon studies using time series data up to the late 1970s. They noted that the bulk of studies developed an empirical approach looking at teenage employment rates (or in some cases unemployment rates) as a function of the minimum wage.[7] Their review claims that eighteen published studies had reached a 'consensus' in line with the orthodox model in that minimum wages are associated with lower employment levels, and the size of the employment effect is more negative for teenagers than for adults. The magnitudes of the effects were such that the elasticity of employment with respect to the minimum wage was in the range of $-0.1$to -0.3: that is, a 10 percent increase in minimum wages would translate into a reduction of 1 to 3 percent in teenage employment.

A revisionist literature has subsequently sprung up which strongly challenges the orthodox model. I think this usefully shows the ways in which economics is able to evolve as a social science subject and its structured framework can offer a flexible means of understanding real world phenomena.

The revisionist work is based upon two prongs, both of which take issue with aspects of the orthodox approach. The first goes back to one of the fundamental premises of the theory by observing that when minimum wages are not set very high then they are less likely to have negative employment consequences. Card and Krueger (1995) re-evaluate the studies surveyed by Brown, Gilroy, and Kohen (1982) in this light by noting that, if one extends the sample into the 1980s and beyond, a very different picture emerges. This is because the real minimum wage was much lower in the 1980s, when the federal minimum wage was not changed at all over most of the Reagan years, and only started to significantly rise again through the 1990s. Card and Krueger (1995) report only a very modest (and statistically insignificant) impact of minimum wages on employment for data from 1954 to 1993 (see Table 6.5 in their book). Given the very small effects they uncover, one can question whether or not the early work really did reach a consensus.

[7] Teenage workers are studied on the grounds that far more of them are relatively low paid and thus their employment/unemployment chances are more likely to be affected by the minimum wage.

The second prong of the revisionist work very strongly reinforces the questioning of reaching a consensual view. It does so by means of adopting a different approach, in line with the theory on minimum wages, about how to evaluate empirically the impact of minimum wage floors. Rather than focusing on macroeconomic time series data, this work uses microeconomic data on individuals or firms and looks at how their behavior is affected by changes in minimum wages. The work tries to use changes in minimum wages as a means to identify employment effects in a quasi-experimental setting. By this I mean that the minimum wage is argued to affect some economics agents (the 'treatment' group) and not others (the 'control' group). Thus one can look at differences in employment rates between treatment and control groups before and after the minimum wage change to evaluate the impact of minimum wages on employment.

This approach has become increasingly popular, and it has been controversial. The most famous paper, by Card and Krueger (1994), looks at what happened to employment before and after a minimum wage hike in New Jersey at the same time as the minimum wage was not altered in an adjacent state, Pennsylvania.[8] In April 1992 the minimum wage in New Jersey was raised from the federal level of $4.25 per hour to $5.05 per hour, while in Pennsylvania the minimum stayed at the federal level. Card and Krueger surveyed fast food restaurants in both states before and after the minimum wage change (in February and November 1992). They found a substantial impact on wage structures: in both states before the New Jersey increase around one-third of restaurants had a starting wage at the $4.25 minimum; after the increase around 90 percent of New Jersey restaurants paid the new $5.05 minimum, while around 35 percent of Pennsylvania restaurants paid the federal minimum of $4.25.

This seems to present a very attractive conceptual means of evaluating the effect of minimum wages on employment since wage costs were significantly raised by the minimum wage increase in New Jersey relative to Pennsylvania. Moreover, the use of a before–after comparison seems to closely resemble the theoretical notion of asking: what happens when one raises a minimum wage? Card and Krueger look at employment effects of minimum wages using two treatment–control settings. In the former the treatment group are New Jersey restaurants and the control group are restaurants in Pennsylvania. In the latter they compare low-wage New Jersey restaurants to a control group of high-wage restaurants that were

[8] This state variation in minimum wages comes about because US states can raise their own minimum wages above the federal minimum.

unaffected by the minimum wage hike. Comparing employment changes in the pre-and post-minimum wage hike periods in the treatment versus control restaurants produced a very strong and robust, but very surprising, finding. There is no evidence of negative employment effects and, if anything, employment actually rose in the treatment group.

This study, and a number of others that adopted a more microapproach (e.g. Card 1992; Machin and Manning 1994) and failed to find negative employment effects, have effectively changed the debate on minimum wages and their economic impact. The question used to be 'how negative is the negative effect?', while it now has become 'is there any employment effect at all?'. This is a good example of how testing first order principles in labor economics has evolved.

One particularly clear example of this is that there is now a thriving body of theoretical work which looks at mechanisms that can explain the lack of employment effects of minimum wages. This ranges from the empirical observation that remains in the competitive framework which states that labor demand is not very sensitive to wage changes (i.e. labor demand is relatively inelastic) through to work where employment is set on the supply side in noncompetitive models where employers have monopsony power, usually induced by labor market frictions, so they can pay wages below marginal products (see Manning 2004 for a very in-depth discussion of monopsony). This said, direct evidence on monopsony existing in modern labor markets remains sparse and is sometimes appealed to on the grounds that other approaches, like the orthodox competitive model, are rejected by the data. Of course, things can become much more complex when one resorts to another explanation simply because a given approach can be rejected, and here particular authors (like Edwards and Gilman 1999 or Gilman et al. 2002) have stressed that it may be desirable to look wider and to study factors like the political aspects of labor markets and wage-setting processes. To do so, for instance by incorporating the notion that wages can act as tools of motivation and control, one loses some of the generality of the economic approach and the move towards more 'realism' evidently makes it harder to try and test between different modeling approaches.

What is more, these findings have fed very strongly into the public policy debate. The UK introduced a National Minimum Wage for the first time in April 1999. These studies, and others, were heavily relied on and influential in discussions about what level at which one should introduce the minimum wage. Rather than thinking minimum wages were bad for jobs, the debate was pitched more around the notion that a minimum wage that was not set too high need not exert a damaging effect on jobs. The empirical evidence testing the basic theory clearly seemed to back this up. Moreover, recent evaluations of the UK minimum wage introduction seems to support this logic as there seems to be little evidence of detrimental employment consequences associated with the introduction (Machin et al. 2003; Stewart 2004).

Human Capital

One very successful area of labor economics has been the development of the human capital approach to education. A particular aspect of interest is its ability to offer a framework that allows one to think about who receives more education, its implications for the quality of the labor force, and for policy to think about trying to design education policies.

The basic premise, initially built up in various pieces of work by Becker (1960, 1962, 1975), Mincer (1958), and Schultz (1961, 1963), is that individuals make a decision about whether to invest in education. While controversial at the time (because of viewing people as capital, like machines) this has now become a standard part of the economics tool kit. The approach states that, when deciding whether to invest in education (or training), individuals carry out a cost–benefit calculation to determine whether there is a positive rate of return to the investment. The benefits come from expected higher labor market earnings; the costs include actual costs of education (like fees) and the opportunity cost of not working while in the education system.

This is an attractive approach, with significant empirical content, for several reasons.[9] First, the concept of a rate of return to education is now widely acknowledged as a highly valuable device and is used not only by economists, but by policymakers, researchers in other disciplines, and by practitioners. Second, the human capital approach also provided a theoretical rationale for the earnings function—now one of the basic tools of economists—by giving a firm theoretical foundation as to why earnings and schooling are linked and by what mechanisms. Third, one can think of trying to define optimal schooling and education levels for economies within the human capital framework. It is evident that this has been widely used by governments across the world in trying to design human capital policies within their education systems.

[9] The book by Polachek and Siebert (1993) provides an excellent overview of many of these issues.

The earnings function is of considerable note for practical economists. There have been literally thousands of estimates of the relation between earnings and education that have been set within this framework. Most household level surveys contain data on earnings and education and many have been used to estimate the rate of return to education.[10] The earnings function has been augmented to be used to estimate many different forms of wage differentials, between different types of individuals: for example, union/nonunion wage differentials, male/female wage differentials, black/white wage differentials and so on. In work that has looked at changes in labor market inequality over time it has been very clearly acknowledged that the rise in wage inequality has come about because wage differentials between different groups of workers have altered and because inequality within those groups has changed. The earnings function clearly shows wage gaps between workers with different education levels and so has been heavily utilized in this literature. This was referred to above in some of the evidence on changing wage structures in Section 2 and an example of the way that educational wage differentials have moved over time is given for the USA and UK in the final column of Table 7.1.

The substantive contribution of the human capital work has been to generate a widespread recognition that the concept of a rate of return to education is a valuable one. In other research areas it was evident that people with higher education levels get paid more, but the reasons why were postulated through a much less structured route than through the human capital approach. It is not surprising therefore that the human capital approach is now firmly in the mainstream, not only in economics, but also among scholars in the education field and for policymakers trying to design efficient, and egalitarian, education systems the world over.

Summary

In this section I have described what I view to be two highly successful research areas in the economic analysis of labor markets. But there are many more. For example, the recent *Handbook of Labor Economics* contains chapters on a very long list of subjects in labor economics.[11] In all of these

[10] There are huge numbers of references here. Some of the useful ones are the cross-country comparisons of Psachoropoulos (1985), Psachoropoulos and Hinchcliffe (1973), and the survey, with a substantive methodological content on how to best estimate the rate of return to education, by Card (1999).

[11] The full list is as follows: Empirical Strategies in Labor Economics; Econometric Methods for Labor Market Analysis; Institutions and Laws in the Labor Market; Changes in the Wage

areas, the economic approach to developing a simple, yet highly predictive framework, has made substantial contributions to research. In many cases there is a mass of empirical work. Many of the key findings have in the past played a key role in defining the agenda in policy circles, and the economic approach is continuing to play a significant role informing policy in many countries of the world. Yet there is still a lot to do. New areas building upon what we already know are emerging. Two good examples that have drawn on the work by labor economists more recently are in the areas of experimental and behavioral economics. These retain some of the key premises and building blocks of orthodox economic theory, but try to push the boundaries further as a means to continue to generate firmer, more robust results in the economic analysis of labor markets.

4. Conclusions

This chapter has set out to show the usefulness of an orthodox economic approach for understanding labor markets and to reveal how this approach can, when set in the right context, be a very good one for looking at contemporary labor markets. It is undeniable that the economic approach has had a significant impact, not only on economists, but much more widely. As a research field, labor economics has had a particularly pronounced impact, most probably because it was the first area in economics to carry out large scale empirical analyses of real world phenomena of interest. That said, there are limitations and clearly some approaches work much better and have much more relevance in some contexts than others.

Structure and Earnings Inequality; Labor Supply; Economic Analysis of Immigration; Intergenerational Mobility in the Labor Market; The Causal Effect of Education on Earnings; The Economics and Econometrics of Active Labor Market Programs; Minimum Wages, Employment and the Distribution of Income; Firm Size and Wages; The Labor Market Implications of International Trade; Individual Employment Contracts; Careers in Organizations; Mobility and Stability: Dynamics of Job Change in Labor Markets; Executive Compensation; Models of Search in the Labor Market; The Analysis of Labor Markets Using Matched Employer-Employee Data; Gross Job Flows; Labor Markets in the Transitional Central and European Countries; Labor Markets in Developing Countries; Labor Markets and Economic Growth; Microeconomic Perspectives on Aggregate Labor Markets; Labor Market Institutions and Economic Performance; Causes and Consequences of Long-Term Unemployment in Europe; Race and Gender in the Labor Market; Economic Analysis of Retirement; Health, Health Insurance and the Labor Market; Transfer Progams Targeted on People With Disabilities; Economics of Crime; Public Sector Labor Markets.

It is also evident that the orthodox economic approach has diversified in many directions, leading to many areas of research, some of which stay close and others which move far away from the basic competitive approach. This is not a recent phenomenon in the labor economics field. For example, there have always been researchers who have tried to weave institutional and historical features into their analysis (see Jacoby's 1990 discussion of 'institutional labor economics'). The methodological approaches embodied in the mainstream economic approach do have some difficulties in fully pursuing this route, as Jacoby's discussion makes very clear. In particular, he emphasizes that the deductivist nature of the orthodox economic approach can limit its ability to study accurately some real world phenomena. The same limiting aspect is true of the skepticism that some economists have of other social science disciplines. Fleetwood (1999) goes further and states that economists would not wish to move away from the notion that predictive power matters for fear of what he refers to as 'a state of theoretical or analytical impotence'.

But it should be acknowledged that these limitations, and taking on board the critical comments made of the orthodox approach, have also acted as a strength to stimulate work in some areas. Labor economics is full of examples that show it to be a developing paradigm that is very much evolving through time. Acknowledgment of the shortcomings of the orthodox approach to modeling the labor market has caused economists to move into areas of study that were not traditionally thought to be part of the economic field of research. Thus interdisciplinary contributions in the areas of economic sociology have emerged (see Chapter 9 by Beamish and Biggart). Economists have generalized noncompetitive labor market models to study aspects of fairness in the workplace, or taken gift exchange models from sociology and applied them to pay determination within firms (see Akerlof 1982). Some of the more recent developments in economic theory, especially in game theory, are also moving in this direction, through interactions with psychologists and doing experimental work on economic behavior (see *inter alia* Fehr and Schmidt 2002).

The strength of the economic approach to analyzing labor markets lies in the fact that the modeling approaches it utilizes are able to generate a range of implications that can be tested with data and hypotheses can be refuted if they do not yield precise enough findings in empirical analysis. In this context, the economic approach is one that has important implications for studying social phenomena in workplaces, firms, and industries. Over the years, there have been many highly successful studies in the economic field that have advanced our knowledge, and informed the policy process. It is hoped that the economic approach to studying labor markets will continue not to stand still and will constructively evolve in the future, in conjunction with other disciplines, to further develop and advance our understanding of the way in which the key actors in the labor market behave.

References

Abowd, J. and Lemieux, T. (1993). 'The Effects of Product Market Competition on Collective Bargaining Agreements: The Case of Foreign Competition in Canada', *Quarterly Journal of Economics*, 108: 983–1014.

Akerlof, G. (1982). 'Labor Contracts as Partial Gift Exchange', *Quarterly Journal of Economics*, 97: 543–69.

—— and Yellen, J. (1990). 'The Fair Wage-Effort Hypothesis and Unemployment', *Quarterly Journal of Economics*, 105: 255–83.

Ashenfelter, O. and Layard, R. (1986). *Handbook of Labor Economics*, vols 1 and 2. Amsterdam: North-Holland.

—— and Card, D. (1999). *Handbook of Labor Economics*, vols 3A, 3B, and 3C. Amsterdam: North-Holland.

Becker, G. (1960). 'Underinvestment in Education', *American Economic Review*, 50: 346–54.

—— (1962). 'Investment in Human Capital: A Theoretical Analysis', *Journal of Political Economy*, 70: 9–49.

—— (1975). *Human Capital: A Theoretical and Empirical Analysis, With Special Reference to Education*. New York: Columbia University Press.

—— and Stigler, G. (1974). 'Law Enforcement, Malfeasance and the Compensation of Enforcers', *Journal of Legal Studies*, 3: 1–18.

Berman, E., Bound, J., and Griliches, Z. (1994). 'Changes in the Demand for Skilled Labor within U.S. Manufacturing Industries: Evidence from the Annual Survey of Manufacturing', *Quarterly Journal of Economics*, 109: 367–98.

—— , ——, and Machin, S. (1998). 'Implications of Skill-Biased Technological Change: International Evidence', *Quarterly Journal of Economics*, 113: 1245–80.

Booth, A. (1995). *The Economics of the Trade Union*. Cambridge: Cambridge University Press.

Borjas, G. (1996). *Labor Economics*. New York: McGraw-Hill.

Brown, C. (1999). 'Minimum Wages, Employment, and the Distribution of Income', in O. Ashenfelter and D. Card (eds.), *Handbook of Labor Economics*, vol 3B. Amsterdam: North-Holland.

—— , Gilroy, C., and Kohen, A. (1982). 'The Effect of the Minimum Wage on Employment and Unemployment', *Journal of Economic Literature*, 20: 487–528.

Brown, J. and Ashenfelter, O. (1986). 'Testing the Efficiency of Employment Contracts', *Journal of Political Economy*, 94: S40–S87.

Card, D. (1992). 'Do Minimum Wages Reduce Employment? A Case Study of California, 1987–89', *Industrial and Labor Relations Review*, 46: 38–54.

—— (1999). 'The Causal Effect of Education on Earnings', in O. Ashenfelter and D. Card, *Handbook of Labor Economics*, vol 3A. Amsterdam: Elsevier–North-Holland.

—— and Krueger, A. (1994). 'Minimum Wages and Employment: A Case Study of the Fast Food Industry in New Jersey and Pennsylvania', *American Economic Review*, 84: 772–93.

—— and —— (1995). *Myth and Measurment: The New Economics of the Minimum Wage*. Princeton, NJ: Princeton University Press.

Edwards, P. and Gilman, M. (1999). 'Pay Equity and the National Minimum Wage: What Can Theories Tell Us?', *Human Resource Management Journal*, 9: 20–38.

Fehr, E. and Schmidt, K. (2002). 'Theories of Fairness and Reciprocity', in D. Matthias, L. Hansen, and S. Turnovsky (eds.), *Advances in Economics and Econometrics – 8th World Congress, Econometric Society Monographs*. Cambridge: Cambridge University Press.

Fleetwood, S. (1999). 'The Inadequacy of Mainstream Theories of Trade Union Behaviour', *Labour*, 13: 445–80.

Freeman, R. (1993). 'How Much Has De-unionization Contributed to the Rise in Male Wage Inequality', in S. Danziger and P. Gottschalk (eds.), *Uneven Tides: Rising Inequality in America*. New York: Russell Sage Foundation.

Gilman, M., Edwards, P., Ram, M., and Arrowsmith, J. (2002). 'Pay Determination in Small Firms in the UK: The Case of the Response to the National Minimum Wage', *Industrial Relations Journal*, 33: 52–67.

Hamermesh, D. (1996). *Labor Demand*: Princeton, NJ: Princeton University Press.

Johnson, G. and Stafford, F. (1999). 'The Labor Market Implications of International Trade', in O. Ashenfelter and D. Card (eds.), *Handbook of Labor Economics*, vol 3B. Amsterdam: North-Holland.

Jacoby, S. (1990). 'New Institutionalism: What Can it learn from the Old?', *Industrial Relations*, 29: 316–40.

Katz, L. and Murphy, K. (1992). 'Changes in Relative Wages, 1963–87: Supply and Demand Factors', *Quarterly Journal of Economics*, 107: 35–78.

—— and Autor, D. (1999). 'Changes in the Wage Structure and Earnings Inequality', in O. Ashenfelter and D. Card (eds.), *Handbook of Labor Economics*, vol 3A. Amsterdam: North-Holland.

Layard, R., Nickell, S., and Jackman, R. (1991). *Unemployment*. Oxford: Oxford University Press.

Lazear, E. (2000). 'Economic Imperialism', *Quarterly Journal of Economics*, 115: 99–146.

—— and Moore, R. (1984). 'Incentives, Productivity and Labor Contracts', *Quarterly Journal of Economics*, 99: 275–96.

Lewis, H. G. (1986). *Union Relative Wage Effects: A Survey*. Chicago, IL: University of Chicago Press.

Lindbeck, A. and Snower, D. (1986). 'Wage Setting, Unemployment and Insider-Outsider Relations', *American Economic Review*, 76: 235–9.

McDonald, I. and Solow, R. (1981). 'Wage Bargaining and Employment', *American Economic Review*, 71: 896–908.

Machin, S. and Manning, A. (1994). 'Minimum Wages, Wage Dispersion and Employment: Evidence from the U.K. Wages Councils', *Industrial and Labor Relations Review*, 47: 319–29.

—— and Van Reenen, J. (1998). 'Technology and Changes in Skill Structure: Evidence from Seven OECD Countries', *Quarterly Journal of Economics*, 113: 1215–44.

—— , Manning, A., and Rahman, L. (2003). 'Where the Minimum Wage Bites Hard: The Introduction of the UK National Minimum Wage to a Low Wage Sector', *Journal of the European Economic Association*, 1: 154–80.

MaCurdy, T. and Pencavel, J. (1986). 'Testing Between Competing Models of Wage and Employment Determination in Unionized Markets', *Journal of Political Economy*, 94: S3–S39.

Malcomson, J. (1999). 'Individual Employment Contracts', in O. Ashenfelter and D. Card (eds.), *Handbook of Labor Economics*, vol 3B. Amsterdam: North-Holland.

Manning, A. (2004). *Monopsony in Motion: Imperfect Competition in Labour Markets*. Princeton, NJ: Princeton University Press.

Mincer, J. (1958). 'Investment in Human Capital and Personal Distribution of Income', *Journal of Political Economy*, 66: 281–302.

Mortensen, D. and Pissarides, C. (1999). 'New Developments in Models of Search in the Labor Market', in O. Ashenfelter and D. Card (eds.), *Handbook of Labor Economics*, vol 3B. Amsterdam: North-Holland.

Nickell, S. and Andrews, M. (1983). 'Unions, Real Wages and Employment in the United Kingdom, 1951–79', *Oxford Economic Papers*, 35: 183–206.

Oswald, A. (1985). 'The Economic Theory of Trade Unions: An Introductory Survey', *Scandinavian Journal of Economics*, 87: S.160–193.

Pissarides, C. (1990). *Equilibrium Unemployment Theory*. Cambridge, MA: MIT Press.

Polachek, S. and Siebert, S. (1993). *The Economics of Earnings*. Cambridge: Cambridge University Press.

Psacharopoulos, G. (1985). 'Returns to Education: A Further International Update and Implications', *Journal of Human Resources*, 20: 583–604.

—— and Hinchcliffe, K. (1973). *Returns to Education: An International Comparison*. Elsevier Scientific.

Schultz, T. (1961). 'Investment in Human Capital', *American Economic Review*, 51: 110–17.

—— (1963). *The Economic Value of Education*. New York: Columbia University Press.

Shapiro, C. and Stiglitz, J. (1984). 'Equilibrium Unemployment as a Worker Discipline Device', *American Economic Review*, 74: 433–44.

Stewart, M. (2004). 'The Impact of the Introduction of the UK Minimum Wage on the Employment Probabilities of Low Wage Workers', *Journal of the European Economic Association*, 2: 67–97.

Stiglitz, J. (2000). 'The Contribution of the Economics of Information to Twentieth Century Economics', *Quarterly Journal of Economics*, 115: 1441–78.
Van Reenen, J. (1996). 'The Creation and Capture of Rents: Wages and Innovation in a Panel of UK Companies', *Quarterly Journal of Economics*, 111: 195–226.
Weiss, A. (1991). *Efficiency Wages: Models of Unemployment, Layoffs and Wage Dispersion*. Princeton, NJ: Princeton University Press.

8

Institutional Economics and the Analysis of Work

Geoffrey M. Hodgson

This essay considers the contribution of the 'old' institutional economics to the analysis of work, work organization, and the production process. By the 'old' institutional economics we refer to a tradition founded in the USA and inspired by Thorstein Veblen, John R. Commons, Wesley Mitchell, and many others. The first section below gives an overview of the nature and history of the 'old' institutionalism. The second section addresses more specifically its contribution to the analysis of work. The third and final section considers some of its weaknesses, but suggests an agenda for future theoretical and empirical enquiry, acknowledging the significant convergences between this tradition and modern 'evolutionary economics' as well as elements within the 'new' institutional economics.

1. The Origins and Nature of Institutional Economics

Institutional economics was one of the most important intellectual movements of the twentieth century. It flourished in the USA in the early decades of the twentieth century. A number of subdisciplines such as economics and law, labor economics, industrial economics, agricultural economics, and industrial relations were highly influenced by institutionalism in the interwar period. A broad and diverse current, it influenced leading social scientists in several disciplines. It also survives globally today and shows signs of revival. One reason for its resurgence is that the importance of institutions in understanding economic processes is becoming increasingly recognized. Accordingly, this tradition of thought has made, and can continue to make, an important contribution to the analysis of the world of production and work.

The 'old' institutional economics should be distinguished from the 'new institutional economics' of Williamson (1975), Posner (1973) and others, although there are now some significant points of convergence between elements of the 'old' and the 'new' traditions. In some respects the 'old' institutional economics is closer to the 'new institutionalism' in sociology (Powell and DiMaggio 1991) and to modern economic sociology (Smelser and Swedberg 1994), although any derivation from or connection with the original institutionalism in economics is rarely acknowledged.

The beginnings of institutional economics can in part be traced to the strong influence of the German historical school on US academia in the last part of the nineteenth century. The German historicists emphasized the historical specificity of economic institutions and the need for economic theory to be sensitive to specific institutional and cultural conditions (Hodgson 2001). The founders of the US Economic Association (AEA) in 1885, including Henry Carter Adams, John Bates Clark and Richard Ely, were strongly influenced by the German historical school and several of them visited Germany to study.

However, the economist who emerged as the leading mentor for US institutionalism was Veblen, whose most important works appeared in the period from 1898 to around the time of World War I. Trained in philosophy as well as economics, and strongly influenced by key figures such as Karl Marx and William James, Veblen (1899, 1914, 1919) imported the core evolutionary principles of Charles Darwin into economic theory, by suggesting that ideas, habits, customs, and institutions were subject to broadly conceived Darwinian principles of competition and selection. However, in contrast to some of his reductionist contemporaries, Veblen did not reduce such socioeconomic entities to biological terms. He argued instead that the core Darwinian principles of variation, inheritance, and selection provided the key to understanding evolutionary processes in society as well as in nature (Hodgson 2004).

For Veblen (1904, 1914), the pecuniary institutions and culture of modern industrial capitalism were at odds with the basic dispositions and instincts that were necessary for the survival of the human species, which had evolved over hundreds of thousands of years. Veblen argued that humans had an instinct to produce useful things for their own survival and this was contradicted by the modern cultural disposition for making money rather than goods. On the other hand, he argued that contact with the mechanized processes of industrial capitalism encouraged a rational and scientific attitude and undermined conservative conventions, including the rights of property. Hence, for his own reasons, he reached a conclusion similar to that found in Marx: capitalism is its own gravedigger. However, the details of Veblen's argument have remained problematic and controversial, both in general theoretical terms (Hodgson 2004), and in the application to the analysis of work (Hoxie 1917). Although many have found these Veblenian ideas attractive, over many years their explanatory promise has remained unfulfilled.

Arguably, the more valuable and enduring parts of Veblen's legacy lie elsewhere. Another prominent and highly relevant element in Veblen's thinking was his insistence that the most important contribution to economic development was neither physical labor nor material capital but knowledge itself. Furthermore, for Veblen (1919) this knowledge was of a collective character, residing in the interlocking habits of thought of a community. It could not readily be broken up into atomistic units, each an object of property with a price tag. Veblen not only provided thereby an acute criticism of the claims of the capitalists on a share of the national income, but also foreshadowed the modern emphasis on the central role of knowledge in economic innovation and growth.

For several reasons, including his relations with women, his unconventional approach to economics and his political radicalism, Veblen never achieved an academic position of high status. Nevertheless, his works became highly influential, he attracted a number of promising students and he became widely recognized as one of the most important economists of the early twentieth century.

Commons was another figure to attain prominence in this period. He was taught by Ely and became intimately aware of the historical school legacy. Commons was elected president of the AEA in 1917 and was one of the most influential economists of the twentieth century. However, Commons was not greatly influenced by Veblen, their personal contacts were infrequent and there are important differences of theoretical approach. For example, Commons rejected Veblen's Darwinian paradigm. In regard to other issues, there are only a few references to Veblen in Commons's works. For some years Commons made no claim to be part of the US institutionalist movement, and he did not embrace the term 'institutional economics' until 1931 (Rutherford 2000, 2001).

For much of his life, Commons and his collaborators (Commons 1909, 1924; Commons et al. 1910–11, 1918–35) were preoccupied with the empirical documentation and theoretical analysis of the legal and customary foundations of the US industrial and commercial system.

In practical terms, he helped to draft a whole series of bills on labor and industrial matters for the State of Wisconsin (Kaufman 1993, 1998, 2003). With his colleagues at the University of Wisconsin, he established the subdiscipline of industrial relations in US academia. As Kaufman (2003: 3) puts it:

> A near consensus exists that the intellectual and policy roots of US industrial relations... are contained in the writings of the early twentieth-century institutional economics of the Wisconsin School, led by John R. Commons.

Kaufman then goes on to examine these roots in detail.

Much of the strength of Commons's writing lies in its empirical richness, particularly in regard to legal and customary processes and precedents. However, with his book on the *Legal Foundations of Capitalism* in 1924, with his *Institutional Economics* of 1934, and with his posthumously published *The Economics of Collective Action* of 1950, Commons turned increasingly to the theoretical and philosophical foundations of institutional economics, and he thus should be credited for attempting the systematic synthesis and presentation of institutionalist ideas that none of his contemporaries had provided. However, he wrote during a period where the original Veblenian foundations of institutionalism, in pragmatist philosophy, Jamesian psychology, and Darwinian principles, were deeply fractured by attacks from positivists, behaviorists and others (Hodgson 2004). Furthermore, his attempts were marred by a lack of definitional and theoretical clarity and precision. For these reasons, many critics regard Commons's valiant attempt at a theoretical synthesis of institutionalist ideas as an idiosyncratic failure.

The third important figure in US institutionalism is Mitchell, who was a student and friend of Veblen. In the interwar period Mitchell became the most prestigious economist in America. From 1913 he was a professor of economics at Columbia University. He became president of the AEA in 1924. In 1920 he helped to set up the National Bureau for Economic Research (NBER), and subsequently was its director. Influenced in part by Veblen's earlier analysis on business cycles (1904), Mitchell and his NBER colleagues devoted much of their efforts to the statistical measurement and theoretical explanation of booms and slumps, and advised successive US governments on countercyclical and job-creating policies. A crucial element in the work of the NBER was its focus on aggregate flows of money as measures of systemic economic activity. This helped to establish modern macroeconomics and in particular influenced and inspired the macroeconomics of John Maynard Keynes.

In 1947 Mitchell was the first recipient AEA Francis A. Walker Medal, awarded every five years 'to the living US economist who in the judgment of the awarding body has during his career made the greatest contribution to economics'. The institutionalist Simon Kuznets, who was Mitchell's former colleague at the National Bureau of Economic Research, won the Nobel Prize in 1971.

Institutionalism was not merely a collection of individuals and ideas. It was a conscious theoretical and policy-oriented movement within US economics, which emerged with a proclaimed label after World War I. The term 'institutional economics' has been traced back to Robert Hoxie in 1916 and Walton Hamilton in 1918 (Rutherford 1997). Hoxie was a student of Veblen who died tragically in 1916. Hamilton was one of the organizers of an officially sponsored movement within the AEA to make its economics theoretically and practically relevant for the world emerging after the end of the war. One of the enduring by-products was the creation of an identity for institutional economics in the interwar period (Dorfman 1974; Barber 1988; Rutherford 2000).

Hamilton (1919) summarized the principles of what he called 'institutional economics' in an essay which may be regarded its original manifesto. In contrast to some modern misconceptions of the 'old' institutionalism as 'atheoretical' or even 'antitheory', Hamilton (1919: 309–11) argued that ' "institutional economics" is "economic theory" '. It 'alone meets the demand for a generalized description of the economic order. Its claim is to explain the nature and extent of order amid economic phenomena'. For Hamilton (1919: 317) the 'most important' omission of the preceding economics was its neglect of 'the influence exercised over conduct by the scheme of institutions under which one lives'. Hamilton saw institutional economics as filling this gap. The influence of institutions was not seen as merely constraining behavior. The idea that institutions form and change individuals—just as individuals form and change institutions—was seen as a central tenet of institutionalism. Hamilton's 'bare outline of the case for institutionalist theory' accepted that 'institutional theory is in process' and stressed the pressing task of relevant, theoretical development.

Hamilton was also responsible for an important account of the nature of institutions. Hamilton (1932: 84) decribed an institution as 'a way of thought or action of some prevalence and permanence, which is embedded in the habits of a group or the customs of a people. . . . Institutions fix the confines of and impose form upon the activities of human beings.' However, the direction of causality is not one-way.

Just as institutions affect individuals, individuals also affect institutions: 'Institutions and human actions, complements and antitheses, are forever remaking each other in the endless drama of the social process' (Hamilton 1932: 89).

Institutional economics, from Veblen to John Kenneth Galbraith (1958, 1969), has consistently emphasized the themes outlined by Hamilton. It has always striven for policy relevance. But, more fundamentally, it has also stressed the role of institutions in economic life, the qualitatively transformative nature of economic activity, and the way in which those institutional and structural changes both affect and reconstitute human purposes, preferences, psychology, and behavior.

Institutionalists do not have a very good record in defining and agreeing among themselves upon the essentials of their approach. I submit, however, that there is a core idea in institutionalism that above all others helps to define its identity. The idea that institutions can be reconstitutive of individuals is arguably the most fundamental characteristic of institutional economics. Obviously, institutions themselves differ, in time and in space. However, individuals themselves are also likely to be radically affected by these differences. Different institutions can act as more than constraints on behavior: they may actually lead to change in the character and beliefs of the individual. In this way, more dimensions of social power are acknowledged. To some degree, individual preferences or habits of thought can be reconstituted by institutional contexts.

As a result, much of the 'new' institutional economics, including that of Williamson (1975), does not go so far as the 'old' institutional economics in analyzing the reconstitution of individual preferences by institutional circumstances. This is because most 'new' institutionalists cling on to an irreducible notion of the rational individual that Veblen, Commons, Mitchell, Hamilton, and others were keen to replace or explain. Much of the 'new' institutionalism sees behavior as 'the result of conscious endeavor by individuals who knew thoroughly their own interests'. But this is Hamilton's own characterization (1919: 316–17) of the very type of economics that institutionalism sought to supersede. For Williamson, for example, the character and purposes of individuals do not change as they move from institution to institution, even from a caring family to a ruthless capitalist firm. Similarly, the 'new' institutionalist Schotter (1981) uses a theory of rational choice within a game-theoretic rubric. The focus is typically on the irreducible and unexplained rational individual. In contrast, 'old' institutional economists stress that institutions and culture can mold individual preferences or purposes. In so far as individuals are rational, the nature and canons of rationality are culturally transmitted, and developed by learning in an institutional context.

However, to presume that individuals are to some extent molded by circumstances is not necessarily to relapse into some version of 'methodological collectivism' where it is presumed that individual capabilities are entirely determined by structures, institutions, and culture. Such a viewpoint would be incapable of adequately explaining individual variation and creativity. On the other hand, if methodological individualism is defined as the view that social phenomena should be explained *entirely* in terms of individuals, then institutionalism is not in accord with this doctrine either. The writings of the founders of US institutional economics avoid the extremes of methodological individualism and methodological collectivism. The clearest statement along these lines, negotiating a position that is away from these two extremes, is in an essay by Veblen, originally published in 1909, and the relevant passage is worthy of inspection in full. Here we confine ourselves to a brief selection. Veblen (1919: 242) pointed out that the assumption of given individuals under given institutional conditions would lead to static outcomes 'since it makes abstraction from those elements that make for anything but a statical result.' Veblen (1919: 242–3) then made it clear that institutions serve not merely as constraints, but they also affect the very wants and preferences of individuals themselves:

> Not only is the individual's conduct hedged about and directed by his habitual relations to his fellows in the group, but these relations, being of an institutional character, vary as the institutional scene varies. The wants and desires, the end and the aim, the ways and the means, the amplitude and drift of the individual's conduct are functions of an institutional variable that is of a highly complex and wholly unstable character.

This statement amounts to a strong assertion of the reconstitutive power of institutions over individuals. Institutional changes affect individual 'wants and desires'. Preferences are endogenous, rather than exogenously given. Nevertheless, he acted immediately to forestall any misunderstanding that this strong downward causation amounted to a methodological collectivism. He did not believe that the social wholes entirely determine the individual parts. Veblen (1919: 243) made it absolutely clear that the individual was still causally effective, that institutions were a product of individuals in a group, and institutions could not exist without individuals:

> The growth and mutations of the institutional fabric are an outcome of the conduct of the individual members of the group, since it is out of the experience of the

> individuals, through the habituation of individuals, that institutions arise; and it is in this same experience that these institutions act to direct and define the aims and end of conduct. It is, of course, on individuals that the system of institutions imposes those conventional standards, ideals, and canons of conduct that make up the community's scheme of life. Scientific inquiry in this field therefore, must deal with individual conduct and must formulate its theoretical results in terms of individual conduct.

Although the above passage emphasizes the role of the individual, it does not amount to an assertion of methodological individualism. Instead, Veblen upheld that individuals could not be removed from the picture, and he placed the individual in its social context. Veblen (1919: 243) insisted that a complete and detailed causal explanation means an explanation of how the individual acquires relevant habits of thought and behavior. Veblen (1919: 243) then went on to criticize those mainstream economists who 'disregard or abstract from the causal sequence of propensity and habituation in economic life and exclude from theoretical inquiry all such interest in the facts of cultural growth'. By emphasizing 'cumulative causation' and 'continuity of cause and effect' Veblen broke from any idea that explanations could ultimately be reduced to one type of entity or level.

In sum, by rejecting both the individual and society as the ultimate unit of explanation, Veblen distanced himself from both methodological individualism and methodological collectivism. His solution was to adopt an evolutionary framework of explanation. More broadly, institutionalists such as Veblen, Commons, and Hamilton saw actors and institutions in an interactive, co-evolving process (Hodgson 2004).

Although he was very much concerned to develop institutional economics as an instrument for 'the problems of control', Hamilton did not define institutional economics in terms of any specific policy stance. In practice, institutionalism was adopted by policymakers from a variety of policy viewpoints, from socialism through social democracy to moderate conservatism. For Hamilton and the other founders of institutionalism, it represented a broad and inclusive theoretical approach, recognizing the importance of institutions and the way they affect individual purposes or preferences. Many leading institutionalists upheld that their approach was compatible with Marshallian price theory, but augmented the Marshallian legacy by bringing the fuller study of institutional, cultural, and technological change into the compass of economics. Economics was thus conceived as a broad subject, devoted to the study of real and evolving economic systems, and drawing ideas from other disciplines, rather than the narrower conception of the discipline as the 'science of choice' that prevails today.

In the interwar period, institutionalism permeated the teaching programs of many US universities. By 1931, more than six comprehensive texts treating economics from an institutionalist standpoint were available, along with several other institutionalist monographs and anthologies. These texts emphasized the economic importance of institutions, that institutions could be changed by policy interventions, that any prevailing institution is not necessarily optimal, that many institutions serve business or pecuniary interests, and that new institutions were required for 'social control' in their era.

However, the institutionalist movement ran into evident theoretical difficulties as early as the 1930s. First, because of the aforementioned shifts in philosophy and psychology, many institutionalists had abandoned the original Veblenian foundations by the time of Veblen's death in 1929. To some degree, institutional economics lost its theoretical bearings (Hodgson 2004). Second, although institutionalists were heavily involved in economic recovery programs after the Great Crash of 1929, to some extent they were blamed for their failure to bring the US economy out of the Great Depression. A younger generation of more technocratic economists—including Paul Samuelson—were attracted by new ideas in mathematical macroeconomics that were not seen as closely associated with institutionalism. Third, the militarization of academia due to World War II transformed economics, giving more precedence to mathematical modeling and optimization techniques (Bernstein 2001; Mirowski 2002).

In the first half of the twentieth century, some US institutionalist ideas spread to Europe, but only to a very limited degree. Strong institutionalist affinities are found among Europeans such as John Hobson, Gunnar Myrdal, and Karl Polanyi, but none of these founded a significant and enduring European institutionalist tradition. By the 1950s, US institutionalism was in steep decline, although its influence persisted in many areas of economics and in industrial relations (Kaufman 1993).

Although it dwindled in size and influence, the old institutionalist tradition nevertheless survived in the USA. The emergence of the 'new' institutional economics in the 1970s once again drew attention to the older tradition, by reviving interest in the nature and importance of institutions.

However, much of the 'new' institutional economics was originally concerned with the study 'of how individual economic agents pursuing their own selfish ends evolve institutions as a means to satisfy them'

(Schotter 1981: 5). In other words, the emphasis was on how the emergence of institutions can be explained, taking individuals and their (allegedly selfish) preferences as given. The aim was to explain how institutions evolved from individuals in an institution-free state of nature. A problem here, however, is that all human interaction involves elemental human institutions, such as language (Hodgson 1998).

By contrast, the 'old' institutionalists recognize that we are all born in a world of historically given institutions. However, institutions are not taken simply as given; Veblen (1899), Commons (1924, 1934) and others developed accounts of how institutions further evolved. Accordingly, the agenda is to understand both the historical evolution of institutions and how institutions may change further through human action and interaction.

In recent years, several 'new' institutional economists have rejected the idea of starting from an institution-free state of nature, and adopted a stance that in some respects is similar to that of the old institutionalism. As signaled by the more recent works of North (1990, 1994) and Aoki (2001), there is some degree of convergence between the two traditions. Nevertheless, Section 2 will concentrate on the contribution of the old institutional economics, and throughout this essay the use of the term 'institutionalism' refers principally to that older tradition.

2. The Contribution of Institutional Economics to the Analysis of Work

Any brief account of the contribution of institutional economics to any field must inevitably be selective, in terms of both the issues and the authors addressed. In regard to social theory, Veblen ranks as the most important of the early institutionalists (Hodgson 2004). Prominent institutionalist contributors to the analysis of work include Veblen, Commons, and Hobson. In contrast, Mitchell, Myrdal, and others devoted more of their efforts to macroeconomic issues. Others made a significant contribution, but not principally to this area. For example, Polanyi's achievement lies principally in economic history and economic anthropology. Galbraith's writing is wide-ranging, but only tangentially touches on social theory and the organization of work at the level of production.

We begin by comparing institutionalism in some respects with Marxism, particularly concerning the theory of motivation of the human agent and the role of habit and custom. The second subsection addresses the substantial contribution of institutionalism concerning the importance of social knowledge and immaterial assets. The third subsection discusses the varying attitudes of institutionalists to Taylorism and trade unions, and discusses some of the theoretical underpinnings of these varying stances.

Similarities and Differences between Institutionalism and Marxism

Like Marxism, the old institutional economics recognizes that the labor process is central to any viable economy, and sees the analysis of this process as vital to the understanding of any socioeconomic system. While neoclassical economics focuses largely on exchange and distribution, both Marxism and institutionalism also stress the central role of production, technological innovation, and the creation of new wealth.

However, one important difference with Marxism emerges at this point. Marxism suggests that the class situation of the workers can itself promote a true understanding of their interests and points to 'false consciousness' when that has not yet occurred. Veblen (1919) observed that the theory of human motivation in Marxism is largely one of rational appraisal of class interest, without any explanation of how the criteria and procedures of rationality themselves evolve. He emphasized that any rational calculation of interests does not itself explain how people acquire their beliefs and seek particular objectives. The class position of an agent—exploiter or exploited—does not itself lead to any particular view of reality or pattern of action. Marxism lacks an explanation of how structures or institutions affected individual purposes or inclinations. It can only point to 'true' interests, in the hope that reason will triumph some day, and they will be revealed to all.

In contrast, institutionalism points to the actual belief systems adopted by workers and others, and attempts to reveal their historical, cultural, and psychological origins. Veblen (1919: 441) argued that the reasoning of agents 'is as much, or more, an outcome of habit and native propensity as of calculated material interest'. This crucial emphasis on habit, as a key mechanism by which social conditions affect individual preferences and beliefs, distinguished Veblen from Marx. The influence of James on Veblen was paramount here. Similarly, Commons (1925) criticized Marxism for its neglect of the role of custom in economic and social life. Veblen convincingly argued that the mere class position of an individual as a wage laborer or a capitalist tells us very little about the specific conceptions or habits of thought, and thereby the likely actions, of the individuals involved. Individual interests, whatever they are, do not necessarily lead to accordant individual actions.

Veblen, Commons, and later institutionalists attempted to fill the explanatory void in Marxism by emphasizing the roles of custom and culture in shaping human behavior. Custom and culture reflect the accumulation of past experience, and the history of the nation, institution, or group. Their development is path dependent, and consequently differences between varieties of (say) capitalism can be traced to differences in their history. While institutionalism and Marxism both emphasize the weight of the past on human perceptions and decisions, institutionalism points more specifically to the role of culture in general and the psychological mechanism of habituation.

Along with a greater recognition of variations in type of capitalist institutions, institutionalists saw culture as a crucial element in the explanation of differences of behavior in different contexts. Accordingly, institutionalism is more sensitive to different varieties of capitalism, such as the differences evidenced today between (say) US, German, or Japanese capitalism, and the importance of differences of organization and subculture at the corporate level (Hodgson 1999).

Immaterial Assets and Social Knowledge

On another highly relevant theme, Veblen, Commons, Hobson, and other institutionalists stress intangible (or immaterial) as well as tangible (or material) assets in the production process. One of the most important of these intangible assets is knowledge. This refers both to knowledge within the production process and reputational knowledge of corporate capabilities such as 'industrial goodwill' (Commons 1919).

The relative importance of the physical means of production in production, compared with knowledge and other intangible assets, has typically been overstressed by mainstream and nonmainstream economists alike. Mainstream economists have long depicted the contribution of physical 'capital', alongside 'labor', to production, treating them both as the principal inputs into a mechanistic function. Although Marx differed in one respect, by seeing labor alone as the source of all 'value', he also stressed tangible rather than intangible assets. Further, in his theory of the falling rate of profit Marx argued that the overall value of the physical means of production would tend to increase, relative to the value of the living labor.

Against this overwhelming trend, Thorstein Veblen was one of the first to stress the relative importance of immaterial assets, including the 'knowledge and practice of ways and means' (Veblen 1919: 343). For Veblen (1919: 185–6) production relied on 'the accumulated, habitual knowledge of the ways and means involved . . . the outcome of long experience and experimentation'. The production and use of all material and immaterial assets depends on elusive, immaterial circumstances and combinations of skills, which are often difficult to identify and own. These capacities reside in the institutions and culture of the socioeconomic system, and they are built up over a long period of time. Accordingly, 'the capitalist employer is . . . not possessed of any appreciable fraction of the immaterial equipment' that is drawn upon every day in the process of production (Veblen 1919: 344).

Veblen invited his readers to consider what would be worse for a community: the loss of all the capital goods used in production, or the loss of all knowledge and skills. The latter sacrifice, he contended, would be much more destructive, because without the relevant knowledge it would not be possible to use much of the remaining equipment. On the other hand, while the loss of capital goods would be substantial and destructive, production could be built up to former levels in a much shorter period of time, using the knowledge retained. Veblen thus argued that 'the substantial core of capital is immaterial wealth, and that the material objects which are formally the subject of the capitalist's ownership are, by comparison, a transient and adventitious matter' (Veblen 1919: 200). As he rejoined in another work:

> This immaterial equipment is, far and away, the most important productive agency in the case; although, it is true, economists have not been in the habit of making much of it, since it is in the main not capable of being stated in terms of price, and so does not appear in the statistical schedules of accumulated wealth. (Veblen 1915: 272)

These important arguments were taken up and developed by Commons (1924: 235–82; 1934: 649–72), who similarly stressed intangible assets. The British institutional economist Hobson (1936: 67) made another related contribution:

> The productivity of workers on the soil or in the factory depends for its amount and quality not entirely and not chiefly upon their working energy, but upon economic conditions under which they work that lie outside their personal control. First and foremost among these conditions is the state of the industrial arts, a rich social inheritance of long accumulation, which is the basis of all skilled workmanship. No living worker or group of workers can properly lay claim to this accumulated knowledge as his private possession, though he is entitled to utilize it in order to increase his productivity.

This expresses the key point that knowledge is a social as well as an individual phenomenon. By contrast, mainstream explanations of economic growth stress changes in owned factor inputs, and sometimes also technological changes driven by research and development. Emphasis on such tangible inputs and measures has often obscured the importance of learning, and the accumulation of social knowledge.

Veblen's insights on the role of knowledge have lost nothing of their significance. Economies such as Germany and Japan lost much of their capital equipment during World War II. But they retained an educated workforce and educational and other institutions that could replicate and enhance technical knowledge. Despite the wartime loss of much of their material capital, by the 1960s in some industries they outperformed the USA. There is evidence concerning different technologies, from light bulb manufacture to nuclear weapons, that mere machines and blueprints are not enough. If tacit knowledge around these productive activities fails to be passed on, or is allowed to decay, then the technology becomes inoperative (Polanyi 1958; MacKenzie 1996).

For Veblen and other institutionalists, institutions were repositories of knowledge. Social groups and institutions carry accumulated knowledge and experiences from the past. Accordingly, Veblen argued that the social complex of interacting individual habits constituted a social stock of largely intangible knowledge that could not be associated with individuals severally. As Veblen (1898: 353–4) put it:

> Production takes place only in society—only through the co-operation of an industrial community. This industrial community... always comprises a group, large enough to contain and transmit the traditions, tools, technical knowledge, and usages without which there can be no industrial organization and no economic relation of individuals to one another or to their environment. The isolated individual is not a productive agent. What he can do at best is to live from season to season, as the non-gregarious animals do. There can be no production without technical knowledge; hence no accumulation and no wealth to be owned, in severalty or otherwise. And there is no technical knowledge apart from an industrial community.

Many economists uphold that production is entirely a result of owned factors of production—such as land, capital, and labor—whose owners can be remunerated accordingly. Veblen developed an enduringly relevant critique of this mainstream notion. Veblen (1921: 28) argued that production depended on a 'joint stock of knowledge derived from past experience' that itself could not become an individually owned commodity, because it involved the practices of the whole industrial community. Veblen (1898: 354) continued:

Since there is no individual production and no individual productivity, the natural-rights preconception that ownership rests on the individually productive labor of the owner reduces itself to absurdity, even under the logic of its own assumptions.

As noted earlier, this led to a devastating critique of the concept of capital in economic theory. For Veblen (1919), instead of 'capital' and 'labor' as 'factors of production', the key to understanding industrial productivity was the repository of knowledge in society at large. Veblen (1919: 348) argued that learning and experience are accumulated within a community:

These immaterial industrial expedients are necessarily a product of the community, the immaterial residue of the community's experience, past and present; which has no existence apart from the community's life, and can be transmitted only in the keeping of the community at large.

Veblen (1914: 103) repeated this point, again and again, here referring to technological knowledge and its storage in the social group:

Technological knowledge is of the nature of a common stock, held and carried forward by the community, which is in this relation to be conceived as a going concern. The state of the industrial arts is a fact of group life, not of individual or private initiative or innovation. It is an affair of the collectivity, not a creative achievement of individuals working self-sufficiently in severalty or in isolation.

Nevertheless, he made it clear that the collective domain of knowledge devalues neither the role of the individual, nor the fact that knowledge is always held by individuals and is a matter of individual experience. As Veblen (1919: 328) put it:

The complement of technological knowledge so held, used, and transmitted in the life of the community is, of course, made up out of the experience of individuals. Experience, experimentation, habit, knowledge, initiative, are phenomena of individual life, and it is necessarily from this source that the community's common stock is all derived. The possibility of growth lies in the feasibility of accumulating knowledge gained by individual experience and initiative, and therefore it lies in the feasibility of one individual's learning from the experience of another.

The individual and the social aspects of knowledge are connected, because the social environment and its 'common stock' of experience provide the means and stimulus to individual learning. The social environment is the result of individual interactions, but without this social environment the individual would be stultified. Learning is thus potentially a process of positive feedback between individual and society. The above quotations make it clear that Veblen saw the social domain as the site of a potential storehouse of knowledge. He took the argument one significant step further when he wrote:

> Any community may be viewed as an industrial or economic mechanism, the structure of which is made up of what is called its economic institutions. These institutions are habitual methods of carrying on the life process of the community in material contact with the material environment in which it lives. When given methods of unfolding human activity in this given environment have been elaborated in this way, the life of the community will express itself with some facility in these habitual directions. The community will make use of the forces of the environment for the purposes of its life according to methods learned in the past and embodied in those institutions. (Veblen 1899: 193–4)

This brought his concept of a social institution into the picture. Veblen stated here that institutions are social structures, involving individual habits and engaged with a material environment. He wrote of members of a community making use of their social and material environment for their purposes, according to methods learned in the past and embodied in their social institutions. The latter quotation is one of his clearest statements that institutions function as repositories of social knowledge.

He also discussed some of the mechanisms and means by which this knowledge is stored. Veblen (1919: 10) wrote of 'habits of thought that rule in the working-out of a system of knowledge' being 'fostered by... the institutional structure under which the community lives'. Veblen not only identified an environment of stored knowledge that is conducive to learning but also saw it as structured and made up of institutions. These institutions are the expression and outcome of the interaction of habituated individual behaviors, but cannot be reduced to the behaviors of individuals alone.

Commons (1934) attempted to develop this interactive aspect further, in his theory of transactions. He contrasted the 'bargaining transactions' of contract and exchange, 'the commands and obedience of managerial transactions', and the 'rationing transactions' carried out through the taxation and expenditure of the state. Commons emphasized that all such transactions involved social interaction and negotiation, with regard to future states of affairs.

However, the institutionalist emphasis on social interaction, social structure, and the social aspects of knowledge, became less popular in economics as the influence of institutionalism declined after World War II. More individualist social scientists would always be wary of terms like 'social memory' and the notion that knowledge could be associated with routines, customs, organizations, and institutions, as well as with individuals. After these early institutionalist appearances, similar conceptions did not begin to become popular again until the 1980s, when in economics Nelson and Winter (1982) described routines as 'organizational memory' and sociologists such as Levitt and March (1988) rehabilitated the concept of 'organizational learning'. But none of these key works from the 1980s refers to Veblen.

Attitudes to Taylorism and Trade Unions

Frederick Winslow Taylor published his *Scientific Management* in 1911. Taylor proposed the detailed empirical analysis of the work process, to gauge the time taken in each operation and to design an appropriate system of incentives to reach production quotas. Contrary to a widespread modern depiction, Taylor was a progressive who believed in higher pay for workers, improved working conditions, and a reduction in working hours. In addition, the Taylorist movement was not generally antiunion. Again contrary to some recent accounts, it had neither the intention, nor achieved the actual outcome, of general workforce deskilling. For many thinkers at the time, Taylorism was a modern, technocratic, empirically grounded, and 'scientific' solution to economic challenges (Tichi 1987; Wrege and Greenwood 1991; Nyland 1996; Guillén 1997; Bruce and Nyland 2001).

Like many of his radical contemporaries, Veblen welcomed Taylorism because he thought that it would help to plan and rationalize production, raise productivity, increase output, and enhance the material conditions of the working classes. Veblen (1904: 313) did not believe that the machine process would lead to deskilling or 'a deterioration or numbing of... intelligence'. He saw this as 'too sweeping a characterization of the change brought on by habituation to machine work'.

But other institutionalists perceived problems in Taylorism and took a more critical view. With the benefit of hindsight and more recent research, we know that Taylorism's overly detailed and mechanical specification of the work process can inhibit workforce motivation and creativity (Vroom and Deci 1970). Hobson noted this possible outcome as early as 1914. In a particularly astute and prescient critique of Taylorism, Hobson (1914:

219–20) noted that even routine work 'still contains a margin for the display of skill, initiative and judgement'. He further argued:

> Indeed, were the full rigour of *Scientific Management* to be applied throughout the staple industries, not only would the human costs of labour appear to be enhanced, but progress in the industrial arts itself would probably be damaged.... The large assistance given to technical invention by the observation and experiments of intelligent workmen, the constant flow of suggestion for detailed improvements, would cease. The elements of creative work still surviving in most routine labour would disappear.

Hobson recognized some matters of motivation and innovation that were neglected in Veblen's account of work and the machine process. Hobson emphasized the zone of discretion and decision-making that is involved in the exercise of all practical skills. He criticized the attempt in Taylorism to separate (managerial) conception entirely from (workforce) execution, on the grounds that if this zone of discretion were undermined, then productivity and creativity would diminish. Hobson suggested that it was neither desirable nor possible for managers to gather together all knowledge relating to the work process, as Taylor had proposed.

This analytical difference within institutionalism, between Veblen and Hobson, hinges in part on the degree to which it is assumed that productive knowledge can be centralized and rationally appraised. Unlike Veblen, Hobson was sceptical of this possibility and aware of its practical limits. Clearly, this dispute carries implications for the possibility or otherwise of a system of comprehensive socialist planning, where all relevant knowledge is gathered together by the (democratic or undemocratic) planning authorities, to form the basis of all planning decisions. Hobson's argument suggests that the scope of such comprehensive planning is limited, by pointing to the existence and importance of localized knowledge and skills, which cannot be fully appraised by any (corporate or other) planning authority.

Symptomatically, other than vague allusions to an undetailed anarcho-syndicalism or a 'Soviet of engineers', Veblen was largely silent on these key questions of economic organization and coordination, relating to the feasibility or otherwise of comprehensive socialist planning. Veblen (1921: 144) wrote minimally of an 'industrial directorate' of experts, 'working in due consultation with a sufficient ramification of sub-centers and local councils' in the apparent belief that obtainable and centralized knowledge and expertise were sufficient to deal with all the problems of conflicting claims and economic allocation in a modern complex economy. Of a possible system to replace capitalism, Veblen provides no more than the haziest outline (Hodder 1956; Rutherford 1992).

The dispute within institutionalism over Taylorism involved other leading figures. Hoxie was asked by Commons in 1914 to write a scientific report for the US Federal Industrial Relations Commission on the merits and demerits of Taylorist 'scientific management'. Taylor believed that workers and trade unions should participate in the detailed study of working time. However, Commons was strongly against any direct form of worker or trade union participation in management on the shop floor. Instead he favored a system of consultation between employers and trade union officials at a representative level (Kaufman 2003). For this reason, and in contrast to Veblen, Commons opposed key aspects of Taylorism. Indebted to Commons, Hoxie felt obliged to slant his report in his direction. Eventually, Commons persuaded a reluctant and dissatisfied Hoxie to publish his draft report. The published report was an equivocal and unconvincing piece of work, in which the arguments in favor of the Taylorist case were inadequately represented (Hoxie 1915). It received a critical review in the prestigious *American Economic Review.* Distraught by his failure, and suffering from intellectual disillusionment, Hoxie cut his own throat from ear to ear (Fishman 1958; McNulty 1973; Nyland 1996; Rutherford 1998).

In the posthumously published *Trade Unionism in the United States,* Hoxie had attempted to test Veblen's argument that engagement with the modern machine process would help to inculcate rational and nontraditional habits of thought. Hoxie (1917) noted that Veblen's argument would imply that trade unionists, being close to the machine process, would be less inclined to accept the 'natural-rights ground of property' than their employers. However, in his studies of US trade unions, Hoxie found that this was not strictly the case. A prominent motive among trade unionists was to secure the maximum possible pecuniary return for their toil. Trade unions entered into the pecuniary world of business and bargained over matters of money. Workers were as much concerned with remuneration as ideas of physical causation. Rutherford (1998: 475) argued that in the face of this critique Veblen (1921) himself modified his views, by placing more emphasis on educated engineers rather than machine workers as possible agents of social change.

The aforementioned differences of opinion between Veblen, Commons, Hoxie, and Hobson, including on matters relating to the organization of work, show that US institutionalism failed to establish a consensus on such key issues. Despite the prescient contribution of Veblen and others on the importance and centrality of knowledge, these earlier problems and disagreements betrayed some basic weaknesses in institutionalism. These will be outlined in the next section.

3. Weaknesses, Omissions, and Potential Revival

Institutional economics is sometimes criticized for its lack of 'theory'. Those that make this charge often identify 'theory' with mathematical models. The bulk of theoretical work in institutional economics is conceptual rather than theoretical, but institutionalists have occasionally made use of mathematics or computer simulations. Hence the charge that institutionalism is 'atheoretical' or 'antitheory' betrays some ignorance of the history of institutional economics (Rutherford 2001; Hodgson 2004).

Another false charge against institutionalism is that it neglects individual agency and falls foul of 'methodological collectivism'. Although some derivative streams of institutionalism were defective in this regard, this charge can be rebutted readily through inspection of the works of founding institutionalists, including Veblen, Commons, and Mitchell. Implicitly rebutting any 'methodological collectivism', Veblen (1919: 243) wrote: 'The growth and mutations of the institutional fabric are an outcome of the conduct of the individual members of the group'.

But this does not mean that institutionalism is immune from criticism. Consider the following test or criterion. When we examine different schools of social thought, we can often point to key, systematic texts that define the approach. Marxists can point to *Capital*, neoclassical economists to Alfred Marshall's *Principles* or Léon Walras's *Elements*, Keynesians to the *General Theory*, and so on. No equivalent and adequate text exists for institutionalists. This intellectual tradition has failed to provide a systematic statement of its approach. In part, this failure is due to the difficulties encountered by institutionalism when the interwar current of academic opinion moved against its original Veblenian foundations in pragmatist philosophy and Jamesian psychology. But it is a serious failure nevertheless.

While Veblen made a brilliant contribution to the understanding of human motivation in its cultural and institutional context, he provided no systematic analysis of one of the central questions of economics. He did not supply sufficient analytical tools in order to understand how past or present systems or organization of production and allocation actually function. Consequently, he provided little guidance on what types of socioeconomic systems were feasible. Key derivative questions, such as the role of markets and the organization of work and incentive structures, were largely ignored.

In contrast, both mainstream economists and new institutional economists (e.g. Williamson 1975) have put great stress on pecuniary incentives and self-interested motivation in the context of all economic activity. Sometimes this emphasis goes too far, by neglecting the role of nonpecuniary incentives, the social and cultural conditioning of self-interest, and the extent of solidaristic or altruistic behavior, at work and elsewhere (Jacoby 1990). There is much empirical evidence of the importance of such matters (e.g. Brown 1954). Nevertheless, the mainstream and new institutionalist traditions have at least attempted to deal with these central questions of incentive structure and motivation, even if the answers are sometimes limited or unsatisfactory.

Consequently, we are faced with an unsatisfactory choice between, on the one hand, the old institutionalist writings that stress the social formation of incentives and preferences, but underestimate the role of pecuniary and other similar incentives, and, on the other hand, mainstream and new institutional economists who overemphasize pecuniary and other matters of self-interest, while neglecting the way in which preferences and motivations can be molded by culture and institutions.

In recent years, however, there have been the beginnings of a conversation between the two institutionalist traditions. For example, the works of North (1990, 1994) pay considerable attention to the way in which perceptions and motives are shaped by culture and ideology, while at the same time seeking an understanding of what structures provide superior incentives and outcomes.

Furthermore, a considerable degree of similarity has been acknowledged between the old institutional economics and the more recent tradition of 'evolutionary economics' inspired in particular by Nelson and Winter (1982). Like the old institutionalists, Nelson and Winter emphasize that institutions and routines act as repositories of knowledge. Much like Veblen, they also attempt to analyze the evolution of institutions and routines as a broadly Darwinian process of variation and selective retention.

These and other significant convergences, including much writing in modern economic sociology (see Chapter 9), provide the occasion for a revival of the old institutionalism, hopefully on a more complete and systematic basis. Furthermore, the intellectual currents of pragmatist philosophy and Jamesian psychology, which formed much of the foundation of Veblen's thought, are themselves enjoying a significant revival (Plotkin 1994; Hands 2001; Hodgson 2004). The intellectual conditions are established for a revived and modernized institutionalist approach, drawing on the insights of the old institutionalists and others.

The grounds for this presumption are not simply the convenient juncture of contemporary intellectual movements. At the ontological level, institutionalism is based on the insight that social reality is structured by systems of social rules, formed as institutions. The relevance of institutions in any adequate analysis of such matters as economic development, the functioning of markets, and the organization of work is now widely acknowledged, including within sociology and mainstream economics. Institutions are the stuff of social life. Although the contribution of the old institutional economics is in several respects incomplete, there are strong grounds to re-examine its deeper and more enduring insights. Its interdisciplinary stance makes it attractive to social scientists from other disciplines. There has been some revival of institutional economics in recent years, notably in Europe as well as elsewhere, and the expectation is that this will continue.

References

Aoki, M. (2001). *Toward a Comparative Institutional Analysis*. Cambridge, MA: MIT Press.

Barber, W. J. (1988). *From New Era to New Deal: Herbert Hoover, the Economists, and American Economic Policy, 1921–1933*. Cambridge: Cambridge University Press.

Bernstein, M. A. (2001). *A Perilous Progress: Economists and Public Purpose in Twentieth-Century America*. Princeton, NJ: Princeton University Press.

Brown, J. A. C. (1954). *The Social Psychology of Industry*. Harmondsworth: Penguin.

Bruce, K. and Nyland, C. (2001). 'Scientific Management, Institutionalism, and Business Stabilization: 1903–1923', *Journal of Economic Issues*, 35(4): 955–78.

Commons, J. R. (1909). 'American Shoemakers, 1648–1895: A Sketch of Industrial Evolution', *Quarterly Journal of Economics*, 24(1): 39–84.

—— (1919). *Industrial Goodwill*. New York: McGraw-Hill.

—— (1924). *Legal Foundations of Capitalism*. New York: Macmillan.

—— (1925). 'Marx Today: Capitalism and Socialism', *Atlantic Monthly*, 686–7.

—— (1934). *Institutional Economics—Its Place in Political Economy*. New York: Macmillan.

—— (1950). *The Economics of Collective Action*. New York: Macmillan.

—— , Phillips, U. B., Gilmore, E. A., Sumner, H. L., and Andrews, J. B. (eds.) (1910–11) *A Documentary History of American Industrial Society*, 10 vols. Cleveland, OH: Arthur H. Clark.

Commons, J. R., Saposs, D. J., Sumner, H. L., Mittleman, H. E., Hoagland, H. E., Andrews, J. B., and Perlman, S. (1918–35) *History of Labor in the United States*, 4 vols. New York: Macmillan.

Dorfman, J. (1974). 'Walton Hamilton and Industrial Policy', in W. H. Hamilton (ed.) (1974) *Industrial Policy and Institutionalism: Selected Essays*, with an introduction by Joseph Dorfman, New York: Augustus Kelley.

Fishman, L. (1958). 'Veblen, Hoxie and American Labor', in D. F. Dowd, (ed.) *Thorstein Veblen: A Critical Appraisal*. Ithaca, NY: Cornell University Press.

Galbraith, J. K. (1958). *The Affluent Society*. London: Hamilton.

—— (1969). *The New Industrial State*. Harmondsworth: Penguin.

Guillén, M. F. (1997). 'Scientific Management's Lost Aesthetic: Architecture, Organization, and the Taylorized Beauty of the Mechanical', *Administrative Science Quarterly*, 42(4): 682–715.

Hamilton, W. H. (1919). 'The Institutional Approach to Economic Theory', *American Economic Review*, 9 (Suppl.): 309–18.

—— (1932). 'Institution', in E. R. A. Seligman and A. Johnson (eds.), *Encyclopaedia of the Social Sciences*, Vol. 8. New York: Macmillan.

Hands, D. W. (2001). *Reflection without Rules: Economic Methodology and Contemporary Science Theory*. Cambridge: Cambridge University Press.

Hobson, J. A. (1914). *Work and Wealth: A Human Valuation*. London: Macmillan.

—— (1936). *Veblen*. London: Chapman & Hall. Reprinted 1991 by Augustus Kelley.

Hodder, H. J. (1956). 'The Political Ideas of Thorstein Veblen', *Canadian Journal of Economics and Political Science*. 22(3): 347–57.

Hodgson, G. M. (1998). 'The Approach of Institutional Economics', *Journal of Economic Literature*, 36(1): 166–92.

—— (1999). *Economics and Utopia: Why the Learning Economy is not the End of History*, London: Routledge.

—— (2001). *How Economics Forgot History: The Problem of Historical Specificity in Social Science*. London: Routledge.

—— (2004). *The Evolution of Institutional Economics: Agency, Structure and Darwinism in American Institutionalism*. London: Routledge.

Hoxie, R. F. (1915). *Scientific Management and Labor*. New York: Appleton.

—— (1917). *Trade Unionism in the United States*. New York: Appleton.

Jacoby, S. M. (1990). 'The New Institutionalism: What Can it Learn from the Old?', *Industrial Relations*, 29(2): 316–59.

Kaufman, B. E. (1993). *The Origins and Evolution of the Field of Industrial Relations in the United States*. Ithaca, NY: Cornell University Press.

—— (1998). 'Regulation of the Employment Relationship: The "Old" Institutional Perspective', *Journal of Economic Behavior and Organization*, 34(3): 349–85.

—— (2003). 'John R. Commons and the Wisconsin School on Industrial Relations Strategy and Policy', *Industrial and Labor Relations Review*, 57(1): 3–30.

Levitt, B. and March, J. G. (1988). 'Organizational Learning', *Annual Review of Sociology*, 14: 319–40.

MacKenzie, D. (1996). (ed.) *Knowing Machines: Essays on Technical Change*. Cambridge, MA: MIT Press.
McNulty, P. J. (1973). 'Hoxie's Economics in Retrospect: The Making and Unmaking of a Veblenian', *History of Political Economy*, 5(3): 449–84.
Mirowski, P. (2002). *Machine Dreams: Economics Becomes a Cyborg Science*. Cambridge: Cambridge University Press.
Nelson, R. R. and Winter, S. G. (1982). *An Evolutionary Theory of Economic Change*. Cambridge, MA: Harvard University Press.
North, D. C. (1990). *Institutions, Institutional Change and Economic Performance*. Cambridge: Cambridge University Press.
—— (1994). 'Economic Performance Through Time', *American Economic Review*, 84(3): 359–67.
Nyland, C. (1996). 'Taylorism, John R. Commons, and the Hoxie Report', *Journal of Economic Issues*, 30(4): 985–1016.
Plotkin, H. C. (1994). *Darwin Machines and the Nature of Knowledge: Concerning Adaptations, Instinct and the Evolution of Intelligence*. Harmondsworth: Penguin.
Polanyi, M. (1958). *Personal Knowledge: Towards a Post-Critical Philosophy*. London: Routledge & Kegan Paul.
Posner, R. A. (1973). *Economic Analysis of Law*, Boston, MA: Little Brown.
Powell, W. W. and DiMaggio, P. J. (eds.) (1991). *The New Institutionalism in Organizational Analysis*. Chicago: University of Chicago Press.
Rutherford, M. H. (1992). 'Thorstein Veblen and the Problem of the Engineers', *International Review of Sociology*, 3: 125–50.
—— (1997). 'American Institutionalism and the History of Economics', *Journal of the History of Economic Thought*, 19(2): 178–95.
—— (1998). 'Veblen's Evolutionary Programme: A Promise Unfulfilled', *Cambridge Journal of Economics*, 22(4): 463–77.
—— (2000). 'Understanding Institutional Economics: 1918–1929', *Journal of the History of Economic Thought*, 22(3): 277–308.
—— (2001). 'Institutional Economics: Then and Now', *Journal of Economic Perspectives*, 15(3): 173–94.
Schotter, A. R. (1981). *The Economic Theory of Social Institutions*. Cambridge: Cambridge University Press.
Smelser, N. J. and Swedberg, R. (eds.) (1994). *Handbook of Economic Sociology*. Princeton, NJ: Princeton University Press.
Taylor, F. W. (1911). *The Principles of Scientific Management*. New York: Harper.
Tichi, C. (1987). *Shifting Gears: Technology, Literature, Culture in Modenist America*. Chapel Hill, NC: University of North Carolina Press.
Veblen, T. B. (1898). 'The Beginnings of Ownership', *American Journal of Sociology*, 4(3): 352–65.
—— (1899). *The Theory of the Leisure Class: An Economic Study in the Evolution of Institutions*. New York: Macmillan.
—— (1904). *The Theory of Business Enterprise*. New York: Charles Scribners.

Veblen, T. B. (1914). *The Instinct of Workmanship, and the State of the Industrial Arts*. New York: Macmillan.

—— (1915). *Imperial Germany and the Industrial Revolution*. New York: Macmillan. Reprinted 1964 by Augustus Kelley.

—— (1919). *The Place of Science in Modern Civilization and Other Essays*. New York: Huebsch.

—— (1921). *The Engineers and the Price System*. New York: Harcourt Brace and World.

Vroom, V. H. and Deci, E. L. (eds.) (1970). *Management and Motivation*. Harmondsworth: Penguin.

Williamson, O. E. (1975). *Markets and Hierarchies: Analysis and Anti-Trust Implications: A Study in the Economics of Internal Organization*. New York: Free Press.

Wrege, C. D. and Greenwood, R. J. (1991). *Frederick W. Taylor, The Father of Scientific Management: Myth and Reality*. Homewood, IL: Irwin.

9

Economic Worlds of Work: Uniting Economic Sociology with the Sociology of Work

Thomas D. Beamish and Nicole Woolsey Biggart

1. Introduction

The economy is the collective production and distribution of resources, that is, the generation and allocation of material goods and services produced by a society in order to sustain it. Work concerns activities that people engage in to support themselves materially and socially within this larger system of production and exchange. To oversimplify, individuals work, and economies are the result. Economies in turn put individuals to work. Given the relationship that exists between work and economy, it is instructive to explore the range of connections that exist between the two and organize them both.

Economic orthodoxy treats work as a commodity, understandable like any other good or service having price or wage fluctuations. This model views market dynamics as organizing the distribution of wages, hence labor, and as inherently separate from other social contexts. Market dynamics are assumed to reflect the aggregate outcome of individual, self-seeking decision-makers, with intact preferences, who calculate and then act to maximize utility. These assumptions, put into practice when the US Federal Reserve, World Bank, International Monetary Fund, and other policy bodies seek to modify economies, have increasingly become the basis for understanding industrial economies, that is, how labor markets are organized and the costs and quality of labor as an industrial input (cf. Stiglitz 1999). Yet, to view work as just a commodity misses much of what organizes laboring as well as what it represents—its meaning—to those engaged in it.

Focusing specifically on laboring, sociological studies fill this void by investigating it as both a personal and collective experience under market conditions. Everett Hughes (1958) and the Chicago School focused on professions and professionalism as they manifested in modern industrial contexts. Attention to professional occupations dominated the post–World War II research agenda in this arena; the interest rested in better understanding the potential relationship between one's occupation and personality traits, levels of alienation, job satisfaction, job mobility, and occupational status (Abbott 1993). Studies of work and stratification have also extensively used structural analysis to assess and track demographic movements within industrial economies (see Blau and Duncan 1967; Braverman 1974; Simpson 1989; Kohn 1990; Abbott 1993). For their part, critical labor studies—a locus of Marxist criticism of capitalist modes of production—have analyzed the change from 'archaic systems,' such as feudalism, to 'modern' industrial systems criticizing them for their alienating, exploitive, and destructive consequences on workers and for the loss of control over work and production processes more generally (Burawoy 1979*a*; Burawoy 1985; Seidman 1991; Vallas 1993). Finally, recent research has focused on trends in work, especially the effect that rapid changes in technology and production are having on workplaces, stressing the changing nature of modern capitalist societies and transformation toward ever more market-based (i.e. commodified) systems of exchange and its reflection in work (Zuboff 1984; Erikson and Vallas 1990; Smith 2001; Vallas 2001).

Economic sociology, in examining the social processes that structure how human societies materially produce, distribute, and consume goods and services,[1] supplies a third view of economic contexts, one that shares a good deal with sociological studies of work, but differs significantly from the suppositions operationalized in economic orthodoxy. Economic sociologists distinguish themselves from their counterparts in economics along three dimensions: (*a*) economic sociologists do not view economic contexts as separate from social and cultural contexts, but rather view them as reflective of and embedded within such contexts; (*b*) economic sociologists view actor preferences and individual actions less as intact, calculated, and about maximizing utility more as ambiguous and affected by socially derived cognitive strategies, substantive rationality, feelings, roles, norms, myths, and expectations that form the basis for

[1] This is also a working definition for economic sociology as a subspeciality within sociology.

interpretation itself and thus even economic decision-making; (*c*) and finally, economic sociologists reject methodological individualism—the idea that the aggregation of individual-level behavior is unproblematic—in favor of models that suggest collections of persons create dynamics different from that which an aggregation of individuals would suggest (see Guillén et al. 2002: 5).

As is obvious, economic sociologists and scholars of work are uniquely positioned to question the assumptions that pervade classical and contemporary accounts of economy and labor and that leaves much of what characterizes exchange and work assumed and unseen. As economic sociologists, we contend that explicit attention to the overlap between the study of economies and work settings, like the actual nexus of economies and work, provides an avenue for a deeper understanding of both.

The quintessential scholar of work and economy, Karl Marx, was the first to theorize explicitly industrial labor relations, noting that price was an inherently distorted means of assessing and understanding the value of work. At the very heart of Marx's 'labor theory of value' (Marx 1967) was his notion that changing economic structures transformed social relations and that the laboring of humans also reflected changing legal, political, and ideological conditions (Marx and McLellan 1977). Yet, in all of his brilliance, even Marx did not predict the numerous forms capitalism would take as it has expanded and both absorbed varied systems of production, exchange, and work, and been transformed in the process. As we know from empirical investigations, capitalist markets, as Marx predicted, have not extinguished all other forms of work and exchange. Rather, capitalism's very expansion has pushed its expression in many different directions and away from a single monolithic shape.

On this front, over the last twenty years, economic sociologists have found that the multiplicity of 'capitalisms' reflects divergent historical contingencies (Collins 1980; Wallerstein 1984; Hamilton 1994), social structures (Granovetter 1985; Baker 1990; Burt 1992; Granovetter 1992; Podolny 1994; Romo and Schwartz 1995; Uzzi 1996; Uzzi 1997; Uzzi 1999) and sociopolitical and cultural milieux (Campbell and Lindberg 1991; Fligstein 1996*a*; Fligstein 1996*b*). Such varieties of capitalism studies by economic sociologists have demonstrated that capitalist societies can be built upon a broad array of organizational and occupational arrangements, yet be resolutely committed to private investment, profit-seeking, free labor, price competition, and other factors we associate with developed capitalist, market-based, or enterprise economies. We know, too, that labor regimes differ depending on the role and structure of states (Burawoy

1979*b*; Campbell and Lindberg 1990; Dobbin 1994; Biggart and Guillén 1999; Dobbin and Dowd 2000), experience with labor organization (Hicks et al. 1978; Cornfield 1991; Stepan-Norris and Zeitlin 1991), and sometimes with the historical experience of colonialism (Fields 1995). For the most part, however, these studies do not examine directly the structure of exchange and how it shapes work relations—economic connections between laborers, ideologies of work, forms of remuneration, and the meaning of work to those who labor.

Taking the 'lessons learned' from the literatures in economic sociology, in this chapter we explore the idea that different structures of exchange affect labor's conceptualization and organization. We utilize research by economic sociologists and related scholarship to illustrate this point. Research by economic sociologists has, in interrogating how economic activity is arranged and understood, provided tools in understanding the context within which work is conceptualized, conducted, organized, and remunerated. In the following pages we:

- Briefly discuss the dominant paradigms that characterize contemporary analysis of economic contexts: economic utility models, conflict models, social structure models, and institutional-cultural models.
- Briefly present a typology of exchange systems that identifies four ideal typifications reflective of the nexus of exchange and work that emerges from the empirical research and theory by economic sociologists and associated scholars. The typology both opens up markets to more critical sociological analysis and extends analysis of economic contexts beyond an exclusive focus on modern markets. Both tacks offer insights relevant to studies of work.
- Reflecting the sociological research and theory of economy and organized by the typology we have found emerges from this research, we review the empirical contributions that economic sociology offers for understanding economies and the implications these hold for understanding work: how it is arranged, performed, changed, and understood by those who are involved in it.
- Finally, we suggest how sensitivity to variations in the way exchange is organized—both within and outside of markets—provides a promising basis for mutually theorizing economic and work studies.[2]

[2] This typology may also have implicatious for the study of organizations, which has obvious overlap with both economic sociology and the sociology of work (see Chapter 11, this volume).

2. Theories of the Economic in Relation to Work

Economic sociologists have made a key distinction that differentiates their approach to economic contexts, broadly defined, from those pursued by classical economics. It centers on exploding the notion of 'exchange' to accommodate social relations, social institutions, and social structures in a way entirely denied by the later group of scholarship (Lie 1992). Exchange as conceived by Max Weber is a 'voluntary agreement involving the offer of any sort of present, continuing, or future utility in exchange for utilities of any sort offered in return' (Weber 1978). It can involve money, goods, and/or services but can also reflect less tangible elements like respect, reciprocity, obligation, duty, and even moral convictions (Polanyi [1944] 1957, 1957). Exchange is one of four basic economic activities, the others being saving, consumption, and production (e.g. laboring) that in practice are typically combined and approached under the overarching term 'market(s)'. Each form of economic action may be subject to organizing, rationalization, and institutionalization and, as we review later, has ramifications for understanding the forms that work takes (Weber 1976). We utilize the more inclusive 'exchange systems' when referring to truck and barter scenarios, as opposed to the usual but specific term market(s). When we do use the term market, we refer only to those economic conditions assumed by classical economics, or to empirical settings that approximate those conditions (much later).

In general, the study of economic contexts in the social sciences has taken five primary forms: neoclassical economic/microeconomic (hereafter neoclassical economic), conflict, network, ecological, and institutional-cultural models. While these distinctions, when sharply drawn, are routinely violated in research practice, they do provide a useful basis for theoretical comparison (for examples of economic analyses that cross these tidy boundaries see North 1981; Akerlof 1984; Coleman 1990). Neoclassical economic theories provide the intellectual bases for contemporary political institutions, social policy, and economic analysis (see Chapter 7). In this perspective, exchange uncorrupted by social influences would appear as a perfect market. A perfect market reflects autonomous or free participants who gauge and strategize their actions based entirely on an assessment of the benefit-to-cost ratio of any given product or service they seek to acquire or trade (Eatwell et al. 1987). Price and its fluctuation is the central mechanism around which the individual makes decisions. Price reflects supply and demand; the differences in offers to buy and sell provoke changes in supply, which in turn theoretically lowers demand and hence price (and vice versa). Finally, in calculating price, economists also assume that the free individual seeks maximum return in any given exchange. Thus conceived, price as a reflection of marginal utility[3] is the mechanism through which order or market equilibrium—Adam Smith's 'invisible hand' (1776)—is achieved and maintained over time. As summarized by Gary Becker, one of the most prolific advocates for a neoclassical model, 'all human behavior can be viewed as involving participants who maximize their utility from stable sets of preferences and accumulate an optimal amount of information and other inputs in a variety of markets' (Becker 1976). While economists recognize that markets are socially real places, with real actors, it is against the presumption of the perfect market that they compare all exchange relations (Becker and Murphy 2000).

Despite the broad scope, consistency, and parsimony of neoclassical economic theory, as well as its widespread policy application to both global and domestic economies—including labor markets—this approach does not provide a realistic analysis of the contexts and conditions under which actual exchange and work take place (Lie 1992, 1997). That is, the gulf between the theoretical presumptions economists employ, and the empirical markets they seek to explain, remains wide. According to economic sociologists, this is at least in part because of the model's failure to take seriously social relations as reflected in affiliations, culture, and institutions and to adequately address inequality and conflict in market contexts (see Reskin and Roos 1990).

Sociologists who study exchange and emphasize conflict—often but not only from the Marxist tradition—focus on the extent to which firms or 'producers' control labor processes and thus set the terms and conditions for work (Burawoy 1979*b*, 1985). Marxists assume that the mode of production that dominates any given society or epoch (currently capitalism), embodies its own logic whose basis is found in various forms of labor exploitation (see Chapter 2). Scholarship of this kind has historicized past and present labor arrangements, noting the conditions under which capitalism, capitalist states, and capitalist firms have exerted their control over labor (Block 1996; Tilly and Tilly 1998) and promoted inequality (Moore 1987) as well as the effect ideology has had on laboring within capitalist systems (Thompson 1964). Sociology of race and feminist

[3] In economics, the worth of a commodity is calculated in terms of its monetary price. The concept of marginal utility holds that value depends on the scarcity and desirability of a commodity as reflected in its exchange and use value. Use value signifies the 'utility' of a given commodity for satisfying a human need and/or desire (Eatwell et al. 1987). Marginal theory is fundamental to modern economic as it points out that both supply and demand–not just supply as postulated by early economists like Ricardo- have an impact on the price a commodity will fetch in the market.

scholarship views production as not only bisected by a capitalist/manager-worker dimension. Conflict theorists see sex and gender, race and ethnicity, and economic development as premised on sex/gender and race/ethnic exploitation (Boserup 1970; Enloe 1990; Cheng and Hsuing 1992; Escobar 1995; see also Chapter 5).

Sociologists who study networks also complicate the assumptions of neoclassical economics, viewing markets as historically developed social structures constituted by concrete social relations—networks of social ties—not merely an aggregation of rational individuals (White 1981; Burt 1982; Baker 1984; Granovetter 1985; Burt 1992; Baker et al. 1998). Network analysts emphasize an anticategorical imperative, in which the attributes of actors (race, class, and gender) are rejected in favor of their roles, positions, and the strength of the ties between them. More than a collection of individuals, according to network analysts, markets reflect the roles, positions, and relationality of participants. Network analysts contend that markets must be understood as independent of specific actor will, belief, and values (Wellman 1983). Network studies of markets as reflecting embedded social ties by Granovetter (1985), Uzzi (1996, 1997, 1999), and others (e.g. Baker 1990; Burt 1992; Granovetter 1992; Romo and Schwartz 1995) have substantially increased our understanding of exchange as influenced by the structural embeddedness of networked individuals.

Sociologists who pursue an ecological view of markets (Freeman et al. 1983; Hannan and Freeman 1984; Barnett and Carroll 1995; Hannan et al. 1995; Barnett and Rivers 1998; Aldrich 1999) take a macro-organizational/firm view that tracks birth and death rates based on competitive-selection processes (see Chapter 11). In some respects, they share a good deal with network theorists in their tracking of the structure of commercial markets and industries, but their unit of analysis, their focus on competition, and attention to the environment as the driving force behind change is sharply divergent from network theory's emphasis and foci. Ecologists view competitive environmental pressure on organizational populations as providing selection pressures in which the 'fit' (i.e. adapted) survive and the unfit disappear from the market. In this conceptualization, strategy and effort have a limited impact; it is the environment, not actors that determine competitive outcomes. Obviously sociality in the form of culture, politics, and relationality have little play in this theoretical perspective (Aldrich and Pfeffer 1976). Ecological models have sensitized economic sociologists to large-scale trends that transform the shape markets take, the shape of firms within markets take, and how diffusion of these forms proceeds. The changes that the ecological view documents have obvious overlap for understanding and predicting the shape work will take in any given 'field' or market where organizational activity takes place.

A fifth approach to understanding exchange and economies, an institutional-cultural view (Zelizer 1988, 1994; Abolafia 1996; Fligstein 2001; Biggart and Delbridge 2004), also shows the importance of social structures in market settings, but emphasizes substantive relations largely ignored by ecological and network theorists (conflict theorists often share this attention to culture and ideology as well). The institutional-cultural view assumes ties must be collectively meaningful (Beamish forthcoming), noting how differing cultures are associated with, and predict, differing exchange relations and hence distinct market logics (Biggart and Hamilton 1992; Biggart and Guillén 1999). Furthermore, from the institutional-cultural perspective, rationality is understood as constrained by conventions, belief, and existing social relations (Biggart and Beamish 2003), and operates on a more limited scale than assumed by economic models. For example, Zukin and DiMaggio (1990) identify three ways that cultural institutions affect economic behavior and, by extension, the forms that work takes: (*a*) by influencing how actors define their own interests, which they call

Table 9.1. Theories of markets

Theories of Exchange	Logics	Foci
Economic model	Asocial forces that posits exchange to reflect autonomous individuals, with stable preferences, optimizing behavior, with price as organizer	Asocial-individualistic, dynamic, strategic-competitive
Critical model	'Producers' and/or the 'Powerful' control exchange processes and set the terms and conditions for the exploitation of labor	Social-structural, dynamic, power-determined
Structural model	Social structures that provide parameters on and thus determine exchange behaviors	Social-structural, static, normative-relational
Ecological model	Reflecting competition for scarce resources, environmental conditions select the most 'fit'	Social-structural, dynamic, competitive-environmental
Institutional-cultural model	Social forces that reflect power, ideology, and socially constructed frameworks that define and direct exchange behaviors	Social-structural, dynamic, interpretive-interactional-relational

constitutive effects; (*b*) by constraining the behavior of exchangers through self-regulation, or regulatory effects; (*c*) by shaping the capacity of groups and individuals to mobilize through the shaping of goals and aspirations conceptually available for enactment.

3. Exchange and Labor: Contribution of Economic Sociology to Understanding Work

While the assumptions of these paradigms studying markets and exchange vary, each identifies constituent elements of systems of exchange that have important implications for understanding the shape work takes and why. The typical economic approach focuses our attention on the rationality of individuals buying and selling labor in a marketplace. The conflict approach illustrates how inequality is systematically reproduced in labor markets and laboring more generally. The social structural approach of network theorists asks us to understand work and labor markets as linked social spheres that influence who gets jobs, promotions, and occupational status. Also structural, the ecological view focuses attention on the larger environment which exerts pressures and pushes selection processes; some firms, sets of firms, populations of firms, and fields of firms survive and prosper passing on traits (strategies, configurations, relations) while others do not survive and thus disappear. Obviously, the shape a firm or population of competing firms takes (i.e. an industry) and whether or not this shape survives to diffuse has a good deal of bearing on work as it has much to do with the forms industrial enterprise takes and thus work within them. Lastly, the institutional-cultural approach reminds us to examine the meaning of work for those working as well as for those who employ workers and how the meaning of exchange and work itself reflects different social settings and different institutional parameters.

These views, collectively, also illustrate how truly intertwined work and economy are—that prevailing systems of work and exchange relations mirror one another. For instance, in Anglo-influenced societies there is an ideological emphasis on exchange governed by utilitarian reasoning, efficiency, and economically calculated relations. These exchange logics are reflected in how the 'typical worker' in many Western industrial economies views his/her labor participation and forms expectations concerning remuneration and obligation to fellow workers and employers. Yet, even as marketized notions of doing business spread, they continue to be founded on, built out of, and imbricated with yet other social systems of meaning and relationality, are inherently context dependant, and require a certain amount of 'switching' as sets of rules that apply to one work space, for example, a factory, are deemed inappropriate to another, for example, a household (see Mische and White 1998). In short, the approaches to economy that we have described make varied assumptions and observations about what organizes labor and economic relations, and we would suggest that all are right. None, however, can make a successful claim to universal correctness.

In this, however, economic sociological arguments do collectively diverge from their classical economic contemporaries in the place they give social relations and substantive rationality in economic contexts. That is, all the economic sociological arguments unite around the view that exchange involves more than just the exercise in formal-rational and calculative behavior, but also reflects substantive relations that differently organize exchange relations. Yet, they also diverge from one another in their research attentions and from their divergent research attentions have emerged observations and corresponding theories that illuminate the diverse basis for human economy. Specifically, a handful of relatively stable systems of exchange have been identified by economic sociologists that cohere over time and across space and that shed light on how work itself is arranged and why. These systems of exchange likewise reveal parallel systems of work and participation that reflect distinctive 'life worlds' (Habermas 1975). Thus, by combining the observations made by economic, conflict, network, ecological, and cultural-institutional approaches to economic organization, we can address more effectively the relationship that work has to exchange and economy.

With this in mind, we offer four ideal-type modes of exchange which have emerged from the empirical record and that have been found to organize differently human economy and, our contention in this chapter, the shape of work both within modern markets and in nonmarket contexts. While these logics can help distinguish *between* dominant systems of exchange, each is also simultaneously at play *within* any given economic system. These are analytic dimensions; concrete social settings involving exchange always involve more than one of these even if one exchange-logic is dominant. The systems of exchange are *market systems, associative systems, communal systems*, and *moral systems* (see Table 9.2). Modern markets, as conventionally conceived by classical economics and many studies by sociologists of economy and work, are but one 'ideal-typical' form of exchange, and even markets are inherently social-structural, cultural, and simultaneously riven by conflict and inequity. The typology identifies

Table 9.2. Economic organization and meaning in worlds of work

Processes	Market	*Systems* Associative	Communal	Moral
Alignment	Instrumental-Universalistic	Instrumental-Particularistic	Substantive-Particularistic	Substantive-Universalistic
Meaning	'You pay and I'll work'.	'I'll work for your benefit, if you'll work for my benefit'.	'I work out of obligation to the group'.	'I work for a higher purpose'.
Remuneration	Wages	Payment	Privilege	Honor
Structure	Market	Network	Collective	Substantive
Differentiation	Individualistic	Relational	In/out group	Ethical
Relation	Contractual	Extended Partnership	Obligatory	Normative
Exit	Final	Breach	Elder status	None

qualitatively different systems of exchange that vary along continuums of *instrumental—substantive* or value-based action and how strongly *universal–particularistic* relations, which represent the social context of participant decision-making. Each case represents a logic to decision-making and action that distinguishes it from the other action logics. Our typology is a model that, like all models, should be judged on its ability as a heuristic device to aid in understanding empirical contexts, not on its 'truth value'.[4]

In brief, in the following pages we outline the contribution economic sociology has made in better understanding exchange in a multitude of settings, both market and nonmarket, and what this suggests about its relationship to the arrangement of work. We organize our efforts by employing the four column systems of exchange typology. In this, we first examine and emphasize research by economic sociologists on contemporary markets as immanently social contexts, revealing their quickly changing shape, and document the widespread effect this is having on work relations in the developed and less developed world. Second, we review economic sociological research on alternative (i.e. nonmarket-based) systems of exchange—represented in *associative, communal,* and *moral* precepts in Table 9.2—that reflect very different understandings of work and hence the action logics that arrange that work differently. We note at the outset that while markets are indeed expanding in their

[4] See Biggart and Delbridge (2004) concerning analogous thoughts on underlying logics and systems of exchange, as well as Fiske (*1993*) and his development of these as underlying the 'Structures of Social Life'.

influence the world over, they are by no means unaffected or entirely extinguishing other forms of exchange.

The Market System and Commodified Labor

Column one elaborates market systems, price-driven exchange arenas that most closely approximate the free-market ideal assumed by traditional economics. That is, for economists any given market is either more or less perfect depending on how closely it resembles or diverges from a set of prescriptive assumptions, including: (*a*) a sufficiently large number of firms/individuals so that no single firm/individual makes more than a negligible contribution to output; (*b*) homogenous goods and services that any single consumer/exchanger would not prefer over any another seller/exchangers; (*c*) socially isolated and independent exchangers; (*d*) exchangers with complete information on which to make decisions regarding their prospective exchange (see Stigler 1968). The ideal typical marketplace operates on universalistic criteria as participants seek to maximize their gains irrespective of the persons with whom they exchange. While economists recognize that no real market conforms to their hypothesized ideal, they do hold that this conceptualization is a useful fiction against which to contrast the functioning of any given real market, tagging deviations as 'imperfections' in need of remedy and movement toward the ideal.

Sociological accounts of markets are typically critical of traditional economic assumptions—that is, methodological individualism, instrumental behavior, and universalistic ideals as explaining behavior in modern markets. However, while they do complicate these assumptions, economic sociologists do not dismiss them entirely, finding that what distinguishes modern markets is their general adherence to many of the precepts economists have identified. Rather, economic sociologists understand that features such as rationality and self-interest are variable across time and space and thus a product of social and cultural construction, not intrinsically universal human conditions (Polanyi 1957; Lie 1992). For example, in Abolafia's (1996) participant observation and comparative analysis of three Wall Street institutions—stock, bond, and futures markets[5]—he argues that the structure of each local exchange supports a particular type of culture (i.e. reflective of substantive forms of rationality) that leads to a distinct orientation towards economic action that includes, for example, utility maximizing behavior, but is not limited to it. He identifies

[5] Wall Street's stock, bond, and futures market are perhaps the closest approximation to classical economic conceptions of 'the market'.

culturally constructed and self-imposed restrictions that mitigate the destabilizing and destructive aspects of pure short-term self-interest. Such collectively constructed yet self-imposed social constraints help to stabilize market interactions and in so doing benefit individuals and the larger collective over the long term. Thus, Abolafia's ethnography does not discount the role that instrumental behavior plays in the work of floor traders or the universalistic ideals these workers espouse when speaking of their behavior on the trading floor, but modifies them by acknowledging their place in an inherently social and relational context. Similarly, Charles Smith (1989) in studying auctions suggests how different types of auction markets lead to different, socially derived, price setting behaviors by antique dealers, horse traders, and others whose work involves buying and selling commodities on an exchange. Thus, while participants on trading floors and auctions continue to evince overridingly instrumental behavioral patterns and pay homage to largely universalistic (i.e. fair) trading and interaction criteria—at least rhetorically—these and other studies like them reveal that there is more at work than just formal, rational, and universal criteria in market settings.

At the level of the firm, industry, and nation-state economic sociologists have also become increasingly aware of differences in how industrial organization and employment relations manifest across national and even regional boundaries even in what are identified as market economies. For example, Maurice, Sellier, and Silvestre (1986: 122) compare German and French industrial systems, noting that neoclassical theories of labor markets cannot explain the differences between these countries. Maurice, Sellier, and Silvestre's research conclusions deny a basic assumption of classical economic doctrine captured in what is called 'convergence theory'—that all market-industrial systems will eventually converge as they excise 'anachronistic' and 'primitive' forms and relations and move towards a single, modern, and advanced market-industrial system (cf. Kaufman et al. 1988; Rostow 1990). In comparing the two industrial systems, Maurice, Sellier, and Silvestre found that social institutional differences by nation in the educational, commercial, and employment relations domains determine how work, society, and markets are constructed, intertwined, and why they differ. Thus, while both Germany and France exhibit modern industrial economies and mature market features, they differ in their distinct social and institutional bases that further reflect distinct social and cultural histories.

Similarly, the importance of social institutions such as those reflected in associative-based systems of exchange (see Table 9.2, column 2) and work are evident in Asian economies. For example, Gerlach's study of Japanese business groups, *Alliance Capitalism* (1992), and Redding's work on Chinese capitalism (1990) both exemplify the nexus of markets and association-based social ties in the conduct of business and the structure of employment relations. In these and parallel research investigations, associative systems—networks of strong and weak ties (Granovetter 1973)—reflect mutual dependence and reciprocity among market participants and exist at the level of the individual (Uzzi 1999), firm (Child and Faulkner 1998), and industry (Hirsch 1985). Examples of 'networked firms' include Japanese keiretsu, Korean chaebol as well as Anglo-American franchises and industry giants such as petrochemical (Yeargin 1991; King and Lennox 2000) and music/entertainment industries (Hirsch 1972; Dowd 2002).[6] In fact, these and other analyses of East Asian, European, and American capitalist exchange systems suggest the limits of economic theory's individualized actor assumptions to conceptualize how particularistic economic relations, in both associative and communal forms, play a part in organizing market economies and work.

The interpenetration of firms, work within firms, markets, and network ties of the communal type (see Table 9.2, column 3) are also born out in Kondo's ethnography (1990) and Dore's case-comparative research (1973) on work, exchange, and economy in Japan and Britain. Dore compared the British industrial system to Japan's in a search for what distinguishes Japan from Western industrial employment systems. Dore, like Maurice, Sellier, and Silvestre (1986), eschewed established explanations of markets such as economic convergence finding that Japan's unique form of employment relations—lifetime employment, intrafirm labor markets with intrafirm career system, intrafirm training, intrafirm-based unions, intrafirm-based welfare, benefits, and collectivist ideology—was itself spreading to more pronounced and 'classical' market economies such as Britain's. Japan's employment relations, according to Dore, reflect a unique blend of paternalism and more universalistic criteria typically associated with advanced market systems. Dore, in drawing these distinctions, labels the Japanese system 'welfare corporatism' and distinguishes this 'organizationally oriented' system from the 'market oriented' one prevalent in Britain (1973: 278). 'Organizationally oriented' captures aspects of a traditional communal system that predates the emergence of

[6] While work within the 'networked' firms may not be very different from that done in the hypothetically 'unaligned firm', executives in networked firms are constrained and influenced by their relationship to others and their need/desire to maintain their personal, firm, and industry-wide connections (i.e., their 'embeddedness' in a network).

industrial markets in Japan and those of the market system ideal prevalent in the West. Dore, however, does not view communal qualities as destined to disappearance as market ideals penetrate deeper into Japanese society. Rather, he surmises that communal ethics fortify Japanese style industrialism and, because of their success (at that time), have a chance to influence Britain's and other European economies.

Kondo (1990) too, in an ethnography of a family owned confectionery in Tokyo that employed thirty full-time and eight half-time workers, provides a picture that illustrates the overlap of cultural idioms of paternalism that interpenetrate with more formal–rational market-based ideals. Kondo, in a revealing example, explores the employer's use of Japan's cultural idiom of 'kinspeople' in addressing his employees as if they were family and also through his sponsorship of group activities while he simultaneously pursued a very shrewd individualistic agenda reflected in his use of management consultants to expand his business and in employing surveillance cameras to assure employee follow through. Ironically, the employees used the 'company as family' idiom to their own advantage when seeking worker empowerment in that factory setting.

Likewise, research on women in national as well as international and global markets has led critical scholars to argue that capitalist industry has systematically exploited female labor—free labor in domestic contexts and low-wage labor in the commercial sector—in ways that distinguishes women's experience (i.e. patricularism) from that of men of equivalent race, ethnic, and class backgrounds. For example, in the European context, while Rubery, Smith, and Fagan (1999) find women's increased labor participation since the 1980s as a striking change in European labor markets, equally conspicuous is the continuing inequality experienced by women in market-based workplaces. These reflect deeply seated social and cultural norms (aka, patriarchy) that coexist with the 'market ideal' that ostensibly emphasizes instrumental and universalistic criteria instead of the particularism inherent to gender discrimination (Scott 1994; see also US parallels Treiman and Roos 1983; Milkman 1987; Ridgeway 1997).

Similarly, research by critical scholars on global economic development has made a strong case that the exploitation of women's labor has, in part, laid the basis for both the industrialization of the west (Engels 1902; Kessler-Harris and Levenson 1982; Matthaei 1982) and the more recent expansion of markets into parts of the developing world (Boserup 1970; Enloe 1990; Cheng and Hsuing 1992; Escobar 1995). Feminist scholars point to Asian Export Processing Zones, Mexican Maquiladoras (Brecher and Costello 1994; Parrado and Zenteno 2001), South and Central American agriculture production (Faber 1993), as well as global sex-tourism (Enloe 1990) to illustrate the gender exploitive exchange relations that arrange the work of women and that characterize the current international division of labor. Theoretical explanations such as *human capital* (Psacharopoulos and Tzannatos 1993), *household strategy* (Gonzalez del la Rocha 1994), and the *new international division of labor* (Nash and Fernandez-Kelly 1983) argue for the important role communal relations, specifically patriarchal family structures play in defining roles, rules, and remuneration and hence in organizing work relations even in ostensibly market driven contexts. Communal ties reflect culturally inscribed gender norms, obligations, constraints, and inducements for women and men that critical sociologists have found provide the substantive basis for lower pay and less power in workplaces for female laborers.

Finally, a handful of authors have also shown the place that morality can play in market places where participants ideally make decisions by calculating costs-to-benefit seemingly devoid of deep substantive convictions. Although economic theory assumes that individuals rationally calculate and in so doing seek to maximize their benefit when making exchange decisions, the concept of benefit typically is left unexplored in the category of 'utility'. Empirical research by economic sociologists shows that actors use moral filters to make choices in some market settings—choices that influence who they will trade with, how they will transact, and even what is considered valuable. Opening up the category of benefit, utility, and even cost reveals the role that substantive, moral categories have on exchange relations. For example, in Biggart's research (1989) on direct selling organizations in the USA, she shows how market behavior involves calculation, but the calculations of Biggart's direct selling informants is infused with meanings that are substantively based and attain a quasi-religious status among direct selling salespersons. Likewise, Charles Smith's work on auctions (already covered above) also reveals that considerations of community and appropriateness shape the actual bidding process and the prices paid by patrons.

These studies and others like them that we outline later, show both the distinctive features of exchange and work in market-based systems that sets them off—especially greater adherence to instrumental and universalistic ideals—even while noting the reality of people who rely on substantive relations and whose relations to one another can reflect systematic inequalities and work relations. We contend that analysis would miss these considerations if it did not challenge traditional economic assumptions concerning the basis of markets.

CHANGING MARKETS

As an ideal typical form, contemporary markets, the world over, are also in a state of rapid transition and transformation (Dicken 1992; Evans 1995; Castells 1996; Guillén 2001; Dicken 2003). Changes to domestic and global markets have broad implications for current and future forms of work. For example, trends in the deregulation of markets and the opening of formerly closed, isolated, and undeveloped markets to outside producers and consumers have resulted in new price and cost pressures. These have translated into increased production speeds, faster product innovation cycles, as well as increases in the variety of products and services that are offered globally (Henderson and Castells 1987). In the main, economic sociologists have identified three interrelated trends in market transformation significant to the study of work. These are: (*a*) the overall expansion and changing shape of markets, (*b*) the changing nature and flow of capital in markets, and (*c*) the dynamic role of deregulation and technological innovation in both fomenting and reflecting these trends and in changing the form and content of work. These shifts, extensively documented by economic sociologists, are dramatically rearranging the relationships that characterize markets: relations between capital, management, and labor, and the character of work itself.

THE CHANGING SHAPE OF MARKETS

The expansion and changing form of markets takes shape in both the internationalization or geographic spread of economic activity across national borders and in globalization, which involves the increased functional integration of what had previously been dispersed economic activity (Reich 1991; Dicken 1992; Gereffi and Korzeniewicz 1994; Evans 1995; Castells 1996; Dicken 2003). Trends in globalization, especially those that have internationalized price competition, have had direct impact on work through the simultaneous lowering of wage structures in some parts of the world and increasing the availability of low wage-work in others (Sassen 1988; Appelbaum and Henderson 1992; Evans 1995). Globalization and associated trends in manufacturing have also led to capital flight both within and between nations towards cheaper locations (Strange 1996). Lower costs come from less expensive material resource inputs, lower taxes and reduced regulatory intervention, and decreased labor costs (Faber 1993). The internationalization of the search for lower cost structures has exerted parallel pressure to innovate and further reduce production process costs, increase competitiveness, and secure survival niches (Fligstein 2001). In short, each of the elements pushing for increased internationalization and global economic integration has dynamically accelerated the rate with which the whole process of economic expansion is occurring (Castells 1996). In this increasingly competitive economic environment, work has been dramatically restructured. For example, certain job categories such as blue collar unskilled and semiskilled manufacturing work has virtually disappeared from the developed world's workforce as it is mechanized out of existence (Bluestone and Harrison 1982; Zuboff 1984) or moves offshore where cheaper nonunion labor is plentiful (Brecher and Costello 1994).

THE CHANGING NATURE AND FLOW OF CAPITAL IN MARKETS

Perhaps the strongest force behind these changes to the global economy and work derives from changes in capital markets themselves, reflected in: (*a*) how capital projects are financed and (*b*) the expectations that these various forms of financing hold for their capital endeavors. There is a direct link between availability and access to capital, the shapes firms have taken, and hence the nature of work in those firms (Chandler 1977; Berk 1994). Economic sociologists and economic historians who have followed the rise of large integrated corporations have found them to reflect nineteenth-century access to tremendous sums of accumulated capital that in turn mirrors the dominant role finance has played in the rise of US style capitalism (Roy 1997; Perrow 2002). Other trends related to the rise of financier driven capitalism include the increased control shareholders and boards of directors have over chief executive officers (Useem 1984; Useem 1993) the volatility of international capital flows (Useem 1996) and the rise of downsizing as a strategy used by executives to provide surges in stock value (Ayling 1997; Naylor and Willimon 1997; Crenson and Ginsberg 2002; Baumol et al. 2003).

Economic sociologists of both the intuitionalist and ecological schools have documented transformations in how corporations are organized and the priorities they pursue reflective of changing economic environments (Zeitlin 1974; Herman 1981; Mizruchi 1982; Schwartz and Mizruchi 1987; Fligstein 1990; Boeker 1991; Hannan et al. 1995; Swaminathan and Carroll 1995; Dobbin and Dowd 1997; Swaminathan and Carroll 2000). Shifts in control of large modern corporations have also been studied extensively by sociologists of the economy and are important to an understanding of work, both as it is experienced and understood. For example, changes in control of

America's largest corporations impacts labor, in both its form and influence, in firm planning, work remuneration, and organization structure.

Studies show that over time, corporate strategy has reflected different conceptions of the firm, the changing terms on which competition takes place, and differing firm 'birth' conditions (Abolafia and Biggart 1991; Leblebici et al. 1991; Baron et al. 1999). Beginning with the industrial revolution through the 1940s, industrial firms were run by owners and then engineer-managers and primarily understood by them as in the business of producing commodities (see Shenhav 1999). Yet, by the close of World War II, as firms increasingly confronted a consumer market premised on replacement, not first time purchase of commodities, sales and marketing specialists began to emerge and hold sway in US corporations. This changed firm strategy away from purely production-based concerns to one that emphasized sales, marketing, and market strategy—what kind and how commodities were produced. This model gave way in the late 1970s as managers and executives with backgrounds in finance, in turn, rose to prominence. These managers brought with them a finance conception of the corporation that viewed them as a bundle of assets (Fligstein 1987; Palmer et al. 1993; Palmer et al. 1995). Finally, recent changes in financial markets have promoted a permutation on this finance conception of the firm towards ever-tighter linkages between shareholder interests, firm performance, and executive decision-making that has had far reaching implications for firms, workers, and the economy more generally. This latest finance-based shareholder conception of the firm views firms not only as a set of assets but as little more than a balance sheet whose basic function is to provide immediate returns (i.e. dividends) to shareholders and where 'assets on balance sheets that [are] underperforming [are] to be sold off, and the profits either dispersed among shareholders or reinvested where higher rates of return might appear' (Fligstein 2001).

This emphasis on finance and shareholder value has de-emphasized the largely unassailable place of formerly dominant key actors: owners, managers, and banks. With the move away from a conception of the corporation as exclusively a commodity producing entity, coupled with the internationalization of production, the concerns of labor have also become less salient to firm strategizing and decision-making (Kolko 1988; Reich 1991; Brecher and Costello 1994; Castells 1996). The finance conception of the firm also directly impacted work by supporting corporate mergers, divestitures, large debt loads, the buying and selling of company stock by corporate pension funds, closing profitable plants for their sale as capital assets, union busting, laying off workers, downsizing, and even strategically employing chapter 11 bankruptcy to 'discipline labor' even when profits were high (Delaney 1992).

Downsizing has been the most contentious cost-reduction tactic widely experienced by the US workforce (Koeber 2002; Knudsen et al. 2003). Initially, in the 1980s, downsizing was publicly rationalized by US corporate managers as a means of reducing redundancy, decreasing costs, and increasing efficiency in production processes (Littler and Innes 2003). Yet, research by economic sociologists over the past two decades has revealed that downsizing better reflects a pre-emptive financial strategy large corporations have used to increase their stock values (Naylor and Willimon 1997). That is, evidence suggests that downsizing generally does not produce the favorable long-term results in efficiency, lower costs, or increases in production that it was initially held to promote, but rather induces a positive but temporary rise in stock prices (Budros 2002). Finally, while the pressures contemporary firms confront have been well researched by economic sociologists, their direct impact on the arrangement, forms, pace, and meaning of work has not been equally well considered and require continued vigorous investigation (see Smith 2001).

THE CHANGING SHAPE OF TECHNOLOGIES AND THE EXPANSION OF MARKET TIME AND MARKET SPACE

Both pushing and reflecting these market changes are corollary trends in deregulation and technological innovation. According to economic sociologists, the deregulation of key industries such as communications, transportation, financial services, utilities, and telecommunications mirror the internationalization of capital as outside investors seek access to local and regional markets (Guillen 2001; Gereffi et al. 2002). Capital expansion, deregulation, functional integration of the global economy, and technological innovation accompany and accelerate the expansion of market systems as described earlier. Innovation in information and communications technologies, biotechnologies, new materials, energy, and space technologies (Freeman 1987 as quoted in Dicken 1992: 469) have decentered some industries such as textiles and apparel and electronic manufacture (Bonacich and Appelbaum 2000; Gereffi et al. 2002) and pushed yet others, such as financial services, banking, consulting, and other specialized services, to agglomerate (Storper and Walker 1989; Sassen 1993, 2001).

These trends have in turn quickened already manifest globalizing tendencies. New, often smaller-scale, competitive ventures characterized by lower cost structures and the latest production technologies do not have the same immobility and sunk costs in outdated technologies and the high wages associated with the more established mass producers. Since the late 1970s mass or 'Fordist' producers—where unionized narrowly skilled workers toil on complex yet rigid single-purpose machinery using standardized inputs to create standardized outputs—have been severely challenged by contemporary flexible and lean production strategies (Shaiken 1993). For example, the steel industry—a former bulwark of US industrial strength and mass productive apparatus—is now dominated by small steel mills known as minimills that rely on highly flexible methods of production characterized by modular and modifiable machinery with fewer multiskilled workers accustomed to multitasking (Henderson and Clark 1990; Utterback 1994; Prechel 1997). This trend in the size and shape the industry takes is also observable in cement, glass, and microcomputer industries (Anderson and Tushman 1990). Finally, even symbol analysts (Reich 1997)—the skilled high-end workers touted as the basis for the developed world's continued affluence and technical dominance—are seeing the migration of jobs and the kinds of work associated with them. Programmers, designers, and other technical-specialist positions, particularly in capital and technology-intensive sectors such as heavy machinery, petrochemicals, computers, and automobiles are beginning to exit developed economies. Countries such as India, Sri Lanka, South Korea, and Taiwan, which have highly educated populations and gain advantage from low-wage structures, are increasingly picking up such jobs (Gereffi et al. 1990; Haggard and Harvard University 1990; Gereffi and Fonda 1992).

Economic sociology, then, while not focusing explicitly on working conditions per se does expose the logic behind firm behavior and consequences for market structuring, which helps illuminate how and why work conditions appear as they do. Economic sociologists have also shown the important part that environment and competition, associations and networks, culture and institutions, and power and inequality play in shaping the market context of work. These accounts have helped us understand the economic contexts within which work is organized and performed (see also Chapter 11). While there is no consensus in economic sociology on the shape or directions contemporary markets will take, there is implicit agreement that firm, industry, and market structures will continue to change dramatically in the near and long-term and with them the nature of laboring in economies globally.

Nonmarket Systems of Exchange: Associational, Communal, and Moral

Economic sociologists provide a much more complicated picture of exchange relations than the theoretical ideal posited by classical economics and operationalized under methodological individualism. As empirical accounts by economic sociologists have repeatedly shown, this holds true even for market contexts where the ideal holds considerable resonance in explaining human behavior and economic transactions, but does not explain all or even most of what occurs in any given market. Yet, for economic sociologists the neoclassical model becomes even more doubtful in its explanatory value when applied outside of exchange arenas that more closely mirror its theoretical assumptions such as the trading floors studied by Abolafia (1996).

In the following, we more explicitly draw attention to systems of exchange that deviate from the market ideal explored above, yet still fall within a broader economic sociological agenda (see statements by Fligstein and Zelizer in Guillén et. al. 2002). Over human history, labor has taken place in three broadly defined settings, only some of them truly 'marketized:' large units such as armies and plantations and, more recently, corporations; local communities such as farms, workshops, and cottage industries; and in the household or domestic sphere (see Tilly and Tilly 1994). These contexts when explored by economic sociologists reveal that association, communal ties, and morality also play roles in organizing exchange now and in the past.

THE ASSOCIATIVE SYSTEM AND ALLIANCE CAPITAL

Economic sociologists who study *networks* and *associations* have developed an understanding of exchange that assumes the opposite of classical economic theory. Transactions are viewed as predicated on the relations or 'ties' that exist between coexchangers and predicted by the strength and/or weakness of the bonds between them. Associative systems (Table 9.2, column 3) appear as networked systems of relations, characterized by strong ties of affiliation in which exchange and hence work are arranged through embedded ties (Uzzi 1996; Uzzi 1997; Gulati and Gargiulo 1999; Uzzi 1999). Sociologists developing structural arguments view social networks as the basis for all social contexts and groupings. The emergence of network explanations of market contexts is a very important theoretical alternative to economic accounts of exchange behavior. Exchange reflects particularism in that participants in associative systems are given preference over nonmembers, but participation is also evocative of instrumentalism, as the pursuit of an end is organized around strategies that have proven effective. As arranged through associative systems of exchange, work is not entirely contingent on price, immediate or direct remuneration, but on the structure of ties between actors. The logic of action in such networks is independent of any given specific actor's will, belief, and/or values, but rather reflects the overall structure of ties (Wellman 1983). In this, network theory has made a strong case for the importance of networks to all human social contexts not just in the exchange of goods and services.

As it relates to laboring, work guilds, cottage industries, unions, alliances, and labor confederations, all exemplify the power that social relations hold for the shape that work takes. Networks appear as nested, overlapping, and interpenetrating associations of both strong and weak ties (Granovetter 1973). They exist at the level of the individual, such as kin networks as well as through less communal forms, for instance professional associations, occupational communities, and communities of practice (Van Maanen and Barley 1984; Wenger 1998; Wenger and Snyder 2000; Mather et al. 2001). Work in associative systems is a mutually defined activity in which one seeks to benefit personally, yet personal benefit is ultimately contingent on the association's success. Associations and alliances between economic actors involve voluntary arrangements that entail work relations based on cooperation, skill sharing, and both material and social coinvestment. Association-based networks appear as alliances and improve the chance of success and reduce the risks to individual member-workers of 'going it alone', even if they simultaneously decrease the potential for particularized distinction and unrestrained success (i.e. individually experienced optimal outcomes). That is, actors in associative systems assume that, over the long run, mutual support and reciprocity—not autonomous self-interest—will result in the best outcome for the parties involved.

Training in associative systems, for example in professional associations and partnerships such as law firms (Mather et al. 2001; Vogel 2001) and medical practice (Hoff and MacCaffrey 1996), are typically organized via mentor–apprentice arrangements that gradually and selectively induct new members into the network and up the social hierarchy. Membership and standing hinge on both exhibiting significant ties and sufficient skill to represent the collective and train potential future members. Remuneration reflects the status and competence of the craftsperson and the object of their efforts, not necessarily hours spent as in (formal) market-based wage system. Exit in an associative system of work entails losing all forms of preferential treatment that come with embeddedness in the community of practice (Wenger 1998; Wenger and Snyder 2000).

THE COMMUNAL SYSTEM AND OBLIGATED WORK

Another variant of associational forms of work and exchange are those based on the logic of collectivity and mutual obligation. Communal systems of work (Table 9.2, column 4) are arranged between parties characterized by particularistic relations, for example those of kinship, ethnic ties, or common membership in a social order, when the substantive value of that relationship either supercedes or heavily influences other considerations (i.e. instrumentalism) and thus structures exchange and work relations. The substantive basis of the relationship—filial piety, consanguinity, and collegiality—sets the terms for exchange, including whether or not the exchange takes place, the prices that are asked and paid, and in fact whether or not direct and/or immediate payment is required at all. In brief, *communal systems* are organized by mutual and obligatory relations. It is the strength of reciprocal and binding relations that comprise and characterize communal systems and their overridingly substantive basis that differentiates them from the instrumental orientation of association-based systems of exchange that are also based on particularistic criteria.

In communal contexts, work reflects membership in a collective where actors share a common identity or have some basis for a shared bond including family, tribe, ethnic group, village, or some other corporate form that if not involving consanguinity requires some alternative basis of emotional or social relation, what Ouchi (1980) and Boisot and Child (1988) refer to as embodying the *clan*. This is the defining aspect of participation: either one is, or is not, a member. The shared tie also identifies whether or not one is obliged preferential treatment (Weber 1978; Schluchter 1981). What is more, because in communal systems remuneration is based, at least in part, on reciprocity and redistribution (Polanyi [1944] 1957) and couched in mutual obligation it is not entirely about price or personal advancement as in markets (i.e. price) or association based systems (i.e. personal advancement).

The basis of work in communal systems is typically dictated by customary rules governing participation and distribution of goods and services. These rules are rooted in substantive rationality and are the source of direction and order in relation between the parties. For example, the group, not an abstract principle, determines what is communally viewed as equitable between clan members given communal ties and member position (senior versus junior members) as well as how loyalty takes shape between segments of the clan—core family, extended family, village, local tribe, regional tribe, tribal diasporas, ethnic identification, and so forth. Nested inside these distinctions, communal relations and hence work can be particularistically arranged by sex difference (patriarchy), lineage (proximity to leadership), or caste (functional differentiation) with laboring reflecting obligation to the larger group. Finally, the communal context precludes true 'exit,' if one is a member by blood. Alternatively, exit may be complete if one is exiled by the group. In short, communal systems create tight rules for membership; one is either inside or outside the familial network.

Case studies have shown work in *communal* or *family networks* reflect the configuration and rules that govern the relational structure. The Sicilian Mafia, Chinese Triads, and Russian Mafiyas fiercely regulate the terms and conditions of work and exchange in part by distinguishing between insiders and outsiders. In the Sicilian Mafia, those outside blood relations can buy services, but are not allowed into the inner recesses of the cabal, where planning and leadership are located (Gambetta 1993; Hess 1998). For example, Gambetta (1993) in his analysis of the Sicilian Mafia found it to be a kin-based economic organization whose chief 'work' was protection. That is, the mafia's chief 'product' is guarantor of economic transactions in a region historically plagued by an absent and ineffective state that does not guarantee contractual relations. What is more, Gambetta found that in contrast to outsider stereotypes of the mafia as violent, unfair, and locally maligned, Sicilians actively seek out its 'services' as a means of assuring smooth transactions in an otherwise unacceptably uncertain environment. This is especially interesting given that the mafia is both *particularistic* (i.e. partial, even unfair) and is *substantively* arranged around kin ties and codes of conduct such as family honor.

In patriarchal social systems, a form of communal structure, female labor is a largely unremunerated and often underappreciated source of material and emotional support in the domestic sphere and revenue in public-commercial sector (Kessler-Harris and Levenson 1982; Matthaei 1982). Feminist scholars have exposed and critiqued both the communal and cultural rationale for the exploitation of female labor, locating it in the character of patriarchal institutions as observed in gender roles and expectations that organize the current and highly sex segregated division of labor (Reskin 1993). For example, research outlining women's commitment to unpaid labor at home (Devault 1991) and their largely unrecognized efforts in volunteer organizations (Daniels 1987) illustrates how exchange and work can be organized according to communal principles—women's roles as 'women-workers' in a patriarchal society.

THE MORAL SYSTEM AND HONORABLE WORK

Finally, sociologists have also identified systems of exchange and work that are arranged via a shared and mutually defined higher purpose. Morally based exchange and work (Table 9.2, column 5) is organized by shared substantive beliefs or higher order principles. Even repugnant values, such as belief in ethnic superiority, can shape exchange relations and hence how work takes form, for example in slave and apartheid-based social systems (Owens 1977; Lazar 1996; Jeeves and Crush 1998). Actors are rational, but only in so far as their actions are oriented towards putting in place a universalistic value or their substantively rational actions are bound by a moral code.[7]

Work within moral systems is organized vis-à-vis a nonmaterial set of rewards—a higher purpose. Of all the systems of exchange and work described thus far, moral systems are most obviously rooted in a substantive logic, relying on initiation rights and socialization as the basis of integration into the social order with honor and recognition supplying a primary mode of remuneration, and shame and dishonor a means of sanction. Differentiation within moral economies is ethically founded and based on universalistic application. Outside of exile or expulsion from the group, or in the individual's repudiation of the moral system's guiding principles, exit is not easy to achieve.

Research that illustrates the moral aspects of work and exchange has taken a number of forms. Institutionalists have identified the shape and valorization of work as a reflection of religious piety (Weber 1976; Collins 1986; Sibler 1993), women's work as an expression of love and personality (Devault 1991) and moral commitment to the concept of family and community (Klatch 1987; Ahlander and Bahr 1995; Stone 1997; Gerson 2002), and in research on communes and communitarian devotion to work as expressing higher principles such as fraternity and equality (Vallier 1962; Barkin and Bennett 1972; Bennett 1975; Simons and Ingram 1997). Weber (1976) wrote the tour de force on the matters of morality, exchange, and work. It is in Protestant asceticism and soteriological anxiety that Weber posits the origin of the intense need for material signs of salvation, the incredible motivation and valorization of work as the means of acquiring such material manifestations, and the subsequent rise of capitalism (Collins 1980). Whether of the physical or liturgical kind,

[7] For a critique of contemporary economic analysis from a 'moral position' see Hausman and McPherson (1996).

laboring holds a central place in Judeo-Christian constructions of moral rectitude and personal discipline (Sibler 1993).

In the case of women's work roles and moral attributions, research by Klatch (1987) on *Women of the Right*—women who embrace traditional values, work roles, and subservience to men—found that in 'acting out her role as woman, as mother, as protector of her children, as moral gatekeeper, the social conservative woman finds affinity between the traditional female role and the adoption of an ideology that rejects narcissism and self-interest for "higher" values of self-sacrifice, faith, devotion and compliance with authority' (Klatch 1987). In this regard, socially conservative women see their gender roles—their submission to the 'natural authority' of patriarchal leadership (in the household, in the community, in the nation, and in God)—as derivative of divine inspiration and thus representative of a divinely ordained hierarchy. Seen through this moral frame, they exchange their labor for a higher order purpose or 'calling' (Klatch 1987).

Conversely, the transformation of gender roles in contemporary society, according to Gerson (2002), has undermined the division of labor and its perceived 'moral legitimacy'. Changes to how exchange structures operate in both familial and economic contexts has produced moral dilemmas for both women and men. This reflects women seeking personal achievement, which is contrary to traditional moral expectations that they seek personal development and relation to others by caring for them. Likewise, men, who in industrial society have traditionally been expected to achieve economically, be nonemotional (i.e. strong) providers and do so by exchanging their labor for wages in the public sphere are increasingly expected to be emotive, investing feeling and care in their relationships with their partners, their children, and even those they work with (Gerson 2002).

Work in communes and communitarian movements (Vallier 1962; Barkin and Bennett 1972; Bennett 1975), monasticism (Sibler 1993), and religious orders (Francis 1950) also provides a view of work pursued for reasons beyond the mundane, entirely instrumental, self-centered, or 'of this world'. That is, life and labor in such contexts involves adhering to an explicitly collectivist and often utopian ideal, guided by a set of moralist principles or canon that seeks simultaneously to embody a higher purpose and promote *gemeinshaft* among participants (Francis 1950; Weber 1976). In the case of the communes, for instance, those based on Jewish and Christian ideals, pietism is embodied in sharing possessions, sharing tasks and decisions with others, minimizing wants, and loving one's brethren.

4. Conclusion: Economic Sociology and the Sociology of Work

Economic sociological research has outlined the dynamically changing nature of macroscopic market conditions, viewable in both the internationalization of markets and in globalizing trends and consequently playing a role in the structure of work. These trends in turn have sensitized scholars of work to the changing conditions of new flexible and lean production regimes, increased firm emphasis on 'time to market', reduction in the number of job classifications, increases in job rotation and multitasking, and increases in workplace teams and joint tasking in the modern workplace, to name but a few, are having on contemporary workplaces in the USA and around the world (Smith 1997; Barley and Kunda 2001). Changes in economic conditions have brought with them new forms and configurations of firms (Powell 1990) that have led to new work arrangements, which in turn require rapidly changing skill requirements for many jobs (Barley and Kunda 2001).

And yet, even given the contemporary emphasis on the transformation and spread of market-based systems of exchange, it has also become apparent from the collective research of critical, network, ecological, and institutional sociologists of both economic and quasi-economic contexts that markets are neither the only recognizable form of exchange to arrange work, nor are they themselves free from the influence of other less 'instrumentally rational' and 'universalistic' action logics. As Lie (1992: 58) states regarding modes of exchange, 'Why should transactions between multinationals be equated with deals in weekend flea markets?'. In this regard, economic sociology has repeatedly illustrated that capitalism is neither singular nor converging on a monolithic form. Rather, capitalism is best conceived as a flexible system of relations whose parameters can accommodate divergent social, cultural, and network elements and still remain 'capitalist'. Nepotism, preferential pricing, patriarchy, morality, networks of association, and the like are viewable and understandable within capitalist and ostensibly market-based systems and outside them as well.

When we *assume* market relations as they are typically characterized, we overlook the ways in which work and economic regimes inform one another, can fundamentally differ in how exchange is conceptualized, and hence in how they are organized by participants. We contend that the relational dynamic between systems of exchange and work create the foundation for how economies themselves are created, conducted, and sustained. We have identified four ideal typical exchange logics that emerge from economic sociology and overlapping research and theory that reflect different assumptions concerning how exchange and work ought to be arranged, conducted, remunerated, and understood. Likewise, systems of work, once articulated, evolve and feed back onto exchange relations and in turn transform them.

By addressing the fundamental building blocks around which economies are built—the logics of exchange—we isolate groups of factors that collectively express different economic ideals and arrangements and as a result, different forms of work organization. This tack could complement current theories of economy and work by unifying their assertions and emphasizing their interpenetrating character. In short, dialogue between economic sociologists and scholars of work will encourage elaboration of formerly unchallenged assumptions by suggesting connections and divergences that would otherwise remain unexamined and hence unexplained.

References

Abbott, A. (1993). 'The Sociology of Work and Occupations', *Annual Review of Sociology*, 19: 187–209.

Abolafia, M. (1996). *Making Markets: Opportunism and Restraint on Wall Street*. Cambridge, MA: Harvard University Press.

—— and Biggart, N. (1991). Competition Perspective', in A. Etzioni and P. Lawrence (eds.), *Socioeconomics: Toward a Synthesis*. Armonk, NY: M. E. Sharpe.

Ahlander, N. R., and Bahr, K. S. (1995). 'Beyond Drudgery, Power, and Equity: Toward an Expanded Discourse on the Moral Dimensions of Housework in Families', *Journal of Marriage and the Family*, 57: 54–68.

Akerlof, G. A. (1984). 'Gift Exchange and Efficiency Wage Theory: Four Views', *American Economic Review Proceedings*, 97: 543–69.

Aldrich, H. E. (1999). *Organizations Evolving*. London: Sage.

—— and Pfeffer, J. (1976). 'Environments of Organizations', *Annual Review Of Sociology*, 2: 79–105.

Anderson, P. and Tushman, M. (1990). 'Technological Discontinuities and Dominant Designs: A Cyclical Model of Technological Change', *Administrative Science Quarterly*, 35: 604–33.

Appelbaum, R. P. and Henderson, J. W. (1992). *States and Development in the Asian Pacific Rim*. Newbury Park, CA: Sage.

Ayling, R. (1997). *The Downsizing of America*. Commack, NY: Nova Science Publishers.

Baker, W. (1984). 'The Social Structure of a National Securities Market', *American Journal of Sociology*, 89(4): 775–811.

—— Faulkner, D. and Fisher, G. A. (1998). 'Hazards of the Market: Continuity and Dissolution of Interorganizational Market Relationships', *American Sociological Review*, 63: 147–77.

—— (1990). 'Market Networks and Corporate Behavior', *American Journal of Sociology*, 96(3): 589–625.

Barkin, D. and Bennett, J. W. (1972). 'Kibbutz and Colony: Collective Economies and the Outside World', *Comparative Studies in Society and History*, 14(4): 456–83.

Barley, S. R. and Kunda, G. (2001). 'Bringing Work Back In', *Organization Science*, 12(1): 76–95.

Barnett, W. P. and Carroll, G. R. (1995). 'Modeling Internal Organizational Change', *Annual Review of Sociology*, 21: 217–36.

Barnett, R. C. and Rivers, C. (1998). *She Works/He Works: How Two-Income Families are Happy, Healthy, and Thriving*. Cambridge, MA: Harvard University Press.

Baron, J. N., Hannan, M. T., and Burton, M. D. (1999). 'Building the Iron Cage: Determinants of Managerial Intensity in the Early Years of Organizations', *American Sociological Review*, 64(4): 527–47.

Baumol, W. J., Blinder, A. S., and Wolff, E. N. (2003). *Downsizing in America: Reality, Causes, and Consequences*. New York: Russell Sage Foundation.

Beamish, T. D. (forthcoming). 'Mental Models', in J. Beckert and M. Zafirovski (eds.), *International Encyclopedia of Economic Sociology*. London: Routledge.

Becker, G. S. (1976). *The Economic Approach to Human Behavior*. Chicago, IL: University of Chicago Press.

—— and Murphy, K. M. (2000). *Social Economics: Market Behavior in a Social Environment*. Cambridge, MA: Belknap Press of Harvard University Press.

Bennett, J. W. (1975). 'Communes and Communitarianism', *Theory and Society*, 2(1): 63–94.

Berk, G. (1994). *Alternative Tracks: The Constitution of American Industrial Order*. Baltimore, MD: John Hopkins University Press.

Biggart, N. (1989) *Charismatic Capitalism*. Chicago, IL: University of Chicago Press.

—— and Beamish, T. (2003). 'The Economic Sociology of Conventions: Habit, Custom, Practice and Routine in Market Order', *Annual Review of Sociology*, 29: 443–64.

—— and Hamilton, G. G. (1992). 'On the Limits of a Firm-Based Theory to Explain Business Networks: The Western Bias of Neoclassical Economics', in N. Nohria and R. G. Eccles (eds.), *Networks and Organizations*. Boston, MA: Harvard Business School Press.

—— and Delbridge, R. (2004). 'Trading Worlds: A Typology of Systems of Exchange', *Academy of Management Review*.

—— and Guillén, M. F. (1999). 'Developing Difference: Social Organization and the Rise of the Auto Industries of South Korea, Taiwan, Spain, and Argentina', *American Sociological Review*, 64(5): 722–47.

Blau, P. M. and Duncan, O. D. (1967). *The American Occupational Structure*. New York: John Wiley & Sons.

Block, F. (1996). *The Vampire State and Other Myths and Fallacies about the U.S. Economy*. New York: New Press.

Bluestone, B. and Harrison, B. (1982). *The Deindustrialization of America*. New York: Basic Books.

Boeker, W. (1991). 'Organizational Strategy: An Ecological Perspective', *Academy of Management Journal*, 34(3): 613–35.

Boisot, M. and Child, J. (1988). 'The Iron Law of Fiefs: Bureaucratic Failure and the Problems of Governance in the Chinese Economic Reforms', *Administrative Science Quarterly*, 33: 507–27.

Bonacich, E. and Appelbaum, R. P. (2000). *Behind the Label: Inequality in the Los Angeles Apparel Industry*. Berkeley, CA: University of California Press.

Boserup, E. (1970). *Women's Role in Economic Development*. New York: St Martins Press.

Braverman, H. (1974). *Labor and Monopoly Capital*. New York: Monthly Review.

Brecher, J. and Costello, T. (1994). *Global Village or Global Pillage: Economic Reconstruction from the Bottom Up*. Boston, MA: South End Press.

Budros, A. (2002). 'The Mean and Lean Firm and Downsizing: Causes of Involuntary and Voluntary Downsizing Strategy', *Sociological Forum*, 17(2): 307–42.

Burawoy, M. (1979*a*). 'The Anthropology of Industrial Work', *Annual Review of Anthropology*, 8: 231–66.

—— (1979*b*). *Manufacturing Consent: Changes in the Labor Process under Monopoly Capitalism*. Chicago, IL: University of Chicago Press.

—— (1985). *The Politics of Production: Factory Regimes under Capitalism and Socialism*. London: Verso.

Burt, R. S. (1982). *Towards a Structural Theory of Action: Network Models of Social Structure, Perceptions, and Action*. New York: Academic Press.

—— (1992). *Structural Holes: The Social Structure of Competition*. Cambridge, MA: Harvard University Press.

Campbell, J. L. and Lindberg, L. (1990). 'Property Rights and the Organization of Economic Activity', *American Sociological Review*, 55: 634–44.

—— and —— (1991). 'The Evolution of Governance Regimes', in J. L. Campbell and J. R. Hollingsworth (eds.), *Governance of the American Economy*. New York: Cambridge University Press.

Castells, M. (1996). *The Rise of the Network Society. The Information Age: Economy, Society, Culture, 1*. Oxford: Blackwell.

Chandler, A. D. (1977). *The Visible Hand: The Managerial Revolution in American Business*. Cambridge, MA: Belknap Press.

Cheng, L. and Hsuing, Ping-Chun. (1992). 'Women, Export Oriented Growth, and the State: The Case of Taiwan', in R. Appelbaum and J. Henderson (eds.), *States and Development in the Asian Pacific Rim*. Thousand Oaks, CA: Sage.

Child, J. and Faulkner, D. (1998). *Strategies of Cooperation: Managing Alliances, Networks, and Joint Ventures*. New York: Oxford University Press.

Coleman, J. (1990). *Foundations of Social Theory*. Cambridge, MA: Belknap.

Collins, R. (1980). 'Weber's Last Theory of Capitalism: A Systematization', *American Sociological Review*, 45(6): 925–42.

—— (1986). *Weberian Sociological Theory.* Cambridge: Cambridge University Press.

Cornfield, D. B. (1991). 'The US Labor Movement: Its Development and Impact on Social Inequality and Politics', *Annual Review of Sociology,* 17: 27–49.

Crenson, M. A. and Ginsberg, B. (2002). *Downsizing Democracy: How America Sidelined its Citizens and Privatized its Public.* Baltimore, MD: Johns Hopkins University Press.

Daniels, A. K. (1987). 'Invisible Work', *Social Problems,* 34(5): 403–15.

Delaney, K. J. (1992). *Strategic Bankruptcy: How Corporations and Creditors Use Chapter 11 to their Advantage.* Berkeley, CA: University of California Press.

Devault, M. (1991). *Feeding the Family: The Social Organization of Caring as Gendered Work.* Chicago, IL: University of Chicago Press.

Dicken, P. (1992). *Global Shift: The Internationalization of Economic Activity,* 2nd edn. New York: Guilford Press.

—— (2003). *Global Shift: Reshaping the Global Economic Map in the 21st Century,* 4th edn. New York: Guilford Press.

Dobbin, F. (1994). *Forging Industrial Policy: The United States, Britain, and France in the Railway Age.* New York: Cambridge University Press.

—— and Dowd, T. J. (1997). 'How Policy Shapes Competition: Early Railroad Foundings in Massachusetts', *Administrative Science Quarterly,* 42(3): 501–29.

—— and Dowd, T. J. (2000). 'The Market That Antitrust Built: Public Policy, Private Coercion, and Railroad Acquisitions, 1825–1922', *American Sociological Review,* 65(5): 631–57.

Dore, R. P. (1973). *British Factory, Japanese Factory: The Origins of National Diversity in Industrial Relations.* Berkeley, CA: University of California Press.

Dowd, T. J. (2002). 'Culture and Commodification: Technology and Structural Power in the Early U.S. Recording Industry', *International Journal of Sociology & Social Policy,* 22(1–3): 106–40.

Eatwell, J., Milgate, M., and Newman, P. (eds.) (1987). *The New Palgrave: A Dictionary of Economics.* London: Macmillan.

Engels, F. (1902). *The Origin of the Family, Private Property and the State.* Chicago, IL: C. H. Kerr & Company.

Enloe, C. H. (1990). *Bananas, Beaches & Bases: Making Feminist Sense of International Politics,* 1st US edn. Berkeley, CA: University of California Press.

Erikson, K. T. and Vallas, S. P. (1990). *The Nature Of Work: Sociological Perspectives.* New Haven, CT: Yale University Press.

Escobar, A. (1995). *Encountering Development: The Making and Unmaking of the Third World.* Princeton, NJ: Princeton University Press.

Evans, P. B. (1995). *Embedded Autonomy: States and Industrial Transformation.* Princeton, NJ: Princeton University Press.

Faber, D. J. (1993). *Environment under Fire: Imperialism and the Ecological Crisis in Central America.* New York: Monthly Review Press.

Fields, K. J. (1995). *Enterprise and the State in Korea and Taiwan.* Ithaca, NY: Cornell University Press.

Fiske, A. P. (1991). *Structures of Social Life: The Four Elementary Forms of Human Relations*. New York/Toronto: The Free Press/Collier Macmillan.

Fligstein, N. (1987). 'The Intraorganizational Power Struggle: The Rise of Finance Presidents in Large Corporations, 1919–1979', *American Sociological Review*, 52: 44–58.

—— (1990). *The Transformation of Corporate Control*. Cambridge, MA: Harvard University Press.

—— (1996*a*). 'How to Make a Market: Reflections on the European Union's Single Market Program', *American Journal of Sociology*, 102: 1–33.

—— (1996*b*). 'Markets as Politics: A Political-Cultural Approach to Market Institutions', *American Sociological Review*, 61: 656–73.

—— (2001). *The Architecture of Markets: An Economic Sociology of Twenty-First-Century Capitalist Societies*. Princeton, NJ: Princeton University Press.

Francis, E. K. (1950). 'Toward a Typology of Religious Orders', *American Journal of Sociology*, 55(5): 437–49.

Freeman, C. (1987). *'The Challenge of New Technologies'*, Paper given at the symposium marking the 25th anniversary of the OECD Interdependence and Cooperation in Tomorrow's World, OECD, Paris.

Freeman, J., Carroll, G. R., and Hannan, M. T. (1983). 'The Liability of Newness: Age Dependence in Organizational Death Rates', *American Sociological Review*, 48(5): 692–710.

Gambetta, D. (1993). *The Sicilian Mafia: The Business of Private Protection*. Cambridge, MA: Harvard University Press.

Gereffi, G. and Fonda, S. (1992). 'Regional Paths of Development', *Annual Review of Sociology*, 18: 419–48.

—— and Korzeniewicz, M. (1994). *Commodity Chains and Global Capitalism*. Westport, CT: Praeger.

—— Wyman, D. L., Cheng, T-J., and Fajnzylber, F. (1990). *Manufacturing Miracles: Paths of Industrialization in Latin America and East Asia*. Princeton, NJ: Princeton University Press.

—— Spener, D., and Bair, J. (2002). *Free Trade and Uneven Development: The North American Apparel Industry after Nafta*. Philadelphia, PA: Temple University Press.

Gerlach, M. L. (1992). *Alliance Capitalism: The Social Organization of Japanese Business*. Berkeley, CA: University of California Press.

Gerson, K. (2002). 'Moral Dilemmas, Moral Strategies, and the Transformation of Gender: Lessons from Two Generations of Work and Family Change', *Gender And Society*, 16(1): 8–28.

Gonzalez del la Rocha, M. (1994). *The Resources of Poverty, Women, and Survival In Mexico City*. Oxford: Blackwell.

Granovetter, M. (1973). 'The Strength of Weak Ties', *American Journal of Sociology*, 78: 1360–80.

—— (1985). 'Economic Action and Social Structure: The Problem of Embeddedness', *American Journal of Sociology*, 91(3): 481–510.

—— (1992). 'Economic Institutions as Social Constructions: A Framework for Analysis', *Acta Sociology,* 35: 3–11.

Guillén, M. F. (2001). 'Is Globalization Civilizing, Destructive, or Feeble? A Critique of Five Key Debates in the Social Science Literature', *Annual Review of Sociology,* 27: 235–60.

—— Collins, R., England, P., and Meyer, M. (2002). *The New Economic Sociology: Developments in an Emerging Field.* New York: Russell Sage.

Gulati, R. and Gargiulo, M. (1999). 'Where do Interorganizational Networks Come From?', *American Journal of Sociology,* 104(5): 1439–93.

Habermas, J. (1975). *Legitimation Crisis,* T. Mccarthy (transl.). Boston, MA: Beacon Press.

Haggard, S. and Harvard University, Center for International Affairs. (1990). *Pathways from The Periphery: The Politics of Growth in the Newly Industrializing Countries.* Ithaca, NY: Cornell University Press.

Hamilton, G. G. (1994). 'Civilization and the Organization of Economies', in Neil Smelser and R. Swedberg (eds.), *Handbook of Economic Sociology.* Princeton, NJ: Princeton University Press.

Hannan, M. and Freeman, J. (1984). 'Structural Inertia and Organizational Change', *American Sociological Review,* 49, 149–64.

Hannan, M. T., Carroll, G. R., Dundon, E. A., and Torres, J. C. (1995). 'Organizational Evolution in a Multinational Context: Entries of Automobile Manufacturers in Belgium, Britain, France, Germany and Italy', *American Sociological Review,* 60(4): 509–28.

Hausman, D. M. and McPherson, M. S. (1990). *Economic Analysis and Moral Philosophy.* Cambridge: Cambridge University Press.

Henderson, J. W. and Castells, M. (1987). *Global Restructuring and Territorial Development.* London: Sage.

Henderson, R. M. and Clark, K. B. (1990). 'Architectural Innovation: The Reconfiguration of Existing Product Technologies and the Failure of Established Firms', *Administrative Science Quarterly,* 35: 9–30.

Herman, E. S. (1981). *Corporate Control, Corporate Power: A Twentieth Century Fund Study.* Cambridge: Cambridge University Press.

Hess, H. (1998). *Mafia and Mafiosi: Origin, Power and Myth.* New York: New York University Press.

Hicks, A., Friedland, R., and Johnson, E. (1978). 'Class Power and State Policy: The Case of Large Business Corporations, Labor Unions and Governmental Redistribution in the American States', *American Sociological Review,* 43(3): 302–15.

Hirsch, P. (1972). 'Processing Fads and Fashions: An Organization-Set Analysis of Cultural Industry Systems', *American Journal of Sociology,* 77(4): 639–59.

—— (1985). 'The Study of Industries', *Research in the Sociology of Organizations,* 4: 271–309.

Hoff, T. J. and MacCaffrey, D. P. (1996). 'Adapting, Resisting and Negotiating', *Work and Occupations,* 23(2): 165–90.

Hughes, E. C. (1958). *Men and their Work*. Glencoe, IL: Free Press.

Jeeves, A. H. and Crush, J. (eds.) (1998). *White Farms, Black Labor: The State and Agrarian Change in Southern Africa, 1910–50*. Portsmouth, NH: Heinemann.

Kaufman, B. E., Dunlop, J. T., Kerr, C., Lester, R. A., and Reynolds, L. G. (1988). *How Labor Markets Work: Reflections on Theory and Practice by John Dunlop, Clark Kerr, Richard Lester and Lloyd Reynolds*. Lexington, MA: Lexington Books.

Kessler-Harris, A. and Levenson, R. (1982). *Out to Work: A History of Wage-Earning Women in the United States*. New York: Oxford University Press.

King, A. and Lennox, M. (2000). 'Industry Self Regulation Without Sanctions: The Chemical Industry's Responsible Care Program', *Academy of Management Journal*, 43: 698–716.

Klatch, R. (1987). *Women of the Right*. Philadelphia, PA: Temple Press.

Knudsen, H. K., Johnson, J. A., Martin, J. K., and Roman, P. M. (2003). 'Downsizing Survival: The Experience of Work and Organizational Commitment', *Sociological Inquiry*, 73(2): 265–83.

Koeber, C. (2002). 'Corporate Restructuring, Downsizing, and the Middle Class: The Process and Meaning of Worker Displacement in the "New" Economy', *Qualitative Sociology*, 25(2): 217–60.

Kohn, M. E. (1990). 'Unresolved Issues in the Relationship between Work and Personality', in K. Erikson and S. P. Vallas (eds.), *The Nature of Work: Sociological Perspectives*. New Haven, CT: Yale University Press.

Kolko, J. (1988). *Restructuring the World Economy*. New York: Pantheon Books.

Kondo, D. K. (1990). *Crafting Selves: Power, Gender and Discourses of Identity in a Japanese Workplace*. Chicago, IL: University of Chicago Press.

Lazar, D. (1996). 'Competing Economic Ideologies in South Africa's Economic Debate', *British Journal of Sociology*, 47(4): 599–626.

Leblebici, H., Salancik, G. R., Copay, A., and King, T. (1991). 'Institutional Change and the Transformation of Interorganizational Fields: An Organizational History of the U.S. Radio Broadcasting Industry', *Administrative Science Quarterly*, 36(3): 333–63.

Lie, J. (1992). 'The Concept of Mode of Exchange', *American Sociological Review*, 57: 508–23.

—— (1997). 'Sociology of Markets', *Annual Review of Sociology*, 23: 341–60.

Littler, C. R. and Innes, P. (2003). 'Downsizing and Deknowledging the Firm', *Work, Employment and Society*, 17(1): 73–100.

Marx, K. (1967) *Capital: A Critical Analysis of Capitalist Production*. New York: International Publishers.

—— and McLellan, D. S. (1977). *Selected Writings*. Oxford: Oxford University Press.

Mather, L. M., Mcewen, C. A., and Maiman, R. J. (2001). *Divorce Lawyers at Work: Varieties of Professionalism in Practice*. New York: Oxford University Press.

Matthaei, J. A. (1982). *An Economic History of Women in America: Women's Work, the Sexual Division of Labor and the Development of Capitalism*. New York/Brighton, Sussex: Schocken Books/Harvester Press.

Maurice, M., Sellier, F., and Silvestre, JJ. (1986). *The Social Foundations of Industrial Power: A Comparison of France and Germany*. Cambridge, MA: MIT Press.
Milkman, R. (1987). *Gender at Work: The Dynamics of Job Segregation by Sex During World War II*. Urbana, IL: University of Illinois Press.
Mische, A. and White, H. (1998). 'Between Conversation and Situation: Public Switching Dynamics across Network Domains', *Social Research*, 65(3): 340–63.
Mizruchi, M. S. (1982). *The American Corporate Network, 1904–1974*. Beverly Hills, CA: Sage.
Moore, B. (1987). *Authority and Inequality under Capitalism and Socialism*. Oxford/New York: Clarendon Press/Oxford University Press.
Nash, J. and Fernandez-Kelly, P. (eds.) (1983). *Women, Men, and the International Division of Labor*. Albany, GA: State University of New York Press.
Naylor, T. H. and Willimon, W. H. (1997). *Downsizing the U.S.A*. Grand Rapids, MI: W. B. Eerdmans.
North, D. (1981). *Structure and Change in Economic History*. New York: W. W. Norton.
Ouchi, W. G. (1980). 'Markets, Bureaucracies and Clans', *Administrative Science Quarterly*, 25: 129–41.
Owens, L. H. (1977). *This Species of Property: Slave Life and Culture in the Old South*. New York: Oxford University Press.
Palmer, D., Barber, B., Zhou, X., and Soyal, Y. (1995). 'The Friendly and Predatory Acquisition of Large U.S. Corporations in the 1960s: The Other Contested Terrain', *American Sociological Review*, 60: 469–99.
——, ——, ——, and —— (1993). *'The Other Contested Terrain: The Friendly and Predatory Acquisition of Large U.S. Corporations in the 1960s'*, Paper given at the American Sociological Association, Miami.
Parrado, E. A. and Zenteno, R. M. (2001). 'Economic Restructuring, Financial Crisis and Women's Work in Mexico', *Social Problems*, 48(4): 456–77.
Perrow, C. (2002). *Organizing America: Wealth, Power and the Origins of Corporate Capitalism*. Princeton, NJ: Princeton University Press.
Podolny, J. M. (1994). 'Market Uncertainty and the Social Character of Economic Exchange', *Administrative Science Quarterly*, 39(3): 458.
Polanyi, K. ([1944] 1957). *The Great Transformation*. Boston, MA: Beacon Press.
—— (1957). 'The Economy as Instituted Process', in K. Polanyi, C. M. Arensberg, and H. W. Pearson, (eds.), *Trade and Market in the Early Empires: Economies in History and Theory*. Glencoe, IL: Free Press.
Powell, W. (1990). 'Neither Market nor Hierarchy: Network Forms of Organization', *Research in Organizational Behavior*, 12: 295–336.
Prechel, H. (1997). 'Corporate Transformation to the Multilayered Subsidiary Form: Changing Economic Conditions and State Business Policy' *Sociological Forum*, 12(3): 405–39.
Psacharopoulos, G. and Tzannatos, Z. (1993). 'Economic and Demographic Effects on Working Women in Latin America', *Journal of Population Economics*, 6: 293–315.
Redding, S. G. (1990). 'The Spirit of Chinese Capitalism'. *De Gruyter Studies in Organization*, 22.

Reich, R. (1991). *The Work of Nations*. New York: Vintage Books.
—— (1997). *The Future of Success: Working and Living in the New Economy*. New York: Vintage Books.
Reskin, B. (1993). 'Sex Segregation in the Workplace', *Annual Review of Sociology*, 19: 241–70.
Reskin, B. F. and Roos, P. A. (1990) *Job Queues, Gender Queues: Explaining Women's Inroads into Male Occupations*. Philadelphia, PA: Temple University Press.
Ridgeway, C. L. (1997). 'Interaction and the Conservation of Gender Inequality: Considering Employment', *American Sociological Review*, 62(2): 218–35.
Romo, F. and Schwartz, M. (1995). 'Structural Embeddedness of Business Decisions: The Migration of Manufacturing Plants in New York State, 1960 to 1985', *American Sociological Review*, 60(6): 874–907.
Rostow, W. W. (1990). *The Stages of Economic Growth: A Non-Communist Manifesto*. 3rd edn. Cambridge: Cambridge University Press.
Roy, W. G. (1997). *Socializing Capital: The Rise of the Large Industrial Corporation in America*. Princeton, NJ: Princeton University Press.
Rubery, J., Smith, M., and Fagan, C. (1999). *Women's Employment in Europe: Trends and Prospects*. London: Routledge.
Sassen, S. (1988). *The Mobility of Labor and Capital: A Study in International Investment and Labor Flow*. Cambridge, Cambridgeshire New York: Cambridge University Press.
—— (1993). 'Rebuilding the Global City: Economy, Ethnicity and Space', *Social Justice*, 20: 32–50.
—— (2001). *The Global City: New York, London, Tokyo*, 2nd edn. Princeton, NJ: Princeton University Press.
Schluchter, W. (1981). *The Rise of Western Rationalism*. Berkeley, CA: University of California Press.
Schwartz, M. and Mizruchi, M. S. (1987). *Intercorporate Relations: The Structural Analysis of Business*. Cambridge: Cambridge University Press.
Scott, A. M. (1994). *Gender Segregation and Social Change: Men and Women in Changing Labour Markets*. Oxford: Oxford University Press.
Seidman, M. (1991). *Workers Against Work*. Berkeley, CA: University of California Press.
Shaiken, H. (1993). 'Beyond Lean Production', *Stanford Law and Policy Review*, 5: 41–52.
Shenhav, Y. A. (1999). *Manufacturing Rationality: The Engineering Foundations of the Managerial Revolution*. Oxford: Oxford University Press.
Sibler, I. F. (1993). 'Monasticism and The "Protestant Ethic": Asceticism, Rationality, and Wealth in the Medieval West', *British Journal of Sociology*, 44(1): 103–23.
Simons, T. and Ingram, P. (1997). 'Organization and Ideology: Kibbutzim and Hired Labor, 1951–1965', *Administrative Science Quarterly*, 42(4): 784–813.
Simpson, I. H. (1989). 'The Sociology of Work', *Social Forces*, 67: 563–81.
Smith, A. (1776). *Inquiry into the Nature and Causes of the Wealth of Nations*. London: Printed for W. Strahan and T. Cadell.
Smith, C. W. (1989). *Auctions: The Social Construction of Value*. New York: Free Press.

—— (1997). 'New Forms of Work Organization', *Annual Review of Sociology*, 23: 315–39.

Smith, V. (2001). *Crossing the Great Divide: Worker Risk and Opportunity in the New Economy*. Ithaca, NY: ILR Press.

Stepan-Norris, J. and Zeitlin, M. (1991). ' "Red" Unions and "Bourgeois" Contracts?', *American Journal of Sociology*, 96(5): 1151–2000.

Stigler, G. J. (1968). *The Organization of Industry*. Homewood, IL: R.D. Irwin.

Stiglitz, J. E. (1999). 'Reforming the Global Economic Architecture: Lessons from Recent Crises', *Journal Of Finance*, 54(4): 1508–21. Papers and Proceedings, Fifty-Ninth Annual Meeting, American Finance Association, New York, January 4–6.

Stone, D. (1997). 'Work and the Moral Woman', *The American Prospect*, 35:78–87.

Storper, M. and Walker, R. (1989). *The Capitalist Imperative: Territory, Technology, and Industrial Growth*. Oxford: Basil Blackwell.

Strange, S. (1996). *The Retreat Of The State: The Diffusion of Power in the World Economy*. Cambridge: Cambridge University Press.

Swaminathan, A. and Carroll, G. (1995). 'Beer Brewers', in G. Carroll and M. Hannan (eds.), *Organizations in Industry. Strategy, Structure, and Selection*. New York: Oxford University Press.

—— and Carroll, G. R. (2000). 'Why the Microbrewery Movement? Organizational Dynamics of Resource Partitioning in the American Brewing Industry after Prohibition', *American Journal of Sociology*, 106: 715–62.

Thompson, E. P. (1964). *The Making of the English Working Class*. London: Victor Gollanz.

Tilly, C. and Tilly, C. (1998). *Work Under Capitalism*. Boulder, CO: Westview Press.

—— and —— (1994). 'Capitalist Work and Labor Markets', in N. J. Smelser and R. Swedberg (eds.), *The Handbook of Economic Sociology*. Princeton, NJ: Princeton University Press.

Treiman, D. J. and Roos, P. A. (1983). 'Sex and Earnings in Industrial Society: A Nine-Nation Comparison', *American Journal of Sociology*, 89(3): 612–50.

Useem, M. (1984). *The Inner Circle: Large Corporations and the Risk Of Business-Political Activity in the US and UK*. New York: Oxford University Press.

—— (1993). *Executive Defense: Shareholder Power and Corporate Reorganization*. Cambridge, MA: Harvard University Press.

—— (1996). *Investor Capitalism: How Money Managers are Changing the Face of Corporate America*. New York: Basic Books.

Utterback, J. M. (1994). *Mastering the Dynamics of Innovation: How Companies can Seize Opportunities in the Face of Technological Change*. Boston, MA: Harvard Business School Press.

Uzzi, B. (1996). 'The Sources and Consequences of Embeddedness for the Economic Performance of Organizations: The Network Effect', *American Sociological Review*, 61: 674–98.

—— (1997). 'Social Structures and Competition in Interfirm Networks: The Paradox of Embeddedness', *Administrative Science Quarterly*, 42(1): 35–67.

—— (1999). 'Embeddedness in the Making of Financial Capital: How Social Relations and Networks Benefit Firms Seeking Financing', *American Sociological Review*, 64(4): 674–705.

Vallas, S. P. (1993). *Power in the Workplace: The Politics of Production at A.T.&T.* Albany, CA: State University of New York Press.

—— (2001). 'The Transformation of Work', *Research in the Sociology of Work*, vo. 10. Amsterdam: JAI Press.

Vallier, I. (1962). 'Structural Differentiation, Production Imperatives and Communal Norms: The Kibbutz in Crisis', *Social Forces*, 40(3): 233–42.

Van Maanen J. V. and Barley, S. R. (1984). 'Occupational Communities: Culture and Control in Organizations', *Research in Organizatinal Behavior*, 6: 287–365.

Vogel, M. E. (2001), 'Lawyering in an Age of Popular Politics: Plea Bargaining, Legal Practice and the Structure of the Boston Bar, 1800–1860', *Sociology of Crime, Law, and Deviance*, 3: 207–52.

Wallerstein, I. M. (1984). *The Politics of The World-Economy: The States, the Movements, and the Civilizations.* New York: Cambridge University Press.

Weber, M. (1976). *The Protestant Ethic and the Spirit of Capitalis.* New York: Scribner.

—— (1978). *Economy and Society: An Outline of Interpretive Sociology*, Berkeley, CA: University of California Press.

Wellman, B. (1983). 'Network Analysis: Some Basic Principles', in R. Collins (ed.), *Sociological Theory.* San Francisco, CA: Jossey-Bass.

Wenger, E. (1998). *Communities of Practice: Learning, Meaning And Identity.* Cambridge: Cambridge University Press.

Wenger, E. C. and Snyder, W. M. (2000). 'Communities of Practice: The Organizational Frontier', *Harvard Business Review*, 78: 139–45.

White, H. (1981). 'Where Do Markets Come From?', *American Journal of Sociology*, 97: 514–47.

Yeargin, D. (1991). *The Prize: The Epic Quest for Oil, Money, and Power.* New York: Touchstone Books.

Zeitlin, M. (1974). 'Corporate Ownership and Control: The Large Corporation and the Capitalist Class', *American Journal Of Sociology*, 79(5): 1073–119.

Zelizer, V. (1988). 'Beyond the Polemics of the Market: Establishing a Theoretical and Empirical Agenda', *Sociological Forum*, 3: 614–34.

—— (1994). *Pricing the Priceless Child: The Changing Social Value of Children*, Princeton, NJ: Princeton University Press.

Zuboff, S. (1984). *In the Age of the Smart Machine: The Future of Work and Power.* New York: Basic Books.

Zukin, S. and DiMaggio, P. (1990). 'Introduction', in S. Zukin and P. DiMaggio (eds.), *Structures of Capital: The Social Organization of the Economy.* New York: Cambridge University Press.

10

Organizational Sociology and the Analysis of Work

Heather Haveman and Mukti Khaire

Organizations are the basic building blocks of modern societies (Coleman 1974; Perrow 1991). They wield great power and distribute many benefits, therefore, they have an enormous impact on many aspects of social life, including work. Indeed, structuralist scholars (Stolzenberg 1978; Baron and Bielby 1980) have proposed that, because most people work in organizations, they play the dominant role in shaping people's work lives. Over the last twenty-five years, sociologists have demonstrated that organizations' task structures, technologies, cultures, power relations, hiring and promotion practices, compensation systems and benefits, and job ladders affect workers' social, psychological, and economic outcomes (see Hodson and Sullivan 2002: 175–95 for a review).[1]

Although we have discovered much about how organizations affect work, far more remains to be learned. There is an intellectual divide between two groups of scholars—those who study organizations and those who study work—that severely limits our understanding. First, most people who study organizations (e.g. those who publish articles in *Administrative Science Quarterly* and *Organization Studies*) examine how

[1] Note that the link between organizations and employees runs in both directions. Fundamentally, people constitute organizations. Psychologists know that 'the situation is not independent of the people in the settings; the situation *is* the people ... structure, process, and culture are the *outcome* of people in organizations, not the cause of the behavior of the organization' (Schneider et al. 1995: 751, emphasis in the original). Organizational cultures and distinctive competencies reflect 'the people who have been in [the organization], the groups it embodies, and the vested interests they have created' (Selznick 1957: 16). Material, informational, and financial resources are valueless unless people are present and motivated to transform them into valued outputs. As Stinchcombe (1997) so aptly put it, people are the 'guts' of formal organizations.

organizational characteristics (size, age, technology, governance structure, and past performance) or environmental forces (state regulation, rivals' locations and actions, technological innovation, and links to supporting organizations) affect organizations themselves, rather than the people who work in them. Only a few investigate what organizations do to and for employees (see Barley and Kunda (2001) for a provocative discussion of this lacuna in organizational theory). Second, when people who study work (e.g. those who publish articles in *Work and Occupations* and *Work, Employment, and Society*) explicitly consider the role of employing organizations, they generally limit their analysis to three issues: segregation of workers by gender and race/ethnicity; technological change in employing organizations; and globalization (specifically, the rise of multinational firms and reliance on international trade). Even within these lines of inquiry, sociologists of work seldom apply insights from organizational analysis.

Our goal in this chapter is to help sociologists of work use theories of organizations to shed light on such important aspects of work as employment and job mobility, wages and benefits, and training. We begin by explaining how research on organizations has evolved over the last forty years and introduce contemporary theories of organizations. Then we show how organizational analysis can inform the sociology of work. In doing so, we both describe past contributions and suggest potentially fruitful lines of future study.

1. Organizational Sociology

Four research traditions dominate organizational sociology today: institutionalism (which has several variants), organizational ecology, resource dependence theory, and social network analysis. All of these research traditions have a common ancestor, contingency theory. In the paragraphs that follow, we first lay out the basic ideas of contingency theory and then introduce contemporary approaches to organizations.

Contingency Theory

This research tradition gets its name from the idea that organizational design choices are contingent on environmental conditions. The theory's basic precepts can be summarized in three sentences:

1. There is no one best way to organize.
2. All ways of organizing are not equally effective.
3. The best way to organize depends on the nature of the environment in which the organization is situated.

Research in this tradition has characterized organizational environments along several dimensions: *complexity*, meaning the number of environmental elements dealt with simultaneously by any organization; *uncertainty*, meaning the variability over time of those elements; and *interdependence*, meaning the extent to which those elements are related to one another.

Contingency theory has three variants. The first, structural contingency theory, emphasized differences in the essential designs and operations of organizations in placid versus rapidly changing environments (Burns and Stalker [1961] 1994; Lawrence and Lorsch 1967 Thompson 1967;). Structural contingency theorists (Blau and Scott 1962; Woodward [1965] 1994; Pugh et al. 1968, 1969) surveyed large numbers of organizations and assessed the interplay among many features of formal organizations, most notably production technology, organizational size, and environmental uncertainty. They viewed environmental conditions as exogenous to organizations and argued that in order to perform well, decision-makers had to adapt their organizations to environments. In contrast, strategic contingency theory (Child 1972) argued that organizational structure and performance are not fully environmentally determined. Instead, powerholders within organizations (usually managers) decide on strategic actions. Not only do managers choose organizational structures, but they also manipulate environmental features and choose relevant performance standards. A third variant, which is most closely associated with Galbraith (1973), stressed the information-processing requirements of environments. As environmental complexity and uncertainty increases, and as the interdependence among the organization's basic tasks increases, so does the amount of information needed to perform those organization's tasks. This, in turn, requires organizations to either reduce the need for information processing (by shifting from process to product structures or creating slack resources) or increase the ability to process information (by strengthening formal hierarchies and forging horizontal ties between units).

Contingency theory was broadly and ambiguously formulated. The precise form of external contingencies was never specified, which made it impossible to test the theory empirically (Schoonhoven 1981). Thus, contingency theory gradually evolved into an orienting strategy for organizational analysis—a meta theory. All research published in the last twenty-five years has recognized explicitly that organizational structure is contingent on external forces and that organizational performance is jointly contingent on structure and environment. Three contemporary lines of research on organizations—organizational ecology, resource-dependence theory, and social network analysis—see organizations' environments as being composed of other organizations. The fourth contemporary approach to organizations, institutionalism, is the most macroscopic, as it also pays considerable attention to environmental forces at the societal level. The following sections describe the basic precepts of these four research traditions and explain their contributions to our understanding of how organizations work.

Organizational Ecology

Organizational ecologists hold that we should study change rather than stability and study populations—collections of organizations that produce similar goods or services and thus depend on similar resources—rather than the individual members of those populations. Toward that end, ecologists have adapted Darwinian models of biological evolution and applied them to explain the evolution of organizational systems; that is, to explain rates of organizational founding and failure in terms of the material and cultural features of organizational environments (e.g. Carroll 1985; Hannan and Freeman 1989). More recently, ecologists have broadened their efforts beyond these population-level processes and have begun to analyze organizational growth, learning, diversification, and retrenchment (e.g. Haveman 1993; Sørensen and Stuart 2000). Ecological explanations highlight competitive and mutualistic interactions between organizations in a single population or, increasingly, between multiple subpopulations defined by characteristics such as size, market niche, technology, and location. Ecological analyses also assess how the attributes of any single organization—especially size, age, technology, and level of specialism or generalism—affect its life chances. For a review of organizational ecology, see Carroll and Hannan (2000).

A central tenet of organizational ecology is that organizations change slowly, if at all, because of strong inertial pressures (Hannan and Freeman 1989: 66–90). Eight constraints on adaptation are proposed, four internal and four external. The internal constraints are investment in plant, equipment, and specialized personnel; limits on the internal information received by decision-makers; internal political constraints supportive of vested interests; and organizational history, which justifies past actions and prevents consideration of alternative strategies. The external pressures for stability are legal and economic barriers to entry into and out of various areas of activity; constraints on the external information gathered by decision-makers; legitimacy considerations; and the problem of collective rationality and the general equilibrium. These pressures favour organizations that offer reliable performance and that can account rationally for their actions, which in turn require that organizational structures be highly reproducible—that is, unchanging (Hannan and Freeman 1989: 70–7). Because inert organizations are favored over changeable ones, inert organizations will be less likely to fail. Note that this structural inertia thesis does not imply that organizations never change; rather, it implies that organizations change *less rapidly* than do external conditions. It also implies that when organizations do change, resources are diverted from operating to reorganizing, reducing the effectiveness of operations and increasing the likelihood of failure. Finally, as mentioned above, recent ecological analysis has investigated the possibility that in some circumstances (e.g., following large scale shifts in environmental conditions) organizations can adapt and has shown that some kinds of change (e.g., related diversification) can be beneficial (e.g. Haveman 1992).

A great strength of this research tradition is its high level of paradigmatic consensus (Pfeffer 1993). Organizational ecologists know what outcomes to study (founding, failure, growth, economic performance, and change), what explanatory factors to consider (the number of organizations of various types, as well as their size, age, location, technology, and identity), and what analytical strategies to employ (quantitative analysis of longitudinal data covering entire industries). Because scholars in this tradition have always built on and refined each other's work, they have produced solidly cumulative knowledge about organizational dynamics.

Analysis of Intra- and Interorganizational Relationships

Scholars in two closely related research traditions—resource dependence and social network analysis—examine how relationships within and between organizations generate opportunities for and constraints on action. Extending ideas from exchange theory (Emerson 1962), resource-dependence theory (Pfeffer and Salancik 1978) posits that organizations' reliance on suppliers of critical resources (including financial and human capital), to customers, to the organizations that control distribution channels, and to governmental and professional oversight agencies makes them vulnerable and generates uncertainty for their decision-makers. To reduce this vulnerability and uncertainty and thereby improve performance, organizations tend to integrate vertically (to take over suppliers or distribution channels), expand horizontally (to diversify and therefore reduce reliance on any set of exchange partners), and enter into partnerships (strategic alliances, joint ventures, and director interlocks).

Social network research on organizations takes as fundamental the idea that organizations' attributes and behaviors can be understood in terms of patterns of ties among individuals and organizations: social relations are primary, while atomistic attributes are secondary. Such relational analysis comes in two stripes: 'macro' and 'micro'. Macrolevel network analysis, which is most similar to resource-dependence research, examines how ties to other organizations—state agencies, competitors, customers, and suppliers—affect organizational structures, actions, performance, and ultimately survival (e.g. Burt 1983). Some macrolevel network studies investigate ties between individuals that span organizational boundaries, notably the long tradition of research on interlocking directorates (see Mizruchi 1996 for a review). Other macro level studies examine ties that are not centred in individuals but rather are truly organizational, such as strategic alliances and joint ventures, supplier/buyer ties, and knowledge flows through patents (e.g. Baker 1990). Both kinds of macrolevel social network analysis focus on the set of opportunities networks open for organizations and the set of constraints networks impose on them.

In contrast, microlevel network research focuses on the social capital of individuals within organization—the resources that people derive from their connections to others, such as ties to kin and school mates, to current and former coworkers, or to counterparts in exchange-partner organizations (Bourdieu 1980; Coleman 1992: 300–21). Social capital improves access to information and material resources, which enhances social status, reduces uncertainty, and improves many individual outcomes. But social capital also creates mutual obligations, which channel action in some predictable directions and foreclose others (see Portes 1998 and Lin 1999 for reviews).

Three features of social networks—size, tie strength, and cohesiveness versus extensiveness—merit discussion. First, organizations' and individuals' social networks vary in the number of others to which to the focal actor is connected. Highly central actors are connected—either directly or indirectly—to many others. Second, social relations can range from very weak to very strong, along several dimensions. Weak ties involve little time, low emotional intensity, little intimacy or trust, or a single currency of exchange, while strong ties involve substantial time, great emotional intensity, great intimacy or trust, or multiple currencies of exchange (Granovetter [1974] 1995). While strong ties are easily activated and offer consistent support, the 'strength' of weak ties is that they provide nonredundant information and access to novel resources. This happens because humans and the organizations they build are subject to homophily—the tendency to be attracted to similar others (McPherson, et al. 2001). Weak ties tend to be to actors who are different from the focal actor and who therefore have different positions in and perspectives on the world. Third, social networks can be arrayed on a continuum from highly cohesive to very extensive. Highly cohesive networks consist of ties to a set of tightly interconnected actors. Very extensive networks, in contrast, bridge many 'structural holes', meaning they link otherwise unconnected groups of organizations or individuals (Burt 1992). Extensive networks offer access to more diverse information and resources, while cohesive networks offer greater support and more coherent demands.

Note the relationships between these features of social networks. First, strong ties require more effort to create and maintain than weak ties; given finite time and resources, individuals and organizations are likely to have fewer strong than weak ties. Thus, the more strong ties there are in an actor's network, the fewer direct ties there will be. Second, a long line of research on individuals has shown that strong ties are cohesive—your friends are friends with each other—while weak ties are the ones that bridge structural holes.

Resource-dependence theory and social network analysis share the great benefit of highlighting power and inequality, which are central concerns of sociology. Thus they return the study of organizations to the center of sociological inquiry. These two research traditions also make explicit the fact that economic action is intrinsically social. Thus they avoid both an undersocialized logic that treats individuals and organizations as akin to self-interested billiard balls, caroming off each other but never penetrating each other's surfaces, and an oversocialized logic that treats relationships between individuals and organizations as fully penetrating their identities and thus wholly determining their actions (Granovetter 1985).

Institutional Approaches to Organizations[2]

Institutionalists have long studied the impact of cultural and political factors on organizational goals, structures, and operations. Selznick's

[2] The chapter by Geoffrey Hodgson assesses the contribution of institutional economics to the study of work. Accordingly, we limit ourselves here to institutional analysis within sociology.

(1949) pioneering work on the Tennessee Valley Authority demonstrated that organizations are constrained by external actors' agendas—in Selznick's study, farmers opposed to government electricity generation—and that when organizations co-opt those actors, organizations' own goals are fundamentally altered. More recently, 'new institutionalists' (Meyer and Rowan 1977; DiMaggio and Powell 1983) have shifted the focus to cognition by investigating how organizations respond to diverse external expectations and revealing how those responses confer legitimacy in the form of taken-for-grantedness, which allows organizational structures and activities to stabilize. Borrowing from economics and rational-choice theory in political science, a third set of scholars (e.g. Brinton and Nee 1998) has begun to attend to how institutions—including single organizations and supra-organizational structures—facilitate exchange relations. These scholars emphasize bounded but intentional rationality, uncertainty, and risk. Ingram and Clay (2000) review the work of this third group of institutionalists, while Scott (2001) surveys the two other varieties of institutionalism in organizational analysis.

One of the most important ideas in institutional analysis is that of isomorphism (literally, 'same shape'). As communities of organizations evolve, a variety of forces (interorganizational power relations, the state and professions, and competition) promote isomorphism within sets of organizations that either are tied directly to each other or play similar roles. Three processes through which organizations become similar to others in their environment have been proposed: mimetic, coercive, and normative isomorphism (DiMaggio and Powell 1983). Mimetic isomorphism is, quite simply, the achievement of conformity through imitation. It can result from efficient responses to uncertainty ('when in doubt, do what other organizations facing the same environment do') or from bandwagon effects ('if many organizations adopt a structure or course of action, then follow their lead'). Coercive isomorphism stems from the pressure imposed by government regulation and administrative guidelines that authorize particular organizational structures and strategies. Finally, normative isomorphism involves pressures imposed by collective actors such as professional and trade associations, bodies that create informal expectations (if not formal rules) about what organizations ought to look like and how they ought to behave.

The strength of the institutionalist perspective is its sweeping reach. Consider the core concepts, *institution* and *institutionalization*. Scholars working in this tradition have claimed that institutionalization is both an outcome, which suggests attention to stability, and an ongoing activity, which suggests attention to change. They have identified structures in which institutions are embedded (the 'carriers' of institutions) at multiple levels in society: the routines, rules, scripts, and schemas that guide the perceptions and actions of individuals and small groups; local, regional, or demographic-group identities and regimes; meso level organizations, occupations, and industries; and society-wide norms and codified patterns of meaning and interpretation (Scott 2001). They have identified a wide array of mechanisms through which institutionalization operates: taken for grantedness, blind, or limitedly rational imitation, appropriateness, accreditation, social obligation, and coercion (Scott 2001). Finally, they have employed a wide array of research designs, ranging from ethnographies and qualitative historical studies to laboratory experiments to statistical analyses of survey and archival data.

Summary

These four contemporary traditions in organizational analysis vary widely. Institutional approaches to organizations are, arguably, the most macroscopic, as they pay most attention to things that pervade whole societies, such as state regulations. Ecological theory, resource-dependence theory, and network analysis operate on a somewhat lower level of analysis, as they are mostly concerned with collections of organizations. Scholars working in these four traditions have divergent understandings of social structure and identity. Resource-dependence theorists and social network analysts view social structure as inherently relational and social identity as being constituted by the ties between organizations and individuals. Organizational ecologists view social structure as inhering in cross-cutting distributions and social identity as deriving from position, absolute or relative, along one or more dimensions of social life, such as organizational age, technology, or strategy. Finally, and most complexly, for institutionalists social structure inheres in the nesting of large organizational communities, individual organizations, small groups, and individuals; it encompasses logics, meanings, and recipes for action. Identity, according to institutionalists, is a social construction—it arises from both relationships (dependencies and networks) and distributional locations.

Having illustrated, albeit briefly, the current state of organizational analysis, we now turn to the issue of how organizational analysis can inform the sociology of work. The next section explains what empirical research on organizations has revealed about several different aspects of work. We also consider obvious but hitherto unstudied implications of organizational theories for people's work lives.

2. Organizational Sociology and Work

Our assessment of how organizations shape people's work lives focuses mainly on intra-organizational forces: formal structures and practices (task structures, internal labor markets, human resources policies, and workforce composition), size, culture, and power. We also pay attention to interorganizational forces, such as state regulations, industry structures and dynamics, labor market structures, the actions of educational institutions, and professionalization projects.[3] For the sake of logical coherence and brevity, we limit ourselves to the socioeconomic effects of organizations on employees: work structures (full-time, part-time, or temporary/contingent work), compensation and nonmonetary rewards, ascriptive (gender, race, and age) segregation and inequality, career mobility, and work/family balance.[4] In the paragraphs that follow, we explain the implications of each perspective on organizations for workers' social and economic outcomes, and describe the findings of empirical research. We also point out many untested links between formal organizations and peoples' work lives.

Organizational Ecology

Organizational ecologists who study work-related phenomena have examined how the demography of organizations within a population (their numbers and size distribution) and organizational size inequality (the number of organizations larger than the focal firm) affect job-shift patterns through matching and reputational processes (Hannan 1988; Greve 1994; Fujiwara-Greve and Greve 2000). Organizational size, for example, has a huge impact on job structures. Large organizations are inevitably more bureaucratic, in the Weberian sense, than their small counterparts:

[3] Note that we leave coverage of one intra-organizational factor, technology, to Chapter 12 by Jacques Bélanger and we leave coverage of one interorganizational factor, professions, to Chapter 13 by Keith Macdonald. Note also that we limit ourselves to contemporary workplaces in developed nations, thereby ignoring longer-term changes in the nature of work in these nations, as well as trends in developing nations. Finally, we spend no time on the effects of unionization and worker organization, as that huge subfield merits separate attention.

[4] Chapter 15 on identity by Robin Leidner will highlight some psychological outcomes for employees.

they have more formal procedures and more managers to oversee people working in more vertically and horizontally differentiated subunits (Blau and Schoenherr 1971). Given these size-based differences in job structures, employees who are poorly matched to their current jobs and firms will look for better matches in smaller or larger firms; for this reason, rates of movement between employing organizations will be high when many firms of all sizes operate and workers can search for organizations that offer the best fit. There is a second nonobvious effect of organizational size: because large organizations tend to offer better rewards than small organizations, workers seeking improved rewards tend to move to large firms; for this reason, greater organizational size inequality increases rates of movement between firms.

Ecologists have also analyzed how vital events in the lives of organizations—founding, growth, contraction, merger, and dissolution—affect job mobility. Founding and growth create jobs wholesale; merger shifts many jobs from one organization to another; contraction, merger, and dissolution destroy huge numbers of jobs (Haveman and Cohen 1994). For instance, foundings create a large proportion of new jobs (Birch 1987). To fill these jobs, people are often hired out of established organizations. The larger the newly founded ventures (the more jobs they have to fill), the bigger the direct impact of founding on job mobility. Organizational dynamics also have indirect effects on job mobility. To continue the example of foundings, the movement of a worker from an established to a new organization creates a vacancy in the established organization. This vacancy is filled when someone new enters that recently vacated position. This second move causes the vacancy to shift to the newcomer's former job. Thus a chain of workers moves in one direction and a chain of job vacancies moves in the opposite direction (White 1970), amplifying the effect of the initial move from the established to the new organization.

Recent ecological research reveals other potentially fruitful paths of inquiry. Organizations that are at high risk of failure (small, low-status, and specialist firms) are also very likely to promote employees because they have little bargaining power (Phillips 2001). On the other hand, firms that occupy robust competitive positions (that operate in sectors that contain few rivals) have a lot of bargaining power and find it easy to recruit employees; hence, they are unlikely to use internal promotions to fill vacancies (Phillips and Sørensen 2003). This line of reasoning has implications for other work outcomes. If organizations in more robust competitive positions have more bargaining power vis-à-vis their employees, then they should be able to recruit better quality employees than their frailer rivals, even if they pay the same wages and offer similar benefits and working conditions. Alternatively, more robust organizations should be able to pay lower wages and offer fewer benefits to attract and retain the same quality employees as their frailer rivals.

Ecological theory can also shed light on the myriad and often indirect effects of one organizational population on another. Consider foundings again. By competing for skilled workers, new ventures may force established rivals to improve working conditions for their own employees. For instance, many high-technology ventures founded in the 1990s developed new work cultures—configurations of practices, norms, and job structures—that tended to be more informal, flexible, egalitarian, and dependent on 'high-powered' incentives such as stock options than were the cultures of established organizations in the same industries (Baron et al. 1996). Caught in tight labor markets (with unemployment rates of less than 3 percent in some regions), established rivals had little choice but to adopt many of these workplace innovations, if they were to keep from losing valuable and scarce employees.

Finally, paying attention to structural inertia—that central tenet of organizational ecology—can help us understand that even the strongest external forces are unlikely to revolutionize work settings. Strong inertia was seen, for example, in East German symphony orchestras after the fall of the Berlin Wall and the subsequent reunification of Germany. Those tremendous shocks had little impact on orchestras' structures and everyday operations (Allmendinger and Hackman 1996). Although players had more say in what was performed in 1991 than in 1990 and were more optimistic about their compensation, nothing else about their work lives changed. Thinking more generally, high levels of structural inertia may make gender- and race-/ethnicity-based segregation and wage inequality resistant to the reforming forces of state regulation, union drives, and shifting labor force demographics.

Resource Dependence and Macrolevel Social Networks: Ties Between Organizations

Resource dependence theory and macrosocial network analysis provide sharp lenses through which to appreciate how organizations' exchange relations shape personnel policies, wages, discrimination, and workforce diversity. For example, resource dependence theory focuses attention on the fact that public sector firms are more dependent on state resources than private sector firms; hence public sector firms are more likely to comply with government regulations on hiring and promotion policies and therefore to meet targets for gender and racial/ethnic composition (e.g. Beehr and Juntenen 1990). And because state funded organizations find it harder than their privately funded peers to resist state policy directives, they are likely to exhibit greater racial/ethnic and gender diversity and lower levels of discrimination.

In a different vein, Fligstein's analysis (1990) of large US corporations demonstrated how three conceptions of control—production, marketing, and finance—followed in quick succession, as a consequence of shifts in government policy. The kinds of people at the top of corporate hierarchies changed in step with external conceptions of control: at first manufacturing executives dominated, then sales and marketing, and finally finance and accounting. According to resource dependence theory, these changes at the top should cascade through the ranks. For instance, having marketing executives dominate the top ranks should confer greater power on all marketing personnel throughout a firm; with greater power comes increased ability to redesign jobs and reward systems and to alter personnel policies. Further, the effects of the marketing function's power should be felt by exchange-partner organizations. Educational institutions, for instance, should expand programs to train students in the dominant field or create finer distinctions within the field (services marketing, industrial marketing, etc.), which in turn should lead to the creation of more complex occupational structures.

Although resource dependence theory usually focuses on power/dependence relations *between* organizations, it can be extended to consider power/dependence relations *within* organizations; that is, relations between a single organization and its employees. Some employees have skills or access to resources that are rare and hard to replicate. The obvious example is highly skilled manual and technical employees. The classic case of resource dependence creating strong and unexpected power relations within an organization is Crozier's study (1964) of a French cigarette factory. The maintenance mechanics, who were low-level employees, were the only ones who could keep the rickety factory machinery operating, so they held considerable sway over their bosses. This logic applies to employees, such as purchasing agents and recruiters, who work in positions that allow (indeed, require) them to develop extensive networks outside their employers. Such well-networked individuals gain control over critical tasks and resources; hence, they gain power over their employers. Resource dependence theory also helps explain why contingent and temporary workers have to put up with 'bad jobs'—those that offer low pay, virtually no opportunity for advancement, and few fringe benefits (Kalleberg et al. 2000). Since contingent and temporary workers can be replaced easily (indeed, their jobs are designed with that outcome in mind), employers are not greatly dependent on them and so need not provide them with the working conditions or benefits that would ensure retention.

Macrolevel network analysis offers similarly novel insights about work. The structure of firms' buyer/supplier networks strongly affects their chances of surviving cyclical downturns. Research on US garment manufacturers shows that firms that have only weak (arm's length) relationships with many subcontractors and those with strong relationships with a few subcontractors are both more likely to fail (and so throw their employees out of work) than firms that have a mix of arm's length and strong relationships (Uzzi 1996). This difference in viability should affect garment manufacturers' relations with their employees. Most basically, having the optimal mixture of relationships with subcontractors should reduce the need to use temporary or part-time workers. Building on the ecological research described above (Phillips 2001; Phillips and Sørensen 2003), having the optimal mix of relationships with subcontractors should also increase bargaining power vis-à-vis employees and allow firms to offer employees lower wages and benefits than rivals that have suboptimal subcontractor networks.

Another example of the importance of interorganizational networks comes from Japan, where *keiretsu*—webs of firms whose ties consist of both interlocking ownership and buyer/supplier relations—create a stratified economy (e.g. Lincoln et al. 1996). Large firms in the core of these networks are buffered from many economic shocks and so can offer their employees 'lifetime' employment, while the smaller, more dependent firms at the peripheries cannot. Business groups are found in many other countries; for example, *chaebol* in Korea, *qiye jituan* in China, and industrial districts in Italy. But the nature of these interorganizational networks varies greatly across societies, because each society constitutes a unique combination of fiscal, political, and social institutions (Orrù et al. 1991). Therefore, the effects of business groups on job structures and working conditions will vary greatly across national contexts.

Microlevel Social Networks: Ties Between Individuals

Many studies show how microlevel social networks affect work life. The most prominent may be Granovetter's research ([1974] 1995) on the importance of weak ties in the job search process. Recall that weak ties (which involve little time, low intensity, or a single currency of exchange) are often to people who are different from you and who have different information about the work world; thus weak ties tend to transmit non-redundant information that may be uniquely useful in your job search. In contrast, strong ties (which involve substantial time, great intensity, or multiple currencies of exchange) are usually to people who are similar to you; you also tend to be tied to each other. Thus strong ties often transmit 'old news'—things you already know. For this reason, weak ties are more likely than strong ties to provide novel (and therefore fruitful) leads regarding available and suitable jobs.

The extent to which employees' social networks bridge 'structural holes', meaning they link otherwise unconnected groups, also shapes work-related outcomes. People with extensive networks are better able to gather information and exert influence at work; this enhances their task performance and career prospects in many settings (Burt 1992). For example, Burt (1997) found that managers in a computer firm whose networks bridged multiple structural holes were more likely to get promoted than those whose networks bridged few or no structural holes. These benefits were strongest for managers who had few peers. Burt (1992) also found that senior employees in a financial services firm whose networks bridged multiple structural holes received higher bonuses than those whose networks bridged few or no structural holes.

Although bridging structural holes enhances access to information and other resources, such loosely connected networks may also generate inconsistent performance demands. Moreover, showing different 'faces' to different parts of a network may generate distrust. Such an effect was found by Podolny and Baron (1997) in their study of employees in a high-technology firm. Employees with few bridges over structural holes in their social networks were faced with more consistent expectations on the job and were trusted more by fellow workers; consequently, they were more likely to be evaluated well and promoted. This study showed that the *content* of individuals' social networks—the 'currencies' that people exchange, such as friendship, task-related information, career advice, and authority to act—matters as much as, if not more than, the *structure* of their networks—whether they consist of weak or strong ties, whether they bridge structural holes or bind people tightly to a small social circle.

Much recent research focuses on the gender and racial/ethnic composition of social networks. Two closely related studies (Fernandez and Weinberg 1997; Petersen et al. 2000) found that the hiring process in a bank's customer service center and a high-technology firm, respectively, was partly meritocratic and partly determined by applicants' ties to current employees. Current employees could give family and friends advice about what recruiters were looking for, which made it easier for those applicants to show recruiters how well they 'fit' the firm and the job. Moreover, in the high-technology firm, which employed mostly whites whose social networks comprised mostly other whites, minority applicants lacked the network access that facilitated getting hired. The social ties that increase the chance people will be hired in the first place also affect their likelihood of exiting the firm: the turn over of referrers from the bank's customer service centre increased the turnover rates of referees (Fernandez et al. 2000). Social ties also affect wages: applicants for jobs in a high-technology firm who knew current employees negotiated higher salaries than those who did not because applicants with friends inside the high-technology firm learned more about the firm's pay practices and their friends lobbied more strongly to have them hired (Seidel et al. 2000). Most employees in this firm were white; since members of racial/ethnic minorities were less likely than whites to be friends with current employees, it was harder for members of racial/ethnic minorities to negotiate high salaries. Thus the ultimate consequence of differential network access was to perpetuate salary gaps between white and nonwhite workers.

Researchers have also considered interactions between social capital (resources derived from social networks) and human capital (personal resources). In a study of income attainment by Dutch managers, Boxman et al. (1991) found that human and social capital were substitutes, albeit with asymmetrical effects: while social capital increased income attainment at all levels of human capital, human capital had no effect on income attainment at the highest levels of social capital. This finding, coupled with that of Seidel, Polzer, and Stewart (2000), may help to explain why researchers observe racial/ethnic segregation and inequality in organizations even after they control statistically for the effects of education and skills. If social contacts improve the chances of getting a good job at high pay, net of individual abilities, workers must have the right social contacts to get ahead. Members of racial/ethnic minorities are less likely than whites to have contacts in organizations with good jobs and so are trapped in low-paying positions.

Finally, social networks shape organizational demography—the distribution of employees along such salient dimensions of social position as gender, race/ethnicity, age, and education—through their effects on job mobility. As described above, weak ties (rather than strong ones), bridges over structural holes (rather than ties to a small clique), and network composition all have huge effects on people's opportunities to move within and across employing organizations. Moreover, individuals' personal resources (their human capital) and networks (their social capital) jointly determine their chances of encountering and seizing opportunities to get better jobs. Over time, the differential mobility of members of various demographic subgroups alters organizational demography. In particular, the universal human tendency toward homophily—to have social ties to similar others—inevitably yields gender and racial/ethnic segregation in employing organizations, unless countered by some exogenous force, such as an official state policy.

Institutional Approaches to Organizations

Institutionalists have conducted scores of studies of the diffusion of organizational structures and practices and their consequences for work. An excellent example is Guillén's (1994) comparative analysis of the spread of three managerial ideologies (scientific management, human relations, and structuralism) in employing organizations in the USA, Britain, Spain, and Germany over the course of the twentieth century. He demonstrated clearly that the adoption or rejection of these models for organizing and controlling workers was not driven by efficiency or technological considerations. Instead, institutional forces such as education (which prepared managers to be more or less receptive to different ideologies), the political actions of professional associations, state policies, and workers' attitudes determined which management paradigms were adopted and which were rejected. Similarly, Maurice, Sellier, and Silvestre (1986) found that, contrary to the expectation that modern societies converge towards a single model of social relations, Germany and France have profoundly different labor management systems. For example, while Germany has a very integrated approach to employee skill formation (with employers, unions, and local and federal governments all playing active roles), France does not. These scholars concluded that such basic things as job descriptions, job categories, and wage rates are created and maintained by particular societal conditions; therefore, they are not easily compared across nations. Finally, Cole (1989) found that the adoption and retention of innovative work group activities (worker participation in management of production processes and quality) varied across three national contexts—Japan, Sweden, and the USA. Labor unions, trade associations, and government agencies all affected the diffusion of these innovations, as well as their effectiveness. Japanese firms adopted these work group activities at higher rates and were more effective than Swedish firms, while Swedish firms both adopted them more widely and used them more effectively than US firms.

Institutionalists view organizational attributes as rationalized myths—widely held beliefs ('everyone knows they are true') concerning what individuals, groups, and whole organizations must do to accomplish their goals—that are played out in all organizations in their quest for legitimacy (Meyer and Rowan 1977). Therefore, institutionalists often study how such powerful entities as the state and the market influence organizations' internal workings, including their personnel practices. The targets of such analysis include civil service reform in city government; due process and grievance procedures; internal labor market structures; pension plans; family, maternity, and medical leave policies; and diversity management practices. A prime example is Dobbin et al.'s (1993) analysis of how US employers responded to the passage of Equal Employment Opportunity (EEO) legislation. They argued that EEO law precipitated a tug-of-war between coercive state pressures and organizational self-interest; personnel practices that supported internal labor markets emerged as the winner of this battle. Over time, these practices were adopted by firms to symbolize their commitment to EEO rather than to reduce actual workplace racial or gender inequality or to promote efficiency. This analysis also showed that human resources managers socially constructed a vague and uncertain mandate from the US government; they were in a position to actually define what was thought to be definitive—'thou shalt not discriminate'—but was really up for specific definition.

Institutional analysis can produce provocative new conclusions about work. For example, Nelson and Bridges' analysis (1999) of pay discrimination lawsuits in the USA showed that standard operating procedures often created pay inequalities between traditionally male jobs (e.g. maintenance mechanic) and traditionally female jobs (e.g. secretary). When employers were sued, they attributed wage rates to 'the market', but in practice they relied on intermediaries, such as personnel managers and compensation consultants, to set pay rates. These intermediaries have biases that are reflected in choices about which jobs are included in comparability surveys. When challenged in the courts, these inequitable wage rates were sanctioned by judges who construed the 'the market' as an objective arbiter of worth rather than a construction of personnel managers and consultants and viewed wage setting as a neutral process rather than a politics ridden effort.

Many institutional analyses explain organizational structure by reference to legitimation. Since formal structure determines the set of jobs in any organization, legitimacy driven adoption of new structures affects who is hired and promoted, how they are socialized and trained, and how their tasks relate to each other. Thus many institutional studies can be extended logically to shed light on job structures and personnel practices. Consider two examples. First, Simons and Ingram (1997) found that ideologies that are deeply entrenched within organizations can determine work practices; but these ideologies, and their attendant work practices, can also be eroded by external pressures. They analyzed Israeli *kibbutzim* — socialist co operatives that originally embraced the ideal of self-reliance. This ideological stance was manifested in a dependence on *kibbutz* members for all labour. After its founding, Israel became increasingly dominated by a capitalist ideology that emphasized efficiency and flexibility. Market competition and cultural expectations both pushed *kibbutzim*, especially those that were highly dependent on banks and those that emphasized a moderate form of socialism and thus de-emphasized political goals, to use more outside labor.

Second, consider the paradox of downsizing in Japan—the country where large corporations long boasted lifetime employment. Ahmadjian and Robinson (2001) found that institutional supports for lifetime employment policies in large, old, and highly reputed Japanese firms broke down as more and more firms downsized in the face of severe economic pressures in the 1990s. The growth of this bandwagon rendered the actions of any single firm less prominent and thus made firms increasingly likely to downsize. Similar trends can be seen in Europe today, where downsizing by large employers began some two decades after it started in the USA.

Finally, institutional analysis can help us develop more nuanced explanations of unexpected empirical results in the study of work. Consider a puzzling finding in research on wages and turnover rates. Although efficiency wage theory suggests that there exists a rational wage level sufficient to recruit employees for any task, Powell, Montgomery, and Cosgrove (1994) showed that paying more than the efficiency wage reduces turnover. This unexpected result can be explained by thinking about wages as institutions: if wages are socially determined and enforced, they cannot be fixed at a single 'efficient' level. Instead, wages and other forms of compensation vary across industries, time periods, and regions.

As Meyer and Rowan (1977: 343) pointed out, 'norms of rationality are not simply general values. They exist in much more specific and powerful ways in the rules, understandings, and meanings attached to institutionalized social structures.' Thus, ideas of what constitute appropriate wage levels will be the same for organizations that face the same environment.

3. Focus on Work–Family Balance

Our discussion has tended to focus more on job mobility than on any other aspect of work, in part because mobility has received the most attention from organizational sociologists. We have also discussed wages and benefits. But many critical issues in the sociological study of work have seldom been informed by organizational analysis. Here, we consider one topic that clearly merits further study: work–family balance. This issue has been around for as long as people have worked outside the home, but, as the number of women in the workforce has increased, it has taken center stage.

Hochschild's pioneering work (1989) revealed that in 80 percent of dual-earner families, women shoulder most of the burden of housework and childcare. Work and family pressures are interdependent: stress from one's work life carries over into the home and vice versa (Zedeck and Mosier 1990). This is increasingly true for men as well as women. A study of one large firm that was publicly committed to family friendly policies showed that as employees spent more time at work, their home life suffered; despite the presence of such benefits as sick-child care, elder-care referral services, and flexible or compressed work days, both male and female employees chose to work longer hours, in part to avoid the tensions of home and family (Hochschild 1997).

Theories of formal organizations—particularly institutional, resource-dependence, and social network—have much to say about practices that make it easier for men and women to balance work and family responsibilities. The institutional perspective is particularly useful for predicting how employers will adapt to changes in government regulations that promote or mandate family friendly practices. This kind of analysis demonstrates that there is often a gap between the law's intentions and its actual impact and that work–family tensions play out in unexpected ways. Resource dependence theory provides complementary insights by predicting which kinds of organizations will be more responsive to legal and other pressures for work–family balance. Finally, analysis of interpersonal networks can illuminate how organizational policies actually operate—their long-term impact on employees' careers.

Kelly's institutional analysis (2003) followed 389 US firms after the passage of the Economic Recovery Tax Act (ERTA) of 1981, which sought to spur employers to create childcare centres at work. Although employer-sponsored childcare programs did diffuse rapidly, dependent-care spending accounts became even more popular. This result is surprising because, in contrast with most US workforce laws (e.g. the EEO laws studied by Dobbin *et al.* 1993), ERTA was concrete and unambiguous. But dependent-care accounts had two advantages over childcare centers: they were less expensive and they were promoted by trusted advisors, namely management consultants. Consultants, like the HR managers studied by Dobbin et al. (1993), were able to manipulate the institutional environment to their own advantage.

For years, researchers considered motherhood to be the prime cause for women's low wages (Budig and England 2001) and for the revolving doors phenomenon that limits women's movement into nonfemale occupations (Jacobs 1989). But institutional analyses of employing organizations' cultures reveal that stereotypes about women's roles in the family have also affected their promotion chances and thus their earnings. Kay and Hagan's institutional analysis (1998), for example, showed that male lawyers in Canada were rewarded with promotions for exhibiting traditional corporate family images (simply having children was a strong predictor of being promoted to partner). In contrast, female lawyers were promoted only when they broke gender stereotypes by giving priority to work outside the home (logging many billable hours), bringing in many new corporate clients, and endorsing the goals of the traditional male law-firm culture.

According to resource dependence theory, organizations will do the most for those employees on whom they depend the most. When women constitute a large fraction of an employing organization's skilled workers, that organization can be expected to attend more to work–family issues. A good example is the US accounting and consulting firm Deloitte and Touche, which in 1991 realized that many women—who constituted just over 50 percent of its entry-level professionals—were leaving the firm before they were considered for promotion to partner (which typically happened after nine to twelve years of service). Troubled by high turnover rates among women, the firm interviewed its professionals and discovered that *both* women and men could not see how to make partner and have a family without the help of a stay-at-home spouse. In response, the firm dramatically overhauled its work structures (e.g. reducing time spent away from the office at the client's site) and personnel policies (e.g. job-assignment procedures); it also invested tremendous effort in changing its culture to be more inclusive of women. This firm is currently trying to diffuse these highly successful changes to its offices outside the USA. A survey of 712 US firms across all industries showed that responsiveness to dependence on valued employees is a general one: firms in industries with larger proportions of female workers were more likely to institutionalize formal sick leave policies to accommodate pregnancies (Guthrie and Roth 1999).

Finally, using social network analysis, Blair-Loy and Wharton (2002) found that ties to supervisors and powerful colleagues increased the chance that employees in a financial service firm would take advantage of family friendly policies such as childcare referral services, short-term leaves of absence (paid and unpaid), flexitime, compressed work weeks, and telecommuting. Connections to prominent individuals also buffered employees from any negative fallout from taking advantage of these policies—for example, from being perceived as entering 'the mommy track'.

4. Conclusion

Efforts to theorize more deeply connections between the features of formal organizations and the lives of the people who work in them will pay off handsomely. In all modern societies, organizations wield tremendous power and distribute innumerable benefits. All interests—economic, political, social, and cultural—are pursued through organizations. Thus, organizations can be deployed to concentrate or disperse power and to increase or decrease equality of opportunity and achievement. If sociologists of work take our suggestions to heart, they will develop more compelling explanations for persistent questions about the creation and maintenance of status orderings and resource distributions at work. Answers to these questions will make it possible for us to improve people's work lives by informing public policy.

By following our suggestions, the sociological study of work will gain in a second way. Most fundamentally, raising the level of analysis from the individual or work group to the organization can provide an entirely new perspective. Both institutional and ecological approaches to organizations emphasize studying work at the societal, sectoral, or individual organizational level, while resource dependence theory and social network approaches emphasize pairs and larger sets of interacting organizations. A more macroscopic focus can reveal many important but often neglected factors that shape individual- and group-level work outcomes.

References

Ahmadjian, C. L. and Robinson, P. (2001). 'Safety in Numbers: Downsizing and the Deinstitutionalization of Permanent Employment in Japan', *Administrative Science Quarterly*, 46: 622–54.

Allmendinger, J. and Hackman, J. H. (1996). 'Organizations in Changing Environments: The Case of East German Symphony Orchestras', *Administrative Science Quarterly*, 41: 337–69.

Baker, W. E. (1990). 'Market Networks and Corporate Behavior', *American Journal of Sociology*, 96: 589–625.

Barley, S. R. and Kunda, G. (2001). 'Bringing Work Back In', *Organization Science*, 12: 76–95.

Baron, J. N. and Bielby, W. T. (1980). 'Bringing the Firms Back In: Stratification, Segmentation, and the Organization of Work', *American Sociological Review*, 45: 737–65.

——, Burton, D., and Hannan, M. T. (1996). 'The Road Taken: Origins and Evolution of Employment Systems in Emerging Companies', *Industrial and Corporate Change*, 5: 239–75.

Beehr, T. A. and Juntenen, D. L. (1990). 'Promotions and Employees' Perceived Mobility Channels: The Effects of Employee Sex, Employee Group, and Initial Placement', *Human Relations*, 43: 455–72.

Birch, D. (1987). *Job Creation in America*. New York: Free Press.

Blair-Loy, M. and Wharton, A. S. (2002). 'Employees' Use of Work–Family Policies and the Workplace Social Context', *Social Forces*, 80: 813–45.

Blau, P. M. and Schoenherr, R. (1971). *The Structure of Organizations*. New York: Basic Books.

—— and Scott, W. R. (1962). *Formal Organizations: A Comparative Approach*. San Francisco, CA: Chandler Publishing.

Bourdieu, P. (1980). 'Le capital sociale: Notes provisaires', *Actes de la recherche en sciences sociales*, 31: 2–3.

Boxman, E. A.W., de Graaf, P. M., and Flap, H. D. (1991). 'The Impact of Social and Human Capital on the Income Attainment of Dutch Managers', *Social Networks*, 13: 51–73.

Brinton, M. C. and Nee V. (eds.) (1998). *The New Institutionalism in Sociology.* New York: Russell Sage Foundation.

Budig, M. J. and England, P. (2001). 'The Wage Penalty for Motherhood', *American Sociological Review*, 66: 204–25.

Burns, T. and Stalker, G. M. ([1961] 1994). *The Management of Innovation*, 3rd edn. Oxford: Oxford University Press.

Burt, R. S. (1983). *Corporate Profits and Co-optation*. New York: Academic Press.

—— (1992). *Structural Holes: The Social Structure of Competition*. Cambridge, MA: Harvard University Press.

—— (1997). 'The Contingent Value of Social Capital', *Administrative Science Quarterly*, 42: 339–65.

Carroll, G. R. (1985). 'Concentration and Specialization: Dynamics of Niche Width in Populations of Organizations', *American Journal of Sociology*, 90: 1262–83.

—— and Hannan, M. T. (2000). *The Demography of Corporations and Industries*. Princeton, NJ: Princeton University Press.

Child, J. (1972). 'Organizational Structure, Environment and Performance: The Role of Strategic Choice', *Sociology*, 6: 1–22.

Cole, R. E. (1989). *Strategies for Learning: Small-Group Activities in American, Japanese, and Swedish Industry*. Berkeley, CA: University of California Press.

Coleman, J. S. (1974). *Power and the Structure of Society*. New York: W. W. Norton.

—— (1992). *Foundations of Social Theory*. Cambridge, MA: Harvard University Press.

Crozier, M. (1964). *The Bureaucratic Phenomenon*. Chicago: University of Chicago Press.

DiMaggio, P. J. and Powell, W. W. (1983). 'The Iron Cage Revisited: Institutional Isomorphism and Collective Rationality in Organizational Fields', *American Sociological Review*, 48: 147–60.

Dobbin, F. R., Sutton, J. R., Meyer, J. W., and Scott, W. R. (1993). 'Equal Opportunity Law and the Construction of Internal Labor Markets', *American Journal of Sociology*, 99: 396–427.

Emerson, R. M. (1962). 'Power-Dependence Relations', *American Sociological Review*, 27: 31–41.

Fernandez, R. M., Castilla, E. J., and Moore, P. (2000). 'Social Capital at Work: Networks and Employment at a Phone Center', *American Journal of Sociology*, 105: 1288–356.

—— and Weinberg, N. (1997). 'Sifting and Sorting: Personal Contacts and Hiring in a Retail Bank', *American Sociological Review*, 62: 883–902.

Fligstein, N. (1990). *The Transformation of Corporate Control*. Cambridge, MA: Harvard University Press.

Fujiwara-Greve, T. and Greve, H. R. (2000). 'Organizational Ecology and Job Mobility', *Social Forces*, 79: 547–86.

Galbraith, J. R. (1973). *Designing Complex Organizations*. Reading, MA: Addison-Wesley.

Granovetter, M. S. (1985). 'Economic Action and Social Structure: The Problem of Embeddedness', *American Journal of Sociology*, 91: 481–510.

—— ([1974] 1995). *Getting a Job: A Study of Contacts and Careers*. Chicago, IL: University of Chicago Press.

Greve, H. R. (1994). 'Industry Diversity Effects on Job Mobility', *Acta Sociologica*, 37: 119–39.

Guillén, M. F. (1994). *Models of Management: Work, Authority, and Organization in a Comparative Perspective*. Chicago, IL: University of Chicago Press.

Guthrie, D. and Roth, L. M. (1999). 'The State, Courts, and Maternity Leave Policies in U.S. Organizations: Specifying Institutional Mechanisms', *American Sociological Review*, 64: 41–63.

Hannan, M. T. (1988). 'Social Change, Organizational Diversity, and Individual Careers', in M. Riley (ed.), *Social Change and the Life Course*, vol 1. Newbury Park, CA: Sage.

—— and Freeman, J. (1989). *Organizational Ecology*. Cambridge, MA: Harvard University Press.

Haveman, H. A. (1992). 'Between a Rock and a Hard Place: Organizational Change and Performance Under Conditions of Fundamental Environmental Transformation', *Administrative Science Quarterly*, 37: 48–75.

—— (1993). 'Organizational Size and Change: Diversification in the Savings and Loan Industry After Deregulation', *Administrative Science Quarterly*, 38: 20–50.

—— and Cohen, L. E. (1994). 'The Ecological Dynamics of Careers: The Impact of Organizational Founding, Dissolution, and Merger on Job Mobility', *American Journal of Sociology*, 100: 104–52.

Hochschild, A. R. (1989). *The Second Shift*. New York: Avon Books.

—— (1997). *The Time Bind: When Work Becomes Home and Home Becomes Work*. New York: Metropolitan Books.

Hodson, R. and Sullivan, T. A. (2002). *The Social Organization of Work*, 3rd edn. Belmont, CA: Wadsworth.

Ingram, P. and Clay, K. (2000). 'The Choice-Within-Constraints New Institutionalism and Implications for Sociology', in K. Cook and J. Hagan (eds.), *Annual Review of Sociology*, 27: 525–46.

Jacobs, J. (1989). *Revolving Doors: Sex Segregation and Women's Careers*. Stanford, CA: Stanford University Press.

Kalleberg, A. L., Reskin, B. F., and Hudson, K. (2000). 'Bad Jobs in America: Standard and Non-Standard Employment Relations and Job Quality in the United States', *American Sociological Review*, 65: 256–78.

Kay, F. M. and Hagan, J. (1998). 'Raising the Bar: The Gender Stratification of Law Firm Human Capital', *American Sociological Review*, 63: 728–43.

Kelly, E. (2003). 'The Strange History of Employer-Sponsored Child Care: Interested Actors, Uncertainty, and the Transformation of Law in Organizational Fields', *American Journal of Sociology*, 109: 606–49.

Lawrence, P. D. and Lorsch, J. W. (1967). *Organizations and Environments*. Boston, MA: Harvard Business School Press.

Lin, N. (1999). 'Social Networks and Status Attainment', *Annual Review of Sociology*, 25: 467–87.

Lincoln, J. R., Gerlach, M. L., and Ahmadjian, C. L. (1996). 'Keiretsu Networks and Corporate Performance in Japan', *American Sociological Review*, 61: 67–88.

McPherson, J. M., Smith-Lovin, L., and Cook, J. M. (2001). 'Birds of a Feather: Homophily in Social Networks', in K. Cook and J. Hagan (eds.), *Annual Review of Sociology*, 27: 415–44.

Maurice, M., Sellier, F., and Silvestre, J. (1986). *The Social Foundations of Industrial Power: A Comparison of France and Germany*. Cambridge, MA: MIT Press.

Meyer, J. W. and Rowan, B. (1977). 'Institutionalized Organizations: Formal Structure as Myth and Ceremony', *American Journal of Sociology*, 83: 340–63.

Mizruchi, M. S. (1996). 'What do Interlocks Do? An Analysis, Critique, and Assessment of Research on Interlocking Directorates', *Annual Review of Sociology*, 22: 271–98.

Nelson, R. L. and Bridges, W. P. (1999). *Legalizing Gender Inequality: Courts, Markets, and Unequal Pay for Women in America*. Cambridge: Cambridge University Press.

Orrù, M., Biggart, N. W., and Hamilton, G. G. (1991). 'Organizational Isomorphism in East Asia', in W. W. Powell and P. J. DiMaggio (eds.), *The New Institutionalism in Organizational Analysis*. Chicago: University of Chicago Press.

Perrow, C. (1991). 'A Society of Organizations', *Theory and Society*, 20: 725–62.

Petersen, T., Saporta, I., and Seidel, M. (2000). 'Offering a Job: Meritocracy and Social Networks', *American Journal of Sociology*, 106: 763–816.

Pfeffer, J. (1993). 'Barriers to the Advancement of Organizational Science: Paradigm Development as Dependent Variable', *Academy of Management Review*, 18: 599–620.

—— and Salancik, G. R. (1978). *The External Control of Organizations: A Resource Dependence Perspective*. New York: Harper & Row.

Phillips, D. J. (2001). 'The Promotion Paradox: Organizational Mortality and Employee Promotion Chances in Silicon Valley Law Firms, 1946–1996', *American Journal of Sociology*, 106: 1058–98.

—— and Sørensen, J. (2003). 'Promoting from a Position of Weakness: Firm Strength and the Rate of Internal Promotion', *Social Forces*, 81: 819–41.

Podolny, J. M. and Baron, J. N. (1997). 'Resources and Relationships: Social Networks and Mobility in the Workplace', *American Sociological Review*, 62: 673–93.

Portes, A. (1998). 'Social Capital: Its Origins and Applications in Modern Sociology', *Annual Review of Sociology*, 24: 1–24.

Powell, I., Montgomery, M., and Cosgrove, J. (1994). 'Compensation Structure and Establishment Quite and Fire Rates', *Industrial Relations*, 33: 229–48.

Pugh, D. S., Hickson, D. J., Hinings, C. R., and Turner, C. (1968). 'Dimensions of Organizational Structure', *Administrative Science Quarterly*, 13: 65–105.

——, Hickson, D. J., and Hinings, C. R. (1969). 'An Empirical Taxonomy of Structures of Work Organizations', *Administrative Science Quarterly*, 14: 115–26.

Schneider, B., Goldstein, H. W., and Smith, D. B. (1995). 'The ASA Framework: An Update', *Personnel Psychology*, 48: 747–73.

Schoonhoven, C. B. (1981). 'Problems with Contingency Theory: Testing Assumptions Hidden within the Language of Contingency "Theory" ', *Administrative Science Quarterly*, 26: 349–77.

Scott, W. R. (2001). *Institutions and Organizations*, 2nd edn. Thousand Oaks, CA: Sage.

Seidel, M. L., Polzer, J. T., and Stewart, K. (2000). 'Friends in High Places: The Effects of Social Networks on Discrimination in Salary Negotiations', *Administrative Science Quarterly*, 45: 1–24.

Selznick, P. (1949). *TVA and the Grassroots*. Berkeley, CA: University of California Press.

—— (1957). *Leadership in Administration*. Berkeley, CA: University of California Press.

Simons, T. and Ingram, P. (1997). 'Organization and Ideology: Kibbutzim and Hired Labor, 1951–1965', *Administrative Science Quarterly*, 42: 784–813.

Sørensen, J. B. and Stuart, T. E. (2000). 'Aging, Obsolescence, and Organizational Innovation', *Administrative Science Quarterly*, 45: 81–112.

Stinchcombe, A. L. (1997). 'On the Virtues of the Old Institutionalism', in J. Hagan (ed.), *Annual Review of Sociology*, 23: 1–18.

Stolzenberg, R. M. (1978). 'Bringing the Boss Back In: Employer Size, Employee Schooling, and Socioeconomic Achievement', *American Sociological Review*, 43: 813–28.

Thompson, J. D. (1967). *Organizations in Action*. New York: McGraw-Hill.

Uzzi, B. (1996). 'The Sources and Consequences of Embeddedness for the Economic Performance of Organizations: The Network Effect', *American Sociological Review*, 61: 674–98.

White, H. C. (1970). *Chains of Opportunity: System Models of Mobility in Organizations*. Cambridge, MA: Harvard University Press.

Woodward, J. ([1965] 1994). *Industrial Organization: Theory and Practice*, 2nd Edn. Oxford: Oxford University Press.

Zedeck, S., and Mosier, K. (1990). 'Work in the Family and Employing Organization', *American Psychologist*, 45: 240–51.

11

Ethics and Work

Karen Legge

Ethics has been defined as a 'systematic attempt to make sense of our individual and social moral experience, in such a way as to determine the rules that ought to govern human conduct, the values worth pursuing, and the character traits deserving development in life' (de George 1995: 19). In the last thirty years there has been an explosion of explicit interest in ethics relating to business and work organizations, reflected in the creation of new journals, academic courses, and posts in 'business ethics'. The intellectual roots of this explicit interest have been attributed variously to the corporate social responsibility movement that emerged during the Cold War, in an attempt to show an 'acceptable face' of capitalism in the face of the Marxist critique (Bowen 1953), to the impact of Rawls's *A Theory of Justice* (1971) (Bowie 2002), and to the feminist and Civil Rights movements in privileging issues of equal opportunity at work. In recent years, concerns about the environment and animal rights, the affects of globalization and, in the wake of corporate scandals, issues of corporate governance, have contributed to that interest (see special issue of *Organization* 1995; *Organization 2003)*.

However, though an explicit interest in business ethics is of relatively recent origin, an implicit concern with ethics at work has a far longer and distinguished pedigree in industrial sociology. At the heart of the work of the founding fathers, Durkheim, Marx, and Weber, lies concern with the ethics of work and society. Thus Durkheim reflected on the problem of social order and normlessness (anomie) in society and pondered on how the breakdown of the mechanical solidarity of primitive society, based on a *conscience collective*, might be replaced by an organic solidarity in industrialized society, founded on the interdependence of economic ties arising out of a specialist division of labor, networks of occupational associations linking individuals to the state, and the emergence within these associations of collectively created moral restraints on individualism. A major concern of Marx was the exploitative nature of work in capitalist societies, where the extraction of surplus value at the point of production inevitably led to worker alienation from the product of his/her labor, the act of production, from his/her human nature and from other people, as social relations were transformed into market relations. Further, he deplored how the logic of capital accumulation results in the commodification of labor as workers' activities are dominated by the requirements of profitability rather than by their own needs. Central to Weber's sociology was not only an anxiety that rationalization, the 'iron cage' of bureaucracy, would crush individual freedom and creativity, but a recognition that different life orders, including bureaucracy, had their own and different moralities. Just as impersonality and neutrality, combined with a technical rationality, were the appropriate values for bureaucracy, so passion and conviction were proper for the political order.

Indeed, a persistent theme in industrial sociology, which stems from the concerns of the founding fathers, is how legitimate social order/change comes about in organizations and society (Burrell and Morgan 1979). Fox's (1966) classic typology of unitary, pluralist, and radical frames of reference embodies competing perspectives on how such order is maintained or challenged in the work place. The interactionists, for example, focus on how the existing order is negotiated; critical theorists on how structural inequalities are both generated and challenged. At the heart of such debates is the assumption that members of organizations have different views about what constitutes the good and the just in society and at work. The definition of what should be 'a fair day's work for a fair day's pay', is central to the struggles over the frontiers of control. The ethics of work are implicated in the major contradiction embedded in capitalist systems: the need to achieve both the control and consent of employees. As Edwards (1990: 44) puts it: '[T]here is a double balance of conflict and co-operation: employers have to control workers while also releasing their creativity; and workers have interests in resisting their own subordination although also needing to co-operate with employers because they rely on them for their livelihoods'. This is reflected in debates about the function of personnel management. Is it, in pluralist terms, about 'achieving both efficiency and justice' (IPM 1963) or, in Marxist terms, about assisting in the exploitation of labor through obscuring its commodity status or, in Weberian terms, about mediating the tensions between instrumental and substantive rationalities?

In reviewing the writing on ethics and work, I will first consider the relevant ethical theories that have guided our thinking about what constitutes a 'good' work experience. I will then show how these may be applied to the analysis of work and employment in different socioeconomic contexts, differentiating between those employed at the 'core' of the organization–managers and knowledge workers–and those at the periphery on nonstandard contracts or even technically not employed by the organization for which they ultimately work (agency and subcontracted labour). Issues about diversity and equality are implicated here. The conclusion that I draw is that the norms derived from general ethical principles are best interpreted in the light of the work and wider social context.

1. Some Ethical Theory

Conventional ethical theory most frequently used in the discussion of work is the premodern, such as Aristotelianism (MacIntyre 1981) and that embodied in religious teaching, such as Judaeo-Christian and Islamic ethics and the modern rationalist ethics of the Enlightenment and beyond, notably Kant's categorical imperative ([1795] 1998), Mill's principle of utility ([1861] 1998), Rawls's difference principle (1971), and Freeman's stakeholder theory (1984). The latter modernist theories depict ethics as comprising collective codes of conduct that exist over and above the individual and which can be used to legitimate independent action.[1] At its most basic, ethical theory is concerned with the identification of what is 'good' and its just or fair distribution. Those of us brought up in the Judaeo-Christian tradition may have vivid memories of the parable of the laborers in the vineyard, where the 'good' was clearly identified (for the laborers, money for their contracted work; for the householder, their labor). What was at dispute was the fair allocation of the good, in that

[1] Partly due to constraints of space in this chapter, I choose not to engage with what has been termed the ethics of 'postmodern constructivism' (Editorial, *Organization*, 1995: 179; Cummings 2000). The point is that the relativism of postmodernism provides no firm basis for devising any generalizable ethical code. All we are left with is 'emotivism', the view that all moral judgements are 'nothing but expressions of preference, expressions of attitude and feeling' (MacIntyre 1981: 11). If, from a postmodern perspective, ethics are a matter of personal choice in the project of the creation and care of an aesthetic personal identity, their utility in guiding *general* evaluations about the ethicality of work and employment is questionable. Bauman's (1993) advocacy of Levinas's (1985) conception of morality as an individual, nonuniversalizable, nonreversible, *unconditional* 'being for the Other', while understandable as a reaction to the modernist collectivist utopias of the twentieth century, appears utopian itself, particularly in the context of global capitalism.

all the laborers received the same sum of money (i.e. one penny), but for different inputs (i.e. different hours of work and levels of effort). Leaving aside the theological message, the workers who had worked all day were aggrieved:

> ... they murmured against the good man of the house.
>
> Saying, 'These last have wrought but one hour, and thou hast made them equal unto us, which have borne the burden and heat of the day.'
>
> But he answered one of them, and said, 'Friend, I do thee no wrong: didst thou not agree with me for a penny? ... Is thine eye evil, because I am good?
>
> Is it not lawful for me to do what I will with mine own?'
>
> (Matthew 20: 11–15)

Here is a clear statement of the laborers' feelings of injustice in a way that mirrors the assumptions of Adam's equity theory of satisfaction (1963) and, indeed, those of distributive justice (lack of fairness in the allocation of outcomes). Juxtaposed is Christ's assertion of procedural justice (the householder had paid them what was agreed at the outset) and of interactional justice (the quality of 'good' treatment that the householder has shown to all) (Folger and Cropanzano 1998). Pushing the example further, one can find echoes of Nozick's (1974) theory of justice as entitlement—the pre-eminence of protecting liberty and, in particular, the right to acquire and transfer property freely, without interference from government or any other pressure group ('Is it not lawful for me to do what I will with my own?').

Major ethical theories by which work and employment may be evaluated divide into basically deontological theories (those that emphasize the rules and principles that should guide action) and teleological theories (those that evaluate all actions in terms of whether they achieve a desired end state or purpose). The theories that are most frequently used when examining the ethicality of work are the deontological theories of Kant, Rawls and stakeholder ethics and the teleological theories of utilitarianism and Aristotelian ethics. I will briefly outline their main propositions.

Kant argues that what makes an action right or wrong is not the sum of its consequences but the fact that it conforms to moral law. Moral laws of duty demand that people act not only in accordance with duty but for the sake of duty. It is not good enough to perform a morally correct action, because this could stem from self-interested motives. Rather an action is moral if it conforms to moral law that is based in pure reason. Reason has three major characteristics: consistency (hence moral actions must not contradict one another); universality (what is right for one person is right for all, therefore do unto others as you would have them do unto you); and a priori derivation (it is not based on experience—hence the morality of an action does not depend on its consequences). Kant developed these ideas into a fundamental moral law that he characterized as the 'categorical imperative'—'categorical' because it is absolutely binding and 'imperative' because it gives instructions about how you should act. For an action to be moral it must (*a*) be amenable to be made consistently universal; (*b*) respect rational beings as ends in themselves, never solely as means to the ends of others; (*c*) stem from and respect the autonomy of rational beings. To treat someone as an end is to offer them a rational argument for acting in a particular way and, assuming their rationality, to leave it to them to evaluate the argument and decide on a course of action. To treat someone as a means is to seek to make that person do something to further one's own purposes by exerting manipulative influence. Hence, what must be avoided is to disregard someone's personhood by exploiting or otherwise using them without regard for their own interests, needs, and conscientious concerns (MacIntyre 1981).

Another form of deontological theorizing focuses less on the rules that might identify what is 'good' in society and organizations and more on what is right (i.e. as already referred to, the just distribution of the good). Much of this theorizing centers on trying to establish universal principles of a just society on the basis of what might be called 'social contracts through experiments'. If we could imagine a situation of no laws, social conventions, or political state, on what principles might rational people agree that might guarantee social order and stability while at the same time place the fewest constraints on individual freedoms? Hobbes, Locke, and Rousseau are the classical social theorists here and the tradition is maintained by Nozick's 'entitlement theory of justice' and the stakeholder and Rawlsian theories of justice (e.g. Rawls 1971; Nozick 1974; Freeman 1984). Popular versions of stakeholder theory assert that organizations should be answerable not just to shareholders, as Friedman (1970), for example, would maintain, but to all those groups, or 'stakeholders'—management, other employees, customers, suppliers, local communities—who potentially benefit from or are harmed by the organization's actions. The stakes of each group are reciprocal, since each can affect the others in terms of harms and benefits as well as rights and duties. From this principle of reciprocity two rules have been derived: (*a*) that the organization should be managed for the benefit of its stakeholders, that their reciprocal rights should be ensured and that they must participate in decisions that substantially affect their interests; (*b*) that management must act in the interests of the stakeholders as their agent and in the interests of the organization to ensure its survival, thus safeguarding the long term stakes of each group.

Rawls's (1971) 'egalitarian theory of justice' is not dissimilar. His approach is very much Kantian in that he attempts to derive principles of distributive justice that should be acceptable to all rational people and, hence, universal. In order to find such principles, Rawls suggests that we perform a thought experiment. Suppose all people were behind a 'veil of ignorance', where we know that we are rational beings and that we value our own good, but we do not know whether we are male or female, black or white, rich or poor, talented or untalented, able-bodied or suffering disability, and so on. What principles would we call just or fair if we did not know what place we had in society/organization? Rawls suggests that we would agree two principles of justice: (*a*) each person should have an equal right to the most extensive basic liberty compatible with like liberty for others; (*b*) social and economic inequalities should only exist where they are (i) reasonably expected to be to everyone's advantage and (ii) attached to positions open to all.

Turning to teleological theories we find, in sharp contrast to a deontological position, utilitarianism. Utilitarianism claims that the morality of actions is to be judged by their consequences. An action is moral if, when compared with any alternative action, it produces the greatest amount of good (or the least possible balance of bad consequences) for the greatest number of people directly or indirectly affected by that action. The 'good' may be variously conceptualized as 'pleasure' (hedonistic utilitarianism), 'happiness' (eudaimonistic utilitarianism), or all 'intrinsically valuable' human goods (ideal utilitarianism). The maximization of the good calls for efficiency. It also allows that people may be treated as a means to an end, if the end is the maximization of the good (or minimization of the bad) for the greatest number.

Finally, we have Aristotelianism and its close cousin, communitarianism (MacIntyre 1981; Etzioni 1995). Aristotelianism is teleological in the sense that it considers that the good life should aim to achieve human beings' innate mental, moral, and social potentialities. Humans are not individualistic but must be understood as part of a broader social community, in which fulfilling one's potential involves developing wisdom, generosity, empathy, courage, and self-restraint, all of which help to make one a good member of the community. This has resonances with communitarianism which focuses on the shared values of individuals within a community of purpose, of which the workplace may be one. In some ways these two ethical theories return us to the roots of personnel management, embedded as it was in a paternalism of employees 'knowing their place' within a rigid social hierarchy in return for owner-managers' exercise, often religiously inspired, of a benevolent social responsibility. If paternalism contradicts Aristotelianism is its marginalizing of employees' right to self-actualization, it is consistent in its emphasis on community, reciprocal loyalties and mutual support (Legge 1999).

Now obviously there are some difficulties with all these theories. It is often said that deontologists covertly appeal to utilitarian consequences in order to demonstrate the rightness of actions, particularly when there is a clash of moral rules. Perhaps, more importantly, Kantian ethics suffer from an 'alienation problem'—that by the very stern and dogmatic standards they impose they can be dismissed out of hand by practitioners as being completely impractical in a capitalist world (Stark 1993). Stakeholder analysis has the problem of short-versus long-term justice, the dangers of pseudo-participation and the real confusion as to whether its message is essentially one of economic democracy or capitalist co-optation (Stoney and Winstanley 2001). Rawls's second principle can be attacked as being too strong (as long as equal opportunities exist, why should rewards have to take account of producing benefit for the least advantaged groups in society?) or too weak (in that it would allow the very, very rich to get much richer as long as the very, very poor got only a little less poor). Utilitarianism has to cope with the problem of lack of knowledge of all (particularly long-term) consequences, of weighing together different kinds of good and evil and of the issue of unjust consequences. Aristotelian ethics face the criticism that it is difficult to demonstrate the assumption that human beings do have specific inherent potentialities and that these are the same for all human beings. Further, some (Hobbes, for one!) might question the assumption that human beings are basically good. Communitarianism runs the criticism of suppressing diversity, while paternalism can be seen as simultaneously encouraging dictatorial authoritarianism and child-like dependency.

In Section 2, I consider the close interrelationships between ethics and work and the nature of the society in which they are embedded.

2. Society and the Ethics of Work and Employment

It could be argued that whether the design of work and of employment contracts reflects ethical principles or not will be a direct reflection of the ethicality of the society and economic system of which they are a part

(Parker 2003). Leaving aside premodern history, this inevitably raises the question of whether capitalism, that great institution of modernism, can be considered ethical. Taking Smith's model ([1776] 1961) from *The Wealth of Nations*, capitalism's core principles of laissez faire and free market competition, in combating the evils of mercantilism and protecting the welfare of the consumer and democracy, in theory at least, could be considered ethical from either a Kantian or utilitarian point of view (Bassiry and Jones 1993). From a Kantian position, capitalism appears ethical as it assumes each person is an autonomous, rational individual, who therefore should be free to make his/her own choices providing they are compatible with like freedom for all (echoes of Rawls here too). From a utilitarian point of view, capitalism is ethical (according to Smith at least) in that it promotes efficiency and social good, reflected in Western capitalist societies' enormous material prosperity. Each person, in pursuing his/her own good, indirectly and unknowing, also promotes the public interest. With this happy combination of individual freedom and productive efficiency, it is hardly surprising that the end of the Cold War has been represented in neoliberal circles as the triumph of the good guys representing democratic capitalism, over the 'evil empire' promoting totalitarian socialism (Fukuyama 1991).

But if capitalism *is* an ethical system, how do we account for work design and employment contracts in capitalist economies that appear to ignore the dignity of the person? From the early twentieth century Rouge River Ford plant at Detroit to the twenty-first century call centers in Scotland, scientific management, Fordism, and associated work practices that give rise to labor intensification have come in for criticism as 'inhuman' systems of work, not least by the early 'human relations' school (e.g. Mayo 1933; Beynon 1973; Hollway 1991; Taylor and Bain 1999). Marx's critique of the crises and contradictions of capitalism, further developed by the labour process theorists, is one explanation for the unethical exploitation of labour and the degradation of work (Braverman 1974; Thompson 1983; Knights and Willmott 1990). But Smith himself saw potential problems with capitalism, many of them stemming from the massive concentration of resources into the hands of a small minority of firms—these days, the global players. Pure capitalism argues that individual free choice (about what to buy, what business to engage in, how much to offer for a commodity or service, at what price to sell your labor) rests on fair transactions. But a transaction is fair only if both parties engage in it freely (without coercion) and if both parties have adequate and appropriate knowledge of the relevant aspects of the transaction. As will be discussed later, it is debatable whether these conditions exist for many people under globalized capitalism.

In the recent past it could be argued that, in the USA and in Northern Europe, the Keynesian settlement, during the period of high Fordism, reflected explicit concerns about social justice and an implicit social contract (Jessop 1994). One example is the mixed economy of the UK 'welfare state' of the 1945 Attlee government and the subsequent pre-1979 corporatist 'one nation' conservative governments. These socioeconomic systems were consciously ethical, based on a pragmatic (if epistemologically somewhat confused) amalgam of Methodism, utilitarianism, and paternalism, laced with Kantian notions about respect for the individual citizen worker and Rawlsian ideas about the 'minimization of regret'. Ethical treatment for the worker boiled down to a commitment to full employment, wages negotiated through 'free' collective bargaining rather than imposed by the employer and supplemented by a social wage provision 'from cradle to grave'. The fact that the social wage was not means tested, but a 'right', stemming from National Insurance contributions, reflected a Kantian respect for the dignity of the person and the principles of consistency and universality. Additionally, by the mid-1970s in the UK and USA, issues about equality of opportunity for women and ethnic groups were at least on the agenda, even if implementation left a lot to be desired (Calas and Smircich 1996).

It was in this period, in the 1950s through to the pre-oil shock mid-1970s, that ethicality in work and employment found particular expression in the research and experimentation in job and socio-technical system work design and in debates about quality of working life (QWL) issues (e.g. Trist et al. 1963; Hackman and Oldham 1976; Gyllenhamer 1977). Such designs, notably the famous experiments at Kalmar and Uddevalla (not surprisingly, in socialist Sweden) aimed to improve worker performance through enhanced motivation resultant on job designs that adhered to the tenets of Hackman and Oldham's job characteristics model (optimizing skill variety, task identity, task significance, autonomy, and feedback), embedded in work system designs that embraced the socio-technical systems principle of joint optimization (very corporatist!). For the action researchers involved in such experiments there was often an explicit commitment to the idea that work should be designed in such a way that workers could fulfill at least some higher order needs and gain intrinsic satisfactions that would enhance their experience of work. But, although Kantian in its respect for the individual, the ethics of QWL were essentially utilitarian, in that the outcomes of job enrichment were also seen in instrumental terms: reduced labor turnover and enhanced productivity from motivated employees.

From the early 1980s to the present day, in the Anglo-American Western world, if to a lesser extent in the Rhenish economies of continental Europe, Right wing governments (including the UK's 'New Labour') have abandoned the Keynesian settlement for neoliberal socioeconomic policies, with the rationale that liberalized markets are necessary to compete in a global economy. The ethical rationale of this position reflects both Adam Smith's liberalism and Nozick's ideas of justice as entitlement and finds expression in Milton Friedman's well known paper, 'The Social Responsibility of Business is to Increase Profit' (1970). 'This 'runaway world' of 'radical modernity' (Giddens 2000) is generally characterized as the product of several interrelated developments: the rise of a globalized capitalism, stimulated by a neoliberal ideology priviliging notions of competitive advantage to be achieved by market liberalization and facilitated by the explosive adoption of information and communication (ICTs) technologies. In the next section I will consider how these recent socioeconomic developments have impacted on the world of work, before examining the ethical implications that such changes have for workers.

3. The 'Runaway World' of the Global Economy

Three major developments may be highlighted that impact directly on the ethicality of work in the twenty-first century

First, the global division of labor has resulted in the developing Third World and erstwhile Eastern Bloc countries specializing as providers of cheap labour and commodities, while the developed First World countries of the so-called triad (Rugman 2000) concentrate on skills that enable the production of high value-added goods and services of all kinds. In the West, this has been reflected in a shift of employment away from labor intensive, commodity goods manufacturing, as such production is outsourced to cheap labor economies, to the service sector, such as financial and business services, retailing, and 'in-person' services (Reich 1991). The service sector comprises three different sorts of work: highly skilled, professional 'knowledge work' (e.g. engineering and IT consultancy, traditional professions); semi-skilled routine back-office work, heavily reliant on operating IT packages (e.g. call centre work, data inputting in financial services); and frontline customer/client facing work, which, not withstanding the often high levels of personal skills and emotional labour involved (e.g., holiday reps, care workers, hairdressers), is generally labelled as semi-or low-skilled.

Second, while *theoretical* rationales about how to achieve sustained competitive advantage might differ, the end result reinforces the message about the desirability of a flexible, 'lean' organization. Thus institutional theorists argue for the tendency towards institutional isomorphism, that organizations imitate what seem to be recipes for success and hence come to resemble each other ('mimetic' isomorphism) (DiMaggio and Powell 1983). The present 'best practice' seems to be the development of the hollowed-out, 'lean' organization, as 'rationalization' has the potential to boost share prices in an Anglo-American culture of 'impatient capital'. Resource-based value theorists argue that keeping up with the leaders does not deliver sustained competitive advantage; rather this depends upon the organization developing its own unique, scarce, and inimitable competencies (Barney 1991). However, in practice, this may lead in not dissimilar directions. One distinctive capability identified by Kay (1993) is the 'architecture' of supplier and employee relations, that is developing appropriate relational forms, be it trust in interpersonal relations or involving subcontracting or networking organizational forms (which may depend on trust or contract). Similarly, if an organization's core competencies relate to employee know-how that cannot just be brought in, but represents job and organizational knowledge that is unique to the organization, can only be learned inside, and is only valuable to the firm itself (e.g. Ohmae's 'transnational organizational man' or woman (1989)), or if it depends on know-how that might be transferable, but is difficult to secure and retain (e.g. Reich's 'symbolic analyst' (1991)), then an appropriate competitive and cost effective organizational form might be a minimalist 'core' supported by a 'periphery' of workers on nonstandard contracts and a network of subcontractors ('outsourcing') and contract labour agencies ('insourcing'), scattered throughout the world. Where this occurs, we see the enactment of Atkinson's model (1984) of the flexible firm writ large.

Third, the achievement of competitive advantage in the global economy is often *pragmatically* associated with responsiveness to the sovereign customer, equated to the speedy delivery of the right product/service, of the right quality, at the right time, and at the right price. 'Rightness' of product/service suggests an understanding of the consumer's needs: hence the need to get closer to the customer via blitzing the slow, unresponsive, long lines of communication of bureaucracy, through business process engineering. In theory, this means a move from function-centered to process-oriented organizational forms and practices; from linear-sequential work organization towards parallel processing and multidisciplinary teamworking; towards integrating previously fragmented tasks so that fewer people take less time to perform the process in question. In practice this is often associated with delayering and downsizing (Knights and Willmott 2000). The achievement of 'right' quality is often associated with the introduction of total quality management (TQM) and (again) functionally flexible teamworking. 'Right' time suggests the introduction of 'just-in-time' (JIT) production of goods and services and the elimination of waste, which may include 'unnecessary' workers. 'Right' price, particularly in relation to relatively standardized, labor intensive products or services, means the reduction of labor costs, by optimizing numerical as well as functional flexibility. Again, the model of 'lean', not to say anorexic organization is reinforced (Sparrow 1998).

The ethicality of such developments in work and employment depend very much on which work roles and employment contracts are evaluated and against which ethical criteria. Clearly, what counts as 'good' work and employment is subjective, but there might be a fair measure of agreement that 'good' work might comprise Hackman and Oldham's (1976) requisite task attributes, combined with developmental opportunities for self-actualization and a collegial organizational climate. This would roughly satisfy both Kantian and Aristotelian principles. 'Good' employment conditions might be defined as a 'fair' relationship between employee inputs (skill, effort, and time) and material outcomes in relation to comparison others (including other employees in the same or comparable organizations and other stakeholders) reached by negotiation and agreement, with the organization additionally committed to a duty of care towards the employee. This would comply with Adam's equity theory of satisfaction and stakeholder theory and would not be incompatible with Rawls's theory of justice. Hodson's ideas (2001: 264) about what constitutes 'dignity at work' make very similar points, in identifying the creation and enforcement of norms which provide both protection from mismanagement and abuse and the creation of bilateral structures of participation that provide opportunities for workers to realize their human potential through creative, meaningful, and productive work.

I will now compare three typical types of work and employment against these criteria, and in terms of utilitarianism: knowledge work at the 'core' of the organization, routine work in commodity manufacturing and in the service sector, and the extreme case of 'peripheral' subcontracted child labor in the Third World.

4. The Ethics of 'Core' and 'Periphery', the 'Haves' and the 'Have-nots'

The Knowledge Worker

Knowledge workers are those who possess either job or organizational knowledge that is recognized as essential to an organization's effectiveness. Thus they may include not only the members of the traditional liberal professions and the professional and managerial elites identified above—'transnational man' [*sic*] (Ohmae 1989) or 'symbolic analysts' (Reich 1991), but any employee who possesses skills and knowledge that cannot easily be bought in or retained and yet on which the organization is highly dependent for achieving success. For example, in lean production systems, with the time-space compression implied in speeding up the order-to-delivery cycle as well as in JIT systems, the very vulnerability of the system creates management dependency on the plant specific knowledge and skills of team-leading direct operatives and on their motivation to apply such skills, through discretionary effort, in managerial interests.

For those knowledge workers that are formally constituted as 'professions', ethical considerations, in theory at least, not only underpin the very content of their work (e.g. justice for the legal, altruism for the medical, and honesty for the accountancy professions), but inform how the work is carried out (ethical codes of practice). But whether or not ethics are so explicitly central to their work, for all knowledge workers there is an implicit ethical contract with both employers and clients. Knowledge work, by its nature, involves high levels of discretion in situations where the non-expert cannot directly evaluate the quality of the work. Hence trust, in theory, is essential in working relationships with knowledge workers.

For such knowledge workers, elements of the good life may be within their grasp: work that is high on Hackman and Oldham's requisite task attributes, offering genuine empowerment, high material rewards, and a reasonable degree of job security. If this implies respect for the employee's skills and knowledge in their own right, the criteria of Kantian ethics is fulfilled; if recognition and career development leads to self-actualization and the achievement of a coherent narrative that renders life meaningful, then such work and employment conditions score highly in Aristotelian terms. If such knowledge workers receive very high material rewards, this might be considered ethical under Rawls's rule; if one believes in a 'trickle down effect' (high pay is necessary to retain high skills, which are necessary for organizational success, that is necessary for economic growth, which in turn is necessary for everyone's advantage). Even if it is recognized that knowledge workers are not respected as ends in themselves, but only instrumentally, as the means to organizational, sustained, competitive advantage, this can still be considered ethical if, in terms of utilitarianism, a case can be made (however difficult to demonstrate) that their work and employment results in the greatest happiness to the greatest number.

But there is a down side. Leaving aside the fact that knowledge workers are more vulnerable to downsizing and delayering than they might have been a generation ago (after all this might be justified in terms of utilitarianism), a common complaint is of heightened pressure through increasingly demanding and shifting targets in the context of restricted resources. This may lead to 'workaholic' lifestyles, 'change fatigue','burn out', and a 'survivor syndrome' of cynicism and mistrust (e.g. Holbeche 1994, 1995; Kettley 1995; Brockett 1988). Further, the potentiality of these outcomes may be exacerbated by the proliferation of auditing activities, in both public and private sectors, replacing the trust traditionally inherent in knowledge working relationships (Power 1997). Not only is the inducement of such behaviors unethical in Kantian terms, but it may be criticized from an Aristotelian standpoint.

MacIntyre (1981) argues that such outcomes reflect three interrelated processes. First, in organizations, we tend to engage with each other not as a whole person, but in terms of our organizational role and, in highly differentiated organizations, this can present only a tiny portion of our full selves. Second, the exigencies of these roles may require us to engage in inauthentic behavior, both manipulating others (thereby contravening Kant's categorical imperative) and allowing others to manipulate us (see Jackall 1988). As MacIntyre (1981: 107) states, 'the most effective manager is the best actor'. Third, a workaholic lifestyle may prevent the development of ourselves in family and community roles that could allow a fuller expression of ourselves as a person. Hence the present maxim: 'No one on their deathbed has said "I wish I'd spent more time at the office"; many have said "I wish I'd spent more time with my family" '. MacIntyre argues that, as a result, we stand no chance of enacting the Aristotelian ideal, as role fragmentation, inauthenticity, and an unbalanced development of potentiality deprive us of the opportunity of developing a substantial, integrated narrative of our lives and, hence, of rendering our lives meaningful to ourselves and to our community as a whole. While MacIntyre focuses on managers, Sennett (1998: 26) sees the 'corrosion of character', which he interprets as resulting from the loss of routine and stability, a changing work ethic, 'illegible' work, and manipulative, inauthentic teamworking consequent on the 'flexibalization' of organizations in the global economy, as a threat to all workers: 'How can a human being develop a narrative of identity and life history in a society composed of episodes and fragments?'

Routine Work in Manufacturing and Service Sectors

The ethicality of routine work in the manufacturing or service sector, to a large extent, rests on whether the 'high' or 'low' road to work design and employment conditions is adopted (Ackroyd and Proctor 1998; Bacon and Blyton 2000; Batt 2000; Delbridge 2003; Holman 2003). Where the 'high' road is adopted, in theory at least, quality of product or service is prioritized and, with it, job enrichment including some degree of empowerment is offered, along with 'high commitment' HRM policies and practices (Pfeffer 1994). In such cases, erstwhile 'routine' work begins to take on some of the characteristics of knowledge working and the arguments developed above apply. However, certainly in the UK, this may be the exception rather than the rule (Ackroyd and Proctor 1998; Cully et al. 1999). Does 'empowerment' really involve an extension of employees' autonomy, choices, and development? Or, is it a question of 'making someone else take the risk and responsibility' (Sisson 1994: 15)? Or is it even a case of 'what is happening is that management is being relieved of some of its "responsibilities of command" by employees converting them into "responsibilities of subordination" ' (Kaler 1996). Interestingly, in the service sector, much employee empowerment focuses on the 'service recovery' of resolving customers' complaints, an activity likely to be stressful and involving emotional labor, rather than on the proactive taking of initiative in the original service offer (Korczynski, 2002: 133). Certainly, the so-called 'empowerment paradox' (Ganz and Bird 1996), whereby empowerment is used to disempower people through their co-optation into a group that represses dissent, would be highly unethical from a Kantian point of view.

Where the 'low' road is adopted, whether in manufacturing or the service sector, the outcome appears to be Tayloristic task design, aimed at cost minimization, along with a stress on surveillance and control (Barker 1993; Sewell 1998; Taylor and Bain 1999). In the service sector, stress associated with labour intensification may be exacerbated by the strains of surface acting associated with emotional labor (Hochschild 1983; Rafaeli and Sutton 1987). Thus, Taylor and Bain (1999: 115), from a labor process perspective, describe operative work in a call centre as comprising

> an uninterrupted and endless sequence of similar conversations with customers she never meets. She has to concentrate hard on what is being said, jump from page to page on screen, making sure that the details entered are accurate and that she has said the right things in a pleasant manner. The conversation ends and as she tidies up the loose ends there is another voice in her headset. The pressure is intense because she knows her work is being measured, her speech monitored, and it often leaves her mentally, physically and emotionally exhausted.

Clearly such work design violates many ethical principles. Kantian ethics would deplore the instrumental, not to say exploitative, use of human labor; Aristotelianism would criticize the failure to provide opportunities for the development of human potentiality, and stakeholder theory might question whether there was mutuality in the treatment of employee vis-à-vis either customer or shareholder. This is particularly the case when such work design is complemented by the use of nonstandard contracts (e.g. part-time work, fixed term contract, zero-hours contract, subcontracting ('outsourcing'), agency working ('insourcing'), temporary and casual working), which may involve the organization loosing its bonds of obligation to its workers when their presence is no longer perceived to be continuously indispensable and, hence, no longer a necessary fixed cost. Such contracts, particularly prevalent for support staff in the growth areas of the service sector, are marked by temporal discontinuity and the treatment of labour as a commodity. 'Outsourcing' and 'insourcing' exacerbates this commodification of labor because the workers are not directly employed by the organization whose policies and decision-making directly affects the quality of their employment. Thus Purcell (1997) cites some overhead transparencies used in a presentation by a major employment agency, suggesting the key advantages to employers of using agency labour, which encapsulates the commodification of labour contractually outside the boundaries of the organization:

1. Enhances flexibility (turn on and off like a tap)
2. No legal or psychological contract with the individual
3. You outsource the management problems associated with noncore staff
4. Greater cost efficiency (on average 15 to 20 percent).

This expresses the very form of instrumental rationality that, Bauman (1989) would suggest, facilitates the removal of people from the realm of moral responsibility, through distancing the Other, leading directly to such evil acts as the Holocaust (cf. du Gay (2000) for a critique of Bauman's argument).

Work in the service sector poses other ethical dilemmas. For example, Korczynski (2002) identifies 'extreme' forms of sales work, characterized by the active stimulation of demand, rather than responding to customers' requests—such as in selling financial products—as particularly vulnerable to ethically questionable practices. Korczynski argues that the practice of paying such salespersons largely by commission, induces an instrumental orientation, whereby customers are perceived purely as a means to an end: profit for the organization and high reward to the salesperson. This results in salespersons, in defiance of Kantian, Rawlsian, and stakeholder ethics, developing an ideology which legitimizes techniques of customer manipulation, either by viewing the customer paternalistically, as someone who needs help to see the true benefits of the product, or by internalizing an image of the customer as dishonest that enables them to justify and rationalize their own manipulation of the customer. To survive, it is suggested, salespersons need to develop a 'will to ignorance' about the tensions between a paternalistic image of customers and their instrumental manipulation (Oakes 1990: 87). However, as Korczynski argues, this 'will to ignorance', combined with a managerial vacuum, consequent on the culture of selling promoting values of entrepreneurial self-reliance among the (largely male) workforce, led directly to the massive and systematic mis-selling of financial products in the UK in the late 1980s and early 1990s. Morally, this broke both the Kantian categorical imperative as well as the ethical imperative of all major religions: 'Thou shalt not steal'.

The instrumentality of capitalism in the pursuit of profit is also at the heart of the colonization and commodification of the emotional labor of service workers (Sturdy and Fineman 2001). As 'quality of service' becomes increasingly the differentiator in achieving competitive advantage, so frontline service workers are required to both manage their own emotions and provide behavioral displays associated with feelings in their interactions with customers (Hochschild 1983; Korczynski 2002). Hochschild argues that this leads to alienation on the part of the service worker as a result of commodificatoin of emotion, structured inequality in relation to customers and managerial imposition of feeling rules. Employees are required not only to act inauthentically through 'surface acting', in contravention of Aristotelian ethics, but to internalize the feelings they are meant to display ('deep acting'). If this involves internalizing an ethic of care towards abusive customers, in order to create profit for the organization, the employee is being abused by management as much as by the customer. If the employee genuinely feels caring towards the abusive customer, perhaps he/she (usually she) might be simultaneously applauded for altruism (caring for someone with a 'problem', as flight attendants are encouraged to redefine a troublesome passenger) and pitied for their false consciousness and eroded autonomy.

However Korczynski (2002) argues that Hochschild's identification of the conditions for *objective* alienation ignores the possibility that emotional labour may be a source of fulfilment, as the natural and spontaneous enactment of an altruistic ethic of care, of respect for others. When employees have some autonomy in their expression of emotional labor, and have socially embedded relationships with customers, as in many of the traditional 'caring' jobs associated with the 'naturally' (or rather socially constructed through patriarchy) caring female labor (Tyler and Taylor 2001), real satisfactions for both parties may result. Indeed, Korczynski points out that tensions may result in what he terms the 'customer-oriented bureaucracy' when employees are constrained by its instrumental rationality from delivering the degree of individual care and attention that they consider to be appropriate.

Nevertheless, a case can be made for the ethicality of routine semi-skilled or unskilled work in manufacturing and service sectors, albeit a weak one. That is, that the worker as a rational, autonomous person freely chooses to engage in that activity and freely enters a contract with the employer that specifies an 'acceptable' effort–reward bargain. While the work may lack Hackman and Oldham's requisite task attributes and be characterized by fragmentation and repetition, or by manipulative, inauthentic behavior, whether on the part of the employee or agents of capital, it may be justified in utilitarian terms by the production of products and services of high use value and low cost to consumer, by the generation of wages to the employee-producer and of dividends to shareholders. Although the work may lack the characteristics to provide for self-actualization, it may deliver some satisfactions to the worker through the rhythms of the activity itself (Baldamus 1961), through social interaction (Roy 1958), and through the collusive game playing that 'manufactures consent' (Burawoy 1979). Further, in Aristotelian terms, by providing the opportunity for the worker to endure such work in exchange for a wage that may support dependents, it enables the expression of altruism. It could also be argued that it is patronising to portray such workers as downtrodden automaton, as much evidence exists of their resistance to surveillance and control in order to protect their autonomy (e.g. Knights and McCabe 1998; Bain and Taylor 2000).

(But, again, can it be ethical to restrict autonomy beyond the extent that Kantian and Rawlsian rules apply?)

A major critique of such a justification is the questionable nature of the assumption that the employee 'freely' enters such an effort–reward bargain. For many people, choice of what work they do and what employment contract they can command is limited by the structural inequalities of their society, by the fact that it does not adhere to Rawlsian principles of a just society. Further, the mantra of 'global competitiveness' encourages First World governments to cut back on employee rights and welfare, as these may be perceived as costs eroding a country's ability to compete in tradables and as encouraging portfolio and foreign direct investment to shift to where such costs are lower. Similarly, even where firms do not outsource jobs to developing countries, the threat of relocation may be used to put a downward pressure on wages (Standing 1999). This has a knock-on effect too. For those entering the labor market without much education, the jobs in manufacturing no longer exist in such plentiful supply and they have to look for temporary or part-time work in low paying service sectors, which are no longer under pressure to raise wages more in line with the (erstwhile better paying) manufacturing sector, owing to the depression of wages and lack of employment in that sector. Hence the income gap, under these conditions and assumptions, inevitably rises between such routine, *disposable* production or in-person service workers (to use Reich's terminology)—generally the young, the old, women, ethnic minorities, and the unskilled—and the core, *indispensable*, knowledge working professional and managerial elites and skilled workers—generally, white, educated, prime age males (if with increasing numbers of women and ethnic minorities).

The best chance of justifying the ethicality of such work and employment practices lies with utilitarianism, *if one can establish that the favoured 'haves' are in the majority.* This may include looking at the balance of 'happiness' of the routine worker as worker *and* as consumer. But, whereas the routine worker may benefit as a consumer as a result of an economic system that exploits him/her as a worker, even the advantages as a consumer are not justly distributed, given the income disparity between knowledge workers and routine workers.

Subcontracted Child Labour in Developing Countries

In a global economy, the longer the supply chain, often stretching to the other side of the world, the more workers are placed contractually outside the boundaries of the outsourcing organization. Then proximity is likely to be replaced by a physical, social, and psychological distance and the danger that responsibility breaks down. It is also more likely that fellow human beings are then transformed into objects different from ourselves for whom we feel no responsibility (Bauman 1989). An extreme case in point is child labor, such as that used in the football manufacturing industry in Sialkot, Pakistan, which supplies about 80 percent of the world's footballs to international companies such as Nike, Reebok, and Adidas. The payment per football at the time of the last World Cup (1998) was 60p per ball, retailing in the West for twenty times that price. In spite of agreements by the multinational manufacturers to ban the use of such labour, it continues. In Sialkot, the alternative employment for children is in more hazardous jobs, such as in tanneries, surgical instruments factories, or prostitution (West 1998). This case may serve as an exemplar for the arguments for and against the ethicality of such work and employment.

The arguments against seem self-evident in Kantian terms. If the international companies that subcontracted such work were motivated by such ideals as treating people with respect and as ends in their own right one might expect either some investment in after-hours schools for the children or the offer of higher, 'fairer' wages (in Western eyes) (as organizations such as 'Traidcraft', allied to aid agencies, advocate and enact). Clearly, too, the contracting companies appear unmoved by stakeholder ethics. In their alliance with retailers, it is not only footballer stitchers that are exploited, but also the customer, through paying an extremely high mark-up on the cost price.

However, the contracting, international companies could conceivably make a case for their actions. Utilitarianism does allow for people to be used instrumentally, as means to ends, if it is to the advantage of the majority. At first sight this may appear to undermine rather than support the companies' case. Surely it is the minority (the shareholders) who benefit most from the use of child labor, not the majority, the workers themselves and the similarly exploited customers? A response might be that, from a Kantian perspective, we must treat customers as autonomous beings capable of making rational choices, who freely choose to buy footballs at a price that the market will bear. Of course, we might question this 'freedom', given large companies' manipulation via the media of our tastes and preferences or, in this case, of our children's insatiable demand for peer-approved fashion items (and are parents acting as responsible, rational adults in acceding to such pressure?) Further, from a utilitarian perspective, the football stitchers (whether adults or children) are better off due to First World investment than they would be without it, given the alternatives of either no paid work or harder, more dangerous, or degrading work in tanneries, instrument factories, or prostitution. It could also be argued that if the international companies had to pay wages approaching those of the developed world, there would be no incentive for them to outsource. In addition, paying First World wages would have an extremely deleterious effect on the local economy.

Taking the spirit of Aristotelianism, that ethics should be based on the achievement of human beings' mental, moral, and social potential, as part of a broader social community, it might even be argued that the money that the children earn contributes not only to their education (as reported) and, therefore to their mental development, but also to their moral development. This would occur through the contribution that their work makes to the survival of their family, particularly to even younger and to older family members who may be unable to earn.

There is a further ethical issue. The part played by large Western companies in the developing world is arguably a form of economic imperialism (Klein 2000). While it may be appropriate to evaluate such organization's actions in terms of Western ethical theory, insofar as they are Western companies, to judge the behaviors of the Third World subcontractors in these terms could be argued to be a form of ethical imperialism, a twenty-first century variant on missionary work, with its paternalistic overtones. A more appropriate position might be one of transcultural relativism: 'When in Rome, do as the Romans do'. The counter argument to this, whether from a Judaeo-Christian or Kantian position, is the absolutist view that moral judgments apply to all members of the moral community and that, if the moral community includes all human beings, then the moral judgment of an action extends to all. Rather than ethical imperialism being implied, it is ethical universalism: 'I am my brothers' and sisters' keeper'.

5. Conclusions

Although the theories considered here allow us to interrogate the notion of the ethicality of work and employment, they do not allow us to reach any certain judgments. Judgment differs depending on which ethical theory one adopts. Most work and employment practices in Western capitalist societies may be justified in terms of utilitarianism, with evidence of increased material prosperity for the majority of workers—even for some workers in developing countries—acting as a rough surrogate that the greatest happiness is being delivered to the greatest number. However, problems of measurement, full knowledge of consequences and the issue of unjust consequences cannot be ignored (global warming as an outcome of economic prosperity being a case in point). Furthermore, general increases in prosperity, at least in the Western world, mask continuing inequalities in the distribution of wealth and opportunity even in the rich West. Discrimination in terms of both pay and opportunity are still the lot of many women and ethnic minority workers, knowledge-based work organizations being no exception (e.g. Special Issue on Gender and Academe, *Gender, Work and Organization*, 2003).

A major problem is the tension between a universalistic, moral objectivism ('the customer is always right') and the translation of such absolutes into specific contexts, where competing rationalities prevail. Workers may agree that pilfering in principle is wrong, but know that in practice management sanctions it in order to avoid paying higher wages. Workers may both agree in principle that 'two wrongs don't make a right', and feel every justification in enacting a 'fair' effort–reward bargain—'working the value of the boat' as Mars's Newfoundland dockers (1982) would put it. This is not to argue that ethics are purely situational, rather that absolute ethical codes are resources upon which all organizational stakeholders draw to justify their actions and further their interests. The ethical theories that provide a justification for capitalism-utilitarianism and Nozick's theory of justice as entitlement may be confronted by Kantian and Rawlsian principles that argue for respect for all people. What prevails as practical ethics in the workplace is the outcome of an ongoing process of negotiation between the different stakeholders, reflecting emergent power/knowledge relationships in which *most* workers are not as powerful as their bosses. Nevertheless, mindful of the circuit of capital, the voices of workers as *consumers* are likely to be more influential in a capitalist society, but at the risk of their co-optation into the ethics of utilitarianism. But, in the long term, the trust-building ethic of 'Do as you would be done by' that may harness workers' productive creativity by providing dignity at work (Hodson 2001) might be the most beneficial to all stakeholders.

References

Ackroyd, S. and Proctor, S. (1998). 'British Manufacturing Organization and Workplace Relations: Some Attributes of the New Flexible Firm', *British Journal of Industrial Relations*, 36(2): 163–83.

Adam, J. S. (1963). 'Towards an Understanding of Inequity', *Journal of Abnormal and Social Psychology*, 67: 422–36.

Atkinson, J. (1984). 'Manpower Strategies for Flexible Organizations', *Personnel Management*, 16(8): 28–31.

Bacon, N. and Blyton, P. (2000). 'High Road and Low Road Teamworking: Perceptions of Management Rationales and Organizational and Human Resource Outcomes', *Human Relations*, 53(11): 1425–58.

Bain, P. and Taylor, P. (2000). 'Entrapped By The "Electronic Panopticon"? Worker Resistance in a Call Centre', *New Technology, Work and Employment*, 15: 2–18.

Baldamus, W. (1961). *Efficiency and Effort*. London: Tavistock.

Barker, J. R. (1993). 'Tightening the Iron Cage: Concertive Control in Self-Managing Teams', *Administrative Science Quarterly*, 38: 408–37.

Barney, J. (1991). 'Firm Resources and Sustained Competitive Advantage', *Academy of Management Journal*, 37: 670–87.

Bassiry, G. R. and Jones, M. (1993). 'Adam Smith and the Ethics of Contemporary Capitalism', *Journal of Business Ethics*, 12: 621–7.

Batt, R. (2000). 'Strategic Segmentation in Front-Line Services: Matching Customers, Employees and Human Resource Systems', *International Journal of Human Resource Management*, 11: 540–61.

Bauman, Z. (1989). *Modernity and the Holocaust*. Cambridge: Polity Press.

—— (1993). *Postmodern Ethics*. Oxford: Blackwell.

Beynon, H. (1973). *Working for Ford*. Harmondsworth: Penguin.

Bowen, H. (1953). *Social Responsibilities of the Businessman*. New York: Harper.

Bowie, N. E. (ed.) (2002). *Business Ethics*. Oxford: Blackwell.

Braverman, H. (1974). *Labor and Monopoly Capitalism*. New York: Monthly Review Press.

Brockett, J. (1998). 'The Impact of Layoffs on Survivors', *Supervisory Management*, February, pp. 2–7.

Burawoy, M. (1979). *Manufacturing Consent*. Chicago, IL: University of Chicago Press.

Burrell, G. and Morgan, G. (1979). *Sociological Paradigms and Organisational Analysis*. London: Heinemann.

Calas, M. and Smircich, L. (1996). 'From "The Woman's" Point of View: Feminist Approaches to Organization Studies', in S.R. Clegg, C. Hardy, and W.R. Nord (eds.), *Handbook of Organization Studies*. London: Sage.

Cully, M., Woodland, S., O'Reilly, A., and Dix, G. (1999). *Britain at Work*. London: Routledge.

Cummings, S. (2000). 'Aesthetics of Existence as an Alternative to Business Ethics', in S. Linstead and H. Hopfl (eds.), *The Aesthetics of Organization*. London: Sage.

De George, R.T. (1995). *Business Ethics*, 4th edn. Englewood Cliffs, NJ: Prentice-Hall.

Delbridge, R. (2003). 'Workers Under Lean Manufacturing', in D. Holman et al. (eds.), *The New Workplace*. Chichester, UK: John Wiley & Sons.

DiMaggio, P. J. and Powell, W. W. (1983). 'The Iron Cage Revisited: Institutional Isomorphism and Collective Rationality in Organizational Fields', *American Sociological Review*, 48: 147–60.

Du Gay, P. (2000). *In Praise of Bureaucracy.* London: Sage.
Edwards, P. K. (1990). 'The Politics of Conflict and Consent', *Journal of Economic Behavior and Organization*, 13: 41–61.
Etzioni, A. (ed.) (1995). *New Comunitarian Thinking: Persons, Virtues, Institutions and Communities*. Charlottesville: University of Virginia Press.
Folger, R. and Cropanzano, R. (1998). *Organizational Justice and Human Resource Management*. Thousand Oaks, CA: Sage.
Fox, A. (1966). 'Industrial Sociology and Industrial Relations', Research Paper No. 3, Royal Commission on Trades Unions and Employers' Associations. London: HMSO.
Freeman, E. (1984). *Strategic Management: A Stakeholder Approach*. Boston, MA: Pitman.
Friedman, M. (1970). 'The Social Responsibility of Business is to Increase Profit', *New York Times Magazine*, September 13.
Fukuyama, F. (1991). *The End of History and the Last Man.* New York: Harper & Row.
Ganz, J. and Bird, F. G. (1996). 'The Ethics of Empowerment', *Journal of Business Ethics, 15: 383–92.*
Giddens, A. (2000). *Runaway World: How Globalization is Reshaping Our Lives*. London: Routledge.
Gyllenhamer, P. G. (1977). *People at Work*. Reading, MA: Addison-Wesley.
Hackman, J. R. and Oldham, G. R. (1976). 'Motivation Through the Design of Work: Test of a Theory', *Organizational Behavior and Human Performance*, 15: 250–79.
Hochschild, A. (1983). *The Managed Heart*. Berkeley, CA: University of California Press.
Hodson, R. (2001). *Dignity at Work*. Cambridge: Cambridge University Press.
Holbeche, L. (1994). *Career Development in Flatter Structures: Raising the Issues*, Report 1. Horsham: Roffey Park Management Institute.
—— (1995). *Career Development in Flatter Structures: Organizational Practices*, Report 2. Horsham: Roffey Park Management Institute.
Hollway, W. (1991). *Work Psychology and Organizational Behaviour.* London: Sage.
Holman, D. (2003). 'Call Centres', in D. Holman et al. (eds.), *The New Workplace.* Chichester, UK: John Wiley & Sons.
IPM (Institute of Personnel Management) (1963). 'Statement on Personnel Management and Personnel Policies', *Personnel Management*, March.
Jackall, R. (1988). *Moral Mazes: The World of Corporate Managers*. New York: Oxford University Press.
Jessop, R. (1994). 'Post-Fordism and the State', in A. Amin (ed.), *Post-Fordism: A Reader.* Oxford: Blackwell.
Kaler, J. (1996). 'Does Empowerment Empower?' Paper presented at the Centre for Organizational and Professional Ethics, Institute of Education, University of London, Workshop on Ethics and Empowerment, September.
Kant, I. ([1795] 1998). *Groundwork for the Metaphysics of Morals*. Cambridge: Cambridge University Press.

Kay, J. (1993). *Foundations of Corporate Success. How Business Strategies Add Value.* Oxford: Oxford University Press.

Kettley, P. (1995). *Employee Morale during Downsizing,* Report 291, Institute of Employment Studies.

Klein, N. (2000). *No Logo.* London: Flamingo.

Knights, D. and McCabe, D. (1998). 'What Happens When the Phones Go Wild? Staff, Stress and Spaces for Escape in a BPR Telephone Banking Call Regime', *Journal of Management Studies,* 35: 163–94.

—— and Willmott, H. (eds.) (1990). *Labour Process Theory.* London: Macmillan.

—— and —— (2000). *The Reengineering Revolution.* London: Sage.

Korczynski, M. (2002). *Human Resource Management in Service Work.* Basingstoke: Palgrave.

Legge, K. (1999). 'Representing People at Work', *Organization,* 6(2): 247–64.

Levinas, E. (1985). *Ethics and Infinity.* Pittsburg, PA: Duquesne University Press.

MacIntyre, A. (1981). *After Virtue.* London: Duckworth.

Mars, G. (1982). *Cheats at Work: An Anthropology of Workplace Crime.* London: Counterpoint.

Mayo, E. (1933). *The Human Problems of Industrial Civilization.* New York: Macmillan.

Mill, J. S. ([1861] 1998). *Utilitarianism.* Oxford: Oxford University Press.

Nozick, R. (1974). *Anarchy, State and Utopia.* New York: Basic Books.

Oakes, G. (1990). *The Soul of the Salesman: The Moral Ethos of Personal Sales.* London: Humanities Press International.

Ohmae, K. (1989). 'Managing in a Borderless World', *Harvard Business Review,* 67(3): 52–61.

Parker, M. (2003). 'Introduction: Ethics, Politics and Organizing', *Organization,* 10(2): 187–203.

Pfeffer, J. (1994). *Competitive Advantage through People.* Boston, MA: Harvard Business School Press.

Power, M. (1997). *The Audit Society. Rituals of Verification.* Oxford: Oxford University Press.

Purcell, J (1997). 'Pulling up the Drawbridge: High Commitment Management and the Exclusive Corporation'. Paper presented to the Cornell Conference on Research and Theory in Strategic HRM: An Agenda for the 21st Century, October.

Rafaeli, A. and Sutton, R. I. (1987). 'Expression of Emotion as Part of the Work Role', *Academy of Management Review,* 12(1): 23–37.

Rawls, J. (1971). *A Theory of Justice.* Oxford: Oxford University Press.

Reich, R. B. (1991). *The Work of Nations.* New York: Knopf.

Roy, D. (1958). 'Banana Time: Job Satisfaction and Informal Interaction', *Human Organization,* 18(1): 156–68.

Rugman, A. (2000). *The End of Globalization.* London: Random House.

Sennett, R. (1998). *The Corrosion of Character.* New York: Norton.

Sewell, G. (1998). 'The Discipline of Teams: the Control of Team-Based Industrial Work Through Electronic and Peer Surveillance', *Administrative Science Quarterly*, 43(2): 397–428.

Sisson, K. (1994). 'Personnel Management: Paradigms, Practice and Prospects', in K. Sisson (ed.), *Personnel Management*, 2nd edn. Oxford: Blackwell.

Smith, A. ([1776] 1961). *The Wealth of Nations*. London: Methuen.

Sparrow, P. (1998). 'New Organisational Forms, Processes, Jobs and Psychological Contracts: Resolving the HRM Issues', in P. Sparrow and M. Marchington (eds.), *Human Resource Management, The New Agenda*. London: FT/Pitman.

Standing, G. (1999). *Global Labour Flexibility, Seeking Distributive Justice*. Basingstoke: Macmillan.

Stark, A. (1993). 'What's Wrong with Business Ethics', *Harvard Business Review*, 71(1): 38–48.

Stoney, C. and Winstanley, D. (2001). 'Stakeholding: Confusion or Utopia? Mapping the Conceptual Terrain', *Journal of Management Studies*, 8(5): 603–26.

Sturdy, A. and Fineman, S. (2001). 'Struggles for the Control of Affect-Resistance as Politics *and* Emotion', in A. Sturdy, I. Grugelis, and H. Willmott (eds.), *Customer Service, Empowerment and Entrapment*. Basingstoke: Palgrave.

Taylor, P. and Bain, P. (1999). 'An Assembly Line in the Head: The Call Centre Labour process', *Industrial Relations Journal*, 30: 101–17.

Thompson, P. (1983). *The Nature of Work*. London: Macmillan.

Trist, E., Higgen, G., Murray, H., and Pollock, A. (1963). *Organisational Choice*. London: Tavistock.

Tyler, M. and Taylor, S. (2001). 'Juggling Justice and Care: Gendered Customer Service in the Contemporary Airline Industry', in A. Sturdy, I. Grugelis, and H. Willmott, H. (eds.), *Customer Service, Empowerment and Entrapment*. Basingstoke: Palgrave.

West, J. (1998). 'Children Still Sweat Over World Cup Footballs', *Sunday Telegraph*, May 10, p. 3.

12

Technology and Work

Jacques Bélanger

After a period when the study of technology became rather outmoded, the information technology revolution has made it an important focus of research again, and led to debates on electronic surveillance and the Panopticon. Drawing on both the classic works and some recent contributions, this chapter discusses these issues but takes some distance from the most alarmist scenarios by insisting on the foremost importance of social relations. It throws light on the structuring influence of technology but also insists there is still much room for agency. At the end, social relations still prevail.

Most social scientists would agree nowadays that technology does not have determining effects on work and on social relations at work more generally. The debate on 'technological determinism' is dead; in fact, the idea is rejected even by those accused of such inclination by other writers. But at least for a while, this 'obsession with technological determinism' (Clark et al. 1988: 11) has inhibited social research on technology. Denying technology a determining role often implied a denial of any role, a position which is no more fruitful.

Itself a result of complex organizational choices, a given technology conditions the range of choices and opportunities within an organization (Thomas 1994). The possibilities or limitations of a given technology play a constructive role, for instance, on the way management controls processes and results, on the form of supervision, as well as on the development of skills and on the resources for collective action or more subtle forms of dissent. These points will be developed by reflecting on some of the influential studies on the structuring influence of technology on work (in Section 1). Section 2 reviews more recent research on the impact of information technology in some of the 'worlds of work', namely manufacturing, call centers, and work outside the confines of the organization. Section 3 argues that the latest generation of technology is already playing a key role in the reshaping of social divisions at work and the development of the so-called 'knowledge organizations'. In such a context, social divisions remain but are redefined in ways which supersede many of the classic distinctions taught in organizational studies and in industrial relations.

1. Approaching the Connection Between Technology and Work

One difficulty concerns the very definition of technology. Many specialists insist that the concept should mean more than machines, tools, and equipment. But beyond that, again, we fall into difficult territory, considering that too broad a definition would make the analysis worthless. Clark et al. (1988: 12–15, 205) suggest that technology can only be understood as part of an 'engineering system'. Technologies 'are not just pieces of hardware and software, but also systems based on certain engineering principles and composed of elements which are functionally arranged (configured) in certain specific ways' (Clark 1988: 13). This is the approach adopted here, by which technology refers to all forms of machinery and equipment, software as well as hardware, used in the design and production of goods and services.

From a scientific viewpoint, there is some continuity in the development of computing technologies, from the huge mainframe computers used in defence and medical research from the 1940s to the most recent development in microelectronics (McLoughlin and Clark 1994: ch. 1). Nevertheless, the advent of information technology represents a major breakthrough. And it is a fairly recent one. If only one date is to be remembered, it should be the invention of the microprocessor in 1971 by an engineer of Silicon Valley (Castells 1998: 65–8; McLoughlin and Clark 1994: 11). With this microprocessor, or 'silicon chip', which captures numerical information, the progress and diffusion of microelectronics became exponential. 'The term information technology was coined probably in the late 1970s to refer to this nexus of computer-based technologies for handling information' (Grauer 2001: 7473). The same expert reports how 'the next period of IT, in the 1980s and the beginning of the 1990s, is characterized by very large-scale integration of circuits, the introduction of the personal computer, and multiple processors in one machine' (Grauer 2001: 7475).[1]

The structure of this chapter is based on the proposition that the current phase of information technology represents a further and distinct phase, at least from the viewpoint of the sociology of work. First, following writers such as Castells (1998), we take the current phase of information technology as a historical period which is distinct from the 'second industrial revolution' which started in the late nineteenth century and, with electricity as the driving source of energy (Björkman 1999), became the industrial basis of the Fordist social compromise (Piore and Sabel 1984).

Second, information technology is different from the phenomenon of 'automation' which, from the early 1950s, became the key word in debates on technology and industry.[2] Information technology has different implications from automation, which is often referred to as continuous process technology, in three main respects. First, a key feature of the phase of automation of the 1950s was that performance was no longer directly dependent upon the immediate intervention of operators, and that work hence became more a matter of maintenance and monitoring. In contrast, most employees using information technology in modern work situations are responsible for the pace and rhythm of production, which is why 'attitudes' and motivation are so high on the management agenda. Second, the automated production process, or at least part of it, had a life of its own; the general flow of production was set by robust technology. With information technology, workstations are usually both autonomous and interconnected as part of a network, which opens the way for work processes which are much more versatile and much less capital intensive. Third, information technology goes a major step further in that, even from an individual workstation, which may be located away from central office, technology supports the process and at the same time generates new information on the process. This was explained eloquently by Shoshana Zuboff:

[1] This author goes on: 'The driving force behind IT in this period of time is described by the so-called Moore's Law, which means that the number of transistors that can fit on a chip doubles every 18 months' (Grauer 2001: 7475). Gordon Moore was Intel President, the leading enterprise of Silicon Valley (Castells 1998: 63, note 40).

[2] Automation, a contraction of 'automatic production', was first used in 1952 (Butera 2001: 993). On the fascination created at the time by the possibilities of an 'automated factory', see the preface to the first edition of *Le travail en miettes*, written in Paris in March 1956 (Friedmann 1964*b*).

> What is it, then, that distinguishes information technology from earlier generations of machine technology? As information technology is used to reproduce, extend, and improve upon the process of substituting machines for human agency, it simultaneously accomplishes something quite different. The devices that automate by translating information into action also register data about those automated activities, thus generating new streams of information....
>
> In this way information technology supersedes the traditional logic of automation. The word that I have coined to describe this unique capacity is *informate*. Activities, events, and objects are translated into and made visible by information when a technology *informates* as well as *automates* (Zuboff 1988: 9–10).

In this context, the underlying search for what Bell ([1960] 1988: 230) called 'engineering rationality', from Frederick Taylor onwards, can now be pursued with much better tools. The possibility to capture and accumulate so much information on day-to-day work activities inevitably leads to questions about electronic surveillance and social domination, which are critical from a sociological perspective. Analyses and interpretations are contrasted about the way employers actually make use of so much information. I will argue that, once more, social and power relations offer the keys to this empirical question. Nevertheless, the conditions which create more room for autonomy and human agency or which, in contrast, lead to excessive management control have to be better documented and understood by social research.

2. Looking Back at Traditional Research Themes

This section reviews some of the lasting contributions on the linkages between technology and work. This review, which is by no means exclusive, draws on both French sociology and some of the more empirical (and sometimes empiricist) contributions which characterize the Anglo-Saxon research tradition.

The French Sociology of Work School

In a classic work entitled *Les Problèmes Humains du Machinisme Industriel*, first published in 1946, Friedmann presented the progress of technology as the driving force in industry and sought to show how it was having harmful effects on the experience of work and on the human condition more generally. This view of technology as the focal point for understanding work was indeed widely shared within the rich school of sociology of work which developed under the intellectual leadership of Friedmann and Naville.[3] The opening sentence of Touraine's chapter on technology and work in *Traité de sociologie du travail* reads as follows: 'Technology and methods of production shape, at least to a large extent, the condition of work in industry' (1964: 387, my translation).

Touraine's important contribution on these matters, and notably the central distinction between three phases of technical development, evolved from a major empirical work, *L'évolution du travail ouvrier aux usines Renault*, published in 1955. The idea is that the evolution of industry, from the universal tools and machines used by craftsmen (phase A), to the specialized machines of mass production (phase B), and then to automation (phase C), is associated with the evolution of work organization and the distribution of skills and qualifications among the workforce. Touraine portrays the linkages between technology and work as complex and discusses them in a subtle way (for instance in his original study, 1955: 175–82). He also insists that the model in three phases should never be interpreted in terms of historical evolutionism, noting the coexistence of different generations of technology at any time in most large organizations, as in a firm like Renault (1955: 174–5, 1964: 392). But such nuances were forgotten by most, and some of the formulations of Touraine's writing had appeal because they suggested a clear pattern. As for instance: the proportion of unskilled and semi-skilled labour in a given workplace grows from phase A to phase B, and then goes down gradually as technology evolves towards phase C (1964: 401).

Touraine's contribution is representative of the dominant line of thinking at the time in French sociology. The leading figures mentioned above were, in different tones and more or less explicitly, influenced by the analysis developed by Marx regarding the evolution of technology and work (Maurice 1980: 23–31). It is also this way of thinking, with emphasis on historical evolution, which led leading French sociologists of this period to be quite optimistic about the possible impact of automation over work. As production would no longer depend directly on physical effort, workers would be freed from the repetitive and tedious character of work and would regain much of the autonomy associated with craftsmanship in the period of artisan production (phase A). Some, such as Mallet

[3] Major empirical studies were conducted, mostly in the 1950s and 1960s, by young scholars like Alain Touraine, Jean-Daniel Reynaud, Michel Crozier, Marc Maurice, and many others who launched their research career in this intellectual environment. They held a very broad view of the realities of 'work', which was by far the most important field of sociological enquiry in France at the time. The classic reference is the *Traité de Sociologie du Travail*, the two volumes on work edited by Friedmann and Naville (1964).

(1969), went a step further and suggested that higher skills and the demand for ever more control over work and decisions would lead the 'new working class' to contest capitalist relations of production more openly.

This way of thinking later led to charges of technological determinism. Reviewing these ideas in a special issue of the journal *Sociologie du travail* after twenty years, Marc Maurice showed in 1980 that this high emphasis on technology as the primary force at play was already something of the past in French sociology. In practice, the focus of research had shifted. Short of a complete explanation of this phenomenon, he notes that this certainly had to do with both theoretical considerations and changes in the real world of work.

Over the last twenty years, in France as elsewhere, scholars became quite worried by any suggestion of 'technological determinism' and research confirmed that various patterns of organization and work could be observed even in automated plants. It became more popular to place the emphasis on complex models of action. In a collective work marking the forty years of the same journal, three contributions confirm this trend which is part of the renewal of sociology of work in France. It is explained that the progressive decline ('déperdition progressive' writes Veltz 2001: 310) of the research approach discussed above relates to theoretical shifts, to the importance of looking beyond the traditional sphere of industrial work (and also of studying services, activities of conception, etc.), and to transformations in the economic sphere (Cochoy 2001; Veltz 2001). Veltz argues that for those who study the evolution of economic competition and its effects on the design and development of products and services, as well as the development of new organizational forms within and between firms, technology is no longer seen as the primary force.

While this is not a movement away from critical sociology, it is certainly a withdrawal from the openly Marxist frames of reference shared by many of the founders of the French sociology of work. Instead, the well-articulated streams of action theory which make the essence of French sociology today look at technology as only one of the forces to be considered for the understanding of social relations in modern organizations.

The Debate on Continuous Process Technology

In Britain and the USA, characteristically, the question was addressed in a more empirical fashion. The work of Joan Woodward (1965) marked a turning point in the ambition to establish empirically, from a detailed survey of 100 firms in south-east Essex and some case studies in some of these, the links between technology and organizational structure. She thus contributed to the foundations of contingency theory: technology, on which she insisted most, but also other contingent factors such as market situation, diversity, and size, 'generate varying degrees of uncertainty and complexity which have to be "coped with" by the development of appropriate structures' (Dawson and Wedderburn 1980: xviii). In short, she sought to show empirically that, contrary to much textbook discussion on management (in the 1960s, but also to a good extent forty years later), a given structure and management approach would 'fit' well in some type of businesses but poorly in others.

A collective work published in 1970 attempted to go further in specifying how different control systems could cope with various types of uncertainty, and suggested that 'the control system may be the underlying variable linking organizational behaviour with technology' (Reeves and Woodward 1970: 55). Working on a two-dimensional model of control systems, categorized as unitary or fragmented, and as personal or mechanical, they seek to account for the evolution of production systems from unit and small batch, to large batch and mass production, and finally to process. Again, we decode an evolution which takes the form of a U-curve and which is akin to those observed by Touraine and by Blauner: unit and process production have something in common, as opposed to mass production (Reeves and Woodward 1970). But while unitary control is of the personal type in the case of unit production, a similar effect is achieved mechanically in the case of processing computer systems. Although *Industrial Organization* (Woodword 1965) became a standard reference, her research objectives have not necessarily been well understood by scholars of following generations, who portrayed her work as a major example of technological determinism, an accusation she would have refuted. Her research is subtler than usually implied. But it remains a rather mechanistic view of the productive organization, with little attention to issues of power and to political processes. As noted by Dawson and Wedderburn in a favorable assessment of her contribution, 'her view of control was essentially apolitical' (1980: xxvi).

The following debate, regarding the potential for automation to reduce alienation, was not always as thorough empirically, but it was certainly more overwhelming and contentious by its theoretical propositions. Launched mainly by Robert Blauner's work, this issue was studied thoroughly by Gallie, who also gave much credit to Mallet. At the time, it was held by many that maintenance craftsmen and technicians would replace semi-skilled production workers as the main figures of the labor force.

Revisiting Blauner's classic work (1964), two observations are striking: the empirical basis is limited (a fact the author readily admits, pp. 12–14), but the structure and thesis are coherent, well written, and easy to grasp. He only conducted fieldwork in one California chemical plant; much of his comparison being based on a secondary source, a large job-attitude survey carried out in 1947.[4] From a comparison of manual work in printing, textile, automobile, and chemical plants, he puts to test the proposition that 'diverse industrial environments result in large variations in the form and intensity of alienation' (Blauner 1964: 4). His conceptual model sees technology as the 'most important single factor that gives an industry a distinctive character' (1964: 6), the other factors being division of labor, social organization, and economic structure.

Direct observation and interviews in this automated context made a lasting influence on Blauner's analysis; it permeates the whole argument of *Alienation and Freedom*. Quite generally, work experience is more favorable in this context: 'as compared to the textile mill and the automobile assembly line, continuous-process technology leads to considerable freedom from pressure, control over the pace of work, responsibility of maintaining a high-quality product, choice of how to do the job, and freedom of physical movement' (1964: 141). He sees this pattern of work as reducing the various dimensions of alienation, such as 'powerlessness' (by giving more control over the immediate work process), 'meaninglessness' (by giving the employee a better view of the whole production system), and 'social alienation' (by fostering occupational communities organized in small crews or teams).

From this basis, Blauner goes a step further and infers that automated production leads to social integration. While his discussion of job autonomy, teamwork, and control over time in this 'calm-and-crisis' work environment is fascinating and generally confirmed by later research, he falls in uncertain territory when suggesting that workers would identify with the company, thus blurring the structural dividing line between them and their employer. With hindsight, patterns of work such as he observed in this chemical plant may arguably reduce alienation, but it is much more ambitious to suggest this leads to 'a social structure with a high degree of consensus between worker and management' (1964: 178). Blauner, finally, makes a further general proposition regarding the historical evolution of

[4] Blauner also notes in the preface that his work as an assembler and as a laborer from 1952 to 1956 (in the electrical and the automative truck industries) contributed to his familiarity with industrial work (1964: ix).

alienation, which follows an inverted U-curve as we evolve from craft production, to assembly-line, and then to automation.[5]

> In the early period, dominated by craft industry, alienation is at its lowest level and the worker's freedom at a maximum. Freedom declines and the curve of alienation (particularly in its powerlessness dimension) rises sharply in the period of machine industry. The alienation curve continues upward to its highest point in the assembly-line industries of the twentieth century. . . .
>
> The alienation curve begins to decline from its previous height as employees in automated industries gain a new dignity from responsibility and a sense of individual function—thus the inverted U. (Blauner, 1964: 182)

This certainly represents an appealing proposition (not least for teaching). The results of Hodson's systematic analysis (1996) of 86 ethnographies, which provides detailed information on the patterns of work in 108 locations, gives partial support for Blauner's U-shaped model. It confirms that craft production offers the highest levels of freedom and 'dignity at work', as opposed to assembly work (Hodson 2001: ch. 5). However, Hodson asserts, 'the culmination of this pattern is associated not with continuous-process automation, but with the increasing organization of the labor process into participative organizations of production' (1996: 734).

There is now almost a consensus among social scientists to guard against such evolutionist schemes of interpretation. Indeed, on the basis of empirical observations which are in many ways similar to those of Blauner as regards automation, Serge Mallet develops contrasting propositions, especially on the question of social integration. In *La Nouvelle Classe Ouvrière*, first published in 1963,[6] Mallet also observes a substantial change in the nature of work and in the way the working-class relates to capitalism in automated industries. This leads to the 'objective integration' of workers in the company, with many advantages as regards wage determination, training and skill levels, and job security (Mallet 1975: 62–6). But as noted by Gallie (1978: 18–19), this analysis, which also reflects historical evolutionism, is sharply different from the notion of social integration developed by Blauner. Mallet sees the improvement in the nature of work as leading to qualitative demands for more and more control on the part of

[5] The parallel with Touraine's three stages of the evolution of technology and manual work, published in 1955 on the basis of in-depth observation at Renault, is striking. Blauner does not refer to Touraine's as he introduces the model of an inverted U-curve, but he does so explicitly earlier in his concluding chapter (1964: 169).

[6] A fourth French edition, published in 1969, includes a new introduction in which Mallet discusses lessons from May 1968; we refer here to the English translation (1975) of this final edition. Mallet died in a car accident in 1973.

the 'new working class', demands which will inevitably lead to more confrontation with capitalist firms.

> Precisely because it is placed in the centre of the most complex mechanisms of organisational capitalism, the new working class is brought to realize more quickly than the other sectors the contradictions inherent in the system.... Its objective situation places it in the position of seeing the deficiencies in modern capitalist organisation, and to arrive at a consciousness of a new way of organising productive relationships, as the only way of satisfying the human needs which cannot be expressed within the present structures. (Mallet 1975: 29)

This debate was the starting point of Gallie's major research (1978) in four refineries of the same company, two in France and two in Britain. His research design is meant to test the ambitious and contrasting conclusions of Blauner and Mallet, who make technology the key factor in the evolution of work and of social relations within capitalism. Noting in passing how 'the data bases on which these theories rest are perilously frail' (1978: 29), Gallie goes through a systematic process of data collection on each site. Somewhat unsurprisingly, at least when we look at it now, he finds much difference between the behavior and attitudes of workers operating similar technologies in France and in Britain, and indeed within each country, as plants were selected in very different regions. This leads the author to emphasize cultural and institutional variables and to develop an interpretation which gives more weight to action theory (1978: 30, 35–6). In short, 'the principal conclusion of the research is that the nature of technology per se has, at most, very little importance for these specific areas of enquiry.... Instead, our evidence indicates the critical importance of the wider cultural and social structural patterns of specific societies for determining the nature of social interaction within the advanced sector' (Gallie 1978: 295; see also pp. 317–18).

Labour Process Theory

A very different line of research and debates, initiated by the work of Harry Braverman (1974) and known as labor process theory, also had much impact in the English-speaking world.[7] Besides the (obsessive) focus on management control, the key point brought home by Braverman (1974)

[7] Interestingly, and although Braverman's book was translated in French and its existence was known by most specialists, his work and the ensuing labour process debate did not have so much impact in France. Of course, ideas do not always travel well between these different intellectual traditions, but a key reason here is that French sociologists felt much of this

and labor process theory was to locate technology as a central element of the capitalist labor process (see in particular Edwards 1979), and to establish some of the foundations for a materialist conception of the employment relationship. From this perspective, technology has a major structuring influence on the pattern of control and on the resources for social cohesion. These ideas have much merit and, for a while, the influence of Braverman was overwhelming.

Nevertheless, even at the time, it was noted that Braverman conceived technology as a rather impersonal or asocial device, more or less as a tool for control in the hands of management, which inevitably reduced or eliminated craft control and the forms of job control developed by semiskilled workers. Lazonick (1983), in particular, was critical of Braverman's account for failing to consider seriously enough the problems of actually controlling workers and making then 'work hard', whatever the sophistication of technology. From his historical background, Lazonick argues that the question of control can only be understood by studying the long-term evolution of capital–labor relations and the impact of institutional arrangements in shaping these relations. Clearly, the problem of control is not 'technical'; it has to do with social relations over time.

Several scholars took the opportunity to assess the legacy of this research tradition, either twenty or twenty-five years after the publication of *Labor and Monopoly Capital* (1974). Reviewing the major American contributions inspired by this book, Smith presented it as a 'paradigmatic breakthrough' (1994: 404). She points out that 'key premises of *Labor and Monopoly Capital* have been turned upside down. Braverman downplayed consent, cooperation, and identity, but a significant number of studies have since persuasively argued that an analysis of labor process transformation is not only partial but, in fact, wrong if it fails to explain how structural change plays on, is limited by, and interacts with subjective experience' (Smith 1994: 416). Her observation regarding the recent focus on subjectivity is accurate, but this shift has become a major issue among those who are part of this research tradition. For some, the drift away from the structural dimensions of the capitalist labour process and the influence of a Foucauldian framework 'supplanting the concept of control with that of surveillance' (Smith and Thompson 1998: 559) have created a new imbalance

ground—and particularly the questions of control and dequalification—had already been covered. Rose (1987: 20–4) discusses the 'intellectual roots of Bravermania' in reference to *Sociologie du travail* in France and points out, in particular, the similarities between Braverman's deskilling thesis and the much earlier studies of Georges Friedmann, who also insisted on the damaging effects of 'modern' technology on craft knowledge.

and are weakening the very essence of labour process theory.[8] Some have pointed out that, as we will see in the following section, the emphasis on technical surveillance sometimes amounts to 'an overdeterministic view of technology' (Smith and Thompson 1998: 558). In other words, the recent move to consider issues of subjectivity and identity, in a voluntarist fashion, ended up with a new form of determinism. It follows that the progress made earlier by labour process theory in the understanding of management control—which remains complex and problematic—is sometimes ignored, and the possibilities for action and resistance (open or subtle) on the part of labour downplayed.

Going through a detailed discussion of labour process theory would bring us beyond the objectives of this chapter. But it is worth stressing that the rich debate evolving from the publication of Braverman's book laid the ground for a materialist line of analysis on workplace relations, particularly during the 1980s. This means, in essence, that the set of social relations people engage in at work is conditioned by the activity of production. This does not mean looking only at the technology per se, but rather studying the process by which labour power (or 'human resources') is 'transformed' to create a different product or a service. Ethnographic studies showed how patterns of management control, effort, and conflict, were tied to the production process, which is at the very same time a social process (for instance Burawoy 1979; Edwards and Scullion 1982). From this perspective, technology is not neutral; it sets a more or less favourable ground for job autonomy, control over effort and working time, and so on. This stream of research made an impact in the fields of industrial relations and industrial sociology, especially in Britain.

General Trends

Two points can be made as regards the linkages of this section to social theory more generally. First, in each of these three streams of research, where technology is seen as the key structural factor, one finds some materialist, when not an openly Marxist, influence. This essentially means that the system of production structures the experience of work, which itself represents a defining feature of the human condition. While

[8] In a vigorous critique of this 'drift away from Braverman and Marxism in labour process theory', Spencer (2000: 224) stresses how 'the Foucauldian preoccupation with the processes involved in the constitution of self-identity not only individualises capitalist social relations, but also conceals the position of capital in the subordination and exploitation of collective labour' (2000: 239).

only some of the contributors to the stream of research on automation, like Mallet, acknowledged Marx's influence, this intellectual tradition is quite obvious in the discussion of French sociology and of labor process theory. In recent decades, sociologists, often influenced by various strands of action theory, have become more inclined to throw light on contingency and the complexities of the modern world, and above all, to fight against any suggestion of a principal determining factor in the experience of work.

Second, and relatedly, models of historical evolution such as Touraine's three stages and Blauner's inverted U-curve are precisely the explanatory devices which have fallen out of fashion in sociological writings. This is certainly so in studies of technology and work, but I suggest it may be a more general trend in social sciences. Again, the emphasis is now on the variability of work experiences, even in comparable technical settings. Studies on the diffusion and effects of information technology, and on the ongoing process of globalization more generally, have exacerbated this general trend of moving away from unidimensional models of explanation. Section 3 will reflect this new way of thinking by illustrating some of the contemporary worlds of work with information technology.

3. Patterns of Work with Information Technology

While information technology changes the nature of work in many ways and creates new possibilities for management control, it is fair to say that it represents more of a break with the past in services and administrative sectors than in manufacturing sectors. For instance, refineries and aluminium smelters operated as a continuous process much before the use of computers, and the successive phases of automation and information technology only made them much more efficient, with much improvement in working conditions. Employees of such industries probably saw a degree of continuity in technological change. In contrast, in administration and services, the flow of production had not been integrated by technical devices, and investment in technology had traditionally been much less important (McLoughlin and Clark 1994: 8–15). In these sectors, information technology represents more of a discontinuity in patterns of work, and more research is needed to assess the extent of its impact.

Since there is no way I could present a satisfactory overview of all the different 'worlds of work' with information technology, the section is structured around three 'faces', or patterns, of work with information technology.

Information Technology in Manufacturing

There is now considerable case study evidence that technology makes a difference as regards the effective development of new forms of work organization. While the constraints of the assembly line inhibit the development of teamwork, continuous process production creates a more favorable terrain for such a development. In routine assembly work, performance depends directly on the volume and quality of output of each employee on a daily basis, and it is more difficult to do away with direct supervision. In contrast, in operations such as metal smelting, oil refineries, or power generation systems, production workers have to monitor technical systems. They have large areas to cover, and performance does not depend directly on 'work pace and effort' on an immediate basis. Employees' attitudes and their will to apply their expertise in order to detect any technical defect or to solve problems without supervision then become vital.

James Barker conducted an ethnographic study in a small American company assembling transmission circuit boards for the telecommunications industry. Self-managing teams had a good deal of autonomy in the organization of work, which consisted of repetitive and monotonous tasks. But he observes that team members were engaged in the construction of a detailed system of rules and norms by which they were constraining themselves, a pattern of 'concertive control' (Barker 1993, 1999).

While Barker does not insist on technology as a tool of control, Graham Sewell portrays the electronic surveillance generated by information technology as the central device. At Kay Electronics, Sewell and Wilkinson observed how the work of teams assigned to the assembling of printed circuit boards was monitored electronically and that, in particular, information on the performance (productivity, quality, attendance) of each worker was displayed for all to see on the shop floor (Sewell and Wilkinson 1992: 283–4; Sewell 1998: 412–13). They argued that 'the development and continued refinement of electronic surveillance systems using computer-based technology can provide the means by which management can achieve the benefits that derive from the delegation of responsibility to teams whilst retaining authority and disciplinary control' (Sewell and Wilkinson 1992: 283). Drawing on this and related research, as well as on Foucault's discussion of the Panopticon, Sewell conceptualizes a model of 'chimerical control' where the dynamics created by a combination of electronic surveillance and peer pressure leaves very little space for autonomy and social resistance. 'The hybrid nature of chimerical control stems from the interaction between its vertical and horizontal dimensions. The vertical dimension relates to panoptic control enacted through the surveillance of individuals, and the horizontal dimension relates to the operation of concertive control supported by peer scrutiny operating within teams' (Sewell 1998: 415).

Zuboff (1988) rather presents information technology as an important but not definite influence on work and power. Over a five year period, she conducted field research on work in eight organizations using computer-based technology, including three pulp and paper mills. Her rich empirical material throws light on the fact that this technology offers a huge potential for detailed management control but could also enhance skills and workers' influence. On the one hand, as noted above, she stresses the 'informating' power of this technology. The tools for collecting and storing data on work activities and minute events are there, and she discusses at some length the idea of the information Panopticon. But on the other hand, she insists on the capacity for information technology to enable and empower workers who were previously excluded from information on production activities, in the days when management considered the exclusive access to such information as a necessary support for the reproduction of authority relations. In short, Zuboff leaves the range of organizational choices open as regards the access to, and control of, the information generated by the production system. She even suggests in the concluding chapter that the empowering dimension of information technology could help transcend the structural divide between management and labor, and lead to 'posthierarchical relationships' (Zuboff 1988: 399–402). On this many would remain sceptical.

Field research we conducted in aluminium smelting indicates how these key organizational choices highlighted by Zuboff are, in the end, conditioned mostly by the social compromise prevailing in a given workplace. In a modern smelter in particular, it was obvious to all that very detailed information on the work activities of every single operator was registered by the production system. But it was understood by all participants that this detailed information would always be used with much circumspection, more or less as a 'safety net', if a problem occurred, and not as a means of excessive control (Bélanger 2001). Any infringement of this understanding by management (against an individual, a team, or more broadly) would be assessed in relation to the general pattern of social relations in the smelter. The extent of self-regulation within each rotating team was considerable, and this is illustrated by the absence of supervisors and managers at night and weekends, that is, for more than 70 percent of production time. There was much social cohesion among these metal workers, most of whom having high seniority with the company; they were proud of their expertise and of their capacity to run the plant efficiently and independently of supervision.

A crucial observation here is that, in spite of a rather sophisticated technology, the reliability of the technical system, and indeed efficiency as such, depended upon a social convention, based on mutual expectations. But in this smelter located at Laterrière, Quebec, the confidence that employees would make the best of their skills to find solutions was not dependent upon the type of social integration suggested by Blauner. It was a social compromise, and the pattern of behavior outlined here was conditioned by the balance of social forces. Indeed, workers and their union had the resources for expressing any discontent, and they certainly used these resources in the recent past. There were reciprocal expectations that all those involved would work to the best of their expertise in spite of the structural division between 'them' and 'us' (Bélanger et al. 2003).

This section indicates a range of ways in which information technology affects work. It suggests that excessive management control is more likely to be observed in routine assembly work. In many work situations, information technology actually has the potential for expanding the range of organizational choices and it does not necessarily reduce management's dependence upon the expertise and tacit skills of their employees (see also de Terssac 1992). But in another respect, as confirmed by recent field research by Vallas (2003) in four pulp and paper mills in the USA, the traditional hierarchical division between management and hourly workers is not at the point of being transcended in capital intensive manufacturing workplaces.

Call Centers: The 'Assembly Line' of Information Technology?

Considering its importance as a sector of employment, and because this whole business is about communication and the management of information, call centers represent the most typical image of work under information technology. Dramatic accounts of 'electronic Panopticon' are frequent among those who have never worked or conducted research there. But such an impressionistic image is not confirmed by ongoing research and, once more, the actual picture appears to be more complex.

While taking the full measure of the potential for control through information technology, critical sociologists have already documented how most call centers remain contested terrains (see for instance Bain and Taylor 2000).[9] I suggest a distinction between two aspects of the experience of work in call centers (aspects which too often remain confused) may help better understand this pattern of work. Research indicates that, on the one hand, customer service representatives (CSRs, the major group of call center workers) are subject to much control by technology but that, on the other hand, their work is not as prescribed and regimented as often expected. This proposition demands some elaboration.

As such workstations integrate telephone and computer technologies (Taylor and Bain 1999: 102, 115), readers will readily figure out the possibilities for technical control which are built up in the system. As noted by Callaghan and Thompson (2001: 21) from their observation in a Scottish call centre:

> Technology is used to control the pace and direction of work in call centers such as Telebank in much the same way as assembly line production. Such ACD [automatic call distribution system] technology systematizes control, with the power to push and pace work flowing not from a boss or supervisor but from the technology. This system of control is strongly embedded in the physical fabric of production and is therefore less obtrusive.

Such technical control is pervasive and focuses primarily on key measures such as 'average handling time' and time spent off the phone, but also generates plenty of information about the way each operator relates to customers on the basis of which various programs of quality assessment, training, and 'coaching' are deployed. As observed by Frenkel et al. (1999: 142), the practices of remote monitoring, by which lines are 'tapped' on a sample basis, usually without the worker's knowledge, and side-by-side monitoring (when a supervisor or manager sits alongside the operator) are usual in many call centers. These practices are presented as means for helping each CSR to improve her/his technique in dealing with customers, but they are also used to assess and reward performance.

These tools for technical control illustrate a key feature of information technology, that is the power to generate and record new data at the very same time as it operates production. However, as pointed out by Frenkel and colleagues (1999: 141): 'The pervasiveness of IT-generated data did not

[9] Hence the final words of Callaghan and Thompson's article: 'The "electronic sweatshop" is good newspaper copy, but is a long way from the still contested reality of the contemporary call centre' (2001: 35).

necessarily mean that workers viewed themselves as trapped in an electronic Panopticon'. Of course, many would simply dismiss this puzzle by pointing out that all this is expected as a natural feature of employment in this sector. But perhaps the operators also find some room for active agency.

The second dimension of our proposition, regarding the extent to which call centre workers have some latitude or must follow a routine, may be subject to more discussion. Of course, it must be stressed how this issue remains an empirical question. There is much diversity among call centers in terms of size, the nature of services provided, market conditions, with many implications on work organization and the routinization of calls (Taylor et al. 2002: 134). In particular, the average duration of calls varies very much and represents a good indicator of complexity; in general, longer voice-to-voice interaction with customers are even more difficult to standardize and 'script'. While impressionistic accounts often present work in call centers as a typical form of unskilled labor, where workers are simply told to 'follow the script', latitude in most cases is much more important. To make any progress with a customer online, a CSR must draw on resources of technical expertise and also some degree of conviviality so that the conversation is perceived as ongoing and satisfying. Managers are well aware that organization performance depends to a considerable extent on social skills and on the quality of these interactions between worker and customer.

On the basis of systematic research in three types of workflows (mass customized service, sales, and knowledge work) for customer-oriented (or 'front-line') employees in the USA, Australia, and Japan, Frenkel and colleagues provide an account of different types of work organization. Their assessment of the work of CSRs, seen as typical of service workers, is balanced if not equivocal. Their results confirm that, in comparison to sales and knowledge workers, customer service workers had more routine tasks. But they 'did not fit the stereotype image of the technologically incarcerated, regimented frontline employee' (Frenkel et al. 1999: 91, also 68–71). They conclude that for each of the three types of workflows, front-line work is becoming more complex. Besides technological and market reasons, the trend toward enhanced customization of services is seen as a major influence. Hence, 'because of the customizing aspect of service work, it requires creativity and hence discretion, which implies the need for learning more than just routinized patterns of behavior' (1999: 270).

Korczynski (2002) portrays service work as a 'customer-oriented bureaucracy' characterized by an inherent tension between a customer orientation, which often is the main motivator for the employee, and the search for rationalization and efficiency on the part of the employer. It is indeed a characteristic feature of service work that relations with customers are both a source of work presssure and strain and often a real source of satisfaction. This dynamic has implications on the very nature of the subordinate relationship between management and labour. This tension is very relevant to an understanding of call centre work: 'management, driven by efficiency requirements, wanted CSRs to relate to a disembodied concept of the customer. CSRs, for whom a central satisfying aspect of the job involved helping specific customers, preferred to identify with embodied customers' (Korczynski et al. 2000: 684).

It follows that, in spite of the 'power of technology', which—we are told by engineers—social scientists tend to overestimate, the space for agency remains significant even here. In many ways, service representatives usually manage to find a balance and 'keep healthy' because, in the end, they are online with another individual: a customer. Field research shows that workers' attitudes are most important. Indeed recruiting and retaining employees with the 'right attitudes' represent a key issue for management (Callaghan and Thompson 2002). CSRs are engaged in 'emotional labour' and, as noted by the same authors, 'far from being passive providers of emotional labour, employees are active and skilled emotion managers in their own right' (2002: 248). In short, management control is high, but 'the space for worker resistance and misbehaviour remains even with a high surveillance context' (Callaghan and Thompson 2001: 34).

Work Outside the Confines of the Organization

A third image of work under information technology relates to the various patterns of work away from the confines of a regular worksite. These patterns are so varied, with so much research to be done, that it is only possible here to uncover some of the features of this limited but growing sphere of employment and work. A common feature of these situations where technology lifts the constraints of space and time seems to be the need to redefine management control and to develop a different conception of the organization.

The notion of 'working at home' refers to quite a variety of situations, both in terms of employment (or self-employment) status and of working conditions. On the basis of data from national surveys in Britain, Felstead and colleagues (2002) were able to establish a useful conceptual distinction between two categories of employees. First, those who have the *option* of working at home, of whom only one in ten will actually work mainly at home. Second, those whose jobs *require* them to work at home, and who are usually in a much more difficult position on the labor market. The data do not allow the authors to compare the economic profile of these two groups as well as they would like. But they did establish the fact that having the option to choose where to work is associated with a privileged position on the labour market. Hence they issue 'a warning regarding the conceptual and empirical fallacy of equating the *practice* of working at home with the *option* of doing so' (Felstead et al. 2002: 205, also 221).

The same research team also conducted a program of interviews with managers and home-located workers in thirteen organizations in Britain. Felstead, Jewson, and Walters (2003) discuss the issues of 'visibility' and 'presence' which, they stress, are among the key resources from which managers construct their mechanisms of control. In particular, absence from the worksite proves to be tricky from an organizational viewpoint because, even when individual output is good, employees can no longer play an active role in normative control, team working, the transmission of tacit knowledge, and the making of an organizational culture more generally. Often, the minority of home workers even feel subtle expressions of resentment from on-site coworkers. 'The weakening of ties between home-located workers and team members in the workplace was seen as having the capacity to generate resentment among on-site coworkers, leading to tension and bad feelings that further disrupted team integration' (Felstead et al. 2003: 254). This study indicates that, contrary to simplistic textbook accounts, some of the limitations associated with these patterns of work raise new issues affecting the social dynamics of the organization. Hence looking at work outside the organisation brings us back, somewhat paradoxically, to the basics of the social relations which also constitute the organization.

An ethnographic study of technicians doing maintenance and repair of photocopiers in the customer's place of business throws light on the networks of social relations which develop outside the boundaries of the large corporation which employs them, namely Xerox (Orr 1996). Two key observations are worth noting. First, Orr conceptualizes this work practice as a triangular relationship between technicians, customers, and machines. Within his/her assigned territory, a technician builds trust relationships and a 'delicate social equilibrium' (1996: 63, also 78–9) with specific customers, a social connection in which even fellow team members should ideally not interfere. Technicians are more comfortable within their geographical and social territory, a phenomenon akin to that observed in shopfloor sociology. Second, it is through the narrative process which evolves within the community of technicians, who like to 'talk about machines', that know-how and expertise are transmitted. Dealing with machines is a complex process of negotiation and creation of tacit meanings. Hence field service technicians represent a fine example of an 'occupational community', as conceptualized by van Maanen and Barley (1984: 314), whose members 'share similar identities and values that transcend specific organizational settings'.

The empirical contributions mentioned here attest that information technology opens the way to a variety of work situations which no longer correspond to the traditional conception of the 'organization'. These changes lead to different patterns of interaction and raise new opportunities but also new concerns for management. In particular, the sharing of know-how among employees and the usual forms of normative control are inhibited.

4. Analytical Issues

The view developed in this chapter is that technology, and particularly the recent phase of information technology, has a major influence on the experience of work. But methodologically and analytically, it is not appropriate to seek to isolate this influence from the changes occurring within organizations, and from social relations more generally. In comparison with the preceding phase of automation associated for instance with refineries, information technology is less robust and less constraining, but it is also more pervasive. It is less 'constraining' in the sense that, in the main, it does not integrate the whole production flow and leaves much room for organizational choice. This is why we observe, as illustrated in Section 2, so much variability in organizational forms under information technology. By 'pervasive' I mean that (*a*) information technology is by no means confined to the workplace but follows the employees in other spheres of life, and (*b*) it has an immense potential for registering information and supporting social control, even when 'you don't see it'. The following pages develop some of the implications of these technical systems for social relations at work.

Technology and Social Divisions

A starting point is to observe that the structural dividing line between management and labour, which Georges Friedmann (1964*a*) saw as the origin of alienation and noncooperation, is not altered by the phenomena discussed in this chapter. This divide is structurally related to the very nature of the employment relationship (Edwards 1986). But much else is changing. First, the technical division of labour appears to be eroding substantially, as the classic idea of specialization, from Adam Smith onwards, is no longer associated with efficiency. Many employees have gained considerable discretion in the organization and execution of their work. Teamwork is only one of the mechanisms through which these changes occur, and the development of multifunctional teams and cellular modes of coordination are now spreading among technicians and professional employees. The point is that different types of work organization can change the form but not the essence of subordination. Second, while the structural divide between management and labor—the traditional focus of industrial relations scholars—remains, we may now have to be less rigid (or more innovative) in defining the concepts and categories to account for the various forms of social divisions at work. Information technology is one of the forces underlying these gradual shifts in the ways social interactions are redefined between supervisors and supervised, between line managers and professionals or technicians of different departments, etc. It follows that 'the rigid separation of mental and material work characteristic of the industrial division of labor and vital to the preservation of a distinct managerial group (in the office as well as in the factory) becomes, not merely outmoded, but perilously dysfunctional' (Zuboff 1988: 393). The general tendency appears to be that hierarchy, the line of authority, has to make more and more compromises in favor of those whose power is based on knowledge of various types.

Information Technology and 'Knowledge Organizations'

At the heart of the traditional idea of the large factory or office was a particular conception of command and control, where the organization appeared to favor unity of space and time, i.e. having most people reporting to work at the same location at similar hours, either for technical reasons (e.g. energy sources, dedicated technology) or because they were working around the same basis of information and expertise. Without falling into any form of futurology, one has to acknowledge that, for many sectors of employment, several of these underlying principles are no longer objective constraints. The diffusion and transfer of the different types of knowledge which make an organization now appear to be the key to efficiency, and this can be achieved through various forms of internal and external networks (Castells 1998; Veltz 2000). Rather than a comprehensive unit with clear boundaries from markets, the organization operates constant linkages with suppliers and customers.

Although by no means the only cause, information technology allows and contributes to these organizational changes. First, while the preceding phase of automation had the characteristic of integrating complete flows of production, or sequences of operations through mechanical devices, information technology has a propensity for creating workstations which are autonomous but nevertheless connected to a centre of information. By superseding the preceding stage of technical integration, it allows for much organizational flexibility. Second, it contributes to the development of so-called knowledge organizations by offering the necessary basis of information and communication for the various networks and related modes of coordination through which employees can operate.

Nevertheless, in most large firms, these possibilities for information technology to play an effective role in supporting networks and innovation are limited by a traditional organizational structure based on hierarchy. Powell notes that for many economists in the USA, the recent technological revolution did not translate so much into productivity increases because of what they saw as a mismatch between worker skills and the demands of technology. He rather argues that the explanation holds in a 'disconnect between organizational form and the new technologies' (Powell 2001: 49). 'If there is a mismatch, then, I contend it is between the capabilities of information technology to handle information and problems whenever and wherever necessary, and the older organizational arrangements that force decisions to be made by a central managerial hierarchy' (2001: 50).

The point is that technology plays a major role in transforming organizations. Before they can properly assess the 'effects of new technology on work', social scientists will have to do more in documenting and understanding these major changes. To give an example with considerable implications: by making the organization no longer necessarily a self-contained place of work, with a unity of space and time, advanced technologies contribute to the broader phenomenon that for so many people, the division between work and leisure, or work and home, is often blurred (Hochschild 1997). While no one contests the enabling possibilities of email, mobile phone, and more and more sophisticated devices, these can be quite invasive and contribute to a further insertion of work into leisure.

Information Technology and Social Domination?

As noted by Zuboff, a characteristic feature of information technology is this capacity to create detailed information about the work activities it is supporting, at the same time and in the same process. This dimension of technology created some of the objective basis for recent debates on social domination and the more or less explicit suggestions of an 'end of resistance'. Hence the references to Foucault and to the Panopticon. The Panopticon is a conceptualization by the moral philosopher Bentham, in the eighteenth century, of an architectural plan by which an observer could oversee without being seen. It was originally discussed in the context of a prison. Michel Foucault saw this as a representation of a society in which surveillance and social control prevailed. As noted by Zuboff (1988: 322), 'information systems . . . would have exceeded even Bentham's most outlandish fantasies'. But as shown by her observation (1988: ch. 9), the extent to which this bulk of raw information is actually used as a tool for the construction of disciplinary powers remains an empirical question. In particular, what are the social conditions by which this might be possible? To what extent do managers follow such a path, at the possible expense of the basis of trust and legitimacy which usually are the preconditions for organizational efficiency? And even more fundamentally, is it possible at all that all forms of social resistance might be eradicated?

Some influential contributions imply that, at least in some social contexts, the answer to this last question might be positive. As noted above, the arguments developed by Barker and by Sewell on the basis of observation of teamwork in equipment manufacturing, certainly suggest forms of control which leave little space for free opposition on the part of labor. Hence, 'concertive control does not free workers from Weber's iron cage of rational rules. . . . The iron cage becomes stronger. The powerful combination of peer pressure and rational rules in the concertive system creates a new iron cage whose bars are almost invisible to the workers it incarcerates' (Barker 1993: 435). At 'Key Electronics', Sewell (1998) notes: 'the extension of surveillance was incremental and, at each stage, it faced little coherent opposition. This does not mean that opposition was absent, but it did appear to be marginalized. This will not always be the case in other research settings, and it remains to be seen whether the unopposed diffusion of chimerical control is a widespread phenomenon' (1998: 423).

While the overall emphasis of Sewell's article clearly is on social domination, this last quote must be taken as a crucial methodological point. The author was, quite rightly, careful not to generalize. Indeed, in spite of the potential of information technology as an instrument of social control, the absence of any form of social cohesion and resistance is always suspect, or likely to cast doubt, from a sociological viewpoint. In most economic and social conditions (at least in advanced economies) so little space for agency is unlikely from a theoretical perspective.

Several British sociologists have felt the need to reiterate this analytical point that, in most social conditions, the eradication of all forms of social resistance at work is unlikely (Thompson and Ackroyd 1995; Knights and McCabe 1998, 2000; Ackroyd and Thompson 1999). As noted by Knights and McCabe in a contribution explicitly aimed at reasserting some analytical balance, 'those authors who follow an overly deterministic and omnipotent conception of power effectively rule out the active subject and provide much grist to the anti-Foucaultian mill that we are anxious to remedy' (Knight and McCabe 2000: 427).

Fleming and Sewell (2002: 864) also see some space for human agency, insisting on the need to consider worker resistance in a more comprehensive mode, including the subtle forms of dissent and of 'active disengagement; the ability to comply without conforming'. They also point out that in order to properly appreciate resistance in the current contexts of work, sociologists must adjust the lenses they were using in the Fordist era and also consider other categories of social behavior. This intuition could be very relevant in light of the analysis we seek to develop here. In traditional organizations, often large and protected by an internal labor market, a 'natural' manifestation of opposition was withdrawal from work, for a short while or once for all, individually or collectively, depending on alternative labor market opportunities, collective resources, and institutional context. Once work becomes less confined to a given place of work with stable work communities, and more dependent upon the application of skills and knowledge, the discretionary use of labor becomes more manifest. Expressing dissatisfaction or dissent may simply mean that one no longer takes emails or remains linked through the cell phone or pager at home, or over the weekend. Or, to give examples from various contexts, suggestions for product development are not made, or an 'appropriate attitude' is not displayed in the case of frontline work. In short, resistance does not necessarily mean overt action; simply not acting may often be a more tactful means of expressing dissent.

5. Conclusion

After reviewing many influential studies on the role of technology in shaping the experience of work, this chapter discussed some of the growing research literature on the impact of information technology. It has highlighted, in particular, the changes currently occurring in so many organizations, as new modes of supervision and coordination are shifting some of the lines of social division at work. However, there is a tendency in the literature to suggest that the organizational changes fostered by information technology will proceed smoothly, almost 'naturally'. I suggest this view is not realistic.

A key limitation is the tension between two different conceptions of production one can observe in most, if not all, organizations. The first has to do with the pursuit of efficiency from a mechanistic or technical perspective, through the use of technology and the development of various management programmes aiming at rationalization and standardization. This drive for 'engineering rationality' has to be interpreted as a 'long wave', from Taylor onwards, with much sophistication since Bell ([1960] 1988) coined this phrase some time ago. Max Weber's conception of rationalization remains the best sociological starting point to study its broader implications on work, and on society more generally. The second conception of production is shaped by those who have learned the trade (*le métier*) and transmitted know-how and empirical knowledge over the years (production workers, frontline employees, etc.). In light of the useful typology of knowledge types and organizational forms developed by Lam (2000: 491–3), I am referring to the tension between the 'embrained' or codified knowledge of the engineers and the tacit or 'embodied' knowledge of most employees, which is more context-specific, more related to the 'tricks of the trade'. Of course, organizational learning and efficiency are improved when connections are established between these two conceptions of production, which are associated to different social and cultural worlds; but social sciences suggest that the development of shared perspectives between these will not be achieved easily.

The very idea of 'engineering rationality', for which the tools have progressed so much over the last century, will always bear some element of a utopia that, in the end, the technical system will run so smoothly that the organizational issues discussed in this chapter will become less of a concern for management. In fact, the problem of consent does not seem to be less crucial than ever before; indeed it is made even more complex. In comparison to various forms of assembly and mass production where cooperation was more 'mechanical', in the sense that it was integrated into the technical system or into the routines suggested by Taylorism (Veltz 2000), it now rests more upon the free will to apply knowledge and ideas and upon relations between various categories of employees at the point of production. As a general rule, the more work stations and human networks are integrated and interconnected, the more production systems are vulnerable and dependent upon such form of cooperation. Veltz (2001) sees this tension between integration and reliability as a natural feature of complex systems of production built on information technology; as he points out, 'as soon as a system has become reliable, one looks for a further degree of integration, hence putting at risk this equilibrium' (2001: 317, my translation). The search for ever more integration is part of this utopia; but to a considerable extent, this makes the working of complex systems dependent upon the autonomy and tacit skills of operators, who are used to the shortfalls of any automated system.

Indeed, students of the employment relationship will add that a fundamental reason why production relations, and the problem of consent, will remain problematic has to do with the structural divide between management and labour. Work has to be socially regulated and, in the end, social relations prevail over any conception of technical determinism.

References

Ackroyd, S. and Thompson, P. (1999). *Organizational Misbehaviour.* London: Sage.

Bain, P. and Taylor, T. (2000). 'Entrapped by the "Electronic Panopticon"? Worker Resistance in the Call Centre', *New Technology, Work and Employment,* 15(1): 2–18.

Barker, J. R. (1993). 'Tightening the Iron Cage: Concertive Control in Self-Managing Teams', *Administrative Science Quarterly,* 38(1): 408–37.

—— (1999). *The Discipline of Teamwork.* Thousand Oaks, CA: Sage.

Bélanger, J. (2001). 'Autorégulation du travail et division sociale: observation dans une aluminerie québécoise', *Sociologie du travail,* 43(2): 159–77.

——, Edwards, P. K., and Wright, M. (2003). 'Commitment at Work and Independence from Management: A Study of Advanced Teamwork', *Work and Occupations,* 30(2): 234–52.

Bell, D. ([1960] 1988). 'Work and its Discontent: The Cult of Efficiency in America', *The End of Ideology.* Cambridge: Harvard University Press, 227–72.

Björkman, T. (1999). 'ABB and the Restructuring of the Electrotechnical Industry', in J. Bélanger et al. (eds.), *Being Local Worldwide.* Ithaca, NY: Cornell University Press.

Blauner, R. (1964). *Alienation and Freedom: The Factory Worker and His Industry.* Chicago, IL: The University of Chicago Press.

Braverman, H. (1974). *Labor and Monopoly Capital: The Degradation of Work in the Twentieth Century.* New York: Monthly Review Press.

Burawoy, M. (1979). *Manufacturing Consent: Changes in the Labor Process under Monopoly Capitalism.* Chicago, IL: The University of Chicago Press.

Butera, F. (2001). 'Automation: Organizational studies', in N.J. Smelser and P.B. Baltes (eds.), *International Encyclopedia of the Social and Behavioral Sciences,* vol 2. New York: Elsevier.

Callaghan, G. and Thompson, P. (2001). 'Edwards Revisited: Technical Control and Call Centres', *Economic and Industrial Democracy,* 22(1): 13–37.

—— and —— (2002). ' "We Recruit Attitude": The Selection and Shaping of Routine Call Centre Labour', *Journal of Management Studies,* 39(2): 233–54.

Castells, M. (1998). *La société en réseaux: l'ère de l'information.* Paris: Fayard.

Clark, J., McLoughlin, I, Rose, H., and King, R. (1988). *The Process of Technological Change: New Technology and Social Choice in the Workplace.* Cambridge: Cambridge University Press.

Cochoy, F. (2001). 'Ce que le détour par la technique nous apprend du travail', in A. Pouchet (ed.), *Sociologie du Travail: Quarante Ans Après.* Paris: Elsevier.

Dawson, S., and Wedderburn, D. (1980). 'Introduction: Joan Woodward and the Development of Organization Theory', in J. Woodward (ed.), *Industrial Organization: Theory and Practice,* 2nd edn. Oxford: Oxford University Press.

De Terssac, G. (1992). *Autonomie dans le Travail.* Paris: Presses Universitaires de France.

Edwards, R. (1979). *Contested Terrain: The Transformation of the Workplace in the Twentieth Century.* New York: Basic Books.

Edwards, P. K. (1986). *Conflict at Work: A Materialist Analysis of Workplace Relations.* Oxford: Blackwell.

—— and Scullion, H. (1982). *The Social Organization of Industrial Conflict: Control and Resistance in the Workplace.* Oxford: Blackwell.

Felstead, A., Jewson, N., Phizacklea, A., and Walters, S. (2002). 'The Option to Work at Home: Another Privilege for the Favoured Few?' *New Technology, Work and Employment,* 17(3): 204–23.

——, Jewson, N., and Walters, S. (2003). 'Managerial Control of Employees Working at Home', *British Journal of Industrial Relations,* 41(2): 241–64.

Fleming, P. and Sewell, G. (2002). 'Looking for the Good Soldier, Svejk: Alternative Modalities of Resistance in the Contemporary Workplace', *Sociology,* 36(4): 857–73.

Frenkel, S. J., Korczynski, M., Shire, K.A., and Tam, T. (1999). *On the Front Line: Organization of Work in the Information Economy.* Ithaca, NY: Cornell University Press.

Friedmann, G. (1946). Les *Problèmes Humains du Machinisme industriel.* Paris: Gallimard.

Friedmann, G. (1964*a*). 'Tendances d'aujourd'hui et perspectives de demain', in G. Friedmann and P. Naville (eds.), *Traité de Sociologie du Travail*, vol 2, 2nd edn. Paris: Armand Colin.

—— (1964*b*). *Le Travail en Miettes*, 2nd edn. Paris: Gallimard.

—— and Naville, P. (eds.) (1964). *Traité de Sociologie du Travail*, 2 vols, 2nd edn. Paris: Armand Colin.

Gallie, D. (1978). *In Search of the New Working Class: Automation and Social Integration within the Capitalist Enterprise*. Cambridge: Cambridge University Press.

Grauer, M. (2001). 'Information Technology', in N.J. Smelser and P.B. Baltes (eds.), *International Encyclopedia of the Social and Behavioral Sciences*, vol 11. New York: Elsevier.

Hochschild, A. R. (1997). *The Time Bind: When Work Becomes Home and Home Becomes Work*. New York: Henry Holt.

Hodson, R. (1996). 'Dignity in the Workplace under Participative Management: Alienation and Freedom Revisited', *American Sociological Review*, 61(5): 719–38.

—— (2001). *Dignity at Work*. Cambridge: Cambridge University Press.

Knights, D. and McCabe, D. (1998). 'Dreams and Designs on Strategy: A Cricical Analysis of TQM and Management Control', *Work, Employment and Society*, 12(3): 433–56.

—— and McCabe, D. (2000). ' "Ain't Misbehavin"? Opportunities for Resistance under New Forms of "Quality" Management', *Sociology*, 34(3): 421–36.

Korczynski, M. (2002). *Human Resource Management in Service Work*. Houndmills: Palgrave.

——, Shire, K., Frenkel, S., and Tam, M. (2000). 'Service Work in Consumer Capitalism: Customers, Control and Contradictions', *Work, Employment and Society*, 14(4): 669–87.

Lam, A. (2000). 'Tacit Knowledge, Organizational Learning and Societal Institutions: An Integrated Framework', *Organization Studies*, 21(3): 487–513.

Lazonick, W. H. (1983). 'Technological Change and the Control of Work: The Development of Capital-Labour Relations in US Mass Production Industries', in H.F. Gospel and C.R. Littler (eds.), *Managerial Strategies and Industrial Relations*. London: Heinemann.

Mallet, S. (1969). *La Nouvelle Casse Ouvrière*. Paris: Seuil.

—— (1975) *The New Working Class*. Nottingham: Spokesman.

Maurice, M. (1980). 'Le déterminisme technologique dans la sociologie du travail (1955–1980). Un changement de paradigme?', *Sociologie du Travail*, 22(1): 22–37.

McLoughlin, I. and Clark, J. (1994). *Technological Change at Work*, 2nd edn. Buckingham: Open University Press.

Orr, J. E. (1996). *Talking about Machines: An Ethnography of a Modern Job*. Ithaca, NY: ILR Press.

Piore, M. and Sabel, C. (1984). *The Second Industrial Divide: Possibilities for Prosperity*. New York: Basic Books.

Powell, W. W. (2001). 'The Capitalist Firm in the Twenty-First Century: Emerging Patterns in Western Enterprise', in P. DiMaggio (ed.), *The Twenty-First-Century Firm*. Princeton, NJ: Princeton University Press.

Reeves, T. K. and Woodward, J. (1970). 'The Study of Managerial Control', in J. Woodward (ed.), *Industrial Organization: Behaviour and Control*. London: Oxford University Press.

Rose, M. (1987). 'Introduction: Retrospection and the Role of a Sociology of Work', in M. Rose (ed.), *Industrial Sociology: Work in the French Tradition*. London: Sage.

Sewell, G. (1998). 'The Discipline of Teams: The Control of Team-based Industrial Work through Electronic and Peer Surveillance', *Administrative Science Quarterly*, 43(2): 397–428.

—— and Wilkinson, B. (1992). ' "Someone to Watch Over Me": Surveillance, Discipline and the Just-in-Time Labour Process', *Sociology*, 26(2): 271–89.

Smith, V. (1994). 'Braverman's Legacy: The Labor Process Tradition at 20', *Work and Occupations*, 21(4): 403–421.

Smith, C. and Thompson, P. (1998). 'Re-Evaluating the Labour Process Debate', *Economic and Industrial Democracy*, 19(4): 551–77.

Spencer, D. A. (2000). 'Braverman and the Contribution of Labour Process Analysis to the Critique of Capitalist Production—Twenty-Five Years On', *Work, Employment and Society*, 14(2): 223–43.

Taylor, P. and Bain, P. (1999). ' "An Assembly Line in the Head": Work and Employee Relations in the Call Centre', *Industrial Relations Journal*, 30(2): 101–17.

——, Mulvey, G., Hyman, J., and Bain, P. (2002). 'Work Organization, Control and the Experience of Work in Call Centres', *Work, Employment and Society*, 16(1): 133–50.

Thomas, R. J. (1994). *What Machines Can't Do: Politics and Technology in the Industrial Enterprise*. Berkeley, CA: University of California Press.

Thompson, P. and Ackroyd, S. (1995). 'All Quiet on the Workplace Front? A Critique of Recent Trends in Brirish Industrial Sociology', *Sociology*, 29(4): 615–33.

Touraine, A. (1955). *L'Évolution du Travail Ouvrier aux Usines Renault*. Paris: Centre National de la Recherche Scientifique.

—— (1964). 'L'organisation professionnelle de l'entreprise: l'évolution du travail ouvrier', in G. Friedmann and P. Naville (eds.), *Traité de Sociologie du Travail*, vol 1, 2nd edn. Paris: Armand Colin.

Vallas, S. P. (2003). 'Why Teamwork Fails: Obstacles to Workplace Change in Four Manufacturing Plants', *American Sociological Review*, 68(2): 223–50.

Van Maanen, J. and Barley, S.R. (1984). 'Occupational Communities: Culture and Control in Organizations', in B.W. Staw and L.L. Cummins (eds.), *Research in Organizational Behavior*, vol. 6, Greenwich, CT: JAI Press.

Veltz, P. (2000). *Le Nouveau Monde Industriel*. Paris: Gallimard.

Veltz, P. (2001). 'La sociologie du travail peut-elle encore parler de la technique?, in A. Pouchet (ed.), *Sociologie du Travail: Quarante Ans Après*. Paris: Elsevier.

Woodward, J. (1965). *Industrial Organization: Theory and Practice*. Oxford: Oxford University Press.

Zuboff, S. (1988). *In the Age of the Smart Machine: The Future of Work and Power.* New York: Basic Books.

13

Professional Work

Keith Macdonald

This chapter deals with 'occupations based on advanced, or complex, or esoteric, or arcane knowledge', or 'formally rational abstract utilitarian knowledge' (Murphy 1988: 245) or what the English-speaking world calls 'professions'. It is important to recognize that 'professional' has a wide range of uses in everyday speech, many of which are value-laden. As Abbott (1988) writes: 'There are so many uses, many of them tendentious, that one has to take as part of one's inquiry the problem of how and why these uses come to exist, and leave the matter of "meaning" to one side.' The chapter will show first how the principal schools of sociological theory have dealt with this topic, leading to the conclusion that some of the most fruitful work on professions has made use of the concept of 'professional project' and endeavoring to show its value in a fuller elaboration as an 'ideal type'. After considering the criticisms to which this approach might be subject, it will be illustrated by summaries of work on three themes within the sociology of the professions—social stratification, knowledge, and patriarchy.

1. Sociological Analysis of the Professions

All the main sociological theories have provided a basis for work on the professions. In the late nineteenth and early twentieth centuries functionalism was very much to the fore, while from the mid-twentieth century Marxian concepts and those of action theory and of symbolic interactionism tended to take over. In the later twentieth century ideas from Foucault and from feminist theory also entered the field.

Functionalism

Professional work is of interest to sociologists because, being knowledge-based, it does not have a tangible product, and so the consumer has to trust the practitioner. Trust may be generated in various ways—having been educated at a famous university, being recognizable as a gentleman or having a licence to practice from the Church. But it is equally important that practitioners make it known that *caveat emptor* does not apply, that they adhere to a code of ethics, and that offenders against it will be punished. These features of professional work led functionalist theorists with their interest in the normative order of society, to focus on professions, with some writers becoming positively eulogistic about them.

Durkheim's theory that work is a major integrative factor in society (when the division of labor is neither forced nor anomic) led to professions being given an important place in functionalist thinking. Durkheim (1957) believed that modern society was threatened by a breakdown in moral authority from which occupational groups could save it. The features of these groups are outlined in the *Division of Labour in Society* (Durkheim 1964: 14), and they are particularly characteristic of the professions, although in their French form professions were more formalized, hierarchical, and closer to the state than an Anglophone reader would expect (Durkheim 1957: 8–14). In the view of Halliday (1987: 18) 'it is clear from his description of the functions to be performed by intermediary bodies (*corps intermediaires)* that they would act in some respects as contemporary professions have done'. Despite the gap between Durkheim's conception of future professions and that of Anglo-American scholars, there is undoubtedly 'a line of intellectual filiation from Durkheim in early twentieth-century France, through Carr-Saunders and Wilson in interwar England, to Parsons and Bell in post-war America' (Halliday 1987: 17). Carr-Saunders and Wilson (1933) saw professions as being one of those stable elements in society which

> inherit, preserve and pass on a tradition.... They engender modes of life, habits of thought and standards of judgement which render them centres of resistance to crude forces which threaten steady and peaceful evolution.... The family, the church and the universities, certain associations of intellectuals, *and above all the great professions*, stand like rocks against which the waves raised by these forces beat in vain. (1933: 497, emphasis added)

Thirty years later this view could still be heard from structural-functionalist sociologists (Lynn 1963: 653; Parsons 1968) who gave professions a prominent place as promoters of social order. (A more moderate and judicious enthusiasm is still current today (Brint 1994; Freidson 2001.) It was out of the functionalist school that the 'traits' approach to the professions arose, which listed the characteristics of an ideal-typical profession, against which occupational groups could be assessed as more or less professional (Goode 1957; Etzioni 1969; Hickson and Thomas 1969). But the functionalist view of the professions was never completely dominant, primarily because, especially in the USA, a quite different variety of sociology was also interested in the professions.

Interactionist Alternatives

The symbolic interactionism school in the USA had always maintained an alternative view, particularly in the sociology of occupations. The studies of Hughes (1958, 1971), Becker et al. (1961), and Freidson (1970*b*, 1973) were the outcome of a tradition which took as its subject matter the actions and interactions of individuals and groups, how they constituted their social worlds as participants, and how they constructed their careers. Professional principles of altruism, service, and high ethical standards were seen as aspects of the everyday world and therefore as somewhat imperfect social constructs rather than the principles of a formal collectivity. Trainee physicians were portrayed as developing cynicism rather than altruism (Becker et al. 1961), doctors appeared as wielders of power, not servants of the social good (Freidson 1970*a*), and most of the professional 'traits' were characterized as ideology (Daniels 1973) or even 'mythology' (McKinlay 1973*b*: 62).

Professional Power

Interactionism gave rise to one version of the 'power' approach that soon came to dominate sociology of the professions (Hall 1983: 11). Although Freidson (1970*b*) had given a strong impetus to this new theme, he considered that some writers had merely replaced the multi-trait approach by 'a single . . . explanatory trait or characteristic' (Freidson 1983: 33)—namely power. Freidson himself makes very little use of the word 'power', preferring the term 'organized autonomy' (1970*b*: 71), reflecting a professions 'licence and mandate' to control its work (Hughes 1958: 78–80), granted by society (or in effect the state) by virtue of winning the support of a political, economic, or social elite (Freidson 1970*b*:188). The main themes in this strand of Freidson's work are how the medical profession in anglophone countries has attained autonomy and 'dominance' over kindred occupations, while resisting outside interference and supervision.

At the same time, Berlant (1975), Parry and Parry (1976), Larson (1977), and others were developing a neo-Weberian line of analysis, which was concerned *inter alia* with power. In Britain, however, a rather different view of power was put forward, deriving from Johnson's (1972) analysis. This approach focused on the relations between producer and consumer of professional services and the extent to which the producer could or could not control the relationship and thereby benefit from it. While Marx is not actually mentioned, the centrality of the 'producers' and their relationships, together with the tenor of other work by this author (e.g. Johnson 1977, 1980), suggests it derived more from a Marxian tradition, which will be dealt with below.

Professions as Social Actors

The 'power approach', was more fruitful than functionalism, but within interactionism another view was emerging—that basically *sociologists were asking the wrong question*; but it was only by degrees that the sociological community realized the significance of what Everett C. Hughes (1963) had written: '[I]n my own studies I passed from the false question "Is this occupation a profession" to the more fundamental one "what are the circumstances in which people in an occupation attempt to turn it into a profession and themselves into professional people"?'

Some sociologists realized that Hughes was saying something radical about the sociology of the professions, but not all of them seemed to understand that Hughes was referring, not to a structure or a system within which *things happen*, but to *people's actions* in a social arena (Jackson 1970; McKinlay 1973*a*: 66). Becker (1970: 91) and Freidson (1983: 27) added to this view the observation that 'profession' is a lay or folk term and that assessing whether an occupation is or is not a profession is what the *folk* do, and it is not the task of sociology to try to do it for them scientifically. Sociology should do something different.

> If 'profession' may be defined as a folk concept, then the research strategy appropriate to it is phenomenological in character. One does not attempt to determine what a profession is in an absolute sense so much as how people in a society determine who is a professional and who is not, how they 'make' or 'accomplish' professions by their activities. (Freidson 1983: 27)

Lay members of society assess the claims of occupational groups and react in ways that affect a 'profession's' standing. This is how 'society' continuously defines and evaluates 'professional traits' or for that matter 'professional power'. What then should sociologists do that is distinct from what the folk do already?

The answer is to be found in the interactionist tradition—in the remark of Hughes (1963) cited above, in the work of Becker and Freidson and explicitly in the research objectives of Larson (1977: xii, xiv); 'Everett C. Hughes and his followers are the principal critics of the 'trait' approach and ask instead '*what professions actually do in everyday life to negotiate and maintain their special position*.... My intention here is to examine *how* the occupations we call professions organized themselves to attain market power' (emphasis added). Larson developed the Chicago interactionist position, and by incorporating the insights of Marx (1958, 1976) Weber and other European social theorists, took the sociological analysis of the professions in a new and rewarding direction.

The Professional Project

From this starting point, Larson's conceptualization builds on the work of Freidson (1970*b*) and draws on his clarification of the nature of professional prestige and the processes by which it is asserted. Freidson emphasizes that the autonomy of a profession depends upon the state and that once a profession has gained autonomy, it can begin to establish a position of social prestige with its own niche in the system of social stratification. It can also develop an ideology and define social reality within its sphere of action.

Larson draws on the Marxian tradition and on the history of professional development (Polyani 1957; Weber 1978; and Parkin 1971). She sees two aspects of modernity as crucial for the emergence of professional groups, namely scientific knowledge and the existence of free markets in societies where qualifications and expertise as well as property are important as 'opportunities for income'. She also emphasizes the need both to obtain such opportunities and to maximize them, while at the same time excluding outsiders (Parkin 1971: 212). The formulation of her research problem follows Freidson (1970*a*, 1970*b*), and draws directly on Weber's view of stratification, his ideas of the economic order and the social order, and the notion that specialist knowledge constitutes an 'opportunity for income' (Weber 1978: 304).

Larson's work emphasizes that social mobility and market control are the outcome of 'the professional project', a term which 'emphasizes the coherence and consistence' of a particular course of action, even though 'the goals and strategies pursued by a given group are not entirely clear or deliberate for all the members' (1977: 6). The market control aspect of the 'project' requires that there should be a body of relatively abstract knowledge, susceptible of practical application, and a market potential. If the possessors of this knowledge can form themselves into a group, which can then begin to standardize and control the dissemination of the knowledge base and dominate the market in knowledge-based services, they will then be in a position to enter into a 'regulative bargain' (Cooper et al. 1988: 8) with the state. This will allow them to standardize their knowledge and restrict access to it, to control their market and supervise the 'production of producers' (Larson 1977: 71)—in short, to achieve a monopoly. These dimensions of market control are interlocked with the dimensions of social prestige to such an extent that Larson describes them as 'two . . . distinct analytical constructs which can be "read" out of the same empirical material' (1977: 66).

Marxian Theory and the Professions

Marxian theory differs from the Weberian and Chicago schools in that it is a sociology of structure and system. In this view, 'processes' are at work that are the consequences of the capitalist mode of production. Marx argues that the basis of stratification, *inter alia*, is to be found in ownership and nonownership of the means of production and the relations of production based on them. It follows that state formation, polarization of social classes, monopolization of the means of production etc. are all *processes* in which the professions are bound up. Marxians see these trends not as the consequences, intended or otherwise, of the actions of individuals and collectivities, but as the working out of the logic of exploitive relations of capitalist production.

Two contributions of Marxian sociology are, first, how professions relate to the state and, second, the thesis of the proletarianization of professional occupations. Johnson (1980), for example, examines the relative merits of Marxian and Weberian analyses of the development of the professions and comes down in favor of the former and sees the professions as an arm of the capitalist state. In later work he gives weight to the 'articulation which involved the interrelated processes of state formation and professionalization' (1982: 188). The importance of the state in relation to the professions is also the concern of Fielding and Portwood (1980), though less overtly Marxian than Johnson, while analyses of the professions in Europe, such as Geison (1984), Cocks and Jarauch (1990), and Krause (1996) also see the state as a dominating actor in the story.

Marxian analyses have also applied the 'labor process' debate to professions, with bureaucratization, the market power of a knowledge base and 'proletarianization' as sub-themes. These are discussed below in Section 3.

Professions or Disciplines

The work of the French ex-Marxist Michel Foucault appeals to the sociologist of the professions because it focuses on the relationship between knowledge and power. Foucault's view is that the emergence of modern society saw both an epistemic shift from a 'classic' to a 'modern' form of knowledge that is organized into 'disciplines' (1977*a*), and a novel capacity of the state for what he terms 'governmentality'. Sovereignty changed from being an exercise in the art of maintaining the power of the prince to the science of the right disposition of all things leading to the welfare of all (Foucault 1979:12). The experts in these new scientific knowledges (or disciplines) were crucial to this governing capacity, and the emergence of independent bodies of professionals in which their expertise was institutionalized, were all part of the emergence of the modern form of sovereignty. The persuasive value of Foucault's terminology should not be overlooked. 'Governmentality' (govern + mentality) and 'discipline' (a system either of control or of knowledge) are examples of how meaning is smuggled in rather than stated.

The originality of Foucault makes it difficult to place his work clearly in any sociological tradition but in certain respects his approach may be seen as having limitations. He has been described as 'brilliant' (Goldstein 1984: 170) and 'penetrating' (Ramsay 1988: 8), but some authors have found him opaque (Goldstein 1984: 171). In Ramsay (1988: 9), Foucault only appears as a source of empirical reference, not as a theorist; the same is true of the papers collected in Geison (1984), Haskell (1984), Cocks and Jarauch (1990), Burrage and Torstendahl (1990), and Torstendahl and Burrage (1990), covering the professions in the USA, Britain, Germany, and Sweden.

The structuralist cast of Foucault's theory gives the impression that although no longer Marxist, his model of society is certainly not action-based, but 'devoid of significant flesh-and-blood actors' (Goldstein 1984: 172–4). Larson (1990) uses Foucauldian structuralist language and dismisses symbolic interactionism as merely studying actions and interactions, failing to reveal the 'lies' of professionals or 'to understand the real significance of the experts' collective appropriation of knowledge'.

There is also an unacknowledged idealism (in the philosophical sense) in Foucault—something not entirely unexpected in an ex-Marxist. This may be seen in his use of metaphors such as 'archive', 'genealogy', or 'gaze' to indicate the nature of his subject matter and the way in which 'discipline', for example, appears to be a metaphysical entity, an element of the *zeitgeist*, manifesting itself in particular social phenomena.

It is probably for such reasons that some sociologists and social historians, such as Ramsay (1984, 1988), acknowledge his work, but do not actually build on it, while others such as Larson (1990) espouse his cause but seem not to have made empirical headway, or like Hopwood (1987) describe their work as 'archaeology' and 'genealogy' but in fact engage in a much more down-to-earth enterprise. Some sociologists have found his work of value in the study of medicine and accountancy, but others see the need to 'provide a corrective to the iconolatrous nature of much sociological literature pertaining to Foucault' (Porter 1996: 76). This work will be considered in Section 3.

Systems, Actors, and Social Closure

While not a follower of Larson, Abbott's (1988) work has affinities with hers. He puts forward a scheme for the study of the professions that aims to shift the emphasis, and which he applies to three case studies of expert 'jurisdictions'—information, law, and personal problems—aiming to 'disentangle the threads of determinants, structures and intentions, then reweave them into an analysis' (1988: 319). His treatment begins with a focus on work: it is the content and the differentiation of work and the desire to control work that gives rise to internal occupational divisions and to conflict with other occupations—conflict over *jurisdiction.*

> The central phenomenon of professional life is thus the link between a profession and its work, a link I shall call jurisdiction. To analyse professional development is to analyse how this link is created in work, how it is anchored in formal and informal social structure and how the interplay of jurisdictional links between the professions determines the history of the individual professions themselves. (1988: 20)

On this basis Abbott puts forward his view of a 'system of professions'. This theoretical destination in (a weak version of) systems theory is conceptually disparate from the work of Freidson and Larson, although his data seem to be as readily analyzable from their perspective as from his own (DiMaggio 1989). Abbott's central theme of 'jurisdiction' is not incompatible with Larson's 'professional project'. Burrage (1988) and Burrage, Jarauch, and Siegrist (1990) also seem to ignore Larson. Burrage (1988) examines the goals pursued by the legal professions in three societies while, in the second, the authors put forward an actor-based framework for the study of the professions; both themes seem to be consistent with Larson's analysis.

Halliday (1987), by contrast, gives monopoly a special emphasis, and gives Larson's work its due. All professions, in their pursuit of monopoly and privilege, have to enter into a special relation with the state, but lawyers in all parts of the division of legal labor have a specific relationship to an arm of the state—the judicature—and in some cases are unambiguously integrated into the state apparatus. This unique situation leads Halliday (1987) to argue that this gives lawyers an interest in the law itself which leads them to act in ways which have nothing to do with the pursuit of monopoly and may in fact be entirely public spirited. Halliday's study focuses on how professional associations construct the authority on which their macrosocial role rests and he analyses the scope of professional action, especially vis-à-vis the state and examines the conditions under which professional bodies may act collectively (1987: xix). He acknowledges the value of the works of Berlant (1975) and of Larson (1984), and most importantly of Weber, noting that they contain lines of thought that may be 'loosely woven into a new conjunction'.

Larson's work is certainly important in this 'new conjunction', not least because it draws on Weber's ideas on the place of occupational groups, especially professions, and of social closure, in the analysis of stratification. Weber observes that, whatever its origins, a group with an interest to pursue will aim to become 'a legally privileged group' with a closed monopoly. 'Its purpose is always the closure of social and economic opportunities to *outsiders*' (Weber 1978: 342; see also Freidson 1970*a*: 159–60).

Weberian sociologists would argue that the realities of social stratification (the actual tactics employed by individuals, families, or collectivities) require the analysis of 'social closure' based not only on property in the means of production but on other criteria as well (Parkin 1979; Collins 1975, 1979, 1986; Murphy 1988). The most important of these criteria is 'credentialism' which is seen as being of the essence of 'collective social mobility' of professions (Hughes 1971). Studies of the 'professional project' are concerned with 'collective social mobility' providing a useful counterbalance to the more usual concerns with individual social mobility (Parry and Parry 1976; Larson 1977; Macdonald 1984).

The Weberian idea of a critical historical analysis of the collective action of professional groups, social closure, and collective social mobility can also be found in Berlant (1975) and in Parry and Parry (1976). Parkin (1971, 1979) and Murphy (1984, 1988) refine and extend the concepts of Weber, while important contributions can also be found in Larkin (1983), Waddington (1984), and Macdonald (1984, 1985*a*, 1985*b*, 1989, 1995), and in Crompton (1987) and Witz (1992), on gender and patriarchy.

A Working Model of the Professions

From the foregoing review of sociological work on the professions it may be concluded that the way forward would emphasize action rather than structure as a means of understanding the social world. It would be Weberian and its nodal point would be 'the professional project' (Larson 1977) which incorporates Weberian notions of conflict and competition.

The heart of the 'professional project' is an occupation's need to strive both economically and socially. First, in what Weber calls the 'social order', the crucial point is that the services provided by a knowledge-based occupation are characteristically different from the goods sold by a manufacturer or a retailer in that they are intangible and the purchaser has to take them on trust. So how can the laity be persuaded to trust the professionals? Knowledge and expertise can be warranted by diplomas, certificates, and degrees, but trust is no less important and will be accorded to those whose outward appearance and manner fits in with accepted notions of repute and respectability. Many writers have documented professionals' motivation and action in this matter (e.g. Berlant 1975; Parry and Parry 1976; Macdonald 1984, 1989). In short, gentlemen wished to have their money, their property, their bodies, and their souls dealt with by gentlemen, and ordinary people followed their example if they could afford to. Professional bodies therefore strove to display their respectability and to achieve upward social mobility. The means adopted varied historically and culturally.

The other element, advantage in the 'economic order', is perhaps, more important, but cannot in the nature of things be separated from the drive for respectability. Economic advantage is pursued in two main areas: the legal closure of the occupation giving a market monopoly; and the exclusive acquisition of the knowledge and education on which the profession is based. While this last aim is 'practical' rather than evaluative, it is also a source of prestige. Possession of education is itself prestigious and its value can enhanced still further if the certification can be obtained from a highly regarded institution—Ivy League, Oxbridge, or *Grande Ecole*.

Finally, in most societies a monopoly can only be granted by the state and therefore the occupation's relation with the state is crucial.

Larson's conceptualization clearly has value for social historians (Geison 1984; Goldstein 1984; Ramsay 1988; Krause 1996) who use it as a general starting point rather than as a research model, while sociologists have followed it in a more detailed fashion (Macdonald (1984, 1985*a*, 1989, 1995) and Witz (1992). Some writers, such as Halliday and Abbott, offer a critique, but then appear to engage in analyses that differ in emphasis rather than in fundamentals.

Conclusion

The concept of a 'professional project' has been shown to be more fruitful than most and promises to continue to be so, although it needs some modification and amplification to handle the breadth of data now available, as follows.

To secure a monopoly, or at least licensure, an occupation must have a special relation with the state, and must strike a 'regulative bargain' (Cooper et al. 1988: 8). But the political culture (Burrage 1988) will strongly affect the style of 'the regulative bargain' and this must be seen as an ever-present feature of the world of a profession occupation.

> Having secured a monopoly an occupation must compete in the marketplace against others who can provide similar or substitute or complementary services. It must, therefore, at the least defend and probably enlarge, the scope of its activities' or its jurisdiction. (Abbott 1988)

As Halliday (1987) points out, professions are not entirely self-seeking. Some of their actions may be mere self-enhancement, economic or social, but far more consist in providing a service for their patients or clients.

The overall strategy of a professional group is best understood in terms of social closure. This concept offers a basis for understanding the progress (or otherwise) of the professional project, the conflicts and interaction between and within occupations, and as a means of analyzing the nature of their discriminatory actions in relation to the structured disadvantages of gender, race, ethnicity, and so on.

If this formulation is thought to be less broadly based that it might be, a corrective may be provided by reading it in conjunction with the recent work of Freidson (2001). This has a much wider theoretical reference than most of his work and aims to set out an 'ideal type' for the study of the professions. This draws on such general institutional concepts as the division of labor, the labor market, bureaucracy, and the state. While the work reviewed above has not ignored these institutions, it is valuable to have a systematic comprehensive treatment of them. Freidson develops his ideal type on the Weberian model, although it is a bit disconcerting to find that this pioneer of an action-based approach to the study of professions sees 'ideal type' as synonymous with 'pipe dream' (implying that 'ideal' refers to perfection rather than to 'idea'). While not in the same class as the functionalism of Parsons or Carr-Saunders, one is inclined to view it in that light because of Freidson's pursuit of both sociological and policy objectives in the same monograph, and his two concluding chapters in vigorous defence of professions. Although readers may even find these chapters 'rather bemusing' Freidson provides an admirably clear and insightful sociological account of professionalism and a defense of the continuing relevance of the professional project (Savage 2003).

Another line of criticism could be that some non-English speaking countries lack a term equivalent to 'profession' (Geison 1984: 3,10), and the models of professions developed by, say, Larson (1977) and Freidson (1970*b*) cannot be applied to them. Critics have felt that the notion of 'a professional project' is too close to its Anglo-American origins and that this so distorts the study of the professions that it is necessary to reformulate the theoretical approach developed in Britain and America (Collins 1990: 15; Burrage et al. 1990; Torstendahl 1990: 59). There is no room here to conduct the review of professions in various societies that would be necessary to evaluate this critique, but a summary of the response to this view would run as follows.

Professions aim for a monopoly of the provision of services of a particular kind, and as monopolies can only be granted by the state, professions have a distinctive relationship with the state; thus the variety of forms the state can take, even within Western industrial society, is a matter of great significance. Basically, the professional project seems best able to prosper where civil society penetrates the state, which in consequence is pluralistic or decentralized: for example, in Britain and the USA. In France and Germany, by contrast, there is a centralized state, less penetrated by civil society. French political ideology is imbued with the notion that allocation of powers to 'lesser governments' would undermine the operation of democracy, so there is little cultural support for such devolution. Germany displays similar elements, but here the statism is much stronger and showed itself in 1932 fatally ready to mutate into dictatorship.

This traumatic lapse has itself left an indelible print on German political culture, which now contains a resolute democraticism.

The way groups achieve social closure will have some fairly direct connection with their societies' institutional and cultural features. Thus, in Britain and the USA, status groups are free to form round their own activities and features, while in France and Germany the tendency is for members of society to use the state structures and its off-shoots such as the universities as the basis for status group formation and for social closure. An interesting comparison historically is between Britain, where professions had the greatest freedom to achieve social closure, and Germany where the 'statist' institutions of Civil Service and University formed the means of socially enclosing a much larger number of people in the *Bildungsburgertum*. But even in the strongly statist culture of Germany, with its 'professionalization from above', there was evidence that showed the desire of members of knowledge-based occupations to achieve autonomy and to embark on a professional project.

It can be argued that the 'professional project' has proven utility in dealing with Britain and the USA. In France and Germany professional groups have existed and striven for professional autonomy; even 'professionalization from above' does not remove the features of market society which permit occupational groups to pursue their project (Siegrist 1990); one can see how it could be applied to most northern European societies (Burrage et al. 1990 and Torstendahl 1990). In the erstwhile communist societies (e.g. USSR) knowledge-based services were provided and regulated entirely by the state (Balzer 1996), but this is no reason to abandon the concept of 'project'. It merely represents the other end of a continuum from a society like Britain, where to all intents and purposes, certain aspects the legal system are in private hands. Societies whose development into modernity occurred in the twentieth or late nineteenth centuries would be expected to have professions showing parallels with those European countries with which they have had colonial or other ties. These links may however have tended to result in more state regulation than obtained in the metropolitan state, as in the case of the former British Empire (Johnson and Caygill 1978). Latin America likewise shows traces of its Iberian ancestry, with the professions having close links to public administration and the universities (De Venanzi 1990), from whom it appears that sociological work on professions in Latin America is not extensive.

The 'professional project' is an 'ideal type', and Weber's original definition of an ideal type states that it contains elements that are 'more or less present and occasionally absent'. So empirical variations do not invalidate the concept, but show that a heuristic concept is doing its job, although the model may require elaboration to continue to function as a research tool.

2. Social Stratification

The sociology of the professions makes an important contribution to the study of stratification (Macdonald and Ritzer 1988), because the history of professional projects sheds light on the development of part of the modern class system and contributes to a dynamic theory of social change. For the present purpose, the important aspect of this is the work on professionals in bureaucracies and the possibility of their 'proletarianization'.

Professions, Bureaucracy, and Proletarianization

There has long been a school of thought that sees bureaucratization as antithetical to professionalism. For example Hall (1968, 1975) concludes that there are many circumstances in which organization rules drive out professional criteria, diminishing professional power and prestige. Another view is that bureaucracies are a means of handling knowledge and therefore pose a threat to professionalism by systematizing professional knowledge in a manner that will remove professional judgment, 'indeterminacy', and ultimately professional power, by rationalizing the corpus of knowledge into bureaucratic procedures and division of labour (Jamous and Peloille 1970).

There is also Braverman's (1974) 'deskilling hypothesis' of which deprofessionalization could be seen as a part. This view, based on Marx's prediction of the proletarianization of the middle class, has probably contributed significantly to the contrary view because it stimulated a plethora of research, the greater part of which disconfirmed the hypothesis. While it is true that many aspects of work have become 'deskilled' in the sense that old crafts and shop-floor know-how have been displaced, the overall composition of the workforce is more, not less, skilled (Littler 1982; Penn 1985; Wood 1982,1989).

The issue of proletarianization of the professions has been debated by sociologists for some time (Oppenheimer 1973; Haug 1973). Braverman (1974) gave the issue particular prominence, and while it reached something of a peak with the publication of *Professionals as Workers*

(Derber 1982), it received further attention from Haug (1988), McKinlay and Arches (1985), and Murphy (1990). The debate centres on three questions: what are the consequences for professionals of their employment in bureaucratic settings with a specialized division of labour? What ensues from the introduction of IT? Is the appearance of 'paraprofessionals' a real innovation or is it merely the normal functioning of the 'system of the professions' (Abbott 1988)?

1. The early research of Hall (1968) throws up a number of consequences of the bureaucratic setting for professionals, and his mature conclusions (1975: 135) emphasize the variety of professional work situations rather than showing any 'deprofessionalization'. In fact the view of Savage et al. (1992) is that professionals in organizations might well have added organizational assets to their class advantages. For example, accountants moving from private practice into organizational employment do not normally disadvantage themselves thereby; any diminution in professional autonomy is often soon offset by managerial privileges and sometimes by promotion to the highest levels.
2. The advent of artificial intelligence and publicly available technical data bases conjures up the visions, on the one hand, of the general practitioner reduced to a keyboard operator, obtaining a computer diagnosis; and on the other, of a lay individual in the public library, getting legal advice from an interactive consultation program. Neither seems plausible. It seems much more probable that the existing professions will be able to incorporate new technology into their existing practice, by one or other of the strategies that they have successfully used in the past to cope with social and technical change.
3. Changes in the jurisdiction and market of a profession may well throw up challenges to the existing arrangements (Haug 1973; Oppenheimer 1973). Today, the evidence for these hypotheses seems to be essentially part of the ebb and flow of professional jurisdictions (Abbott 1988). Such challenges are far more likely to be deflected or absorbed by the existing occupations and, if successful, there is a good chance that they are mounted by a specialist group within an existing profession, as in Halpern (1988) on the case of paediatrics in the USA. Haug (1988) is one of a few sociologists with any faith in the deprofessionalization hypothesis, and although she admits that there is insufficient evidence to retain it, Freidson (2001)

has recently lent his weight to it. Derber et al. (1990), however, have thrown their weight in the other direction by theorizing professionals as 'the new class' whose monopolization of knowledge as an economic resource has deskilled and proletarianized a whole stratum of workers below them.

This research could be used to argue that the position of the established professions in Britain, USA, and probably in the rest of the Western world is not seriously threatened. Even if one acknowledges the force of Murphy's (1988) arguments, that their knowledge-base and indeed their whole situation is contingent on being owners of capital assets, it seems that their existing class advantages may not only enable them to resist the challenges of social and technical change, but even to turn them to advantage. Their greatest danger is perhaps the state, which has attempted to increase both regulation and market competition of professions (Savage et al. 1992: 73); but they seem to have been able to accommodate these pressures. The occupations which have lost some of their class advantage are those that Johnson (1972) terms 'mediative professions', i.e. those that are dependent on public sector provision of the service that gives them employment–school teachers, nurses, social workers, etc. On the other hand there is the view, strongly expressed by Freidson (2001: 209), drawing *inter alia* on Abbott (1988) and on Brint (1994), that there is a process at work whereby 'recent jurisdictional boundaries will be altered by reassigning many now professional tasks to less qualified workers'. In writing in this way, Freidson seems to have abandoned his original action theory position in favor of a 'process' in which professionals are 'transformed', which indeed is not unexpected in view of his aim of exploring the institutional logic of how work can be organized and controlled. A comparative sociological history, using an action-based approach, would see the relinquishing of technically routinized tasks as having been in the nature of the professional project for over a century at least.

Conclusion

The professional project is intended to secure for its members economic and social advantage, resulting in upward social mobility. To relate this to the social stratification of the society in which the project is pursued should widen our understanding of class formation and the working of the structure of inequality as a whole. It also allows for the development of a conceptualization of social class that explicitly theorizes the middle-class and middle-class formation, against a societal background of historical development and change, and which provides insight into the capacities of middle-class people to establish their new positions in a modernizing society and to achieve individual and collective upward social mobility.

3. Knowledge

Sociological studies of the professions emphasize knowledge as a 'core generating trait' of professionalism (Larson 1977: 40; Halliday 1987: 29; Abbott 1988: 9). Modern knowledge may be defined as *formally rational abstract utilitarian knowledge, systematic, codified, and generalized* (Murphy 1988: 246–7) and like all modern scientific knowledge, it is in the public realm, and may be challenged or compared or linked up with knowledge of other professions, sciences, or specialisms. Nonetheless, modern professions attempt to maintain the maximum control over their knowledge.

The knowledge that provides the basis for professional practice is that which is *certified and credentialed* (Weber 1978). A claim to professionalism is credentialed by a relatively high level qualification, typically a degree, or by a relatively high-ranking establishment, including a professional body with high entry standards. Weber sees such knowledge as the base on which an occupation can establish social closure and enhance its social status, and this is possible largely because *the means of production for their line of business is in their heads*, at least at the time of their establishment. It follows that in banking, for example, where the means of production is essentially a large sum of money, what is in the heads of the members of the Institute of Bankers does not enable them to embark on a professional project.

Work, Knowledge, Abstraction, and Indeterminacy

Although an occupational monopoly of knowledge is a sine qua non of a claim to professional standing, Abbott (1988: 19, 31) emphasizes that in understanding professions, the starting point must be professional *work*. The content and control of professional work, differentiation in types of work, and the jurisdiction that the profession attempts to claim for its work are the heart of the matter. But in addition, the quality that characterizes professional work (and here we get back to the topic of knowledge) is *abstraction*. This is the quality that will allow an occupation to achieve public acknowledgement of their jurisdiction: 'the jurisdictional claims that create these subjective qualities have three parts: claims to classify a problem, to reason about it, and to take action on it: in more formal terms, to diagnose, to infer, and to treat. Theoretically these are the three acts of professional practice' (Abbott 1988: 40).

Abbott (1988: 58) focuses not only on work but on the connection between work and knowledge, and the 'cultural work' that has to be carried out:

> [B]ehind the world of professional work lies a rationalizing, ordering system that justifies it with cultural values, at the same time generating new means for professional work. As custodian of professional knowledge in its most abstract form, this academic centre is uniquely situated to claim new jurisdictions. But the claims are cognitive only. They cannot become recognized jurisdictions without concrete social claims and legitimating responses. Interprofessional competition, that is, takes place before public audiences.

In addition to the emphasis on professional work, Abbott also gives an important place to theoretical knowledge (1988: 102). He establishes the significance of the polarity between abstraction and concreteness, and he reviews the forces that 'push abstraction in professional knowledge towards an equilibrium between extreme abstraction and extreme concreteness'. At either extreme, the profession tends to lose credibility; too great abstraction appears to be mere formalism, too great concreteness is judged to be no more than a craft. At some nicely chosen spot in between, the possessor of knowledge and technique can successfully exercise professional judgment, which is a notion akin to that put forward by Jamous and Peloille (1970:113) of cognitive *indetermination*. For Jamous and Peloille the distinction is between 'indetermination' and 'technicality', and they put forward the idea that those occupations that claim successfully to be professions need to be high on indeterminacy. This enables their members to assert the right to exercise professional judgment and thus to put themselves and their actions and their decisions beyond the scrutiny of their clients and the lay public. While this view of professional knowledge is often quoted, it is difficult to see how a body of professionals could maintain their knowledge base at a high level of indeterminacy indefinitely, because they would have to acknowledge the primacy of scientific knowledge if they were to maintain their legitimacy in the modern world. Recent trends, especially in medicine, would indicate that 'professional judgment' is a less robust shield than it once was. Indeterminacy is also linked to another of Abbott's points, namely the location of knowledge. Modern knowledge has always been associated with the printed word, which has been one way that knowledge becomes 'concrete', but it could also come to be located in organizations which professionals do not control. At the present time the possibility is always present that professional knowledge, and how to apply it, can be located in machines, i.e. computers.

Foucault on Power and Knowledge

Foucault ([1966] 1973) is often regarded as having important insights about the nature of knowledge and its relation to professions, especially medicine. Arney (1982) for example believes that his conceptualizations have generated new perspectives on professional knowledge, practice, and power, and applies them to obstetrics. This lead was followed by Armstrong (1983, 1987) on medicine and Nettleton (1992) on dentistry. All three conclude that medical knowledge is knowledge about individuals and is concerned with a discourse whereby the patient is constituted as an object of medical enquiry and is therefore tied up with surveillance and discipline. Arney (1982) in *Power and the Profession of Obstetrics* elaborates Foucault's idea about the development of modern knowledge by introducing an additional stage in the early twentieth century, which subjects the individual to emotional constraints in a system of rules which is no less intrusive than those of conventional medicine. Arney (1982: 231), like other Foucaultians, draws on the notion of the Panopticon, which implies continuous supervision (of a prisoner, in the original plan), in such a way that the subject knows he/she is under observation; a condition which leads the inmate to cooperate in their own discipline (Foucault 1977*b*). By contrast, Porter's (1996: 76) research shows that 'clients of the New Nursing have gained considerably more in terms of their own knowledge and autonomy than they have lost in terms of the nurses' knowledge of them'.

Johnson (1994, 1995) uses Foucault's (1979, 1980) notion of 'governmentality' in the study of the professions. This is 'the gaze' applied not to individuals, but to populations, and is allied to Foucault's notion of 'surveillance'. Johnson's analysis leads to the same conclusion as his earlier work that relied on Marxian concepts—that the professions are best understood as a manifestation or articulation of the state; but Johnson no longer sees this as part of the logic of capitalism, but as an example of the disembodied spirit of control that runs the Foucauldian world. 'Governmentality' has an attractive ring to it, but it is as much a rhetorical device as an analytical concept and it may well be a sort of pun, because it is also referred to as 'a certain *mentality*' (Foucault 1979: 20).

The above authors confirm Foucault's conception of the development of knowledge, but they also show how modern professional knowledge has taken another turn since the 1930s moving, it is argued, in a more 'social' and even humanitarian direction, but one which has also achieved even greater compliance by clients in their own surveillance and powerlessness. On the other hand it should be noted that these changes have provided opportunities for a level of health that is far beyond that possessed by any previous society. As for the loss of freedom, this would appear to be as nothing compared to the degree of constraint that existed in classical society, according to another French scholar, Fustel de Coulanges. 'The citizen was subordinate in everything, and without any reserve, to the city; he belonged to it body and soul' ([1864] 1955: 219).

The problem in taking Foucault as a starting point is that he was neither a sociologist nor a social historian but a philosopher, who used aspects of historical and sociological knowledge to pursue his interests in epistemology and ontology. This may be gauged from the references to be found in the 'Afterword' by Gordon (1980) to *Power-Knowledge*, in which there are twice as many references to philosophers as to any anyone who could remotely be described as a social scientist. To many, it was his talents as a *performer* (on the page or in the flesh), rather than the coherence of his ideas that captured minds (Baudrillard 1977; Kellner 1989; Jay 1993). Perhaps one should bear in mind Baudrillard's (1977) title—*Oublier Foucault*.

Conclusion

Professional knowledge is only what the occupational group can annexe and hold on to. The advantages they derive from it are only those that their professional project can achieve in a particular historical context.

4. Patriarchy

The professional project provides the basis for the discussion of patriarchy, which is taken to refer 'to a societal-wide system of gender relations of male dominance and female subordination... [and] the ways in which male power is institutionalized within different sites in society' (Witz 1992: 11).

The professions have played a part in patriarchy's stubborn resistance against the struggle of women to improve their position. Social closure, as part of the professional project, is valuable in explaining the operation of patriarchy. Parkin (1979), Collins (1985), and Murphy (1988), make some use of it in relation to gender, but it is in the work of Crompton and Sanderson (1989) and especially in Witz (1992) that a full development can be found.

Witz applies the social closure model to professions and patriarchy in conjunction with an emphasis on 'discursive strategies', that is to say, the 'discourse' of everyday interaction and especially the terms in which those with power express what they say and write. This is often extremely important in the maintenance of existing relations, such as those of gender: for example, the power of the medical profession in the nineteenth century in relation to women who aspired to become doctors was reinforced, or even embedded in, the language they (and everybody else) spoke. 'Discursive strategies' may be seen as a link between the concepts of ideology and closure practices, and the cases Witz (1992: 7) cites (of paramedical occupations) provide convincing examples.

Witz develops the use of the concept of social closure drawing on the work of Parkin (1979) and Murphy (1988) and characterizes it as follows.

Exclusionary closure is the exercise of power by an occupational association in a downwards direction primarily by defining membership in ways that exclude those regarded as 'ineligibles' (Parkin 1979: 450) or 'outsiders' (Weber 1978: 342) but includes those already practicing, framing criteria in a manner acceptable to the state.

Demarcationary closure extends exclusion by specifying the boundaries between subordinate occupations, in order to maintain an advantage over practitioners in allied fields. Doctors for example, have played a crucial role in defining the areas of competence of paramedical groups, deciding whether or not a skill shall be hived off to a subordinate group.

Inclusionary closure is the counterpart of exclusionary closure and covers the actions of those who attempt to make themselves eligible, either by devising ways to acquire the necessary characteristics or to force the professional body, or the credentialing educational establishments, or the state, to change the rules which disadvantage them.

Dual closure deals with those practitioners who, having been denied access to a professional body, strive to carve out their own occupational field, distinguishing it from that of other, probably dominant, groups but establishing at the same time their own exclusionary practices: they do not emulate or aim for parity or eventual amalgamation with the dominant group.

Nursing and Midwifery

Witz sees dual closure as the means by which groups such as midwives and nurses undertook their gendered professional projects in the late nineteenth century. They were subjected to demarcatory strategies by the medical profession and responded by marking out the best territory they could by their own exclusions and boundaries of practice.

Nursing has several features inimical to its professional project. First, its practice was dependent on or mediated by other organizations—originally charitable foundations, and later, local and central government. Second, the emphasis on practice, and especially the practice of caring, made it hard to lay claim to the possession of esoteric knowledge or the indeterminacy which legitimates the use of 'professional judgment'. Lastly, practice based on caring allowed opponents to throw doubt on their objectivity, because caring could be said to exclude objectivity. All these factors were incorporated into the discursive practices that hindered the nurses' professional project.

Nursing, in Britain, is an example of a 'dual closure' project, which employed complementary exclusion and usurpation, aimed at removing the authority of male doctors over female nurses, and the control of hospitals over nursing labor. Nurses wished to achieve both authority and autonomy in their work and this 'dual closure' professional project was pursued by both credentialist and legalistic tactics. These features and their outcomes may be summarized as follows:

1. Exclusionary aims
   (*a*) Centralized control over occupation, established by legislation (legalistic)
   (*b*) Self-government by means of majority of nurses on governing body (legalistic)
   (*c*) One-portal entry controlled by governing body (credentialist)

2. Usurpationary aims
   (*a*) Training: challenge to the autonomy of voluntary hospitals on content and standards
   (*b*) Employment: undermining of the relationship between hospitals and nursing labour and obtaining some influence over pay and conditions
   (*c*) Formalizing the relation between medicine and nursing in a way that would give nursing both recognition and some measure of autonomy

Centralized control by the General Nursing Council was indeed created but it neither contained a majority of nursing members nor was it given control over those issues listed above because decisions had to be ratified by the minister. So the attainment of 1(*a*) above actually involved failure on 1(*b*), while the Nurses Registration Act specified multiple portals of entry and allowed for the creation of more. The usurpationary aims were only achieved in a limited way, while the power of the state was enhanced. Witz (1992: 167) concludes that 'credentialist tactics, which pivoted round the one-portal system of entry, were subverted and legalistic tactics of state sponsorship backfired on nurses. At this critical historical juncture, nurses' professional project had failed.'

In the years since that failure, developments have confirmed the importance of the factors that shaped the outcome just described; namely the dominant position of the medical profession and the inaccessibility of the organizational structure of the hospital, increasingly provided by the state. The powerful forces of medicine constantly seek to control nursing's professional milieu in the hospitals, and given this situation, nursing has achievements to be proud of. Some kind of accommodation with medicine was necessary, but the acceptance of the patriarchal dominance of medicine contributed to what Etzioni (1969) calls 'the caste-like subservience' of nursing to medicine; a simile that nicely catches that pervasiveness of patriarchal practice and discourse that makes it appear 'natural'.

Midwifery and the medical profession were also involved with a lengthy contest that was made more complex by differences of opinion within obstetricians. There is no space to recount these conflicts, but in Britain it resulted in an accommodation similar to that achieved by nursing. In North America, especially in Canada, obstetricians achieved much greater dominance and it is only in recent decades that midwives have obtained some independence (Rushing 1993).

Law and Accountancy

In the standard works on the professions there is a resounding silence on the subject of women and this reflects the way in which professions such as law and accountancy treated women (Macdonald 1995). An important part of the social closure that they had achieved in the nineteenth century was that they were 'gentlemen' and therefore women were axiomatically ineligible. The force of the arguments of the women's movement made this axiom look increasingly fragile and in response professions developed quite elaborate discursive practices. Their formal, public aspect defined professional practice and the characteristics of women in ways that made the two incompatible, in order to justify exclusionary practices; but discursive practice is also embedded in everyday interaction and it provides the mechanism that men employ and women experience in the maintenance of patriarchy. This is admirably demonstrated in a study by Spencer and Podmore (1987), which explores the ways in which women solicitors are marginalized in their profession by their male colleagues.

In the legal profession, discrimination against women is particularly pronounced, partly because the career structure is extended by the addition of the judiciary at the upper end; thus in Britain only 2 or 3 percent of judges are women, and it was not until 2003 that the first woman was appointed Lord of Appeal in ordinary—the other eleven Law Lords are all men. In accountancy likewise, it is only in the last twenty years that women have reached the upper levels of the profession and English accountants have now actually had a woman as president. In the USA the door was opened to women much earlier, but for some time there was only a trickle passing through it. The first woman received her CPA certificate in 1899, but by 1909 the total had only risen to ten. By 1924, fifty-four women had become CPAs, but the tactics of patriarchal exclusion by firms kept them out of public practice. An editorial in the *Journal of Accountancy* (December 1923), while acknowledging the ability of women accountants, asserted that

> women are not wanted on the staff of practising public accountants, because of
> The need to be ready to serve whenever and wherever called on to do so.
> The requirement to travel with groups of staff members.
> Working at night in places of difficulty and inconvenience.
> Embarrassment caused by working with heterogeneous personnel.
> Objections by some clients to women.

These specious objections are similar to those of British lawyers in the 1980s, but as frequently happens, if there is a labor shortage, women suddenly become quite acceptable. Such a change took place in World War II, and may be epitomized by the case of Pearl A. Scherer, who started off as an a clerk in the Army Corps of Engineers, worked her way up to responsibility for the first computer installation on the West Coast and at the end of the war was posted to the Philippines as Chief Accountant, responsible for the reclamation of all equipment and supplies from the battle zones.

Patriarchal practices and discourse have deep roots and are all the harder to eradicate because they are part of women's as well as men's socialization. But, as Witz (1992: 207–10) observes, female projects have a better chance of success in relation to the state than elsewhere, for the state is (nominally at least) based on legal-rational principles and should therefore be open to institutional change that can erode the multiple inequalities from which women still suffer.

5. Conclusion

Occupations that are regarded as professions are those that have succeeded in achieving the objectives of their project—a monopoly in the provision of services based on their specialist knowledge. The counterpart of this, the quest for enhanced social status, must also have been attained.

What does the profession do next? In the same way that the rewards of the professional project are attained by steady, constant effort on the part of members and their organization, they are only retained by comparable exertion. The condition of professional monopoly, like that of liberty, is eternal vigilance. The key tasks for the continued success of any profession are to maintain control over its knowledge base, to find ways to combat the ever-present tendency for knowledge to become located in organizations or machines rather than in their members, to hold its own vis-à-vis the state, and to resist attempts at incursion into its jurisdiction by other occupations. The key concept for the sociologist wishing to analyze these activities is 'the professional project'.

Nonetheless, some recent writers have argued that the 'neo-Weberian approach' (which is largely synonymous with the professional project) fails to provide the concepts to handle the changes that the professions face in the twenty-first century. For example, Saks (2003) feels that it gives insufficient attention to one of the institutions in Freidson's (2001) perspective, the division of labor—especially in the field of medicine. Saks offers a critique, but others, such as McKinley and Marceau (2002) suggest that, for medicine, the current orthodoxy is altogether too limited to analyze the extrinsic changes arising from the growing power of the state and corporatization of doctoring, and the intrinsic changes in the medical division of labour. 'A future sociology of the professions can no longer overlook the now pervasive macrostructural influences on provider behavior (corporate dominance)'.

Even further from the spirit of the ideal type of the professional project is the advocacy by Hartley (2002) of 'the countervailing powers framework', illustrating how the relationships among relevant parties in the health care system (of 'competing' health care providers, the state, corporate and consumer forces) can best be understood as a *system of alignments* (emphasis in the original). Proponents of the professional project, however, would see these factors as falling within the ambit of that concept, and that to move to an emphasis on *system* is to risk a return to the structuralism, whether functionalist or Marxian, that loses sight of the motives of actors, both collective and individual.

The strength of the professional project as a concept is that it has drawn systematically on a number of important themes in sociology. This has not been mere eclecticism, but more in the nature of a dialectic between the poles of function and action, of structure and agency. Its origins in the functionalism of Durkheim and Parsons were subject to critique and development by Hughes and others of the Chicago school that drew out the motives and actions of individuals and groups from the manifold structures of the functionalist treatments. Larson's development of the idea of a professional project drew on the structuralism of Marx and the action orientation of Weber, using them to theorize the professions in relation to work, stratification, the state, and modern rational scientific knowledge. This last emphasis led sociologists to find the ideas of Foucault attractive, which gave rise to some valuable empirical work, although the theoretical payoff was less impressive. More significant perhaps is the way that feminist theories have been combined with the professional project to demonstrate the operation of patriarchal practices and discourse by the professions, and to show how predominantly female occupations strive to fulfil their ambitions. Freidson's (2001) ideal type of the institutional setting of the professional project is an authoritative endorsement.

References

Abbott, A. (1988). *The System of the Professions.* London: University of Chicago Press.

Armstrong, D. (1983). *Political Anatomy of the Body.* Cambridge: Cambridge University Press.

—— (1987). 'Bodies of Knowledge: Foucault and the Problem of Human Anatomy', in G. Scambler (ed.), *Sociological Theory and Medical Sociology.* London: Tavistock.

Arney, W.R. (1982). *Power and the Profession of Obstetrics.* London: University of Chicago Press.

Balzer, H. D. (ed.) (1996). *Russia's Missing Middle Class: The Professions in Russian History.* Armonk, NY: M. E. Sharpe.

Baudrillard, J. (1977). *Oublier Foucault*. Paris: Editions Galilee.

Becker, H.S. (1970). *Sociological Work*. Chicago, IL: Aldine.

—— , Greer, B., Hughes, E. C., and Strauss, A.L. (1961). *Boys in White*. Chicago, IL: University of Chicago Press.

Berlant J.L. (1975). *Professions and Monopoly: A Study of Medicine in the United States and Great Britain*. Berkeley, CA: University of California Press

Braverman, H. (1974). *Labour and Monopoly Capital: The Degradation of Work in the Twentieth Century*. New York: The Monthly Review Press.

Brint, S. (1994). *In an Age of Experts: The Changing Role of Professionals in Politics and Public Life*. Princeton NJ: Princeton University Press.

Burrage, M. (1988). 'Revolution and the Collective Action of the French, American and English Legal Professions', *Law and Social Enquiry, Journal of the American Bar Foundation*, 13(2): 225–77.

—— and Torstendahl, R. (eds.) (1990). *Professions in Theory and History*. London: Sage.

—— Jarauch, K., and Siegrist,H. (1990). 'An Actor-based Framework for the Study of the Professions', in M. Burrage and R. Torstendahl (eds.), *Professions in Theory and History*. London: Sage.

Carr-Saunders A.M. and Wilson P.A. (1933). *The Professions*. Oxford: Clarendon Press

Cocks, G. and Jarauch, K. H. (eds.) (1990). *German Professions 1800–1950*. Oxford: Oxford University Press.

Collins, R. (1975). *Conflict Sociology; Towards an Explanatory Science*. New York: Academic Press.

—— (1979). *The Credential Society: An Historical Sociology of Education and Stratification*. New York: Academic Press.

—— (ed.) (1985). *Three Sociological Traditions*. Oxford: Oxford University Press.

—— (1986). *Weberian Sociological Theory*. Cambridge: Cambridge University Press.

—— (1990). 'Changing Conceptions in the Sociology of the Professions', in R. Torstendahl and M. Burrage (eds.), *The Formation of Professions: Knowledge, State and Strategy*. London: Sage.

Cooper, D., Lowe, A., Puxty, A., Robson, K., and Willmott, H. (1988). Regulating the U.K. Accountancy Profession: Episodes in the Relation Between the Profession and the State. Paper presented at ESRC Conference on Corporatism at Policy Studies Institute, London, January.

Crompton, R. (1987). 'Gender, Status and Professionalism', *Sociology*, 21: 413–28.

—— and Sanderson, K. (1989). *Gendered Jobs and Social Change*. London: Unwin Hyman.

Daniels, A. K. (1973). 'Professionalism in a Formal Setting', in J. B. McKinlay (ed.), *Processing People*. London: Holt, Reinhart and Winston.

De Coulanges, F. ([1864] 1955). *The Ancient City*. New York: Doubleday Anchor Books.

De Venanzi, A. (1990). *La Sociologia de las Profesiones y la Sociologia como Profession.* Caracas: Universidad Central de Venezuela.

Derber, C. (ed.) (1982). *Professionals as Workers: Mental Labour in Advanced Capitalism.* Boston, MA: G. K. Hall.

Derber, C., Schwartz, W. A., and Magrass, Y. (1990). *Power in the Highest Degree.* New York: Oxford University Press.

DiMaggio, P. (1989) 'Review of Abbott (1988)', *American Journal of Sociology,* 95(2): 534–5.

Dingwall, R and Lewis, P. (eds.) (1983). *The Sociology of the Professions.* London: Macmillan.

Durkheim, E. (1957). *Professional Ethics and Civic Morals.* New York: Free Press. (Originally published 1950 as *Leçons de Sociologie: Physique des Moeurs et du Droit*).

—— (1964). *The Division of Labour in Society.* New York: Free Press.

Etzioni, A. (1969). *The Semi-Professions and their Organization: Teachers, Nurses and Social Workers.* New York: Free Press.

Fielding, A. and Portwood D. (1980). 'Professions and the State—Towards a Typology of Bureaucratic Professions', *Sociological Review,* 28(1): 23–54

Foucault, M. ([1966] 1973). *The Order of Things.* New York: Vintage Books.

—— (1977*a*). *The Archaeology of Knowledge.* London: Tavistock.

—— (1977*b*). *Discipline and Punish: The Birth of the Prison.* London: Allen Lane, The Penguin Press.

—— (1979). 'On Governmentality', *Ideology and Consciousness,* 6: 5–22.

—— (1980). *Power-Knowledge.* Brighton: The Harvester Press.

Freidson, E. (1970*a*). *The Profession of Medicine.* New York: Dodd, Mead and Co. ('Afterword' added 1988).

—— (1970*b*). *Medical Dominance.* Chicago: Aldine-Atherton.

—— (1973). *Professions and their Prospects.* New York: Sage.

—— (1983). 'The Theory of the Professions: The State of the Art', in R. Dingwall and P. Lewis (eds.), *The Sociology of the Professions.* London: Macmillan.

—— (2001). *Professionalism: The Third Logic.* Cambridge: Polity Press.

Geison, G.W. (ed.) (1984). *French Professions and the State, 1700–1900.* Philadelphia, PA: Pennsylvania University Press.

Goldstein, J.(1984). 'Foucault Among the Sociologists: The "Disciplines" and the History of the Professions', *History and Theory,* 170–92.

Goode, W. J. (1957). 'Community within a Community: The Professions', *American Sociological Review,* 22: 194–200.

Gordon, C. (1980). 'Afterword', in M. Foucault, *Power-Knowledge.* Brighton: Harvester Press.

Hall, R. H. (1968). 'Professionalization and Bureaucratization', *American Sociological Review,* 33(1): 92–104.

—— (1975). *Occupations and the Social Structure,* 2nd edn. Englewood Cliffs, NJ: Prentice-Hall.

Hall, R.H. (1983). 'Theoretical Trends in the Sociology of Occupations', *Sociological Quarterly*, 24: 5–23.

Halliday, T.C. (1987). *Beyond Monopoly*. London: University of Chicago Press.

Halmos, P. (ed.) (1973). *Professionalization and Social Change*, Sociological Review Monograph No. 20, University of Keele.

Halpern, S. A. (1988). *American Pediatrics: The Social Dynamics of Medicine*. London: University of California Press.

Hartley, H. (2002). 'The System of Alignments Challenging Physician Professional Dominance: An Elaborated Theory of Countervailing Powers', *Sociology of Health & Illness*, 24(2), 178–207.

Haskell, T. L. (1984). *The Authority of Experts*. Bloomington, IN: University of Indiana Press.

Haug, M. R. (1973). 'Deprofessionalization: An Alternative Hypothesis for the Future', in P. Halmos (ed.), *Professionalization and Social Change*, Sociological Review Monograph No. 20, University of Keele.

—— (1988). 'A Reexamination of the Hypothesis of Physician Deprofessionalization', *Millbank Quarterly*, 66 (suppl. 2).

Hickson, D.J. and Thomas, M.W. (1969). 'Professionalization in Britain: a Preliminary Measure', *Sociology*, 3: 37–53.

Hopwood, A. G. (1987). 'The Archaeology of Accounting Systems', *Accounting, Organizations and Society*, 12(3): 207–34.

Hughes, E. C. (1958). *Men and Their Work*. New York: Free Press.

—— (1963). 'Professions', *Daedalus*, 92: 655–68.

—— (1971). *The Sociological Eye*. New York: Aldine.

Jackson, J. A. (ed.) (1970). *Professions and Professionalization*. Cambridge: Cambridge University Press.

Jamous, H. and Peloille, B. (1970). 'Changes in the French University Hospital System', in J. A. Jackson (ed.), *Professions and Professionalization*. Cambridge: Cambridge University Press.

Jay M. (1993). *Downcast Eyes*. London: University of California Press.

Johnson T.J. (1977). 'Professions in the Class Structure', in R. Scase (ed.), *Class, Cleavage and Control*. London: Allen and Unwin.

—— (1980). 'Work and Power', in G. Esland and G. Salaman (eds.), *The Politics of Work and Occupations*. Milton Keynes: Open University Press.

—— (1982). 'The State and the Professions: Peculiarities of the British', in A. Giddens, and G. Mackenzie (eds.), *Social class and the Division of Labour: Essays in Honour of Ilya Newstadt*. Cambridge: Cambridge University Press.

Johnson, T. (1972). *Professions and Power*. London: Macmillan.

—— (1994). 'Expertise and the State', in M. Gane and T. Johnson (eds), *Foucault's New Domains*. London: Routledge.

—— (1995). 'Governmentality and the Institutionalization of Expertise', in T. Johnson, G. Larkin, G., and M. Saks (eds.), *Health Professions and the State in Europe*. London: Routledge.

Johnson, T. and Caygill, M., (1978). 'The Development of Accountancy Links in the Commonwealth', in Parker, R. H. (ed.) *Readings in Accountancy and Business Research, 1970–71*. London: ICAEW

Kellner, D. (1989). *Jean Baudrillard: From Marxism to Postmodernism and Beyond*. Cambridge: Polity Press.

Krause, E. A. (1996). *Death of the Guilds: Professions, States and the Advance of Capitalism, 1930 to the Present*. New Haven, CT: Yale University Press.

Larkin, G. (1983). *Occupational Monopoly and Modern Medicine*. London: Tavistock.

Larson, M. S. (1977). *The Rise of Professionalism*. London: University of California Press.

—— (1984). 'The Production of Expertise and the Constitution of Expert Power', in T. L. Haskell (ed.), *The Authority of Experts*. Bloomington IN: Indiana University Press.

—— (1990). 'On the Matter of Experts and Professionals and How it is Impossible to Leave Anything Unsaid', in R. Torstendahl and M. Burrage (eds.), *The Formation of Professions: Knowledge, State* and Strategy. London: Sage.

Littler, C. R. (1982). *The Development of the Labour Process in Capitalist Society*. London: Heinemann.

Lynn, K. (1963). 'Introduction to the Professions', *Daedalus* (Fall).

Macdonald, K. M. (1984). 'Professional Formation: The Case of Scottish Accountants', *British Journal of Sociology*, 35(2): 174–89.

—— (1985*a*). 'Social Closure and Occupational Registration', *Sociology*, 19(4): 541–56.

—— (1985*b*). 'Professional Formation: A Reply to Briston and Kedslie', *British Journal of Sociology*, 38(1): 106–11.

—— (1989). 'Building Respectabilty', *Sociology*, 23(1): 55–80.

—— (1995). *The Sociology of the Professions*. London: Sage.

—— and Ritzer, G. (1988). 'The Sociology of the Professions: Dead or Alive?' *Work and Occupations*, 15(3): 251–72.

McKinlay, J.B. (1973*a*). 'On the Professional Regulation of Change', in P. Halmos (ed.), *Professionalization and Social Change*, Sociological Review Monograph No. 20, University of Keele.

—— (1973*b*). 'Clients and Organizations', in J. B. MckKinlay (eds.), *Processing People*. London: Holt, Reinhart and Winston.

—— and Arches, J. (1985). 'Towards the Proletarianization of Physicians', *International Journal of Health Services*, 15: 161–95.

—— and Marceau L. D. (2002). 'The End of the Golden Age of Doctoring', *International Journal of Health Services*, 32 (2), 379–416.

Marx, K. (1958). 'Manifesto of the Communist Party', in K. Marx and F. Engels (eds.), *Selected Works*, vol I. Moscow: Foreign Languages Publishing House.

—— (1976). *Capital*. Harmondsworth: Penguin.

Murphy, R. (1984). 'The Structure of Closure: A Critique and Development of the Theories of Weber, Collins and Parkin', *British Journal of Sociology*, 35(3): 547–67.

—— (1988). *Social Closure*. Oxford: Clarendon Press.

Murphy, R. (1990). 'Proletarianization or Bureaucratization: The Fall of the Professional?', in R. Torstendahl and M. Burrage (eds.), *The Formation of Professions: Knowledge, State and Strategy*. London: Sage.

Nettleton, S. (1992). *Power, Pain and Dentistry*. Buckingham: Open University Press.

Oppenheimer, M. (1973). 'The Proletarianization of the Professional', in P. Halmos (ed.), *Professionalization and Social Change*, Sociological Review Monograph No. 20, University of Keele.

Parkin, F. (1971). *Class Inequality and Political Order*. London: McGibbon and Kee.

—— (1979). *Marxism and Class Theory: A Bourgeois Critique*. London: Tavistock.

Parry, N.C.A. and Parry J. (1976). *The Rise of the Medical Profession: A Study of Collective Social Mobility*. London: Croom Helm.

Parsons, T. (1968). 'Professions', *International Encyclopedia of the Social Sciences*, Vol XII. Glencoe, IL: Free Press.

Penn, R. (1985). *Skilled Workers in the Class Structure*. Cambridge: Cambridge University Press.

Polyani, K. (1957). *The Great Transformation*. Boston, MA: Beacon Press.

Porter, S. (1996). 'Contra-Foucault: Soldiers, Nurses and Power', *Sociology*, 30 (1): 59–78.

Ramsay, M. (1984). 'The Politics of Professional Monopoly in Nineteenth-Century Medicine: The French Model and its Rivals', in G. Geison (ed.), *French Professions and the State, 1700–1900*. Philadelphia, PA: Pennsylvania University Press.

—— (1988). *Professional and Popular Medicine in France 1770–1830: The Social World of Medical Practice*. Philadelphia, PA: Pennsylvania University Press.

Rushing, B. (1993). 'Ideology in the Re-emergence of North American Midwifery', *Work and Occupations*, 20(1): 46–67

Saks, M. (2003). 'The Limitations of the Anglo-American Sociology the Professions: A Critique of the Current Neo-Weberian Orthodoxy', *Knowledge, Work & Society*, 1(1).

Savage, M. (2003). 'Review of Freidson (2001)', *Sociological Review*, 51 (1): 166–7.

——, Barlow, J., Dickens, P., and Fielding, T. (1992). *Property, Bureaucracy and Culture: Middle-class Formation in Contemporary Britain*. London: Routledge.

Siegrist, H. (1990). 'Public Office or Free Profession; German Attorneys in the Nineteenth and Early Twentieth Centuries', in G. Cocks and K. H. Jarausch (eds.), *German Professions 1800–1950*. Oxford: Oxford University Press.

Spencer, A. and Podmore, D. (1987). *In a Man's World*. London: Tavistock.

Torstendahl, R. (1990). 'Essential Properties, Strategic Aims and Historical Development: Three Approaches to Theories of Professionalism', in M. Burrage and R. Torstendahl (eds.), *Professions in Theory and History*. London: Sage.

—— and Burrage, M. (eds.) (1990). *The Formation of Professions: Knowledge, State and Strategy.* London: Sage.
Waddington, I. (1984). *The Medical Profession in the Industrial Revolution.* London: Humanities Press.
Weber, M. (1978). *Economy and Society.* London: University of California Press.
Witz, A. (1992). *Professions and Patriarchy.* London: Routledge.
Wood, S. (ed.) (1982). *The Degradation of Work?* London: Hutchinson.
—— (ed.) (1989). *The Transformation of Work?* London: Unwin Hyman.

14

Towards a Theory of Dominant Interests, Globalization, and Work

Stephen J. Frenkel[1]

Globalization is a controversial concept. This is partly because it encompasses a wide variety of economic, political, and social processes, whose relative importance varies according to the perspective of the scholar's discipline and interests. Anthropologists explore changing social networks and consumption patterns while economists are more likely to focus on trade and investment flows. These varying perspectives give rise to different evaluations: globalization may be seen as a complex process of influence by Western cultures but also appropriation and reinterpretation by host societies. On the other hand, it can also be viewed as a reorganizing process as economies restructure in the face of increasing international competition with some economies benefiting more than others. Evaluating globalization is further complicated by varying levels and forms of analysis. Ethnographic studies of communities over several years will yield data and conclusions that are likely to differ significantly from international, cross-sectional, economic analyses. These remarks suggest a need for clarity in establishing an argument about the nature and impact of globalization in any particular domain while cautioning against any generalizations that go beyond that area of enquiry. In the present context this means we need to be clear about the meaning of both globalization and work and to draw conclusions based on theorizing that relationship.

The chapter is organized in five sections. In Section 1, I clarify the meaning of globalization and work and briefly review five perspectives on this rela-

[1] I would like to thank Paul Edwards and Anthony Ferner for useful comments on a previous draft. The paper also benefitted from discussion at seminars held at University College, Dublin, the University of Warwick, and the University of Witwatersrand.

tionship. I favor a dominant interests approach which posits that multinational corporations (MNCs), supported by governments, succeed in shaping the political economy at international and national levels and directly influence work systems. Section 2 uses empirical evidence to explain dominant interests theory in more detail. Section 3 discusses the power, structure, and processes of MNCs, especially as these relate to influencing work systems' design. Section 4 illustrates how globalization contributes to what Katz and Derbishire (2000) refer to as convergent divergence in work systems, i.e. the adoption of fewer, similar types of work system models while simultaneously promoting divergence or differences within these models. Case study evidence drawn from four global industries—apparel, software, airline, and pharmaceuticals—support this proposition. In Section 5, I argue that dominant interests theory is not simply a framework for explanation, it is also a tool for intervening in the globalization process. With both theory and practice in mind, the chapter concludes with three brief research proposals.

1. Perspectives on Globalization and Work

Although globalization is multifaceted in its processes and its impacts, it essentially describes growing interdependence between people in different countries. This may be mediated through economic (trade and investment), political (supra-national institutions such as the EU) and social mechanisms (mass media, tourism, migration). Work is one important way in which interdependence occurs. For example, over the last twenty years the decline in developed country manufacturing reflects technical progress and the growing manufacturing capability of many newly industrialized and developing countries, particularly in Asia.

Work is conceived as formal employment—typically, but not invariably, implying an employer–employee relationship.[2] Work, however, is more than an economic contract defined by the tasks undertaken in exchange for pay and other substantive conditions of employment. It includes the way tasks

[2] This helps to restrict the scope of this chapter. It is not meant to deny the importance of the informal economy. Indeed, in developing countries between 30 and 80 percent of the working population participate in this sector (Munck 2002: 112). The relationship between globalization and changes in the informal economy are controversial and merit detailed investigation, particularly in regard to the participation of women and children (Munck 2002: 114). While company cost-reducing strategies may encourage an informalization of formal employment relations (Webster and Omar 2003: 210), the growing emphasis on quality and supply reliability in many industries may deter companies from relying on small, undercapitalized work units.

Table 14.1. Alternative globalization theories and work

Theory type	Primary drivers of globalisation	Nature and role of governments	Power and role of MNCs	Work system implications
Hyperglobalizers	Economic	Diminishing	Increasing domination by global companies	Global best practice predominates; convergence on high road, HRM systems as less effective systems lose competitive edge
Skeptics	Political and economic	Slightly diminishing but continuing to shape economies	Power of home-centred or regionally based MNCs increasing	Divergence as local contexts exert continuing influence; coexistence of innovation and quality-oriented systems mainly in advanced countries and cost-reducing systems in developing countries.
Transformationalists	Technology, economic and social	Diminishing with authority diffused between institutions at various levels	Increasing but unevenly distributed and constrained by opposition movements and NGOs	Difficult to predict: divergence where local context dominates and convergence where global forces—ideology (e.g. favoring labor flexibility) and technology (enabling similar forms of production or service delivery) influence firms competing in international markets.
Global ethnographers	Social, historical, political, economic, and technological	Varies depending on location; diminished power of the state encourages intrusion of global interests into local contexts	Increasing with variable effects mediated by history and local norms	Divergence as norms and practices are negotiated informally in local settings that are variously influenced by global forces and networks involving reconstructed identities
Dominant interests	Political, economic and social	Rising power of MNCs supported by governments pursuing mainly neoliberal policies in the 1993–2003 period	Increasing with considerable diversity but with tendency towards global, network organizational form	Converging divergence with tendency towards uniformity based on five work system models, particularly models permitting management control over labor with little or no union representation. The sources of divergence derive from various market, institutional, and MNC-related factors

are systematically organized by management and the manner in which conflicts over these aspects are addressed by legally or socially sanctioned rules. In other words, work can be regarded as a more or less coherent arrangement or system comprising task organization and employee regulation.

With few exceptions, theorists have not systematically analyzed the impact of globalization on work. Nevertheless, it is possible to draw relevant implications from their analyses. I do this by summarizing (and by necessity, simplifying) five perspectives on globalization. These are outlined in Table 14.1. In addition, the ensuing discussion highlights the merits of dominant interests theory.

Hyperglobalizers argue that economic forces are reflected in the rise of the global corporation and the decline of the nation state (Ohmae 1990, 1995). Welfare states are particularly under threat as companies urge governments to reduce expenditure in order to ease the tax burden and increase labor market flexibility. Supra-national institutions are emerging to regulate international competition. Two implications for work are worth noting. First, employment comes to depend increasingly on the comparative attractiveness of different economies and sectors to MNCs. Second, as markets become globalized, competition will increasingly be based on quality and innovation rather than simply on price. Thus, work systems are likely to converge on what is considered 'best practice'. Currently, this mainly takes the form of systematic attempts to align organization and employee expectations through the practice of human resource management (HRM).

Skeptics are represented by the work of Hirst and Thompson (1996) who argue that globalization is a myth and that governments remain important architects of the emerging world order. Increasing disparities between the rich North and poor South reflect continuity in world politics rather than change. MNCs are increasingly powerful however they vary in resource endowments and compete in different markets. Pursuing diverse strategies, these organizations assume various forms, which in part reflect different stages in their development and different businesses in home and host countries. Consequently, work systems under MNC control are characterized more by diversity than uniformity, with a tendency for MNCs in the advanced countries to pursue the high road, quality-based work systems compared to cost-based, low road strategies more commonly found in developing countries.

Transformationalists argue that globalization is a significant force strongly influenced by digital technology and political-economic changes that open societies to international resource flows and cultural interchange which facilitate construction of new cultures and identities

(Giddens 1999). The opening of countries to external influences is uneven. West European countries, for example, are closely enmeshed in flows of trade, investment, and individual mobility (via tourism or migration), in contrast to many African countries who largely remain outside the globalization process, except perhaps as price takers in global commodity markets. Transformationalists observe that 'globalization from above'—the role played by MNCs and governments is resisted from 'below' by social movements and NGOs opposing various practices, e.g. the use of sweatshop labor in producing big brand sportswear and, until recently, defending the high prices of life-saving drugs in developing countries.

Castells (1996) restricts his predictions about the effects of globalization on work to broad labor market tendencies, for example, changes in occupational and industrial structures and the rise of nonstandard employment. Pessimists like Beck (2000) and Munck (2002) are more inclined to emphasize negative consequences as noted below, although differences in national contexts and contingencies caution against predicting and hence generalizing the effects of globalization.[3] In the case of work systems, different combinations of global forces and local circumstances are likely to lead to divergence. However, where global forces predominate, in the form of economic policy ideas (neo-liberalism), common technology (e.g. silicon chip manufacture that requires high quality standards) and widely accepted management systems (e.g. Just in Time and Six Sigma), convergence is more likely. This might take the form of 'best practice' HRM or Japanese-inspired work systems. Alternatively, as theorists like Beck (2000) and Munck (2002) have argued, globalization encourages management to relinquish obligations to provide any security of employment for employees. The burden of risk is shifted to the worker who receives little protection from trade unions or governments. Labor flexibility *qua* numerical flexibility signals the race to the bottom, which is particularly serious when this threatens basic labor standards as in developing countries (Munck 2002: 128–34). These theorists argue that it can only be

[3] Transformationalists tend to underplay the historical, political antecedents of globalization in favor of structural tendencies. For example, in quoting approvingly of Held et al. (1999: 85), Munck (2002: 56) claims that: 'we are witnessing a move away from state-centric politics to a new more complex form of multilayered global governance.' Later he observes that: 'Workers across the world live under the aegis of the same neoliberal discourses, work under similar labour regimes characterized by 'flexibilisation' and often watch the same television programmes' (p. 56). The first statement which refers to the changing structure of politics remains unconnected to the second which points to an emerging dominant managerial ideology. The reason workers share the common experience to which Munck refers is explained by the dominant interests theory as explained below.

countered through building institutions 'from below' and engaging in political action.

Global ethnographers have focused on the experience of work as a way of understanding the dynamics and effects of globalization (George 2000; Ó Riain 2000; Collins 2002). Globalization is conceived in a threefold, interrelated way: as forces (social, political, technological, etc.) influencing a community or social group; as social contacts or networks that develop with the intrusion of global influences into local society; and together, as a means of enabling individuals to construct meaning and new identities from past and present experience (Gille and Ó Riain 2002). Identifying these dynamics and their outcomes is said to require a grounded, ethnographic analysis. Although this methodology precludes generalization, evidence generated in this way can lead to theory development and hypothesis formulation. Hence the proposition in Table 14.1 that posits work divergence as the most likely outcome as workers develop their own meaning systems, norms, and identities in the process of negotiating and accommodating to work.

Dominant interests theory is an idea in the making, so I concentrate here on its main features. This differs from global ethnography in adopting the concept of work system rather than workers' subjective experiences as the *explicandum*, as discussed in more detail later. In essence, the idea of work system implies the study of a relationship—between management and workers, oriented towards comparative analysis. Moreover, unlike global ethnography, which stresses the cultural dynamics of globalization, dominant interests theory views globalization mainly as a political-economic phenomenon accompanied by technological and social processes. Contra the hyperglobalizers, it is a multi-tiered theory of governance based on a coincidence of interests (albeit incomplete and varying over time) between dominant corporations based in the dominant nation, and the government of that country. In the contemporary world this is the US.

The government receives political support from MNCs (and other US employers) including legitimacy and resources (via taxation) from economic growth. Dominance is typically negotiated or imposed, depending on the relative power of competitors, and is supported with superior military power. US influence is apparent in transnational institutions (e.g. IMF and WTO) and forums (e.g. Davos and G8 meetings) and in bilateral agreements on aid, trade, and defence. Globalization is a means of pursuing a common interest between the government and large corporations in extending US economic influence. This includes political and military strategies to foster stability in developing countries and efforts to enlarge markets by privatization of public utilities, and to ensure market access through lowering of trade barriers. Pressure is applied on foreign governments directly and through transnational organizations like the IMF and OECD to reduce 'market imperfections' more generally, including demands for greater financial transparency, equal treatment of foreign investors, and elimination of corruption in business transactions.

US-based MNCs exert influence in three main ways. First, as noted above, they exercise substantial political influence. Second, MNCs attempt to shape consumer identity and consciousness through marketing and consumer credit provision. Third, MNC influence is exercised directly on employees through the impact of corporate or regional headquarters' strategies and policies on subsidiaries, suppliers and competitors. US MNCs are at the forefront, making concerted efforts to transfer so-called 'best practices'. At the same time, in attempts to secure investment or new business, coercive performance comparisons are made between subsidiaries and between contractors. This process encourages learning and continuous improvement and hence similarity in work patterns. US consulting companies are also significant creators, carriers, and implementers of new business ideas.[4] The success of these efforts to transfer practices cannot however be taken for granted as local managers, employees, and civil society interest groups vary in their receptivity and power to oppose change (Smith and Meiskins 1995; Almond et al. 2005).

In contrast to the tranformationalists, dominant interests theory acknowledges historical contingencies and changes in dominance. In this regard, it is noteworthy that, as argued by the hyperglobalizers, some MNCs are becoming transnational or global although the extent to which this threatens to break the link between these MNCs and their country of origin is unclear. Where MNCs continue to retain a home country nexus, it is possible that US-based MNCs may lose their relative influence as MNCs based in other countries (Europe, Japan, Korea, and perhaps China) begin to compete more effectively in international markets. Dominant MNC policies and priorities may therefore begin to diverge from the neoliberal agenda that is currently in favour. This will have implications for work systems, particularly if the logic of employment-income protection (Frenkel and Kuruvilla 2002) begins to assert itself through growing distrust of MNCs and governments (see later) leading to popular demands for greater protection from globalization's effects. These include chronically high

[4] Smith and Meiskins (1995: 257) note that McKinsey & Co. was responsible for reorganising the structures of over half the top 100 companies in Britain in the 1960s.

Table 14.2. Growing patterns of workplace practices

Low Wage	HRM	Project-Based	Japanese-Oriented	Joint Team-based
Managerial discretion with informal procedures	Corporate culture and extensive communication	Individual and group dialogue and negotiation	Standardized procedures	Joint decision making
Hierarchical work relations	Directed teams	Temporary project teams, tightly coordinated	Problem-solving teams	Semi-autonomous work groups
Low wages with piece rates	Above-average wages with contingent pay	Base-pay plus performance and reputation-based supplements	High pay linked to seniority and performance appraisals	High pay with pay-for-knowledge
High turnover	Individualized career development	Short-duration employment; reputation-based career	Employment stabilization	Career development
Strong anti-union animus	Union substitution	Occupational community and/or union	Enterprise unionism	Union and employee involvement

Source: Katz and Darbishire (2000: Fig. 1.1; Marsden 2004; Table 1).

levels of unemployment, insecure jobs, and a race to the bottom in wages and conditions fuelled by cost-based competition in some sectors.

While MNCs influence work systems indirectly, through political influence as noted above, and through a demonstration effect, that is by taking decisions, for example on pay, that influence other employers in local labor markets, these organizations directly impact work systems through the introduction of specific human resource strategies. Employing workers in different occupations who differ according to their contribution and uniqueness means that MNCs (and employers more generally) have had to develop work system strategies. As shown in Table 14.2, the consequent patterns assume five main forms depending on the strategic power of employees and institutional characteristics (Katz and Derbishire 2000: 9–15; Marsden 2004: 88–9).

At one extreme is the *low wage model*, characterized by jobs generally regarded as low-skilled where workers are substitutable as in mass production and where work is often based on part-time and/or temporary female or young workers as in mass services (Milkman 1991; Frenkel, forthcoming). Typically, there are few procedures limiting managerial discretion. This model thrives under three conditions: where management subscribe to neoliberal ideology; where local labor markets are lightly regulated; and where competition is mainly cost-based. At the opposite extreme is the nonunion *HRM model* where workers are valued for their creativity, knowledge, and scarce skills. Under these conditions, work systems are more likely to reflect workers' expectations as management attempt to ensure high workplace performance and employee retention by rewarding and developing workers' competencies and providing a satisfying work environment (Katz and Derbishire 2000: 190–208). Where MNC host country tradition (as in the USA) and home country institutional environment (as in China) militate against independent trade unions, the HRM model tends to prevail. Managerial prerogative is enshrined in a strong corporate culture, teamwork, and other features shown in Table 14.2 that encourage worker identification with the firm. The *Project-based model* is less widespread than its HRM counterpart but shares with it a basis in creative, autonomous, highly skilled work. A major difference is the temporary nature of work engagements, exemplified by work in the film, music, and media industries but also found in construction and information technology sectors. Coordinating firms are relatively small and locally based while workers are specialists possessing considerable tacit 'know-how' to provide a successful collective performance. In addition, coordination is achieved through dialogue and influence by the director or leader. Although pay and careers in these industries are based on individual performance and acquired reputation (resulting in large pay inequalities), there is usually a strong collective foundation. A union or professional body typically negotiates minimum rates according to occupational standards agreed with employers, and such a body may also provide employment services. Access to work is often highly dependent on involvement in fluid occupational community networks where reputation is the critical currency.

The *Japanese-oriented model* arose in large manufacturing workplaces where management acknowledged the need to provide some security of employment and incentives to workers employed largely on routine work. In addition, the advantages of direct participation in work-related decisions and representation of worker interests are recognized in the form of quality circles and enterprise unionism respectively. These mechanisms enable management to coordinate employee and employer interests. This model is standard practice among Japanese companies operating in Just-In-Time Total Quality Management (JIT-TQM) manufacturing environments. US and European MNC competitors, most notably in the auto industry, have sought to emulate their successful Japanese counterparts (Kochan et al. 1997). Where workers enjoy greater strategic power based on a collective tradition, the *Joint Team-based model* is likely to predominate. Based on the pluralist principle, implying joint decision-making, consultation, and a central role for the union, such arrangements tend to be confined to industries and countries where unions remain powerful, e.g. the German metalworking and telecommunications sectors. However, as neoliberal ideology and attendant policies have become more influential in recent years, the viability of this model is being strongly challenged.

These five types of work system are interpreted and implemented in different ways according to variations in corporate and business unit strategy, the objectives and capabilities of local management, and extant institutional arrangements and norms. These factors encourage diversity both within and between MNCs and are sufficiently powerful to justify the argument elaborated by Katz and Derbishire (2000) that although work systems are converging (i.e. becoming more similar in broad terms); they are diverging (i.e. becoming more diverse)—in matters of detail.

2. Globalization as a Political Project

World trade is estimated to have grown at more than double the annual rate of world production (7 percent compared to 3 percent) over the 1992–2002 period (United Nations 2001: 4) and between 1991 and 2000 there were 1,185 regulatory changes in national foreign direct investment regimes across the world. Almost all (95 percent) of these changes facilitated foreign investment (UNCTAD 2001: xvii–xv). Not only do these economic facts summarize key aspects of globalization in the contemporary period, they also hint at a neoliberal project that has been vigorously pursued by US MNCs supported by the US government and key international agencies. Attracting MNCs investment and promoting exports has meant constructing lightly regulated labor markets or moving in that direction. I will proceed by describing the neoliberal or laissez-faire (Hutton 2002) ideology to which most US MNC managers and leaders of key international institutions subscribe, and then investigate their labor market preferences, noting the extent to which policies associated with these ideas are implemented.

The law of comparative advantage and the theory of perfect competition provide an economic rationale for globalization. It is not simply a matter of reducing trade protection or permitting MNCs to enter domestic markets, a longer term policy framework needs to guarantee private property rights and the operation of markets as free of impediments as possible. This neoliberal approach to economic development implies 'a level playing field' so that foreign investors are not discriminated against, and corrupt business practices are eliminated. Government influence over allocation of capital including subsidies to state enterprises and support for infant industries is discouraged.[5] In addition, trade unions should not interfere in determining the price of labour. This so-called free market economy is intended to foster entrepreneurship and is therefore accompanied by a low level of direct taxation, relying instead on regressive, indirect forms. This means that although governments may favor raising health, education, and social insurance standards, social welfare is typically subordinated to the interests of capital.[6]

Arguing that US MNCs play a strong proactive role in influencing public policy, Robert Kuttner (2000: 149) maintains that:

> [T]he trick was to have a workforce and a national regulatory climate congenial to multinational enterprise. Thus did these giant corporations become bearers not just of goods and services, but an ideology. And their commitment to this ideology was hardly armchair philosophy. They also worked politically to elect ideological confreres, to influence policy and to carry out global rules of engagement that made congenial habitats for themselves. They won allies in the financial press and in the economics profession. They invested large sums to promote compatible scholarship.

Fostering a neoliberal globalization ideology has been something of a one-way street. As Joseph Stiglitz (2003: 235)–a nobel laureate and chief economist at the World Bank between 1997 and 2000–has noted, US companies through their political influence have adversely impacted third world producers, particularly in agriculture.[7]

[5] Ironically, according to Chang (2004), neither the USA nor any other advanced country developed on the basis of this neoliberal strategy. This raises the question of whether the pursuit of the neoliberal agenda reflects the interests of the USA and other advanced countries in perpetuating the subordination of the developing countries or is this simply a case of economists and policy-makers being misled by a theory that happens to legitimate the myth of the free-market US model?

[6] Hutton (in Giddens and Hutton 2000: 156) goes further, claiming that 'The very existence of laissez-faire unravels the safety-net. Social programmes are expensive and require either high levels of taxation or public borrowing, both of which are anathema to laissez-faire capital.'

[7] For example, in 2002 around 25,000 US farming companies accounted for a third of total global output in spite of their costs being twice the international price of cotton per pound (Stiglitz 2003: 207). This was made possible by subsidies to the tune of $3.9 billion (three times the US aid budget for Africa) which reduced world prices by around 26 percent at the expense of some 10 million African farmers (Monbiot 2003: 190).

Evidence for the view that contemporary globalization means the molding of national economic systems into forms compatible with US interests comes from several sources. Stiglitz, the insider, claims the existence of a dominant ideology known as 'the Washington Consensus'. This ideology, upheld by senior officials at the IMF, the World Bank, and the US Treasury, defines the 'right' policies for developing countries.[8] It includes fiscal austerity, privatization, and market liberalization (Stiglitz 2002: 53)–policies that reflect the key commercial and financial interests of developed country MNCs, especially those headquartered in the US. Reflecting on his experience as a senior US official, Stiglitz suggests that:

> America pushed the ideology of the free market and tried hard to get access for U.S. companies overseas. In doing so, we in the Clinton administration too often put aside the kinds of principles for which we should have stood. We did not think about the impact of our policies on the poor in the developing countries, but on job creation in America. We believed in liberalizing capital markets but didn't think about how it might lead to great global instability.... While we talked about democracy, we did everything we could to maintain our control of the global economic system, and to make sure that it worked for our interests, or more accurately, for the financial and corporate interests that dominated this part of our political life. (Stiglitz 2003: 204)

Hutton (2002) concurs with this interpretation of globalization, arguing that the IMF and World Bank 'have become de facto agents of the US Treasury in its quest to sustain American financial hegemony and policy prescriptions irrespective of the consequent contradictions and strains' (p. 193).[9] Moreover, he suggests that 'over the 80s and 90s a parallel axis to that between the US Treasury and the IMF and World Bank grew up between the US Department of Commerce and first GATT and latterly the World Trade Organisation–and for similar reasons' (2002: 202). In this regard, it is noteworthy that the US has been the dominant voice in these and other international institutions including the Bank for International Settlements. In the IMF and World Bank, decision-making rights are tied to the amount of stock held by different countries. With more than 15 percent of total stock in these institutions held by the USA, American officials 'can block a resolution supported by every other state'

[8] Hutton (2002: 197) refers to journalist Blustein's observation of US Treasury and IMF teams checking into the same hotel in South Korea and negotiating in tandem with the Korean ministry of finance.

[9] While acknowledging the World Bank's attempt to pursue a different course, Hutton (2002) suggests that Stiglitz's resignation from the World Bank in November 1999 is evidence that the Bank's 'scope for manoeuvre was very limited' (p. 199).

(Monbiot 2003: 16). In the WTO, although each member country has a vote, 'its principal decisions are made during the "Green Room" negotiations, which are convened and controlled by the European Union, the United States, Canada, and Japan' (Monbiot 2003: 16–17).

Economic and associated institutional prerequisites for successful globalization are not sufficient. Political change is also necessary. According to President George W. Bush:

> The great struggles of the 20th century between liberty and totalitarianism ended with a decisive victory for the forces of freedom–and a single sustainable model for national success: freedom, democracy and free enterprise. Today, the US enjoys a position of unparalleled military strength, and great economic and political influence.... We seek to create a balance of power that favours human freedom.... The US will use this opportunity to spread the benefits of freedom across the globe.... We will make freedom and the development of democratic institutions key themes in our bilateral relations. (Bush, 21 September 2002, quoted in Nolan 2003: 74)

This proselytizing sentiment is echoed by a former chairman of the US Stock Exchange who stated that: 'in matters of finance and politics, if not culture, we are becoming the world and much of the world wants to become us' (quoted in Hutton 2002: 79).

Petras and Veltmeyer (2001) believe that US foreign policy differs from the past but nevertheless retains its highly partisan character. They speak of a new imperial order that does not support authoritarian, militaristic regimes, as in the past, but favors 'combining electoral processes and individual freedoms with highly elitist decision-making structures' (p. 70). This form of government is intended to provide legitimacy without giving voters much real influence on policy. Indeed, the more economies are opened to trade and foreign investment, the more they come to depend on foreign capital, the more the sentiments of bankers and the views of MNC leaders and senior international officials matter.[10] The new imperial order thus links back to the US as the dominant international power and to other developed countries as allies or accomplices. Stiglitz (2002) sums up this situation as: 'Global governance without global government, one in which a few institutions–the World Bank, the IMF, the WTO–and a few players–the finance, commerce, and trade ministries, closely linked to certain financial and commercial interests–dominate

[10] As the transformationalists maintain, globalization's impact is uneven. Countries that attract FDI and trade internationally typically possess natural resources or have other advantages (low costs, proximity to markets, political stability, etc). MNCs and their home country governments become embroiled in political conflict when important investments or trading relationships are threatened by hostile host country governments or by civil war.

the scene, but in which many of those affected by their decisions are left almost voiceless' (p.21–2).

Hutton (2002: 183) attributes US success in shaping globalization to the pursuit of three principles: exercising power unilaterally where possible; focusing aggressively and unilaterally on promoting US interests in important markets; and favouring market solutions to solve economic problems. Nevertheless, US power should not be exaggerated: the EU in the future may become a possible counter social democratic capitalist model (Marginson and Sisson 2004), and China and India appear to be on the ascendant.[11]

Before considering the impact of this new imperial order on work, we must ask what the leaders of MNCs and international regulatory institutions deem to be desirable labour markets. Criteria and priorities can be inferred from MNC investment decisions. One important criterion is market access, particularly in large population countries, and total factor productivity. Cooke's (2003*a*: chap. 4) analysis of four recent studies of investment behaviour by US and OECD member firms highlights the relevance of appropriate industrial relations (IR) institutional contexts. He argues that:

> MNCs have chosen to invest in countries whose IR systems offer (1) greater net comparative unit labour cost advantages and (2) greater flexibility to either diffuse or create preferred Human Resource Management/Labour Relations practices. As such, host country IR systems marked by lower compensation cost for skills sought, by less imposing government workplace regulations, and by less extensive union representation and decentralized collective bargaining structures attract greater FDI. (p.82)

This quotation leaves unsaid a preference for slack rather than tight labour markets in order to facilitate employee hiring, ease retention problems, and encourage workforce discipline. This increases employment insecurity and enables labour flexibility (Standing 1999: 159), thereby dovetailing neatly with neoconservative government policy on restraining inflation by managing aggregate demand well below the full employment level.

The proclivity towards lightly regulated labour markets is not confined to US MNCs.[12] In a regression analysis of FDI flows between the EU and the

[11] For the first time, the US (and EU) faced organized opposition by developing countries at the Cancun 2003 WTO meeting. This effectively stalled further multilateral trade liberalization until the needs of developing countries are satisfactorily addressed (*Economist* 2003*b*: 11).

[12] MNCs and employers more generally believe that lightly regulated labour markets enhance labour flexibility, however as Rubery and Grimshaw (2003) observe: 'Deregulatory policies that reduce employment protection and weaken social security benefits may act as a disincentive to employees to press for wage gains or to seek more attractive employment opportunities in other organisations. The heightened discipline factor may thus generate new rigidities in the labour market' (146–7).

US and vice versa during the decade ending 1995, Kleiner and Ham (2003) demonstrate that not only are the levels of FDI much greater from the EU to the US than the reverse, but that a key reason for this is the difference in US and EU labour market arrangements. Reinforcing this point, Cooke (2003*b*) notes that 'union penetration among foreign-owned [mainly EU and Japan] subsidiaries in the United States dropped from nearly 30 percent in 1980 to below 15 percent by 1998 show[ing] that it is not only US-based MNCs that attempt to bolster their relative power by aggressively avoiding unionization, as well as closing and downsizing foreign operations that have been unionized.' (p. 408) In short, both EU and US-based MNCs favour labour markets where management's discretion is restricted only by legally enforceable minimum standards endorsed by the International Labour Organization (ILO 1999) and where pay rates and employment conditions are determined by market and performance criteria. The drive to establish such conditions comes about *indirectly* by political means–attempting to influence governments to create or restructure labour markets in this image, including withdrawal of support for tripartism,[13] and *directly*, through MNCs (and other employers) introducing employment systems that embody these principles. Where strongly institutionalized social market models exist (mainly in Western Europe), there has been pressure to shake off so-called Euroscelerosis in favour of more labor market flexibility. Sometimes, as in France and Germany, this has entailed new regulations, particularly over working time. Where labor markets already provide considerable flexibility, as in the US, UK, and Ireland, governments have been reluctant to pass new laws or regulations that limit labor flexibility. The same is true of many developing countries, where Stiglitz (2002) suggests that although the notion of flexible labor markets 'sounds like little more than making the labour market work better but as applied [to developing countries] it has been simply a code for lower wages, and less job protection' (p. 84). Labor market structuring is only part of the story. Later I discuss MNC work system strategies, bearing in mind that these companies often play a leadership role in local labor markets.

Having argued that labor market flexibility and associated practices form part of the broader globalization project promoted by MNCs and

[13] The largest MNCs seem to prefer to influence directly governments rather than working through employer organizations. This contributes to the relative weakness of the ILO in international affairs, for the latter is based on a tripartite structure that provides for employer organization and not direct MNC representation. Nevertheless, the influence of MNCs within transnational employer organizations deserves more research.

senior US and international bureaucrats, I now examine the role, power, and structure of MNCs in the world economy.

3. Multinational Corporations: Globalization's Software

In this section I examine the significance of MNCs in the world economy, particularly US MNCs. I then consider the organizational implications of US MNC dominance.

Currently, of the largest 100 economies in the world, approximately thirty are MNCs, the remainder are countries (UNCTAD 2002; de Grauwe and Camerman 2003). In terms of added value, thirty-seven of the largest 100 economic entities are MNCs (Legrain 2002: 140). MNCs account for at least 20 percent of world GDP and in 1998 directly employed about 86 million workers (Köhler 2003: 33). If suppliers to MNCs are included, the GDP figure rises to 40 percent (Ruigrok and van Tulder 1995). This is an understatement since it excludes service companies that depend on MNCs for most of their business. Examples include local transport, communications, legal, accounting, and consulting firms. Moreover, MNCs frequently account for a large and growing share of employment in important sectors. In the UK, foreign affiliates of MNCs accounted for 13.7 percent of manufacturing employment in 1985 rising to 18.2 percent in 1992 and in Sweden growth was even more dramatic: 7.7 percent in 1985 and 18 percent in 1996. Even in Germany, where host country institutions may be thought to limit MNC penetration, the proportion of foreign affiliate employment rose from 6.6 percent in 1985 to 13 percent in 1996 (Muller-Camen et al. 2001: 436).

MNCs play a significant role in the export sectors of many countries. According to Cooke (2003*b*: 414), MNCs account for between two thirds and three quarters of the world's exports. In today's leading developing country, China, MNCs generated nearly 41 percent of that country's primary and secondary goods' exports over the period 1995 to 1997 (UNCTAD 1999:410). Moreover, since FDI in China has been growing strongly, making it the world's largest recipient of FDI in 2002 (*Economist* 2003*a*: 64), this figure is likely to have increased markedly in recent years. This point underscores a more general observation: MNCs are employing proportionately more of their workforces in host country affiliates. This is especially important to developing countries where very high unemployment typically prevails. Currently, around a third of MNC affiliate employment is located in the third world (Köhler 2003: 36).[14] In addition, overseas markets are not only important to MNCs but they are of growing significance. Thus, according to Petras and Voltmeyer (2001: 67): 'Between 1980 and 1993, among the top 100 TNCs, those earning more than 50 percent of their profits overseas increased from 27 percent to 33 percent of the total' (p.67). MNCs are also a major source of imports. A half of total US imports are sourced from US subsidiaries or affiliates (Hutton 2002: 200). Moreover, a substantial proportion of short-term money flows–speculative capital that contributes to exchange rate volatility and hence adversely impacts on economic growth and employment in many countries–emanates from sentiment and decisions taken by leading US investment banks.

The importance of US-based MNCs can be inferred from data on the 500 largest MNCs (Forbes 2003). The combined sales revenue of these MNCs in 2003 was US$11,584 billion. US-based MNCs account for 48 percent of the total 500, and 54 percent of the largest 50 MNCs. European companies account for 31 percent of the top 500, followed by Japan (11 percent), other Asian countries (6 percent) and other countries (4 percent). US MNCs are at the forefront of FDI, expenditure on R&D, and sustainable competitive advantage (Nolan 2004: 314–16).[15]

Stimulated by fast changing and volatile markets and enabled by digital technology, MNCs seek flexible, integrated operations implying changes in form, with consequences for the way employees are managed. Many MNCs have developed from loose-knit combinations of relatively autonomous units serving several domestic markets to more centralized forms that exploit a common set of technologies, attempting to create worldwide brands (Rubery and Grimshaw 2003: 201–5). This global form co-exists with other MNCs characterized by network structures that disperse power more widely and emphasize collaboration and knowledge sharing in order to increase profits and market share by

[14] In recent years both low-end and high-end service work have been transferred from developed to developing countries. Call centres and software design have been growing in India and the Philippines, and Caribbean data processors process information for US firms. According to IBM executives, up to 3 million service jobs are expected to be transferred from first-world to third-world countries. Significantly lower labor costs (more than ten times lower in some cases) provide a strong incentive (Greenhouse 2003).

[15] The USA's share of total world FDI outflows rose to 27 percent in 1997, nearly doubling since the 1986–91 period. In 1997 135 of the top 300 companies by R&D expenditure were based in North America, while the rate of growth was relatively high. Of 238 companies identified as 'world leaders' by Morgan Stanley DeanWitter, 134 were North American.

taking advantage of innovations created in, or across, different parts of the organization.[16]

Responsiveness to opportunities and idiosyncrasies of local markets have led MNCs to seek growth by rationalizing and closing down unprofitable business units and acquiring potentially profitable new units that generate new products or services. In order to limit liability for losses while retaining control over local business units, MNCs have created legally independent entities in which they have a controlling shareholding and over which they exercise control with the assistance of information technology. This type of network structure is variously known as the federated (Standing 1999: 122–4) or multilayered subsidiary form (Prechel 2002: 62).

These developments highlight both the growing influence of MNCs and their adaptability. Two further characteristics worth noting are, first, that MNCs are constantly in flux. The bulk of FDI activity comprises mergers and acquisitions, giving contemporary MNCs a temporary, hybrid quality.[17] Second, MNC power is paradoxical. While the resources at their disposal have increased significantly in recent years, their legitimacy, as evidenced by public trust, has been declining.[18] Firms associated with global brands are especially vulnerable (Klein 2000). Suspicion has been fanned by illegal behaviour (e.g. Enron, WorldCom, Microsoft), allega-

[16] Network organizations develop in response to market volatility and uncertainty which encourage firms to concentrate on a core set of competences and to outsource peripheral functions. Project-based work systems are appropriate to these conditions, particularly where products or services are highly customized and perishable (i.e. have a short life-span). In some industries, notably those dominated by professional services such as law, accounting, and consulting, the internally focused network organization comprises a partnership whose local units are linked internationally through circulation of personnel and knowledge management systems. These mechanisms help to create and reproduce useful practices, including work systems, across countries. In many other industries, networking has an external orientation aimed at improving supply chain efficiency. This externally focused network organization is dominated by key producers–for example, in manufacturing, by the leading auto and consumer electronics firms–or by buyers in large-scale retailing, or design and marketing companies in fashion-dominated industries. Interfirm networks often span national borders as manufacturing strategy is determined by the global MNC and increasingly located in low cost, lightly regulated countries or regions (Borrus et al. 2000; Wilkinson et al. 2001). Finally, it is worth noting that MNCs may restructure to develop their internal and external networking capabilities simultaneously.

[17] Singh et al. (2003: 49–50) claim that the last decade has witnessed 'a gigantic international merger wave' (p.49), likely to have been the largest ever recorded for the UK and USA, the two countries with the best historical data.

[18] For example, a recent UK Mori poll undertaken by the *Financial Times* (2003) revealed that 'four out of five people said directors of large companies could not be trusted to tell the truth. Almost the same proportion thought directors were paid too much'.

tions of exploitation of third world labour and environmental degradation, excessive senior management remuneration,[19] and continuous restructuring that is often associated with large-scale lay-offs and subsequent adverse employment effects.[20] Hence demands for a new corporate citizenship paradigm (Waddock 2002), a subject to which I return in the concluding section.

4. Multinational Corporations and Work: Divergence Within Limits

The study of MNC work systems presents several challenges. Three deserve special mention. First, the object of enquiry is contestable. Work may be viewed as simply a set of interrelated tasks undertaken for payment, a narrow so-called objective definition because it excludes workers' subjective experience. Alternatively, as noted earlier, global ethnographers focus on particular types of workers, exploring how globalization affects their social networks and how this influences their consciousness and identity, including the meaning of globalization (Burawoy et al. 2000; Collins 2002; Gille and Ó Riain 2002). A third alternative, which I prefer, is the notion of work systems. As indicated earlier, this implies a set of interdependent policies and practices around formal employment. This broader concept of work is intended to work at the middle range of analysis, consistent with an operationalized concept of globalization. This has its antecedents in theories of industrialization (Kerr et al. 1964) and changes in advanced capitalism (Piore and Sabel 1984; Gordon et al. 1992; Boyer and Durand 1997). These theories sought to explain changes in work systems by reference to economic and political forces, which is analogous to the present enterprise.

In pursuing this objective, epistemological problems are posed by issues of scale, place, and connectivity. MNCs are typically large, with control

[19] According to Kevin Murphy, since 1970, CEO pay increased from 25 times to 90 times the pay of the average US worker. Total compensation, including stock options measured at grant value, increased from slightly over 25 times average worker pay in 1970 to about 360 times average worker pay (Academy of Management Issues Forum, 2003:9). Regarding the UK, *The Guardian Weekly* (August 7–13, 2003: 8) reported that although share prices had declined for three consecutive years, falling by 24 percent in 2002, the earnings of directors of Britain's 100 largest companies (according to the FTSE-100 index) rose by 23 percent in the same year while average earnings rose by three percent, slightly exceeding the inflation rate.

[20] According to Hutton (2000: 29), re-entry jobs—jobs acquired following a corporate restructuring—offer pay rates around 20 percent less than the employee's previous job.

widely dispersed through subsidiaries and contractors that include multiple workplaces. In addition, projects may often involve cross-site, international collaboration. How can one obtain valid knowledge about work systems in these circumstances? Inevitably, one must be selective, basing decisions on explicit criteria. Theoretical sampling is one possible route. However, this presupposes a guiding theory or fairly well developed set of ideas that may need to be framed in anticipation of what is possible, in other words, within limitations set by access and resource constraints. At present there are no strong theories that connect globalization and work–strong, in the sense of clearly articulated models and operationalized variables that enable hypothesis testing. This leads to the third, methodological issue: what kinds of methodologies are most appropriate to the problem at hand? Some academics may avoid the problem of engagement with the real world by concentrating on theory development. Others may follow the positivist paradigm to generate theory and test hypotheses. I prefer what might be called a grounded architectural approach. This takes theory (the site-inspired, architectural plan) as a guide, using it to select research sites to undertake multiple in-depth case studies using qualitative and quantitative methods (constructing the building in the light of practical problems and professional criteria). This approach engages with the emergent theory by refining it in the light of empirical enquiry by developing conjectures for further exploration.

From the standpoint of assessing the dominant interests theory of globalization, existing research on MNC work systems presents three difficulties. First, the findings are almost exclusively based on case studies that are unsuitable for drawing conclusions on the relative impact of multiple variables and cannot yield generalizations (Rubery and Grimshaw 2003: 217). Second, there has been a preoccupation with HR management policies and formal practices. Only limited attention has been given to workplace dynamics and outcomes associated with actual MNC practices. Third, in exploring similarities and differences in MNC work system practices, varying levels of abstraction suggest different answers. Thus, at a low level of abstraction, work practices might look very different (e.g., various kinds of teamwork), while at a higher level they appear similar (teamwork compared to individual work assignments). These problems aside, available evidence indicates that MNCs are subject to a variety of factors, some of which encourage work system convergence, while others contribute to divergence. Consistent with dominant interests theory, I will argue that globalization encourages both convergence and divergence with the latter continuing to have the upper hand.

5. Convergent Forces

Four factors associated with globalization have been promoting the adoption of similar work system practices *within* any particular MNC. First, there is what Frenkel and Kuruvilla (2002) refer to as the logic of competition. Globalization invites new entrants to markets and makes it easier for foreign firms to compete. More intense competition means that firms are constantly seeking to limit risk, contain costs, improve quality, and market new products or services. Converting labor from a fixed to a variable cost appeals to management. A second factor noted earlier is relevant here–the tendency towards lightly regulated labour markets. Together, these two factors encourage MNCs (and other employers) to introduce various forms of labor flexibility. Corporate characteristics, especially strategy, structure, and culture, is a third factor. Corporate integration is sometimes viewed as a strategic imperative, particularly where global branding is paramount. MNCs that have a common technology or whose processes are highly interdependent have an incentive to support integrative practices (e.g., centralized financial control or knowledge management systems) and pursue synergies across subsidiaries including the development of similar work system policies (Edwards 2000; Muller-Camen et al. 2001). Where corporate culture is strong and work systems are based on common principles, there will be a tendency to transfer work practices to subsidiaries (Bèlanger et al. 1999; Royle 2002). The fourth factor is employment of expatriate managers in key positions across the corporation. Japanese MNCs are well known for using this device to exercise corporate control and to transfer important practices to overseas subsidiaries (Doeringer et al. 2003).

The first three factors mentioned above also contribute to similarities in work systems *between* MNCs. Four further factors contribute to interfirm convergence. These are: the influence of dominant country practices; international regulation; sectoral distinctiveness; and enhanced management power. While the first three factors reflect the process of globalization, the fourth factor, which relates to particular industries, has a paradoxical quality that we note below.

At present, the US and to a lesser extent Japan are the main sources of influential management and work practices (Katz and Derbishire 2000; Edwards and Ferner 2002) which as mentioned earlier, are deliberately transferred and circulate more generally via consultants, the business media, and management schools. International work regulation is less common worldwide, although the ILO's core labor standards now stand as a minimum floor of workers' rights (ILO 1999) and MNCs based in member countries are expected to comply with the OECD's revised guidelines on MNC behaviour (OECD 2000). Within trading blocs, international regulation is beginning to exert some influence.[21] The European Works Council directive which applies to MNCs employing 1,000 or more workers, and more than 150 workers in two or more EU or European Economic Area countries. It requires consultative structures that promote cross-country, and intrafirm dialogue (Muller-Camen et al. 2001; Bain and Hester 2003; Beaupain et al. 2003).

The third factor encouraging interfirm convergence in work systems is the growth of management power vis-à-vis employees in many labor markets. This is indicated by the lack of union influence in many countries (Frenkel 2003: 142). It has enabled management to adopt combinations of various forms of labor flexibility (Standing 1999: 83–127; Kalleberg 2003),[22] and to implement systematic, formal processes for managing employees, particularly where collective discipline is required (as in JIT-TQM or Six Sigma systems), or where profitability is highly dependent on worker creativity, skills, and knowledge. In effect, formalization permits comparisons to be more easily made across work systems in company subsidiaries and it encourages stronger management policy coordination. These developments are evident in the relative growth of Japanese-oriented and HRM work systems (Katz and Derbishire 2000), illustrating the 'co-operative dependent' character of much contemporary workplace relations (Frenkel 1994, 1995).

[21] From the point of view of convergence and divergence of national systems of employment relations, the growth of the EU market and institutions has been significant. For example, the Euro company and European regional tiers of global corporations have become more important. This has encouraged the adoption of common practices within companies across the EU. Company level bargaining is undermining sector-level bargaining in several European countries thereby contributing to growing convergence of employment relations arrangements within companies but increased diversity within countries (Marginson and Sisson 2004).

[22] In addition to organizational flexibility, Standing (1999: 83–127) has analysed five types of labor flexibility. These are: (1) job structure flexibility–the decomposition of bureaucracies into organizations that are subdivided into specialized craft or Taylorist forms; (2) income flexibility–declining state benefits and a higher proportion of contingent to fixed pay; (3) nonwage labor cost flexibility–training, coordination, welfare or labour protection, and labour turnover costs that can be reduced by employing part-time temporary staff who receive little training or welfare support; (4) numerical flexibility–employment of various kinds of labor that are closely matched to variations in demand for the product or service, e.g., casuals, part-timers, and self-employed contractors; and (5) work process/function flexibility–e.g., working time adjustments (flexitime, shift working, short-time working, and annualized hours schemes) and changes in jobs (skill enlargement and multiskilling).

Finally, sectors or industries tend to have distinctive technological and market features that lead to common pressures and similar work practice responses. For example, in the aftermath of September 11 and the SARS epidemic, MNCs in the airline industry experienced substantially reduced demand for their services. The companies moved to reduce labor costs in similar ways (Clarke et al. 2002). Likewise, in the athletic shoe industry, widely publicized allegations of substandard labor conditions in some contractor factories have encouraged MNCs to introduce strict guidelines and monitoring practices to ensure that minimum standards are upheld (Frenkel 2000). The paradox is that sectoral distinctiveness contributes to convergence in work systems within sectors while promoting divergence between work systems across sectors (Colling and Clark 2002; Edwards and Ferner 2002).

6. Divergent Forces

Divergence within and between MNC work systems arise when conditions obtain that are contrary to some of those mentioned above. These include barriers to global competition, whether intentional (e.g., tariffs) or unintentional (e.g., highly differentiated, low volume markets), government labor market policies that protect workers' rights to training and employment as in Sweden, and corporate diversification, especially rapid growth by merger and acquisition. The relative absence of international regulation has also contributed to diversity. Six further globalization factors contribute to work system divergence.

First, there is the country of origin or home country effect. MNCs headquartered in different countries transfer business and work practices to distant subsidiaries. This process is well documented for US (Edwards and Ferner 2002) and Japanese firms (Elger and Smith 1998), but appears to be complicated by the dominant country effect in the case of European firms (Ferner and Quintanilla 1998; Hayden and Edwards 2001; Kurdelbusch 2002).[23] A second factor is the host country effect which is associated with the proposition that business systems vary significantly across countries (Whitley 1999) and that such differences influence the work systems of MNC subsidiaries (Frenkel and Kuruvilla 2002; Brewster and Tregaskis

[23] Compared to their US and Japanese counterparts, the largest European MNCs locate considerably more of their direct investment outside the home country (Edwards and Ferner 2002: 96). This may encourage greater decentralization and more work system diversity across subsidiaries in different countries.

2003; Kenney and Tanaka 2003). Third, MNC subsidiaries vary in resources, capabilities, and proximity to markets. Subsidiaries develop different relationships with headquarters and specialize in satisfying different markets (Frenkel and Royal 1998; Colling and Clark 2002). Some subsidiaries may be highly innovative leading to 'reverse diffusion' (Edwards 2000), while others may implement new production principles such as JIT-TQM less successfully than anticipated, either because they have been unable or unwilling to learn, or because they lack appropriate flexibility and motivational spirit required to make the transition (Kochan et al. 1997: 309). Note that the strategic position of subsidiaries and relations with corporate headquarters change over time resulting in oscillations in the extent to which local managers can shape subsidiary work systems.

A fourth source of intrafirm work system diversity concerns subsidiary or contractor firm interpretation and implementation of common rules and norms established at MNC headquarters. Policies are interpreted and implemented in a variety of ways depending on subsidiary or contractor management goals and culture, taking into account local circumstances. For example, in the athletic shoe industry, global firms' relations with Taiwanese and Korean contract suppliers vary in the extent of trust and collaboration. This results in different work systems at contractor factories. This is in spite of a common adherence to minimum labor standards required by the MNCs codes of labor practice (Frenkel and Scott 2002; Mamic 2003). Fifth, the constant flux occasioned not only by mergers and acquisitions as noted earlier, but by joint ventures, out-sourcing arrangements, rationalization, and technological change disrupts work systems. These changes contribute to fragmentation of established internal labor markets and the rise of hybrid forms that reflect large-scale employer influence in both external and internal labour markets (Royal and Althauser 2003). Sixth, and finally, in the midst of intense competition and technological change, management are unsure of what constitutes sustainable 'best practice' so that in many cases there is continuous experimentation. This tends to disrupt work system coherence (Katz and Derbishire 2000: 273).

7. Variations in Work Systems

In the real world the elements of work systems are rarely perfectly aligned, operating as a smooth, interdependent whole. Changes in production systems and introduction of new practices—e.g., pay structures, task reconfigurations, etc.—are frequently contested and lead to compromises thereby contributing to variations in work systems. In addition, as noted earlier, work system divergence arises from a variety of factors related to increasing opportunities for MNCs to operate with greater discretion in lightly regulated labor markets and where decision-making is decentralized to business units whose strategic position and capabilities vary significantly. It is therefore not surprising to find that work systems are complex and varied, as illustrated by the cases shown in Table 14.3. These represent some of the few MNC studies that extend into the workplace.

Before interpreting these data, there are three caveats. First, the studies are selective. They focus on global industries and they probably overrepresent unionized firms and underrepresent service organizations, at least in the advanced countries. And they do not include all work systems under the control of the relevant MNCs. Second, because the aims of each study differ, the processes and outcomes are not always easy to compare. Third, the studies do not focus solely on US MNCs, and in one case (Airlines), the firms are UK-owned.

Bearing these limitations in mind, several observations can be made. To begin with, each case has features that liken it to one or more of the five patterns outlined earlier. Thus, in the Apparel case, there is a tendency towards the Japanese-oriented model co-existing with a stronger trend toward the low-pay work system. The Software development work system resembles the project-based system, characterized by short-term employment, team-based work, and worker dependence on networks for future employment. However, in two respects the software work system is similar to the HRM model: employment is with a spin-off of an MNC whose pay and conditions are relatively good.

In the Airline workplaces, pilots resemble the joint team-based approach, however this appears to be the product of industrial action by the union rather than cooperation between workers and management. By contrast, the cabin crew work system is similar to the low-pay model, except that these workers receive some, albeit limited, union protection. In the Pharmaceutical cases, a joint team-based approach was evident in the UK, except that workplace change was dominated by a proactive management, with the unions accommodating to, rather than embracing, change resulting in low workforce morale. In the South African workplace there was a tendency toward the Japanese-oriented model but with limited

Table 14.3. Work systems in apparel, software development, airline, and pharmaceutical industries

Industry, home country and source	Strategy	Work system practices	Workers' responses and effects *Procedural*	*Substantive*
***Apparel*, mainly US (Taplin and Winterton 2002)**	Quality and market responsiveness–niche production or cost reduction via outsourcing alliances to low cost producers and internal reorganization	Manufacturing restructuring–JIT and focus on higher value products; relocation of sites to Asia or via contracting	JIT-related new technology and teamwork limited; lean retailing puts premium on market responsiveness; squeeze by concentrated retailers and textile suppliers means cost cutting while maintaining high quality. Neo-Taylorism dominates in context of low unionization	Job reductions, insecurity, work intensification, and low pay in developed countries; job creation in some developing countries. Some increased job satisfaction with new production systems but JIT coupled with teamwork uncommon, especially in developing countries
***Software development*, US (Ó Riain 2000)**	High quality, rapid product design testing; contract between Irish affiliate and partially owned, small spin-off US design company partly based on cost advantage	Six-member team under virtual control from US; subordinate status re. software work; high autonomy; individuals working under different contracts but favourable pay and conditions reflect workers' strategic power	Project of several months' duration; strict deadlines; work rhythm sequence normal, hectic, relaxed. Team orientation varies in relation to deadlines; inward looking, pre-deadline cohesion with intense focus on project completion, and outward-oriented, post-deadline fragmentation and relaxation while seeking new work. Local team solidarity against remote management	Insecurity of employment–team pitched for new work that they lacked the skills to complete–subcontracted out. Thereafter, design work shifted to USA–team virtually disbanded. Employability important–continual search for new work hence importance of local and global networks; local culture with global awareness based on common workplace; individualism reasserts itself when project completed and individuals must find new work
***Airlines*, UK (Blyton et al. 2002)**	Labour cost reduction and higher performance in response to increasing global competition; increased alliance-building	Restructuring aimed at increasing productivity; occupational differences re. job security, career opportunities and pay	Unionized, collective agreements–threatened/actual industrial action–positive outcome of negotiations with pilots but not for cabin crew	Pilots and cabin crew: increasing work intensity and longer hours; changed pay system. Pilots: pay improved overall; increased career opportunities; opposite for cabin crew

(*Contd.*)

Table 14.3. *(Contd.)*

Industry, home country and source	Strategy	Work system practices	Workers' responses and effects *Procedural*	*Substantive*
***Pharmaceuticals*, US (Frenkel and Royal 1998)**	Corporate restructuring, cost reduction and performance improvement. UK plant–key specialist supplier to European market cf. South African plant serving smaller local market–alliance-building for lower cost generics	Downsizing and plant closings; selective restructuring and new investment–applied to UK cf. SA workplace	Two unionized workplaces; UK plant rationalized, more specialized and efficient producer; partnership unions. Negotiated job demarcation reduced via teams, new pay and job evaluation structure and fewer bargaining units. SA workplace–drive to increase efficiency supported by increased communication and shop steward participation under weak, conservative union control	UK workplace–job insecurity; low morale; team working–plant closed down seven years later. SA workplace–higher morale and less job insecurity but uncertainty re. corporate strategy and union representation, and lack of resources restricting scope of change

Note: Authors of cases in each industry are indicated in the first column of the table.

introduction of supporting practices. In short, most of the work systems described in the cases are hybrids that reflect complex combinations of global and local improvisation. This supports the argument that divergence is a stronger tendency than convergence.

Nevertheless, the cases do show some common work system features. These include substantial competitive pressure on MNCs to cut costs and improve performance. This apparently led firms to focus on their core competence, developing alliances and contracting relations with other companies. Work systems have also had to change. Work restructuring is a common denominator and so are job losses, with workplace closures occurring in all four cases, although in Airlines this is not evident from the table but is supported by recent evidence (Clarke et al. 2002: 452). Note that with the exception of Apparel, team working is a common work practice. That is, if one makes the reasonable assumption that team working is normal practice in Airlines. This suggests that MNCs use both functional and numerical flexibility in seeking higher workplace performance. Although there is little detailed evidence of common strategies being used to effect change, management had been on the offensive. In the two sets of unionized workplaces (Airlines and Pharmaceuticals), consultation and negotiation seems to have been used, leading to union cooperation in most instances. For workers, the substantive effects have been painful: employment and income insecurity, and increasing pay inequities between individuals (Software development), between workers in different plants (Apparel and Pharmaceuticals), and between occupational groups (Airlines), probably sharpening the division between winners and losers (Hayman 1999:104–5). Work intensification is also evident, although in Software this occurred as part of the development cycle. Finally, there is evidence of workplace mobility as MNCs sought more cost-effective locations for Apparel production, Software development, and Pharmaceutical manufacturing, where UK capacity was subsequently absorbed, mainly by the company's larger French plants.

In addition to a sector effect, most clearly evident in Software development and Airlines, local institutional contexts and unions were strong influences, although the union impact has probably declined since the research was undertaken. Variations in outcomes are directly attributable to the relative power of developers in Software and pilots in Airlines, in contrast to the limited power of semiskilled Apparel workers. In Pharmaceuticals, trade unions were being weakened, however, they continued to provide a channel for consultation and negotiation.

In summary, this overview leads to two observations: first, while there is evidence for particular work system models exerting an influence on management thinking, reality is complex, with divergence being the predominant tendency. Second, the work systems that we examined demonstrated management's ascendancy regarding power over workers, evident in the growing flexibility required of employees. This is consistent with the neoliberal ideology of lightly regulated labour markets that facilitate managerial control of labour in various ways. Depending on strategy and context, US MNCs are likely to embrace any one or more of four models discussed in the chapter. The only model that they oppose is the Team-based approach with union representation, although strategically placed workers such as pilots have sometimes forced management's hand in this regard.

8. Conclusion

In this chapter I have proposed a dominant interests framework to explain the relationship between globalization and work. This approach views contemporary globalization as a neoliberal political project that reflects MNC interests in promoting international trade and investment and political-economic environments that are conducive to these activities. US MNCs have played a dominant role in this process, helping to create and sustain lightly regulated labour markets and fostering Low wage, HRM, Project-based, and Japanese-oriented types of work systems, while limiting the growth of Joint Team-based forms of work organization. This tendency toward convergence in work systems has however been accompanied by increased diversity arising from a variety of contextual and firm-related factors. Dominant interests theory is thus a framework that is sensitive to contingencies that produce converging divergence in work systems.

Once again it is worth emphasizing that globalization and its consequences are historically contingent and path dependent. MNCs, governments, and social organizations reappraise existing policies and learn to address old problems in new ways. They also develop novel strategies as new conditions emerge. Indeed currently, the neoliberal variant of globalization is being challenged by governments side-lined by the USA, and by NGOs and unions mobilizing popular opinion. Demands for a stronger voice at the globalization table are being made at the WTO and governments in several countries–Argentina, Mexico, the Philippines, South Korea, and Thailand–are being called to account for deep recessions and/or stalled growth associated with globalization and IMF-inspired reform measures. Meanwhile, there is support in the EU for retaining the social market model in a more flexible form.

In response to these and other pressures globalization is taking on new characteristics. The US has retreated to pursuing trade and investment liberalization through bilateralism, and demands for greater corporate social responsibility are being institutionalized in the form of rapidly growing ethical investment funds, and labour and environmental monitoring arrangements. A UN-sponsored Global Compact has over 1,000 MNCs signed up (less than 5 percent US-based) to work with worker and environmental groups for a sustainable future. These developments are likely to have significant consequences for work systems, indeed they may inspire a new model of stakeholder capitalism that challenges and supersedes the prevailing shareholder-capitalism model with its management dominated work systems.

Turning to research, the objectives of dominant interest theory is twofold: to explain contemporary work systems and provide a tool for realizing an emancipatory vision of globalization which would include strategies for change. With these goals in mind, there is a need to theorize and explore more systematically the relationship between political and economic interests of the dominant nation (the USA) and how these affect work systems. This major endeavour should have a historical dimension and extend to other competitor nations or political entities such as the EU. At a less abstract level, deeper analysis is needed regarding the manner and extent to which MNCs, particularly US MNCs, exert political influence in shaping labor market policy. Home and host governments, and international institutions could be targeted. It is also necessary to provide further information and analysis of MNC work systems, perhaps by undertaking a representative survey of MNCs, identifying their work systems, and testing hypotheses concerning the factors promoting convergence and divergence referred to earlier in this chapter. Finally, we need to know more about the effects of different work system configurations. This might be obtained by systematically comparing work systems over time within MNC subsidiary workplaces, with the selection of MNCs and subsidiaries being guided by an appropriately developed theory. The results of a research program based on projects similar to those outlined above are likely to refine the dominant interests framework as an explanation of the relationship between globalization and work while holding out the prospect of developing concepts and strategies that will prove useful in promoting the interests of the working majority.

References

Academy of Management Issues Forum (2003). *What Should be Done About CEO Pay?* http://myaom.pace.edu/octane8admin/websites/ProfessionalDevelopment/default.asp?id=128

Almond, P., Edwards, T., Colling, T. et al. (2005). 'Unraveling Home and Host Country Effects: An Investigation of the HR Policies of an American Multinational in Four European Countries', *Industrial Relations*, 44(2): 276–306.

Bain, R. and Hester, K. (2003). 'Carrot or Stick? How MNCs Have Reacted to the European Works Council Directive', in W. N. Cooke (ed.), *Multinational Companies and Global Human Resource Strategies*. Westport, Connecticut: Quorum Books.

Beaupain, T., Jefferys, S. and Annand, R. (2003). 'Early Days: Belgian and U.K. Experiences of European Works Councils', in Cooke, W. N. (ed.), *Multinational Companies and Global Human Resource Strategies*. Westport, CT: Quorum Books.

Beck, U. (2000). *The Brave New World of Work*. London: Polity Press.

Bélanger, J., Edwards, P., and Wright, M. (1999). 'Best HR Practice and the Multinational Company', *Human Resource Management Journal*, 9(3): 53–70.

Blyton, P., Lucio, M., McGurk, J., and Turnbull, P. (2002). 'Globalization, Restructuring and Occupational Labour Power: Evidence from the International Airline Industry', in Y. A. Debrah and I. G. Smith (eds.), *Globalisation, Employment and the Workplace*. London: Routledge.

Borrus, M., Ernst, D., and Haggard, S. (2000). *International Production Networks in Asia: Rivalry or Riches?* London: Routledge.

Boyer, R. and Durand, J-P. (1997). *After Fordism*. Houndmills: Macmillan.

Brewster, C. and Tregaskis, O. (2003). 'Convergence or Divergence of Contingent Employment Practices? Evidence of the Role of MNCs in Europe', in W. N. Cooke (ed.), *Multinational Companies and Global Human Resource Strategies*. Westport, CT: Quorum Books.

Burawoy, M., Blum, J., George, S. et al. (2000). *Global Ethnography: Forces, Connections and Imaginations in a Postmodern World*. Berkeley: University of California Press.

Castells, M. (1996). *The Rise of the Network Society*. Oxford: Blackwell.

Chang, H-J. (2004). *Kicking Away the Ladder: Development Strategy in Historical Perspective*. London: Anthem Press.

Clark, I., Colling, T., Aomond, P. et al. (2002). 'Multinationals in Europe 2001-2: Home Country, Host Country and Sector Effects in the Context of Crisis', *Industrial Relations Journal*, 33(5): 446–64.

Colling, T. and Clark, I. (2002). 'Looking for 'Americanness': Home-Country, Sector and Firm Effects on Employment Systems in as Engineering Services Company', *European Journal of Industrial Relations*, 8(3): 301–24.

Collins, J. (2002). 'Deterritorialization and Workplace Culture', *American Ethnologist*, 29(1): 151–71.

Cooke, W. (2003*a*). 'The Influence of Relations System Factors on Foreign Direct Investment', in W. Cooke (ed.), *Multinational Companies and Global Human Resource Strategies*. Westport, CT: Quorum Books.

—— (2003*b*). 'The Role of Power and Implications for Transnationals Workplace Outcomes', in W. N. Cooke (ed.), *Multinational Companies and Global Human Resource Strategies*. Westport, CT: Quorum Books.

De Grauwe, P. and Camerman, F. (2003) 'How Big are the Big Multinational Companies?', www.econ.kuleuven.ac.be/ew/academic/intecon/Degrauwe

Doeringer, P. B., Lorenz, E. and Terkla, D. G. (2003). 'The adoption and diffusion of high-performance management: lessons from Japanese multinationals in the West'. *Cambridge Journal of Economics*, 27, 265–86.

Economist (2003*a*). 'Is the Wakening Giant a Monster?', February 15: 63–5.

Economist (2003*b*). 'Cancun's Charming Outcome', September 20: 11.

Edwards, T. (2000). 'Multinationals, international integration and employment practice in domestic plants'. *Industrial Relations Journal*, 31/2, 115–29.

Edwards, T. and Ferner, A. (2002). 'The renewed 'American Challenge': a review of employment practice in US multinationals'. *Industrial Relations Journal*, 33/2, 94–111.

Elger, T. and Smith, C. (1998). 'Exit, Voice and 'Mandate': Management Strategies and Labour Practices of Japanese Firms in Britain'. *British Journal of Industrial Relations*, 36/2, 185–207.

Ferner, A and Quintanilla, J. (1998). 'Multinationals, National Business Systems and HRM: the Enduring Influence of National Identity or a Process of "Anglo-Saxonisation" '. *International Journal of Human Resource Management*, 9/4, 710–31.

Ferner, A. and Quintanilla, J. (2002). 'Between Globalization and Capitalist Variety: Multinationals and the International Diffusion of Employment Relations'. *European Journal of Industrial Relations*, 8/3, 243–50.

Financial Times (2003). 'No Confidence in British Business–Company Directors are Seen as Untrustworthy and Overpaid', June 30: 18. Available on http://80-global.factiva.com.proxy

Forbes (2003). *The Global 500*. 21 July, Forbes.com.

Frenkel, S. J. (1994). 'Patterns of Workplace Relations in the Global Corporation: Toward Convergence?' in J. Bélanger, P. Edwards, and L. Haiven (eds.), *Workplace Industrial Relations and the Global Challenge*. Ithaca: ILR Press, 240–74.

Frenkel, S. J. (1995). 'Workplace Relations in the Global Corporation: A Comparative Analysis of Subsidiaries in Malaysia and Taiwan', in Frenkel, S. and Harrod, J. (eds.), *Industrialization and Labor Relations: Contemporary Research in Seven Countries*. Ithaca: ILR Press, 179–215.

Frenkel, S. J. (2000). 'Globalization, Athletic Footwear Commodity Chains and Employment Relations in China'. *Organization Studies*, 22/4, 531–62.

Frenkel, S. J. (2003). 'The Embedded Character of Workplace Relations'. *Work & Occupations*, 30/2, 3–21.

Frenkel, S.J. (2004). 'Service Workers in Search of Decent Work', in S. Ackroyd, R. Batt, P. Tolbert, P. Thompson, et al. (eds.) *Handbook of Work & Organization*, Oxford: Oxford University Press.

Frenkel, S. J. and Kuruvilla, S. (2002). 'Logics of Action, Globalization, and Changing Employment Relations in China, India, Malaysia, and the Philippines'. *Industrial and Labor Relations Review*, 55/3, 387–412.

Frenkel, S. J. and Royal, C. (1998). 'Corporate-Subsidiary Relations, Local Contexts and Workplace Change in Global Corporations'. *Industrial Relations*, 53/1, 154–85.

Frenkel, S. J. and Scott, D. (2002). 'Compliance, Collaboration, and Codes of Labor Practice: The *adidas* Connection'. *California Review Management*, 45/1, 29–49.

George, S. (2000). 'Dirty Nurses and "Men Who Play": Gender and Class in Transnational Migration', in M. Burawoy, J. Blum, S. George et al. (eds.), *Global Ethnography: Forces, Connections and Imaginations in a Postmodern World*. Berkeley: University of California Press.

Giddens, A. (1999). *Runaway World*. London: Reith Lectures. Available at http://www.abc.net.au/rn/events/reith99.htm

Giddens, A. and Hutton, W. (2000) 'In Conversation', in Hutton, W. and Giddens, A. (eds.) *On the Edge: Living with Global Capitalism*. London: Jonathan Cape.

Gille, Z. and Ó Riain, S. (2002). 'Global Ethnography', *Annual Review of Sociology*, 28: 271–95.

Gordon, D., Edwards, R., and Reich, M. (1992). *Segmented Work, Divided Workers: The Historical Transformation of Labor in the United States*. Cambridge: Cambridge University Press.

Greenhouse, S. (2003). 'IBM Explores Shift of White-Collar Jobs Overseas', *NY Times.com Article*, July 22.

Guardian Weekly (2003). 'Big-firm Directors Earn Fat-Cat Label', August 7–13: 8.

Hayden, A. and Edwards, T. (2001). 'The Erosion of the Country of Origin Effect', *Relations industrielles*, 56(1): 116–40.

Hayman, R. (1999). 'Imagined Solidarities: Can Trade Unions Resist Globalization?', in P. Leisink (ed.), *Globalization and Labour Relations*. London: Edward Elgar.

Held, D., McGrew, A., Goldblatt, D., and Perraton, P. (1999). *Global Transformations: Politics, Economics and Culture*. Cambridge: Polity Press.

Hirst, P. and Thompson, G (1996). *Globalization in Question: The International Economy and the Possibilities of Governance*. Cambridge: Polity Press.

Hutton, W. (2002). *The World We're In*. London: Little, Brown.

Hutton W. and Giddens, A. (eds.) (2000). *On the Edge: Living with Global Capitalism*. London: Jonathan Cape.

ILO (International Labour Organization) (1999). Decent Work, International Labour Conference, 87th Session, Report of the Director-General, Geneva.

Kalleberg, A. L. (2003). 'Flexible Firms and Labor Market Segmentation: Effects of Workplace Restructuring on Jobs and Workers', *Work and Occupations*, 30(2): 154–75.

Katz, H. C. and Derbishire, O. (2000). *Converging Divergences: Worldwide Changes in Employment Systems*. Ithaca: ILR Press/Cornell University Press.

Kenney, M. and Tanaka, S. (2003). 'Transferring the Learning Factory to America? The Japanese Television Assembly Transplants', in W. N. Cooke (ed.), *Multinational Companies and Global Human Resource Strategies*. Westport, CT: Quorum Books.

Kerr, C., Dunlop, J. T., Harbison, F., and Myers, C. (1964). *Industrialism and Industrial Man: The Problems of Labour and Management in Economic Growth*. New York: Oxford University Press.

Klein, N. (2000). *N. Logo*. London: Harper Collins.

Kleiner, M. and Ham, H. (2003). 'The Effect of Different Industrial Relations Systems in the United States and the European Union on Foreign Direct Investment Flows', in W. N. Cooke (ed.), *Multinational Companies and Global Human Resource Strategies*. Westport, CT: Quorum Books.

Kochan, T., Lansbury, R., and MacDuffie, J. (1997). *After Lean Production: Evolving Employment Practices in the World Auto Industry*. Ithaca: ILR/Cornell University Press.

Köhler, G. (2003). 'Foreign Direct Investment and its Employment Opportunities in Perspective: Meeting the Great Expectations of Developing Countries?', in W. N. Cooke (ed.), *Multinational Companies and Global Human Resource Strategies*. Westport, CT: Quorum Books.

Kurdelbusch, A. (2002). 'Multinational and the Rise of Variable Pay in Germany', *European Journal of Industrial Relations*, 8(3): 325–49.

Kuttner, R. (2000). 'The Role of Governments in the World Economy', in W. Hutton, and A. Giddens (eds.), *On the Edge: Living with Global Capitalism*. London: Jonathan Cape.

Legrain, P. (2002). *Open World: The Truth about Globalization*. London: Abacus.

Mamic, I. (2004). Implementing Codes of Conduct. Sheffield: Greenleaf.

Marginson, P. and Sisson, K. (2004). *European Integration and Industrial Relations. Multi-level Governance in the Making*. London: Palgrave.

Marsden, D. (2004). 'Employment Systems: Workplace HRM Strategies and Labor Institutions,' in B. Kaufman (ed.) *Theoretical Perspectives on Work and the Employment Relationship*, IRRA. Urbana-Champaign: University of Illinois.

Milkman, R. (1991). *Japan's California Factories: Labor Relations and Economic Globalization*. Los Angeles: UCLA Institute of Industrial Relations.

Monbiot, G. (2003). *The Age of Consent: A Manifesto for a New World Order*. London: Flamingo.

Muller-Camen, M., Almond, P., Gunnigle, P., Quintanilla, J., and Tempel, A. (2001). 'Between Home and Host Country: Multinationals and Employment Relations in Europe', *Industrial Relations Journal*, 32(5): 435–48.

Munck, R. (2002). *Globalisation and Labour: The New 'Great Transformation'*. London: Zed Books.

Nolan, P. (2003). *China at the Cross-Roads*. Cambridge: Polity Press.

Nolan, P. (2004) 'Industrial Policy in the Early 21st Century: The Challenge of the Global Business Revolution', in Ha-Joon Chang (ed.), *Rethinking Development Economics*. London: Anthem Press.

Ó Riain, S. (2000) 'Net-Working for a Living: Irish Software Developers in the Global Workplace', in M. Burawoy, J. Blum, S. George et al. *Global Ethnography: Forces, Connections and Imaginations in a Postmodern World*. Berkeley: University of California Press.

OECD (2000). *Guidelines for Multinational Enterprises*. Available at http://www.oech.org

Omae, K. (1990) *The Borderless World: Power and Strategy in the Interlinked Economy*. New York: Harper Row.

Omae, K. (1995). *The Evolving Global Economy: Making Sense of the New World Order*. Boston: Harvard Business School Press.

Petras, J. and Veltmeyer, H. (2001). *Globalization Unmasked*. London: Fernwood Publishing & Zed Books.

Piore, M. and Sabel, C. (1984). *The Second Industrial Divide: Possibilities for Prosperity*. New York: Basic Books.

Prechel, H. (2002). 'The Labor Process and the Transformation of Corporate Control in the Global Economy', in B. Berberoglu (ed.), *Labor and Capital in the Age of Globalization: The Labor Process and the Changing Nature of Work in the Global Economy*. New York: Rowman & Littlefield.

Royle, R. (2002). 'Multinational Corporations, Employers' Associations and Trade Union Exclusion Strategies in the German Fast-food Industry', *Employee Relations*, 24(4): 437–60.

Royal, C. and Althauser, R. (2003). 'The Labor Markets of Knowledge Workers: Investment Bankers. Careers in the Wake of Corporate Restructuring', *Work and Occupations*, 30(2): 214–233.

Rubery, J. and Grimshaw, D. (2003). *The Organization of Employment: An International Perspective*. London: Palgrave Macmillan.

Ruigrok, W. and van Tulder, R. (1995). *The Logic of International Restructuring*. London: Routledge.

Singh, A., and Weisse, B. (2003). 'Corporate Governance, Competition, the New International Financial Architecture and Large Corporations in Emerging Markets', *Management of Capital Flows: Comparative Experiences and Implications for Africa*. New York: United Nations.

Smith, C, and Meiskins, P. (1995). 'System, Society and Dominance Effects in Cross-National Analysis', *Work, Employment and Society*, 9(2): 241–67.

Standing, G. (1999). *Global Labour Flexibility: Seeking Distributive Justice*. London: Macmillan.

Stiglitz, J. E. (2002). *Globalization and its Discontents*. New York: W. W. Norton & Company.

Stiglitz, J.E. (2003). *The Roaring Nineties: A New History of the World's Most Prosperous Decade*. New York: W.W. Norton.

Taplin, I. M. and Winterton, J. (2002). 'Responses to Globalized Production: Restructuring and Work Reorganization in the Clothing Industry of High-wage Countries', in Y. A. Debrah and I. G. Smith (eds.), *Globalization, Employment and the Workplace*. London: Routledge.

UNCTAD (United Nations Conference on Trade and Development) (1999). *Foreign Direct Investment and the Challenge of Development*. New York: United Nations.

UNCTAD (United National Conference on Trade and Development) (2001). *World Investment Report 2001 Promoting Linkages*. New York: United Nations.

UNCTAD (United National Conference on Trade and Development) (2002). 'Are Transnationals Bigger than Countries?', *TAD/INF/PR/47*, August 12. Available at www.unctad.org

United Nations (2001). *World Economic and Social Survey 2001*. New York: United Nations.

Waddock, S. (2002). *Leading Corporate Citizens: Vision, Values, Value Added*. Boston: McGraw Hill.

Webster, E. and Omar, R. (2003). 'Work Restructuring in Post-Apartheid South Africa', *Work and Occupations*, 30(2): 194–213.

Whitley, R. (1999). *Divergent Capitalisms: The Social Structuring and Change of Business Systems*. Oxford: Oxford University Press.

Wilkinson, B., Gamble, J., Humphrey, J., Morris, J., and Anthony, D. (2001). 'The New International Division of Labour in Asian Electronics: Work Organization and Human Resources in Japan and Malaysia', *Journal of Management Studies*, 38(5): 675–95.

World Bank (2000). *World Development Indicators 2000*. Washington, DC: World Bank.

15

Identity and Work

Robin Leidner[1]

Theoretical interest in the nature of identity has boomed in both the social sciences and the humanities.[2] However, relatively few contemporary theorists have put work at the center of their analyses of identity in late or post modernity. Some argue that other dimensions of life, such as consumption, have displaced work as a crucial arena for identity construction. Other theorists have simply focused analytical attention elsewhere. For example, much recent theorizing on collective identities has emphasized race, nationality, gender, or sexuality rather than occupation or class, while theories of subjectivity that focus on the exercise of power through diffuse discursive processes tend not to give workplace relations special priority. Nonetheless, work remains an important basis of identity. It can be an arena for self-development, a source of social ties, a determinant of status, and a shaper of consciousness. For all these reasons, people's relation to work contributes to their sense of self and the sense that others have of them.

In an oft-quoted passage of his 1951 essay 'Work and Self', Everett Hughes asserted that 'a man's work is one of the things by which he is judged, and certainly one of the more significant things by which he judges himself'. How he makes a living, Hughes ([1951*a*]: 1984 338–9) goes on, 'is one of the more important parts of his social identity, of his self; indeed of his fate in the one life he has to live'. Hughes's insistence that sociologists attend to the significance of work to identity remains relevant, but many aspects of his formulation require reconsideration.

[1] I am grateful to Sam Kaplan, Silke Roth, and the editors of this book for their advice and assistance.

[2] For overviews and guides to the literature, see Hogg et al. (1995), Elliott (2001), Callero (2003), May and Cooper (1995), Cerulo (1997), and Howard (2000).

Perhaps most obviously, the ambiguous use of 'man' begs the questions of how gender affects the salience of work to identity and of how specific work identities can come to be gendered. Moreover, while theorizing about identity has been flourishing, many contemporary theorists of identity have little to say about work or explicitly call its centrality to identity into question. If, even for men, the significance of work to identity is more variable than Hughes assumed, that variability needs to be accounted for, both in terms of the conditions of work and of available alternative bases of identity. In particular, sociologists must attend to social changes that affect the possibility or desirability of basing one's identity in work.

A variety of interrelated trends and structural changes have reshaped the world of work since Hughes wrote. Some of these involve shifts in the composition of the labor force. Women have entered paid labor in unprecedented numbers; as increasingly mobile capital relocates production, new populations become wage laborers; large numbers of people travel great distances in search of work. In many nations whole sectors of the economy are staffed by immigrants, while workers around the globe compete for jobs more directly than ever before. How the meaning of work for identity varies among differently situated workers requires empirical investigation, as do the effects of these changes on patterns of collective identification.

Other major trends affecting the relation of work to identity concern what kinds of work people do. In the most advanced economies, the decline in manufacturing jobs and rise in service jobs continue apace, and service workers often face different kinds of challenges to the self than do manufacturing workers. Rapid technological change creates new kinds of work and makes others obsolete, destabilizing work identities and affecting the possibilities for maintaining other anchors of identity, such as community and family. Within organizations, changing managerial strategies reconfigure tasks and responsibilities. Consequently, management may seek to shape workers' subjectivities to suit shifting economic conditions and business plans.

In addition, processes of economic restructuring have brought about major changes in how work is organized. Employers increasingly seek to hire exactly the kind and amount of labor they need at a given moment. Rather than seeking to bind workers to the organization, many employers create temporary jobs, hire consultants, subcontract work, and otherwise limit their obligations to workers. If, for many people, work is indeed 'one of the most important parts' of individual identity, as Hughes argued, increasingly fluid relations of work pose significant challenges to identity.

In recent years, then, the division of labor, structures of work, and employment relations have all been undergoing rapid change, necessarily affecting the possibilities for constructing identity through work. As structural changes alter the place of work in many people's lives, employers, government officials, mass media, and other sources of guidance and instruction proffer or impose new understandings of how people should orient themselves to work. These developments prompt reconsideration of familiar approaches to understanding work and identity.

The word 'identity' encompasses a somewhat paradoxical combination of meanings. One primary set of meanings focuses on individuality, the life history, and set of social relations that constitute the person. Another set of meanings concerns collectivity, patterns of shared identification. The term 'identity politics' exemplifies this usage. Race and ethnicity, nationality, gender, sexuality, and class are the most frequently referenced bases of identity, singly and in combination. While emphases differ, each set of meanings can apply both to self-conception and to how one is regarded and treated by others. Virtually all sociologists regard the sense of self as socially structured, so personal identity and social identity are inevitably intertwined, but theoretical traditions vary in the degree to which they emphasize individual and collective identities.

The thinkers whose work formed the foundations of sociological theory considered the nature of the relationship between work and identity key to understanding social solidarity, power, and historical change. Since the era of Marx, Durkheim, and Weber, sociologists have debated how social and economic transformations have altered the links between work and identity or undermined their significance. This essay outlines both the changing ways that sociologists have approached this subject and some of the historical transformations that have inspired theoretical innovation. It begins with an overview of principal theoretical approaches, tracing shifting claims about why—or whether—work is central to understanding identity. The chapter proceeds by considering workers' experiences and understandings in relation to various levels of social organization, starting with the significance of work to a person's moral standing. This section highlights the changing relevance of gender to cultural judgments about work and character. The next section takes up the implications for identity of doing a particular kind of work, the focus of much research on occupational cultures and on social interaction. Occupations have declined in importance as bases for identity, however, as work has increasingly been situated within organizations. Following Marx and Weber, sociologists have emphasized how organizations construct and manipulate workers' identities, drawing on labor process theory and poststructuralism to analyze the ways employers use their power to constrain and dominate identity formation. Yet work organizations are embedded in a changing social and economic landscape that has eroded the possibilities for basing identity on long-term employment relations. The final section of this essay examines the challenge which contemporary developments in the organization of work pose for sociologists concerned with the opportunities and obstacles workers face in making and sustaining an identity.

1. Theorizing Work and Identity

Many contemporary analyses of work rely on a comparison, implied or explicit, with forms of work, particularly craft work and professions, that traditionally provided stable, lifelong identities, strong communities, and satisfying meanings. In these forms of work (especially in idealized, nostalgic images of them) the occupational group has exclusive mastery of a set of skills and knowledge, full membership requires an extended period of training and socialization, individual practitioners exercise substantial autonomy, and occupation shapes many aspects of workers' social lives.

Durkheim ([1893] 1984: 338–9), who considered strong occupational communities central to social solidarity, saw specialization based on the division of labor as an inevitable consequence of social density and therefore did not believe it could be reversed. But precisely because specialization makes interdependence obvious, Durkheim looked to the division of labor to provide social cohesion as societies become more differentiated and individualistic. Generations of sociologists interested in work have taken up his concern with whether and how occupational groups could generate and sustain a shared morality and with the kinds of social relations that provide individuals with a sense of meaning.

However, the major trends of the nineteenth and twentieth centuries brought work increasingly under the control of organizations rather than occupational and professional groups. Marx and Engels's work on the social relations of capitalism and Weber's on rationalization, particularly bureaucratization, help account for the historical processes that undermined these ways of organizing work and the forms of work-based identity associated with them.

Marx and Engels identified work as the primary arena in which people become who they are. Ideally it could be the sphere in which they develop their full capacities and become most fully human. Marx ([1932] 1978:

160) envisioned a communist society in which, unlimited by enforced specialization, one could 'do one thing today and another tomorrow, to hunt in the morning, fish in the afternoon, rear cattle in the evening, criticise after dinner... without ever becoming hunter, fisherman, shepherd or critic'. Under capitalism, however, exploitive relations of production and the intensive division of labor alienate people from their work and its products, drain work of meaning, and stunt proletarians forced to submit to industrial discipline. But the logic of capitalism that drives workers to wage labor and deprives them of control over work also erodes differences among them, thus clarifying that their true interests are opposed to those of capitalists. Since class defines one's position in the central conflict shaping historical change, work-based identity—class consciousness—is of primary importance even as work itself is deprived of meaning.

Much of Weber's writing concerns the circumstances under which work can be personally meaningful and the degree to which group identities and conflicts center on economic position. He did not share Marx's belief in the inherent priority of work as a potential source of meaning and self-development, but he showed how religious beliefs could imbue work with deep meaning. He also revealed, however, how the development of capitalism tended to deprive work of meaning, making it an 'iron cage' (Weber [1904–5] 1958: 181). Weber acknowledged that class is a crucial basis for collective identification and struggles over power, but his recognition of the importance of status and of the role of the state broadened the range of concerns that could be brought to the study of work and work-based identity. Weber's analysis of forms of authority and of the steady progress of rationalization emphasized the distinctive significance of bureaucratic organization for identity. Rationalized organizations differentiate the work role (the office) from other bases of identity and they structure work so that formal rules minimize individual judgment in favor of ends determined by hierarchical superiors (Weber [1922] 1979).

While Marxian and Weberian theory highlight how the organization of work was transformed in ways that separated workers' activity from their own intentions and goals, the American microsociological tradition shows how people actively construct meaning and identity at work. Symbolic interactionism, which developed from the theoretical approach of Mead (1934) and other pragmatists, and Goffmanian analysis, which drew as well on Durkheim's work on ritual, have considerably enriched the study of work, notably by examining the processes through which identity is created and presented.[3] Sociologists in these traditions often analyze patterns of interaction and self-presentation as integral to struggles for status and autonomy by individuals or occupational groups.

Ethnographic investigations of particular occupations form the main body of work in this tradition, exemplified by the Chicago School of research on work initiated by Everett Hughes in the late 1930s. Inquiry centers on the management of self-presentation and of relations with others, on meanings of work, and on symbols of membership and status. This approach addresses issues of power and inequality primarily by exploring individual and collective struggles for status, dignity, and autonomy, giving relatively little attention to class identification or macrolevel economic structures as determinants of work-based identities.

During the 1950s and 1960s, other sociologists questioned the degree to which identity was based on work. The answer, broadly speaking, was 'not much'. Dubin's (1956) attempt to measure the 'central life interest' of US industrial workers; the influential Affluent Worker Project's investigation of the class identification of well-paid factory workers in an English community (Goldthorpe 1968, 1969); and Mills's (1951) assessment of the meaning of work for middle-class Americans all led to the same conclusion: workers' approach to their jobs was generally instrumental. Despite some variation in their interpretations, these writers held that changes in the conditions of work meant that for most people, work is 'a sacrifice of time, necessary to building a life outside of it' (Mills 1951: 228), a possible source of extrinsic rewards—income, status, or power—but not of intrinsic meaning, which is unavailable to people not in control of their own work.

More recent assessments of the centrality of work to identity generally focus less on changes in the world of work than on broader changes in the organization of society, especially modes of exercizing power, and on associated cultural shifts. Several important contemporary theorists argue that given the breakdown of taken-for-granted life patterns and of the cohesive communities that enforced them, people must choose who to be. Identity becomes a project, something people are responsible for working on (Rose 1990; Giddens 1991; Bauman 2001; Beck and Beck-Gernsheim 2002). This line of argument generally minimizes the significance of work as an arena of self-construction and expression, and much

[3] A second, more structural approach to symbolic interactionism conceptualizes individual identity in terms of relationships organized by social roles. From this perspective, known as 'identity theory', the relevance of work to identity would depend on the relative number, importance, and salience of relations with others based on work role, as compared with relations based on other role identities (Hogg et al. 1995; Howard 2000).

contemporary theory claims explicitly that consumption has replaced production as the sphere in which people define their identities (Baudrillard [1970] 1998; Bauman 1998; Smart 2003; Zukin and Maguire 2004).

However, the increase in choice about who one is going to be generates insecurity, making people susceptible to the effects of what Foucault calls 'technologies of power' that provide instructions for working on the self and pressures to do so. Mass media, professional discourses, self-improvement programs, and capitalist enterprise encourage self-expression, normalize self-discipline, and contribute to self-consciousness about identity. Products and services available for purchase appear to provide the means for realizing one's individuality and exercising choice.

These arguments notwithstanding, work still structures the daily lives of most people and significantly shapes their identities. While it is true that many people devote themselves to self-fashioning through therapeutic scrutiny, consumer choices, voluntaristic relationships, and work on the body, the social and economic resources obtained from work constrain their access to and interest in the sorts of cultural practices and discourses said to shape identity in late or post-modernity. Furthermore, those with the greatest economic and educational resources, who presumably are most able to determine the shape of their lives, often exercise choice by investing heavily in a work-based identity, as the cultural concern about 'workaholism' reveals. For most women, the decline in traditional limitations has meant a dramatic increase in the importance of paid work for self-identity, not a decline, and while the choice of occupations has expanded for many women, the option of staying out of the paid labour force has become less available. And some social critics have asserted that more people have turned to work for recognition, meaning, and a sense of belonging as families have become more fragile and stressful and communal ties have weakened (Hochschild 1983; Hochschild 1997; Philipson 2002).

Moreoever, extensive research on work and personality has demonstrated that work can shape identity in crucial ways whether or not workers regard it as a central or meaningful part of their lives (summarized in Kohn 1990). Both longitudinal studies and cross-sectional studies in several countries find that conditions of work have substantial effects on adults' 'values, self-conceptions, orientations to social reality, and cognitive functioning' and that control over work is particularly significant. The most important of the measured features of work are the 'structural imperatives of the job . . . that determine how much opportunity, even necessity, the worker has for exercising occupational self-direction', factors such as closeness of supervision, degree of routinization, and substantive complexity (Kohn 1990: 40–2).

Furthermore, theorizing about identity as a project intersects with the sociology of work in several ways. First, much self-discipline and cultivation are oriented to presenting oneself as a desirable commodity on the job market (Entwistle 2000, cited in Zukin and Maguire 2004; Wellington and Bryson 2001). That market includes many kinds of work that require projecting a particular image and enacting a particular kind of personality (see Mills 1951 on 'The Personality Market'). Biggart (1983), in an analysis of trends in best-selling self-help manuals, links changes in the job market and other economic conditions to changing beliefs about the kinds of personal traits that contribute to success.

Second, the notion of career guides many decisions about how to organize one's life and shape one's identity, particularly for middle-class people. Beginning in childhood, people learn to think of their activities in terms of their relevance to career success: how will this activity look on a university application? What sorts of experiences will provide skills, information, or contacts that could prove useful? What modes of self-presentation create a desirable image and what kinds of relationships will prove helpful (see Grey 1994; Lareau 2003)?

Third, it is important to remember that the various cultural discourses, disciplinary practices, and consumer choices said to shape identity do so through the work of various kinds of professionals, bureaucrats, marketers, and practitioners. The work they do which shapes others' identities is itself subject to study.

Finally, the roles of worker and consumer are not necessarily distinct. Korczynski et al. (2000) demonstrate that customer service representatives are trained to call on their own experiences as consumers to motivate them to provide good service. Others contend that the model of the 'enterprising subject' who takes initiative and accepts responsibility for constructing his/her own identity applies not only to consumers but also, at least in managerial discourse, to workers, who are urged to approach work as one more arena for self-development, self-expression, and identity construction (Du Gay 1996: 80).[4]

Though contemporary theories of identity have de-emphasized work, some of their ideas and premises have proved useful for analyzing the significance of work in people's lives. For instance, appreciation of

[4] Korczynski et al. (2000) and May and Cooper (1995) question the actual prevalence of such an orientation to work and of management practices guided by this ideology.

the importance of gender, race, ethnicity, and sexuality as salient bases of identity and political mobilization has generated research and theorizing that call attention to the two-way flow of influence between work and identity: not only are workers' identities shaped by the work they do, but workers' (or intended workers') identities affect the design of jobs, workplace relations, and the exercise of power at work. Relatively few contemporary researchers assume that class consciousness can be understood as independent of these other bases of identity and inequality. Poststructuralist theory emphasizing the fluidity, multiplicity, and incoherence of identity and the discursive construction of subject positions has inspired new kinds of readings of workers' subjectivities. The boundary between the sociology of work and the sociology of culture has been blurred as researchers pursue shared interests in identity.

How work relates to identity remains a fascinating question for sociological investigation and theorizing. Several important theorists foresee a dramatic change in that relation, arguing that societies will have to develop modes of identity, morality, social integration, and citizenship that are not based on paid work (Rifkin [1995] 2004; Gorz 1999; Beck 2000). Given the multiple levels at which work affects identity, the stakes of such a transformation are high.

2. Work, Moral Worth, and Identity

Seventeenth-century Puritans were not alone in treating work as a measure of individual worth (Weber [1904–5] 1958). Whether or not one works for a living remains a key factor in moral assessment in many cultures and therefore an important element of self-identity. In the USA, for example, national ideology links life outcomes firmly to individual effort and treats work as a measure of self-reliance, responsibility, pride, and social contribution. Mainstream American culture treats willingness to work as a basic marker of adult status and worthy citizenship. Governmental and media discourses that brand those who won't accept available work as lazy and parasitical bolster this moral understanding of work. While some advice does warn that work should not crowd out other moral obligations, such as those to family or religion, for the most part religious and family obligations do not contradict the moral necessity of work. Rather, accepting the obligations of work may be an ideological or practical necessity for meeting religious or familial obligation.

Alternative discourses dispute the moral centrality of work, particularly when the work available can be regarded as exploitative, demeaning, or meaningless. Yet ethnographic evidence suggests that mainstream work ideology shapes the self-conceptions even of those most likely to be regarded as unwilling to work or as disdaining honest work in favor of criminal activity. Edin and Lein (1997) report that the poor women in their sample preferred working to receiving public welfare, though some could not afford to accept low-wage work because the added expenses of employment left them worse off. Jobless people sometimes feel that the only honest work available to them would be more damaging to the self than not working (Snow and Anderson 1987), but Edin and Nelson (2001: 386) found that poor men who could earn money through irregular or illegal work often aspired to honest, steady work, not only for its practical benefits but also because they saw it as providing respectability and a sense of full participation in society, and Liebow (1967) discovered that men on the far margins of the workforce, however much they justified the avoidance of work, suffered a loss of self-respect as a result.

Exceptions to the rule obliging adults to work vary over time and are subject to disagreement, but they typically include the elderly, people with disabilities, and those receiving education or training. Yet some people past normative retirement age or with disabilities have fought for the right to work because they are eager to be treated as full members of society rather than as pitiable dependents (Engel and Munger 2003).

Gender complicates the story. The question of whether women are obliged to work does not arise, except for women of the most affluent classes, in times and places where procuring and preparing food, producing and maintaining clothing, gathering fuel and water, and other life-sustaining tasks are heavily labor-intensive. However, when the burdens of household production and reproduction are lessened—by infrastructural development, institutional differentiation, commodification of goods and services, or, for the privileged, simply access to servants—the status of unpaid household responsibilities as work becomes more ambiguous. Much that women do at home seems unlike work because it is no longer physically onerous or because it is essentially nurturant, sociable, aesthetic, or organizational and assumed to be a natural expression of femininity, requiring no effort.

Functionalist sociologists classified women's role in families (and hence in society) as 'expressive' rather than 'instrumental' (Parsons and Bales 1955). However, cooking, cleaning, laundering, and childrearing remain time-consuming responsibilities, to which have been added the challenges of obtaining and coordinating the goods and services available on the market or from public institutions. Marxist feminists took the lead in analyzing such unpaid domestic labor as part of the broader political economy (Hartmann 1981; Sargent 1981). Other scholars have applied the term 'work' to the less tangible effort required to create and sustain families, homes, and emotionally healthy adults and children (Daniels 1987; Hochschild 1989; DeVault 1991). Much research has demonstrated that women's relation to domestic labor varies greatly by class, frequently structured by distinctions based on race, nationality, citizenship, or rural/urban origins (e.g. Glenn 2002).

As the proportion of women, including mothers, who work for pay has risen dramatically, the strain of doing domestic work as well has become apparent, since the structures of most jobs, careers, and workplaces reflect the assumption that someone other than the worker attends to these matters (Acker 1990). The rise in women's paid employment has not been matched by a proportional rise in men's domestic work, in part because of how closely much of this work is linked to gender identity. Cultural definitions of such effort as the expression of maternal love, wifely affection, womanly sensibility, or individual personality mean that many women's self-regard rests on handling these responsibilities well, and even those who are not so invested are subject to others' judgments about their care of home and family in ways that men are not. Many men, in contrast, regard doing such work as inconsistent with masculinity and feel entitled to have it done for them and to their liking (Berk 1985; Hochschild 1989; DeVault 1991).

Caring for home and family, whether understood as work or as an alternate form of social contribution, once unquestionably exempted women from a moral obligation to work for pay unless their earnings were essential to support their families. Its current status is much less clear. Certainly some women do devote themselves to domestic work full-time for at least part of their lives, but rather than being a taken-for-granted life pattern, being a housewife is increasingly viewed as a choice or even a luxury (Gerson 2002). In the USA, changes in welfare policy mean that the choice is no longer state-supported for poor mothers. Women therefore frequently face competing imperatives. They are held responsible for adequately performing domestic work, especially mothering, even while holding a paying job which makes achieving that standard extremely difficult (Edin and Lein 1997; Garey 1999; Kurz 2002).

Many women consider holding a paying job or doing a specific kind of work central to their identities. However, not being able to earn a living does not necessarily threaten their identities as women, and working for pay sometimes contradicts rather than enhances the identities of 'good wife' and 'good mother'. In contrast, paid work is not only consistent with masculinity and with the identities of 'good husband' and 'good father', it is widely regarded as essential to them (Gerson 1993; Townsend 2002). Men who are unwilling to work to support their families face moral censure and sometimes legal sanctions. Those who are unable to do so often struggle with self-condemnation as well as with unsympathetic social judgments. When only insecure, poorly paid jobs or none at all are available to men, judgments of individuals may be less severe, but men still face increased risk for depression, alcoholism, and drug abuse, and community problems escalate. Social scientists diagnose these outcomes not just as general effects of poverty, but also as crises of masculinity (Wilson 1987, 1996; see especially McDowell 2003). Much literature on social problems suggests that when men are unable to validate their masculinity through work, at least some seek to gain money and status through illegal means or to demonstrate their autonomy, authority, and efficacy through violence ranging from domestic abuse to terrorism.

Many men now face more pressure to participate in 'second shift' work at home than previous generations did and they do not necessarily perceive it as undermining masculinity, though few see full-time unpaid work as providing an adequate basis for masculine identity. For most, 'providing' remains the sine qua non of adequate fatherhood and of adult masculinity, and limited involvement in family life does not challenge definitions of masculinity as it does femininity (Wajcman and Martin 2002).

Regular employment not only provides important confirmation of moral worth, but also creates and sustains identity for both men and women in other ways. Work organizes daily life, immerses workers in networks of relationships, and provides the means to pay for things significant to self-definition. But whether work enhances or undermines self-respect, status, and dignity depends on the specifics of the work, its social organization, and the actions and interpretation of the workers themselves (see Hodson 2001).

3. Occupation and Identity

The particular kind of work people do is frequently central both to their self-identity and to the identity others ascribe to them. The sociology of occupations and professions has been especially attentive to these issues in studies of occupational cultures, patterns of interaction, and struggles over status and autonomy.

Certainly some elements of identity can derive from the experience of work itself, the satisfactions of feeling oneself competent to accomplish one's intentions, overcome difficulties, create something—or, conversely, the frustrations of feeling oneself incompetent to do these things or of not being allowed to do them. Some kinds of work can be experienced as deeply expressive of identity, as 'callings' or 'labors of love' (Freidson 1990; Menger 1999), especially when there are cultural supports for such interpretations (as there are for artists, clergy, and health care workers, for example). In many cases, work can be seen to provide evidence of personal qualities, such as courage for fire fighters, rationality for engineers, and empathy for psychotherapists. When the worker views such qualities positively, work can be central to identity. On the other hand, those doing work that conveys discreditable connotations may do their best to distance their identities from their work roles or to provide counter interpretations (Goffman 1961*c*; Hughes [1951*a*] 1984; Rollins 1985). Often the capacity to accomplish particular kinds of work becomes embodied over time, making knowledge and skill indistinguishable and deepening the connection between work and self (Zuboff 1988; Attewell 1990).

The significance of particular kinds of work for identity frequently comes not only from the experience of doing the work but also from participation in an occupational culture. Such cultures develop around the sets of tasks and forms of knowledge within the purview of given groups of workers. Some occupational cultures have developed over centuries; new ones come into being as new kinds of expertise and areas of work develop; all are subject to change or even extinction based on technological and organizational innovations and shifting configurations of power. Participation in an occupational culture frequently involves an explicit reframing of self-identity as well as development of a new collective identification.

Processes of initiation into an occupation vary in their intensity, length, and form, but in well-defined occupations they are explicitly intended to transform the identity of the initiate. Novices gain skills and a body of practical and, sometimes, abstract knowledge. When socialization is successful they also learn and internalize the occupation's ideology, ethos, traditions, and norms, including criteria for judgment, craft pride, and rules for interacting among themselves and with various others. Through formal education, apprenticeships, on-the-job interactions, stories, tests, teasing, and other means, newcomers learn from more experienced members of the occupation what it means to join them. In the process, initiates are expected to take on the ways of thinking and behaving characteristic of the occupation or profession, to learn to distinguish themselves from outgroup members, and to feel loyalty to each other and to the values of the group. Rituals along the way may mark the newcomers' progress, or demonstrate how far they have to go, culminating in induction ceremonies, ranging from licensing to violent hazing, which may confer such symbols of full membership as titles and rights to wear particular clothing (Freidson 1970; Haas and Shaffir 1982; Trice 1993).

Like many cultural and functional analyses, accounts of socialization to occupational cultures run the risk of overstating the unity of cultures and their positive aspects. Scholars have demonstrated that socialization can fail, that while many aspects of occupational culture serve useful functions for the group and for society they may well have dysfunctional aspects (such as creating rigidities and generating self-serving ideologies and behavior) and that occupational values may be internally inconsistent as well as inconsistent with other social values important to the public good.

One aspect of occupational cultures that has received substantial attention from scholars is their tendency to reproduce patterns of exclusion. Sexism, racism, and ethnocentrism flourish in many occupations, especially those with relatively strong cultures in which collective identities as members of the occupation overlap with collective identities based on gender, race, and ethnicity (e.g. Hartmann 1976). Explicitly discriminatory policies were common before they were legally challenged, and informal but intentional patterns of discrimination frequently remain, such as refusal to 'show the ropes' to outgroup members, outright harassment, and social isolation. In addition to deliberate practices, occupational cultures may generate exclusion by maintaining practices, values, and norms that make it less likely that outsiders will feel welcome, pass informal tests of acceptability, or identify strongly with the occupation. Such ethnocentrism may be expressed through practices as trivial as choice of music in the workplace and as serious as firefighters' differentially valuing the safety of different neighborhoods (Chetkovich 1997). Similarly, occupational cultures are frequently highly gendered, making it difficult for those in the minority to meld gender identity with occupational identity, as studies of occupations ranging from policing to litigation have demonstrated (Martin 1980; Pierce 1995). The evidence indicates that men value and defend the gendered identity of male-dominated occupations far more intensely than women do female-dominated ones, suggesting that for many men work that expresses masculinity is a significant basis for gender identity (Williams 1989, 1995).

Studies of the development of occupational identity in the microsociological tradition focus less on culture and more on the processes by which individuals' identities are transformed. For instance, studies of medical training provide striking examples of how painful experiences with superiors and with patients and their families challenge novices to reshape their identities to cope with accepting responsibility for routinely handling emotionally difficult matters effectively (Haas and Shaffir 1984; Bosk [1979] 2003).

Ethnographic investigations of particular occupations form the main body of work in this tradition, but Hughes strongly encouraged his students and colleagues to search out parallel processes across the full range of types of work, 'the humble and the proud', even as they elaborated the distinctive features of particular forms of work (Hughes [1951*a*] 1984, [1951*b*] 1984, [1952] 1984). A strength of this comparative approach was its determination to look beyond the ideological claims used to justify occupational practices, especially those in the professions, often with the effect of deflating the pretensions of the proud by showing the similarity between their concerns and intentions and those of the humble. The aim of exploring how similar themes play out in different settings was not to minimize the importance of difference and inequality, but to identify and explain patterns of variation.

The efforts of workers to construct, present, and defend a favorable identity in their own eyes and in the eyes of others animate what Hughes called 'the social drama of work'(Hughes [1951] 1984*a*). The stakes of that drama—workers' dignity and self-regard—are matters people in every line of work consider worth struggling over. They do so, for example, by trying to exercise control over how much effort they will expend, to contest others' right or capacity to judge the quality of their work, to get someone else to handle whatever is considered dirty work, and to enhance the prestige of their occupations or contest the relevance of stigmatized work to their identities (Hughes [1951*a*] 1984, [1959] 1984). Goffman elaborated the focus on drama by using the language of theater to describe how people stage self-presentations and respond to others' performances. His dramaturgical approach illuminates the efforts of workers to shape the impressions others hold of them in ways that bolster their own importance and counter demeaning interpretations of what their work implies about their identities. Goffman's distinction between frontstage and backstage behavior, for example, provides a conceptual lens for examining how all kinds of workers try to represent themselves and their occupations creditably before relevant audiences despite wide variation in the resources they have available for impression management (Goffman 1959).

The theoretical and methodological underpinnings of this ethnographic approach provide several key advantages for analyzing work and identity. First, the conceptualization of identity as rooted in interaction and as an object of ongoing contestation undermines the assumptions that the self has a stable core, unitary and consistent over time. Rather, it problematizes identity, taking for granted that selves are social constructions and that identities are multiple, situational, fluid, and discursive, just as poststructuralists assert. Sociologists working in this vein do assume that people generally act to preserve and enhance their self-regard, but without taking for granted that they aim for any particular balance of individuation and conformity, prestige and social contribution, or other bases of evaluation. The focus on how people infuse their work with meaning allows for investigation of the effects of various ideological influences on their subjectivity without assuming the priority of any given discourse.

Second, the focus on social interaction alerts sociologists of work to pay attention to the full range of people with whom workers engage. Rather than assuming that work-based identity is necessarily constructed primarily in relation to employers, researchers analyze workers' interactions with various kinds of co-workers, with customers and clients, with occupational groups that have related mandates, and with the general public, as well as with workplace superiors, noting patterns of variation in which sets of interactants are most salient. Struggles over control and dignity, efforts to resist and outwit, and bonds of solidarity and support can be found within all of these relations and are not solely determined by lines of class cleavage.

Third, because they do not start with the assumption that any particular kind of work provides a model for work in general, sociologists in this tradition tend neither to make sweeping generalizations about contemporary work nor to be blinkered by preconceived categorizations of types of work. Rather, they think comparatively, using detailed case studies as a basis for making limited generalizations about processes that operate in occupations with shared features and for specifying sources of variation. A memorable illustration of the usefulness of this habit of mind is Goffman's elaboration of the challenges and strategies common to people in 'the tinkering trades', whether they are psychiatrists or auto mechanics (Goffman 1961*a*).

Fourth, attention to the specifics of interaction, to concerns with status, and to processes of identification makes obvious the ongoing relevance of other bases of identity to occupational identity. Hughes raised these issues in his 1945 discussion of the processes contributing to the marginalization of the 'lady engineer' and the 'Negro physician' (Hughes [1945] 1984). Interactions with co-workers, customers, and others at work will be affected by the gender, class, race, and other social characteristics of the participants. Hochschild's (1983) description of the differential deference passengers accord male and female flight attendants highlights the point. In fact, the status of an occupation, its culture, and the patterns and quality of interactions among members are entwined with the identities of the majority of jobholders, reflecting their socially constructed attributes and reinforcing the dominant employment pattern. At the same time, the association of particular groups with particular jobs shapes the meanings of racialized or ethnic masculinities and femininities (e.g. Kanter 1977; Cockburn 1985; Weston 1990; Glenn 1992; Collinson and Hearn 1996; Anderson 1999). Interactive factors do not wholly explain such patterns, but they are key to understanding workers' experiences, explaining resistance to change, and accounting for many kinds of workplace outcomes.[5]

The combination of these factors has helped ethnographers make significant progress in detailing the characteristic dynamics of important categories of work, including 'interactive service work' (Leidner 1991), domestic service, 'care work,' and unpaid work in households. Work in these overlapping categories typically incorporates or makes distinctive kinds of demands on workers' identities, requires emotion work, and draws on and reinforces constructions of race, gender, and ethnicity (relevant works include Hochschild 1983; DeVault 1991; Diamond 1992; Glenn 1992; Leidner 1993; Wrigley 1995; Himmelweit 1999; Steinberg and Figart 1999; Hondagneu-Sotelo 2001; Cancian et al. 2002). In short, it engages workers' selves in complex ways that cannot by captured by overly generalized or one-sidedly structural theoretical perspectives.

The relative weaknesses of sociological approaches to work and identity that focus on occupational cultures and workplace interaction concern their capacity to analyze large-scale structures and processes of historical

[5] Inequality of work opportunities based on considerations of gender, race, ethnicity, or nationality paradoxically protects the self-identities of those who bear the brunt of such inequality in one respect: they are less susceptible to the self-blame that meritocratic ideology breeds in those who do not achieve career success (Sennett and Cobb 1972; contrast Rollins 1985; Lamont 2000).

change satisfactorily. Those active in this tradition are not oblivious or indifferent to these concerns. Hughes recognized the importance of analyzing how occupations are linked into systems, of situating contemporary studies within the context of broad historical trends, and of paying attention to processes of change in the ways occupations come into being, in their degree of independence from business enterprises and state institutions, and in the apportionment of responsibilities, tasks, and status among related occupations. But macrosociological forces are not the focus in this tradition.

4. Work, Identity, and Organizations

With the development of organizational forms that undercut the power of occupational groups to exercise control over work, fewer workers experience occupation as a stable anchor of identity. While that shift led some sociologists to question the significance of work for identity, others consider the power of organizations to shape workers' identities a crucial mode of domination.

For many people, 'I work for IBM' or 'I'm with the city government' more aptly expresses work identity than does 'I'm a mechanic' or 'I'm an accounts receivable clerk', since everything from material well-being to status to future prospects may depend on the worker's association with a particular employer. Organizations often strenuously promote such identification, hoping to build loyalty and motivate dedicated work by providing benefits, using the language of 'family' or 'team', or otherwise emphasizing the shared interests of members of the organization. Enthusiasm for policies emphasizing such unity and mutuality waxes and wanes in managerial ideology. Early twentieth-century welfare capitalism, mid-century human relations approaches, and late twentieth-century efforts to manage corporate culture each aimed to generate feelings of inclusion and connection.

Strong identification with an organization does not necessarily extinguish oppositional identity (Hareven 1982), but many sociologists have doubted the capacity of employees to sustain identities that are not dominated by organizational efforts to manage their behavior and shape their consciousness. Whyte's *The Organization Man* (1956) described an increasingly conformist culture, crystallizing anxiety about the social costs of the willingness of white-collar workers to relinquish independent judgment. Much subsequent theorizing and research has concerned collective rather than individual identity, with the question of how changing managerial ideologies and practices affect the development of class consciousness an important focus of inquiry.

Labor process theory, originally formulated by Braverman in *Labor and Monopoly Capital* (1974), carries forward Marx's analysis of labor under capitalism by focusing on control over work. Braverman's deskilling thesis held that capital wrested control of production from workers by expropriating their knowledge and skill and building it into systems of production and technology under managerial control. Routinizing work processes made workers' craft knowledge and skill increasingly irrelevant, allowing managers to hire less skilled, relatively interchangeable workers who could neither command high wages nor exercise leverage based on their exclusive expertise. Separating the conception of work from its execution robbed workers of opportunities for exercising judgment, developing mastery, and creating finished products, thus also robbing them of their occupational identities as skilled workers and of their capacity to take pride in work they experienced as an extension of themselves. Routinization simultaneously undermined the traditionally strong collective identity of craft workers, which was built and sustained through apprenticeships, craft-based unions, and cultural traditions.

Subsequent research and theorizing in the labor process tradition explored both the significance of workers' consciousness in determining workplace outcomes and managerial attempts to shape that consciousness. 'Resistance' emerged as a key concept linking workers' self-understandings, management's strategies, and the dialectics of class conflict. Edwards (1979) recast the workplace as 'contested terrain' in which workers struggle to resist managerial control over the labour process, in turn prompting employers to develop different control strategies. Workers' motivation and capacity to resist managerial control depend in part on the strength of workplace cultures that reflect their class, occupational, gender, and ethnic identities. Such cultures can provide space for workers to express values contrary to management's, to share strategies of resistance, and to derive status on their own terms (Halle 1984; Benson 1986; Trice 1993; Strangleman and Roberts 1999), though their effects may be paradoxical (Burawoy 1979; Westwood 1984; Hossfeld 1993).

Though Braverman argued that managerial attempts to manipulate workers' subjective experience of work were mere window-dressing, subsequent research on workplace control has strongly emphasized managerial strategies designed to displace workers' cultures and reshape their consciousness. Such approaches have two main advantages from managers' point of view. First, compared with more overtly coercive control strategies, they generate relatively little resistance even as they extend employers' control to include more aspects of workers' selves. Second, unlike deskilling, they allow employers to draw on workers' intelligence and creativity, an important benefit since most jobs cannot be routinized so thoroughly that no initiative or judgment is necessary (see Friedman 1977).

Edwards (1979) describes bureaucratic control as extending managerial jurisdiction to include workers' values and personalities. Within a system of extensive rules geared to internal labor markets, managers differentially reward workers for disciplined, dedicated work and for conformity to the organization's standards, promoting organizational rather than class identification and loyalty. But many scholars concerned with the transformation of workers' subjectivity stress the contrast rather than the continuity between bureaucratic approaches and newer ones aimed explicitly at managing workplace culture and altering workers' values, attitudes, and self-understandings. Indeed, the latter often accompany the introduction of participatory work structures that partly contravene key precepts of bureaucracy, such as hierarchy and specialization.[6] These methods seek to modify workers' frames of reference so that they don't merely consent to behave in ways that further organizational goals, but go further and commit themselves to the organization's values. Theorists speak of employers' undertaking 'corporate culturism' (Willmott 1993), 'normative control' (Kunda 1992), 'post-Fordist hegemonic control' (Graham 1995), 'cultural cleansing' (Strangleman and Roberts 1999), or 'corporate colonization' (Willmott 1993; Casey 1995). They do so in response to changing competitive conditions that demand organizational flexibility, to the challenges of managing different kinds of work, to fads in management theory, or simply to the ongoing pressure to devise the most effective means of harnessing employees' labor power. Corporate culture campaigns cultivate workers' sense of belonging and reinforce the values said to make the organization distinctively admirable. Typically, the ideology which workers are pressured—or seduced—to embrace centers on every worker striving for excellence and accepting responsibility for the organization's success by displaying flexibility and taking initiative to solve problems (Willmott 1993). In addition to eliciting workers' commitment to organizational values, employers institute intensive forms of

[6] Biggart (1989) describes the highly elaborated cultures of direct sales organizations, whose control systems are based on charismatic rather than bureaucratic authority.

monitoring and surveillance to reshape workers' consciousness. Barker (1993) argues that participative work structures like self-managing teams add peer pressure to other forces of surveillance and persuasion, creating 'concertive control' (see also Chapter 3, this volume).

To analyze these sorts of practices, sociologists increasingly draw on Foucault's work on the creation of self-disciplining subjects, and more generally on poststructuralist theoretical frameworks that emphasize the centrality of discourse to the exercise of power and the construction of subjectivity. Such accounts differ from materialist labor process approaches in their emphasis on issues of meaning and identity in explaining workers' behavior. They differ from the symbolic interactionist tradition in their theoretical underpinnings and their focus on employers' power. One of the most influential approaches, developed by Knights and Willmott (1989), argues that the potency of employers' strategies for shaping workers' subjectivity and engaging their agency derives from the intersection of those strategies with the 'identity work' required in a context of rapid change and proliferating choices (Giddens 1991; Beck et al. 1994). The anxiety people feel about sustaining a sense of autonomy and of continuous selfhood helps explain workers' acceptance of the subject positions made available to them in employer-controlled cultures, but also their determined allegiance to other social structures and practices that support valued aspects of their identities (Knights and Willmott 1989).

Claims about the significance of cultural control of organizations have generated debate about its novelty, prevalence, and efficacy. Critics such as Thompson and Findlay (1999) note that some analysts influenced by the cultural turn in scholarship have been far too ready to leap from analyses of management texts or ethnographies of single firms to claims about a general shift in workplace control strategies, which are said to correspond to broader social changes associated with late modernity or postmodernity (Rose 1990; Casey 1995; Du Gay 1996). In addition to pointing out that the majority of workers have not been subjected to such methods, skeptics have questioned the degree to which 'the gaze has been truly internalized' by workers who have experienced them (Thompson and Ackroyd 1995: 624, commenting on Barker 1993). In line with the focus of labor process theory on worker/management struggles and with Foucauldian concern about disciplinary power, a great deal of debate has centered on how successfully management has colonized workers' subjectivities.

Casey (1995) considers the hegemonic power organizations exercise through cultural control potent enough to create 'designer employees' who suit the organization's requirements. Many sociologists have argued, however, that workers do not unambiguously commit themselves to the values promoted by management (e.g. Thompson and Ackroyd 1995). Some point out that the appropriate standard for judging the effectiveness of efforts to colonize workers' subjectivity is not whether workers resist overtly but whether they adopt management's values and point of view. The empirical record demonstrates the pervasiveness of psychological distancing as a response to organizational cultures designed to create true believers. Workers frequently respond to such normative pressure with mistrust, using irony, cynicism, and guile rather than open contestation to establish an independent stance (Thompson 1990; Kunda 1992; Knights and McCabe 1998; Thompson and Findlay 1999). In a rare comparative study of similar industrial work units that differed on the presence of team-based work initiatives, Vallas (2003) found little evidence to support the view that such measures cause workers to internalize managerial viewpoints. On the contrary, they introduced 'significantly counter-hegemonic effects' that led to open, collective resistance to managerial authority:

> In cognitive terms, the introduction of team systems seems to disrupt or de-naturalize existing authority relations by encouraging workers to adopt an increasingly demanding, intrinsic orientation toward their jobs. Structurally, team systems appear to foster patterns of solidarity and mutual support that enable workers to contest or recast managerial initiatives. Finally, and in more cultural or discursive terms, by introducing the language of participation into the workplace, team systems provide workers with a legitimate rhetorical framework with which to claim decision-making powers they have previously been denied. (Vallas 2003: 120)

Nonetheless, the failure of normative control measures to win workers' full commitment does not mean that they are necessarily ineffective in undermining active opposition in some settings. Kunda (1992) found that while managerial employees of a high tech firm typically used ironic and parodic expressions of company values to signal their autonomy, they complied with those values, in part because the company's toleration of such distancing paradoxically reinforced its message of openness and freedom. More significantly, Kunda argues that the stance employees adopted to signal their psychological independence generated a pervasive cynicism and sense of meaninglessness. Willmott (1993: 538–9) describes the process:

> In the absence of a well-organized, supportive counter-culture, the very process of devaluing corporate ideals tends to produce confusion and emptiness, thereby

making employees enduringly vulnerable to the (precarious) sense of stability and identity provided by a dramaturgical, cynical, instrumental compliance with corporate values.

The application of poststructuralist ideas to organizational control strategies has reoriented the approach to workers' subjectivity that labor process theory stimulated in several ways. First, to some extent it has shifted attention away from collective identity, particularly class consciousness, to individual identity, which it presents as highly problematic. Second, since the pressure to engage in identity work is seen as originating outside the workplace, workers' attachment to identities and practices that reinforce inequality need not be interpreted merely as false consciousness or as compensation for degraded work (Knights and Willmott 1989). The workplace is a significant site of power relations and of identity work, but the drive to sustain a secure and autonomous work identity derives from conditions that extend beyond the workplace. Third, poststructuralist ideas have broadened discussion of workers' subjectivities beyond issues of resistance, contributing to an account of compliance with organizational manipulation of subjectivity that does not represent workers as simply reactive to managerial strategy. Even workers who do not resist the subjectivities promoted by management do exercise agency in the form of identity work (Knights and Willmott 1989). Fourth, poststructuralist ideas challenge the assumption that workers' resistance represents the expression of an authentic humanity struggling for freedom. Rather, they treat individuals' anxiety to establish an autonomous identity as itself a product of immersion in relations of power (Willmott 1993).

British work that develops labor process theory or applies poststructuralist ideas to work and identity has generally been quite removed from the American microinteractionist tradition. Strikingly, the basic assumptions of that approach appear as promising innovations in Thompson and Findlay's recommendation (1999: 176) for opening up investigation into what motivates identity work:

> [O]ur starting point is simply that we can observe that workplace actors as knowledgeable agents draw on *symbolic resources* in their relations of contestation and co-operation ... to assert their own identities or shape others [']within struggles over power and resources, to legitimate their own actions or delegitimate others[']; or as a means of surviving and developing satisfactions from particular conditions of work and employment.... [W]e believe that the notion of symbolic resources can go some way to enabling us to understand the experience of culture change in the workplace. (emphasis in original)

The insights of poststructuralist thoughts do cast the emphasis of symbolic interactionists on individuals' struggle to enhance their status and infuse their work with meaning in quite a different light: compare Hughes's eagerness ([1951*a*] 1984: 342) 'to understand the social and social-psychological arrangements and devices by which men make their work tolerable, or even make it glorious to themselves and others' with Knights and Willmott's reference (1989: 554) to the 'power-induced technologies by which we are captured in our everyday grasping at the straws that confirm our sense of independence and importance'. Yet Hughes's mid-century certainty about the ubiquity of such identity work calls into question the claim that it is induced by social pressures characteristic of late modernity or postmodernity. As Thompson and Findlay suggest above, the emphasis theorists of the subjective experience of work have put on managerial manipulation of people's assumed need to stabilize a precarious identity has drawn attention away from the range of ways that work can be meaningful. The satisfaction some workers take in demonstrating competence, in finding opportunities for self-development, status, and connection, even in providing good service (see Korczynski et al. 2000), all can contribute to their investment of energy and identification in their work, and all can be manipulated by management. Surely workers drew meaning from such aspects of work even when identities were strongly based in traditional communities, and they continue to be relevant aspects of many workers' subjectivity, whether or not management actively incites and exploits them.

The research on organizational manipulation of workers' identities described so far deals largely with how workers' self-understandings and attitudes relate to the control system, not to the work itself. That is, the focus of research has been on workers' willingness to work hard, do their best, and act in the organization's interest, not on their ability to complete tasks satisfactorily. Sociologists who have brought together elements of labor process theory and microinteractionism in studies of 'interactive service work' (Leidner 1991) have pointed to the specific techniques involved in the standardization of human interactions, especially to organizations' assertions of control over many aspects of workers' identities. Hochschild (1983) identified 'emotional labor' as a distinctive element of labor processes intended to produce an emotional response in the people buying (or otherwise subjected to) an organization's services. She showed that when particular kinds of interactions are part of the 'product' being sold or are otherwise integral to accomplishing the work, employers very explicitly assert authority over workers' emotions and related aspects of their presentation of selves. Hochschild's work laid out many issues that have been developed in subsequent research on interactive service work: how workers take on the personae they are required to present on the job; the effects on workers of having to manage their emotions and the emotions of the often recalcitrant targets of their efforts; the forms of resistance available to workers; and the significance of gender to many aspects of the work, including hiring, the content and style of service interactions, the relative power of workers and those receiving services, and workers' reactions to their jobs. Sociologists responding to Hochschild extended the analysis of emotion work to a variety of settings, not all of them involving direct service or routinization, and elaborated the range of possible effects (e.g. Wouters 1989; Pierce 1995; Steinberg and Figart 1999; Sharma and Black 2001; Bolton and Boyd 2003; Williams 2003). Studies of interactive service work identified the many aspects of workers' selves over which employers could claim authority (words, looks, moods, facial expressions, feelings, patterns of thought, self-concepts) and their means of controlling them (scripts, uniforms, regulations about appearance, interactive rules, incentives, surveillance, solicitation of customer evaluation, programs of character transformation) (e.g. Van Maanen and Kunda 1989; Fuller and Smith 1991; Leidner 1993; Macdonald and Sirianni 1996).

Analyses of workers' responses to employers' manipulation of their identities raise complications for labor process and poststructuralist approaches to the subject. The 'identity work' argument concerning workers' vulnerability to the cultural control of organizations seems to take for granted that the identities held out by employers are attractive to workers and would uphold their sense of themselves as autonomous individuals. But not only do most organizational efforts to standardize interactive service work straightforwardly undermine workers' assertion of autonomy or individuality, they also frequently situate workers in interactions in which they must behave or be treated as people they do not want to be. Goffman (1961*b*: 186) described organizations as 'place[s] for generating assumptions about identity', and these assumptions are frequently unflattering or personally objectionable to workers. Employers often offer interpretations and narratives intended to make these aspects of the work more palatable, for example by framing manipulative and pushy behavior as necessary to providing an important service or by arguing that not taking disrespectful treatment personally is a mark of 'professionalism' (Hochschild 1983; Leidner 1993). Moreover, the acceptance by interactive service workers of all or some elements of the identity employers ask them to enact need not be explained either by anxiety about identity generated outside the workplace or by commitment to management's point of view. Interactive service work is distinctive in that the labor process involves nonemployees and is therefore structured by the efforts of workers, managers, and service-recipients to exercise control. In some situations workers acquiesce to or even embrace managerially prescribed modes of self-presentation and interaction because they enhance their capacity to control service interactions or to protect themselves from service-recipients' assertions of power (Leidner 1993).

A somewhat different approach to the identity of service workers draws on theory asserting the centrality of images, signs, and symbols in postmodernity to argue that 'service workers must be increasingly conceptualized as cultural sign vehicles' (Wellington and Bryson 2001: 934). Much research along these lines emphasizes that employers try to hire, shape, and sell particular constructions of gender, especially eroticized femininity, requiring extensive 'body work' or 'aesthetic labour' on the part of employees (Adkins 1995; McDowell 1995; Adkins and Lury 1999; Warhurst et al. 2000).

But not only do organizations that employ service workers take advantage of and shape aspects of gender identity beyond the aesthetic, other kinds of employers also participate in the construction of workers' gender identities. For example, analysts have noted many manufacturers' preference for hiring women workers, especially young women from cultures or in countries perceived as producing female docility. Some manufacturers, in fact, make decisions about where to locate factories based on the availability of such a labor force. But several studies have highlighted the role of employers in creating and sustaining the desired forms of femininity—or at least the appearance thereof—through their hiring practices, control systems, and other policies, which they base on stereotyped notions about gender, race, and culture (Hossfeld 1994; Mohanty 2003). Salzinger (2003) found that employers in the same industry, in the same country intent on hiring docile female workers—garment manufacturers in Mexico—created workforces who enacted femininity in quite different ways within distinctive employer-dominated workplace cultures. Other research has documented the role of organizations in cultivating specific forms of masculinity (Margolis 1979; Leidner 1991; Collinson 1992; Collinson and Hearn 1996).

As the reference to employers' choosing the countries in which to locate their plants indicates, organizations are embedded in a broad context of economic and social dynamics. Trends at this level constrain the role organizations play in constructing work-based identities and shape the cultural narratives and material prospects that define the place of work in individuals' identities.

5. Changing Structures of Employment

The themes that have dominated postmodern and poststructuralist accounts of individual identity—destabilization, discontinuity, fluidity—now characterize the discussion of work as well. 'Constant revolutionizing of production, uninterrupted disturbance of all social conditions, everlasting uncertainty and agitation' are hardly new elements of capitalism (Marx and Engels [1948] 1978: 476), but this dynamism is more evident than ever as businesses, industries, and states face stepped-up pressure for rapid adaptation and transformation. The combination of technological innovation and neoliberal economic policy has generated broad-scale economic restructuring. New technologies make some products, plants, skills, and workers obsolete, and the new opportunities that arise often benefit populations other than the ones that were harmed. The ease with which both capital and production can be shifted around the world has attenuated the capacity of states to regulate capitalism and to ameliorate its effects. Many people find that 'all that is solid melts into air' as economic change disrupts the attachments to place, job, organization, occupation, and career that had supported their identities. They are asked to embrace this new reality.

> Change, on all fronts, personal, social, and institutional, is the mantra of our times; we are reminded—endlessly and relentlessly—that the only constant is change. To survive, we must come to terms with turbulent environments, thrive on rampant chaos, welcome rapidly changing markets, adjust to high degrees of uncertainty, and celebrate seemingly perpetual technological revolutions. (Kunda and Maanen 1999: 65)

Organizations have responded to enhanced competition, quickened product cycles, fast-moving technological change, and general uncertainty with strategies that enhance their flexibility. These strategies, which typically include cutting jobs, finding cheaper labor, and limiting commitment to workers, have significantly altered labor market prospects and working conditions. Managerial, technical, and professional workers have been affected, as well as production, clerical, and service workers who had previously had some expectation of long-term employment. Large corporations have 'downsized' to create 'leaner' organizations with fewer layers of management. When mergers and acquisitions have created duplication of function, they have cut redundant departments. They have closed plants that are insufficiently profitable or when they can move production to places with cheaper labor and less regulation. Businesses now outsource many kinds of work formerly done by employees, everything from janitorial, security, and food services to production, training, and legal work. In addition to contracting work out to other businesses, corporations have altered their relation to many workers they hire directly, using short-term contracts with professionals, creating part-time jobs, relying on temporary workers, and treating workers as 'independent contractors'. These changes all limit organizations' obligations to workers, often eliminating job benefits as well as job security for those they do employ and allowing them to hire only as much labor, with just the desired skills, as they need at any given time. As organizations change shape from fixed bureaucratic pyramids to loose, shifting networks, employees are expected to become more flexible, too. Many are required to learn new skills, to work on project teams that often include temporary workers, to take on new responsibility for outcomes, and to accept that there is no guarantee of ongoing employment.

Corporate cultures intended to produce workers' full commitment to and identification with their employers are hardly suitable means of labour control for organizations that disavow any promise of job security so that they can change the size and make-up of their workforce at any time. Not all organizations have abandoned efforts to shape workers' identities, but rather than trying to integrate them into a unified culture, many minimize the distinction between the organizational environment and the free market, urging workers to be entrepreneurial, independent, open to change, and comfortable taking risks. More and more people are disciplined directly by market forces. Others who do have regular jobs are continually reminded, by the presence of temporary workers, demands for contract concessions, and news of layoffs, that their protection from those forces is precarious. Not only assembly workers but also clerical workers, programmers, customer service representatives, and many others in advanced economies are well aware that companies can hire or contract for less expensive workers in other parts of the world to do their jobs.

Given this changed environment, many sociologists interested in work and identity now focus less on the domination of workers' subjectivity and more on the loss of structures that provide a basis for stable identity. Gorz (1999: 53) writes:

> [T]he central figure of our society—and the 'normal' condition within that society... is becoming... the figure of the insecure worker, who at times 'works' and at times does not 'work', practises many different trades without any of them actually being a trade, has no identifiable profession or, rather, whose profession it is to have no profession, and cannot therefore identify with his/her work....

For this 'central figure', neither organizational attachment nor commitment to an occupation can anchor identity. Are other kinds of work-based identities available? And what are the effects of instability in economic conditions, employment structures, and demand for labor on bases for identity other than paid work? Those who lose out economically have less leeway to define themselves through consumption choices, and they may also find that identities based on family are harder to create or sustain. Those forced or enticed to move to improve their work situation give up community ties that can sustain identity, and many international migrants sacrifice close family ties as well. Whether these structural changes also open up new resources for identity construction and decrease constraints on it is a matter of ongoing debate (see Elliott 2001). On one hand, some observers emphasize the creativity and freedom made possible by structures of work that allow people to design their own careers, change directions, choose where and how much to work rather than being corporate drones. Florida (2002), for example, describes a 'creative class' that regards stability as constraint, preferring loose connections and stimulating change. People who have skills that are in high demand, especially those with few community ties, can indeed benefit from the opportunities that open up in an increasingly individualized labor market. Sennett (1998), however, stresses the costs of the new high-risk world of work even for those who can compete in it successfully. In his view, a work life characterized by short-term jobs, reshuffling project teams, and frequent geographical moves allows for only transient attachments which provide no basis for character or for a coherent life narrative.

Careful empirical research complicates such broad generalizations by showing the varied, often contradictory effects of ongoing structural change on the experiences and identities of workers in different social and geographic locations. For example, consider the fates of managerial and professional workers. Wajcman and Martin (2002: 988), who studied managers in Australian companies representative of the 'new capitalism', found that both men and women used individualistic market narratives in their optimistic accounts of their 'portfolio careers'. Even in this elite group, however, women were much less able than men to integrate commitment to family into their work identities, and therefore less able to tailor a life to suit themselves. Those on the wrong side of the changes wrought by economic restructuring find it much harder to sustain coherent life narratives. Newman (1988) and Smith (2001) describe the personally devastating declines in status, material well-being, and sense of self experienced by formerly successful American professionals and managers. As Newman (1988: 93–4) puts it, 'To be a downwardly mobile executive is first to discover that you are not as good a person as you thought you were and then to end up not sure who or what you are.' The identity disorientation these people suffer differs from that of professionals from nations losing out in the new global economy who migrate to wealthier nations to work in low-status jobs (e.g. Diamond 1992; Hondagneu-Sotelo 2001). The latter may experience less self-blame for their loss of status, but they often suffer isolation, prejudice, and guilt about leaving children and other family members. Managers, professionals, and highly-skilled technical workers have gotten a disproportionate share of attention in the literature on economic transformation, as have footloose individuals able to negotiate their own conditions of work. Smith (2001: 158) provides a useful reminder of the larger picture:

> The majority of workers . . . create the infrastructure that makes it possible for free agents to prosper. . . . Most workers continue to be located in subordinate positions in hierarchies based on unequal power and to have their activities, efforts, and outcomes measured, evaluated, and disciplined.

Her case studies of three US workplaces that have implemented employment practices that enhance organizational flexibility and promote worker flexibility, and of a job search club for unemployed professionals, reveal a complex reality in which workers perceive opportunity as well as heightened risk. Their willingness to accept new demands on them at work and to commit to the kind of personal transformation they are told is necessary to succeed in the new economy varies but is generally high, sometimes reflecting desperation, sometimes reflecting manipulation by employers, but sometimes sustained by experiences of enhanced personal efficacy. Workers who did not previously have access to stable or well-paying jobs or to the cultural capital that allowed them to feel in control of interactions benefited from new kinds of work opportunities and from training in interpersonal skills. Others tried to adapt to changed circumstances and hoped that they would be among the winners in an economic environment in which workers bear much of the risk formerly shouldered by organizations. Some gambled that they could keep their plant from closing by accepting new work practices; some committed themselves to temporary work for a thriving company in hopes of becoming regular employees; others recast their resumés to minimize long-term industry-specific experience that might signal inflexibility or unreasonable expectations to potential employers. Whether and how workers' investments in new kinds of work identities pay off depends in large part on local and regional factors, as well as on how their race, gender, class, and nationality position them in the opportunity structure.

Workers in other parts of the world face different sorts of opportunities, risks, and uncertainties as jobs come and go based on the relative attractions of local labor forces, regulatory environments, and other factors. The coercive labor regimes and poor working conditions imposed on workers in less-developed countries by multinational firms and their surrogates have been widely decried (Klein 1999; Gray 1998; Smart 2003). Nonetheless, in some cases export-oriented jobs do compare favorably to available alternatives or provide new possibilities for identity construction that workers can use, individually or collectively, to enhance their status and autonomy. Freeman's account (2000) of Barbadian women doing clerical work for foreign companies vividly illustrates the creativity with which workers can fashion new identities that both draw on and reshape local gender and class distinctions.

One set of theorists, including Gorz (1999), Beck (2000), and Rifkin ([1995] 2004), argues that the technological and economic developments that have altered the availability and conditions of work are so profound that 'we must dare to prepare ourselves for the Exodus from "work-based society"; it no longer exists and will not return' (Gorz 1999: 1). Beck (2000:14) points out a destabilizing contradiction in contemporary life: 'on the one hand, work is the centre of society around which everything and everyone revolve and take their bearings; on the other hand, everything is done to eliminate as much work as possible'. Therefore, 'everyone, unemployed and potentially insecure workers alike, is urged to fight for a share of the "work" capital is abolishing all around him/her' (Gorz 1999: 53), while the gap between those whose skills can command high wages and those who struggle to find enough work to support themselves and their families increases (Castells 1996; Smart 2003). Given the reality that a smaller proportion of the world's population than ever before is needed to produce necessary goods and services, these theorists believe that it is fruitless to hope for full employment and that workplaces, law, politics, and culture need to reflect that reality. 'The idea that social identity and status depend only upon a person's occupation and career must be taken apart and abandoned,' Beck (2000: 57) argues, 'so that social esteem and security are really uncoupled from paid employment'. Accomplishing that transformation would require new ways of distributing opportunities for paid work, leisure, civic engagement, self-development, and care for others, as well as a new basis for apportioning income and rights.

Generations of sociologists and other social theorists have analyzed the significance of work for identity and critiqued the social and economic arrangements that structure what possibilities work provides for establishing a stable sense of self, developing one's abilities, attaining material well-being, and achieving moral standing. Recent descriptions of major transformations in the structures of employment call into question whether work can be a primary source of identity, purpose, community, status, or security for most people. If available work opportunities are increasingly precarious and short-term, can the same be said for identities?

Theorists contemplating changes in the nature of contemporary identity—whether consumption has replaced work as the key site for constructing identity; whether identities are increasingly self-determined and increasingly ephemeral—have differed in whether they stress the potential for liberation or the potential for devastation in these developments. So too have theorists contemplating changes in the organization of work (see Beck 2000: 36–66 for a range of future scenarios). As they assess how economic restructuring affects the relation of work to identity, sociologists would do well to keep in mind some lessons of earlier investigations. First, sweeping claims about new developments can obscure the persistence of older patterns of thought, behavior, and organization. Just as new forms of labor control co-exist with earlier ones rather than displacing them entirely (Edwards 1979), long-term attachments to career, occupation, and employer will continue to organize many people's lives though others are denied these possibilities. Second, stable and rewarding work experiences have always been unevenly distributed, so a decline in the centrality of work as a basis for identity would be a welcome change for some, a frightening loss for others. While work can be a source of pride, solidarity, rewarding relationships, and meaning, for many it is a realm of domination, indignity, and emptiness, the significance of which for identity they would gladly renounce. Finally, both political struggle and individual creativity help to determine the place of work in society and in people's lives. If opportunities for building a life around paid work actually are declining, the result could be a disaster or a boon. But we may be sure the outcome will depend on the capacity of societies to develop alternative sources of economic security, social integration, meaning, and positive self-identity.

References

Acker, J. (1990). 'Hierarchies, Jobs, Bodies: A Theory of Gendered Organizations', *Gender & Society*, 4(2): 139–58.

Adkins, L. (1995). *Gendered Work: Sexuality, Family and the Labour Market*. Buckingham: Open University Press.

—— and Lury, C. (1999). 'The Labour of Identity: Performing Identities, Performing Economies', *Economy and Society*, 28(4): 598–614.

Anderson, E. (1999). 'The Social Situation of the Black Executive: Black and White Identities in the Corporate World', in M. Lamont (ed.), *The Cultural Territories of Race: Black and White Boundaries*. Chicago, IL, New York: University of Chicago Press, Russell Sage Foundation.

Attewell, P. (1990). 'What Is Skill?' *Work and Occupations*, 17(4): 422–48.

Barker, J. R. (1993). 'Tightening the Iron Cage: Concertive Control in Self-Managing Teams', *Administrative Science Quarterly*, 38: 408–37.

Baudrillard, J. ([1970] 1998). *The Consumer Society: Myths and Structures*. London: Sage.

Bauman, Z. (1998). *Work, Consumerism and the New Poor*. Buckingham: Open University Press.

—— (2001). *The Individualized Society*. Cambridge, Malden, MA: Polity Press, Blackwell.

Beck, U. (2000). *The Brave New World of Work*. Cambridge: Polity Press.

—— and Beck-Gernsheim, E. (2002). *Individualization: Institutionalized Individualism and its Social and Political Consequences*. London: Sage.

——, Giddens, A., and Lash, S. (1994). *Reflexive Modernization: Politics, Tradition and Aesthetics in the Modern Social Order*. Cambridge: Polity Press.

Benson, S. P. (1986). *Counter Cultures: Saleswomen, Managers, and Customers in American Department Stores, 1890–1940*. Urbana, IL: University of Illinois Press.

Berk, S. F. (1985). *The Gender Factory: The Apportionment of Work in American Households*. New York: Plenum Press.

Biggart, N. W. (1983). 'Rationality, Meaning, and Self-Management: Success Manuals, 1950–1980', *Social Problems*, 30(3): 298–311.

—— (1989). *Charismatic Capitalism: Direct Selling Organizations in America*. Chicago IL: University of Chicago Press.

Bolton, S. C. and Boyd, C. (2003). 'Trolley Dolly or Skilled Emotion Manager?: Moving on from Hochschild's Managed Heart', *Work, Employment And Society*, 17(2): 289–308.

Bosk, C. L. ([1979] 2003). *Forgive and Remember: Managing Medical Failure*. Chicago, IL: University of Chicago Press.

Braverman, H. (1974). *Labor and Monopoly Capital: The Degradation of Work in the Twentieth Century*. New York: Monthly Review Press.

Burawoy, M. (1979). *Manufacturing Consent: Changes in the Labor Process under Monopoly Capitalism*. Chicago, IL: University of Chicago Press.

Callero, P. L. (2003). 'The Sociology of the Self', *Annual Review of Sociology*, 23: 115–33.

Cancian, F. M., Kurz, D., and Reviere, R. (2002). *Child Care and Inequality: Rethinking Carework for Children and Youth*. New York: Routledge.

Casey, C. (1995). *Work, Self, and Society: After Industrialism*. London: Routledge.

Castells, M. (1996). *The Rise of the Network Society*. Cambridge, MA: Blackwell.

Cerulo, K. A. (1997). 'Identity Construction: New Issues, New Directions', *Annual Review of Sociology*, 23: 385–409.

Chetkovich, C. A. (1997). *Real Heat: Gender and Race in the Urban Fire Service*. New Brunswick, NJ: Rutgers University Press.

Cockburn, C. (1985). *Machinery of Dominance: Women, Men, and Technical Know-How*. London: Pluto Press.

Collinson, D. (1992). *Managing the Shopfloor: Subjectivity, Masculinity, and Workplace Culture*. Berlin: W. de Gruyter.

—— and Hearn, J. (1996). *Men as Managers, Managers as Men: Critical Perspectives on Men, Masculinities, and Managements*. London: Sage Publications.

Daniels, A. K. (1987). 'Invisible Work', *Social Problems*, 34(5): 403–15.

DeVault, M. L. (1991). *Feeding the Family: The Social Organization of Caring as Gendered Work*. Chicago, IL: University of Chicago Press.

Diamond, T. (1992). *Making Gray Gold: Narratives of Nursing Home Care*. Chicago, IL: University of Chicago Press.

Du Gay, P. (1996). *Consumption and Identity at Work*. London: Sage Publications.

Dubin, R. (1956). 'Industrial Worker's Worlds: A Study of the Central Life Interests of Industrial Workers', *Social Problems*, 131–42.

Durkheim, E. ([1893] 1984). *The Division of Labor in Society*. New York: Free Press.

Edin, K. and Lein, L. (1997). *Making Ends Meet: How Single Mothers Survive Welfare and Low-Wage Work*. New York: Russell Sage Foundation.

—— and Nelson, T. J. (2001). 'Working Steady: Race, Low-Wage Work, and Family Involvement among Noncustodial Fathers in Philadelphia', in E. Anderson and D. S. Massey (eds.), *The Problem of the Century: Racial Stratification in the United States*. New York: Russell Sage Foundation.

Edwards, R. (1979). *Contested Terrain: The Transformation of the Workplace in the Twentieth Century*. New York: Basic Books.

Elliott, A. (2001). *Concepts of the Self*. Cambridge: Polity Press.

Engel, D. M. and Munger, F. W. (2003). *Rights of Inclusion: Law and Identity in the Life Stories of Americans with Disabilities*. Chicago, IL: University of Chicago Press.

Entwistle, J. (2000). 'Fashioning the Career Woman: Power Dressing as a Strategy Off Consumption', in M. R. Andrews and M. M. Talbot (eds.), *All the World and Her Husband: Women in Twentieth-Century Consumer Culture*. London: Cassell.

Florida, R. L. (2002). *The Rise of the Creative Class: And How It's Transforming Work, Leisure, Community and Everyday Life*. New York: Basic Books.

Freeman, C. (2000). *High Tech and High Heels in the Global Economy: Women, Work, and Pink-Collar Identities in the Caribbean*. Durham, NC: Duke University Press.

Freidson, E. (1970). *Professional Dominance: The Social Structure of Medical Care*. New York: Atherton Press.

—— (1990). 'Labors of Love in Theory and Practice: A Prospectus', in K. Erikson and S. P. Vallas (eds.), *The Nature of Work: Sociological Perspectives*. New Haven, CT: American Sociological Association Presidential Series and Yale University Press.

Friedman, A. L. (1977). *Industry and Labour: Class Struggle at Work and Monopoly Capitalism*. London: Macmillan.

Fuller, L. and Smith, V. (1991). 'Consumers' Reports: Management by Customers in a Changing Economy', *Work, Employment and Society*, 15: 1–16.

Garey, A. I. (1999). *Weaving Work and Motherhood*. Philadelphia, PA: Temple University Press.

Gerson, K. (1993). *No Man's Land: Men's Changing Commitments to Family and Work*. New York: Basic Books.

—— (2002). 'Moral Dilemmas, Moral Strategies, and the Transformation of Gender: Lessons from Two Generations of Work and Family Change', *Gender & Society*, 16(1): 8–28.

Giddens, A. (1991). *Modernity and Self-Identity: Self and Society in the Late Modern Age*. Stanford, CA: Stanford University Press.

Glenn, E. N. (1992). 'From Servitude to Service Work: Historical Continuities in the Racial Division of Paid Reproductive Labor', *Signs*, 18(1): 1–43.

—— (2002). *Unequal Freedom: How Race and Gender Shaped American Citizenship and Labor*. Cambridge, MA: Harvard University Press.

Goffman, E. (1959). *The Presentation of Self in Everyday Life*. Garden City, NY: Doubleday.

—— (1961*a*). 'The Medical Model and Mental Hospitalization: Some Notes on the Vicissitudes of the Tinkering Trades', *Asylums; Essays on the Social Situation of Mental Patients and Other Inmates*. Garden City, NY: Anchor Books.

—— (1961*b*). 'The Underlife of a Public Institution: A Study of Ways of Making out in a Mental Hospital', *Asylums; Essays on the Social Situation of Mental Patients and Other Inmates*. Garden City, NY: Anchor Books.

—— (1961*c*). 'Role Distance', *Encounters: Two Studies in the Sociology of Interaction*. Garden City, NY: Anchor Books.

Goldthorpe, J. H. (1968). *The Affluent Worker, Industrial Attitudes and Behaviour*. Cambridge: Cambridge University Press.

Goldthorpe, J. H. (1969). *The Affluent Worker in the Class Structure*. Cambridge: Cambridge University Press.

Gorz, A. (1999). *Reclaiming Work: Beyond the Wage-Based Society.* Cambridge, UK, Malden, MA: Polity Press, Blackwell.

Graham, L. (1995). *On the Line at Subaru-Isuzu: The Japanese Model and the American Worker.* Ithaca, NY: ILR Press.

Gray, J. (1998). *False Dawn: The Delusions of Global Capitalism.* New York: The New Press.

Grey, C. (1994). 'Career as a Project of the Self and Labour Process Discipline', *Sociology,* 28(2): 479–97.

Haas, J. and Shaffir, W. (1982). 'Ritual Evaluation of Competence: The Hidden Curriculum of Professionalization in an Innovative Medical School Program', *Work and occupations,* 9(2): 131–54.

—— and —— (1984). 'The "Fate of Idealism" Revisited', *Urban Life,* 13(1): 63–81.

Halle, D. (1984). *America's Working Man: Work, Home, and Politics among Blue-Collar Property Owners.* Chicago, IL: University of Chicago Press.

Hareven, T. K. (1982). *Family Time and Industrial Time: The Relationship between the Family and Work in a New England Industrial Community.* Cambridge: Cambridge University Press.

Hartmann, H. (1976). 'Capitalism, Patriarchy, and Job Segregation by Sex', in M. Blaxall and B. Reagan (eds.), *Women and the Workplace: The Implications of Occupational Segregation.* Chicago, IL: University of Chicago Press,

—— (1981). 'The Family as the Locus of Gender, Class, and Political Struggle: The Example of Housework', *Signs,* 6(3): 366–94.

Himmelweit, S. (1999). 'Caring Labor', *Annals of the American Academy of Political and Social Science,* 561: 27–38.

Hochschild, A. R. (1983). *The Managed Heart: Commercialization of Human Feeling.* Berkeley, CA: University of California Press.

—— (1989). *The Second Shift: Working Parents and the Revolution at Home.* New York: Viking.

—— (1997). *The Time Bind: When Work Becomes Home and Home Becomes Work.* New York: H. Holt/Metropolitan Books.

Hodson, R. (2001). *Dignity at Work.* Cambridge: Cambridge University Press.

Hogg, M. A., Terry, D. J., and White, K. M. (1995). 'A Tale of Two Theories: A Critical Comparison of Identity Theory with Social Identity Theory', *Social Psychology Quarterly,* 58(4): 255–69.

Hondagneu-Sotelo, P. (2001). *Doméstica: Immigrant Workers Cleaning and Caring in the Shadows of Affluence.* Berkeley, CA: University of California Press.

Hossfeld, K. (1993). '"Their Logic against Them": Contradictions in Sex, Race, and Class in Silicon Valley', in A. Jaggar and P. Rothenberg (eds.), *Feminist Frameworks: Alternative Theoretical Accounts of the Relations between Women and Men.* New York: McGraw-Hill.

Hossfeld, K. (1994). 'Hiring Immigrant Women: Silicon Valley's "Simple Formula" ', in M. B. Zinn and B. T. Dill (eds.), *Women of Color in U.S. Society.* Philadelphia, PA: Temple University Press.

Howard, J. A. (2000). 'Social Psychology of Identities', *Annual Review of Sociology*, 26: 367–93.

Hughes, E. C. ([1945] 1984). 'Dilemmas and Contradictions of Status', *The Sociological Eye; Selected Papers*. New Brunswick, NJ: Transaction Books.

—— ([1951*a*] 1984). 'Work and Self', *The Sociological Eye: Selected Papers*. New Brunswick, NJ: Transaction Books.

—— ([1951*b*] 1984). 'Mistakes at Work', *The Sociological Eye: Selected Papers*. New Brunswick, NJ: Transaction Books.

—— ([1952] 1984). 'The Sociological Study of Work: An Editorial Forward', *The Sociological Eye, Selected Papers*. New Brunswick, NJ: Transaction Books.

—— ([1959] 1984). 'The Study of Occupations', *The Sociological Eye; Selected Papers*. New Brunswick, NJ; London: Transaction Books.

Kanter, R. M. (1977). *Men and Women of the Corporation*. New York: Basic Books.

Klein, N. (1999). *No Space, No Choice, No Jobs, No Logo: Taking Aim at the Brand Bullies*. New York: Picador USA.

Knights, D. and Willmott, H. (1989). 'Power and Subjectivity at Work: From Degradation to Subjugation in Social Relations', *Sociology*, 23(4): 535–58.

—— and McCabe, D. (1998). 'Dreams and Designs on Strategy: A Critical Analysis of TQM and Management Control', *Work, Employment And Society*, 12(3): 433–56.

Kohn, M. L. (1990). 'Unresolved Issues in the Relaionship between Work and Personality', in K. Erikson and S. P. Vallas (eds.), *The Nature of Work: Sociological Perspectives*. New Haven, CT: American Sociological Association Presidential Series and Yale University Press.

Korczynski, M., Shire, K., Frenkel, S., and Tam, M. (2000). 'Service Work in Consumer Capitalism: Customers, Control and Contradictions', *Work Employment and Society*, 14(4): 669–87.

Kunda, G. (1992). *Engineering Culture: Control and Commitment in a High-Tech Corporation*. Philadelphia, PA: Temple University Press.

—— and Maanen, J. V. (1999). 'Changing Scripts at Work: Managers and Professionals', *Annals of the American Academy of Political and Social Science*, 561: 64–80.

Kurz, D. (2002). 'Caring for Teenage Children', *Journal of Family Issues*, 23(6): 748–67.

Lamont, M. (2000). *The Dignity of Working Men: Morality and the Boundaries of Race, Class, and Immigration*. New York: Russell Sage Foundation Cambridge, MA Harvard University Press.

Lareau, A. (2003). *Unequal Childhoods: Class, Race, and Family Life*. Berkeley, CA: University of California Press.

Leidner, R. (1991). 'Serving Hamburgers and Selling Insurance: Gender, Work, and Identity in Interactive Service Jobs', *Gender & Society*, 5(2): 154–77.

Leidner, R. (1993). *Fast Food, Fast Talk: Service Work and the Routinization of Everyday Life*. Berkeley, CA: University of California Press.

Liebow, E. (1967). *Tally's Corner: A Study of Negro Streetcorner Men*. Boston, MA: Little.

Macdonald, C. L. and Sirianni, C. (1996). *Working in the Service Society*. Philadelphia, PA: Temple University Press.

McDowell, L. (1995). 'Body Work: Heterosexual Gender Performance in City Workplaces', in D. Bell and G. Valentine (eds.), *Mapping Desires: Geographies of Sexualities*. London: Routledge.

—— (2003). *Redundant Masculinities?: Employment Change and White Working Class Youth*. Malden, MA: Blackwell.

Margolis, D. R. (1979). *The Managers: Corporate Life in America*. New York: Morrow.

Martin, S. E. (1980). *Breaking and Entering: Policewomen on Patrol*. Berkeley, CA: University of California Press.

Marx, K. ([1932] 1978). 'The German Ideology', Part I, in R. C. Tucker (ed.), *The Marx-Engels Reader*. New York: Norton & Company.

—— and Engels, F. ([1948] 1978). 'Manifesto of the Communist Party', in R. C. Tucker (ed.) *The Marx-Engels Reader*. New York: Norton & Company.

May, C. and Cooper, A. (1995). 'Personal Identity and Social Change: Some Theoretical Considerations.' *Acta Sociologica*, 38(1): 75.

Mead, G. H. (1934). *Mind, Self, and Society: From the Standpoint of a Social Behaviorist*. Chicago, IL: University of Chicago Press.

Menger, P-M. (1999). 'Artistic Labor Markets and Careers', *Annual Review of Sociology*, 25(1): 541–74.

Mills, C. W. (1951). *White Collar: The American Middle Classes*. New York: Oxford University Press.

Mohanty, C. T. (2003). 'Women Workers and the Politics of Solidarity', *Feminism without Borders: Decolonizing Theory, Practicing Solidarity*. Durham: Duke University Press.

Newman, K. S. (1988). *Falling from Grace: The Experience of Downward Mobility in the American Middle Class*. New York: Free Press.

Parsons, T. and Bales, R. F. (1955). *Family, Socialization and Interaction Process*. Glencoe, IL: Free Press.

Philipson, I. J. (2002). *Married to the Job: Why We Live to Work and What We Can Do About It*. New York: Free Press.

Pierce, J. L. (1995). *Gender Trials: Emotional Lives in Contemporary Law Firms*. Berkeley, CA: University of California Press.

Rifkin, J. ([1995] 2004). *The End of Work: The Decline of the Global Labor Force and the Dawn of the Post-Market Era*. New York: Jeremy P. Tarcher/Penguin.

Rollins, J. (1985). *Between Women: Domestics and Their Employers*. Philadelphia, PA: Temple University Press.

Rose, N. S. (1990). *Governing the Soul: The Shaping of the Private Self*. London: Routledge.

Salzinger, L. (2003). *Genders in Production: Making Workers in Mexico's Global Factories*. Berkeley, CA: University of California Press.
Sargent, L. (1981). *Women and Revolution: A Discussion of the Unhappy Marriage of Marxism and Feminism*. Boston, MA: South End Press.
Sennett, R. (1998). *The Corrosion of Character: The Personal Consequences of Work in the New Capitalism*. New York: W. W. Norton.
—— and Cobb, J. (1972). *The Hidden Injuries of Class*. New York: Knopf.
Sharma, U. and Black, P. (2001). 'Look Good, Feel Better: Beauty Therapy as Emotional Labour', *Sociology*, 35(4): 913–31.
Smart, B. (2003). *Economy, Culture and Society: A Sociological Critique of Neo-Liberalism*. Buckingham: Open University Press.
Smith, V. (2001). *Crossing the Great Divide: Worker Risk and Opportunity in the New Economy*. Ithaca, NY: ILR Press.
Snow, D. A. and Anderson, L. (1987). 'Identity Work among the Homeless: The Verbal Construction and Avowal of Personal Identities', *American Journal of Sociology*, 92(6): 1336–71.
Steinberg, K. and Figart, D. (1997). Emotional Labor Since *'The Managed Heart', Annals of the American Academy of Political and Social S* 561: 8–26.
Strangleman, T. and Roberts, I. (1999). 'Looking through the Window of Opportunity: The Cultural Cleansing of Workplace Identity', *Sociology*, 33(1): 47–67.
Thompson, P. (1990). 'Crawling from the Wreckage: The Labour Process and the Politics of Production', in D. Knights and H. Willmott (eds.), *Labour Process Theory*. London: Macmillan.
—— and Ackroyd, S. (1995). 'All Quiet on the Workplace Front? A Critique of Recent Trends in British Industrial Sociology', *Sociology*, 29(4): 615–33.
—— and Findlay, P. (1999). 'Changing the People: Social Engineering in the Contemporary Workplace', in L. Ray and A. Sayer (eds.), *Culture and Economy after the Cultural Turn*. London: Sage.
Townsend, N. W. (2002). *The Package Deal: Marriage, Work, and Fatherhood in Men's Lives*. Philadelphia, PA: Temple University Press.
Trice, H. M. (1993). *Occupational Subcultures in the Workplace*. Ithaca, NY: ILR Press.
Vallas, S. P. (2003). 'The Adventures of Managerial Hegemony: Teamwork, Ideology, and Worker Resistance', *Social Problems*, 50(2): 204–25.
Van Maanen, J. and Kunda, G. (1989). '"Real Feelings": Emotional Expression and Organizational Culture', in L. L. Cummings and B. M. Staw (eds.), *Research in Organizational Behavior*. Greenwich, CT: JAI Press.
Wajcman, J. and Martin, B. (2002). 'Narratives of Identity in Modern Management: The Corrosion of Gender Difference?' *Sociology*, 36(4): 985–1002.
Warhurst, C. N., Dennis, Witz, A., Cullen, A. M. (2000). 'Aesthetic Labour in Interactive Service Work: Some Case Study Evidence from the 'New' Glasgow', *Service Industries Journal*, 20(3): 1–18.
Weber, M. ([1904–05] 1958). *The Protestant Ethic and the Spirit of Capitalism*. New York: Charles Scribner's Sons.

—— ([1922] 1979). 'Bureaucracy', in H. H. Gerth and C. W. Mills (eds.), *From Max Weber: Essays in Sociology*. New York: Oxford University Press.

Wellington, C. A. and Bryson, J. R. (2001). 'At Face Value? Image Consultancy, Emotional Labour and Professional Work', *Sociology*, 35(4): 933–46.

Weston, K. (1990). 'Production as Means, Production as Metaphor: Women's Struggle to Enter the Trades', in F. D. Ginsburg and A. L. Tsing (eds.) *Uncertain Terms: Negotiating Gender in American Culture*. Boston, MA: Beacon Press.

Westwood, S. (1984). *All Day, Every Day: Factory and Family in the Making of Women's Lives*. London: Pluto Press.

Whyte, W. H. (1956). *The Organization Man*. New York: Simon and Schuster.

Williams, C. (2003). 'Sky Service: The Demands of Emotional Labour in the Airline Industry', *Gender, Work and Organization*, 10(5): 513–50.

Williams, C. L. (1989). *Gender Differences at Work: Women and Men in Nontraditional Occupations*. Berkeley, CA: University of California Press.

—— (1995). *Still a Man's World: Men Who Do 'Women's' Work*. Berkeley, CA: University of California Press.

Willmott, H. (1993). 'Strength Is Ignorance; Slavery Is Freedom: Managing Culture in Modern Organizations', *Journal of Management Studies*, 30(4): 515–52.

Wilson, W. J. (1987). *The Truly Disadvantaged: The Inner City, the Underclass, and Public Policy*. Chicago, IL: University of Chicago Press.

—— (1996). *When Work Disappears: The World of the New Urban Poor*. New York: Knopf.

Wouters, C. (1989). 'The Sociology of Emotions and Flight Attendants: Hochschild's *Managed Heart*'. *Theory, Culture and Society*, 6: 95–123.

Wrigley, J. (1995). *Other People's Children*. New York: Basic Books.

Zuboff, S. (1988). *In the Age of the Smart Machine: The Future of Work and Power*. New York: Basic Books.

Zukin, S. and Maguire, J. S. (2004). 'Consumers and Consumption', *Annual Review of Sociology*, 30: 173–97.

16

Conclusions: Change at Work and the Opportunities for Theory

Peter Cappelli

The previous chapters have outlined a range of interesting and important theoretical frameworks across the discipline of sociology that have been or could be used to examine work and workplace issues. The purpose of this concluding chapter is in some ways to work backward from theory, to begin with some of the important phenomena of the contemporary workplace, the facts that need to be explained, and then consider how the various theoretical frameworks outlined earlier might be used to examine them.

The place to begin such as discussion is with a series of caveats. What one considers to be important in terms of developments in work and in the workplace is colored by the lenses that one uses. Economists, for example, quite clearly focus on markets, and so for them, the most important developments in the workplace are those associated with labor markets, specifically labor market outcomes, such as wages and job losses. It is probably fair to say that these aspects of the workplace get a disproportionate amount of attention in part because they tend to affect large groups of people and the economy as a whole. They also can be measured in relatively straightforward ways, which makes it easy to examine how they have changed over time.

Psychologists, the second major field with an interest in workplace issues, concern themselves with the individual and their relationships with the workplace. These would include individual attributes (knowledge, skills, abilities, personality, etc.) and their effects on organizational outcomes but especially worker reactions and responses to the workplace context and to particular employment practices, such as training and selection systems. Some of these clearly do change over time. But the focus of the field is primarily on understanding variation across individuals, and less so on changes in those responses over time.[1] And systematic information on employee and workplace attitudes across representative samples is not readily available and is even more difficult to come by over time. As a result, it is somewhat difficult for psychologists who study the workplace to have a unique take on 'what is new' at work or in the workplace. Their answers likely focus on the changing context at work, which might affect employee responses—new technology, new working conditions, new patterns of employment, etc.—and the data for those answers are likely to come from other fields.

Sociologists appear to have the broadest set of interests concerning workplace phenomena. They are interested in all of the labor market outcomes that are the focus of economists, some of the employee responses that concern psychologists, and all aspects of social behavior at work. But most importantly and uniquely, sociologists are concerned with the institutions and organizations of the workplace, perhaps especially the practices and arrangements that operate inside organizations. Along with fields such as industrial relations, they examine employee relationships and the changes in employers and other organizations (e.g. unions and workplace intermediaries) that influence those relationships. Given this very broad set of interests, it is difficult for a review of changes and contemporary issues affecting work and the workplace to be exhaustive in terms of the issues of concern to sociologists. The set of issues discussed below is, as a result, highly selective.

The second great complication in reviewing important developments in the workplace is the difficulty in determining 'which workplace?'. As with cartography, an outline of any phenomenon can reveal almost infinite differences the closer one is willing to look, while local variations tend to disappear and similarities pop up as one moves away and towards a more general description of situations. Writing a survey of developments in the overall society or economy necessarily glosses over important variations in the experiences across occupations, industries, and sectors of the workplace. Changes in the experiences of call centers over time, for example,

[1] The other conceptual difficulty with respect to examining changes in employee responses over time, especially attitudinal data, is the tendency for responses to renorm over time. Individual responses have a strong dispositional aspect to them (e.g. variations in job satisfaction levels have a strong individual component to them that persists over time even as individuals change jobs and circumstances), and individuals also get used to changes in their context and adjust their responses to them. What passes for 'normal' changes over time.

which appear to reflect the growing influence of scientific management, are radically different from those in information technology, which appear to have moved towards open markets, or production work, which seems to have moved closer to empowered teams. And those variations pale in comparison to the difficulty in describing trends across countries and regions. Because of the great variation in circumstances across occupations, across industries, and across countries and the difficulty of choosing from among those variations, it makes sense to present only the most general stories that seem to apply across most contexts. An important issue illustrated above that falls by the wayside, then, is the question of how work is organized since the variations across contexts seem to overshadow the similarities.

In choosing among important developments to consider, the bias in this chapter is straightforward and reflects the underlying base of research and knowledge in the academic world as it exists now. By objective standards, for example, the most important developments in the world at work as we move into the new millennium are those taking place in China and India, not only because they affect the most people but because they affect global labor markets in profound ways. Yet we know relatively little in any systematic way about those changes and much more about developments in Europe and especially the USA, because those are the regions where researchers have been the most busy studying the workplace and where data are available to do so.

A third issue is to decide what is truly a contemporary issue. Many of the most important developments shaping work around the world reflect trends that have been underway for sometime. For example, the workplace changes associated with industrialization cut across virtually all issues that concern modern sociology and are also happening in many countries. While it is tremendously important, it is hardly a new issue. The shift from industrial to service work is another important trend and one that has been underway for decades in the developed world. Finally, the influence of technology is a perennial favorite in lists of 'new developments', but there is nothing fundamentally new about the fact that technologies change, altering work and workers in the process.

The admittedly subjective list of important and contemporary workplace developments below leaves out many worthy contenders. Among them is changes in the nature of work organization, specifically, a move away from Fordist systems towards alternatives that make greater use of behavioral principles, especially teamwork and employee empowerment more generally. Yet identifying the extent to which this is truly a trend requires acknowledging that there are also moves in the opposite direction, especially attempts to isolate measures of individual performance and manage to those. This is particularly noticeable in call centers, where principals of scientific management (e.g. breaking down jobs into component parts, providing 'scripts' and other ways of performing those tasks, measuring and rewarding on a piecerate system) are pervasive.

The decline of trade unions is another possible contender, although that decline is much less pronounced outside the USA and UK and seems tied in terms of factors driving it to more general issues of corporate restructuring. The use of off-shoring and the more general practice of outsourcing is another contender for the list of contemporary workplace concerns. Outsourcing matters because it is one of the drivers of job loss and insecurity about jobs. It is not per se a workplace issue, however, and has arguably more to do with changing the boundaries of the firm than with workers. Work and jobs that move out of a given company may end up in organizations that offer 'worse' or 'better' jobs. Off-shoring in the sense that jobs move overseas is a new issue only to the extent that new and different jobs can be moved offshore than previously, although the movement of jobs clearly does have effects on those that remain (Feenstra and Hansen 1996).

The arguments that follow, therefore, represent a very selective view of contemporary workplace issues that cut across occupations, industries, and industrial societies. They represent relatively new trends, ones that research has documented but not yet explained in detail. As such, they can be thought of as raw material for applying the theoretical frameworks discussed in earlier chapters. As each trend is discussed, specific insights from the previous chapters are indicated. In addition, a final section of the chapter examines ways in which different social theories may approach these five trends holistically. While some theories are aimed specifically at explaining workplace phenomena, others address underlying processes that shape such developments. The writings of Marx, Weber, and Durkheim, for example, focused on the operation of capitalism and such large issues as class, bureaucracy, and the nature of social cohesion and social solidarity. These theories aim to locate 'work' much more generally in an understanding of human social organization. As Burrell puts it in discussing postmodern analysis, 'the postmodern turn is less about economics, production and work than it is about philosophy, consumption and leisure'. The purpose here is to show how even the most abstract theories have a purchase on concrete trends.

Contemporary Issues at Work and in the Workplace

Given the caveats above, the following five headings represent issues of real practical importance across workplaces, ones that challenge assumptions and long-held beliefs about work and especially about employment.

The Changing Attachment of Employees to Employers

In the early days of industrialization, employee relationships with employers were, for the most part, extremely casual, and turnover rates of 300 percent or so per year were common. The rise of assembly lines changed those relationships by creating a need to reduce turnover. The deskilling literature drew attention to the fact that assembly lines and Fordist methods of production based on scientific management reduced the need for skilled workers. But in the process, it also converted most manual work from unskilled labor to semiskilled. As illustrated by Henry Ford's famous $5 per day wage, reducing turnover became of paramount importance with assembly line work because quits and dismissals had a profoundly negative effect on quality and productivity.[2]

As more industrial employers accepted the need to stabilize employment and union-based rules of job control enforced job security, employment moved towards a 'lifetime' model. The export of scientific management to the UK, and to a lesser extent Europe, produced somewhat similar developments, although employment relations had never been as casual there as in the USA. Employment policy in the USA and, indeed, most of the industrial world, was built on the model that employment relationships between employers and employees were long term. Indeed, this was the case. In the 1970s, for example, average job tenure in the USA, despite assumptions about geographic and occupational mobility as well as 'at will' employment, equaled that of Japan, the home of explicit lifetime employment policies.

Exactly what caused the change in employee attachment is beyond the scope of this chapter, but it is fair to say that it was driven by employers and how they operate businesses in particular. The biggest manifestation of the change in employee attachment was changes in the pattern of unemployment. Before the mid-1980s, the US government did not track permanent job losses because the assumption was that workers who lost their jobs did so because of downturns in business and would be rehired

[2] The development of these practices is outlined in Peter Cappelli (2000).

when business returned. The Bureau of Labor Statistics' new 'displaced worker' survey, begun after then, started to track the causes of job losses and their more permanent nature.

The biggest change reflected by this survey is the fact that job losses are now associated with factors other than business cycle-related downturns. Controlling for differences in the business cycle, the risk of job loss actually appeared to be greater in the 1990s than in the 1980s, and the earnings loss that displaced workers experience once they move on to alternative employers has also been growing (Farber 1999). During periods of economic expansion, job losses are offset by new hiring; in downturns, they are not. The most important cause of permanent job losses since the mid-1980s has been plant closures, unlike in previous decades where recession-related downturns in business were the biggest factor. Further, those who lose their jobs now stay unemployed longer, reflecting the fact that they are no longer rehired when business improves, as was the case in earlier generations (Vallenta 1996).

In Europe, unemployment levels rose sharply in the 1970s from what had been persistently low levels, and increased through the 1980s. The largest economies in the European Union, Germany, France, Italy, and Spain, have had the highest unemployment rates. The duration of unemployment has for some time been longer throughout Europe than in the USA. That is, the move for job losses to be permanent happened sooner in Europe. The high and persistent rates of unemployment in Europe remain a puzzle, but attention has focused on the role that institutions—union agreements and regulations—have played in raising the fixed costs of employment, thus restricting employer's interests in hiring (see Blanchard 2004 for a review of European unemployment experience). The improved unemployment picture in the UK beginning in the 1990s, along with its employers securing much greater latitude to lay off and restructure, raised the intriguing question of whether the lack of such latitude also explains the lack of improvement in European unemployment.

DECLINING TENURE

Employee tenure represents the amount of time that an employee stays with an employer and is one very important measure of attachment. It is driven by employee turnover, which has two aspects: employer initiated, typically through layoffs, and employee initiated, through quits. (Dismissals for cause account for a trivial amount of turnover.) Quits account for about two-thirds of turnover. They move cyclically with the business cycle, rising when the economy expands and falling when it contracts, whereas layoffs move counter-cyclically.

Temporary layoffs associated with recessions stretched but did not break employees' relationships with their employer. Most laid-off employees were rehired when economic growth picked up again. In terms of tenure and other measures of the employment relationship, the rehired employee was judged to be in a continuous relationship even having once been laid-off. Permanent layoffs obviously end the relationship. Whether or not tenure had declined in the USA was hotly debated in the mid- and late 1990s as anecdotal information suggested that layoffs, employee quits, and outside hiring should be reducing turnover. But this effect was not showing up in studies of aggregate tenure using government data. The chart below shows the decline in men's tenure and the increase in women's over the past two decades in the USA. The changes are modest. Women's tenure appears to have risen for reasons that do not necessarily reflect changes in employment practices (i.e. a reduction in the need to quit when married and having children), while men's tenure has declined in a noticeable but less than dramatic fashion.

One interpretation of the controversy was that the trends had yet to appear because the data lagged the current period by several years, so it was possible that changes had occurred but had yet to show up. The change from 1996 to 1998, for example, is about as big as the change from 1983 to 1991 (see Figure 16.1). Another possibility was that something else was going on in the work force. One candidate was that the workforce was also aging in this period, and one normally expects tenure to rise with an older workforce as workers settle in having found good 'matches', and layoffs, which were typically seniority-related, decline in their impact as workers age. When one looks within age group, effectively controlling for age, declines in tenure are much more dramatic (see Figure 16.2).

A quick summary of the above suggests that the nature of the attachment between employers and employees has changed considerably. It has weakened in that job losses are more common and are more likely to be permanent. The causes of job loss have also become less predictable, less related to overall economic conditions, and more likely to be traced to developments originating from within the firm, ostensibly within the control of the executive team. Overall, as a result, job tenure, the amount of time that employers and employees stay together, has also declined. These developments raise interesting questions for research:

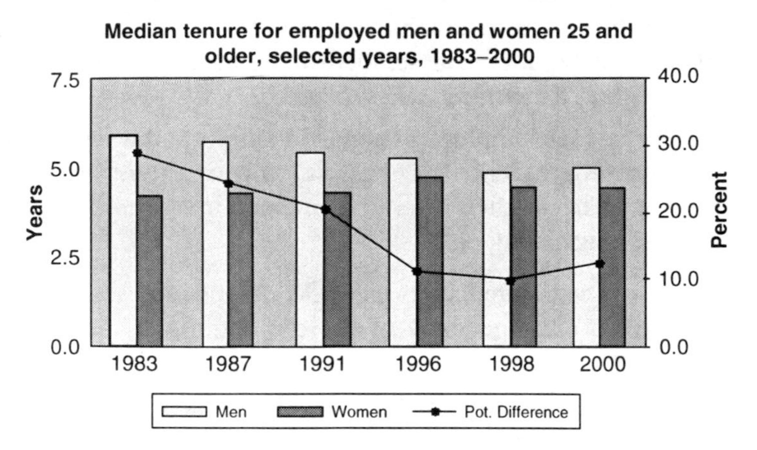

Figure 16.1

Source: 'The Editor's Desk', *Monthly Labor Review*, August 2003, 'Median Tenure Declines Little in Recent Years'.

Figure 16.2

Source: 'The Editor's Desk', *Monthly Labor Review*, September 2000, 'Median Tenure Declines Among Older Men, 1983–2000'.

- What factors have driven the decline in tenure—how much has been initiated by employers and how much reflects the greater willingness and ability of employees to quit?
- What are the consequences of the decline in attachment? How does it affect the attitudes of employees toward their employer? Does it lead to a decline in commitment, citizenship, and other pro-employer behaviors that in the past were thought to derive from deeper attachment between employees and employers?

- How does the decline in attachment affect the role that employees see for themselves? If, for example, identification with the employer has declined, what, if anything, takes its place?
- Has the behavior of employers changed in important ways in response to declining attachment? For example, to what extent has declining attachment reduced their interest in making investments in training and developing employees?

A wide range of the theoretical frameworks described in earlier chapters might be used to examine some of these questions. In particular, the arguments used to examine issues of workplace identity described by Leidner in Chapter 15 could be used to examine how the changes in employee attachment to employers have affected their attitudes towards work, towards their employer, and towards themselves. An obvious hypothesis to explore is whether declines in attachment and in identification with employers are offset by increased identification in other domains. Specifically, is there an increasing attempt to professionalize jobs and fields that is driven by reduced employer attachments?

Rising Inequality of Income

The second change in work and workplace issues has been the sharp increase in inequality associated with wages and other forms of employment-based compensation. This development is often described in labor economics as the most important change in the workplace because it is so well documented. After some initial debates in the late 1980s, a consensus emerged rather quickly that inequality had grown in the USA since 1980 after having declined sharply during and after World War II (see Levy and Murnane 1992 for the seminal discussion) as has the inequality of wealth (Wolff 1992). Similar increases in wage inequality have been observed across virtually all the developed economies of the world (see Edwards and Whalley 2002). The basic pattern of the increase in wage inequality has been the relative decline in income for less educated, less skilled workers. This has led to the view that something has changed about the nature of the demand for labor, a bias towards more skilled workers (more appropriately, a bias against less skilled workers) and the descriptive phrase that became popular in economics, 'skilled biased technological change'. Exactly what that something is has not been established, although the speculation clearly leans towards information technology and the changing skill requirements associated with it as one component. Among the other prominent explanations is the finding that declines in unionization accounts for a large proportion of the rise in wage inequality in the USA, the UK, and Canada (Card et al. 2003). But a great deal of inequality remains to be explained.

The causes of the rise in wage inequality are numerous and vary somewhat country by country. Whether they point to common, underlying causes remains to be seen but is a question of fundamental importance. Especially from the perspective of sociology, it is important to understand the extent to which inequality results from factors underway inside firms and other employer organizations. For example, to what extend does rising inequality result from changes such as decreased use of seniority systems and job-based pay systems and greater use of merit-based pay, 'broad-banding,' discretionary bonuses and other arrangements that allow pay to vary by the individual? And how much is associated with changing policies towards the pay of managers and executives that have led to dramatic increases in their compensation? To what extent is it driven by broader society-level changes that play themselves out through politics and government policies, such as relative declines in minimum wages, union power, and other supports for low-wage workers? And finally, to what extent is the rise in inequality truly due to the factors of primary interest to economists, such as changes in the basic production function linking labor to products and services that affects the relative demand for different kinds of labor?

The consequences of increases in inequality have been even less explored than the causes. Because income drives consumption patterns, we should expect that rising income inequality will begin to produce sharp changes in other aspects of society, such as changes in housing patterns (e.g. greater separation between rich and poor), changes in patterns of college attendance (e.g. declining attendance among lower income groups and changes in the public/private nature of the schools they attend), and greater stratification in other aspects of society.

These developments in the rewards from work lead to another important set of research questions:

- To what extent are these changes in inequality the result of forces that are beyond the control of individual employers, such as changing production functions or patterns of international trade? And how much of the changes result from decisions within their control, such as greater efforts to identify and link individual pay to individual performance, essentially increasing inequality within groups of otherwise apparently similar workers?

- To what extent, if any, has the decline in real and relative earnings of lower-skill workers changed the identification of those workers and how they see themselves? Has it, for example, altered the way they think about class and the groups to which they identify themselves? Has it changed how they view other groups in society, especially those who are wealthy?
- How has the rising inequality of income affected communities and their social structures? What has been the effect on inequality of housing and education patterns within communities?

Questions concerning the causes of rising inequality could benefit considerably from being addressed through the older institutional economics approaches described by Hodgson (see Chapter 8). Specifically, can we look within individual organizations to see how changes in practices concerning wage setting have affected income inequality in those settings—how much is within the control of individual employers? While economists have used the term 'technology' as a synonym for a black box of potential changes in how business is done that might affect the demand for labor, it would be especially useful to pursue the approach suggested by Bélanger in Chapter 12 and consider specific types of technology and their effects not only on skill requirements that affect supply and demand but also on factors such as wage setting institutions.

In Chapter 7 Machin shows how economics has developed explanations for some of these issues, such as skill-biased technological change and analyses concerning minimum wages and human capital. As Machin shows, economics has not limited itself to purely competitive models of the labor market, but it is also clear that economics sets tight boundaries on the depth of explanations it offers and typically stays away from issues such as the institutions and employer practices that shape labor market outcomes. Other approaches aim to go deeper. A classic example is the definition of human capital. As Gottfried shows in Chapter 5, feminist research has argued that what is defined as capital is shaped by gender processes. Similarly, Beamish and Biggart (Chapter 9) show that economic exchange is connected to other systems of exchange, so that the ways in which people are inserted into labor markets is shaped by family, community, and other institutions. In Chapter 10 Haveman and Khaire detail how several of the developments discussed here are shaped by organizational contexts. For example, they show that the mobility of employees between organizations is influenced by the size of organizations, and also the size *distribution*: because large organizations offer greater rewards than small ones, size inequality will increase rates of mobility. Thus, to the extent that size distributions are shifting, there will be one explanation for mobility flows. As Haveman and Khaire also explain, rates of the founding of new organizations are also important. When, as among internet companies in the late 1990s, many new firms are established, there will be influences on labor market behavior as people are recruited into these firms. Organizational sociology has generated specific hypotheses, based in a model of the ecology and politics of organizations, to explain such developments.

Rise in Nonstandard Work and Contingent Labor

The third important issue associated with work and the workplace is the greater use of employment relationships that are 'nonstandard', in other words, rather than regular, full-time employment. Since the New Deal in the USA, employment policies have been based on the assumption that virtually all employees work in full-time jobs with a regular employer where the attachment is long-term, if not lifetime. In the UK and Europe, employment policies and regulations enforced this norm even more strongly, with some countries banning outright other employment arrangements. Temporary help, the nonstandard arrangement that has received the most attention recently, had been around since the 1930s, but it began to grow at a sharp and noticeable rate in the USA in the 1980s. Although the use of agency-based temporary help in the USA is small in absolute terms (2 to 3 percent of the workforce), it had increased very rapidly in this period, by a factor of three to five times depending on the estimates. In European countries, the share of workers in temporary or contract work status in periods during the late 1980s and early 1990s rose as high as one-quarter because these arrangements represented a way around the restrictive regulations governing full-time employees.

The sharp increase in temp work in particular focused attention in the policy and research community on alternative employment arrangements more generally, of which temporary help is the leading example. Most involve explicit labor market intermediaries, such as agencies that stand between the client 'employer' and the workers and that separate the location of work from the management of work; others, like independent contractors, create a market-based rather than a traditional employment relationship.

The belief that temp jobs in particular were worse on many dimensions and that employers were systematically shifting jobs from 'regular' arrangements to ones that were less permanent helped the term 'contingent work' to became a popular synonym for all of these alternative arrangements. The consensus early on seemed to be that the rise of contingent work was driven by employers' interest in cutting costs, an interest that shifted somewhat over time towards an emphasis on flexibility. By the 1990s, however, it became clear that not all workers in these alternative arrangements had jobs that seemed to be worse off. At the same time, many workers in full-time and ostensibly permanent employment relationships perceived their jobs to be contingent in the sense that they saw the jobs per se, hours of work, or pay as unstable. The US Bureau of Labor Statistics acknowledged this view with a new survey that defined 'contingent work' as the perceptions of employees that their jobs might not last, something that could occur even in the context of a regular, full-time job.

Researchers also began to be more aware of alternative arrangements to temporary help. Most involved labor market intermediaries where workers were performing tasks for an organization that was not their employer. Contract or leased employees, for example, look very much like temporary help except that the relationships are often long-term. Some, like professional employer organizations (PEOs), see a third party becoming the legal employer of one's current workforce and seem to be about altering just the legal nature of the employment relationship (i.e., legal liability for compliance with laws and regulations) without necessarily affecting the employees or their day-to-day management. Other arrangements, such as having a vendor provide services on one's premises, transfer management responsibilities but do not necessarily lead to contingent work for the employees of the vendor whose jobs are often regular and permanent. They may represent the interface between what is an alternative work arrangement and what is a strategic business decision about the boundary of the firm.

Independent contractors represent yet another arrangement that seems close to contingent work in that the relationships are short-term. But unlike temporary help, there is no intermediary between worker and employer. Instead, a market relationship substitutes for an employment relationship.

Although they are typically grouped together, these various arrangements differ considerably. There are some common themes, however. First, in contrast to regular, full-time employment, they all represent diminished obligations by employers and offer employers greater ease in adjusting their labor supply. Second, with the exception of part-time work, they all involve intermediaries, such as temp agencies, staffing firms, or, in the case of independent contractors, the outside labor market.

Estimates of the level of nonstandard work are reasonably consistent and suggest that about 30 percent of the workforce in the USA has one of these relationships (see Segal and Sullivan 1997). Because these individuals are not working every day, however, the proportion of workers in nonstandard arrangements in a given establishment on any particular day is much less, about 14 percent (Cappelli 2003). Nonstandard work, especially temporary help and leased employees, has also been on the rise in Europe in large measure because these arrangements made it possible for employers to avoid restrictive regulations governing regular employment. In the 1990s, countries like the Netherlands and Spain had as much as a quarter of their workforces involved in temporary help or leased employment (see de Ruyter and Burgess 2000; and Connelly and Gallagher 2004 for surveys of research across countries).

Exactly why these nonstandard workplace arrangements have increased is a topic of some debate, although it clearly seems associated with employer demands for these practices. Why and how employers use these different arrangements is perhaps the central question in this area. Among the other important questions that seem especially oriented to sociological analyses are:

- What is the role of intermediaries in the labor market? How do they function? How do they affect clients on both sides (employers and workers) of the relationship?
- What is the experience of a nonstandard worker? How does it affect their notions of identity to have a weak attachment to the place where they work? In other cases, what is the effect of having a separation between where they work and who their actual employer is?
- How does this new relationship affect commitment? Earlier research on 'dual allegiance' between employers and unions might be revisited in the context of employers and temp agencies or staffing firms to see, for example, whether there are conflicts between the types of attachment that workers feel to their legal employer, who signs their paychecks, and the place and people with whom they work?

Many of these questions relate to the issue of identity discussed earlier to the extent that the nature of workers' identity affects how they view their tasks, how they see the entity that employs them, and how they feel towards the entity for which they are performing tasks. Several concepts from earlier chapters could also be applied to these questions. For example, while nonstandard work seems to be on the rise around the world, the patterns in growth rates and types of practices differ considerably across countries and raise interesting questions for the frameworks proposed by Frenkel (Chapter 14) on globalization. What role have multinational employers played in shaping these patterns? Have they spread nonstandard work or actually restrained it by maintaining a greater than average distribution of traditional jobs? To what extent has technology made it easier to identify and measure individual job tasks in ways that allow performance standards to be easily maintained and work to be shifted away from traditional employees who are bound to the firm with employment relationships that increase their ommitment?

Barley and Kunda (2004) have examined these issues in the context of one reasonably unique situation, high-end information technology work. They find, among other things, that intermediaries do much more than play broker and essentially determine the structure of the relationships between contractors and clients.

Changes in the Executive Function, Especially in For-Profit Organizations

Virtually all of the research concerning work and workplaces has historically focused on production workers and, more recently, 'frontline' workers whose ranks include customer contact jobs. Research on executives in sociology has historically been directed at examining aspects of their socioeconomic background as they relate to issues of mobility and social class. To the extent to which there is research on executive jobs and work, it has been the preserve of economic-based research directed at incentive structures (executive compensation) and related models of board structure.

The executive function has changed in important and powerful ways, however, that have important implications not just for the individuals in those jobs but also for the organizations that they run. Among the most important, which plays out themes associated with issue the above (the changing attachment of employees to employers), is the declining attachment of executive talent to organizations. The popular view of the relationship between executives and their companies, which is coded in important aspects of employment legislation, is that managers and particularly executives have stronger and deeper ties to their employers than other employees.[3] The idea that executives built careers by climbing job ladders within

[3] For example, in the USA, managers and executives are 'exempt' from the wage and hour requirements of employment law and cannot unionize on the grounds that, because they in some ways 'are' the organization, they do not need the same protection from it that other employees do.

their own organizations is almost enshrined in models of careers. Yet there is increasing evidence that this is no longer the case. Managers in the 1990s were more likely to be displaced than other employees (Cappelli 1992), top executive turnover has increased, and tenure decreased since the 1980s (Cappelli and Hamori 2005). Executive search firms and outside search, rather than human resource departments and internal development, now play the central role in determining which executives get which jobs. We have moved towards a completely different relationship. Whether executives see themselves and begin to operate more like professions as their attachment to individual employers weakens is but one of the questions worth exploring. There is at least anecdotal evidence suggesting that functions like human resources and finance have actively worked through professional organizations to turn those jobs into something like professions with standardized approaches and credentials that cut across employers.

Similarly, and arguably more importantly, executive compensation and governance have changed to make executives largely accountable to shareholders. The notion that the executive role was to balance the stakeholders of the corporation—employees, customers, the community, and shareholders—has given way to a model where executives have only one constituency, the shareholders. These developments have played out across countries in very different ways, reflecting path dependence associated with legal frameworks in place before corporations (Morck and Steier 2005). Understanding how corporate governance is adapting around the world to the pressure from global capital markets for shareholder value is an important question worth exploring, as will be how those adaptations affect the operation of firms. Changes in executive compensation designed to treat top executives in particular more like shareholders by compensating them with stock and shareholder-based instruments raises another important question as to whether those developments and the incentives they produce will seek to separate executives from other managers, eroding further the notion of 'unitary' organizations with consistent organizational cultures. In addition to these questions, other obvious issues for research include:

- Has the social identity of executives changed because of their greater mobility across organizations, and has their ability to direct organizational culture eroded as well?
- To what extent do executives now see themselves as a separate class from other managers; has executive compensation made them see themselves as investors more than managers?

- How has the move towards shareholder value-based systems of governance changed the way firms manage the workplace on issues that divide the interests of shareholders and employees, such as policies towards layoffs?

Several chapters have placed these issues in context. Beamish and Biggart (Chapter 9) show how economic sociology throws light on the flow of capital and markets and the rise of the shareholder value movement. Haveman and Khaire (Chapter 10) similarly demonstrate the evolution of different conceptions of corporate control, based on production, marketing, and finance, in the USA. They go on to spell out the implications for different managerial professions and for the way in which the occupational structure develops. The current emphasis on shareholders thus sets a context for the degree to which certain occupations can gain power and influence. And Chapter 13 by Macdonald on the professions makes two parallel contributions. First, it focuses specifically on occupations labeled as professions to show how claims to power and prestige have been negotiated as capitalism has evolved. As it concludes, the study of such questions is likely to re-emerge as 'empirical reality' changes; developments discussed here illustrate this changing reality. Second, the conceptual analysis of professions in terms of claims to expertise and so forth can surely be applied to other 'nonprofessional' occupations, as with the claims to expert knowledge of computer and bioscience companies. The current obsession with 'knowledge management', for example, provides a rich terrain for analyses informed by studies of professions. Similarly, Bélanger's discussion of information technology (Chapter 12) suggests how a long-standing tradition of analysis, of the impact of technology on work relations, can be developed as new technical systems emerge. The very different traditions discussed by Macdonald and Bélanger might be brought into constructive engagement with each other.

Changes in Work–Life Balance

The balance of time and energy between work and nonwork activities and how it might be changing over time is the final issue in this short list of important workplace issues. This question is especially important in sociology because it cuts across many topics of traditional interest, such as gender roles, family structure and demography more generally, work and nonwork roles, and so on. The important factor driving interest in work–life balance questions, at least in modern times, has been the increased labor force participation of women, which has added to their traditional role as caregivers, especially for children, and created the problem of balance. Long-run patterns of economic development beginning with industrialization and the move away from agrarian societies affect work–life issues by lowering rates of childbearing. These patterns are not new but continue to play out around the world. Among industrialized countries and particularly in the USA, the social changes affecting work–life balance have had more to do with declining real wages, which helped create the demand for two-career families, and changes in norms, expectations, and regulations concerning appropriate roles for women that have allowed them greater access to more aspects of the labor force and to keep jobs longer (Goldin 2004).

The most important component of the change in labor force participation of women, especially in the USA, has been for women with children at home. The rate of labor force participation of such women rose from about 47 percent in the mid-1970s to 73 percent by 2000 (Fullerton 1999). That jump was especially great for single mothers, and part of the explanation may be changes in the tax code (the Earned Income Tax Credit) that increased the returns to low-wage work (Meyers and Rosenbaum 2001). The fact that single parent households have risen especially in Europe but in the USA as well has made the challenges of work–family balance more pressing as the conflicts are concentrated on a single individual. An examination of UK and German rates of employment for women finds that the increase in employment over time is accounted for in part by rising part-time employment and accompanied by more interruptions in careers that are associated with problems balancing family activities (Fitzenberger and Wunderlink 2004).

The obvious effect of the expansion of work effort by women, especially those with children, is to make it more difficult for them to perform the other tasks that they have traditionally carried out. Because the number of hours in the day are fixed, something has to give when paid employment is added to the list of demands. Exactly what 'gives'—whether husbands take on more family responsibilities in married households, whether childcare and other responsibilities are pushed outside the family, possibly 'outsourced' to other care providers or reduced altogether, and so on—are some of the very important issues that need to be examined. A partial attempt to accommodate the additional demands is simply to sleep less (!), and research suggests that working parents do indeed spend less time sleeping than nonparents (Bianchi 2000).

Studies have consistently shown that being married improves the labor market outcomes of men, as does having children once married. The argument here is that the additional responsibilities of providing for a family force them to become more serious and reliable, essentially refocusing their attention on work and presumably away from nonwork activities (e.g. bowling). For women, however, something like the opposite has been true. Marriage per se neither helps nor hurts their labor market outcomes, but having children does hurt them, and the more children, the greater the negative effect. Presumably women with children cannot increase their focus on work if they are maintaining their traditional nonwork roles.

Efforts to help employees accommodate both work and nonwork tasks has become something of a cottage industry in the field of management with a wide variety of books and articles offering advice on how this can be handled. For the most part, these arguments focus on getting employers to concentrate on important tasks and goals and back off from less essential ones, typically by giving employees greater flexibility as to when they perform tasks. These efforts can be very helpful at addressing problems caused when competing demands occur at exactly the same time. They do little to address problems caused by the fact that the total demands from work and family may be excessive and cannot be accommodated simply by sequencing them differently.

Although there is a growing body of research on work–life balance issues in other fields, notably organizational behavior, there are a number of topics that are uniquely suited for further sociological analysis, including:

- How are family roles changing as a result of workplace demands?
- What effect are family demands having on workplace outcomes? Specifically, how are patterns of job-related success, such as career advancement, changing for those with family demands—are they improving for women, for example, and declining for men, in response to changing roles at home?
- What are the effects of formal programs to help workers balance work and family demands, both legislative, such as family leave requirements, and corporate policies?

These issues and others associated with work–life balance obviously intersect questions of gender in fundamental ways. Chapter 5 by Gottfried and its discussion of family wages, preference theory, and constructs associated with labor market structures are excellent frameworks to begin examining work–family balance questions.

Cross-cutting Themes

Several themes from the earlier chapters suggest approaches that could be applied to better understand all of the issues raised above. The brief discussion below of these cross-cutting themes is embedded in an understanding of three levels at which social theory addresses empirical phenomena.

The first level comprises those theories that offer specific explanations of concrete phenomena. The chapters by Machin and by Haveman and Khaire, for example, lay out the detailed results of programs of research with clear-cut hypotheses that are derived from formal bodies of theory. Machin stresses the need to abstract from the world in order to make testable predictions. In the words of the latter chapter, such research tends to rest on 'paradigm consensus'. Haveman and Khaire, in particular, ask us to take what we know about organizations more seriously in understanding workplace outcomes. Some of these perspectives, such as network analyses and institutionalization, are already well-established but could be extended further into understanding the dynamics of the workplace. The ecological perspective is one that matters and has been underused: as Neumark and Reed (2002) find, jobs that are in the fastest growing industries, presumably the newest jobs, have systematically different attributes with respect to issues such as work organization, compensation, and tenure than do jobs that have been in existence longer.

Second, and to a degree overlapping with the first, are theories that address the question neatly posed by the British industrial sociologist W. G. Baldamus, 'what determines the determinants?' (quoted in Nichols, 1997: 90). What social and political processes create the proximate factors, such as what aspects of human capital are valuable or what constitutes a profession? Chapter 3 by Sewell and Barker raises the importance of ideas in shaping the social order and, particularly, in changing it. A common approach to understanding workplace changes, especially in economics, is to see them as driven by some exogenous and somewhat amorphous development, such as competition or technology. In fact, the actors who respond to and play out the pressures from even exogenous forces always have some discretion, and how that discretion is exercised depends a great deal on beliefs about what is appropriate. The decline of unions and union power, the declines in worker protections more generally, and the erosion of the system of mutual obligations embedded in traditional non-union employment practices are phenomena where the influence of values and ideas would seem to be paramount. The role of politics broadly defined in shaping the workplace, through government regulations as well as unilateral actions, has been a dramatically underresearched topic.

Within this second level of analysis, Beamish and Biggart (Chapter 9) also illustrate several key ways in which the five trends outlined above can be addressed. First, it highlights 'varieties of capitalism' and thus points to varying national contexts which will shape, for example, the meaning of the work–life balance. State welfare systems in such countries as France and Sweden affect the choices open to family members and create different choice sets from those in the USA. Second, markets are socially constructed, so that apparently market-driven trends such as rising inequality can be understood in terms of the institutional context in which markets are embedded. Gottfried explains the gender processes underlying such ideas as human capital, and Macdonald explains the ways in which notions of professions have been negotiated as capitalism has evolved.

Hodgson (Chapter 8) also raises the importance of economic and social institutions in shaping workplace outcomes. The early studies of workplace issues from the Wisconsin School and the Industrial Relations approach emphasized the important roles that unions, collective bargaining, local labor markets, and other institutions played in shaping virtually all aspects of the workplace, from work organization to turnover rates. Despite the fact that decades of studies have demonstrated the explanatory power of these institutions, research interest in them has eroded sharply as the industrial relations tradition has faded along with union influence and the rise of the individual incentives approach of neoclassical economics.

Overall, this second group clearly contains work with established paradigms or problematics, for example the French sociology of work school discussed by Bélanger (Chapter 12). But there are also differences of theory and method, and a much less clearly articulated formal framework than is the case with the first group of analyses.

Third come theories that address very broad issues of meaning in social development. Here, paradigms are often in tension with each, and the goal is not to produce specific hypotheses for workplace phenomena. Yet such theories also powerfully speak to the nature of work. This is very clear in Hyman's discussion (Chapter 2) of Marxism. First, this tradition offers some insights into the concrete trends noted above. For example, the ways in which the Marxist perspective has examined issues of skill in prior research has much to say about the idea of skill-biased technical change. Second, there is understanding of the relationships, or in Marxist analysis, contradictions, between different developments in the workforce. One of the most important of these contradictions is between 'empowerment' (as in teams for routine employees and responsibility and devolution for managers) and 'degradation' (limited autonomy and risks of job loss for workers; tighter control systems, and also job loss, for managers). Third, traditions such as Marxism address the long-term dynamics of capitalism that play out in specific results such as wage inequality. At this level, Weberian analysis also opens up such issues as the rationalization of society. Ideas here speak powerfully to the pressures on individuals to conform, and also to the ways in which relations between work and nonwork spheres may themselves have been rationalized. The idea of a work–life balance, for example, suggests a planned and technical optimization, whereas Weber would underline the ambiguities and the 'dark side' of rationalization.

As Burrell demonstrates in Chapter 6, work in the postmodern tradition addresses similar issues, notably through such concepts as the Panopticon and the disciplinary society. As he also shows, this tradition offers perspectives that inform analyses at the second level of analysis identified above. The themes of identity and sexuality in organizations stand out here as well. Yet there is also a concern to understand deeper conditions of existence. As Burrell, Hyman, and Sewell and Barker demonstrate, there are strongly differing views about the readings of Foucault, Marx, and Weber and of the degrees to which the relevant traditions are compatible with each other. But each tradition offers strong perspectives on work in its concrete manifestations. For those who see parallels, combined perspectives may also be feasible.

Overall, at each of these levels of analysis, there is considerable potential for social theories covered in this book to be used in addressing the five contemporary issues highlighted above. In the process, both social theory and our understanding of the evolving workplace will be enriched.

References

Barley, S. R. and Kunda, G. (2004). *Gurus, Hired Guns, And Warm Bodies: Itinerant Experts in a Knowledge Economy.* Princeton, NJ: Princeton University Press.

Bianchi, S. (2000). Maternal Employment and Time with Children: Dramatic Change or Surprising Continuity?, *Demography*, 37(4): 401–14.

Blanchard, O. J. (2004). 'Explaining European Unemployment', *NBER Reporter* (Summer).

Cappelli, P. (1992). 'Examining Management Displacement', *Academy of Management Journal*, 35(1): 203–17.

Cappelli, P. (2000). 'Market-Mediated Employment: The Historical Context', in M. Blair and T. A. Kochan (eds.), *The New Relationship: Human Capital in the American Corporation*. Washington, DC: The Brookings Institution.

—— (2003). *A Study of the Extent and Causes of Non-Standard Work: A Report to the Russell Sage Foundation*. New York: Russell Sage.

—— and Hamori, M. (2005). 'The New Path to the Top: Changes in the Attributes and Careers of Corporate Executives, 1980 to 2001', *Harvard Business Review* (January).

Card, D., Lemieuz, T., and Riddell, W. C. (2003). *Unionization and Wage Inequality: A Comparative Study of the U.S., U.K., and Canada*. NBER Working Paper No. w9473.

Connelly, C. E. and Gallagher, D. G. (2004). 'Emerging Trends in Contingent Work', *Research Journal of Management*, 30(6): 959–83.

De Ruyter, A. and Burgess, J. (2000). 'Part-time Employment in Australia: Evidence for Globalization?' *International Journal of Manpower*, 21(6): 452–63.

Edwards, T. H. and Whalley, J. (2002). *Short and Long Run Decompositions of OECD Wage Inequality Changes*. NBER Working Paper w9265.

Farber, H. S. (1999). 'Job Loss in the United States, 1981–2003', *Journal of Labor Economics*, 17(4): S142–S169.

Feenstra, R. C. and Hansen, G.H. (1996). 'Globalization, Outsourcing, and Wage Inequality', *American Economic Review* 86(2): 240–5.

Fitzenberger, B. and Wunderlink, G. (2004). 'The Changing Life Cycle Pattern of Female Employment: A Comparison of Germany and the UK', *Scottish Journal of Political Economy*, 51(3): 302–28.

Fullerton, H. N., Jr. (1999). 'Labor Force Participation: 75 Years of Change, 1950–1998 and 1998–2025', *Monthly Labor Review*, 122(12).

Goldin, C. (2004). *From the Valley to the Summit: The Quiet Revolution that Transformed Women's Work*. NBER Working Paper No. 10335.

Levy, F. and Murnane, R. (1992). 'U.S. Earnings Levels and Earnings Inequality: A Review of Recent Trends and Proposed Explanations', *Journal of Economic Literature*, 1333–81.

Meyers, D. D. and Rosenbaum, D.T. (2001). 'Welfare, Earned Income Tax Credit, and the Labor Supply of Single Mothers', *Quarterly Journal of Economics* 116(3): 1063–113.

Morck, R. K. and Steier, L. (2005). *The Global History of Corporate Governance: An Introduction*. NBER Working Paper No. 11062.

Neumark, D. and Reed, D. (2002). *Employment Relationships in the New Economy*. NBER Working Paper 8910.

Nichols, T. (1997) *The Sociology of Industrial Injury*. London: Mansell.

Segal, L. M. and Sullivan, D. G. (1997). 'The Growth of Temporary Service Work', *Journal of Economic Perspectives*, 11(2): 117–36.

Valenta, R. G. (1996). 'Has Job Security in the US Declined?' *Federal Reserve Bank of San Francisco Weekly Letter*, No. 90–107, February 16.

Wolff, E. N. (1992). 'Changing Inequality of Wealth', *The American Economic Review*, 82(2): 552–9.

Index

Lightning Source UK Ltd.
Milton Keynes UK
UKOW04f1010200614

233770UK00001B/7/P

9 780199 285983